Third
Edition

Economics
for Managers

Paul G. Farnham
Georgia State University

PEARSON

Boston   Columbus   Indianapolis   New York   San Francisco   Upper Saddle River
Amsterdam   Cape Town   Dubai   London   Madrid   Milan   Munich   Paris   Montréal   Toronto
Delhi   Mexico City   São Paulo   Sydney   Hong Kong   Seoul   Singapore   Taipei   Tokyo

Editor in Chief: Donna Battista
AVP/Executive Editor: David Alexander
Senior Editorial Project Manager:
  Lindsey Sloan
Director of Marketing: Maggie Moylan
Executive Marketing Manager:
  Lori Deshazo
Senior Marketing Assistant:
  Kimberly Lovato
Managing Editor: Jeffrey Holcomb

Art Director: Jayne Conte
Cover Designer: Suzanne Duda
Cover Art: Newart/Shutterstock
Media Director: Lisa Rinaldi
Production Manager: Meghan DeMaio
Full-Service Project Management:
  Integra Software Services, Pvt Ltd.
Printer/Binder: RR Donnelley
Cover Printer: RR Donnelley
Text Font: ITC Century Std

Credits and acknowledgments borrowed from other sources and reproduced, with permission, in this textbook appear on the appropriate page within text.

Microsoft® and Windows® are registered trademarks of the Microsoft Corporation in the U.S.A. and other countries. Screen shots and icons reprinted with permission from the Microsoft Corporation. This book is not sponsored or endorsed by or affiliated with the Microsoft Corporation.

Library of Congress Cataloging-in-Publication Data

Farnham, Paul G.
  Economics for managers / Paul G. Farnham, Georgia State University.—Third Edition.
    p. cm
  Includes bibliographical references and index.
  ISBN-13: 978-0-13-277370-6 (alk. paper)
  ISBN-10: 0-13-277370-8 (alk. paper)
  1. Economics. 2. Management. I. Title.
  HB171.5.F2487 2013
  330.024'658—dc23
                                                      2012051034

10 9 8 7 6 5
V0UD

ISBN 10: 0-13-277370-8
ISBN 13: 978-0-13-277370-6

Dedication

To my friend and colleague, Dr. Jon Mansfield, who continues to excel at teaching economics for managers.

Brief Contents

Contents

Managerial Rule of Thumb: Competition Means Little Control Over Price   182

Managerial Rule of Thumb: Adopting Strategies to Gain Market Power in Competitive Industries   189

MARKET STRUCTURE: MONOPOLY AND MONOPOLISTIC COMPETITION   196

CASE FOR ANALYSIS: Changing Market Power for Eastman Kodak Co.   197

Managerial Rule of Thumb: Using Lock-In as a Competitive Strategy   211

Managerial Rule of Thumb: Understanding Antitrust Laws   221

Managerial Rule of Thumb: Maintaining Market Power in Monopolistic Competition   226

MARKET STRUCTURE: OLIGOPOLY   230

CASE FOR ANALYSIS: Oligopoly Behavior in the Airline Industry   231

Preface

The third edition of *Economics for Managers* builds on the strengths of the first two editions, while updating the case studies and examples, the data, and the references supporting the discussion. *Economics for Managers*, Third Edition, does not attempt to cover all the topics in traditional principles of economics texts or in intermediate microeconomic and macroeconomic theory texts. As in the previous editions, the goal of this text is to present the fundamental ideas of microeconomics and macroeconomics and then integrate them from a managerial decision-making perspective into a framework that can be used in a single-semester course for Master of Business Administration (MBA), Executive MBA (EMBA), and other business students.

What's New in This Edition?

This edition has been completely revised to update the industry cases and examples in the microeconomics section and the data and analysis in the macroeconomics section.

- Twelve of the sixteen chapters have entirely new cases, while the cases in the remaining four chapters have been updated extensively.
- New cases include: Micro- and Macroeconomic Influences on the Global Automobile Industry; Demand Elasticity and Procter & Gamble's Pricing Strategies; The iPhone in China; Changing Market Power for Eastman Kodak Co.; Airline Pricing Strategies: Will They Start Charging for the Use of the Lavatories?; Mixed Signals on the U.S. Economy in Summer 2012; The Chairman's Quandary; and Strong Headwinds for McDonald's.
- Linkage to the marketing literature, particularly in Chapter 4, Techniques for Understanding Consumer Demand and Behavior, and in Chapter 10, Pricing Strategies for the Firm, has been increased.
- The macroeconomics section of the text has been completely rewritten, given the changes in the macroeconomy since 2008, when the second edition was drafted.
- The macroeconomic data in the tables have been updated to 2011, and the data in the figures show trends from 2000 to first quarter 2012.
- The macroeconomics discussion, which makes extensive use of Federal Reserve Monetary Policy Reports to Congress and reports and analyses by the Congressional Budget Office, includes recent policy issues such as the impact of the American Recovery and Reinvestment Act of 2009, the fiscal cliff debates in 2012, and the Federal Reserve's use of nontraditional policy tools to stimulate the economy.
- An extensive discussion of the situation in the European Union from 2010 to 2012, which includes the banking, sovereign debt, and growth crises and the impact of these events on managerial decision making, is presented.

Motivation for the Text

Most micro/managerial economics and intermediate macroeconomics texts are written for economics students who will spend an entire semester using each text. The level of detail and style of writing in these texts are not appropriate for business students or for the time frame of a single-semester course. However, business students need more than a principles of economics treatment of these topics because they have often been exposed to that level of material already. The third edition of *Economics for Managers* will continue to present economic theory that goes beyond principles of economics, but the text is not as detailed or theoretical as a standard intermediate economics text given the coverage of both micro- and macroeconomics and the additional applications and examples included in this text. The compactness of the text and the style of writing are more appropriate for MBA students than what is typically found in large, comprehensive principles texts.

As in the previous editions, each chapter of *Economics for Managers*, Third Edition, begins with a "Case for Analysis" section, which examines events drawn from the current news media that illustrate the issues in the chapter. Thus, students begin the study of each chapter with a concrete, real-world example that highlights relevant economic concepts, which are then explained with the appropriate economic theory. Numerous real-world examples are used to illustrate the theoretical discussion. This approach appeals to MBA students who typically want to know the relevance and applicability of basic economic concepts and how these concepts can be used to analyze and explain events in the business environment.

Intended Audience

This text is designed to teach economics for business decision making to students in MBA and EMBA programs. It includes fundamental microeconomic and macroeconomic topics that can be covered in a single quarter or semester or that can be combined with other readers and case studies for an academic year course. The book is purposely titled *Economics for Managers* and not *Managerial Economics* to emphasize that this is *not* another applied microeconomics text with heavy emphasis on linear programming, multiple regression analysis, and other quantitative tools. This text is written for business students, most of whom will not take another course in economics, but who will work in firms and industries that are influenced by the economic forces discussed in the text.

A course using this text would ideally require principles of microeconomics and macroeconomics as prerequisites. However, the text is structured so that it can be used without these prerequisites. Coverage of the material in this text in one semester does require a substantial degree of motivation and maturity on the part of the students. However, the style of writing and coverage of topics in *Economics for Managers* will facilitate this process and are intended to generate student interest in these issues that lasts well beyond the end of the course.

Economics for Managers can be used with other industry case study books, such as *The Structure of American Industry* by James Brock. These books present extensive discussions of industry details from an economic perspective. Although they focus primarily on microeconomic and managerial topics, these texts can be used with *Economics for Managers* to integrate influences from the larger macroeconomic environment with the microeconomic analysis of different firms and industries.

Organization of the Text

The text is divided into three parts. Part 1, Microeconomic Analysis, focuses on how individual consumers and businesses interact with each other in a market economy. Part 2, Macroeconomic Analysis, looks at the aggregate behavior of different sectors of the economy to determine how changes in behavior in each of these sectors influence the overall level of economic activity. And finally, Part 3, Integration of the Frameworks, draws linkages between Parts 1 and 2.

Although many of the micro- and macroeconomic topics are treated similarly in other textbooks, this text emphasizes the connections between the frameworks, particularly in the first and last chapters. Changes in macroeconomic variables, such as interest rates, exchange rates, and the overall level of income, usually affect a firm through microeconomic variables such as consumer income, the price of the inputs of production, and the sales revenue the firm receives. Managers must be able to analyze factors relating to both market competition and changes in the overall economic environment so they can develop the best competitive strategies for their firms.

To cover all this material in one text, much of the detail and some topics found in other micro and macro texts have been omitted, most of which are not directly relevant for MBA students. There is no calculus in this text, only basic algebra and graphs. Algebraic examples are kept to a minimum and used only after the basic concepts are presented intuitively with examples. Statistical and econometric techniques are covered, particularly for demand estimation, at a very basic level, while references are provided to the standard sources on these topics. The text places greater emphasis than other texts on how managers use nonstatistical and marketing strategies to make decisions about the demand for their products, and it draws linkages between the statistical and nonstatistical approaches.

Economics for Managers, Third Edition, includes little formal analysis of input or resource markets, either from the viewpoint of standard marginal productivity theory or from the literature on the economics of organization, ownership and control, and human resource management. The latter are interesting topics that are covered in other texts with a focus quite different from this one. The macroeconomics portion of this text omits many of the details of alternative macro theories discussed elsewhere. Students are given the basic tools that will help them understand macroeconomics as presented in business sources, such as the *Wall Street Journal*, that emphasize how the national government and the Federal Reserve manage the economy to promote full employment, a stable price level, and economic growth.

Chapter-by-Chapter Breakdown: What's New in This Edition?

Part 1: Microeconomic Analysis

The third edition of *Economics for Managers* includes new and updated cases from 2010 to 2012 that introduce each chapter. In some chapters, the cases are on the same topic as in previous editions (e.g., the copper industry in Chapter 2) to facilitate the transition for current users of the text.

Chapter 1 introduces an entirely new case on the global automobile industry, which includes a discussion of the microeconomic factors influencing competition among the major players in the industry, and the impact of macroeconomic changes on the entire industry. The chapter focuses on the competition between Japanese and American auto makers, how the American industry has been making a comeback in recent years, and how that change intensified competition among the American producers. I also discuss the impact of the 2011 earthquake and tsunami on the Japanese auto industry and the effect of the 2010 recall and quality issues on Toyota. Automobile production and demand changes in China are major issues in this chapter. Moreover, the role of China regarding both individual firms' strategies and in the larger macroeconomic environment will be a significant factor throughout this text.

Another theme introduced in this chapter is the impact of the global financial crisis and recession on managerial strategies. General Motors and Chrysler received a bailout from the U.S. government to help them survive. The ongoing economic crisis in Europe, which I discuss throughout the text, created major challenges for all players in the global automobile industry. I also discuss the role of currency exchange rates, particularly the impact of the strong yen on the Japanese auto industry.

As in previous editions, this chapter presents the frameworks for the microeconomic and macroeconomic analyses used throughout the text. I introduce the role of relative prices and discuss the different models of market competition. I also present the circular flow macroeconomic model that focuses on consumption (C), investment (I), and government spending (G), and spending on exports (X) and imports (M). I introduce macro policy issues, including the U.S. Federal Reserve policy since 2008 of targeting historically low interest rates and fiscal policy issues such as the American Recovery and Reinvestment Act of 2009.

These microeconomic and macroeconomic issues will be discussed again in the context of the fast-food industry in Chapter 16. The use of two well-known industries to frame both the microeconomic and macroeconomic discussion is a unique feature of *Economics for Managers*, Third Edition.

Chapter 2 updates the case on the copper industry that introduces the concepts of demand and supply and shows the extreme volatility of prices in a competitive industry. The current discussion highlights the issues of the global demand for copper, the particular influence of China, and the problem of copper thefts due to its high price. I have retained much of the discussion of the copper industry from previous editions to illustrate the impact of these changes over time. Even though this chapter focuses on the microeconomic concepts of demand and supply, the copper industry has been given the name "Dr. Copper," because strong demand and high prices can indicate the overall health of the economy.

New examples of the non-price factors influencing demand include (1) the impact on the Zippo Manufacturing Co. of changing attitudes on cigarette smoking; (2) the Chinese demand for pecans; (3) the effect of the Japanese earthquake on the demand for luxury goods in that country; (4) the increased marketing of beer and other products to the Hispanic community; (5) the return of the practice of layaway in department stores; and (6) the effect of substitutes on Nestle bottled water.

New examples of the non-price factors influencing supply include (1) the effect of new technology on pecan growers; (2) the impact of high pecan prices as inputs for bakers; (3) the impact of high oil prices on the supply of natural gas; and (4) the effect of Chinese demand on the number of lumber producers. The extensive numerical example on the copper industry that is used throughout Chapter 2 has been updated to reflect recent events in the copper industry.

Chapter 3 begins with a new case on the relationship between Procter & Gamble's pricing strategy and the price elasticity of demand. I have updated information on price elasticity for airline prices, gasoline, and illegal substances such as cocaine and heroin. The discussion of income elasticity now includes the demand for wines, while the cross-elasticity discussion includes the relationship between airline and automobile travel, which influenced the regulation of child airline safety seats, and consumer demand for wireline and wireless phones. I have updated Table 3.7 with recent estimates of demand elasticity for food, water, and higher education. I have also increased the discussion of the relationship between the economic and marketing approaches to consumer demand, and I have updated an earlier marketing demand elasticity study included in previous editions.

Chapter 4 presents a new case on how firms use cable television and Visa/MasterCard information to better understand and impact consumer behavior. Although successful from the firm's viewpoint, these strategies have raised concerns over the invasion of consumer privacy. In the discussion of marketing techniques to estimate consumer demand, I have drawn extensively on two major marketing references: Vithala R. Rao, *Handbook of Pricing Research in Marketing*, 2009, and Thomas T. Nagle et al., *The Strategy and Tactics of Pricing, 5th ed.*, 2011. I have also updated the econometric references on estimating consumer demand, and I added a new case, "Case Study III: The Demand for Cheese in the United States." I retained the case study of automobile demand and the illustrations of the use of consumer market data in econometric demand studies from the previous editions.

In Chapter 5, I updated the opening case, "Production and Cost Analysis in the Fast-Food Industry," by adding a discussion of fast-food delivery in various parts of the world. New productivity examples in the chapter include (1) the use of additional workers versus robots by Amazon and Crate & Barrel; (2) eliminating diminishing returns in hospital emergency rooms; (3) a discussion of Toyota's quality problems; and (4) an updated discussion of overall industry productivity increases.

Chapter 6 begins with a new case, "The iPhone in China," that focuses on the long-run decisions of Apple Inc. to produce iPhones in China and the controversy that followed over working conditions in those Chinese factories. I also discuss the location and production decisions of smaller manufacturers such as Standard Motor Products of North Carolina. New examples of long-run production and cost decisions include (1) the use of robots in mining operations and hospitals; (2) crowdsourcing or farming out production tasks to the general public; (3) law firms' increased use of software for the discovery process; (4) the trade-off between airline use of smaller jets to cut costs and increased time for refueling; and (5) the decreased use of bags in grocery stores. I also describe the limits of lean production that arose during the Japanese earthquake and tsunami, and I update the discussion of the use of nurse-to-patient ratios to regulate hospital staffing decisions.

Chapter 7 begins with an update of the case of the potato industry from the previous editions of the book. Earlier editions focused on how potato farmers attempted to move away from the competitive market, where they had very little control over price. They formed farmers' cooperatives to help control production and keep prices high. These moves recently faced consumer challenges as price-fixing arrangements. I discuss other recent influences on the potato industry, including obesity concerns resulting from potato consumption and a move to eliminate white potatoes from federally subsidized school breakfasts and lunches. I also update the analysis of competitive strategies in the broiler chicken, red meat, milk, and trucking industries. The red meat industry discussion includes both the issues of "pink slime" and the National Cattlemen's Beef Association's MBA or Master of Beef Advocacy, a training program to promote and defend red meat. The theme in all of these cases is how firms deal with the volatility of the competitive market.

Chapter 8 begins with a new case, "Changing Market Power for Eastman Kodak Co.," which illustrates how the changing markets for cameras and film eroded the market power of this well-known company. In the section on the sources of market power, I have updated the discussion of mergers in the banking, beer, and airlines industries and examined mergers among pharmacy-benefit managers and law firms. New licensing examples include the case of interior decorators and the controversy over who can perform teeth whitening. I have updated the patent discussion with the case of Pfizer's blockbuster drug Lipitor and the patent infringement case between Apple Inc. and Samsung Electronics Co. The changing market power section now includes a discussion of how bricks-and-mortar retailers are fighting showrooming and the consumer use of phone apps to compare prices and then purchase online.

I have updated the antitrust section with a discussion of the August 2010 revisions in the antitrust guidelines and the use of the Herfindahl-Hirschman Index (HHI). I also provided new references on the guidelines. Although the Microsoft antitrust case was an important illustrative example in the two previous editions of the text, it has become dated. I replaced this case with a discussion of the failed merger of AT&T and T-Mobile in 2011. This case clearly illustrates for students the controversies over the existence and use of market power. This discussion is extended in the monopolistic competition section with an update on the cases of independent drugstores and booksellers.

The opening case in Chapter 9 builds on the previous case of interdependent airline pricing behavior by adding current examples of oligopolistic strategies. I have also updated the examples of oligopolistic behavior between Coke and Pepsi; in the doughnut industry; and among DHL, Federal Express, and UPS. I added a discussion of the predatory pricing case of Spirit Airlines versus Northwest Airlines, included new references on cartel behavior, and updated the discussion of OPEC and the diamond cartel.

Chapter 10 begins with the case, "Airline Pricing Strategies: Will They Start Charging for the Use of the Lavatories?" This case illustrates revenue or yield management strategies where the airlines have unbundled their services and are charging separately for different services based on demand elasticity and consumer willingness to pay. I have extended this discussion throughout the chapter and have drawn extensively on articles in the *Journal of Revenue and Pricing Management*, a source that would be very useful for MBA students. As in Chapter 4, I have included more linkages with the marketing literature by including examples and citations from Vithala R. Rao, *Handbook of Pricing Research in Marketing*, and Thomas T. Nagle et al., *The Strategy and Tactics of Pricing, 5th ed.* I updated the discussion of major league baseball ticket pricing and peak load pricing with smart electric meters, and I added an example of revenue management by the Atlanta Symphony Orchestra. At the end of the chapter, I added material to the discussion of the macro impacts on pricing in 2011–2012.

Part 2: Macroeconomic Analysis

Part 2, Macroeconomic Analysis, continues with the framework in the second edition. After introducing the macroeconomic variables in Chapter 11, the text discusses real spending by individuals, firms, and governments ($C + I + G + X - M$) in Chapter 12. This material draws on the analyses students see daily in the *Wall Street Journal* and other business publications. A discussion of money, money markets, and Federal Reserve policy is presented in Chapter 13. These elements are combined using the aggregate demand–aggregate supply (*AD–AS*) model in Chapter 14. Monetary and fiscal policy implementation issues are also presented in this chapter. Chapter 15 continues to focus on exchange rate and balance of payments issues and presents an updated discussion of controversies over the role of the euro and the Chinese yuan. The text continues to describe the impacts of policy changes in these areas on the U.S. and foreign economies. However, *as in the previous editions, and unlike the presentation in other texts, Economics for Managers*, Third Edition, has an extensive discussion in both Chapters 14 and 15 of the impact of macro policy changes on the competitive strategies of both domestic and international firms. *This is a unique feature of this textbook*, which makes it most appropriate for MBA students who will probably never make macroeconomic policy, but who will work in firms and industries influenced by these policy changes.

The macro section of the second edition of *Economics for Managers* was revised just as the U.S. economy was slipping into recession in 2008. Given that the third edition was revised in 2012, I rewrote most of the macro discussion to reflect the substantial economic and policy changes during that period. I updated the references for the national income and product accounts and for the underground economy (Chapter 11). I used 2011 data for all the tables, while the figures show trends from 2000 to the first quarter of 2012. I updated the discussion of each component of GDP with recent data and events (Chapter 12), and I made extensive use of Federal Reserve Monetary Policy Reports to Congress and the reports and analyses by the Congressional Budget Office. All of the cases reflect the uncertainty about the U.S. and global economies in 2011–2012 and the slow recovery from the recession of 2007–2009. In the case in Chapter 13, "The Chairman's Quandary," I discuss the dilemma facing Federal Reserve officials in summer 2012 as they made decisions on future monetary policy. This discussion includes issues related to the continuation of historically low targeted interest rates, Operation Twist, future bond buying, and the use of public statements to achieve monetary policy goals. I also refer students to Federal Reserve Chairman Ben Bernanke's 2012 College Lecture Series, The Federal Reserve and the Financial Crisis.

In Chapter 14, I discuss recent fiscal policy issues, including the American Recovery and Reinvestment Act of 2009, the fiscal cliff debate in 2012, the impacts of fiscal multipliers and how they are estimated, the role of automatic stabilizers, and the interactions between fiscal and monetary policies. On the supply side, I updated the discussion of productivity growth and the natural rate of unemployment. I kept the section on the use of the aggregate macro model to explain changes in the economy from 2007 to 2008, but I added a similar discussion for the period 2011–2012. I also added a summary of the U.S. auto bailout in 2008–2009, and I discussed the impact of the uncertain economic recovery on managerial decisions in 2011–2012.

Chapter 15, which is built around the opening case, "Uncertainty in the World Economy in 2012," focuses on the U.S. economy and international issues from 2010 to 2012. The chapter includes an analysis of the weakness in the Chinese economy, the worsening situation in Europe, and capital flows among industrialized and emerging economies. I have updated all tables and figures, included balance of payments data for 2011, and I updated the discussion and references on balance of payment issues and the role of fixed versus flexible exchange rates. I include a discussion and extensive references on the euro zone situation that involves the banking crisis, the sovereign debt crisis, the growth crisis, and the issue of the sustainability of the euro, and I show the impact of the euro crisis on managerial decision making. I also updated the discussion of the Southeast Asia crisis from the second edition, and I have included recent policy issues related to the Chinese yuan.

Part 3: Integration of the Frameworks

As noted earlier in this section, in Part 3 we return to the issues first discussed in Chapter 1, the relationship between microeconomic and macroeconomic influences on managerial decision making. Chapter 16 presents the case, "Strong Headwinds for McDonald's," which examines the effects of changes in the microeconomic and macroeconomic environment on McDonald's competitive strategies. I discuss current challenges facing the company and how these challenges were met in the past. I then broaden the discussion to include McDonald's major rivals in the fast-food industry, Burger King, Subway, Wendy's, and Starbucks, and I discuss the opportunities and challenges facing all of these companies as they enter emerging markets. I have added a discussion of how these companies are facing public health concerns over obesity, and I present a detailed discussion of the impact of regulations requiring calorie counts on menus. I have also kept a statistical study of fast-food industry demand that was included in previous editions of the text. I discuss macroeconomic influences on the fast-food industry with details from the International Monetary Fund Global Economic Report in October 2012.

The text ends by emphasizing its major theme: *Changes in the macro environment affect individual firms and industries through the microeconomic factors of demand, production, cost, and profitability.* Firms can either try to adapt to these changes or undertake policies to try to modify the environment itself. This theme is particularly important in this third edition of *Economics for Managers*, given the impact of the slow recovery from the 2007–2009 recession on the overall economy and on the strategies of different firms operating in this environment.

Unique Features of the Text

Chapter Opening Cases for Analysis

Each chapter begins with a "Case for Analysis" section, which examines a case drawn from the current news media that illustrates the issues in the chapter. Thus, students begin the study of each chapter with a concrete, real-world example that highlights relevant economic issues, which are then explained with the appropriate economic theory. For example, Chapter 2 begins with a case on the copper industry that illustrates forces on both the demand and supply sides of the market that influence the price of copper and have caused that price to change over time. This example leads directly to a discussion of demand and supply functions and curves, the concept of equilibrium price and quantity, and changes in those equilibria. Within this discussion, I include numerous real-world examples to illustrate demand and supply shifters. The chapter concludes by reviewing how formal demand and supply analysis relates to the introductory case. Students thus go from concrete examples to the relevant economic theory and then back to real-world examples.

Interdisciplinary Focus

Economics for Managers, Third Edition, continues to have an interdisciplinary focus. For example, Chapter 3 presents demand price elasticity estimates drawn from both the economics and marketing literature. Empirical marketing and economic approaches to understanding consumer demand are both discussed in Chapter 4. The production and cost analysis in Chapters 5 and 6 relates to topics covered in management courses, while the pricing discussion in Chapter 10 draws extensively on the marketing literature. Thus, the third edition of *Economics for Managers* is uniquely positioned to serve the needs of instructors who are trying to integrate both micro- and macroeconomic topics and who want to relate this material to other parts of the business curriculum.

Focus on Global Issues

Global and international examples are included in both the microeconomic and macroeconomic sections of the text. For example, Chapter 2 discusses how demand from China, an earthquake in Chile, and the financial crisis in Europe affected the copper industry. I revisit these international issues again in Chapters 15 and 16. Analyses of the impact of changing consumer demand, new production technologies, and rising input costs on both U.S. and international firms are included in many of the microeconomic chapters. Chapters 14 and 15 include discussions of the effects of U.S. and international macroeconomic policy changes on firms located around the world.

As noted previously, *Economics for Managers*, Third Edition, takes the unique approach in Chapters 1 and 16 to discuss the impact of both microeconomic and macroeconomic factors on firms' competitive strategies in international markets. The analysis of the global automobile industry in Chapter 1 and the fast-food industry in Chapter 16 helps students see how economic and political issues around the world impact managerial decision making. This *integration of micro and macro tools* in the global setting has been a key feature of all editions of *Economics for Managers*.

Managerial Decision-Making Perspective

Economics for Managers is developed from a firm and industry decision-making perspective. Thus, the demand and elasticity chapters focus on the implications of elasticity for pricing policies, not on abstract models of consumer behavior. To illustrate the basic models of production and cost, the text presents examples of cost-cutting and productivity-improving strategies that firms actually use. It discusses the concept of input substitution intuitively with examples, but places the formal isoquant model in an appendix to Chapter 6. The text then compares and contrasts the various models of market behavior, incorporating discussions and examples of the measurement and use of market power, most of which are drawn from the current news media and the industrial organization literature.

Throughout the chapters you will find "Managerial Rule of Thumb" features, which are shortcuts for using specific concepts and brief descriptions of important issues for managers. For example, Chapter 3 contains several quick approaches for determining price and income elasticities of demand. Chapter 4 includes some key points for managers to consider when using different approaches to understanding consumer behavior.

Macroeconomics presents a particular challenge for managers because the subject matter is traditionally presented from the viewpoint of the decision makers, either the Federal Reserve or the U.S. Congress and presidential administration. Although *Economics for Managers*, Third Edition, covers the models that include this policy-making perspective, the text also illustrates how the actions of these policy makers influence the decisions managers make in various firms and industries. This emphasis is important because most students taking an MBA economics course will never work or make policy decisions for the Federal Reserve or the U.S. government, but they are or will be employed by firms that are affected by these decisions and policies.

End-of-Chapter Exercises

As you will see, some of the end-of-chapter exercises are straightforward calculation problems that ask students to compute demand-supply equilibria, price elasticities, and profit-maximizing levels of output, for example. However, many exercises are broader analyses of cases and examples drawn from the news media. These exercises have a managerial perspective similar to the examples in the text. The goal is to make students realize that managerial decisions usually involve far more analysis than the calculation of a specific number or an "optimal" mathematical result. One of the exercises at the end of each chapter is related to the "Case for Analysis" discussed at the beginning of that chapter.

Instructor Resource Center

Economics for Managers is connected to the Instructor Resource Center available at **www.pearsonhighered.com/farnham**. Instructors can access a variety of print, digital, and presentation resources available with this text in downloadable format. Registration is simple and gives you immediate access to new titles and new editions. As a registered faculty member, you can download resource files and receive immediate access and instructions for installing course management content on your campus server. If you ever need assistance, our dedicated technical support team is ready to help with the media supplements that accompany this text. Visit **http://247pearsoned.custhelp.com/** for answers to frequently asked questions and toll-free user support phone numbers. The following supplements are available to adopting instructors:

- Instructor's Manual
- Test Item File also available in TestGen software for both Windows and Mac computers
- PowerPoint Presentations containing all figures and tables from the text

Acknowledgments

As with any major project, I owe a debt of gratitude to the many individuals who assisted with this book.

I first want to thank my friend and colleague, Jon Mansfield, who worked with me in developing materials for the book. Jon and I have discussed the integration of microeconomics and macroeconomics for business students for many years as we both experimented with new ideas for teaching a combined course. We even team-taught one section of the course for EMBA students so that we could directly learn from each other. Jon is a great teacher, and his assistance in developing this approach has been invaluable.

I next want to thank the generations of students I have taught, not only in the MBA and EMBA programs, but also in the Master of Public Administration, Master of Health Administration, and Master of Public Health programs at Georgia State. They made it quite clear that students in professional master's degree programs are different from those in academic degree programs. Although these students are willing to learn theory, they have insisted, sometimes quite forcefully, that the theory must always be applicable to real-world managerial situations.

I also want to thank my colleagues Professors Harvey Brightman and Yezdi Bhada, now retired from Georgia State's Robinson College of Business, for their teaching seminars and for backing the approach I have taken in this book. I always knew that business and other professional students learned differently from economics students. Harvey and Yezdi provided the justification for these observations.

I want to acknowledge the following graduate research assistants supported by the Department of Economics, Georgia State University, for their contributions to various editions of the text: Mercy Mvundura, Djesika Amendah, William Holmes, and Sarah Beth Link. They provided substantial assistance in finding the sources used in the text and in developing tables and figures for the book.

The Prentice Hall staff has, of course, been of immense help in developing the third edition of the text. I would especially like to thank David Alexander, Executive Editor, Pearson Economics, for his support and Lindsey Sloan, Senior Editorial Project Manager, Economics, Pearson Higher Education, who has been available to answer all my questions at every step of the project. I would also like to thank Fran Russello, Pearson Production Manager, and Anand Natarajan, Project Manager at Integra Software Services, for their assistance in producing the text.

I would like to thank all those who assisted with supporting materials. Professor Leonie Stone of SUNY Geneseo contributed to the end-of-chapter questions in the micro section of the text. I also want to acknowledge the assistance of all the reviewers of the various drafts of the text. These include:

Gerald Bialka, *University of North Florida*; John Boschen, *College of William and Mary*; Vera Brusentsev, *University of Delaware*; Chun Lee, *Loyola Marymount University*; Mikhail Melnik, *Niagara University*; Franklin E. Robeson, *College of William and Mary*; Dorothy R. Siden, *Salem State College*; Ira A. Silver, *Texas Christian University*; Donald L. Sparks, *The Citadel*; Kasaundra Tomlin, *Oakland University*; Doina Vlad, *Seton Hill University*; John E. Wagner, *SUNY-ESF*; E. Anne York, *Meredith College*.

Finally, I want to thank my wife, Lynn, and daughters, Ali and Jen, for bearing with me during the writing of all editions of this text.

—*Paul G. Farnham*

About the Author

Paul G. Farnham is Associate Professor Emeritus of Economics at Georgia State University. He received his B.A. in economics from Union College, Schenectady, New York, and his M.A. and Ph.D. in economics from the University of California, Berkeley. For over 30 years, he specialized in teaching economics to students in professional master's degree programs including the Master of Business Administration and Executive MBA, Master of Public Administration, Master of Health Administration, and Master of Public Health. He has received both teaching awards and outstanding student evaluations at Georgia State. Dr. Farnham's research focused first on issues related to the economics of state and local governments and then on public health economic evaluation issues where he has published articles in a variety of journals. He co-authored three editions of *Cases in Public Policy Analysis* (1989, 2000, and 2011), contributed to both editions of *Prevention Effectiveness: A Guide to Decision Analysis and Economic Evaluation* (1996, 2003), and wrote a chapter for the *Handbook of Economic Evaluation of HIV Prevention Programs* (1998). He is currently a Senior Service Fellow in the Division of HIV/AIDS Prevention at the Centers for Disease Control and Prevention in Atlanta. Dr. Farnham can be reached at pfarnham@gsu.edu.

Economics
for Managers

1 Managers and Economics

Why should managers study economics? Many of you are probably asking yourself this question as you open this text. Students in Master of Business Administration (MBA) and Executive MBA programs usually have some knowledge of the topics that will be covered in their accounting, marketing, finance, and management courses. You may have already used many of those skills on the job or have decided that you want to concentrate in one of those areas in your program of study.

But economics is different. Although you may have taken one or two introductory economics courses at some point in the past, most of you are not going to *become* economists. From these economics classes, you probably have vague memories of different graphs, algebraic equations, and terms such as *elasticity of demand* and *marginal propensity to consume*. However, you may have never really understood how economics is relevant to managerial decision making. As you'll learn in this chapter, managers need to understand the insights of both *microeconomics*, which focuses on the behavior of individual consumers, firms, and industries, and *macroeconomics*, which analyzes issues in the overall economic environment. Although these subjects are typically taught separately, this text presents the ideas from both approaches and then integrates them from a managerial decision-making perspective.

As in all chapters in this text, we begin our analysis with a case study. The case in this chapter, which focuses on the global automobile industry, provides an overview of the issues we'll discuss throughout this text. In particular, the case illustrates how the automobile industry is influenced by both the microeconomic issues related to production, cost, and consumer demand and the larger macroeconomic issues including the uncertainty in global economic activity, particularly in Europe, and the value of various countries' currencies relative to the U.S. dollar.

Case for Analysis

Micro- and Macroeconomic Influences on the Global Automobile Industry

In September 2012, U.S. automobile sales increased to 1.19 million cars and light trucks per month, a 12.8 percent increase from a year earlier. This increase represented an annualized rate of 14.94 million vehicles, the highest sales rate since March 2008 before the recession began in the United States. Much of the increase was driven by passenger car sales at Toyota Motor Corp., Honda Motor Co., and Chrysler Group LLC. There was a significant increase in sales for Toyota and Honda from the previous year, as both companies were recovering from the earthquake that hit Japan in March 2011.[1] Analysts noted similar increases in August 2012 that were attributed to pent-up consumer demand for replacing aging vehicles and the low-interest financing and other incentives Japanese auto makers offered to regain market share lost in 2011 due to the lack of availability of their cars.[2]

Automobile production in the United States had expanded in 2012, given favorable foreign exchange rates and a plentiful supply of affordable labor. Toyota, Honda, and Nissan Motor Co. all increased their production capacity in the United States with the goal of shipping automobiles to Europe, Korea, the Middle East, and other countries. The strong value of the yen, and conversely the weak U.S. dollar, gave Japanese producers the incentive to produce cars in the United States for export around the world. This investment by foreign automobile producers helped the U.S. economy that was still struggling to recover from the recession of 2007–2009. Automobile industry employment in the United States was estimated to increase from 566,400 in 2010 to 756,800 in 2015. Although these estimates were well below the 1.1 million automobile workers employed in 1999, they indicated that the economic recovery was moving forward. General Motors Co., which had once encouraged auto parts suppliers to relocate in low-wage countries, now encouraged them to locate near U.S. auto plants.[3]

U.S. auto producers, who had once essentially lost the competition to their Japanese rivals in the 1980s and 1990s and who went through government-backed (GM and Chrysler) or private (Ford) restructurings during the U.S. recession, regained profitability and invested in the engineering and redesign of their cars. Several Fords were designed with a voice-operated Sync entertainment system, and the Chevrolet Cruze that was launched in 2010 came with 10 air bags compared with 6 for the Toyota Corolla. As the U.S. economy recovered, Americans also began purchasing more trucks and sport-utility vehicles (SUVs), which helped to restore profits and market share for the Detroit auto makers. Trucks and SUVs made up 47.3 percent of the U.S. market in 2009, 50.2 percent in 2010, and 50.8 percent in 2011. This segment of the market had been hit particularly hard during the U.S. recession.[4]

As the U.S. automobile industry revived, the competition between Ford and GM again became more intense. In 2008, Ford supported the government bailout for GM and Chrysler because Ford was worried that a collapse of these companies would also impact the auto parts industry. As the domestic auto industry recovered, Ford, which had often focused just on Toyota as its key competitor, began developing strategies to counter GM. Ford realized that customers who had long been loyal to Asian brands were again looking at U.S. cars, given the generally perceived quality increases in the U.S. auto industry.[5]

---

[1] Jeff Bennett, "Corporate News: Passenger Cars Lift U.S. Sales—Big Gains for Toyota, Honda, Chrysler: Pickup Weakness Weighs on GM, Ford," *Wall Street Journal (Online)*, October 3, 2012.

[2] Christina Rogers, "August U.S. Car Sales Surge," *Wall Street Journal (Online)*, September 4, 2012.

[3] Joseph B. White, Jeff Bennett, and Lauren Weber, "Car Makers' U-Turn Steers Job Gains," *Wall Street Journal (Online)*, January 23, 2012; Neal Boudette, "New U.S. Car Plants Signal Renewal for Manufacturing," *Wall Street Journal (Online)*, January 26, 2012.

[4] Mike Ramsey and Sharon Terlep, "Americans Embrace SUVs Again," *Wall Street Journal (Online)*, December 2, 2011; Jeff Bennett and Neal E. Boudette, "Revitalized Detroit Makes Bold Bets on New Models," *Wall Street Journal (Online)*, January 9, 2012.

[5] Sharon Terlep and Mike Ramsey, "Ford and GM Renew a Bitter Rivalry," *Wall Street Journal (Online)*, November 23, 2011.

Japanese auto makers in 2011 and 2012 faced managerial decisions that were influenced both by the nature of the competition from their rivals and by macroeconomic conditions, most importantly the value of the exchange rate between the yen and the U.S. dollar.[6] Production by both Toyota and Honda was hit by the earthquake and tsunami in Japan in March 2011 and by subsequent flooding in Thailand that disrupted the supply of electronics and other auto parts made there. Toyota sales were also influenced by the recall and quality issues in 2010 related to the gas pedal and floor mat design. Honda's redesigned 2012 Civic was criticized for its technology and less-than-luxurious interior. The car was dropped from Consumer Reports' recommended list in August 2011. Honda officials acknowledged that they had underestimated the competition from U.S. producers.

The strong yen, which made exports from Japan less price competitive, also gave the Japanese producers the incentive to produce their cars in the United States. Honda, which had produced 1.29 million vehicles in North America in 2010, planned to open a new plant in Mexico and expand production in all seven of its existing assembly plants to 2 million cars and trucks per year. Production abroad was a particular issue for Toyota, which made half of its automobiles in Japan, compared to Honda and Nissan, which produced about one-third of their output in Japan. The president of Toyota, Akio Toyoda, grandson of the company founder, had made a public commitment to build at least 3 million cars in Japan annually, half of which would be for export. Some company officials argued for streamlining production in Japan by decreasing production without raising costs, essentially redefining the economies of scale in the company's production process. These officials believed the company could meet domestic goals with high-precision production, cost-cutting, and collaboration on new technology with parts suppliers.

Auto producers also focused on China during this period, although there was concern about the slowing Chinese economy.[7] Auto sales in China increased only 2.5 percent in 2011 compared with increases of 46 percent in 2009 and 32 percent

in 2010. However, the size of the Chinese economy continued to be the major incentive for expansion in that country. In April 2012, Ford announced that it would build its fifth factory in eastern China as part of its plan to double its production capacity and sales outlets in the country by 2015. This production increase would make the company capable of producing 1.2 million passenger cars in China, approximately half of the number of cars it built in North America in 2011. Ford lagged behind other major auto producers in entering the world's largest car market. Ford's strategy was to build cars from platforms developed elsewhere to minimize costs. However, these platforms might not provide enough space in the back seats to appeal to affluent Chinese, who often employed drivers. General Motors developed a partnership with Chinese SAIC Motor Corp. to become the dominant foreign competitor in China. This partnership resulted in production changes such as designing Cadillacs with softer corners, dashboards with more gadgets, and increasing the comfort of the rear seats to appeal to Chinese consumers. The challenge for GM was that SAIC could also use GM's expertise and technology to make itself a major competitor with the U.S. company. In 2012, the Chinese automobile industry began increasing exports, although these were not thought to be a threat in developed markets in the United States and Europe, given perceived quality issues including lack of air-conditioning and power windows. However, Chinese producers were making inroads into emerging markets in Africa, Asia, and Latin America.

The other major influence on the global auto industry in 2011 and 2012 was the recession and economic crisis in Europe.[8] In October 2012, Ford announced a plan to cut its operating losses in Europe by closing three auto-assembly and parts factories in the region, reduce its workforce by 13 percent, and decrease automobile production by 18 percent. Ford predicted a loss of $1.5 billion in Europe in 2012 and a similar loss in 2013. The cost-cutting in Europe was combined with the introduction of several new commercial vans and SUVs and the introduction of the Mustang sports car for the first time. All European auto makers faced decreased car sales and chronic overcapacity at this time. Daimler AG, maker of Mercedes-Benz automobiles, announced that it would not achieve its profit targets, while PSA Peugeot Citroen SA announced a government bailout of its financing arm and a cost-sharing pact with General Motors. There had been a smaller decrease in auto-producing capacity in Europe since the 2008 financial crisis compared with that during the restructuring of the U.S. auto industry that was influenced by the federal government bailout.

[6]The following discussion is based on Jeff Bennett and Neal E. Boudette, "Revitalized Detroit Makes Bold Bets on New Models"; Mike Ramsey and Yoshio Takahashi, "Car Wreck: Honda and Toyota," *Wall Street Journal (Online)*, November 1, 2011; Chester Dawson, "For Toyota, Patriotism and Profits May Not Mix," *Wall Street Journal (Online)*, November 29, 2011; Mike Ramsey and Neal E. Boudette, "Honda Revs Up Outside Japan," *Wall Street Journal (Online)*, December 21, 2011; and Yoshio Takahashi and Chester Dawson, "Japan Auto Makers on a Roll," *Wall Street Journal (Online)*, April 22, 2012.
[7]This discussion is based on Andrew Galbraith, "Car Makers Still Look to China," *Wall Street Journal (Online)*, April 19, 2012; Sharon Terlep and Mike Ramsey, "Ford Bets $5 Billion on Made in China," *Wall Street Journal (Online)*, April 20, 2012; Chester Dawson and Sharon Terlep, "China Ramps Up Auto Exports," *Wall Street Journal (Online)*, April 24, 2012; and Sharon Terlep, "Balancing the Give and Take in GM's Chinese Partnership," *Wall Street Journal (Online)*, August 19, 2012.

[8]This discussion is based on Sharon Terlep and Sam Schechner, "GM, Peugeot Take Aim at Europe Woes," *Wall Street Journal (Online)*, July 12, 2012; Mike Ramsey, David Pearson, and Matthew Curtin, "Daimler Warns as Europe Car Makers Cut Back," *Wall Street Journal (Online)*, October 24, 2012; and Marietta Cauchi and Mike Ramsey, "Ford to Shut 3 Europe Plants," *Wall Street Journal (Online)*, October 25, 2012.

Two Perspectives: Microeconomics and Macroeconomics

As noted above, **microeconomics** is the branch of economics that analyzes the decisions that individual consumers and producers make as they operate in a market economy. When microeconomics is applied to business decision making, it is called **managerial economics**. The key element in any market system is pricing, because this type of system is based on the buying and selling of goods and services. As we'll discuss later in the chapter, **prices**—the amounts of money that are charged for different goods and services in a market economy—act as signals that influence the behavior of both consumers and producers of these goods and services. Managers must understand how prices are determined—for both the **outputs**, or products sold by a firm, and the **inputs**, or resources (such as land, labor, capital, raw materials, and entrepreneurship) that the firm must purchase in order to produce its output. Output prices influence the revenue a firm derives from the sale of its products, while input prices influence a firm's costs of production. As you'll learn throughout this text, many managerial actions and decisions are based on expected responses to changes in these prices and on the ability of a manager to influence these prices.

Managerial decisions are also influenced by events that occur in the larger economic environment in which businesses operate. Changes in the overall level of economic activity, interest rates, unemployment rates, and exchange rates both at home and abroad create new opportunities and challenges for a firm's competitive strategy. This is the subject matter of **macroeconomics**, which we'll cover in the second half of this text. Managers need to be familiar with the underlying macroeconomic models that economic forecasters use to predict changes in the macroeconomy and with how different firms and industries respond to these changes. Most of these changes affect individual firms via the pricing mechanism, so there is a strong connection between microeconomic and macroeconomic analysis.[9]

In essence, macroeconomic analysis can be thought of as viewing the economy from an airplane 30,000 feet in the air, whereas with microeconomics the observer is on the ground walking among the firms and consumers. While on the ground, an observer can see the interaction between individual firms and consumers and the competitive strategies that various firms develop. At 30,000 feet, however, an observer doesn't see the same level of detail. In macroeconomics, we analyze the behavior of individuals aggregated into different sectors in the economy to determine the impact of changes in this behavior on the overall level of economic activity. In turn, this overall level of activity combines with changes in various macro variables, such as interest rates and exchange rates, to affect the competitive strategies of individual firms and industries, the subject matter of microeconomics. Let's now look at these microeconomic influences on managers in more detail.

Microeconomics
The branch of economics that analyzes the decisions that individual consumers, firms, and industries make as they produce, buy, and sell goods and services.

Managerial economics
Microeconomics applied to business decision making.

Prices
The amounts of money that are charged for goods and services in a market economy. Prices act as signals that influence the behavior of both consumers and producers of these goods and services.

Outputs
The final goods and services produced and sold by firms in a market economy.

Inputs
The factors of production, such as land, labor, capital, raw materials, and entrepreneurship, that are used to produce the outputs, or final goods and services, that are bought and sold in a market economy.

Macroeconomics
The branch of economics that focuses on the overall level of economic activity, changes in the price level, and the amount of unemployment by analyzing group or aggregate behavior in different sectors of the economy.

---

[9]Note that the terms *micro* and *macro* are used differently in various business disciplines. For example, in *Marketing Management, The Millennium Edition* (Prentice Hall, 2000), Philip Kotler describes the "macro environment" as dealing with *all* forces external to the firm. His examples include both (1) the gradual opening of new markets in many countries and the growth in global brands of various products (microeconomic factors for the economist) and (2) the debt problems of many countries and the fragility of the international financial system (macroeconomic problems from the economic perspective). In each business discipline, you need to learn how these terms and concepts are defined.

Microeconomic Influences on Managers

The discussion of the global automobile industry in the opening case illustrates several microeconomic factors influencing managerial decisions. In 2012, Japanese auto makers used low-interest financing and other incentives to regain market share lost in previous years. Toyota had to recover from the impact of its recall and negative quality issues in 2010, while Honda stumbled on the redesign of its 2012 Civic by not incorporating features offered by its competitors. U.S. auto makers reengineered and redesigned their production processes to add features with greater customer appeal. They also responded to the increased demand for trucks and SUVs, a market segment that had been negatively impacted by the recession. Ford and GM began reengaging in their traditional market rivalry. All producers who planned to sell in China, the world's largest automobile market, had to recognize the difference in tastes and preferences of Chinese consumers, such as the desire for larger back seats.

Relative prices
The price of one good in relation to the price of another, similar good, which is the way prices are defined in microeconomics.

Decisions about demand, supply, production, and market structure are all microeconomic choices that managers must make. Some decisions focus on the factors that affect consumer behavior and the willingness of consumers to buy one firm's product as opposed to that of a competitor. Thus, managers need to understand the variables influencing consumer demand for their products. Because consumers typically have a choice among competing products, these choices and the demand for each product are influenced by **relative prices**, the price of one good in relation to that of another, similar good. Relative prices are the focus of microeconomic analysis. The Japanese auto makers' use of low-interest financing and other pricing incentives noted above is an example of a strategy based on influencing relative prices. All auto makers discussed in the case had to respond to changing consumer demand over time and to variations in consumer tastes and preferences that influenced demand in different countries.

Production technology and the prices paid for the resources used in production influence a company's final costs of production. The relative prices of these resources or factors of production will influence the choices that managers make among different production methods. Whether a production process uses large amounts of plant and equipment relative to the amount of workers and whether a business operates out of a small office or a giant factory are microeconomic production and cost decisions managers must make. As noted in the case, Ford Motor Co. used production platforms developed elsewhere to minimize its production costs as it entered the Chinese market. However, this cost-minimizing strategy was not appropriate for producing cars with larger back seats that appealed to affluent Chinese customers. General Motors also had to redesign its Cadillac to meet Chinese demand.

Markets

Markets
The institutions and mechanisms used for the buying and selling of goods and services. The four major types of markets in microeconomic analysis are perfect competition, monopolistic competition, oligopoly, and monopoly.

All of the auto makers in the opening case made strategic decisions in light of their knowledge of the market environment or structure. **Markets**, the institutions and mechanisms used for the buying and selling of goods and services, vary in structure from those with hundreds or thousands of buyers and sellers to those with very few participants. These different types of markets influence the strategic decisions that managers make because markets affect both the ability of a given firm to influence the price of its product and the amount of independent control the firm has over its actions.

There are four major types of markets in microeconomic analysis:

1. Perfect competition
2. Monopolistic competition
3. Oligopoly
4. Monopoly

Large Number of Firms			Single Firm
Perfect Competition ----- Monopolistic Competition ----- Oligopoly ----- Monopoly			

FIGURE 1.1
Market Structure

These market structures can be located along a continuum, as shown in Figure 1.1. At the left end of the continuum, there are a large number of firms in the market, whereas at the right end of the continuum there is only one firm. (We'll discuss other characteristics that distinguish the markets later in the chapter.)

The two market structures at the ends of the continuum, perfect competition and monopoly, are essentially hypothetical models. No real-world firms meet all the assumptions of perfect competition, and few could be classified as monopolies. However, these models serve as benchmarks for analysis. All real-world firms contain combinations of the characteristics of these two models. Managers need to know where their firm lies along this continuum because market structure will influence the strategic variables that a firm can use to face its competition.

The major characteristics that distinguish these market structures are

1. The number of firms competing with one another that influences the firm's control over its price
2. Whether the products sold in the markets are differentiated or undifferentiated
3. Whether entry into and exit from the market by other firms is easy or difficult
4. The amount of information available to market participants

The Perfect Competition Model

The model of **perfect competition**, which is on the left end of the continuum in Figure 1.1, is a market structure characterized by

1. A large number of firms in the market
2. An undifferentiated product
3. Ease of entry into the market
4. Complete information available to all market participants

In perfect competition, we distinguish between the behavior of an individual firm and the outcomes for the entire market or industry, which represents all firms producing the product. Economists make the assumption that there are so many firms in a perfectly competitive industry that no single firm has any influence on the price of the product. For example, in many agricultural industries, whether an individual farmer produces more or less product in a given season has no influence on the price of these products. The individual farmer's output is small relative to the entire market, so the market price is determined by the actions of *all* farmers supplying the product and *all* consumers who purchase the goods. Because individual producers can sell any amount of output they bring to market at that price, we characterize the perfectly competitive firm as a **price-taker**. This firm does not have to lower its price to sell more output. In fact, it cannot influence the price of its product. However, if the price for the entire amount of output in the market increases, consumers will buy less, and if the market price of the product decreases, they will buy more.

In the model of perfect competition, economists also assume that all firms in an industry produce the same homogeneous product, so there is no product differentiation. For example, within a given grade of an agricultural product, potatoes or peaches are undifferentiated. This market characteristic means that consumers do not care about the identity of the specific supplier of the product they purchase. They may not even know who supplies the product, and that knowledge would be irrelevant to their purchase decision, which will be based largely on the price of the product.

Perfect competition
A market structure characterized by a large number of firms in an industry, an undifferentiated product, ease of entry into the market, and complete information available to participants.

Price-taker
A characteristic of a perfectly competitive firm in which the firm cannot influence the price of its product, but can sell any amount of its output at the price established by the market.

Profit
The difference between the total revenue that a firm receives for selling its product and the total cost of producing that product.

Market power
The ability of a firm to influence the prices of its products and develop other competitive strategies that enable it to earn large profits over longer periods of time.

Imperfect competition
Market structures of monopolistic competition, oligopoly, and monopoly, in which firms have some degree of market power.

Monopoly
A market structure characterized by a single firm producing a product with no close substitutes.

Barriers to entry
Structural, legal, or regulatory characteristics of a firm and its market that keep other firms from easily producing the same or similar products at the same cost.

Monopolistic competition
A market structure characterized by a large number of small firms that have some market power as a result of producing differentiated products. This market power can be competed away over time.

Oligopoly
A market structure characterized by competition among a small number of large firms that have market power, but that must take their rivals' actions into account when developing their own competitive strategies.

The third assumption of the perfectly competitive model is that entry into the industry by other firms is costless. This means that if a perfectly competitive firm is making a **profit** (earning revenues in excess of its costs), other firms will also enter the industry in an attempt to earn profits. However, these actions will compete away excess profits for all firms in a perfectly competitive industry.

The final assumption of the perfectly competitive model is that complete information is available to all market participants. This means that all participants know which firms are earning the greatest profits and how they are doing so. Thus, other firms can easily emulate the strategies and techniques of the profitable firms, which will result in greater competition and further pressure on any excess profits.

While the details of this process will be described in later chapters, these four assumptions mean that perfectly competitive firms have no **market power**—the ability to influence their prices and develop other competitive strategies that allow them to earn large profits over longer periods of time. All of the other market structures in Figure 1.1 represent **imperfect competition**, in which firms have some degree of market power. How much market power these firms have and how they are able to maintain it differ among the market structures.

The Monopoly Model   At the right end of the market structure continuum in Figure 1.1 is the **monopoly** model, in which a single firm produces a product for which there are no close substitutes. Thus, as we move rightward along the continuum, the number of firms producing the product keeps decreasing until we reach the monopoly model of one firm. A monopoly firm typically produces a product that has characteristics and qualities different from the products of its competitors. This product differentiation often means that consumers are willing to pay more for this product because similar products are not considered to be close substitutes.

In the monopoly model, there are also **barriers to entry**, which are structural, legal, or regulatory characteristics of the market that keep other firms from easily producing the same or similar products at the same cost and that give a firm market power. However, while market power allows a firm to influence the prices of its products and develop competitive strategies that enable it to earn larger profits, a firm with market power cannot sell any amount of output at a given market price, as in perfect competition. If a monopoly firm raises its price, it will sell less output, whereas if it lowers its price, it will sell more output.

The Monopolistic Competition and Oligopoly Models   The intermediate models of monopolistic competition and oligopoly in Figure 1.1 better characterize the behavior of real-world firms and industries because they represent a blend of competitive and monopolistic behavior. In **monopolistic competition**, firms produce differentiated products, so they have some degree of market power. However, because these firms are closer to the left end of the continuum in Figure 1.1, there are many firms competing with one another. Each firm has only limited ability to earn above-average profits before they are competed away over time. In **oligopoly** markets, a small number of large firms dominate the market, even if other producers are present. Mutual interdependence is the key characteristic of this market structure because firms need to take the actions of their rivals into account when developing their own competitive strategies. Oligopoly firms typically have market power, but how they use that power may be limited by the actions and reactions of their competitors.

The opening case of this chapter did not explicitly discuss the market structure of the major auto producers. However, because all of these firms are large multinational companies that sell globally, they obviously have substantial market power and are located far from the model of perfect competition on the continuum in Figure 1.1. The case noted that U.S. automobile sales were at an annualized rate of 14.94 million vehicles in 2012.

Large national or multinational companies typically find themselves operating in multiple markets, making the analysis of market structure more complicated as the market environment may differ substantially among these markets. Each of these markets has its own characteristics in terms of the number and size of the competitors and product characteristics. Differences between the Chinese and U.S. markets were discussed throughout the case.

The Goal of Profit Maximization   In all of the market models we have just presented, we assume that the goal of firms is **profit maximization**, or earning the largest amount of profit possible. Because profit, as defined above, represents the difference between the revenues a firm receives for selling its output and its costs of production, firms may develop strategies to either increase revenues or reduce costs in an effort to increase profits. Profits act as a signal in a market economy. If firms in one sector of the economy earn above-average profits, other firms will attempt to produce the same or similar products to increase their profitability. Thus, resources will flow from areas of low to high profitability. As we will see, however, the increased competition that results from this process will eventually lead to lower prices and revenues, thus eliminating most or all of these excess profits.

Profitability is the standard by which firms are judged in a market economy. Profitability affects stock prices and investor decisions. If firms are unprofitable, they will go out of business, be taken over by other more profitable companies, or have their management replaced. Subsequently, we model a firm's profit-maximization decision largely in terms of static, single-period models where information on consumer behavior, revenues, and costs is known with certainty. Real-world managers must deal with uncertainty in all of these areas, which may lead to less-than-optimal decisions, and managers must be concerned with maximizing the firm's value over time. The models we present illustrate the basic forces influencing managerial decisions and the key role of profits as a motivating incentive.

> **Profit maximization**
> The assumed goal of firms, which is to develop strategies to earn the largest amount of profit possible. This can be accomplished by focusing on revenues, costs, or both.

Managerial Rule of Thumb

Microeconomic Influences on Managers

To develop a competitive advantage and increase their firm's profitability, managers need to understand:

- How consumer behavior affects their revenues
- How production technology and input prices affect their costs
- How the market and regulatory environment in which managers operate influences their ability to set prices and to respond to the strategies of their competitors ∎

Macroeconomic Influences on Managers

The discussion of the impact of the global recession, the continued problems in Europe's financial recovery, and the role of currency exchange rates in the case that opened this chapter can be placed within the **circular flow model** of

> **Circular flow model**
> The macroeconomic model that portrays the level of economic activity as a flow of expenditures from consumers to firms, or producers, as consumers purchase goods and services produced by these firms. This flow then returns to consumers as income received from the production process.

FIGURE 1.2
GDP and the Circular Flow
C = consumption spending
I = investment spending
G = government spending
X = export spending
M = import spending
Y = household income
S = household saving
T_P = personal taxes
T_B = business taxes

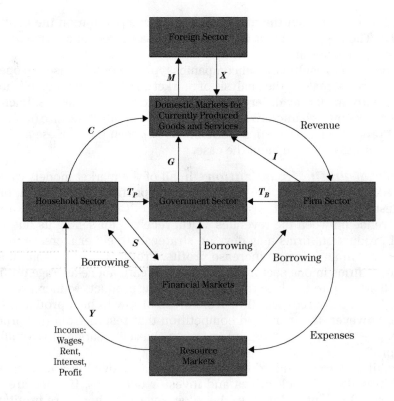

macroeconomics, shown in Figure 1.2. This model portrays the level of economic activity in a country as a flow of expenditures from the household sector to business firms as consumers purchase goods and services currently produced by these firms and sold in the country's output markets. This flow then returns to consumers as income received for supplying firms with the inputs or factors of production, including land, labor, capital, raw materials, and entrepreneurship, which are bought and sold in the resource markets. These payments, which include wages, rents, interest, and profits, become consumer income, which is again used to purchase goods and services—hence, the name *circular flow*. Figure 1.2 also shows spending by firms, by governments, and by the foreign sector of the economy. Corresponding to these total levels of expenditures and income are the amounts of output produced and resources employed.

The levels of expenditures, income, output, and employment in relation to the total capacity of the economy to produce goods and services will determine whether resources are fully employed in the economy or whether there is unemployed labor and excess plant capacity. This relationship will also determine whether and how much the absolute price level in the economy is increasing. The **absolute price level** is a measure of the *overall* price level in the economy as compared with the microeconomic concept of relative prices, which refers to the price of one particular good compared to that of another, as we discussed earlier.

Economists use the circular flow model in Figure 1.2 to define and analyze the spending behavior of different sectors of the economy, including

- **Personal consumption expenditures (C)** by all households on durable goods, nondurable goods, and services
- **Gross private domestic investment spending (I)** by households and firms on nonresidential structures, equipment, software, residential structures, and inventories

Absolute price level
A measure of the overall level of prices in the economy.

Personal consumption expenditures (C)
The total amount of spending by households on durable goods, nondurable goods, and services in a given period of time.

Gross private domestic investment spending (I)
The total amount of spending on nonresidential structures, equipment, software, residential structures, and business inventories in a given period of time.

- Federal, state, and local **government consumption expenditures and gross investment (G)**
- **Net export spending (F)** or total **export spending (X)** minus total **import spending (M)**

Consumption spending (C) is largely determined by consumer income (Y), but it is also influenced by other factors such as consumer confidence, as noted below. Much business investment spending (I) is derived from borrowing in the financial markets and is, therefore, affected by prevailing interest rates. The availability of funds for borrowing is influenced by the amount of income that consumers save (S) or do not spend on goods and services.[10] Some consumer income (Y) is also used to pay personal taxes (T_P) to the government sector to finance the purchase of its goods and services. The government also imposes taxes on business (T_B). If government spending (G) exceeds the total amount of taxes collected ($T = T_P + T_B$), the resulting deficit must be financed by borrowing in the financial markets. This government borrowing may affect the amount of funds available for business investment, which in turn may cause interest rates to change, influencing firms' costs of production.

The foreign sector also plays a role in a country's circular flow of expenditures because some currently produced goods and services are purchased by residents of other countries, exports (X), while a given country's residents use some of their income to purchase goods and services produced in other countries, imports (M). Net export spending (F), or export spending (X) minus import spending (M), measures the net effect of the foreign sector on the domestic economy. Import spending is subtracted from export spending because it represents a flow of expenditures out of the domestic economy to the rest of the world.[11]

Spending by all these sectors equals **gross domestic product (GDP)**, the comprehensive measure of overall economic activity that is used to judge how an economy is performing. Gross domestic product measures the market value of all currently produced final goods and services within a country in a given period of time by domestic and foreign-supplied resources. GDP equals the sum of consumption spending (C), investment spending (I), government spending (G), and export spending (X) minus import spending (M).

Government consumption expenditures and gross investment (G)
The total amount of spending by federal, state, and local governments on consumption outlays for goods and services, depreciation charges for existing structures and equipment, and investment capital outlays for newly acquired structures and equipment in a given period of time.

Net export spending (F)
The total amount of spending on exports (X) minus the total amount of spending on imports (M) or (F = X − M) in a given period of time.

Export spending (X)
The total amount of spending on goods and services currently produced in one country and sold abroad to residents of other countries in a given period of time.

Import spending (M)
The total amount of spending on goods and services currently produced in other countries and sold to residents of a given country in a given period of time.

Gross domestic product (GDP)
The comprehensive measure of the total market value of all currently produced final goods and services within a country in a given period of time by domestic and foreign-supplied resources.

Factors Affecting Macro Spending Behavior

In macroeconomics, we develop models that explain the behavior of these different sectors of the economy and how changes in this behavior influence the overall level of economic activity, or GDP. These behavior changes arise from

1. Changes in the consumption and investment behavior of individuals and firms in the private sector of the economy
2. New directions taken by a country's monetary or fiscal policy-making institutions (its central bank and national government)
3. Developments that occur in the rest of the world that influence the domestic economy

[10]Households also borrow from the financial markets, but they are net savers on balance.
[11]If a country's export spending and import spending do not balance, there will be a flow of financial capital among different countries. This flow will affect a country's currency exchange rate, the rate at which one country's currency can be exchanged for another (Chapter 15).

Changes in Private-Sector Behavior   Although there are many factors that influence consumption spending (C) and investment spending (I), credit availability, consumer wealth in the housing and stock markets, and confidence on the part of both consumers and businesspeople were extremely important factors influencing the U.S. economy in the recession of 2007–2009 and the slow economic recovery since that time.

Monetary Policies   In response to the slowing U.S. economy in 2007, the Federal Reserve, the central bank in the United States, began lowering its targeted interest rate, which had been 5.25 percent since June 2006. In December 2008, the Federal Reserve cut the targeted rate to historic lows of between 0 and 0.25 percent. This policy has been maintained up through the writing of this chapter. These rate changes were reactions to sluggish growth in consumer spending, employment and manufacturing activity, continued turmoil in the housing and financial markets, and sharp drops in the stock market. Managers in any economy must be aware of the **monetary policies** of their country's central bank that influence interest rates and the amount of funds available for consumer and business loans.

Monetary policies
Policies adopted by a country's central bank that influence the money supply, interest rates, and the amount of funds available for loans, which, in turn, influence consumer and business spending.

Fiscal policy
Changes in taxing and spending by the executive and legislative branches of a country's national government that can be used to either stimulate or restrain the economy.

Fiscal Policies   To respond to the recession and financial crisis in the United States, Congress passed the American Recovery and Reinvestment Act (ARRA) in February 2009. This legislation represented changes in **fiscal policy**—taxing and spending policies by a country's national government that can be used to either stimulate or restrain the economy ($T = T_P + T_B$ and G in the circular flow model in Figure 1.2). Fiscal policy decisions are made by a country's executive and legislative institutions, such as the president, his or her administration, and the Congress in the United States. As a result, fiscal policy actions may be undertaken to promote political as well as economic goals.

The ARRA had numerous spending and revenue provisions that can be grouped as follows: (1) providing funds to states and localities, including aid for education and support for transportation projects; (2) supporting people in need through measures such as extending unemployment benefits; (3) purchasing goods and services including construction and other investment activities; and (4) providing temporary tax relief for individuals and businesses.[12]

Changes in the Foreign Sector   The opening case for this chapter noted that the strong yen, which made exports from Japan less price competitive, gave Japanese producers the incentive to produce cars in the United States. This was a strategic problem for Toyota, whose president had made a public commitment to build at least 3 million cars in Japan annually. The value at which a country's currency can be exchanged for another currency affects the flow of imports and exports to and from the country and the level of economic activity in the country. Policies to keep that exchange rate at a certain level can have negative effects on other economic goals and can be offset by the actions of currency traders in financial markets. Exchange rate policies need to be coordinated with monetary and fiscal policies to maintain the proper rate of economic growth.

---

[12]Congressional Budget Office. *Estimated Impact of the American Recovery and Reinvestment Act on Employment and Economic Output from April 2012 Through June 2012.* August 2012. Available at www.cbo.gov.

Managerial Rule of Thumb

Macroeconomic Influences on Managers

Changes in the macro environment affect individual firms and industries through the microeconomic factors of demand, production, cost, and profitability. Managers don't have control over these changes in the larger macroeconomic environment. However, managers must be aware of the developments that will have a direct impact on their businesses. Managers sometimes hire outside consultants for reports on the macroeconomic environment, or they ask in-house staff to prepare forecasts. In any case, they need to be able to interpret these forecasts and then project the impact of these macroeconomic changes on the competitive strategies of their firms. Although overall macroeconomic changes may be the same, their impact on various firms and industries is likely to be quite varied. ■

Summary

In this chapter, we discussed the reasons why both microeconomic and macroeconomic analyses are important for managerial decision making. *Microeconomics* focuses on the decisions that individual consumers and firms make as they produce, buy, and sell goods and services in a market economy, while *macroeconomics* analyzes the overall level of economic activity, changes in the price level and unemployment, and the rate of economic growth for the economy. All of these factors affect the decisions managers make in developing competitive strategies for their firms.

We illustrated these issues by discussing the challenges and problems facing the global automobile industry in 2011 and 2012. Some of these challenges arose from changes in consumer preferences and demand over time, while others resulted from differences in preferences in various markets. However, all automobile producers were affected by the slow global economic recovery at this time and by fluctuating values of currency exchange rates.

We then briefly introduced the concept of market structure and presented the four basic market models: *perfect competition, monopolistic competition, oligopoly,* and *monopoly.* We also showed how the economic activity between consumers and producers fits into the aggregate *circular flow model* of macroeconomics, and we defined the basic spending components of that model: *consumption, investment, government spending,* and *spending on exports and imports.* We illustrated the effects of changes in *monetary policy* by a country's central bank and changes in *fiscal policy* by the national administrative and legislative institutions on the overall level of economic activity.

We will next analyze these issues in more detail. We first focus on the microeconomic concepts of demand and supply, pricing, production and cost, and market structures (Chapters 2 through 10). We'll then turn our attention to macroeconomic models and data (Chapters 11 through 15). We return to integrate these issues further where we'll look at more examples of the combined impact of both microeconomic and macroeconomic variables on managerial decision making (Chapter 16).

Key Terms

absolute price level, p. 10

barriers to entry, p. 8

circular flow model, p. 9

export spending (*X*), p. 11

fiscal policy, p. 12

government consumption
   expenditures and gross
   investment (*G*), p. 11

gross domestic product (GDP), p. 11

gross private domestic investment
   spending (*I*), p. 10

imperfect competition, p. 8

import spending (*M*), p. 11

inputs, p. 5

macroeconomics, p. 5

managerial economics, p. 5

market power, p. 8

markets, p. 6

microeconomics, p. 5

monetary policies, p. 12

monopolistic competition, p. 8

monopoly, p. 8

net export spending (*F*), p. 11

oligopoly, p. 8

outputs, p. 5

perfect competition, p. 7

personal consumption
   expenditures (*C*), p. 10

prices, p. 5

price-taker, p. 7

profit, p. 8

profit maximization, p. 9

relative prices, p. 6

Exercises

Technical Questions

1. What are the differences between the microeconomic and macroeconomic perspectives on the economy?
2. Explain the differences between the inputs and outputs of a production process.
3. What are the four major types of markets in microeconomic analysis? What are the key characteristics that distinguish these markets?
4. Why do economists assume that firms are price-takers in the model of perfect competition? How does this pricing behavior differ from that in the other market models?
5. In macroeconomics, what are the five major categories of spending that make up GDP? Are all five categories added together to determine GDP?
6. Discuss the differences between fiscal and monetary policies.

Application Questions

1. Give illustrations from the opening case in this chapter of how both microeconomic and macroeconomic factors influence the global automobile industry.
2. In each of the following examples, discuss which market model appears to best explain the behavior described:
   a. Corn prices reached record highs in the United States in August 2012, given the worst drought in decades. However, by October these prices started to drop again as countries including China, Japan, and South Korea began to purchase from producers in other countries such as Argentina and Brazil.[13]
   b. In 2012, Staples Inc., OfficeMax Inc., and Office Depot Inc. were all closing many stores, decreasing the size of their stores, and focusing more on online operations. All three chains struggled to deal with changing consumer shopping habits as consumers tested equipment in the stores and then made purchases online.[14]

[13]Andrew Johnon Jr., "Weak Exports Hurt Corn," *Wall Street Journal (Online)*, November 2, 2012.
[14]Ann Zimmerman and Shelly Banjo, "New Web Victim: Office-Supply Store," *Wall Street Journal (Online)*, September 25, 2012.

c. In fall 2012, T-Mobile announced it was close to a merger with its smaller rival MetroPCS. This merger would strengthen T-Mobile's position as the fourth-largest wireless operator in the United States. The merger would allow the combined company to cut costs and operate on a larger scale.[15]

d. Chinese cooking is the most popular food in America that isn't dominated by big national chains. Chinese food is typically cooked in a wok that requires high heat and a special stove. Specialized chefs are also required. Small mom-and-pop restaurants comprise nearly all of the nation's 36,000 Chinese restaurants, which have more locations than McDonald's, Burger King, and Wendy's combined.[16]

3. In current business publications, find examples of firms whose strategies to increase profits focus primarily on generating more revenue. Compare these cases with firms that are trying to cut costs to increase profits.

4. The slow recovery from the recession of 2007–2009 forced many firms to develop new competitive strategies to survive. Find examples of these strategies in various business publications.

[15]Anton Troianovski, "T-Mobile Finds a New Lifeline," *Wall Street Journal (Online)*, October 2, 2012.
[16]Shirley Leung, "Big Chains Talk the Talk, But Can't Walk the Wok," *Wall Street Journal*, January 23, 2003.

2

Demand, Supply, and Equilibrium Prices

n this chapter, we analyze demand and supply—probably the two most famous words in all of economics. *Demand*—the functional relationship between the price of a good or service and the quantity demanded by consumers in a given period of time, all else held constant—and *supply*—the functional relationship between the price of a good or service and the quantity supplied by producers in a given period of time, all else held constant—provide a framework for analyzing the behavior of consumers and producers in a market economy. Managers need to understand these terms to develop their own competitive strategies and to respond to the actions of their competitors. They also need to understand that the role of demand and supply depends on the environment or market structure in which a firm operates.

We begin our discussion of demand and supply by focusing on an analysis of the copper industry from 1997/98 to 2011. In our case analysis, we'll discuss how factors related to consumer behavior (demand) and producer behavior (supply) determine the price of copper and cause changes in that price. In the remainder of the chapter, we'll look at how the factors from the copper industry fit into the general demand and supply framework of economic theory. We'll develop a conceptual analysis of demand functions and demand curves; discuss the range of factors that influence consumer demand; analyze how demand can be described verbally, graphically, and symbolically using equations; and look at a specific mathematical example of demand. We'll then describe the supply side of the market and the factors influencing supply in the same manner. Finally, we'll discuss how demand- and supply-side factors determine prices and cause them to change.

Case for Analysis

Demand and Supply in the Copper Industry

The copper industry illustrates all the factors on the demand and supply side of a competitive market that we discuss in this chapter. Shifts in these factors can cause current and expected future prices of copper to change rapidly. In addition, the copper industry serves as a signal for the status of the global economy. Because copper is used in so many industries around the world, the metal has been given the name "Dr. Copper," since a strong demand and high prices for it can indicate that the overall economy is healthy.[1]

In February 2011, copper prices reached an all-time high of $4.62 per pound, having almost quadrupled after a two-year series of increases. At that time there was a fear that this rally in prices had stopped, given speculation about events in China. Previously, traders and industry observers had thought that China had an insatiable demand for the metal. However, rising interest rates in China could have forced speculators to sell copper to reduce their financing costs, while consumers kept their inventories low to save capital. At this time previously unreported stockpiles of copper were also discovered in China, many of which were in bonded warehouses where traders stored goods before moving them in or out of the country. Analysts observed that these supplies could easily have been moved into the market.[2]

In April 2011, copper analysts worried about further decreases in prices. The worldwide economic downturn had caused demand to decrease in key markets, such as housing and construction. Copper consumers had reacted to previous high prices by seeking cheaper alternative substitute materials, such as aluminum and plastic.[3] In June 2011, analysts reported that copper prices surged to the highest level in two weeks due to the reporting of better-than-expected Chinese industrial production data. Unfavorable U.S. economic data and concern over Chinese inflation had caused prices to decrease, but the industrial output report indicated that demand could increase again.[4] However, later that month concerns over economic conditions in Europe, an important consumer of copper for plumbing and electrical wiring, put further downward pressure on prices.[5]

During the summer of 2011, copper prices increased in response to a U.S. Department of Labor report that new claims

for unemployment benefits fell for the first time in three weeks. The widespread use of the metal in construction and manufacturing meant that any changes in unemployment could impact copper prices. There was also concern on the supply side, given that recent severe winter weather in Chile and a potential strike at a large copper plant could disrupt production.[6]

The extreme volatility of the copper market was illustrated in September 2011. On September 27 the *Wall Street Journal* reported that copper prices rose sharply, given a report that the European Union might expand its support of the Euro zone's troubled banks and a Federal Reserve Bank of Chicago report showing increased manufacturing output in the Midwest region of the United States.[7] However, one day later it was reported that price declines had erased the previous market increase of more than 5 percent as investors continued to worry about the European financial crisis and whether previously anticipated strong imports into China might not occur.[8]

Unforeseen events have also influenced the copper market. Copper prices reached a seven-week high after a massive earthquake hit Chile in March 2010. There were concerns that supply from the world's largest copper producer would be impacted by the quake. Analysts attempted to determine as quickly as possible how much the country's infrastructure had been damaged.[9]

Similar factors affected the copper market in 2006 and 2007.[10] Analysts predicted a decrease in the supply of copper in 2007 after many strikes limited production in 2006. This decreased production along with strong worldwide demand caused the price of copper to remain at historic highs during that year. Much of this demand was stimulated by the economic growth in China. A lack of new mining projects also limited supply, given that many large, known copper deposits were in areas with unstable governments or were difficult to reach.[11] Another impact of the high prices was the increased theft of copper coils in air-conditioning units, copper wires, and copper pipes used for plumbing in homes and businesses

[1]Carolyn Cui and Tatyana Shumsky, "Dr. Copper Offers a Mixed Prognosis," *Wall Street Journal (Online)*, April 11, 2011.
[2]Cui and Shumsky, "Dr. Copper Offers a Mixed Prognosis."
[3]Andrea Hotter, "Lofty Copper Prices Remain at Risk," *Wall Street Journal (Online)*, April 28, 2011.
[4]Matt Day, "Copper Rises on China Industrial-Production Data," *Wall Street Journal (Online)*, June 14, 2011.
[5]Amy D'Onofrio, "Copper Falls on Uncertainty Over Global Economy," *Wall Street Journal (Online)*, June 20, 2011.

[6]Matt Day, "Copper Surges on Improved U.S. Labor Market View," *Wall Street Journal (Online)*, July 7, 2011.
[7]Matt Day, "Copper Continues Gains as Global Markets Rally," *Wall Street Journal (Online)*, September 27, 2011.
[8]Matt Day, "Copper Slides to a 13-Month Low on Worries About Demand," *Wall Street Journal (Online)*, September 28, 2011.
[9]Allen Sykora, "Copper Prices Rise Following Quake," *Wall Street Journal (Online)*, March 1, 2010.
[10]Allen Sykora, "Copper Surplus is Foreseen in '07," *Wall Street Journal*, February 28, 2007.
[11]Patrick Barta, "A Red-Hot Desire for Copper," *Wall Street Journal*, March 16, 2006.

in many parts of the United States.[12] Thefts, even of cemetery bronze vases containing large amounts of copper, continued with the relatively high prices of copper in subsequent years.[13]

Analysts predicted that increased quantities of copper would be available in 2007 due to several factors. (1) The strikes that occurred in 2006 were not expected to continue the next year. (2) The higher copper prices encouraged companies to mine lower-grade copper that would not have been economically feasible with lower prices. However, the high copper prices also gave many copper users the incentive to find substitutes for the metal. Aluminum producers benefited from the high copper prices, and these prices stimulated the increased use of plastic piping in home construction.

Forecasts of future prices and production can be very uncertain, given the variety of factors operating on both the demand and supply side of the market. One report estimated a surplus of 108,000 metric tons for the first 11 months of 2006, while another estimated a surplus of 40,000 metric tons for the entire year. The extent of substitution with other products was also difficult to estimate, as was the substitution with scrap metal.[14] Moreover, in February 2007, the first impacts of the slowing housing market on the U.S. economy were just beginning to appear. This is another example of changes in the macroeconomy impacting this industry, leading to the name "Dr. Copper."

Copper prices continued to be influenced by the demand from China. This demand slowed in 2008 as the Chinese drew down their inventories when global prices were high and shut down some industrial activity preceding the Olympics in August 2008. The slowing Chinese economy in fall 2008 also impacted the world copper market where prices continued to fall.[15]

An analysis of a substantial decline in copper prices 10 years earlier from November 1997 to February 1998 illustrated many of these same factors.[16] The 1997 financial crisis and recession in Southeast Asia had a significant impact on the copper industry, as did uncertain demand from China and the increased use of copper in communications technology in North America. Expectations also played a role as many copper users were hesitant to buy because they thought prices might continue their downward trend.

On the supply side, the low price of copper forced mining companies to decide whether certain high-cost mines should be kept in operation. However, a new mining process called "solvent extraction" also allowed some companies to mine copper at a lower cost, which permitted more copper mines to stay in business.

We can see from this discussion that a variety of factors influence the price of copper and that these factors can be categorized as operating either on the demand (consumer) side or the supply (producer) side of the market. Sometimes the influence of one factor in lowering prices is partially or completely offset by the impacts of other factors that tend to increase prices. Thus, the resulting copper prices will be determined by the magnitude of the changes in all of these variables.

Note also that the case discusses *general* influences on the copper industry. There is no discussion of the strategic behavior of individual firms. This focus on the entire industry is a characteristic of a perfectly or highly competitive market, where there are many buyers and sellers and the product is relatively homogeneous or undifferentiated. Prices are determined through the overall forces of demand and supply in these markets. All firms, no matter where they are located on the market structure continuum, face a demand from consumers for their products. The factors influencing demand, which are discussed in this chapter, thus pertain to firms operating in every type of market. However, the demand/supply framework and the resulting determination of equilibrium prices apply only to perfectly or highly competitive markets. We'll now examine the concepts of demand and supply in more detail to see how managers can use this framework to analyze changes in prices and quantities of different products in various markets.

[12]Sara Schaefer Munoz and Paul Glader, "Copper and Robbers: Homeowners' Latest Worry," *Wall Street Journal*, September 6, 2006.

[13]Joe Barrett, "Sky-High Metal Prices Lead to a Grave Situation," *Wall Street Journal (Online)*, November 22, 2011.

[14]Sykora, "Copper Surplus is Foreseen in '07."

[15]Allen Sykora, "China Copper Need Set to Rise," *Wall Street Journal*, August 25, 2008; James Campbell and Matthew Walls, "China Drags Down Metals: Slump in Real Estate: Export Industries May Keep Lid on Oil Prices, *Wall Street Journal*, October 29, 2008; Allen Sykora, "Copper Is Vulnerable to Falling Further," *Wall Street Journal*, November 24, 2008.

[16]Aaron Lucchetti, "Copper Limbo: Just How Low Can It Go?" *Wall Street Journal*, February 23, 1998.

Demand

Although demand and supply are used in everyday language, these concepts have very precise meanings in economics.[17] It is important that you understand the difference between the economic terms and ordinary usage. We'll look at demand first and turn our attention to supply later in the chapter.

[17]Even basic terms such as **demand** may be defined differently in various business disciplines. For example, in *Marketing Management, The Millennium Edition* (Prentice Hall, 2000), Philip Kotler defines **market demand** as "the total volume that would be bought by a defined customer group in a defined geographical area in a defined time period in a defined marketing environment under a defined marketing program" (p. 120). Since advertising and marketing expenditures are the focus of this discipline, demand is defined to emphasize these issues rather than price.

Demand is defined in economics as a functional relationship between the price of a good or service and the quantity demanded by consumers in a given period of time, *all else held constant.* (The Latin phrase *ceteris paribus* is often used in place of "all else held constant.") A **functional relationship** means that demand focuses not just on the current price of the good and the quantity demanded at that price, but also on the relationship between different prices and the quantities that would be demanded at those prices. Demand incorporates a consumer's willingness *and* ability to purchase a product.

Nonprice Factors Influencing Demand

The demand relationship is defined with "all else held constant" because many other variables in addition to price influence the quantity of a product that consumers demand. The following sections summarize these variables, many of which were discussed in the opening case on the copper industry.

Tastes and Preferences   Consumers must first desire or have tastes and preferences for a good. For example, in the aftermath of the September 11, 2001, terrorist attacks on New York and Washington, D.C., the tastes and preferences of U.S. consumers for airline travel changed dramatically. People were simply afraid to fly and did not purchase airline tickets regardless of the price charged. In October 2001, most of the major airlines began advertising campaigns to increase consumer confidence in the safety of air travel. United Airlines' advertisements featured firsthand employee accounts, while American Airlines encouraged people to spend time with family and friends over the upcoming holidays and beyond.[18]

Changing attitudes toward cigarette smoking have had a major impact on Zippo Manufacturing Co., which produced "windproof" cigarette lighters for 78 years. Annual lighter sales decreased from 18 million in 1998 to 12 million in 2010. The company tried to influence consumer behavior with new lighter designs, including those with images of Elvis Presley and the Playboy logo. However, the company also developed new products including a men's fragrance, casual clothing, watches, and camping supplies as a response to these changes in preferences.[19]

The U.S. pecan industry has been impacted by changing Chinese preferences for these nuts. China bought one-quarter of the U.S. crop in 2009, whereas the country had little demand five years earlier. A belief that eating pecans would help ward off Alzheimer's disease and influence the brain development of babies helped generate this demand.[20]

The Japanese earthquake in March 2011 influenced the demand for luxury goods in that country. Although Japanese consumers traditionally were willing to pay some of the world's highest prices for fashion and other luxury goods, surveys following the quake showed that many consumers believed that showing off luxury goods was in bad taste. Sales of expensive fashion items and accessories in Japan were second only to that in the United States before the quake.[21]

Socioeconomic variables such as age, gender, race, marital status, and level of education are often good proxies for an individual's tastes and preferences for a particular good, because tastes and preferences may vary by these groupings and products are often targeted at one or more of these groups. Beer brewers have targeted Hispanics who will account for 23 percent of the nation's legal-drinking-age

Demand
The functional relationship between the price of a good or service and the quantity demanded by consumers in a given time period, *all else held constant.*

Functional relationship
A relationship between variables, usually expressed in an equation using symbols for the variables, where the value of one variable, the independent variable, determines the value of the other, the dependent variable.

---

[18]Melanie Trottman, "Airlines Launch New Ad Campaigns Using Emotion to Restore Confidence," *Wall Street Journal*, October 24, 2001.
[19]James R. Hagerty, "Zippo Preps for a Post-Smoker World," *Wall Street Journal (Online)*, March 8, 2011.
[20]David Wessel, "Shell Shock: Chinese Demand Reshapes U.S. Pecan Business," *Wall Street Journal (Online)*, April 18, 2011.
[21]Mariko Sanchanta, "Japan Grows Leery of Luxury," *Wall Street Journal (Online)*, May 27, 2011.

population in 2030, particularly given the decline in overall sales due to high unemployment among men ages 21–34. Corona developed Spanish- and English-language advertisements focusing on luxurious beach settings to convey the brand's premium status. It also developed a 32-ounce bottled version of the beer designed for family gatherings that was targeted on states with large Hispanic populations, such as Arizona and California. MillerCoors began a campaign to promote its products to Mexican soccer fans.[22]

Similarly, Procter & Gamble Co. retargeted its marketing, changed its mix of celebrity spokeswomen, and increased the amount of Spanish on its products. This was part of its competitive strategy particularly in the U.S. toothpaste market where Colgate-Palmolive Co. built a dominant position based on its strength in Latin American markets. Procter & Gamble found that Hispanic customers were more likely to use fragrances in their homes than other sociodemographic groups. Hispanic households spent more on cleaning and beauty products and were more loyal to their brands than the average U.S. customer. Procter & Gamble also used actress Eva Mendes and singer-actress Jennifer Lopez as spokeswomen to promote its products in the Hispanic community.[23]

Economic theory may also suggest that one or more of these socioeconomic variables influences the demand for a particular good or service. For example, persons with more education are believed to be more knowledgeable about using preventive services to improve their health. Marital status may influence the demand for acute care and hospital services because married individuals have spouses who may be able to help take care of them in the home.[24] Thus, tastes and preferences encompass all the individualistic variables that influence a person's willingness to purchase a good.

Income   The level of a person's income also affects demand, because demand incorporates both willingness and ability to pay for the good. If the demand for a good varies directly with income, that good is called a **normal good**. This definition means that, all else held constant, an increase in an individual's income will increase the demand for a normal good, and a decrease in that income will decrease the demand for that good. If the demand varies inversely with income, the good is termed an **inferior good**. Thus, an increase in income will cause a consumer to purchase less of an inferior good, while a decrease in that income will actually cause the consumer to demand more of the inferior good. Note that the term *inferior* has nothing to do with the quality of the good—it refers only to how purchases of the good or service vary with changes in income.

Normal Goods   In many cases, the effect of income on particular goods and services is related to the general level of economic activity in the economy. Although jewelers used the transition from the year 1999 to 2000 to influence consumer tastes and preferences for jewelry, the strong economy and the booming stock market in 1999 also played a role in influencing demand.[25] On the other hand, the loss of both jobs and stock market wealth in fall 2008 caused retail spending to decline below already-weak forecasts.[26] This frugality continued throughout the recession and the slow recovery in the subsequent years. Wal-Mart noted an increase in paycheck-cycle shopping where consumers stocked up on products soon after getting

Normal good
A good for which consumers will have a greater demand as their incomes increase, all else held constant, and a smaller demand if their incomes decrease, other factors held constant.

Inferior good
A good for which consumers will have a smaller demand as their incomes increase, all else held constant, and a greater demand if their incomes decrease, other factors held constant.

---

[22]David Kesmodel, "Brewers Go Courting Hispanics," *Wall Street Journal (Online)*, July 12, 2011.
[23]Ellen Bryon, "Hola: P&G Seeks Latino Shoppers," *Wall Street Journal (Online)*, September 15, 2011.
[24]The demand for health and medical services is discussed in Donald S. Kenkel, "The Demand for Preventive Medical Care," *Applied Economics* 26 (April 1994): 313–25; and in Rexford E. Santerre and Stephen P. Neun, *Health Economics: Theories, Insights, and Industry Studies*, 4th ed. (Mason, OH: Thomson South-Western, 2007).
[25]Rebecca Quick, "Jewelry Retailers Have Gem of a Holiday Season," *Wall Street Journal*, January 7, 2000.
[26]Ann Zimmerman, "Retailers Wallow and See Only More Gloom," *Wall Street Journal*, November 7, 2008.

paid and moved toward smaller product sizes toward the end of the month when their cash ran low. Wal-Mart customers also demanded a return of a Depression-era strategy, layaway, which the company had cancelled in 2005. Target, which attracts more affluent customers than Wal-Mart, found that its sales rebounded more quickly to prerecession patterns than did Wal-Mart.[27]

Both increases in income and changes in tastes and preferences have resulted in an increased demand for gourmet pet food, especially for dogs. The head of Del Monte's food and pet division said in 2006 that "the humanization of pets is the single biggest trend driving our business."[28] Changes in tastes in human food spill over into the pet food market. However, the demand for gourmet pet food was also driven by the change in pet ownership from parents of small children, who had neither the time nor money to spend lavishly on their pets, to childless people ranging from gay couples to parents whose children have left home. These couples have larger incomes and treat their pets as they would their children.

Inferior Goods   Firms producing inferior goods do not benefit from a booming economy. One such example is the pawnshop industry, which suffered during the economic prosperity of the late 1990s and 2000, as fewer people swapped jewelry and other items for cash to cover car payments and other debts.[29] Although pawnshops have always suffered from a somewhat disreputable image, the strong economy provided an income effect that further hurt the business and caused many chains to incur large losses.

Dollar stores' sales increased during the 2007 recession and moderated only somewhat during the slow recovery. These stores experienced increases in the number of customers who traded down out of economic necessity and who could have gone elsewhere but were still exercising frugality.[30] Payday lenders also increased their business during the recession. Although these companies often charged interest rates of more than 500 percent on their loans, they developed strategies to lure customers away from traditional banks by appealing to people with substandard credit records. The 22 payday loan offices in West Palm Beach, Florida made $328.9 million in loans in fiscal year 2010, an increase of 119 percent from fiscal year 2008.[31]

In the health care area, it is argued that tooth extractions are an example of an inferior good. As individuals' incomes rise, they are able to afford more complex and expensive dental restorative procedures, such as caps and crowns, and they are able to purchase more regular preventive dental services. Thus, the need for extractions decreases as income increases.[32]

Prices of Related Goods   There are two major categories of goods or products whose prices influence the demand for a particular good: substitute goods and complementary goods.

Substitute Goods   Products or services are **substitute goods** for each other if one can be used in place of another. Consumers derive satisfaction from either good or service. If two goods, X and Y, are substitutes for each other, an increase in the price of good Y will cause consumers to decrease their consumption of

Substitute goods
Two goods, X and Y, are substitutes if an increase in the price of good Y causes consumers to *increase* their demand for good X or if a decrease in the price of good Y causes consumers to *decrease* their demand for good X.

---

[27]Ann Zimmerman, "Frontier of Frugality," *Wall Street Journal (Online)*, October 4, 2011.

[28]Deborah Ball, "Nothing Says, 'I Love You, Fido' Like Food with Gourmet Flair," *Wall Street Journal*, March 18, 2006.

[29]Kortney Stringer, "Best of Times Is Worst of Times for Pawnshops in New Economy," *Wall Street Journal*, August 22, 2000.

[30]Zimmerman, "Frontier of Frugality."

[31]Jessica Silver-Greenberg, "Payday Lenders go Hunting: Operations Encroach on Banks during Loan Crunch; 'Here, I Feel Respected,' " *Wall Street Journal (Online)*, December 23, 2010.

[32]Rexford E. Santerre and Stephen P. Neun, *Health Economics: Theories, Insights, and Industry Studies*, rev. ed. (Orlando, FL: Dryden, 2000), 90.

good Y and increase their demand for good X. If the price of good Y decreases, the demand for substitute good X will decrease. Thus, changes in the price of good Y and the demand for good X move in the same direction for substitute goods. The amount of substitution depends on the consumer's tastes and preferences for the two goods and the size of the price change.

By 2006 the abundance and relatively low prices of cell phones, iPods, and laptop computers resulted in many teens and young adults no longer purchasing wristwatches. In 2005, sales of watches priced between $30 and $150, the type most often purchased by these age groups, declined more than 10 percent from 2004.[33] In response to this threat from substitute products, watchmakers developed new models that do much more than tell time, including watches with earbuds that play digital music files, watches with programmable channels, and models with compasses and thermometers.

In 2007, large increases in the price of platinum resulted in an increased demand for palladium, a lesser-known platinum-group metal. The price of an ounce of platinum was approximately $1,190 compared with $337 for an ounce of palladium. Because the two metals have a similar look and feel, many jewelers offered palladium to customers as a less expensive alternative, particularly for wedding and engagement rings. World demand for palladium in jewelry was 1.12 million ounces in 2006 compared with 1.74 million ounces for platinum.[34]

There are many substitutes for a given brand of bottled water, including both other types of drinks and other brands of water. Customers bought less of Nestle's bottled water during the 2007 recession, due to both the loss of income and the switch to the large number of cheaper private-label brands launched by supermarkets. Nestle responded by pushing Pure Life, a lower-priced water derived from purified municipal sources.[35]

Complementary goods

Two goods, *X* and *Y*, are complementary if an increase in the price of good *Y* causes consumers to *decrease* their demand for good *X* or if a decrease in the price of good *Y* causes consumers to *increase* their demand for good *X*.

Complementary Goods **Complementary goods** are products or services that consumers use together. If products X and Y are complements, an increase in the price of good Y will cause consumers to decrease their consumption of good Y and their demand for good X, since X and Y are used together. Likewise, if the price of good Y decreases, the demand for good X will increase. Changes in the price of good Y and the demand for good X move in the opposite direction if X and Y are complementary goods.

As prices of personal computers have dropped over time, there has been an increased demand for printers and printer cartridges. This complementary relationship has allowed Hewlett-Packard Company to actually sell its printers at a loss that it recouped through its new ink and toner sales. Analysts estimated that in 2005 the company earned at least a 60 percent profit margin on both ink and toner cartridges and two-thirds of the company's profits were derived from these sales. In 2006, Walgreen Company, the drugstore chain, announced plans for an ink-refill service in 1,500 of its stores with a price at less than half the cost of buying new cartridges.[36] OfficeMax and Office Depot also offered these services. This example shows how a complementary relationship between two goods can create a profit opportunity for a firm, which then may still be competed away by the development of substitute goods.

Future Expectations Expectations about future prices also play a role in influencing current demand for a product. If consumers expect prices to be lower in the future, they may have less current demand than if they did not have those

---

[33]Jessica E. Vascellaro, "The Times They Are a-Changin'," *Wall Street Journal*, January 18, 2006.
[34]Elizabeth Holmes, "Palladium, Platinum's Cheaper Sister, Makes a Bid for Love," *Wall Street Journal*, February 13, 2007.
[35]Deborah Ball, "Bottled Water Pits Nestle vs. Greens," *Wall Street Journal (Online)*, May 25, 2010.
[36]Pui-Wing Tam, "A Cheaper Way to Refill Your Printer," *Wall Street Journal*, January 26, 2006.

expectations. In 2011, steel prices fell due to decreased demand arising from unrest in the Middle East, the impact of Japan's earthquake and tsunami, and relatively high supply. Yet some buyers, including Moscow-based Central Steel Co., held off on further purchases, given an expectation that prices would drop another 2–5 percent in the following weeks. A U.K.-based steel consulting firm noted that many Western European customers with adequate stockpiles were also waiting on the sidelines for future price decreases.[37]

Likewise, if prices are expected to increase, consumers may demand more of the good at present than they would without these expectations. In fall 2007, world grain prices were surging from major demand increases stimulated by U.S. government incentives encouraging businesses to turn corn and soybeans into motor fuel, increased incomes from the growing economies of Asia and Latin America, and a growing middle class in these areas that was eating more meat and milk, increasing the demand for grain to feed the livestock. Even though U.S. corn farmers expected a record harvest, which should have had a moderating effect on grain prices, traders in the futures markets for corn were already betting that the price of corn would increase from $3.25 per bushel to more than $4.00 in March 2008 and would stay above that level until 2010.[38]

Number of Consumers   Finally, the number of consumers in the marketplace influences the demand for a product. A firm's marketing strategy is typically based on finding new groups of consumers who will purchase the product. In many cases, a country's exports may be the source of this increased demand. Although the U.S. timber industry continued to be depressed in 2011 from the weakness in the U.S. housing market, exports to China surged, particularly from mills in the Pacific Northwest. Russia increased tariffs on its exports to China in 2007, so Chinese buyers turned to the United States and Canada to satisfy the demand arising from that country's construction boom. The number of U.S. logs shipped to China increased more than 10 times between 2007 and 2010.[39]

The effect of growing populations on demand and grain prices was discussed above in the "Future Expectations" section of the chapter. Both increases in the size of the population in Asian and Latin American economies and growth in the middle-class segments of these economies had a stimulating effect on the demand for many types of grain.

Demand Function

We can now summarize all the variables that influence the demand for a particular product in a generalized demand function represented as follows:

$$2.1 \quad Q_{XD} = f(P_X, T, I, P_Y, P_Z, EXC, NC, \ldots)$$

where

Q_{XD} = quantity demanded of good X

P_X = price of good X

T = variables representing an individual's tastes and preferences

I = income

P_Y, P_Z = prices of goods Y and Z, which are related to the consumption of good X

EXC = consumer expectations about future prices

NC = number of consumers

---

[37]Robert Guy Matthews, "Steel Price Softens as Supply Solidifies," *Wall Street Journal (Online)*, April 10, 2011.
[38]Scott Kilman, "Historic Surge in Grain Prices Roils Market," *Wall Street Journal*, September 28, 2007.
[39]Jim Carlton, "Chinese Demand Lifts U.S. Wood Sales," *Wall Street Journal (Online)*, February 8, 2011.

Equation 2.1 is read as follows: The quantity demanded of good X is a function (f) of the variables inside the parentheses. An ellipsis is placed after the last variable to signify that many other variables may also influence the demand for a specific product. These may include variables under the control of a manager, such as the size of the advertising budget, and variables not under anyone's control, such as the weather.

Each consumer has his or her own **individual demand function** for different products. However, managers are usually more interested in the **market demand function**, which shows the quantity demanded of the good or service by *all* consumers in the market at any given price. The market demand function is influenced by the prices of related goods, as well as by the tastes and preferences, income, and future expectations of all consumers in the market. It can also change because more consumers enter the market.

Demand Curves

Equation 2.1 shows the typical variables included in a demand function. To systematically analyze all of these variables, economists define demand as we did earlier in this chapter: the functional relationship between alternative prices and the quantities consumers demand at those prices, all else held constant. This relationship is portrayed graphically in Figure 2.1, which shows a **demand curve** for a given product. Price (P), measured in dollar terms, is the variable that is explicitly analyzed and shown on the vertical axis of the graph. Quantity demanded (Q) is shown on the horizontal axis. The other variables in the demand function are held constant with a given demand curve, but act as **demand shifters** if their values change.

As we just mentioned, demand curves are drawn with the price placed on the vertical axis and the quantity demanded on the horizontal axis. This may seem inconsistent because we usually think of the quantity demanded of a good (dependent variable) as a function of the price of the good (independent variable). The dependent variable in a mathematical relationship is usually placed on the vertical axis and the independent variable on the horizontal axis. The reverse is done for demand because we also want to show how revenues and costs vary with the level of output. These variables are placed on the vertical axis in subsequent analysis. In mathematical terms, an equation showing quantity as a function of price is equivalent to the inverse equation showing price as a function of quantity.

Demand curves are generally downward sloping, showing a **negative or inverse relationship** between the price of a good and the quantity demanded at that price, all else held constant. Thus, in Figure 2.1, when the price falls from P_1 to P_2, the quantity demanded is expected to increase from Q_1 to Q_2, if nothing else changes. This is represented by the movement from point A to point B in Figure 2.1. Likewise, an increase in the price of the good results in a decrease in quantity demanded, all else held constant. Most demand curves that show real-world behavior exhibit this

Individual demand function
The function that shows, in symbolic or mathematical terms, the variables that influence the quantity demanded of a particular product by an individual consumer.

Market demand function
The function that shows, in symbolic or mathematical terms, the variables that influence the quantity demanded of a particular product by all consumers in the market and that is thus affected by the number of consumers in the market.

Demand curve
The graphical relationship between the price of a good and the quantity consumers demand, with all other factors influencing demand held constant.

Demand shifters
The variables in a demand function that are held constant when defining a given demand curve, but that would shift the demand curve if their values changed.

Negative (inverse) relationship
A relationship between two variables, graphed as a downward sloping line, where an increase in the value of one variable causes a decrease in the value of the other variable.

FIGURE 2.1
The Demand Curve for a Product
A demand curve shows the relationship between the price of a good and the quantity demanded, all else held constant.

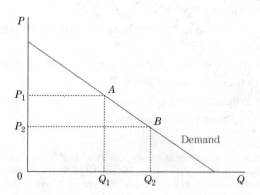

inverse relationship between price and quantity demanded. (We'll later discuss the economic model of consumer behavior that lies behind this demand relationship.) (Chapter 3 appendix.)

Change in Quantity Demanded and Change in Demand

The movement between points *A* and *B* along the demand curve in Figure 2.1 is called a **change in quantity demanded**. It results when consumers react to a change in the price of the good, all other factors held constant. This change in quantity demanded is pictured as a movement along a given demand curve.

It is also possible for the entire demand curve to shift. This shift results when the values of one or more of the other variables in Equation 2.1 change. For example, if consumers' incomes increase, the demand curve for the particular good generally shifts outward or to the right, assuming that the good is a normal good. This shift of the entire demand curve is called a **change in demand**. It occurs when one or more of the variables held constant in defining a given demand curve changes.

This distinction between a change in demand and a change in quantity demanded is very important in economic analysis. The two phrases mean something different and should not be used interchangeably. The distinction arises from the basic economic framework, in which we examine the relationship between two variables while holding all other factors constant.

An increase in demand, or a rightward or outward shift of the demand curve, is shown in Figure 2.2. We've drawn this shift as a parallel shift of the demand curve, although this doesn't have to be the case. Suppose this change in demand results from an increase in consumers' incomes. The important point in Figure 2.2 is that an increase in demand means that consumers will demand a larger quantity of the good *at the same price*—in this case, due to higher incomes. This outcome is contrasted with a movement along a demand curve or a change in quantity demanded, where a larger quantity of the good is demanded *only at a lower price*. This distinction can help you differentiate between the two cases.

Changes in any of the variables in a demand function, *other than the price of the product*, will cause a shift of the demand curve in one direction or the other. Thus, the relationship between quantity demanded and the first variable on the right side of Equation 2.1 (price) determines the slope of the curve (downward sloping), while the other right-hand variables cause the curve to shift. In Figure 2.2, we assumed that the good was a normal good so that an increase in income would result in an increase in demand, or a rightward shift of the demand curve. If the good was an inferior good, this increase in income would result in a decrease in demand, or a leftward shift of the curve. An increase in the price of a substitute good would cause the demand curve for the good in question to shift rightward, while an increase in the price of a complementary good would cause a leftward

Change in quantity demanded
The change in quantity consumers purchase when the price of the good changes, all other factors held constant, pictured as a movement along a given demand curve.

Change in demand
The change in quantity purchased when one or more of the demand shifters change, pictured as a shift of the entire demand curve.

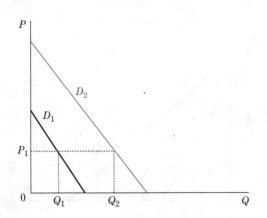

FIGURE 2.2
Change (Increase) in Demand
A change in demand occurs when one or more of the factors held constant in defining a given demand curve changes.

shift of the demand curve. A change in consumer expectations could also cause the curve to shift in either direction, depending on whether a price increase or decrease was expected. If future prices were expected to rise, the current demand curve would shift outward or to the right. The opposite would happen if future prices were expected to decrease. An increase in the number of consumers in the market would cause the demand curve to shift to the right, while the opposite would happen for a decrease in the number of consumers.

Individual Versus Market Demand Curves

The shift in the market demand curve as more individuals enter the market is illustrated in Figure 2.3, which shows how a market demand curve is derived from individual demand curves. In this figure, demand curve D_A represents the demand for individual A. If individual A is the only person in the market, this demand curve is also the market demand curve. However, if individual B enters the market with demand curve D_B, then we have to construct a new market demand curve. As shown in Figure 2.3, individual B has a larger demand for the product than individual A. The demand curve for B lies to the right of the demand curve for A, indicating that individual B will demand a larger quantity of the product at every price level.

Horizontal summation of individual demand curves
The process of deriving a market demand curve by adding the quantity demanded by each individual at every price to determine the market demand at every price.

To derive the market demand curve for both individuals, we do a **horizontal summation of individual demand curves**. This means that for every price we add the quantity that each person demands at that price to determine the market quantity demanded at that price. At prices above P_1, only individual B is in the market, so demand curve B is the market demand curve in that price range. Below price P_1, we need to add together the quantities that each individual demands. For example, at a zero price, individual A demands quantity Q_2, and individual B demands quantity Q_3, so the quantity demanded by the market (both individuals) at the zero price is Q_4, which equals Q_2 plus Q_3. The market demand curve, D_M, is derived in the same manner by adding the quantities demanded at other prices.

Based on the information in Figure 2.3, we can infer that if another individual, C, came into the market, the market demand curve would shift further to the right. Thus, a market demand curve can shift as individuals enter or leave a market.

Linear Demand Functions and Curves

Linear demand function
A mathematical demand function graphed as a straight-line demand curve in which all the terms are either added or subtracted and no terms have exponents other than 1.

The demand curves in Figures 2.1, 2.2, and 2.3 have been drawn as straight lines, representing a **linear demand function**. A linear demand function is a specific mathematical relationship of the generalized demand function (Equation 2.1) in which all terms are either added or subtracted and there are no exponents in any terms that take a value other than 1. The graph of a linear demand function has a constant slope. This linear relationship is used both because it simplifies the analysis and

FIGURE 2.3
Individual Versus Market Demand Curve
A market demand curve is derived from the horizontal summation of individual demand curves; that is, for every price, add the quantity each individual demands at that price to determine the market quantity demanded at that price.

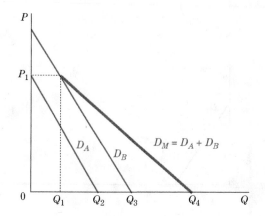

because many economists believe that this form of demand function best represents individuals' behavior, at least within a given range of prices. However, not all demand functions are linear. We will later discuss the implications of a particular type of demand function for consumer behavior in greater detail (Chapter 3).

Mathematical Example of a Demand Function

Although we have been discussing demand functions and demand curves in verbal, symbolic, and graphical terms, these relationships can also be expressed as a mathematical equation. In this section, we begin a hypothetical numerical example based on the copper industry articles that we have used throughout the chapter. For simplicity, we assume that our demand and supply functions are both linear.

Suppose that the demand function for copper at the beginning of 2010 is represented by Equation 2.2:

$$2.2 \quad Q_D = 3 - 2P_c + 0.2I + 1.6TC + 0.04E$$

where

Q_D = quantity demanded of copper (millions of pounds)

P_C = price of copper ($ per pound)

I = consumer income index

TC = telecom index showing uses or tastes for copper in the telecommunications industry

E = expectations index representing purchasers' expectations of a lower price over the following six months

We assume here that the quantity demanded of copper is a function only of P_C, the price of copper; I, consumer income; TC, the telecom index; and E, the expectations index. An economist or market analyst would develop this model of demand and derive the actual values of the constant term and coefficients of the variables in Equation 2.2 from real-world data using various empirical methods (Chapter 4).

The negative coefficient on the P_C variable shows the inverse relationship between price and quantity demanded of copper. If the price of copper increases, the quantity demanded decreases. This represents a typical downward sloping demand curve. We can see from this demand function that copper is a normal good because the income variable, I, in Equation 2.2 has a positive coefficient. Increases in income result in increases in the demand for copper. The positive coefficient on the TC variable means that as improved technology and higher demand for telecom services in North America and Europe create more uses for copper in the telecommunications industry, the overall demand for copper increases. The expectations index, E, represents consumers' expectations of a lower price over the following six months, where a lower index number implies that more purchasers expect a lower price. This expectation decreases the current demand for copper. Equation 2.2 is a mathematical representation of the conceptual relationships developed earlier in the chapter.

To define a specific demand curve for copper, we need to hold constant the level of consumer income, the telecom index, and the expectations index. Suppose that $I = 20$, $TC = 2.5$, and $E = 100$. Substituting 20 for I, 2.5 for TC, and 100 for E in Equation 2.2 gives us Equation 2.3:

$$2.3 \quad Q_D = 3 - 2P_C + 0.2(20) + 1.6(2.5) + 0.04(100)$$

or

$$Q_D = 15 - 2P_C \text{ or } [P_C = 7.5 - 0.5Q_D]$$

We can clearly see the meaning of the expression *all else held constant* in Equation 2.3. In that equation, the effects of consumer income, the telecom index, and the expectations index are embodied in the constant term 15. If we change the values of any of these three variables, the constant term in Equation 2.3 changes, and we have a change in demand or a new demand equation that graphs into a different demand curve. A change in quantity demanded in Equation 2.3 is represented by substituting different values for the price of copper and calculating the resulting quantity demanded at those prices. Equation 2.3 also shows the inverse demand function, with price as a function of quantity. These equations are equivalent mathematically.

Managerial Rule of Thumb

Demand Considerations

Managers need to understand the factors that influence consumer demand for their products. Although product price is usually important, other factors may play a significant role. In developing a competitive strategy, managers need to determine which factors they can influence and how to handle the factors that are beyond their control. ■

Supply

Supply
The functional relationship between the price of a good or service and the quantity supplied by producers in a given time period, *all else held constant.*

We now examine producer decisions to supply various goods and services and the factors influencing those decisions. **Supply** is the functional relationship between the price of a good or service and the quantity that producers are willing and able to supply in a given time period, *all else held constant.*

Nonprice Factors Influencing Supply

Although supply focuses on the influence of price on the quantity of a good or service supplied, many other factors influence producer supply decisions. These factors generally relate to the cost of production.

State of Technology   The state of technology, or the body of knowledge about how to combine the inputs of production, affects what output producers will supply because technology influences how the good or service is actually produced, which, in turn, affects the costs of production. For example, the discussion of the copper industry noted that a change in mining technology allowed companies to produce copper at a lower cost, keeping more of them in business. This change in technology contributed to a decrease in mining costs of 30 percent between the 1980s and the 1990s.[40]

In the nickel industry, most of the world's production has come from deposits that were relatively easy to exploit. However, these deposits comprise only about 40 percent or less of the world's remaining reserves. During the 1990s companies tried to develop a process called "high pressure acid leaching" to remove nickel from other rock deposits. The hope was that this new technology would open large new deposits of nickel. Although the initial equipment failed to stand up to the extreme heat and pressure of the process, more recent changes in the technology have increased its reliability and usefulness.[41]

Pecan growers were able to respond to the increased demand of the nut described earlier in the chapter, given the development of machines to shake the nuts from

---

[40]Lucchetti, "Copper Limbo: Just How Low Can It Go?"
[41]Patrick Barta, "With Easy Nickel Fading Fast, Miners Go After the Tough Stuff," *Wall Street Journal,* July 12, 2006.

the trees and sweep them off the ground. In the shelling plants, upgraded technology resulted in the use of machines to wash the nuts in hot water to kill bacteria, crack and separate the meat from the shells, separate halves from smaller pieces, skim out any worms, and roast, chop, and sort the pieces by size and color.[42]

Input Prices   Input prices are the prices of all the inputs or factors of production—labor, capital, land, and raw materials—used to produce the given product. These input prices affect the costs of production and, therefore, the prices at which producers are willing to supply different amounts of output. For broiler chickens, feed costs represent 70–75 percent of the costs of growing a chicken to a marketable size. Thus, changes in feed costs are so important that market analysts often use them as a proxy to forecast broiler prices and returns to broiler processors.[43]

Although the higher prices for pecans noted earlier in the chapter benefited growers, they represented increased costs for bakers and ice cream makers. Pecans are a key ingredient in fruitcakes, accounting for 27 percent of the weight in many varieties. Bakers worried that consumers would react to the higher prices of their products resulting from these increased costs of production.[44] One of the factors influencing the 2011 decrease in steel prices noted earlier in the chapter was falling prices for major raw ingredients in steel production. Prices for iron ore decreased 9.5 percent from February to March 2011.[45]

Prices of Goods Related in Production   The prices of other goods related in production can also affect the supply of a particular good. Two goods are substitutes in production if the same inputs can be used to produce either of the goods, such as land for different agricultural crops. Between 2005 and 2007, U.S. tobacco acreage increased 20 percent with tobacco being planted in areas such as southern Illinois that had not grown any substantial amount since the end of World War I. Even though corn prices were at near-record levels of $4.00 per bushel during this period, they were not high enough to compete with tobacco planting. Even with higher labor and other costs, one farmer in Illinois estimated that he netted $1,800 per acre from his 150 acres of tobacco compared with $250 per acre for corn and that planting tobacco had increased his annual income by 35 percent over the previous three years.[46]

Companies use the same type of rigs to drill for oil and natural gas. Therefore, they allocate equipment according to the price and profitability of each fuel. Given that the price of oil increased significantly between 2010 and 2011 from unrest in Northern Africa and the Middle East, the number of land rigs in the U.S. drilling for natural gas decreased 8 percent while oil rigs increased 81 percent. One major gas producer spent 90 percent of its $5 billion budget on oil drilling.[47]

There can also be complementary production relationships between commodities. As more oil and natural gas are produced, the supply of sulfur, which is removed from the products, also increases. Sixty-foot-high blocks of unwanted sulfur were reported in Alberta, Canada, and Kazakhstan in 2003.[48] Likewise, if the demand for and price of white-meat chicken increases, there will be an increase in the supply of dark-meat chicken.

[42]David Wessel, "Shell Shock: Chinese Demand Reshapes U.S. Pecan Business."
[43]Richard T. Rogers, "Broilers: Differentiating a Commodity," in *Industry Studies*, 2nd ed., ed. Larry L. Duetsch (Armonk, NY: Shapiro, 1998), 71.
[44]David Wessel, "Shell Shock: Chinese Demand Reshapes U.S. Pecan Business."
[45]Robert Guy Matthews, "Steel Price Softens as Supply Solidifies."
[46]Lauren Etter, "U.S. Farmers Rediscover the Allure of Tobacco," *Wall Street Journal*, September 18, 2007.
[47]Daniel Gilbert, "As Natural Gas Prices Fall, the Search Turns to Oil," *Wall Street Journal (Online)*, May 23, 2011.
[48]Alexei Barrionuevo, "A Chip off the Block Is Going to Smell Like Rotten Eggs," *Wall Street Journal*, November 4, 2003.

Future Expectations   Future expectations can play a role on the supply side of the market as well. If producers expect prices to increase in the future, they may supply less output now than without those expectations. The opposite could happen if producers expect prices to decrease in the future. These expectations could become self-fulfilling prophecies. Smaller current supplies in the first case could drive prices up, while larger current supplies in the second case could result in lower prices. Expectations may not always be correct. Given the high demand and lumber prices in summer 2004, lumber manufacturers expected that demand would start to drop as interest rates rose. When this did not happen, prices continued to climb.[49]

Number of Producers   Finally, the number of producers influences the total supply of a product at any given price. The number of producers may increase because of perceived profitability in a given industry or because of changes in laws or regulations such as trade barriers. For example, the lumber market was reported to be exceedingly strong in January 1999, largely due to demand from the booming U.S. housing market. However, quotas on the amount of wood that Canada could ship into the United States also played a role in keeping the price of lumber high in the United States in January of that year.[50]

Similarly, in November 2004, tariffs on 115 Chinese producers of wooden bedroom furniture were lowered from 12.9 to 8.6 percent. Because these companies accounted for 65 percent of the bedroom furniture imported to the United States from China, the resulting increased supply lowered prices for consumers and put more competitive pressure on U.S. furniture makers who had already closed dozens of factories in North Carolina and Virginia in the previous four years.[51]

In 2010, the Canadian lumber industry was revived by increased demand from China. Numerous producers reopened recently shuttered mills and called back workers to respond to the increased Chinese demand. Owners estimated that one new mill of Western Forest Products, Inc., which was about to start production, would send half of its output to China.[52]

Supply Function

A supply function for a product, which is defined in a manner similar to a demand function, is shown in Equation 2.4:

$$\text{2.4} \quad Q_{XS} = f(P_X, TX, P_I, P_A, P_B, EXP, NP, \dots)$$

where

Q_{XS} = quantity supplied of good X

P_X = price of good X

TX = state of technology

P_I = prices of the inputs of production

P_A, P_B = prices of goods A and B, which are related in production to good X

EXP = producer expectations about future prices

NP = number of producers

Equation 2.4 shows that the quantity supplied of good X depends on the price of good X, the other variables listed above, and possibly variables peculiar to the firm

[49]Avery Johnson, "Sticker Shock at the Lumberyard," *Wall Street Journal*, August 11, 2004.

[50]Terzah Ewing, "Lumber's Strength Defies Bearish Trend," *Wall Street Journal*, January 26, 1999.

[51]Dan Morse, "U.S. Cuts Tariffs on Imports of China's Bedroom Furniture," *Wall Street Journal*, November 10, 2004.

[52]Joel Millman, "Canada's Mills Lumber Back to Life, Fueled by Chinese," *Wall Street Journal (Online)*, November 2, 2010.

or industry that are not included in the list, as indicated by the ellipsis. As with the demand function, we can distinguish between an individual supply function and a market supply function. The **individual supply function** shows, in symbolic or mathematical terms, the variables that influence an individual producer's supply of a product. The **market supply function** shows the variables that influence the overall supply of a product by all producers and is thus affected by the number of producers in the market.

Supply Curves

We graph a **supply curve** in Figure 2.4, showing price (P) on the vertical axis and quantity supplied (Q) on the horizontal axis. For simplicity, all supply curves in this chapter will represent market supply functions. The supply curve in Figure 2.4 shows the relationship between price and quantity supplied, holding constant all the other variables influencing the supply decision (all variables beside P_X on the right side of Equation 2.4). Changes in these variables, the **supply shifters**, will cause the supply curve to shift.

As you can see in Figure 2.4, a supply curve generally slopes upward, indicating a **positive or direct relationship** between the price of the product and the quantity producers are willing to supply. A higher price typically gives producers an incentive to increase the quantity supplied of a particular product because higher production is more profitable. The supply curve in Figure 2.4 represents a **linear supply function** and is graphed as a straight line. Not all supply functions are linear, but we will use this type of function for simplicity. Keep in mind that a supply curve does not show the actual price of the product, only a functional relationship between alternative prices and the quantities that producers want to supply at those prices.

Change in Quantity Supplied and Change in Supply

Figure 2.4 shows a given supply curve defined with all other factors held constant. If the price increases from P_1 to P_2, the quantity supplied increases from Q_1 to Q_2. This movement from point A to point B represents a movement along the given supply curve, or a **change in quantity supplied**. Some factor has caused the price of the product to increase, and suppliers respond by increasing the quantity supplied. This supply response is by the existing suppliers, since the number of suppliers is held constant when defining any given supply curve.

Figure 2.5 shows a shift of the entire supply curve. This represents a **change in supply**, not a change in quantity supplied. The supply curve shifts from S_1 to S_2 because one or more of the factors from Equation 2.4 held constant in supply curve S_1 changes. The increase in supply, or the rightward shift of the supply curve in Figure 2.5, shows that producers are willing to supply a larger quantity of output at any given price. Thus, the quantity supplied at price P_1 increases from Q_1 to Q_2. This differs from the movement along a supply curve, or a change in quantity supplied, shown in Figure 2.4, where the increase in quantity supplied is associated

Individual supply function
The function that shows, in symbolic or mathematical terms, the variables that influence the quantity supplied of a particular product by an individual producer.

Market supply function
The function that shows, in symbolic or mathematical terms, the variables that influence the quantity supplied of a particular product by all producers in the market and that is thus affected by the number of producers in the market.

Supply curve
The graphical relationship between the price of a good and the quantity supplied, with all other factors influencing supply held constant.

Supply shifters
The other variables in a supply function that are held constant when defining a given supply curve, but that would cause that supply curve to shift if their values changed.

Positive (direct) relationship
A relationship between two variables, graphed as an upward sloping line, where an increase in the value of one variable causes an increase in the value of the other variable.

Linear supply function
A mathematical supply function, which graphs as a straight-line supply curve, in which all terms are either added or subtracted and no terms have exponents other than 1.

Change in quantity supplied
The change in amount of a good supplied when the price of the good changes, all other factors held constant, pictured as a movement along a given supply curve.

FIGURE 2.4
The Supply Curve for a Product
A supply curve shows the relationship between the price of a good and the quantity supplied, all else held constant.

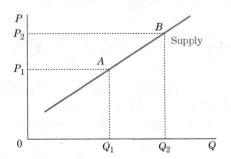

FIGURE 2.5

Change (Increase) in Supply

A change in supply occurs when one or more of the factors held constant in defining a given supply curve changes.

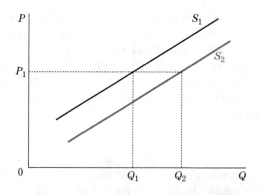

Change in supply

The change in the amount of a good supplied when one or more of the supply shifters change, pictured as a shift of the entire supply curve.

with a higher price for the product. This distinction between a change in quantity supplied and a change in supply is analogous to the distinction between a change in quantity demanded and a change in demand. We use the same framework—the relationship between two variables (price and quantity), all else held constant—on both the demand and the supply sides of the market.

Developing new technology typically causes an increase in supply, or a rightward shift of the supply curve, because technology changes usually lower the costs of production. The same result holds for a decrease in the price of any of the inputs of production, which lowers the costs of production and causes the supply curve to shift to the right. Any increase in the price of inputs increases the costs of production and causes the supply curve of the product to shift to the left.

The effect of a change in the price of a related good on the supply of a given good depends on whether the related good is a substitute or complement in production. An increase in the price of a substitute good causes the supply curve for the given good to shift to the left. A decrease in the price of a substitute good causes an increase in the supply of the given good. The opposite set of relationships holds for goods that are complements in production. If the price of the complementary good increases, the supply of the given good increases.

Producer expectations of lower prices cause the supply curve of a good to shift to the right. The supply increases in anticipation of lower prices in the future. The opposite holds if producers expect prices to increase. There would be a smaller current supply than without those expectations.

Finally, an increase in the number of producers results in a rightward shift of the supply curve, while a decrease results in a leftward shift of the supply curve. A given supply curve shows how prices induce the current number of producers to change the quantity supplied. Any change in the number of producers in the market is represented by a shift of the entire curve.

Mathematical Example of a Supply Function

To continue the mathematical example we began in the demand section, we assume that the supply function for copper is represented by Equation 2.5. (Note that real-world supply functions are empirically estimated from data in different firms and industries.)

$$2.5 \quad Q_S = -5 + 8P_C - 0.5W + 0.4T + 0.5N$$

where

Q_S = quantity supplied of copper (millions of pounds)

P_C = price of copper ($ per pound)

W = an index of wage rates in the copper industry

T = technology index

N = number of active mines in the copper industry

In Equation 2.5, we assume that the quantity supplied of copper is a function only of the price of copper, wage rates in the copper industry (the price of an input of production), the technology index, and the number of firms in the industry. The positive coefficient on the P_C variable shows the positive relationship between the price of copper and the quantity supplied. A higher price will elicit a larger quantity supplied. This relationship represents a normal, upward sloping supply curve. The other variables in Equation 2.5 cause the supply curve to shift. The wage rate index, W, has a negative coefficient. As wage rates increase, the supply of copper decreases because an increase in this input price represents an increase in the costs of production. The technology index (T) and the number of active mines variable (N) both have positive coefficients, indicating that an increase in technology or in the number of active mines will increase the supply of copper.

To define a specific supply curve, we need to hold constant the wage rate index, the technology index, and the number of firms in the copper industry. Suppose that $W = 100$, $T = 50$, and $N = 20$. Substituting these values into Equation 2.5 gives Equation 2.6.

2.6 $Q_S = -5 + 8P_C - 0.5(100) + 0.4(50) + 0.5(20)$

or

$Q_S = -25 + 8P_C$ or $[P_C = 3.125 + 0.125Q_S]$

As with the demand curve in Equation 2.3, the supply curve in Equation 2.6 shows the relationship between the price of copper and the quantity supplied, all else held constant. The constant term, –25, incorporates the effect of the wage and technology indices and the number of firms in the industry. Any changes in these variables change the size of the constant term, which results in a different supply curve.[53]

Summary of Demand and Supply Factors

Table 2.1 summarizes the factors influencing both the demand and the supply sides of the market. Notice the symmetry in that some of the factors—including the prices of related goods, future expectations, and the number of participants—influence both sides of the market.

TABLE 2.1 Factors Influencing Market Demand and Supply

DEMAND	SUPPLY
Price of the product	Price of the product
Consumer tastes and preferences	State of technology
Consumer income:	Input prices
Normal goods	
Inferior goods	
Price of goods related in consumption:	Prices of goods related in production
Substitute goods	Substitute goods
Complementary goods	Complementary goods
Future expectations	Future expectations
Number of consumers	Number of producers

[53]If we rewrite the supply equation with price as a function of quantity supplied, we get $P = 3.125 + 0.125Q_S$, as shown in Equation 2.6. This equation implies that producers must receive a price of at least $3.125 per pound to induce them to supply any copper.

Managerial Rule of Thumb

Supply Considerations

In developing a competitive strategy, managers must examine the technology and costs of production, factors that influence the supply of the product. Finding ways to increase productivity and lower production costs is particularly important in gaining a strategic advantage in a competitive market where managers have little control over price. ■

Demand, Supply, and Equilibrium

As we discussed earlier in the chapter, demand and supply are both functional relationships between the price of a good and the quantity demanded or supplied. Neither function by itself tells us what price will actually exist in the market. That price will be determined when the market is in equilibrium.

Definition of Equilibrium Price and Equilibrium Quantity

Equilibrium price

The price that actually exists in the market or toward which the market is moving where the quantity demanded by consumers equals the quantity supplied by producers.

Equilibrium quantity (Q_E)

The quantity of a good, determined by the equilibrium price, where the amount of output that consumers demand is equal to the amount that producers want to supply.

In a competitive market, the interaction of demand and supply determines the **equilibrium price**, the price that will actually exist in the market or toward which the market is moving. Figure 2.6 shows the equilibrium price (P_E) for good X. The equilibrium price is the price at which the quantity demanded of good X by consumers equals the quantity that producers are willing to supply. This quantity is called the **equilibrium quantity (Q_E)**. At any other price, there will be an imbalance between quantity demanded and quantity supplied. Forces will be set in motion to push the price back toward equilibrium, assuming no market impediments or governmental policies exist that would prevent equilibrium from being reached.

Lower-Than-Equilibrium Prices

The best way to understand equilibrium is to consider what would happen if some price other than the equilibrium price actually existed in a market. Suppose P_1 is the actual market price in Figure 2.7. As you see in the figure, price P_1 is lower than the equilibrium price, P_E. You can also see that the quantity of the good demanded by consumers at price P_1 is greater than the quantity producers are willing to supply. This creates a shortage of the good, shown in Figure 2.7 as the amount of the good between Q_D and Q_S. At the lower-than-equilibrium price, P_1, consumers demand more of the good than producers are willing to supply at that

FIGURE 2.6
Market Equilibrium
Market equilibrium occurs at that price where the quantity demanded by consumers equals the quantity supplied by producers.

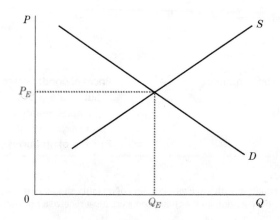

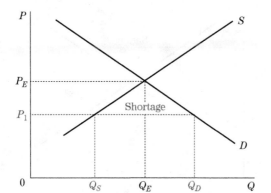

FIGURE 2.7
A Lower-Than-Equilibrium Price
A shortage of a good results when the market price, P_1, is below the equilibrium price, P_E.

price. Because there is an imbalance between quantity demanded and quantity supplied at this price, the situation is not stable. Some individuals are willing to pay more than price P_1, so they will start to bid the price up. A higher price will cause producers to supply a larger quantity. This adjustment process will continue until the equilibrium price has been reached and quantity demanded is equal to quantity supplied.

Price and rent controls are examples of the imbalances between demand and supply that result from lower-than-equilibrium prices. In New York City, which used rent controls for many years for certain apartments, the excess demand for these apartments meant that many of them never actually appeared on the market. They were either kept by the current occupants or transferred to those with connections to the occupants.[54] Rent controls often led to decreased maintenance in the controlled units and increased rents in the noncontrolled sector.[55] You can also observe lower-than-equilibrium prices being charged for tickets to the Super Bowl and many other sporting and entertainment events where scalpers sell tickets for prices far exceeding the stated price. The quantity demanded of tickets at the stated price is greater than the quantity supplied at that price, so people will pay much more than the stated price for these tickets. Recognizing this excess demand, the producers of the hit Broadway show *The Producers* began, in October 2001, setting aside at least 50 seats at every performance to sell at $480 per ticket, a price far exceeding the top regular charge of $100. This was a strategic move to tap into the excess demand and ensure that the creators of the play, and not the scalpers, received a bigger share of the royalties.[56] This trend increased both on Broadway and with other performing arts organizations over the next decade.[57]

Notre Dame University conducts a lottery every year to parcel out the 30,000 seats available to contributors, former athletes, and parents for football games in its 80,000-seat stadium. In September 2006, the university had 66,670 ticket requests for the 30,000 seats for the Notre Dame–Penn State game. Individuals and businesses take advantage of the excess demand during game weekends. Houses for visitors rent for $3,000 or more, motel rooms normally renting for $129 per night sell out at $400, parking passes are sold on eBay for $500, and $59 tickets can fetch a price of $1,600.[58]

[54]Richard Arnott, "Time for Revisionism on Rent Control?" *Journal of Economic Perspectives* 9(1) (Winter 1995): 99–120.

[55]Blair Jenkins, "Rent Control: Do Economists Agree?" *Econ Journal Watch* 6(1) (January 2009): 73–112.

[56]Jessie McKinley, "For the Asking, $480 a Seat for 'The Producers,'" *New York Times*, October 26, 2001.

[57]Patrick Healy, "Broadway Hits Make Most of Premium Pricing," *The New York Times (Online)*, November 24, 2011.

[58]Ilan Brat, "Notre Dame Football Introduces Its Fans to Inflationary Spiral," *Wall Street Journal*, September 6, 2006.

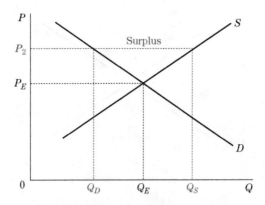

Higher-Than-Equilibrium Prices

Figure 2.8 shows the opposite case, a higher-than-equilibrium price. At price P_2, the quantity supplied, Q_S, is greater than the quantity demanded, Q_D, at that price. This above-equilibrium price creates a surplus of the good and sets into motion forces that will cause the price to fall. As the price falls, the quantity demanded increases and the quantity supplied decreases until a balance between quantity demanded and quantity supplied is restored at the equilibrium price. Thus, the existence of either shortages or surpluses of goods is an indication that a market is not in equilibrium.

In this chapter, we have used several agricultural examples to illustrate the forces shifting demand and supply curves because agricultural markets exhibit many competitive characteristics. These markets also provide good examples of non-equilibrium prices and imbalances between demand and supply, given the extensive government agricultural subsidization programs that have been in operation over the years. These crop subsidy programs kept the price of many agricultural products above equilibrium, which resulted in an excess quantity supplied compared with quantity demanded. During the 1990s, the U.S. government began eliminating or cutting back many of these subsidy programs. As prices for their crops have fallen, many farmers have gone out of business.

The choices among crops to be planted are often influenced by the pattern of federal subsidies. The *Wall Street Journal* reported in April 1999 that U.S. farmers intended to plant a record 73.1 million acres of soybeans that spring, even in the face of declining prices for this product.[59] Although this move was likely to cause soybean prices to fall even further, farmers were responding to a soybean subsidy that was higher than those for other crops. This increased level of planting by U.S. farmers, combined with large harvests from other countries, was expected to push soybean prices to under $4 a bushel, the lowest level since the 1980s. However, under a U.S. Department of Agriculture marketing-loan program, U.S. farmers could expect a price of $5.26 per bushel of soybeans. In response, they were expected to produce 2.9 billion bushels of soybeans, up 5 percent from the previous year's harvest.

The tobacco subsidy program guaranteed farmers a minimum price for their crops and allocated quotas stating how many acres could be planted. Growers who did not own a quota had to purchase or rent one from current owners. This system increased prices and limited production to narrow geographic areas and to plots of land that were typically not larger than 10 acres. When the system was disbanded in 2004, thousands of farmers stopped growing tobacco. In 2005, acreage dropped

---

[59]Scott Kilman, "Farmers to Plant Record Soybean Acres Despite Price Drop, as a Result of a Subsidy," *Wall Street Journal*, April 4, 1999.

27 percent from the previous year, and tobacco prices fell from $1.98 to $1.64 per pound. However, over time tobacco production has increased again, given that farmers no longer have to purchase quotas and can plant much more acreage. Tobacco production has shifted to large tracts of land where the crop can be grown more efficiently.[60]

By 2011, many crop prices had increased so significantly that they were too high to trigger payouts under a price support formula. Global grain markets shifted in 2006 when the federal government required that the oil industry mix billions of gallons of corn-derived ethanol with gasoline each year. The increase in middle-class consumers in emerging economies such as China also increased the demand for corn. In 2011, corn sold for $7 per bushel, far above the target price of $2.63, and soybeans sold for $13 per bushel compared with a target price of $6. Economists estimated that commodity prices would not fall back to target levels for at least another decade.[61]

Mathematical Example of Equilibrium

We can illustrate the concept of equilibrium with the mathematical example of the copper industry we have been using throughout the chapter. So far, we have defined the demand and supply curves for copper in Equations 2.3 and 2.6:

2.3 $Q_D = 15 - 2P_C$

2.6 $Q_S = -25 + 8P_C$

Equilibrium in a competitive market occurs at the price where quantity demanded equals quantity supplied. Since Equation 2.3 represents quantity demanded as a function of price and Equation 2.6 represents quantity supplied as a function of price, we need an equilibrium condition to find the solution in the market. The equilibrium condition is shown in Equation 2.7 where we set the two equations equal to each other and solve for the equilibrium price and quantity.

2.7 $Q_D = Q_S$

$$15 - 2P_C = -25 + 8P_C$$

$$40 = 10P_C$$

$P_C = P_E = \$4.00$ and $Q_E = 7$ (by substituting $4.00 into either equation)

Thus, the equilibrium price of copper in this example is $4.00 per pound, and the equilibrium quantity is 7 million pounds. This is the only price–quantity combination where quantity demanded equals quantity supplied. At a price lower than $4.00 per pound, the quantity demanded from Equation 2.3 will be greater than the quantity supplied from Equation 2.6, and a shortage of copper will result. At a price higher than $4.00 per pound, the quantity demanded will be less than the quantity supplied, and a surplus of copper will occur.

Changes in Equilibrium Prices and Quantities

Changes in equilibrium prices and quantities occur when market forces cause either the demand or the supply curve for a product to shift or both curves shift. These shifts occur when one or more of the factors held constant behind a given demand

---

[60]Etter, "U.S. Farmers Rediscover the Allure of Tobacco."
[61]Scott Kilman, "Crop Prices Erode Farm Subsidy Program," *Wall Street Journal (Online)*, July 25, 2011.

FIGURE 2.9

Change in Demand

A change in demand, represented by a shift of the demand curve, results in a movement along the supply curve.

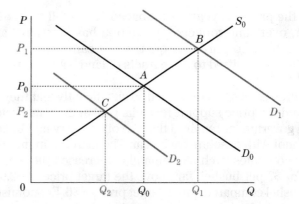

or supply curve change. Much economic analysis focuses on examining the changes in equilibrium prices and quantities that result from shifts in demand and supply.

Change in Demand   Figure 2.9 shows the effect of a change in demand in a competitive market. The original equilibrium price, P_0, and quantity, Q_0, arise from the intersection of demand curve D_0 and supply curve S_0. An increase in demand is shown by the rightward or outward shift of the demand curve from D_0 to D_1. This increase in demand could result from a change in one or more of the following nonprice variables: tastes and preferences, income, prices of related goods, expectations, or number of consumers in the market, as we discussed earlier in the chapter. This increase in demand results in a new higher equilibrium price, P_1, and a new larger equilibrium quantity, Q_1, or in the movement from point A to point B in Figure 2.9. This change represents a movement along the supply curve or a change in quantity supplied. Thus, a change in demand (a shift of the curve on one side of the market) results in a change in quantity supplied (movement along the curve on the other side of the market).

The opposite result occurs for a decrease in demand. In this case, the demand curve shifts from D_0 to D_2 in Figure 2.9, and the equilibrium price and quantity fall to P_2 and Q_2. This change in demand also causes a change in quantity supplied, or a movement along the supply curve from point A to point C.

Change in Supply   Figure 2.10 shows the effect of a change in supply on equilibrium price and quantity. Starting with the original demand and supply curves, D_0 and S_0, and the original equilibrium price and quantity, P_0 and Q_0, an increase in supply is represented by the rightward or outward shift of the supply curve from S_0 to S_1. As we discussed earlier in the chapter, this shift could result from a

FIGURE 2.10

Change in Supply

A change in supply, represented by a shift of the supply curve, results in a movement along the demand curve.

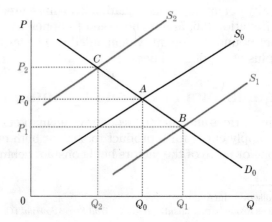

change in technology, input prices, prices of goods related in production, expectations, or number of suppliers. The result of this increase in supply is a new lower equilibrium price, P_1, and a larger equilibrium quantity, Q_1. This change in supply results in a movement along the demand curve or a change in quantity demanded from point A to point B.

Figure 2.10 also shows the result of a decrease in supply. In this case, the supply curve shifts leftward or inward from S_0 to S_2. This results in a new higher equilibrium price, P_2, and a smaller equilibrium quantity, Q_2. This decrease in supply results in a decrease in quantity demanded or a movement along the demand curve from point A to point C.

Changes on Both Sides of the Market   As in the copper case discussed at the beginning of this chapter, most outcomes result from changes on *both* sides of the market. The trends in equilibrium prices and quantities will depend on the size of the shifts of the curves and the responsiveness of either quantity demanded or quantity supplied to changes in prices.

In some cases, we know the direction of the change in equilibrium price, but not the equilibrium quantity. This result is illustrated in Figures 2.11 and 2.12, which show a decrease in supply (the shift from point A to point B) combined with an increase in demand (the shift from point B to point C). Both shifts cause the equilibrium price to rise from P_0 to P_2. However, the direction of change for the equilibrium quantity (Q_0 to Q_2) depends on the magnitude of the shifts in the curves. If the decrease in supply is less than the increase in demand, the equilibrium quantity will rise, as shown in Figure 2.11. The equilibrium quantity will fall if the increase in demand is less than the decrease in supply, as shown in Figure 2.12.

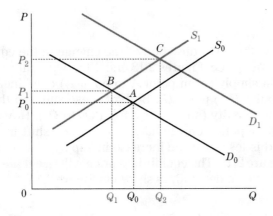

FIGURE 2.11
Decrease in Supply and Increase in Demand: Increase in Equilibrium Quantity
These changes in demand and supply result in a higher equilibrium price and a larger equilibrium quantity.

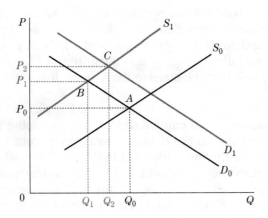

FIGURE 2.12
Decrease in Supply and Increase in Demand: Decrease in Equilibrium Quantity
These changes in demand and supply result in a higher equilibrium price and a smaller equilibrium quantity.

FIGURE 2.13
Increase in Supply and Increase in Demand: Lower Equilibrium Price
These changes in demand and supply result in a lower equilibrium price and a larger equilibrium quantity.

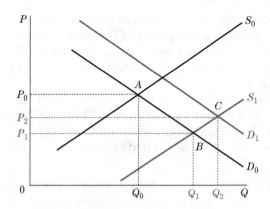

FIGURE 2.14
Increase in Supply and Increase in Demand: Higher Equilibrium Price
These changes in demand and supply result in a higher equilibrium price and a larger equilibrium quantity.

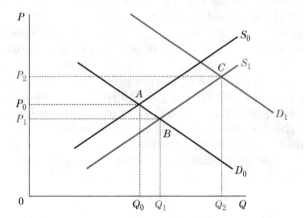

In other cases, we know the direction of the change in the equilibrium quantity, but not the equilibrium price. Figures 2.13 and 2.14, which illustrate this situation, show an increase in supply (from point A to point B) combined with an increase in demand (from point B to point C). Both of these shifts in the curves result in a larger equilibrium quantity (an increase from Q_0 to Q_2). However, the direction of the price change depends on the magnitude of the shift in each curve. If the increase in demand is less than the increase in supply, the equilibrium price will fall, as shown in Figure 2.13. The equilibrium price will rise if the increase in supply is less than the increase in demand, as shown in Figure 2.14.

Mathematical Example of an Equilibrium Change

In Equation 2.7, we solved for the equilibrium price and quantity of copper with demand Equation 2.3 and supply Equation 2.6. This resulted in an equilibrium price of $4.00 per pound and an equilibrium quantity of 7 million pounds. We now show how a change in the equilibrium price and quantity from the beginning of 2010 to the end of 2011 resulted from changes in the factors discussed in the beginning of this chapter.

Suppose the recession in the United States and the turmoil in European financial conditions resulted in the cancellation of copper-using projects and there was no offsetting increase in the demand for copper from China. Assume that this change caused the income index (I) in demand Equation 2.3 to decrease from 20 to 14. The uncertain demand for telecommunications services in North America and Europe caused the telecom index to decrease from 2.5 to 1.875. The expectations index (E) decreased over the period from 100 to 80, given that a larger number of purchasers expected a lower price over the following six months. These changes give a new demand function, as shown in Equation 2.8.

$$2.8 \quad Q_{D2} = 3 - 2P_C + 0.2I + 1.6TC + 0.04E$$
$$= 3 - 2P_C + 0.2(14) + 1.6(1.875) + 0.04(80)$$
$$= 12 - 2P_C \text{ or } [P_C = 6 - 0.5Q_D]$$

Also suppose that the wage index, W, decreased slightly from 100 to 98 over this period due to the economic slowdown. Assume that improvements in physical capital increased the technology index (T) from 50 to 55 and that China released some of its previously undiscovered stockpiles of copper, which had the effect of increasing the value of N from 20 to 28. These changes gave a new supply function, as shown in Equation 2.9.

$$2.9 \quad Q_{S2} = -5 + 8P_C - 0.5W + 0.4T + 0.5N$$
$$= -5 + 8P_C - 0.5(98) + 0.4(55) + 0.5(28)$$
$$= -18 + 8P_C \text{ or } [P_C = 2.25 + 0.125Q_S]$$

The new equilibrium price and quantity are derived in Equation 2.10 by setting the new demand function, Equation 2.8, equal to the new supply function, Equation 2.9.

$$2.10 \quad Q_{D2} = Q_{S2}$$
$$12 - 2P_C = -18 + 8P_C$$
$$30 = 10P_C$$
$$P_C = P_E = \$3.00 \text{ and } Q_E = 6$$

The resulting equilibrium price is $3.00 per pound of copper, and the equilibrium quantity is 6 million pounds.

Figure 2.15 shows the original and final equilibrium in the copper industry example (original $P_E = \$4.00$ per pound, $Q_E = 7$ million pounds; final $P_E = \$3.00$ per pound, $Q_E = 6$ million pounds, respectively). Both the demand and the supply curves are graphed from the equations showing price as a function of quantity. We can see that both the demand curve shift and the supply curve shift resulted in a lower equilibrium price.

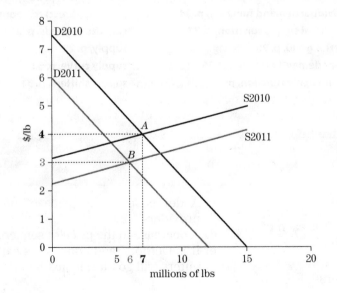

FIGURE 2.15
Copper Industry Example
This figure illustrates the changes in demand and supply in the copper industry discussed in the opening case of the chapter. Both the demand and the supply shifts resulted in a downward trend in copper prices.

Summary

In this chapter, we discussed how the forces of demand and supply determine prices in competitive markets. In the case of the copper industry, we saw how both demand- and supply-side factors influenced copper prices. We also discussed how both microeconomic factors, such as a change in the technology of copper production, and macroeconomic factors, including changes in the Chinese economy and the U.S. recession that began in 2007, affected the prices charged, the profitability, and the competitive strategies of firms in the copper industry.

We examined these changes with the economic model of demand and supply. *Demand* is defined as the relationship between the price of the good and the quantity demanded by consumers in a given period of time, all other factors held constant. *Supply* is defined as the relationship between the price of the good and the quantity supplied by producers in a given period of time, all other factors held constant. The equilibrium price, or the price that actually exists in the market, is that price where quantity demanded equals quantity supplied and is represented by the intersection of given demand and supply curves. When the factors held constant behind a particular demand or supply curve change, equilibrium prices respond to these demand and supply shifters. We provided numerous examples of these shifters throughout the chapter and discussed the effect of these demand and supply changes on prices in the copper industry.

We'll later examine the quantitative concept of elasticity, which economists have developed to measure the amount of consumer response to changes in the variables in market demand functions. We'll also examine what impact elasticity has on a firm's revenues and pricing policies (Chapter 3).

Key Terms

change in demand, p. 25
change in quantity demanded, p. 25
change in quantity supplied, p. 31
change in supply, p. 32
complementary goods, p. 22
demand, p. 19
demand curve, p. 24
demand shifters, p. 24
equilibrium price, p. 34

equilibrium quantity (Q_E), p. 34
functional relationship, p. 19
horizontal summation of individual demand curves, p. 26
individual demand function, p. 24
individual supply function, p. 31
inferior good, p. 20
linear demand function, p. 26
linear supply function, p. 31

market demand function, p. 24
market supply function, p. 31
negative (inverse) relationship, p. 24
normal good, p. 20
positive (direct) relationship, p. 31
substitute goods, p. 21
supply, p. 28
supply curve, p. 31
supply shifters, p. 31

Exercises

Technical Questions

1. Consider the demand for computers. For each of the following, state the effect on demand:

   a. An increase in consumer incomes

   b. An increase in the price of computers

   c. A decrease in the price of Internet service providers

   d. A decrease in the price of semiconductors

   e. It is October, and consumers expect that computers will go on sale just before Christmas.

2. Consider the supply of computers. For each of the following, state the effect on supply:

   a. A change in technology that lowers production costs
   b. An increase in the price of semiconductors
   c. A decrease in the price of computers
   d. An increase in the wages of computer assembly workers
   e. An increase in consumer incomes

3. The demand curve is given by

   $$Q_D = 500 - 5P_X + 0.5I + 10P_Y - 2P_Z$$

   where

   Q_D = quantity demanded of good X
   P_X = price of good X
   I = consumer income, in thousands
   P_Y = price of good Y
   P_Z = price of good Z

   a. Based on the demand curve above, is X a normal or an inferior good?
   b. Based on the demand curve above, what is the relationship between good X and good Y?
   c. Based on the demand curve above, what is the relationship between good X and good Z?
   d. What is the equation of the demand curve if consumer incomes are $30,000, the price of good Y is $10, and the price of good Z is $20?
   e. Graph the demand curve that you found in (d), showing intercepts and slope.
   f. If the price of good X is $15, what is the quantity demanded? Show this point on your demand curve.
   g. Now suppose the price of good Y rises to $15. Graph the new demand curve.

4. The supply curve is given by

   $$Q_S = -200 + 20P_X - 5P_I + 0.5P_Z$$
   where
   Q_S = quantity supplied of good X
   P_X = price of good X
   P_I = price of inputs to good X
   P_Z = price of good Z

   a. Based on the supply curve above, what is the relationship between good X and good Z?
   b. What is the equation of the supply curve if input prices are $10 and the price of Z is $20?
   c. Graph the supply curve that you found in (b), showing intercepts and slope.
   d. What is the minimum price at which the firm will supply any of good X at all?
   e. If the price of good X is $25, what is the quantity supplied? Show this point on your supply curve.
   f. Now suppose the price of inputs falls to $5. Graph the new supply curve.

5. Suppose the demand and supply curves for a product are given by

   $$Q_D = 500 - 2P$$
   $$Q_S = -100 + 3P$$

   a. Graph the supply and demand curves.
   b. Find the equilibrium price and quantity.
   c. If the current price of the product is $100, what is the quantity supplied and the quantity demanded? How would you describe this situation, and what would you expect to happen in this market?
   d. If the current price of the product is $150, what is the quantity supplied and the quantity demanded? How would you describe this situation, and what would you expect to happen in this market?
   e. Suppose that demand changes to $Q_D = 600 - 2P$. Find the new equilibrium price and quantity, and show this on your graph.

6. Graph representative supply and demand curves for the breakfast cereal market, labeling the current equilibrium price and quantity. Then show the effect on equilibrium price and quantity of each of the following changes (consider each separately):

   a. The price of muffins rises, assuming muffins and breakfast cereals are substitutes.
   b. The price of wheat, an input to cereal production, rises.
   c. Consumers expect that cereal prices will be higher in the future.
   d. There is a change in technology that makes production less expensive.
   e. New medical reports indicate that eating breakfast is less important than had previously been thought.

7. Consider the market for automobiles, and draw representative supply and demand curves.

   a. Suppose that the price of gasoline rises, and at the same time, the price of steel (an input to automobile production) falls. Show this on your graph. If you have no other information, what can you say about the change in equilibrium price and quantity?
   b. Now suppose that you have the additional information that the rise in gasoline prices has been relatively large, while the reduction in steel costs has been relatively small. How would this change your answer to (a)?

8. Consider the market for hamburger, and draw representative supply and demand curves.

   a. Assume that hamburger is an inferior good. Suppose that consumer incomes fall, and at the same time, an improvement in technology lowers production costs. Show this on your graph. If you have no other information, what can you say about the change in equilibrium price and quantity?

b. Now suppose that you have the additional information that the change in consumer incomes has been relatively small, while the reduction in production costs has been relatively large. How would this change your answer to (a)?

Application Questions

1. Using the facts in the opening case, the discussion in the chapter, and demand and supply curves, show the impacts of the events in the case on the price and quantity of copper. Clearly distinguish between changes in demand and supply and changes in the quantity demanded and the quantity supplied.

2. Using data sources from business publications and the Internet, discuss significant trends in both demand and supply in the copper industry that have influenced the price of copper since September 2011. What are the implications of these trends for managerial decision making in the copper industry?

3. Consider the following facts.[62]

   a. Easing drought conditions in the Black Sea wheat belt are causing world wheat production to recover.

   b. China is consuming nearly a quarter of the U.S. soybean crop to feed its hogs and chickens that are demanded by its expanding middle class.

   c. Farmers have typically responded to high prices by planting more land.

   d. The USDA predicts that U.S. farmers will increase the land used for the nation's eight largest crops by 9.8 million acres, the biggest change in 15 years.

   e. Possible civil war in cocoa-producing Ivory Coast increased prices to the highest levels in 32 years despite increased production last year.

   f. Weather problems in major wheat-producing countries such as Canada and Russia caused world wheat production to drop 5.5 percent.

Using standard demand and supply curves, describe and illustrate the effect on equilibrium price and quantity of each of these changes in the particular commodity market.

4. The following facts are about the peanut and peanut butter industry.[63]

   a. Another hot, dry summer has devastated the 2011 peanut crop. Although peanuts are typically planted between mid-April and June, farmers had to wait several weeks after that period for rain.

   b. Many peanut butter producers looked for ways to cut costs in other areas, such as shipping and warehousing.

   c. Some farmers had already planted cotton in place of peanuts, given the high price of cotton.

   d. The scorching heat singed many peanut plants, leaving more peanuts to be processed for oil rather than used for peanut butter.

Using demand and supply analysis, describe the effects of these changes on both the peanut and peanut butter industries.

5. Consider the following discussion.[64]

   It has been a tough year in the poultry business, with supply outpacing demand and feed-grain prices rising substantially. But producers are hoping all that changes when the summer cook-out season starts.

   The seasonal upswing in chicken consumption, along with the anticipated jump in spot-market poultry prices, could bring some relief to producers whose profit margins have been slashed by surging corn and soybean-meal costs.

   Rising feed-grain prices, accelerated by the diversion of corn to make ethanol, have pushed up the cost of producing a live chicken by as much as 65 percent over the past two years.

---

[62]Scott Kilman, "U.S. Farmers Head into Key Stretch for Harvests," *Wall Street Journal (Online)*, March 7, 2011.

[63]Paul Ziobro, "Peanut-Butter Makers Face Crunch," *Wall Street Journal (Online)*, October 10, 2011.
[64]"Chicken Producers in Price Pinch," *Wall Street Journal*, May 21, 2008.

Three factors make analysts more optimistic: Companies are cutting production, weekly egg-set numbers are declining (egg sets are fertile eggs placed in incubators), and prices are responding positively to the decreasing supply.

The production slowdown is a response to the surge in feed-grain prices last fall.

Profit margins at producers will not improve unless spot-market prices for chicken move up fast enough to cover costs paid for corn and soybean meal to feed chicken flocks.

Production cutbacks and seasonal demand have helped fuel a 20-cent increase in boneless, skinless breast-meat prices to $1.46 a pound. Prices are expected to reach at least $1.80 by summer 2008.

a. Use demand and supply analysis to illustrate the changes in chicken prices described in the above article.
b. Describe what has happened in the corn and soybean-meal markets and how that has influenced the chicken market.

3 Demand Elasticities

I n this chapter, we explore the concept of demand in more detail. We focus on the downward sloping demand curve, which shows an inverse relationship between the price of the good and the quantity demanded by consumers, all else held constant. This demand curve applies to the entire market or industry in a perfectly competitive market structure, even though individual firms in this market are price-takers who cannot influence the product price.

All firms in the other market structures—monopolistic competition, oligopoly, and monopoly—face downward sloping demand curves because they have varying degrees of market power. These firms must lower the price at which they are willing to sell their product if they want to sell more units. If the product price is higher, consumers will buy fewer units. Thus, product price is a strategic variable that managers in all real-world firms must choose. Managers must also develop strategies regarding the other variables influencing demand, including tastes and preferences, consumer income, the price of related goods, and future expectations. This chapter focuses on the quantitative measure—demand elasticity—that shows how consumers respond to changes in the different variables influencing demand.

We begin this chapter with a case that discusses Procter & Gamble Co.'s pricing strategies and consumer responsiveness to the demand for its products as the company navigated the economic downturn from 2009 to 2011. We then formally present the concept of price elasticity of demand and develop a relationship among changes in prices, changes in revenues that a firm receives, and price elasticity. Next we illustrate all elasticities with examples drawn from both the economics and the marketing literature.

The chapter appendix presents the formal economic model of consumer behavior, which shows how both consumer tastes and preferences and the constraints of income and product prices combine to influence the consumer's choice of different products.

Case for Analysis

Demand Elasticity and Procter & Gamble's Pricing Strategies

Like many other companies, Procter & Gamble Co. (P&G) had to constantly alter its pricing strategies as it faced declining and shifting consumer demand for many of its products from 2009 to 2011. Although the recession that began in December 2007 officially ended in June 2009, P&G managers continued to face consumer cutbacks even on basic household staples. Rather than purchase P&G premium-priced brands, such as Tide detergent and Pampers diapers, consumers chose less-expensive brands, including Gain detergent and Luvs diapers. The P&G chief executive noted at the time that consumers were trying more private-label and retailer brands than they would in more normal economic times.[1]

Because the company also faced higher commodity prices and global currency swings, P&G officials raised prices in the first quarter of 2009, developed new products, and increased advertising to emphasize why their brands offered more value than the competition. Officials reported that the higher prices hurt sales volume but increased total sales revenues by 7 percent. However, industry analysts wondered if the deceased sales volume would eventually cause the company to lower prices and increase promotions.[2]

By spring 2010, P&G had reversed course and was engaged in a market-share war by cutting prices, increasing product launches and spending more on advertising. The company's goal was to win back market share lost during the recession to lower-priced rivals even at the expense of profitability. P&G lowered prices on almost all of its product categories during early 2010.[3]

This strategy continued into the summer of 2010, although there were concerns at that point that the company had missed industry analyst profit estimates even though it had increased market share. Although the company announced that it intended to raise prices in the first half of 2011, officials debated whether consumers had become accustomed to the lower prices. Industry analysts argued that the company needed to sell more products in the lower-priced categories.[4]

The ongoing discounting reduced P&G's profits, which decreased 12 percent in the second quarter of 2010, because sales revenue rose less than P&G expected. To offset the negative effects of the lower prices, P&G introduced new products including Gillette razors that promised a less irritating shave, Crest toothpaste with a "sensitive shield," and Downy fabric softener that advertised keeping sheets smelling fresh for a week. The company also began moving into emerging markets such as Brazil, where its research showed that Brazillians took more showers, used more hair conditioner, and brushed their teeth more often than residents of any other country. The company planned to enter the Brazillian market in several new product categories at once, such as Oral B toothpaste and Olay skin cream.[5]

Given continued lower-than-expected revenue and slow sales in early 2011, P&G announced that it would cut costs but would also try to raise prices on goods to offset the higher costs. P&G announced initiatives to eliminate some manufacturing lines and sell off smaller brands. However, private-label brands continued to post larger sales gains than brand names.[6]

In April 2011, the company announced a 7 percent increase in prices for its Pampers diapers and a 3 percent increase in the price of wipes. Surveys indicated that customers were less likely to switch to a cheaper baby product than for items such as bleach, bottled water, and liquid soap. The company hoped that parents would be willing to pay higher prices for diapers, even if they cut back elsewhere, in the belief that the higher-priced products were better for their baby's comfort or development. P&G also raised the price of its Charmin toilet paper and Bounty paper towels. One industry analyst concluded that brands that had the highest market share, were purchased infrequently (such as sunscreen or light bulbs), were necessities, had few competitors, or where it would be difficult to reduce consumption

[1]Ellen Byron, "P&G, Colgate Hit by Consumer Thrift—Household Products Makers See Sales Weakening, Raise Prices to Keep Quarterly Profits from Plunging," *Wall Street Journal (Online)*, May 1, 2009.

[2]Byron, "P&G, Colgate Hit by Consumer Thrift—Household Products Makers See Sales Weakening, Raise Prices to Keep Quarterly Profits from Plunging."

[3]Ellen Byron, "P&G Puts Up Its Dukes Over Pricing—Consumer-Products Makers Risk Margins to Grab Market Share from Rivals and Cheap Store Brands," *Wall Street Journal (Online)*, April 30, 2010.

[4]John Jannarone, "The Hefty Price of Procter's Gambet," *Wall Street Journal (Online)*, August 12, 2010.

[5]Ellen Byron, "P&G Chief Wages Offensive Against Rivals, Risks Profits," *Wall Street Journal (Online)*, August 19, 2010.

[6]Ellen Byron, "Earnings: P&G Feels the Pinch of Rising Costs," *Wall Street Journal (Online)*, January 28, 2011.

(toilet paper) were most likely to be the products whose prices could be increased. P&G, with its distinctive items, including beauty products, pet food, and toothpaste, was likely to be better able to raise prices than Kimberly-Clark and Clorox that operated in highly competitive product categories with large commodity cost pressures.[7]

By fall 2011, P&G reported solid sales growth and that it had successfully raised prices even though some of its competitors held back on their price increases. P&G had more ability to raise prices on its premium products because company officials observed that higher-end consumer spending had held up better than that of lower-income shoppers, who were still affected by continuing unemployment. P&G lost some market share in North America and Western Europe because its competitors did not immediately follow its price increases. However, company officials expected that the competitors would soon follow P&G on its higher prices.[8]

This case illustrates how a company's pricing policies depend on how consumers respond to price changes. In the first quarter of 2009, P&G raised prices and then reported declining sales volume but increased sales revenues. In subsequent years, the company lowered prices, which increased sales volume, but did not increase revenue as much as expected so that there was a negative effect on profits. Because the company was concerned about consumer adjustment to lower prices over time, it also adopted other strategies to increase profitability, such as developing new products and entering new markets.

Thus, it appears from the above case that consumer responsiveness to a company's price changes is related to

1. Tastes and preferences for various quality characteristics of a product as compared to the impact of price
2. Consumer income and the amount spent on a product in relation to that income
3. The availability of substitute goods and perceptions about what is an adequate substitute
4. The amount of time needed to adjust to change in prices

To examine these issues in more detail, we first define demand elasticity, and we relate this discussion to the variables influencing demand.

---

[7]Ellen Byron and Paul Ziobro, "Whoa Baby, Prices Are Jumping for Diapers, Other Family Basics," *Wall Street Journal (Online)*, April 25, 2011.

[8]Paul Ziobro, "P&G Says Costs Will Curb Current Quarter," *Wall Street Journal (Online)*, October 28, 2011.

Demand Elasticity

Demand elasticity

A quantitative measurement (coefficient) showing the percentage change in the quantity demanded of a particular product relative to the percentage change in any one of the variables included in the demand function for that product.

A **demand elasticity** is a quantitative measurement (coefficient) showing the percentage change in the quantity demanded of a particular product relative to the percentage change in any one of the variables included in the demand function for that product. Thus, an elasticity can be calculated with regard to product price, consumer income, the prices of other goods and services, advertising budgets, education levels, or any of the variables included in a demand function.[9] The important point is that an elasticity measures this responsiveness in terms of *percentage changes in both variables*. Thus, an elasticity is a number, called a *coefficient*, that represents the *ratio* of two percentage changes: the percentage change in quantity demanded relative to the percentage change in the other variable.

Percentage changes are used so that managers and analysts can make comparisons among elasticities for different variables and products. If absolute changes were used instead of percentage changes and the quantities of products were measured in different units, elasticities could vary by choice of the unit of measurement. For example, using absolute values of quantities, managers would find it difficult to compare consumer responsiveness to demand variables if the quantity of one product is measured in pounds and another is measured in tons, because they would be comparing changes in pounds with changes in tons.

---

[9]Although we can also calculate supply elasticities from a product supply function in a comparable manner, we will postpone our discussion of this issue until we present the model of perfect competition (Chapter 7).

Price Elasticity of Demand

The **price elasticity of demand (e_p)** is defined as the percentage change in the quantity demanded of a given good, X, relative to a percentage change in its price, all other factors assumed constant, as shown in Equation 3.1.[10] A percentage change in a variable is the ratio of the absolute change ($Q_2 - Q_1$ or ΔQ; $P_2 - P_1$ or ΔP) in that variable to a base value of the variable, as shown in Equation 3.2.

Price elasticity of demand (e_P)
The percentage change in the quantity demanded of a given good, X, relative to a percentage change in its own price, all other factors assumed constant.

$$3.1 \quad e_P = \frac{\% \Delta Q_X}{\% \Delta P_X}$$

$$3.2 \quad e_P = \frac{\dfrac{\Delta Q_X}{Q_X}}{\dfrac{\Delta P_X}{P_X}} = \frac{\dfrac{Q_2 - Q_1}{Q_X}}{\dfrac{P_2 - P_1}{P_X}}$$

where

e_P = price elasticity of demand

Δ = the absolute change in the variable: ($Q_2 - Q_1$) or ($P_2 - P_1$)

Q_X = the quantity demanded of good X

P_X = the price of good X

Price elasticity of demand is illustrated by the change in quantity demanded from Q_1 to Q_2 as the price changes from P_1 to P_2, or the movement along the demand curve from point A to point B in Figure 3.1. Because we are moving along a demand curve, all other factors affecting demand *are assumed to be constant*, and we are examining only the effect of *price* on quantity demanded. All demand elasticities are defined with the other factors influencing demand assumed constant so that the effect of the given variable on demand can be measured independently.

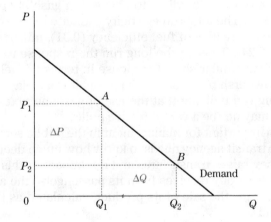

FIGURE 3.1
Price Elasticity and the Movement Along a Demand Curve
Price elasticity is measured as a movement along a demand curve from point A to point B.

---

[10]Price elasticity is sometimes called the "own price elasticity of demand" because it shows the ratio of the percentage change in the quantity demanded of a product to the percentage change in its *own* price.

The Influence of Price Elasticity on Managerial Decision Making

Price elasticity of demand is an extremely important concept for a firm because it tells managers what will happen to revenues if the price of a product changes. It can also help firms develop a pricing strategy that will maximize their profits.

The demand for airline travel changed substantially between 1999 and 2006 due to the following factors. Although business travelers have always been less price sensitive than tourists because they have less ability to postpone a trip or search for alternatives, they have become more price sensitive due to improvements in electronic communications and increased restrictions on travel reimbursement. Tightened security restrictions at airports have resulted in travelers having an increased preference for direct flights. The option of purchasing tickets on the Internet has reduced customer search costs and increased their knowledge about alternative fares. It has been estimated that the price elasticity of demand for tourists increased in absolute value from 0.78 to 1.05 and for business travelers from 0.07 to 0.10 over the period 1999 to 2006. The price elasticity was 31 percent larger for tourists and 43 percent larger for business travelers. The connection semi-elasticity, or the percentage reduction in quantity demanded if a direct flight became a connecting flight, increased in absolute value from 0.55 to 0.75 for business travelers and from 0.75 to 0.80 for tourists. Thus, both business travelers and tourists exhibited a stronger preference for direct flights in 2006.[11] The airlines use knowledge about these different elasticities to develop a complex schedule of prices for different groups of travelers and varying types of flights.

Information on the price elasticity of demand for gasoline affects managerial decisions in the automobile industry. In response to a price increase, consumers may travel less by car, either switching to alternative modes of transport or by traveling less in general. Consumers may also sell their cars, buy more efficient models, or change the usage of various household models. Thus, changes in gasoline prices affect the quantity demanded of gasoline though fuel efficiency, mileage per car, and car ownership. Consumers will typically drive less in the short run and then consider ownership changes in the long run.[12]

In an analysis based on data from 43 other studies, researchers estimated a short-run price elasticity of gasoline demand of –0.34 and a long-run elasticity of –0.84. Consumers have more options to adjust to changes in gasoline prices in the long run than in the short run. The long-run elasticity estimate can be decomposed into estimates of the price elasticities of fuel efficiency (0.31), mileage per car (–0.29), and car ownership (–0.24). Thus, in the long run the response to changes in gasoline prices is driven by a similar size of response in terms of fuel efficiency, mileage per car, and car ownership. These relatively small price elasticities in both the short run and the long run indicate that the use of gasoline taxes to decrease the demand for gasoline may not be a very effective policy.[13]

Elasticities are also important for management in the public sector. For example, a manager at a public transit agency needs to know how much decrease in ridership will result if the agency raises transit fares and the impact of this fare increase on the **total revenue** the agency receives from its passengers (the amount of money received by a producer for the sale of its product, calculated as the price per unit times the quantity sold).

Total revenue
The amount of money received by a producer for the sale of its product, calculated as the price per unit times the quantity sold.

---

[11]Steven Berry and Panle Jia, "Tracing the Woes: An Empirical Analysis of the Airline Industry," *American Economic Journal: Microeconomics* 2 (August 2010): 1–43.

[12]Martijn Brons, Peter Nijkamp, Eric Pels, and Piet Rietveld, "A Meta-Analysis of the Price Elasticity of Gasoline Demand: A SUR Approach," *Energy Economics* 30 (2008): 2105–22.

[13]Brons et al., "A Meta-Analysis of the Price Elasticity of Gasoline Demand: A SUR Approach."

Price Elasticity Values

The calculated value of *all* price elasticities for downward sloping demand curves is a negative number, given the inverse relationship between price and quantity demanded. If price increases, quantity demanded decreases and vice versa. Therefore, it is easier to drop the negative sign and examine the absolute value $(|e_P|)$ of the number to determine the size of the price elasticity. This procedure leads to the definitions shown in Table 3.1.

As shown in Table 3.1, demand is elastic if the coefficient's absolute value is greater than 1 and inelastic if the coefficient's absolute value is less than 1. For **elastic demand**, the percentage change in quantity demanded by consumers is greater than the percentage change in price. This implies a larger consumer responsiveness to changes in prices than does **inelastic demand**, in which the percentage change in quantity demanded by consumers is less than the percentage change in price. In the case of **unitary elasticity**, where $|e_P| = 1$, the percentage change in quantity demanded is exactly equal to the percentage change in price.

Elasticity and Total Revenue

The fourth column of Table 3.1 shows the relationship among price elasticity, changes in prices, and total revenue received by the firm, which, as noted above, is defined as price times quantity $[(P)(Q)]$. If demand is *elastic*, higher prices result in lower total revenue, while lower prices result in higher total revenue. This outcome arises because the percentage change in quantity is greater than the percentage change in price. If the price increases, enough fewer units are sold at the higher price that total revenue actually decreases. Likewise, with elastic demand, if price decreases, total revenue increases. Even though each unit is now sold at a lower price, there are enough more units sold that total revenue increases. Thus, for elastic demand, changes in price and the resulting total revenue move in the opposite direction. A higher price causes total revenue to decrease, while a lower price causes total revenue to increase.

These relationships for elastic demand are illustrated for the demand curve shown in Figure 3.2.[14] For this demand curve, at a price of $10, 2 units of the product are demanded, and the total revenue the firm receives is $10 × 2 units, or $20. If the price decreases to $9, the quantity demanded increases to 3 units, and the total revenue increases to $27. Demand is elastic in this range because total revenue increases as the price decreases.

Elastic demand
The percentage change in quantity demanded by consumers is greater than the percentage change in price and $|e_P| > 1$.

Inelastic demand
The percentage change in quantity demanded by consumers is less than the percentage change in price and $|e_P| < 1$.

Unitary elasticity (or unit elastic)
The percentage change in quantity demanded is exactly equal to the percentage change in price and $|e_P| = 1$.

TABLE 3.1 Values of Price Elasticity of Demand Coefficients

VALUE OF ELASTICITY COEFFICIENT	ELASTICITY DEFINITION	RELATIONSHIP AMONG VARIABLES	IMPACT ON TOTAL REVENUE
$|e_P| > 1$	Elastic demand	$\%\Delta Q_x > \%\Delta P_x$	Price increase results in lower total revenue.
			Price decrease results in higher total revenue.
$|e_P| < 1$	Inelastic demand	$\%\Delta Q_x < \%\Delta P_x$	Price increase results in higher total revenue.
			Price decrease results in lower total revenue.
$|e_P| = 1$	Unit elastic or unitary elasticity	$\%\Delta Q_x = \%\Delta P_x$	Price increase or decrease has no impact on total revenue.

---

[14]This demand curve is also the basis for the numerical example in the next section of the chapter.

FIGURE 3.2

Elastic Demand and Total Revenue

If demand is elastic, a decrease in price results in an increase in total revenue, and an increase in price results in a decrease in total revenue.

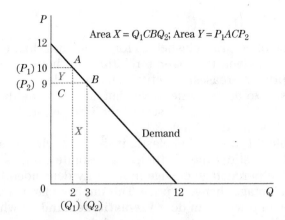

Area $X = Q_1CBQ_2$; Area $Y = P_1ACP_2$

This change in total revenue is illustrated graphically in Figure 3.2. If the price of $10 is labeled P_1 and the quantity of 2 units is labeled Q_1, the total revenue of $20 is represented by the area of the rectangle $0P_1AQ_1$. Likewise, if the price of $9 is labeled P_2 and the quantity of 3 units is labeled Q_2, the total revenue of $27 is represented by the area of the rectangle $0P_2BQ_2$. The change in revenue is represented by a comparison of the size of the rectangle P_1ACP_2 (rectangle Y) with that of the rectangle Q_1CBQ_2 (rectangle X). The first rectangle, Y, represents the loss in revenue from selling the original 2 units at the lower price of $9 instead of the original price of $10. This loss of revenue is 2 units times $1 per unit, or $2. The second rectangle, X, represents the gain in revenue from selling more units at the lower price of $9. This gain in revenue is 1 unit times $9 per unit, or $9. We can see both numerically and graphically that the gain in revenue (rectangle X) is greater than the loss in revenue (rectangle Y). Therefore, total revenue increases as the price is lowered when demand is elastic.

The opposite result holds for *inelastic* demand. In this case, if the price increases, total revenue also increases because the percentage decrease in quantity is less than the percentage increase in price. With a price increase, enough units are still sold at the higher price to cause total revenue to increase because each unit is sold at the higher price. Likewise, if price decreases, total revenue will decrease. All units are now being sold at a lower price, but the quantity demanded has not increased proportionately, so total revenue decreases. Thus, for inelastic demand, changes in price and the resulting total revenue move in the same direction. A higher price causes total revenue to increase, while a lower price causes total revenue to decrease.

Figure 3.3 illustrates this relationship for inelastic demand. For this demand curve, at a price of $4, 8 units are demanded, and the firm receives $32 in revenue. If the price falls to $3 per unit, the quantity demanded is 9 units, and the firm takes in $27 in revenue. Thus, as the price decreases, total revenue decreases, illustrating inelastic demand. In Figure 3.3, as in Figure 3.2, you can see the change in total revenue by comparing rectangle P_1ACP_2 (rectangle Y) with rectangle Q_1CBQ_2 (rectangle X). When the price is lowered from $4 to $3, the 8 units that were formerly sold at the price of $4 are now sold for $3 each. The associated revenue loss is $1 per unit times 8 units, or $8. The revenue gain is the one additional unit that is now sold at a price of $3, or $3. It can be seen both graphically and numerically that the revenue gain (rectangle X) is less than the revenue loss (rectangle Y). Therefore, as the price decreases with inelastic demand, total revenue decreases.

If demand is *unit elastic*, changes in price have no impact on total revenue because the percentage change in price is exactly equal to the percentage change

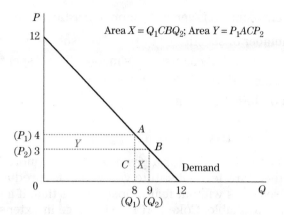

FIGURE 3.3
Inelastic Demand and Total Revenue
If demand is inelastic, a decrease in price results in a decrease in total revenue, and an increase in price results in a increase in total revenue.

in quantity. The effects on price and quantity are equal and offsetting. Rectangles X and Y in Figures 3.2 and 3.3, representing the gain and loss of revenue, would be exactly the same size if demand was unit elastic.

Managerial Rule of Thumb

Estimating Price Elasticity

The examples of point elasticity and changes in revenue can be converted into managerial rules of thumb for estimating price elasticity.[15] Managers can get a ballpark estimate of price elasticity by asking their customers two questions:

1. What do you currently pay for my product? (Call this price P_1.)
2. At what price would you stop buying my product altogether? (Call this price P_2.)

Price elasticity can then be calculated as $P_1/(P_1 - P_2)$. The intuition behind this rule is that the higher the value of P_2, the higher the price the customer is willing to pay rather than do without the product, and the lower the price elasticity. This rule of thumb is based on an implicit linear demand function and the point price elasticity formula given in Equation 3.5 later in this chapter.

For the second rule, managers should ask themselves the following questions regarding a proposed 10 percent drop in the price of the firm's product:

1. By how much will the sales revenue increase as a result of the higher volume of sales? (Call this amount X.)
2. By how much will the sales revenue decrease as a result of a lower price on each unit sold? (Call this amount Y.)

The price elasticity of demand is the ratio of X/Y. This rule of thumb is based on the changes in revenue with elastic and inelastic demand illustrated in Figures 3.2 and 3.3. A large price elasticity coefficient means that X will be large relative to Y, whereas a small price elasticity coefficient means that Y will be large relative to X. ∎

Determinants of Price Elasticity of Demand

Three major factors influence the price elasticity of demand and cause it to differ among products:

1. The number of substitute goods
2. The percent of a consumer's income that is spent on the product
3. The time period under consideration

---

[15]This discussion is drawn from Shlomo Maital, *Executive Economics* (New York: Free Press, 1994), 186–88.

All else held constant, demand is generally more inelastic or less responsive to price.

* The fewer the number of substitutes or perceived substitutes available
* The smaller the percent of the consumer's income that is spent on the product
* The shorter the time period under consideration

We'll look at each of these factors in turn.

Number of Substitute Goods

If there are few substitute goods for a given product or, more important, if consumers *perceive* there are few substitute goods for the product, managers have more ability to raise prices without fear of losing sales than if a greater number of substitute goods are available. Coke and Pepsi engage in extensive advertising to convince their customers that the other product is not an adequate substitute. Each company wants to shift out the demand curve for its product and make it relatively more inelastic. This is a constant struggle, given the availability of a wide range of substitute drinks: other soft drinks, teas, fruit drinks, sports beverages, and even water. Coke and Pepsi have, of course, expanded into these other markets, so that each company owns a number of substitute products for the basic cola.

In response to the expansion in the speciality-coffee market by McDonald's Corp., which impacted consumers' price sensitivity for Starbucks' coffee, Starbucks announced a plan in May 2010 to sell Seattle's Best Coffee in 30,000 fast-food outlets, supermarkets, and coffee houses. During the recession of 2007 to 2009, Starbucks suffered a decline in same-store sales and closed hundreds of stores, while McDonald's expanded with its lower-priced coffees. Seattle's Best was a former competitor that Starbucks acquired in 2003.[16]

In addition to the differences between business and leisure travel noted previously in the chapter, airline demand elasticities also depend on the length of the trip. Because cars, buses, and trains are substitutes for shorter airline flights, these flights should have a larger price elasticity of demand. Research studies have estimated the following price elasticities: long-haul international business, –0.26; long-haul international leisure, –0.99; long-haul domestic business, –1.15; and long-haul domestic leisure, –1.52.[17] These estimates confirm expectations about the role of distance (international vs. domestic flights) and the differing elasticities for business versus leisure travel.

The role of substitutes in influencing price elasticity of demand means that the price elasticity of demand for the product of a specific producer will be larger than the price elasticity for the product in general. All other producers of that same product are substitutes for the specific producer. We discuss several examples later in the chapter where the price elasticity of demand for the product is inelastic, whereas it is elastic for the output of a specific producer.

Percent of Consumer's Income Spent on the Product

Items that cost little tend to have more inelastic demands. If the price of your local newspaper doubles tomorrow, going from 50 cents to $1, you may not even notice the price increase, or perhaps you will choose to buy the paper four rather than five times per week. If the price of the European vacation you have planned for next summer doubles, you may consider traveling to a destination closer to home.

---

[16]Kevin Helliker, "Starbucks Targets Regular Joes: Firm to Offer Second Coffee Brand—Its Seattle's Best— in Fast-Food Outlets, Supermarkets, Machines," *Wall Street Journal (Online)*, May 11, 2010.

[17]David W. Gillen, William G. Morrison, and Christopher Stewart, *Air Travel Demand Elasticities: Concepts, Issues, and Measurement* (Ottawa: Department of Finance, 2002).

In this case, your quantity demanded decreases to zero, whereas there was only a slight decrease for the newspaper case. As you would guess, consumers tend to be more sensitive to changes in the prices of goods that represent a large percent of their incomes.

Time Period

The shorter the time period, the less chance consumers have of finding acceptable substitutes for a product whose price has risen, and the more inelastic the demand. Over time, consumers can find a greater number of substitutes, and elasticities tend to be larger. We noted these differences in the earlier discussion of short- and long-run price elasticities of demand for gasoline.

Numerical Example of Elasticity, Prices, and Revenues

We are now ready to explore the issues presented in Table 3.1 in more detail through the use of a numerical example that illustrates the relationships among elasticities, changes in prices, and changes in revenues to a firm. However, we first discuss a problem that arises in the calculation of price elasticities.

Calculating Price Elasticities

A problem occurs during the calculation of price elasticities because there are different sources of data available for these calculations. We may have data on actual quantities and prices, or we may have a demand equation that shows the functional relationship between price and quantity demanded.

Arc Price Elasticity   We first analyze the case with data on quantities and prices. In Figure 3.1, we illustrated a large price change that resulted in a large change in quantity demanded. If the price falls from P_1 to P_2, all else assumed constant, the quantity demanded increases from Q_1 to Q_2. Because points Q_1 and Q_2 may be significantly different from each other, a different value for the percentage change in quantity may result, depending on whether Q_1 or Q_2 is used for the base quantity in Equation 3.2. If we are measuring the effect of a price decrease from P_1 to P_2, which causes the quantity demanded to increase from Q_1 to Q_2, we will tend to use Q_1 as the base because that is our beginning quantity. If we are measuring the decrease in quantity demanded resulting from a price increase from P_2 to P_1, we will tend to use quantity Q_2 as the base quantity. The same problem occurs when we are measuring the percentage change in price. We will tend to use P_1 as the base for price decreases and P_2 as the base for price increases because these are the current prices of the product.

Because an elasticity coefficient is just a number, it is useful to have that coefficient the same for an increase or a decrease in quantity demanded. However, that result might not occur with the example in Figure 3.1 because dividing the absolute change in quantity (ΔQ) by Q_1 could result in a quite different number than dividing it by Q_2. For example, if $Q_1 = 10$ and $Q_2 = 20$, $\Delta Q = 10$. $\Delta Q/Q_1 = 10/10 = 1.0$, or a 100 percent increase in quantity. However, $\Delta Q/Q_2 = 10/20 = 0.5$, or a 50 percent decrease in quantity. The percentage increase in quantity is substantially different from the percentage decrease in quantity.

This issue is *not* a problem with the definition of price elasticity; instead, it is a numerical or calculation problem that arises for elasticity of demand when the starting and ending quantities and prices are significantly different from each other, as in Figure 3.1. We are calculating elasticity over a region or arc on the demand

Arc price elasticity of demand
A measurement of the price elasticity of demand where the base quantity or price is calculated as the average value of the starting and ending quantities or prices.

curve (point A to point B in Figure 3.1). The calculation problem can also arise if a manager does not know the shape of the entire demand curve, but simply has data on several prices and quantities.[18]

The conventional solution to this problem is to calculate an **arc price elasticity of demand**, where the base quantity (or price) is the average value of the starting and ending points, as shown in Equation 3.3.

$$3.3 \quad e_P = \cfrac{\cfrac{(Q_2 - Q_1)}{(Q_1 + Q_2)}}{\cfrac{2}{\cfrac{(P_2 - P_1)}{(P_1 + P_2)}{2}}}$$

Point Price Elasticity   A price elasticity is technically defined for very tiny or infinitesimal changes in prices and quantities. In Figure 3.1, if point B is moved very close to point A, the starting and ending prices and quantities are also very close to each other. We can then think of calculating an elasticity at a particular point on the demand curve (such as point A). This can be done in either of two ways: using calculus or using a noncalculus approach.

Equation 3.4 shows the formula for **point price elasticity of demand** where d is the derivative from calculus showing an infinitesimal change in the variables.

Point price elasticity of demand
A measurement of the price elasticity of demand calculated at a point on the demand curve using infinitesimal changes in prices and quantities.

$$3.4 \quad e_P = \cfrac{\cfrac{dQ_X}{Q_X}}{\cfrac{dP_X}{P_X}} = \cfrac{dQ_X P_X}{dP_X Q_X}$$

If you have a specific demand function, you can use calculus to compute the appropriate derivative (dQ_X/dP_X) for Equation 3.4.

However, because we do not require calculus in this text, we'll use a simpler approach for a linear demand function. The point price elasticity of demand can be calculated for a linear demand function as shown in Equation 3.5.

$$3.5 \quad e_P = \frac{P}{(P - a)}$$

> *where*
> P = the price charged
> a = the vertical intercept of the plotted demand curve (the P-axis)[19]

Thus, for any linear demand curve, a point price elasticity can be calculated for any price by knowing the vertical intercept of the demand curve (as plotted on the P-axis) and using the formula in Equation 3.5.

---

[18]If a manager has data only on prices and quantities, he or she needs to be certain that all other factors are constant as these prices and quantities change to be able to correctly estimate the price elasticity of demand. This is the major problem in estimating demand functions and elasticities (Chapter 4).

[19]Following S. Charles Maurice and Christopher R. Thomas, *Managerial Economics*, 7th ed. (McGraw-Hill Irwin, 2002), 92, the derivation of this result is as follows. For a linear demand curve,

$P = a + bQ$ or $Q = [(P - a)/b]$

$b = (\Delta P/\Delta Q)$ and $1/b = (\Delta Q/\Delta P)$

$e_P = (\Delta Q/Q)/(\Delta P/P) = (\Delta Q/\Delta P)(P/Q) = (1/b)[P/(P - a)/b] = [P/(P - a)]$

Numerical Example

Table 3.2 presents a numerical example using a linear, or straight-line, downward sloping demand curve. Demand curves may be either straight or curved lines, depending on how people actually behave. Throughout most of this text, we use *linear* downward sloping demand curves for our examples. These are the simplest types of curves to illustrate mathematically. They are also good representations of consumer behavior in different markets (Chapter 4).

The Demand Function

The demand function in Table 3.2 shows a relationship between quantity demanded (Q) and price (P), with all other factors held constant. The effect of all the other variables influencing demand is summarized in the constant term of 12.[20] Demand functions such as the one in Table 3.2 are estimated from data on real-world consumer behavior (Chapter 4).

The first row in Table 3.2 shows that the demand function can be stated either as quantity as a function of price or as price as a function of quantity. Mathematically, the two forms of the relationship are equivalent. In a behavioral sense, we usually think of quantity demanded as being a function of the price of the good. However, we use the inverse form of the relationship, price as a function of quantity, to plot a demand curve and to calculate the point price elasticity of demand, as shown in Equation 3.5.

Other Functions Related to Demand

Given the demand function in Table 3.2, we can derive a **total revenue function**, which shows the total revenue (price times quantity) received by the producer as a function of the level of output. To find total revenue, we can calculate the quantity demanded at different prices and multiply the terms together, or we can use the formal total revenue function given in Table 3.2.

Average revenue is defined as total revenue per unit of output. The **average revenue function** shows how average revenue is related to the level of output. Because total revenue equals $(P)(Q)$, average revenue equals the price of the product by definition. This is shown in the third line of Table 3.2. Thus, at any level of output, the average revenue received by the producer equals the price at which that output is sold.

Total revenue function
The functional relationship that shows the total revenue (price times quantity) received by a producer as a function of the level of output.

Average revenue
Total revenue per unit of output. Average revenue equals the price of the product by definition.

Average revenue function
The functional relationship that shows the revenue per unit of output received by the producer at different levels of output.

TABLE 3.2 Numerical Example of Demand, Total Revenue, Average Revenue, and Marginal Revenue Functions

Demand function	$Q = 12 - P$ or $P = 12 - Q$
Total revenue function	$TR = (P)(Q) = (12 - Q)(Q) = 12Q - Q^2$
Average revenue function	$AR = \dfrac{TR}{Q} = \dfrac{(P)(Q)}{Q} = P$
Marginal revenue function	$MR = \dfrac{\Delta TR}{\Delta Q} = \dfrac{TR_2 - TR_1}{Q_2 - Q_1}$
	$MR = \dfrac{dTR}{dQ} = 12 - 2Q$

---

[20]If we had a demand function that explicitly included another variable such as income, once we put in a specific value for income (to hold it constant), that number would become part of the constant term of the equation.

Marginal revenue
The additional revenue that a firm takes in from selling an additional unit of output or the change in total revenue divided by the change in output.

Marginal revenue function
The functional relationship that shows the additional revenue a producer receives by selling an additional unit of output at different levels of output.

Marginal revenue is defined as the additional revenue that a firm receives from selling an additional unit of output or the change in total revenue divided by the change in output. It can be calculated in discrete terms if you have data on the total revenue associated with different levels of output, as shown in the fourth line of Table 3.2. If you have a mathematical total revenue function, the **marginal revenue function** can be calculated by taking the derivative of the total revenue function with respect to output. (Because calculus is not required in this text, we will supply any marginal revenue functions that you need.)

The numerical values for the functional relationships in Table 3.2 are given in Table 3.3. The first two columns of Table 3.3 show the values of the demand function and the inverse relationship between price and quantity demanded. Column 3 presents total revenue for the different levels of output. Column 4 shows marginal revenue calculated in discrete terms, which represents the change in total revenue between one and two units of output, between two and three units of output, and so on. Column 5 shows marginal revenue calculated from the marginal revenue function presented in the last line of Table 3.2. In this case, marginal revenue is calculated for an infinitesimal change in output that occurs at a given level of output. Thus, Column 5 shows marginal revenue calculated precisely at a given level of output compared with the Column 4 calculations of marginal revenue between different levels of output. You will notice that the values in Columns 4 and 5 are very similar. The differences between Columns 4 and 5 are similar to the differences between the arc and point price elasticities of demand we discussed earlier in the chapter. Remember that these are differences in the calculation of the numbers, not in the definition of the concepts.

Calculation of Arc and Point Price Elasticities

Table 3.4 illustrates arc and point price elasticity calculations from the demand functions in Tables 3.2 and 3.3. Table 3.4 illustrates both the differences in the calculation methods for arc and point price elasticities and the similarities in the

TABLE 3.3 Numerical Values for the Functional Relationships in Table 3.2

(1) Q	(2) P	(3) $TR = (P)(Q)$	(4) $MR = \Delta TR/\Delta Q$	(5) $MR = dTR/dQ$
0	12	0		12
1	11	11	11	10
2	10	20	9	8
3	9	27	7	6
4	8	32	5	4
5	7	35	3	2
6	6	36	1	0
7	5	35	−1	−2
8	4	32	−3	−4
9	3	27	−5	−6
10	2	20	−7	−8
11	1	11	−9	−10
12	0	0	−11	−12

TABLE 3.4   Arc Price Elasticity Versus Point Price Elasticity Calculations (Data from Tables 3.2 and 3.3)

ARC ELASTICITY: ELASTIC DEMAND

$P_1 = \$10; Q_1 = 2; TR_1 = \$20$

$P_2 = \$9; Q_2 = 3; TR_2 = \$27$

$$e_P = \dfrac{\dfrac{Q_2 - Q_1}{Q_1 - Q_2}}{\dfrac{P_2 - P_1}{P_1 + P_2}} = \dfrac{\dfrac{3-2}{2+3}}{\dfrac{9-10}{10+9}}$$

$$e_P = \dfrac{\dfrac{\frac{1}{5}}{2}}{\dfrac{-1}{19}} = \dfrac{\frac{2}{5}}{\frac{-2}{19}} = \dfrac{-19}{5} = -3.80$$

POINT ELASTICITY: ELASTIC DEMAND

$$e_P = \dfrac{P}{(P-a)}$$

where $a = 12$

$P = \$10$

$$e_P = \dfrac{10}{(10-12)} = \dfrac{10}{-2} = -5.00$$

POINT ELASTICITY: UNIT ELASTIC DEMAND

$$e_P = \dfrac{P}{(P-a)}$$

where $a = 12$

$P = \$6$

$$e_P = \dfrac{6}{(6-12)} = \dfrac{6}{-6} = -1.00$$

ARC ELASTICITY: INELASTIC DEMAND

$P_1 = \$4; Q_1 = 8; TR_1 = \$32$

$P_2 = \$3; Q_2 = 9; TR_2 = \$27$

$$e_P = \dfrac{\dfrac{Q_2 - Q_1}{Q_1 + Q_2}}{\dfrac{P_2 - P_1}{P_1 + P_2}} = \dfrac{\dfrac{9-8}{8+9}}{\dfrac{3-4}{4+3}}$$

$$e_P = \dfrac{\dfrac{\frac{1}{17}}{2}}{\dfrac{-1}{7}} = \dfrac{\frac{2}{17}}{\frac{-2}{7}} = \dfrac{-7}{17} = -0.41$$

POINT ELASTICITY: INELASTIC DEMAND

$$e_P = \dfrac{P}{(P-a)}$$

where $a = 12$

$P = \$4$

$$e_P = \dfrac{4}{(4-12)} = \dfrac{4}{-8} = -0.50$$

results. In this example, the arc price elasticity of demand between a price of $10 and a price of $9 is –3.80, while the point price elasticity calculated precisely at $10 is –5.00. The arc price elasticity calculated between a price of $4 and a price of $3 is –0.41, while the point price elasticity at $4 is –0.50.

Price Elasticity Versus Slope of the Demand Curve

We can see in Table 3.4 that the price elasticity of demand is not constant along this linear demand curve. At prices above $6, the demand is elastic, whereas the demand is inelastic at prices below $6. The demand is unit elastic at a price of $6. We'll explore these relationships in more detail in the next section of the chapter. However, this analysis does show us that elasticity and slope are *not* the same concepts. A linear demand curve, like any straight line, has a constant slope, but the price elasticity of demand varies along this demand curve. Thus, for a linear demand function, the price elasticity coefficient must be calculated for a specific price and quantity demanded on that curve because the coefficient is smaller at lower prices than at higher prices.[21]

Demand Elasticity, Marginal Revenue, and Total Revenue

The relationships among demand, total revenue, and marginal revenue in Tables 3.2 and 3.3 are summarized in Figures 3.4 and 3.5. The inverse demand curve, $P = 12 - Q$, is plotted in Figure 3.4 along with the corresponding marginal revenue curve. Values of the total revenue function are plotted in Figure 3.5.

A firm is always constrained by its demand curve. In the case of the linear demand curve in Figure 3.4, a price of $12 drives the quantity demanded to 0, and, at a price of $0, the quantity demanded is 12 units. Thus, total revenue (price times quantity) in Figure 3.5 begins and ends at zero at each end of the demand curve in Figure 3.4.

In the top half of the demand curve in Figure 3.4, when managers lower the price, total revenue in Figure 3.5 increases. This means that demand is elastic in this range of the demand curve, as a decrease in price results in an increase in total revenue. At a price of $6 and a quantity demanded of 6 units, total revenue is maximized at $36, as shown in Figure 3.5. Demand at this point is unit elastic. In the bottom half of the demand curve, below a price of $6, a decrease in price causes total revenue to fall as quantity demanded increases from 6 to 12 units of output. This means that demand is inelastic for this portion of the demand curve. The decrease in total revenue between 6 and 12 units of output is illustrated in Figure 3.5.

The marginal revenue curve is also plotted with the demand curve in Figure 3.4. The marginal revenue curve begins at the point where the demand curve intersects the price axis and then has a slope twice as steep as the demand curve. This can be seen in the equations in Table 3.2, where the demand function is expressed as $P = 12 - Q$ and the marginal revenue function is $MR = 12 - 2Q$. This relationship between the demand and the marginal revenue function holds for all linear downward sloping demand curves. Once you draw the demand curve, you can draw the corresponding marginal revenue curve, even if you do not have specific equations for the curves.

FIGURE 3.4
Demand and Marginal Revenue Functions
The demand, marginal revenue, and total revenue functions are interrelated, as shown in Figures 3.4 and 3.5.

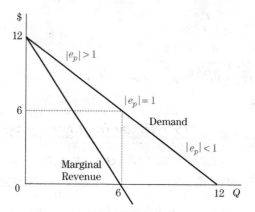

---

[21]Equation 3.2 can be simplified to show price elasticity as follows:

$$3.2 \quad e_p = \frac{\dfrac{\Delta Q_X}{Q_X}}{\dfrac{\Delta P_X}{P_X}} = \frac{(\Delta Q_X)(P_X)}{(\Delta P_X)(Q_X)}$$

The first ratio of variables in Equation 3.2 (Q_X/P_X) is a slope term. It shows the absolute change in quantity divided by the absolute change in price and is constant for a linear demand function. To calculate price elasticity, however, we must multiply this slope term by the ratio of a given price and quantity demanded, the second ratio of variables in Equation 3.2 (P_X/Q_X). While the slope term remains constant along the demand curve, the second term does not. As you move down the demand curve, price decreases and quantity demanded increases, so the ratio and, thus, the price elasticity of demand decrease.

FIGURE 3.5
The Total Revenue Function

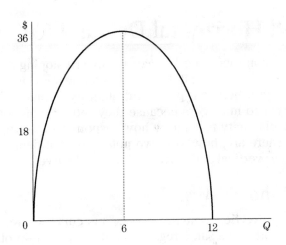

We can also see a relationship between marginal revenue and price elasticity in Figure 3.4. Marginal revenue is positive, but decreasing in value, between a price of $12 and a price of $6 (or between 0 and 6 units of output). This means that as price is lowered in that range, total revenue increases, but at a decreasing rate.[22] Figure 3.5 shows that total revenue increases from $0 to $36 as output increases from 0 to 6 units. However, the rate of increase lessens and the total revenue curve becomes flatter as output approaches 6 units. Because the top half of the demand curve is the elastic portion, marginal revenue must be a positive number when demand is elastic.

Decreases in the price below $6 cause the marginal revenue curve in Figure 3.4 to become negative. The additional revenue that the firm takes in from selling an additional unit of output is negative. The total revenue function in Figure 3.5 starts to decrease after 6 units of output are sold. We already established that the bottom half of the demand curve is the inelastic portion of that curve. Thus, when demand is inelastic, lowering the price decreases total revenue, so that marginal revenue is negative.

At the exact midpoint of the demand curve, marginal revenue equals zero. This is also the point where total revenue reaches its maximum value. In Figure 3.5, total revenue is at a maximum of $36 at a quantity of 6 units of output and a price of $6. And as we established, demand is unit elastic at this price. Any small change in price at this point will have no impact on total revenue. Table 3.5 summarizes all of these relationships for a linear downward sloping demand curve.

TABLE 3.5   Relationships for a Linear Downward Sloping Demand Curve

ELASTICITY	IMPACT ON TOTAL REVENUE	MARGINAL REVENUE
Elastic $\lvert e_P \rvert > 1$ Upper half of demand curve	$\downarrow P \Rightarrow \uparrow TR$ $\uparrow P \Rightarrow \downarrow TR$	Positive (for increases in Q)
Inelastic $\lvert e_P \rvert < 1$ Lower half of demand curve	$\downarrow P \Rightarrow \downarrow TR$ $\uparrow P \Rightarrow \uparrow TR$	Negative (for increases in Q)
Unit Elastic $\lvert e_P \rvert = 1$ Midpoint of demand curve	$\downarrow P \Rightarrow$ No change in TR $\uparrow P \Rightarrow$ No change in TR TR is at its maximum value	Zero

[22]This can be explained mathematically because marginal revenue is the slope of the total revenue function. The slope of the total revenue curve in Figure 3.5 decreases as output increases to 6 units.

Vertical and Horizontal Demand Curves

The previous discussion focused on *linear* downward sloping demand curves. We use these examples to represent all downward sloping demand curves that exhibit an inverse relationship between price and quantity demanded. These demand curves are important to managers because they reflect typical consumer behavior, with the price elasticity measuring how responsive quantity demanded is to changes in price. There are, however, two polar cases of demand curves that we should also consider: vertical and horizontal demand curves.

Vertical Demand Curves

Figure 3.6 presents a vertical demand curve. This curve shows that the quantity demanded of the good is the same regardless of the price—in other words, there is no consumer responsiveness to changes in the price of the good. This vertical demand curve represents **perfectly inelastic demand**, where the elasticity coefficient is zero ($e_P = 0$).

Perfectly inelastic demand
Zero elasticity of demand, illustrated by a vertical demand curve, where there is no change in quantity demanded for any change in price.

Can you guess what, if any, types of goods would have such a demand curve? Students often suggest products that are produced by only one supplier, such as the electricity supplied by a local power utility in a state where there has been no deregulation of electricity. Yet this answer is incorrect. Even if people can buy their electric power from only one source, and even if they usually will not be very responsive to price, they typically will not be totally *unresponsive* to changes in price. If the price of electricity increases, people may choose to run their air conditioners less in the summer or be more careful about how many lights they light up in their houses. Thus, they are decreasing the quantity demanded of electricity in response to a higher price and therefore do not have a vertical demand curve for electricity.

A vertical demand curve would pertain to a product that is absolutely necessary for life and for which there are no substitutes. Insulin for a diabetic might be a reasonable example, although this answer relates to the product insulin in general and not to a particular type of insulin produced by a specific drug company. You would think that illegal, addictive drugs or other addictive substances would have very low elasticities of demand, even if they are not zero. However, the evidence is not clear even for these products. Researchers have estimated the price elasticity of demand for marijuana to lie between –1.0 and –1.5, while that for opium to be approximately –0.7 over shorter time periods and around –1.0 over longer periods. In a study of persons arrested for cocaine and heroin use in 42 large cities from 1988 to 2003, cocaine price elasticity estimates ranged from –0.07 to –0.17 and that for heroin use was estimated at –0.1. The estimates were slightly lower for drug offenders compared with nondrug offenders (–0.12 to –0.13 vs. –0.16 to –0.19 for cocaine use and –0.09

FIGURE 3.6
Vertical Demand Curve
A vertical demand curve represents perfectly inelastic demand.

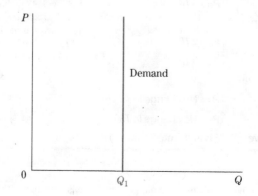

to –0.14 vs. –0.12 to –0.28 for heroin use). Cigarette smoking price elasticities have been estimated at –0.75 for adults, while teenage smoking elasticities may be greater than 1 in absolute value.[23] Thus, even for addictive substances, the price elasticities may not be close to zero. The key issues for perfectly inelastic demand are that the product is necessary for life and there are no substitutes.[24]

Horizontal Demand Curves

The other polar case, the horizontal demand curve, is shown in Figure 3.7. This is the example of **perfectly (or infinitely) elastic demand** ($e_P = \infty$). Any increases in price above P_1 in Figure 3.7 would cause the quantity demanded to decrease to zero, while any price decreases below P_1 would cause the quantity demanded to increase tremendously. This demand curve does not have any exact applications in reality, although estimates of the price elasticity of demand for the output of individual farmers are extremely large. Estimated absolute values of the demand elasticities for individual producers of common fruits and vegetables range from 500 to 21,000, with most values greater than 2,000.[25] These values are not infinite in size, but they are extremely large compared with normal elasticity values.

The perfectly elastic demand curve plays a very important role in economic theory because it represents the demand curve facing an individual firm in the model of perfect competition. In this model, the individual firm is one of a large number of firms producing a product such that no single firm can influence the price of the product. If such a firm tried to raise its price, its quantity demanded would fall to zero.

> **Perfectly (or infinitely) elastic demand**
> Infinite elasticity of demand, illustrated by a horizontal demand curve, where the quantity demanded would vary tremendously if there were any changes in price.

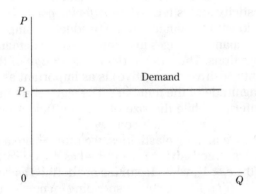

FIGURE 3.7
Horizontal Demand Curve
A horizontal demand curve represents perfectly or infinitely elastic demand.

[23]Charles T. Nisbet and Firouz Vakil, "Some Estimates of Price and Expenditure Elasticities of Demand for Marijuana Among U.C.L.A. Students," *Review of Economics and Statistics* 54 (November 1972): 473–75; Jan C. Van Ours, "The Price Elasticity of Hard Drugs: The Case of Opium in the Dutch East Indies, 1923–1938," *Journal of Political Economy* 103 (1995): 261–79; Dhaval Dave, "Illicit Drug Use Among Arestees, Prices, and Policy," *Journal of Urban Economics* 63 (2008): 694–714; Gary S. Becker, Michael Grossman, and Kevin M. Murphy, "An Empirical Analysis of Cigarette Addiction," *American Economic Review* 84 (June 1994): 396–418; Frank J. Chaloupka and Michael Grossman, *Price, Tobacco Control, and Youth Smoking*, NBER Working Paper Series, no. 5740 (Cambridge, MA: National Bureau of Economic Research, 1996); Frank J. Chaloupka and Henry Wechsler, "Price, Tobacco Control Policies, and Smoking Among Young Adults," *Journal of Health Economics* 16 (June 1997): 359–73; David P. Hopkins, Peter A. Briss, Connie J. Ricard, Corinne G. Husten, Vilma G. Carande-Kulis, Jonathan E. Fielding, Mary O. Alao et al., "Review of Evidence Regarding Interventions to Reduce Tobacco Use and Exposure to Environmental Tobacco Smoke," *American Journal of Preventive Medicine* 20 Suppl 1 (2001): 16–66.
[24]Although the individual demand curve for insulin might be perfectly inelastic, the market demand curve would have a nonzero elasticity coefficient. For every user of insulin, there is some maximum price they are willing and able to pay. When this price is exceeded, these users drop out of the market, causing quantity demanded to vary with price.
[25]Dennis W. Carlton and Jeffrey M. Perloff, *Modern Industrial Organization*, 4th ed. (New York: Pearson Addison-Wesley, 2005).

Thus, each firm is a price-taker and faces a horizontal demand curve. Individual agricultural producers come close to fitting this definition. That is why the estimated demand elasticities presented above, while not infinite, are very large in size.

Income and Cross-Price Elasticities of Demand

Although price elasticity of demand is of great importance, managers also need to know the size of the other elasticities in the demand function for a given product. Two other common elasticities are the income elasticity and the cross-price elasticity of demand.

Income Elasticity of Demand

Income elasticity of demand

The percentage change in the quantity demanded of a given good, X, relative to a percentage change in consumer income, assuming all other factors constant.

The **income elasticity of demand** shows how consumers change their demand for a particular product in response to changes in income. The elasticity coefficient is defined as the percentage change in the quantity demanded of the good relative to the percentage change in income, holding all other factors constant. This change in income could be a change for an individual consumer resulting from a raise or new job, or it could arise from a change in the general level of economic activity in the overall economy affecting all consumers.

If an increase in income results in an increase in the demand for the good or if declining income causes consumers to decrease their demand, the good has a *positive* income elasticity of demand and is called a *normal good*. Thus, changes in income and the demand for normal goods move in the same direction. If an increase in income results in a decrease in demand or vice versa, the good has a *negative* income elasticity and is termed an *inferior good*. As you've learned, this term has nothing to do with the quality of the product; it simply denotes a negative income elasticity of demand. Changes in income and the demand for inferior goods move in opposite directions. Thus, the *mathematical sign* of the income elasticity of demand coefficient (positive or negative) is as important as the *size* of the elasticity coefficient (magnitude of the number). The sign tells a manager whether the good is normal or inferior, while the size of the coefficient measures the responsiveness of the demand to changes in income.

Necessity

A good with an income elasticity between 0 and 1, where the expenditure on the good increases less than proportionately with changes in income.

Luxury

A good with an income elasticity greater than 1, where the expenditure on the good increases more than proportionately with changes in income.

For goods with positive income elasticities, we often make a distinction between necessities and luxuries. **Necessities** are defined as goods with an income elasticity between 0 and 1 ($0 < e_I < 1$), while **luxuries** are defined as goods with an income elasticity greater than 1 ($e_I > 1$). Consumer spending on necessities does not change substantially as income changes, whereas spending on luxury goods changes more than proportionately with changes in income.

Table 3.6 summarizes these concepts. For income elasticity of demand, the percentage change in quantity is the change between the two quantities demanded divided by the base quantity; the same is true for the percentage change in income. As with price elasticity, income elasticities can be calculated either for discrete changes in income and quantities (arc elasticity) or for infinitesimal changes (point elasticity).

A study based on scanner data for wine purchases in U.S. retail outlets over the years 2002 to 2005 estimated that the income elasticities of demand for white wines (2.996 to 3.003) were twice as large as those for red wines (1.285 to 1.312). A similar result occurred when wines under and over $10 per bottle were analyzed separately. When wines were analyzed by both price point and varietal, all income elasticities were estimated to be positive with Rielsing over $10 per bottle having a significantly large elasticity value of 9.9. Thus, wines are generally luxury goods with some fairly large income elasticities.[26]

[26]Steven S. Cuellar, Tim Colgan, Heather Hunnicutt, and Gabriel Ransom, "The Demand for Wine in the USA," *International Journal of Wine Business Research* 22 (2010): 178–90.

TABLE 3.6   Income Elasticity and Cross-Price Elasticity of Demand Coefficients

ELASTICITY NAME	ELASTICITY DEFINITION	VALUE OF ELASTICITY COEFFICIENT	IMPACT ON DEMAND
Income elasticity: e_I	$$\frac{\%\Delta Q_X}{\%\Delta I} = \frac{\frac{\Delta Q_X}{Q_X}}{\frac{\Delta I}{\Delta I}}$$	$e_I > 0$: Normal good	Increase in income results in increase in demand
		$0 < e_I < 1$: Necessity	Decrease in income results in decrease in demand
		$e_I > 1$: Luxury	
		$e_I < 0$: Inferior good	Increase in income results in decrease in demand
			Decrease in income results in increase in demand
Cross-price	$$\frac{\%\Delta Q_X}{\%\Delta P_Y} = \frac{\frac{\Delta Q_X}{Q_X}}{\frac{\Delta P_Y}{\Delta P_Y}}$$	$e_C > 0$: Substitute good	Increase in the price of good Y results in increase in the demand for good X
			Decrease in the price of good Y results in decrease in the demand for good X
Elasticity: e_C		$e_C < 0$: Complementary good	Increase in the price of good Y results in decrease in the demand for good X
			Decrease in the price of good Y results in increase in the demand for good X

Managerial Rule of Thumb

Calculating Income Elasticity

The following is a simple rule of thumb for calculating the income elasticity of demand for a product based on two questions for a consumer:

1. What fraction of your total budget do you spend on Product X?
2. If you earned a bonus of an additional $1,000, what part of that bonus would you spend on Product X?

   The ratio of the answer to question 2 to the answer to question 1 is the income elasticity of demand.[27] Applying this rule to different products will give managers a quick means of determining how changes in income will affect the demand for various products. ∎

Cross-Price Elasticity of Demand

The **cross-price elasticity of demand** measures how the demand for one good, X, varies with changes in the price of another good, Y. The elasticity coefficient is defined as the percentage change in the quantity demanded of good X relative to the percentage change in the price of good Y, holding all other factors constant. Two goods with a *positive* cross-price elasticity of demand coefficient are said to be *substitute goods*. An increase in the price of good Y causes consumers to demand more of good X because they are substituting good X for good Y. Coffee and tea are substitute goods, as an increase in the price of coffee will cause some people to switch to drinking tea. If two goods have a *negative* cross-price elasticity of demand coefficient, they are called *complementary goods*. An increase in the price of good Y results in a decrease in the demand for good X if the two goods are used together or are complements. Coffee and cream are complements because an

Cross-price elasticity of demand

The percentage change in the quantity demanded of a given good, X, relative to the percentage change in the price of good Y, all other factors held constant.

---

[27]This example is drawn from Shlomo Maital, *Executive Economics* (New York: Free Press, 1994), 195. The answer to question 1 is X/Y, where X is the amount of good X purchased and Y is income. The answer to question 2 is $(\Delta X)/(\Delta Y)$. The ratio of answer 2 to answer 1 is $(\Delta X/\Delta Y)/(X/Y)$, which can be converted to $(\Delta X/X)/(\Delta Y/Y)$, the definition for the income elasticity of demand.

increase in the price of coffee causes people to drink less coffee and, therefore, use less cream. Goods that have a zero cross-price elasticity of demand are unrelated in terms of consumption.

Thus, both the mathematical sign and the magnitude or size of the cross-price elasticity coefficient are important concepts for managers. The sign of the coefficient tells whether the goods are substitutes or complements, and the size of the cross-price elasticity measures the extent of the relationship between the goods. These relationships are summarized in the bottom part of Table 3.6.

In 1986, the Federal Trade Commission (FTC) filed suit to block a merger between the Coca-Cola Company and the Dr. Pepper Company in order to maintain competition and, thus, lower prices in the carbonated soft drink market.[28] The size of the relevant market, the number of substitutes, and, therefore, the implied cross-price elasticities of demand between Coke and other beverages were key issues in these proceedings. The FTC's argument that the carbonated soft drink market was the relevant market was based on evidence that soft drink pricing and marketing strategies focused on the producers of other soft drinks, not fruit juices, milk, coffee, tea, or other beverages. Documents indicated that Coke officials gathered information on the prices and sales of other carbonated soft drink producers, not producers of other beverages. Although Coca-Cola argued that the company competed against all other beverages, which were, therefore, actual or potential substitutes for carbonated soft drinks, the judge in the case ruled for the FTC and accepted its argument regarding the narrower number of relevant substitutes.

Estimates of the cross-price elasticity of demand influenced the decision by the Federal Aviation Administration (FAA) in 2005 not to mandate the use of child safety seats on commercial airlines. An FAA analysis indicated that if families were forced to purchase additional seats for infants under two years of age, they might opt to drive rather than fly. The increase in the price of airline fares could cause families to substitute relatively risky automobile travel for relatively safe air travel. It has been estimated that such a mandate would save 0.3 infant lives per year in the air, but, given a positive cross-price elasticity of 0.356 between the price of air travel and the quantity of road travel, would result in an additional 11.5 deaths on the nation's roads.[29]

The cross-price elasticity between land- or wireline and wireless telephone services has also played a role in the communications industry. Regulation of landline services regarding price increases is influenced by the amount of substitution between these services and other modes of communication. The U.S. Department of Justice and the Federal Communications Commission have generally been skeptical that the availability of wireless phones constrains the ability of landline carriers to raise prices. Because many U.S. households have a landline connection and at least one wireless telephone, it is also not clear whether these two services are substitutes or complements.

A study of state data from 2001 to 2007 indicated that a 1 percent increase in the price of wireline service was estimated to increase the demand for wireless service by approximately 0.48 to 0.69 percent, while the cross-price elasticity of wireline demand with respect to the wireless price was estimated to lie between 1.25 and 1.32. The cross-price elasticity between the demand for cable television and the price of direct broadcast satellite has been estimated to be between 0.3 and 0.5, so that consumers appear to view wireless telephones to be at least as interchangeable with wirelines as

---

[28]This discussion is based on Lawrence J. White, "Application of the Merger Guidelines: The Proposed Merger of Coca-Cola and Dr. Pepper (1986)," in *The Antitrust Revolution: The Role of Economics*, eds. John E. Kwoka Jr. and Lawrence J. White, 2nd ed. (New York: HarperCollins, 1994), 76–95.

[29]Shane Sanders, Dennis L. Weisman, and Dong Li, "Child Safety Seats on Commercial Airliners: A Demonstration of Cross-Price Elasticities," *Journal of Economic Education* 39 (Spring 2008): 135–44.

cable television is with direct broadcast satellite service. Thus, wireless telephones appear to have evolved as a strong substitute for traditional landline service.[30]

In the previously discussed study of the demand for wine, the cross-price elasticity of white wine for red wine was estimated to be positive but less than one, while the cross-price elasticity of red wine for white wine was positive and greater than two. Thus, red wine drinkers are more likely to switch to white wine than white wine drinkers are to switch to reds. The cross-price elasticities of most wine varietals were positive, indicating substitutability among varietals.[31]

Elasticity Estimates: Economics Literature

Table 3.7 presents estimates of elasticity of demand coefficients derived in the economics literature for various products. These estimates show how elasticities differ among products, groups of consumers, and over time. Remember that price elasticity coefficients are reported as negative numbers even though we look at their absolute values to determine the size of the coefficients.

TABLE 3.7   Estimates of Demand Elasticities

PRODUCT	PRICE ELASTICITY COEFFICIENT	INCOME ELASTICITY COEFFICIENT	CROSS-PRICE ELASTICITY COEFFICIENT
CHICKEN/AGRICULTURAL PRODUCTS/ OTHER FOOD			
Broiler chickens	−0.2 to −0.4	+1.0 (1950) +0.38 (1980s)	+0.20 (beef) +0.28 (pork)
Cabbage	−0.25	N.A.	
Potatoes	−0.27	+0.15	
Eggs	−0.43	+0.57	
Oranges	−0.62	+0.83	
Cream	−0.69	+1.72	
Apples	−1.27	+1.32	
Fresh tomatoes	−2.22	+0.24	
Lettuce	−2.58	+0.88	
Fresh peas	−2.83	+1.05	
Individual producer	−500 to −21,000		
Food away from home	−0.81		
Soft drinks	−0.79		
Juice	−0.76		
Cereals	−0.60		
Milk	−0.59		
Fish	−0.50		
Cheese	−0.44		
Sweets/sugars	−0.34		

(continued)

[30]Kevin W. Caves, "Quantifying Price-Driven Wireless Substitution in Telephony," *Telecommunications Policy* 35 (2011): 984–98.
[31]Cuellar et al., "The Demand for Wine in the USA."

TABLE 3.7   *Continued*

PRODUCT	PRICE ELASTICITY COEFFICIENT	INCOME ELASTICITY COEFFICIENT	CROSS-PRICE ELASTICITY COEFFICIENT
BEER			
Commodity	−0.7 to −0.9		
72-oz. packages	−5.07		
144-oz. packages	−5.008		
288-oz. packages	−4.543		
WATER DEMAND	−0.33	+0.13	
THE TOBACCO INDUSTRY (CIGARETTES)			
College students	−0.906 to −1.309		
Secondary school students	−0.846 to −1.450		
Adults, long-run, permanent change in price	−0.75		
Adults, short-run, permanent change in price	−0.40		
Adults, temporary change in price	−0.30		
HEALTH CARE			
Primary care	−0.1 to −0.7	$0.0 < e_I < +1.0$	
Total/elective surgery	−0.14 to −0.17		
Physician visits	−0.06		
Dental care	−0.5 to −0.7		
Nursing homes	−0.73 to −2.40		
Inpatient/outpatient hospital services	N.A.		+0.85 to +1.46
Individual physicians	−2.80 to −5.07		
HIGHER EDUCATION TUITION			
Any university	−0.05 to −0.40		
Individual university	−2.17 to −5.38		

Sources: Richard T. Rogers, "Broilers: Differentiating a Commodity," in *Industry Studies*, ed. Larry L. Duetsch, 2nd ed. (Armonk, NY: Sharpe, 1998); Tatiana Andreyeva, Michael W. Long, and Kelly D. Brownell, "The Impact of Food Prices on Consumption: A Systematic Review of Research on the Price Elasticity of Demand for Food," *American Journal of Public Health* 100 (February 2010): 216–22; Daniel B. Suits, "Agriculture," and Kenneth G. Elzinga, "Beer," in *The Structure of American Industry*, eds. Walter Adams and James W. Brock, 11th ed. (Upper Saddle River, NJ: Prentice Hall, 2005); Dennis W. Carlton and Jeffrey M. Perloff, *Modern Industrial Organization*, 4th ed. (New York: Pearson Addison-Wesley, 2005); Jeremy W. Bray, Brett R. Loomis, and Mark Engelen, "You Save Money When You Buy in Bulk: Does Volume-Based Pricing Cause People to Buy More Beer?" *Health Economics* 18 (2009): 607–18; Sheila M. Olmstead, W. Michael Hanemann, and Robert N. Stavins, "Water Demand Under Alternative Price Structures," *Journal of Environmental Economics and Management* 54 (2007): 181–98; Frank J. Chaloupka and Henry Wechsler, "Price, Tobacco Control Policies and Smoking Among Young Adults," *Journal of Health Economics* 16 (June 1997): 359–73; Frank J. Chaloupka and Michael Grossman, *Price, Tobacco Control, and Youth Smoking*, NBER Working Paper Series, no. 5740 (Cambridge, MA: National Bureau of Economic Research, 1996); Gary S. Becker, Michael Grossman, and Kevin M. Murphy, "An Empirical Analysis of Cigarette Addiction," *American Economic Review* 84 (June 1994): 396–418; Rexford E. Santerre and Stephen P. Neun, *Health Economics: Theories, Insights, and Industry Studies*, 4th ed. (Mason, OH: Thomson SouthWestern, 2007); Sherman Folland, Allen C. Goodman, and Miron Stano, *The Economics of Health and Health Care*, 3rd ed. (Upper Saddle River, NJ: Prentice Hall, 2001); Robert E. Carter and David J. Curry, "Using Student-Choice Behavior to Estimate Tuition Elasticity in Higher Education," *Journal of Marketing Management* 27 (2011): 1186–207.

Elasticity and Chicken and Agricultural/Food Products

As shown in Table 3.7, broiler chickens have a low price elasticity of demand, as do many other agricultural products. This low demand elasticity accounts for the wide swings in the income of farmers, particularly in response to bumper crops, or large increases in supply. Farm production is subject to many factors outside producer control, such as the weather and attacks by insects. Crops are grown and then thrown on the market for whatever price they will bring. If there is a bumper crop, this increase in supply drives farm product prices down. Because quantity demanded does not increase proportionately, given the inelastic demand, total revenue to the producers decreases. This is the essence of the "farm problem" that has confronted U.S. policy makers for many years.[32]

Table 3.7 shows that not all farm products have inelastic demands, however. Customers are much more responsive to the price of fresh tomatoes, lettuce, and fresh peas, with the elasticity of demand exceeding 2.00 in absolute value for these products. Table 3.7 also shows the difference between the elasticity of demand for the product as a whole and that for an individual producer of the product. While the elasticity of demand for many agricultural products is inelastic or less than 1 in absolute value, the elasticities of demand for individual producers are extremely large, ranging from –500 to –21,000. Farming can be considered a perfectly competitive industry, given the huge elasticities of demand for the individual producers of farm products. This is why we use the infinitely elastic or horizontal demand curve to portray the individual firm in perfect competition and the downward sloping demand curve for the output in the entire market.

Agricultural products are generally necessities, with income elasticities less than 1. However, the larger income elasticities for apples and cream mean that consumption will increase more than proportionately with increases in income. Broiler chickens have changed from a luxury good in the 1950s to a necessity today, as evidenced by the decrease in the size of their income elasticity. And, as expected, chicken is a substitute good with beef and pork, because chicken has a positive cross-price elasticity of demand with both of these products.

The price elasticity estimates in Table 3.7 for the categories "food away from home" to "sweets/sugars" were derived from a review of U.S. studies published from 1938 to 2007 with average values of the most recent estimates reported.[33] Although all of these estimates indicated inelastic demand, estimates for "soft drinks" and "juice" were relatively less inelastic while those for "sweets/sugars" were relatively more inelastic. "Food away from home" had the highest elasticity among these categories. Although the average price elasticity estimate for the "milk" category was –0.59, the study also reported estimates for "skim milk," 1 percent, and for "whole milk" ranging from –0.75 to –0.79, whereas the average elasticity for 2 percent milk was –1.22. Cross-price elasticities indicated that consumers were more likely to switch to reduced- or low-fat milk than skim milk when the price of whole milk increased. The authors of the study did not find any studies of price elasticities or cross-price elasticities that would predict how consumers would shift between healthier and less healthy food categories, such as whole grain and refined flour breads, brown and white rice, baked and regular chips, and reduced-fat and regular cheese.

Elasticity and Beer

The price elasticities of demand for beer also differ for the overall commodity and individual brands. Price elasticity estimates for beer as a commodity are less than 1 in absolute value, whereas estimates for individual brands are reported to be quite elastic, as there are many more substitutes among brands of beer than for beer as a product. The package size price elasticities in Table 3.7 represent substitution

---

[32]This discussion is drawn from Daniel B. Suits, "Agriculture," in *The Structure of American Industry*, eds. Walter Adams and James Brock, 11th ed. (Upper Saddle River, NJ: Prentice Hall, Inc., 2005), 1–22.

[33]Tatiana Andreyeva, Michael W. Long, and Kelly D. Brownell, "The Impact of Food Prices on Consumption: A Systematic Review of Research on the Price Elasticity of Demand for Food," *American Journal of Public Health* 100 (February 2010): 2216–22.

with a different package size of the same brand of beer or with another brand in response to price changes, so they would be expected to be large.[34] Results of the same study indicated that consumers are more likely to buy a larger-volume package in response to a price change than they are to buy a smaller-volume package or to switch brands. Although this study did not explicitly examine the extent of substitution from beer to wine or liquor, other research has indicated that many wine and liquor drinkers will switch to beer when faced with a price increase, but that few beer drinkers will switch to wine or liquor. They are more likely to switch package size for their beer.

Water Demand

Because water managers have often argued that consumers do not respond to changing prices, demand management has often been implemented through restrictions on water uses or requirements for the adoption of specific technologies.[35] However, a review of studies between 1963 and 1993 indicated that the average price elasticity of demand was –0.51, the short-run median was –0.38, and the long-run median was –0.64, with 90 percent of all estimates between zero and –0.75. Estimating the demand for water is complicated because water is typically priced either with a uniform marginal price, increasing block prices where the marginal price increases with the quantity consumed, or decreasing block prices. One study of 11 urban areas in the United States and Canada that took these pricing strategies into account estimated a price elasticity of –0.33. This somewhat lower estimate may be related to consumers keeping consumption at a kink point of one of the blocks or reacting to changes in the block prices. The estimated income elasticity of demand (+0.13) was also low compared with other studies where results ranged from 0.2 to 0.6. This difference may have resulted from the statistical estimation techniques used in the study.

Elasticity and the Tobacco Industry

The price elasticity of demand for cigarettes is of interest to the tobacco industry, state and federal policy makers, and public health advocates.[36] Legislators and public health advocates have long used cigarette taxation as a policy to attempt to limit smoking, particularly among teenagers. We noted earlier in the chapter that cigarette price elasticity of demand for adults is inelastic, but not zero. The estimates in Table 3.7 also show that teenagers and college students have a larger price elasticity of demand for cigarettes than adults. This result is expected for several reasons. Teenagers are likely to spend a greater proportion of their disposable income on cigarettes than adults. There are also substantial peer pressure effects operating on young people. Increased cigarette taxes and prices have a direct negative effect on consumption, as shown by the elasticity estimates.[37] Using taxes to reduce teenage smoking is an effective policy overall because few people begin smoking after the age of 20. The tobacco industry has long been aware of these price effects on smoking behavior and has lobbied to limit cigarette tax increases.

[34]Jeremy W. Bray, Brett R. Loomis, and Mark Engelen, "You Save Money When You Buy in Bulk: Does Volume-Based Pricing Cause People to Buy More Beer?" *Health Economics* 18 (2009): 607–18.

[35]This discussion is based on Sheila M. Olmstead, W. Michael Hanemann, and Robert N. Stavins, "Water Demand Under Alternative Price Structures," *Journal of Environmental Economics and Management* 54 (2007): 181–98.

[36]This discussion is based on George M. Guess and Paul G. Farnham, *Cases in Public Policy Analysis*, 3rd ed. (Washington, DC: Georgetown University Press, 2011).

[37]David P. Hopkins, Peter A. Briss, Connie J. Ricard, Corinne G. Husten, Vilma G. Carande-Kulis, Jonathan E. Fielding, Mary O. Alao et al., "Reviews of Evidence Regarding Interventions to Reduce Tobacco Use and Exposure to Environmental Tobacco Smoke," *American Journal of Preventive Medicine* 20 Suppl 1 (2001): 16–66.

The cigarette data also illustrate the differences between behavior in the near future and behavior over longer periods of time and between temporary and permanent price changes. Consumers are more price sensitive if they believe a price change is going to be permanent. As noted earlier in the chapter, consumers also have larger price elasticities over longer periods of time because they are able to search out more substitutes for the product in question. In response to higher cigarette prices, smokers may also switch to brands with higher tar and nicotine contents, inhale more deeply, reduce idle burn time, or switch to the use of smokeless tobacco.[38]

Elasticity and Health Care

The price elasticity estimates for health care are important because arguments are often made that the demand for these services is medically driven (people "need" health care). Table 3.7 shows that consumers are price sensitive to medical care goods and services. Although the demand is relatively inelastic, it is not perfectly inelastic, as the "needs" argument suggests. As the table shows, the demand for primary care is more inelastic than the demand for more discretionary services, such as dental care and nursing homes. The income elasticity of demand for health care services is generally less than +1.00, indicating that most consumers consider these services to be necessities. Inpatient and outpatient hospital services are generally thought to be substitute goods, as shown by the positive cross-price elasticities in Table 3.7, particularly because there has been a trend to perform many services on an outpatient basis that previously had been done in the hospital. However, some studies have derived negative cross-price elasticity estimates, indicating that these services might be complements in certain cases because some procedures done in the hospital may require follow-up outpatient visits. This example shows that economic theory alone may not be able to predict the sign of an elasticity and that elasticity coefficients need to be estimated from data on consumer behavior.

The differences in health care elasticities for overall primary care (–0.1 to –0.7) and for services provided by individual physicians (–2.80 to –5.07) again illustrate the principle that demand can be much more elastic for the individual producer of a product than for the product in general. Although these differences between product and individual producer elasticities are not as large as those between agricultural products and their producers, they still indicate that individual physicians are considered substitutes for one another.

Tuition Elasticity in Higher Education

Tuition pricing decisions in higher education are complex strategies based on pressures to maintain student enrollment; hire and retain faculty, administrators, and athletic coaches; and to maintain and build physical plant.[39] University administrators need to understand student response to tuition pricing decisions. Most studies have estimated tuition price elasticities ranging from –0.05 to –0.40. However, these studies were typically based on aggregate or national data that showed student response in terms of their decision to attend any college or university in their home country.

One study analyzed how students make decisions between a school's tuition level and the "non-tuition elements" including available housing, food service,

[38]Micheal Grossman and Frank J. Chaloupka, "Cigarette Taxes: The Straw to Break the Camel's Back," *Public Health Reports* 112 (July/August 1997): 291–97; Matthew C. Farrelly, Christina T. Nimsch, Andrew Hyland, and K. Michael Cummings, "The Effects of Higher Cigarette Prices on Tar and Nicotine Consumption in a Cohort of Adult Smokers," *Health Economics* 13 (2004): 49–58; Jerome Adda and Francesca Cornaglia, "Taxes, Cigarette Consumption, and Smoking Intensity," *American Economic Review* 96 (2006): 1013–28.
[39]This discussion is based on Robert E. Carter and David J. Curry, "Using Student-Choice Behaviour to Estimate Tuition Elasticity in Higher Education, " *Journal of Marketing Management* 27 (October 2011): 1186–207.

recreational facilities, and perceptions of campus life. This study used an online experiment to manipulate tuition levels at multiple universities to see which schools students at the focal university selected. Researchers estimated tuition elasticities for each of the 11 colleges in the focal university, which ranged from –2.17 in pharmacy to –5.38 in business. As expected, these elasticities for individual university choice were elastic and much larger compared with the aggregate national level estimates. The study also found that in-state residents were relatively more price sensitive than nonresidents and that undergraduates were more price sensitive than graduate students. Elasticity estimates varied substantially by academic division, indicating that university administrators could implement differential pricing policies based on these elasticities.

Managerial Rule of Thumb

Price Elasticity Decision Making

Which demand elasticity, the one for the entire product or the one for the individual producer, is appropriate for decision making by the firm? In markets where firms have some degree of market power, that answer depends on the assumption made about the reaction of other firms to the price change of a given firm. If all firms change prices together, the product demand elasticity is relevant. However, if one firm changes price without the other firms following, the larger elasticities for individual producers shown in Table 3.7 are appropriate. ∎

Elasticity Issues: Marketing Literature

Marketing brings greater detail to the basic economic analysis of price elasticity by examining such issues as the demand for specific brands of products and the demand at the level of individual stores. Marketing also takes a somewhat different approach to pricing and consumer behavior than economics, where buyers' responses to price changes are based on the economic model of rational consumer choice, which is described in Appendix 3A.[40] Although behavioral economics, which relaxes many consumer choice assumptions, is becoming more important in the economics discipline, marketing has traditionally relied on insights borrowed from psychology. These include the common belief that consumers treat price as an indicator of product quality, that buyers tend to perceive price differences in proportional rather than in absolute terms, that buyers perceive prices from left to right and calculate differences between pairs of prices taking into account only the more important digits on the left, and that the presentation of prices can affect consumers' reference prices or those prices that buyers' consider to be reasonable or fair.

Advertising elasticity of demand
The percentage change in the quantity demanded of a good relative to the percentage change in advertising dollars spent on that good, all other factors held constant.

Marketers are also concerned about the size of the price elasticity of demand compared with the **advertising elasticity of demand**, as both price and advertising are strategic variables under the control of managers. Changes in product price cause a movement along a given demand curve, while increases in advertising can cause changes in consumer preferences and bring new consumers into the market, thus shifting the entire demand curve. A key issue for managers is which strategy has the greatest impact on product sales. Table 3.8 presents the results of three major marketing studies, all of which we'll look at in more detail in the remainder of this section. We will also discuss a more recent study that updates the results of this earlier work.

---

[40]This discussion is based on Thanos Skouras, George J. Avlonitis, and Kostis A. Indounas, "Economics and Marketing on Pricing: How and Why Do They Differ?" *Journal of Product & Brand Management* 14 (2005): 362–74.

TABLE 3.8 Elasticity Coefficients from Marketing Literature

STUDY	PRODUCT	PRICE ELASTICITY COEFFICIENT	ADVERTISING ELASTICITY COEFFICIENT
Tellis (1988)	Detergents	−2.77	
	Durable goods	−2.03	
	Food	−1.65	
	Toiletries	−1.38	
	Others	−2.26	
	Pharmaceutical	−1.12	
Sethuraman and Tellis (1991)	All products	−1.61	0.11
	Durables	−2.01	0.23
	Nondurables	−1.54	0.09
	Product life cycle—early	−1.10	0.11
	Product life cycle—mature	−1.72	0.11
Hoch et al. (1995)	Soft drinks	−3.18	
	Canned seafood	−1.79	
	Canned soup	−1.62	
	Cookies	−1.60	
	Grahams/saltines	−1.01	
	Snack crackers	−0.86	
	Frozen entrees	−0.77	
	Refrigerated juice	−0.74	
	Dairy cheese	−0.72	
	Frozen juice	−0.55	
	Cereal	−0.20	
	Bottled juice	−0.09	
	Bath tissue	−2.42	
	Laundry detergent	−1.58	
	Fabric softener	−0.79	
	Liquid dish detergent	−0.74	
	Toothpaste	−0.45	
	Paper towels	−0.05	

Sources: Gerard J. Tellis, "The Price Elasticity of Selective Demand: A Meta-Analysis of Econometric Models of Sales," *Journal of Marketing Research* 25 (November 1988): 331–41; Raj Sethuraman and Gerald J. Tellis, "An Analysis of the Tradeoff Between Advertising and Price Discounting," *Journal of Marketing Research* 28 (May 1991): 160–74; Stephen J. Hoch, Byung-Do Kim, Alan L. Montgomery, and Peter E. Rossi, "Determinants of Store-Level Price Elasticity," *Journal of Marketing Research* 32 (February 1995): 17–29.

Marketing Study I: Tellis (1988)

The first group of elasticities, analyzed by Tellis, is from a meta-analysis or survey of other econometric studies of selective demand. Selective demand was defined by Tellis as "demand for a particular firm's branded product, measured as its sales or market share."[41] It differs from the demand for the overall product category, which is the focus of most of the economic studies of price elasticity in Table 3.7. The term *brand* was used generically by Tellis "to cover the individual brand, business unit, or firm whose sales or market share is under investigation."[42]

Tellis's study included 367 elasticities from 220 different brands or markets for the period 1961 to 1985. For all products in his study, Tellis found a mean price elasticity of −1.76. Therefore, on average for these firms and products, a 1 percent change in price results in a 1.76 percent change in sales in the opposite direction. The mean price elasticities for all product groups were also greater than 1 in absolute value. Tellis found that the demand for pharmaceutical products is relatively more inelastic than those for the other categories, given that safety, effectiveness, and timing considerations may be more important than price in influencing consumer demand. Pharmaceuticals requiring prescriptions are likely to be covered by health insurance for many consumers, which would make these individuals less price sensitive because part of that price is paid by a third party. The results of the Tellis analysis are important because they are based on numerous empirical studies of the price elasticity of demand of many different brands of products.

Marketing Study II: Sethuraman and Tellis (1991)

The second group of elasticities in Table 3.8 is derived from a meta-analysis of 16 studies conducted from 1960 to 1988 that estimated both price and advertising elasticities. This sample was different from the first meta-analysis described in the table because the studies surveyed in this analysis were required to have estimated both price and advertising elasticities. There were 262 elasticity estimates representing more than 130 brands or markets in this survey.

For this sample, Sethuraman and Tellis found a mean price elasticity of −1.609 (rounded to −1.61) and a mean short-term advertising elasticity of +0.109 (rounded to +0.11). Thus, the ratio of the two elasticities was 14.76, which means that the size of the average price elasticity is about 15 times the size of the average advertising elasticity. Pricing is obviously a powerful tool influencing consumer demand.

In Table 3.8, the price elasticity for durable goods is greater than that for nondurables. However, Sethuraman and Tellis argued that these estimates were not significantly different, while the differences in advertising elasticity estimates between durable and nondurable goods (0.23 vs. 0.09) were significant. These researchers also argued that durable goods might have a lower price elasticity than nondurables because consumers will pay a higher price for the higher perceived quality associated with known brands of durable goods, while customers will be more likely to shop around for a low price on nondurable goods. Advertising elasticities are likely to be higher for durable goods because consumers generally seek much information before the purchase of these goods.

Marketers have also focused on the stages in a product's life cycle—Introduction, Growth, Maturity, and Decline.[43] When a new product is introduced, there is usually a period of slow growth with low or nonexistent profits, given the large fixed costs often associated with product introduction. In the Growth period, the product is more widely accepted, and profits increase. When the product reaches Maturity, sales slow because the product has been accepted by most potential customers, and profits slow or decline because competition has increased. Finally, in the period of Decline, both sales and profits decrease. Marketers have hypothesized

---

[41]Gerard J. Tellis, "The Price Elasticity of Selective Demand: A Meta-Analysis of Econometric Models of Sales," *Journal of Marketing Research* 25 (November 1988): 331.
[42]Ibid.
[43]This discussion is based on Philip Kotler, *Marketing Management: The Millennium Edition* (Upper Saddle River, NJ: Prentice-Hall, 2000), 303–16.

that the price elasticity of demand increases over the product life cycle. Consumers are likely to be better informed and more price conscious about mature products, and there is likely to be more competition at this stage. Those who adopt a product early, during the Introduction and Growth stages, are likely to focus more on the newness of the product rather than its price. These expected differences in elasticities are shown in the estimates in Table 3.8.

Tellis also found that the ratio of the median price elasticity to advertising elasticity is three times higher for the United States than for Europe (19.5 vs. 6.2).[44] Thus, consumers may be more price sensitive than advertising sensitive in the United States compared with Europe. This difference could mean that the level of advertising is too high in the United States or that there is less opportunity for price discounting in Europe than in the United States.

Marketing Study III: Hoch et al. (1995)

The third set of elasticities in Table 3.8 comprises store-level price elasticities estimated from scanner data from Dominick's Finer Foods, a major chain in the Chicago metropolitan area. Table 3.8 shows large differences in price elasticities among product categories. Hoch et al. also found that the elasticities differed by store location. They analyzed how the elasticities were related to both the characteristics of the consumers in the market area and the overall competitive environment. Their results are summarized as follows:[45]

* More-educated consumers have higher opportunity costs, so they devote less attention to shopping and, therefore, are less price sensitive.
* Large families spend more of their disposable income on grocery products, and, therefore, they spend more time shopping to garner their increased returns to search; they are also more price sensitive.
* Households with larger, more expensive homes have fewer income constraints, so they are less price sensitive.
* Black and Hispanic consumers are more price sensitive.
* Store volume relative to the competition is important, suggesting that consumers self-select for location and convenience or price and assortment.
* Distance from the competition also matters. Isolated stores display less price sensitivity than stores located close to their competitors. Distance increases shopping costs.

Marketing Study Update

Bijmolt et al. updated the 1988 study by Tellis in a 2005 meta-analysis, which included 1,851 price elasticities from 1961 to 2004.[46] This study examined brand and stockkeeping-unit (SKU) elasticities only and excluded sales elasticities, analyzed elasticities for a single brand or SKU and not averages across items, considered only price elasticities based on actual purchase or sales data as opposed to experimental or judgment data, and limited the analysis to business-to-consumer markets.

These researchers found an average price elasticity of −2.62 that was substantially larger than the value of −1.76 in the Tellis study. This difference could have resulted

---

[44]Gerald J. Tellis, *Effective Advertising: Understanding When, How, and Why Advertising Works* (Thousand Oaks, CA: Sage Publications, Inc., 2004).

[45]Stephen J. Hoch, Byung-Do Kim, Alan L. Montgomery, and Peter E. Rossi, "Determinants of Store-Level Price Elasticity," *Journal of Marketing Research* 32 (February 1995): 28.

[46]Tammo H. A. Bijmolt, Harald J. Van Heerde, and Rik G. M. Pieters, "New Empirical Generalizations on the Determinants of Price Elasticity," *Journal of Marketing Research* XLII (May 2005): 1441–56.

from differences in sample sizes and estimation methods in the two studies and from changes in the underlying determinants of elasticities over time. However, Bijmolt et al. reconfirmed that the price elasticity of demand for durable goods was greater than for other products. They no longer found significant price elasticity differences between countries or between estimation methods. They did find that price elasticities were significantly larger in the Introduction/Growth stage than in the Mature/Decline stage, a result opposite to that of Tellis. Bijmolt et al. also found that inflation led to substantially larger price elasticities, especially in the short run, and that there were differences between the price elasticities for the short-run promotion of products versus longer-run price changes.

These researchers concluded that consumers seemed to base their purchase timing and quantity decisions increasingly on price promotions. If price elasticities were largest in the growth stage of product categories, starting with a low-price strategy might be the most effective approach for managers. The lack of effect of brand ownership on price elasticities meant that manufacturing brands were not necessarily more differentiated than private labels. Finally, the absence of price elasticity differences by country might mean that similar pricing strategies could be developed across developed countries. Bijmolt et al. noted that all these results pertained to bricks-and-mortar selling, and that price elasticities on the Internet could be significantly different.

Managerial Rule of Thumb

Elasticities in Marketing and Decision Making

You will most likely pursue these issues raised by the marketing literature in more depth in your marketing courses. The major point for business students is to recognize the importance of price elasticity of demand and the linkages between economics and marketing. Managers must be familiar with the fundamentals of demand and consumer responsiveness to all variables in a demand function because their marketing departments will build on these concepts to design optimal promotion and pricing strategies. ■

Summary

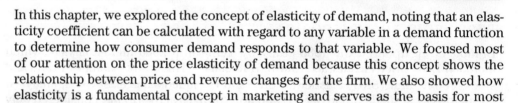

In this chapter, we explored the concept of elasticity of demand, noting that an elasticity coefficient can be calculated with regard to any variable in a demand function to determine how consumer demand responds to that variable. We focused most of our attention on the price elasticity of demand because this concept shows the relationship between price and revenue changes for the firm. We also showed how elasticity is a fundamental concept in marketing and serves as the basis for most pricing and promotion strategies.

We can now see how price elasticity relates to Procter & Gamble's pricing strategies discussed in the opening case of the chapter. When P&G increased prices in the first quarter of 2009, sales volume or quantity demanded decreased but sales revenues increased. Thus, the company faced inelastic demand for its products at that time. In the next few years when P&G cut prices to regain market share, consumer response and price elasticity were less than expected, so there was a negative effect on profits. The case discussed varying elasticities among P&G products, where consumers had more elastic demand for products with more substitutes and greater competition. We also noted that, in addition to changing its pricing strategy, P&G attempted to increase demand (shift the demand curve) by developing new products and entering emerging markets.

In the following appendix, we present the standard economic model of consumer choice. This model incorporates the concepts of consumer tastes and preferences, income, and the market prices of goods and services to show how consumer decisions change in the face of changing economic variables. The underlying assumption is that consumers maximize the utility they receive from consuming different goods and services subject to a budget constraint that incorporates both income and the prices of these goods and services. The end products of this model are the consumer demand curve and its relevant elasticities that we have been studying in this chapter.

Appendix 3A Economic Model of Consumer Choice

Economists have developed a formal model of consumer choice that focuses on the major factors discussed in this chapter that influence consumer demand: tastes and preferences, consumer income, and the prices of the goods and services. We briefly review this model to show how it can be used to derive a consumer demand curve and to illustrate reactions to changes in income and prices.

Consumer Tastes and Preferences

In this model, we assume that consumers are faced with the choice of different amounts of two goods, X and Y (although the model can be extended mathematically to incorporate any number of goods or services). We need to develop a theoretical construct that reflects consumers' preferences between these goods. Consumers derive *utility*, or satisfaction, from consuming different amounts of these goods. We use an *ordinal measurement of utility* in which consumers indicate whether they prefer one bundle of goods to another, but there is no precise measurement of the change in utility level or how much they prefer one bundle to another. Ordinal measurement allows our utility levels to be defined as one "being greater than another," but not one "being twice as great as another."

We also make the following assumptions about consumer preference orderings over different amounts of the goods:

1. Preference orderings are complete. Consumers are able to make comparisons between any combinations or bundles of the two goods and to indicate whether they prefer one bundle to another or whether they are indifferent between the bundles.
2. More of the goods are preferred to less of the goods (i.e., commodities are "goods" and not "bads"). Preferences are transitive. If bundle A is preferred to bundle B, and bundle B is preferred to bundle C, then bundle A is preferred to bundle C.
3. Consumers are selfish. Their preferences depend only on the amount of the goods they directly consume.
4. The goods are continuously divisible so that consumers can always purchase one more or one less unit of the goods.

From these assumptions, we develop a consumer's *indifference curve* that shows alternative combinations of the two goods that provide the same level of satisfaction or utility. We show in Figure 3.A1 that such an indifference curve must be downward sloping if the above assumptions about preferences hold.

In Figure 3.A1, point A represents an initial bundle of goods X and Y, with X_1 amount of good X and Y_1 amount of good Y. All combinations of the two goods are represented as points in Figure 3.A1. According to the above preference assumptions, the bundle of goods represented by point A must be preferred to any bundle of

FIGURE 3.A1

Derivation of a Consumer Indifference Curve

The indifference curve through point A must lie in the nonshaded areas of the quadrant.

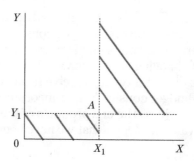

goods in the shaded rectangle to the southwest of point A because point A contains either more of both goods or more of one good and no less of the other. Likewise, any bundle of goods in the shaded area northeast of point A must be preferred to the bundle of goods at point A. We can, therefore, conclude that the indifference curve through point A must lie in the nonshaded areas of Figure 3.A1. Only in these areas of the figure will there be other combinations of goods X and Y that provide the consumer with the same satisfaction or utility as that provided at point A.

Figure 3.A2 illustrates such an indifference curve through point A. This indifference curve must be downward sloping, given the above discussion. Facing a choice between the bundle of goods represented by point A (X_1, Y_1) and point B (X_2, Y_2), the consumer is indifferent between these bundles because they both provide the same level of utility (U_1). Other bundles of goods, such as point C (X_3, Y_3), provide greater levels of utility because they lie on indifference curves farther from the origin. Thus, utility levels increase as we move in the direction of the arrow (northeast from the origin).

Looking at points B and A on indifference curve U_1, we can see that if the consumer gives up a certain amount of good Y, he needs an additional amount of good X to keep the utility level constant. If he gives up the amount of good Y represented by $Y_2 - Y_1$ or ΔY, he needs $X_1 - X_2$ or ΔX to keep his utility level constant. The ratio $\Delta Y / \Delta X$, which shows the rate at which the consumer is willing to trade off one good for another and still maintain a constant utility level, is called the *marginal rate of substitution* (MRS_{XY}). Mathematically, it is the slope of the indifference curve.

An indifference curve is typically drawn convex to the origin or as shown in Figures 3.A2 and 3.A3.

The slope of the convex indifference curve in Figure 3.A3 decreases as you move down the curve. This result implies that an individual has a diminishing marginal rate of substitution. When the individual is at point A (X_1, Y_1), with only a small amount of good X, he is willing to trade off a large amount of good Y, or $Y_1 - Y_2$, to gain an additional amount of X and move to point B (X_2, Y_2). However, starting

FIGURE 3.A2

Illustration of Consumer Indifference Curves

The consumer is indifferent between the bundles of goods, X and Y, represented by points A and B. These points lie on the same indifference curve, U_1. Point C represents a bundle of goods with a greater level of utility, U_3. Consumer preferences are represented by the marginal rate of substitution ($\Delta Y/\Delta X$) or the rate at which the consumer is willing to trade off one good for the other.

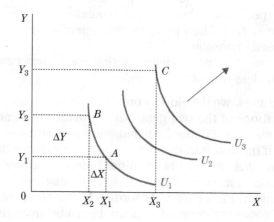

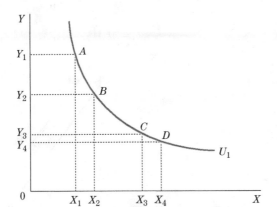

FIGURE 3.A3
A Convex Indifference Curve
An indifference curve is typically drawn convex to the origin, representing a diminishing marginal rate of substitution.

at point C (X_3, Y_3), the individual is willing to give up a much smaller amount of good Y, or $Y_3 - Y_4$, to obtain the additional amount of good X and move to point D (X_4, Y_4). This diminishing marginal rate of substitution reflects the principle of *diminishing marginal utility*. The additional or marginal utility that an individual derives from another unit of a good decreases as the number of units the individual already has obtained increases. When an individual has only X_1 units of good X, he is willing to trade off more units of good Y to obtain an additional unit of good X than when he already has a large amount of good X (X_3).

The behavioral assumption behind the consumer choice model is that the consumer wants to maximize the utility derived from the goods and services consumed (goods X and Y, in this case). However, the consumer is constrained by his level of income and by the prices he faces for the goods. We need to illustrate the effect of this constraint and then show how the consumer solves this *constrained maximization problem*.

The Budget Constraint

The consumer's budget constraint is represented by Equation 3.A1:

3.A1 $I = P_X X + P_Y Y$

> *where*
>> I = level of consumer's income
>> P_X = price of good X
>> X = quantity of good X
>> P_Y = price of good Y
>> Y = quantity of good Y

Equation 3.A1 shows that a consumer's income (I) can be spent either on good X [(P_X)(X)] or on good Y [(P_Y)(Y)]. For simplicity, we assume that all income is spent on the two goods.

With given values of I, P_X, and P_Y, we can graph a budget line, as shown in Figure 3.A4. The budget line shows alternative combinations of the two goods that can be purchased with a given income and with given prices of the two goods.

The budget line intersects the X-axis at the level of good X that can be purchased (X_1) if the consumer spends all his income on good X. The level of income (I) divided by the price of good X (P_X) gives this maximum amount of good X. Likewise, the budget line intersects the Y-axis at the level of good Y that can be

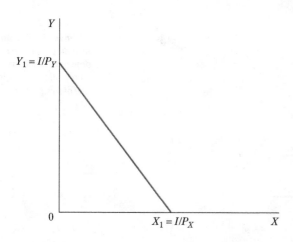

FIGURE 3.A4
The Budget Line
The budget line shows alternative combinations of the two goods, X and Y, that can be purchased with a given income and with given prices of the goods.

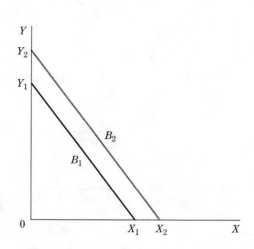

FIGURE 3.A5
Change (Increase) in Income (Prices Constant)
A change in income, assuming prices are constant, is represented by a parallel shift of the budget line.

purchased (Y_1) if all income is spent on good Y. This amount of good Y is determined by dividing the level of income (I) by the price of good Y (P_Y). The slope of the budget line is distance $0Y_1/0X_1 = (I/P_Y)/(I/P_X) = P_X/P_Y$. Thus, the slope of the budget line is the ratio of the relative prices of the two goods.

We illustrate a change in income, holding prices constant, in Figure 3.A5. Because the slope of the budget line is the ratio of the prices of the two goods and because prices are being held constant, a change in income is represented by a parallel shift of the budget line. If income increases from level I_1 to I_2, the budget line shifts out from B_1 to B_2, as shown in Figure 3.A5. This increase in income allows the consumer to purchase more of both goods, more of one good and the same amount of the other, or more of one good and less of the other.

We illustrate a decrease in the price of good X, holding both income and the price of good Y constant, in Figure 3.A6. The budget line swivels out, pivoting on the Y-axis. Because the price of good Y has not changed, the maximum quantity of Y that can be purchased does not change either. However, the price of good X has decreased, so good X has become cheaper relative to good Y. Budget line B_2 has a flatter slope because the slope of the line is the ratio of the prices of the two goods, which has changed.

FIGURE 3.A6
Change (Decrease) in the Price of Good *X* (All Else Constant)
A decrease in the price of good X is represented by a swiveling of the budget line around the intercept on the Y-axis.

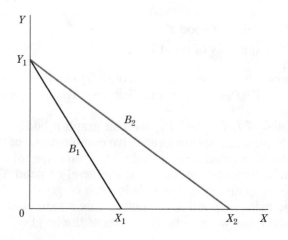

The Consumer Maximization Problem

We illustrate the solution to the consumer problem of maximizing utility subject to the budget constraint in Figure 3.A7. Point A, with X_1 amount of good X and Y_1 amount of good Y, is the solution to the consumer maximization problem. This point gives the consumer the highest level of utility (the indifference curve farthest from the origin), while still allowing the consumer to purchase the bundle of goods with the current level of income and relative prices shown in the budget line. Compare point A with point B (X_2 amount of good X and Y_2 amount of good Y). Point B lies on the budget line, so it represents a bundle of goods that the consumer could purchase. However, it would lie on an indifference curve closer to the origin (not pictured). This curve would represent a lower level of utility, so the consumer would not be maximizing the level of utility. Point C, corresponding to X_3 amount of good X and Y_3 amount of good Y, lies on the same indifference curve as point A and, therefore, provides the same level of utility as the goods represented by point A. However, point C lies outside the current budget line. It is not possible for the consumer to purchase this bundle of goods with the given income and prices of the goods.

   Point A is characterized by the tangency of the indifference curve farthest from the origin with the budget line. The slopes of two lines are equal at a point of tangency. The slope of the indifference curve is the marginal rate of substitution between goods X and Y, while the slope of the budget line is the ratio of the prices of the two goods. Thus, point A, or *consumer equilibrium*, occurs where $MRS_{XY} = (P_X/P_Y)$.

Changes in Income

We can now use the concept of consumer equilibrium to illustrate changes in consumer behavior in response to changes in economic variables. Figure 3.A8 shows an increase in income, all else held constant. The original point of consumer equilibrium is point A, with X_1 amount of good X and Y_1 of good Y. The increase in income is represented by an outward parallel shift of the budget line. To maximize utility with the new budget line, the consumer now moves to point B and consumes X_2 of good X and Y_2 of good Y. In this case, we can see that both X and Y are normal goods because the consumer increases the quantity demanded of each good in response to an increase in income, all else held constant.

   Figure 3.A9 is a similar example showing an increase in income. However, we can see in this example that good X is an inferior good. In Figure 3.A9, the original

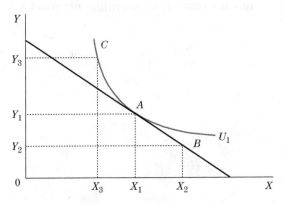

FIGURE 3.A7
The Consumer Maximization Problem
Point A represents the combination of goods where the consumer maximizes utility subject to the budget constraint.

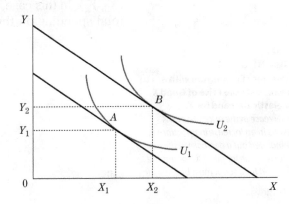

FIGURE 3.A8
Consumer Equilibrium with a Change in Income (Two Normal Goods)
To maximize utility, the consumer moves from point A to point B as income increases, consuming more of both goods.

FIGURE 3.A9

Consumer Equilibrium with a Change in Income (One Normal and One Inferior Good)
To maximize utility, the consumer moves from point A to point B as income increases, consuming more of good Y and less of good X.

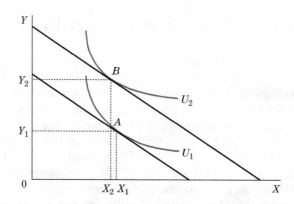

equilibrium occurs at point A (X_1, Y_1), while the new equilibrium after the income increase occurs at point B (X_2, Y_2). As income increases, the quantity demanded of good Y increases, but the quantity demanded of good X decreases. Thus, Y is a normal good in this example, while X is an inferior good.

Changes in Price

Figure 3.A10 shows a decrease in the price of good X, all else held constant. The original consumer equilibrium in Figure 3.A10 occurs at point A, with X_1 of good X and Y_1 of good Y. The decrease in the price of good X, all else held constant, is represented by the swiveling of the budget line with a new consumer equilibrium at point B (X_2, Y_2). Thus, the movement from point A to point B represents a movement along the consumer's demand curve for good X because a decrease in the price of good X results in an increase in the quantity demanded.

If we think of good Y as a *composite good* representing all other goods and services, we can see in Figure 3.A10 that the decrease in the price of good X caused expenditure on good X to decrease because spending on the composite good Y increased. Decreased expenditure on good X is equivalent to decreased total revenue for the producers of good X. Thus, in Figure 3.A10, a decrease in the price of good X results in a decrease in the total revenue for good X, so that the demand for good X must be inelastic. We illustrate the opposite case of elastic demand for good X in Figure 3.A11.

In Figure 3.A11, the original consumer equilibrium occurs at point A (X_1, Y_1), and the equilibrium after the decrease in the price of good X occurs at point B (X_2, Y_2). In this case, the quantity demanded of good X has increased so much that total spending on the composite good, Y, has decreased, so spending on good X

FIGURE 3.A10

Consumer Equilibrium with a Decrease in the Price of Good *X* (Inelastic Demand for *X*)
A decrease in the price of good X results in an increase in the quantity demanded but a decrease in the total revenue for good X, so that the demand for good X must be inelastic.

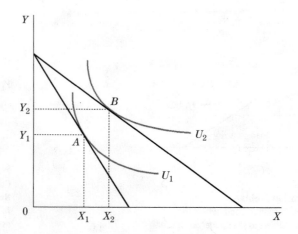

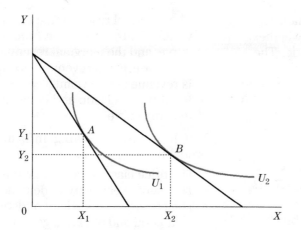

FIGURE 3.A11

Consumer Equilibrium with a Decrease in the Price of Good X (Elastic Demand for X)

A decrease in the price of good X results in an increase in the quantity demanded and in the total revenue from good X, so that the demand for good X must be elastic.

has increased. A decrease in the price of good X has resulted in an increase in expenditure on X and, therefore, in the total revenue to the firm producing X. When a decrease in price results in an increase in total revenue, demand is elastic.

If we think of good Y as simply another good and not a composite good, Figures 3.A10 and 3.A11 illustrate the cross-price elasticity of demand. In Figure 3.A10, a decrease in the price of good X results in an increase in the quantity demanded of good Y. Thus, the two goods in this figure must be complements in consumption because the cross-price elasticity of demand is negative. The opposite case holds in Figure 3.A11, where a decrease in the price of good X results in a decrease in the quantity demanded of good Y. Here goods X and Y are substitute goods with a positive cross-price elasticity of demand.

Key Terms

advertising elasticity of demand, p. 72

arc price elasticity of demand, p. 56

average revenue, p. 57

average revenue function, p. 57

cross-price elasticity of demand, p. 65

demand elasticity, p. 48

elastic demand, p. 51

income elasticity of demand, p. 64

inelastic demand, p. 51

luxury, p. 64

marginal revenue, p. 58

marginal revenue function, p. 58

necessity, p. 64

perfectly (or infinitely) elastic demand, p. 63

perfectly inelastic demand, p. 62

point price elasticity of demand, p. 56

price elasticity of demand (e_p), p. 49

total revenue, p. 50

total revenue function, p. 57

unitary elasticity (or unit elastic), p. 51

Exercises

Technical Questions

1. For each of the following cases, calculate the *arc* price elasticity of demand, and state whether demand is elastic, inelastic, or unit elastic.

   a. When the price of milk increases from $2.25 to $2.50 per gallon, the quantity demanded falls from 100 gallons to 90 gallons.

   b. When the price of paperback books falls from $7.00 to $6.50, the quantity demanded rises from 100 to 150.

   c. When the rent on apartments rises from $500 to $550, the quantity demanded decreases from 1,000 to 950.

2. For each of the following cases, calculate the *point* price elasticity of demand, and state whether demand is elastic, inelastic, or unit elastic. The demand curve is given by

$$Q_D = 5,000 - 50P_X$$

   a. The price of the product is $50.
   b. The price of the product is $75.
   c. The price of the product is $25.

3. For each of the following cases, what is the expected impact on the total revenue of the firm? Explain your reasoning.

   a. Price elasticity of demand is known to be –0.5, and the firm raises price by 10 percent.
   b. Price elasticity of demand is known to be –2.5, and the firm lowers price by 5 percent.
   c. Price elasticity of demand is known to be –1.0, and the firm raises price by 1 percent.
   d. Price elasticity of demand is known to be 0, and the firm raises price by 50 percent.

4. The demand curve is given by

$$Q_D = 500 - 2P_X$$

   a. What is the total revenue function?

   b. The marginal revenue function is $MR = 250 - Q$. Graph the total revenue function, the demand curve, and the marginal revenue function.
   c. At what price is revenue maximized, and what is revenue at that point?
   d. Identify the elastic and inelastic regions of the demand curve.

5. You have the following information for your product:

   - The price elasticity of demand is –2.0.
   - The income elasticity of demand is 1.5.
   - The cross-price elasticity of demand between your good and a related good is –3.5.

   What can you determine about consumer demand for your product from this information?

6. You have the following information for your product:

   - The price elasticity of demand is –0.9.
   - The income elasticity of demand is 0.5.
   - The cross-price elasticity of demand between your good and a related good is 2.0.

   What can you determine about consumer demand for your product from this information?

Application Questions

1. In March 2010, Mc Donald's Corp. announced a policy to increase summer sales by selling all soft drinks, no matter the size, for $1.00. The policy would run for 150 days starting after Memorial Day. The $1.00 drink prices were a discount from the suggested price of $1.39 for a large soda. Some franchisees worried that discounting drinks, whose sales compensate for discounts on other products, could hurt overall profits, especially if customers bought other items from the Dollar Menu. McDonald's managers expected this promotion would draw customers from other fast-food chains and from convenience stores such as 7-Eleven. Additional customers would also help McDonald's push its new beverage lineup that included smoothies and frappes. Discounted drinks did cut into McDonald's coffee sales in previous years as some customers chose the drinks rather than pricier espresso beverages. Other chains with new drink offerings, such as Burger King and Taco Bell, could face pressure from the $1.00 drinks at McDonald's.[47]

   a. Given the change in price for a large soda from $1.39 to $1.00, how much would quantity demanded have to increase for McDonald's revenues to increase? (Use the arc elasticity formula for any percentage change calculations.)
   b. What is the sign of the implied cross-price elasticity with drinks from McDonald's competitors?
   c. What are the other benefits and costs to McDonald's of this discount drink policy?

---

[47]Paul Ziobro, "McDonald's Bets Pricing Drinks at $1 Will Heat Up Summer Sales," *Wall Street Journal (Online)*, March 18, 2010.

2. In the second half of 2002, several major U.S. airlines began running market tests to determine if they could cut walk-up or unrestricted business fares and maintain or increase revenues. Continental Airlines offered an unrestricted fare between Cleveland and Los Angeles of $716, compared with its usual $2,000 fare, and found that it earned about the same revenue as it would have collected with the higher fare. Making similar changes on its routes from Cleveland to Houston, Continental found that the new fare structure yielded less revenue, but greater market share. On the Houston–Oakland route, the new fare structure resulted in higher revenue.[48]

   a. What did these test results imply about business traveler price elasticity of demand on the Cleveland–Los Angeles, Cleveland–Houston, and Houston–Oakland routes for Continental Airlines?
   b. How did these results differ from the discussion of airline elasticity in this chapter?
   c. What factors caused these differences?

3. Based on the elasticity data in Table 3.7, discuss why public health officials generally advocate the use of cigarette taxes to reduce teenage smoking, while state and local governments often use these taxes to raise revenue to fund their services.

4. The price elasticity of demand for urban transit fares has been estimated to lie between –0.1 and –0.6. Based on these results, what is the economic argument for raising transit fares? What political arguments might local governments and transit authorities encounter in opposition to these economic arguments?

5. Develop a case study of a retailer that uses rewards or loyalty programs to influence demand and price elasticity of demand for their products. How do these programs influence both current and future demand?

6. Why would we expect that the price elasticity of demand for the product of an individual firm would typically be greater than the price elasticity of demand for the product overall? Illustrate your answer with examples from this chapter.

7. Find examples in the current business news media of how eBay and other online sellers obtain information about the price elasticity of demand by making unannounced temporary adjustments to their prices and fee structures.

8. Priority Mail has been one of the most profitable products for the U.S. Postal Service, growing six times faster than first-class deliveries over the period from 1995 to 1999 and accounting for almost 8 percent of the Postal Service's mail revenue. Because the Postal Service lost $480 million in the fiscal year ending September 30, 2000, it adopted the strategy of raising Priority Mail rates by 16 percent to help offset this loss. Bear Creek Corporation planned to ship 15 to 20 percent fewer Priority Mail packages in response to the rate increase. If this corporation's response is typical for Priority Mail customers, will the Postal Service meet its goal of reducing its deficit with this policy?[49]

[48]Scott McCartney, "Airlines Try Business-Fare Cuts, Find They Don't Lose Revenue," *Wall Street Journal*, November 22, 2002.
[49]Rick Brooks, "Priority Mail Is Prey for Rivals after Raising Rates a Steep 16%," *Wall Street Journal*, January 24, 2001.

Techniques for Understanding Consumer Demand and Behavior

In this chapter, we explore how both managers and economists use marketing and other consumer data to analyze the factors influencing demand for different products. Many firms, particularly large corporations, hire economists who employ sophisticated statistical or econometric techniques to estimate demand functions or to forecast future demand. Most managers, however, will *not* be involved with forecasting and undertaking the complex statistical analyses performed by business economists. Managers are more likely to work with marketing and consumer research departments to profile and understand a company's customers and to try to anticipate changes in consumer behavior.

We begin this chapter with a case that focuses on the use of new technologies to understand consumer purchasing behavior and to target advertising precisely to different groups of consumers. We then illustrate and evaluate the techniques managers and marketing departments typically use to obtain this information. Next we look briefly at how economists use the econometric technique of multiple regression analysis to empirically estimate demand functions. The goal of this discussion is not to train you as business economists who produce these statistical analyses, but to help you become better consumers of this type of work and to see its usefulness for *managerial* decision making. We end the chapter by illustrating the interrelationships between the marketing/consumer research approach to analyzing consumer demand, which managers favor, and the formal econometric approach used by economists.

Case for Analysis

The Use of New Technology to Understand and Impact Consumer Behavior

Although we focus in this chapter on traditional methods used by marketers and economists to understand and analyze consumer behavior, companies are increasingly using data from consumers' television-viewing behavior and credit card purchases to better understand purchasing decisions and to target advertising messages based on these decisions.[1] Data-gathering firms match information on consumers' TV-viewing behavior with other personal data to help advertisers buy ads targeted to shows watched by different groups of consumers. In addition, cable companies are developing new systems designed to show highly targeted ads based on much more detailed consumer characteristics.

Traditionally, advertisers bought commercials on shows that were popular with different age and socioeconomic groups. New data from cable TV boxes combined with other household data now allow advertisers to target audience segments more narrowly, such as Chicago residents shopping for plane tickets to Los Angeles. Companies such as Simulmedia obtain information from cable company boxes on when channels are changed. They then bundle these data into different groups of viewers, such as "wild n' crazies" (young males) and "hecklers" (stand-up comedy), which are then used for advertising campaigns.

Cable companies such as Cablevision Systems Corp. are also developing systems that can show different commercials at the same time to different households viewing the same program. This technology was first used by the U.S. Army to target varying recruitment ads to different groups of viewers. The technology anonymously matches names and addresses of Cablevision's subscribers with data provided by advertisers. However, all of these approaches face potential backlash from consumers or regulatory groups over concerns regarding the invasion of privacy and the use of personal information.

Visa, Inc. and MasterCard, Inc. use similar approaches to sell their consumer-purchasing data for use in online advertising.[2] These companies own some of the world's largest databases of sales transactions, which include 43 billion annual credit and debit card transactions for Visa and 23 billion for MasterCard. Given the hundreds of companies tracking consumers' online behavior, information, such as gender, age, location, income, and interests, is now a commodity. Future strategies focus on merging data about consumer's online behavior with activities in real marketplaces. One example would be to target a weight-loss ad to a person who had just made a purchase at a fast-food chain and then follow up to see if the individual bought the advertised products. MasterCard proposed such a strategy in 2011, but then tabled the idea given concerns and regulations on the use of consumer data by financial-services companies. All of these strategies incorporate inherent conflicts between technologies that allow the collection and sale of new, detailed personal information on consumer behavior for profit-making activities and concerns over the invasion of privacy.

Retailer Target also faced this dilemma as it developed statistical methods to be able to identify women who were pregnant before other retailers knew the baby was on the way.[3] Target marketers learned from neuroscience research that it is difficult to change consumer buying habits once they are ingrained. However, there are brief periods, such as around the birth of a child, when old routines fall apart and buying habits are in flux. Using data from its baby shower registry, Target researchers analyzed purchases of 25 products that allowed them to develop a "pregnancy prediction" score and to estimate a woman's due date. This allowed the company to send coupons timed to specific stages of a pregnancy with the expectation that these women would purchase other items as well as baby products and become regular Target customers. Because this approach could easily be considered an invasion of women's privacy, Target began mixing coupons for baby products with advertisements for all types of products that pregnant women would never buy. They found that women would use the coupons as long as the baby ads looked random.

---

[1]This discussion is based on Jessica E. Vascellaro, "TV's Next Wave: Tuning in to You," *Wall Street Journal (Online)*, March 7, 2011.

[2]This discussion is based on Emily Steel, "Using Credit Cards to Target Web Ads," *Wall Street Journal (Online)*, October 25, 2011.

[3]Charles Duhigg, "How Companies Learn Your Secrets," *The New York Times (Online)*, February 16, 2012.

Understanding Consumer Demand and Behavior: Marketing Approaches

The opening case illustrates current and proposed uses of new technology to gather additional data about consumer behavior and to profit from the sale of these data. These new approaches build on methods that marketing departments have traditionally used to analyze consumer behavior such as

1. Expert opinion
2. Consumer surveys
3. Test marketing and price experiments
4. Analyses of census and other historical data
5. Unconventional methods

Much of the discussion of these nonstatistical approaches to learning about demand and consumer behavior is found in the marketing literature.[4] We briefly summarize this literature—which is usually covered more extensively in marketing courses—and then relate these approaches to statistical or econometric demand estimation, the approach used most often by economists.

Analyzing demand and consumer behavior involves the study of what people say, what they do, or what they have done.[5] Surveys of consumers, panels of experts, or the sales force working in the field can provide information on how people say they behave. Test marketing and price experiments focus on what people actually do in a market situation. Analyses of census and other historical data and statistical or econometric demand estimation are based on data showing how consumers behaved in the past. These studies then use that behavior as the basis for predicting future demand. Some of these techniques are implemented in an uncontrolled marketing environment, whereas others are used in a controlled research framework. Let's start by looking at the role of expert opinion.

Expert Opinion

Expert opinion

An approach to analyzing consumer behavior that relies on developing a consensus of opinion among sales personnel, dealers, distributors, marketing consultants, and trade association members.

Sales personnel or other experts, such as dealers, distributors, suppliers, marketing consultants, and members of trade associations, may be interviewed for their **expert opinion** on consumer behavior. At least 10 experts from different functions and hierarchical levels in the organization should be involved with making an expert judgment on a particular product. For example, large appliance companies and automobile producers often survey their dealers for estimates of short-term demand for their products. This approach is especially useful in multiproduct situations, where other strategies may be prohibitively expensive.

The inherent biases of this approach are obvious, as sales personnel and others closely related to the industry may have strong incentives to overstate consumer interest in a product. These individuals may also have a limited view of the entire set of factors influencing product demand, particularly factors related to the

---

[4]Kent B. Monroe, *Pricing: Making Profitable Decisions*, 2nd ed. (New York: McGraw-Hill, 1990); Robert J. Dolan and Hermann Simon, *Power Pricing: How Managing Price Transforms the Bottom Line* (New York: Free Press, 1996); Financial Times, *Mastering Marketing: The Complete MBA Companion in Marketing* (London: Pearson Education, 1999); Philip Kotler, *Marketing Management: The Millennium Edition* (Upper Saddle River, NJ: Prentice Hall, 2000); Vithala R. Rao (ed.), *Handbook of Pricing Research in Marketing* (Cheltenham, UK: Edward Elgar, 2009); Thomas T. Nagle, John E. Hogan, and Joseph Zale, *The Strategy and Tactics of Pricing*, 5th ed. (Upper Saddle River, NJ: Prentice-Hall, 2011).

[5]The following discussion of the marketing approaches used to understand consumer behavior is based largely on Kotler, *Marketing Management: The Millennium Edition*; Dolan and Simon, *Power Pricing: How Managing Price Transforms the Bottom Line*; Rao (ed.), *Handbook of Pricing Research in Marketing*; and Nagle, Hogan, and Zale, *The Strategy and Tactics of Pricing*.

overall level of activity in the economy. Therefore, this approach works better in business-to-business markets, where there are fewer customers and where experts are likely to know the markets well.

Consumer Surveys

Consumer surveys include both direct surveys of consumer reactions to prices and price changes, and conjoint analyses of product characteristics and prices.

In **direct consumer surveys**, consumers are asked how they would respond to certain prices, price changes, or price differentials. Questions may include the following:

- At what price would you definitely purchase this product?
- How much are you willing to pay for the product?
- How likely are you to purchase this product at a price of $XX?
- What price difference would cause you to switch from Product X to Product Y?[6]

Direct consumer surveys
An approach to analyzing consumer behavior that relies on directly asking consumers questions about their response to prices, price changes, or price differentials.

These surveys are easily understood and less costly to implement than other approaches to analyzing consumer behavior. Surveys have the greatest value when there are a relatively small number of buyers who have well-defined preferences that they are willing to disclose in a survey format. Surveys are most useful for new products, industrial products, and consumer durables that have a long life, as well as for products whose purchase requires advanced planning. In these surveys, market researchers may also collect information on consumer personal finances and consumer expectations about the economy.

Limitations to this approach include the issue of whether consumer responses to the questions reflect their actual behavior in the marketplace. This problem is particularly important regarding reactions to changes in prices. Can consumers know and accurately respond to questions on how they *would* behave when facing different prices for various products? Surveys also tend to focus on the issue of price in isolation from other factors that influence behavior. There may be response biases with this approach because interviewees may be reluctant to admit that they will not pay a certain price or that they would rather purchase a cheaper product. Surveys also typically ask for a person's response at a time when they are not actually making the purchase, so they may not give much thought to their answer.

Consumer surveys are not always successful in obtaining accurate information. In one survey conducted by a major hotel chain that covered all aspects of the hotel's operations, including the prices, guests were asked what price was considered too high, as well as what the highest acceptable price was.[7] The results of this survey indicated that the hotel chain's prices in various cities were about as high as business guests would pay. Managers realized there was a bias in the survey because respondents were also asked what price they were currently paying for the hotel rooms. Respondents were unwilling to tell the hotel management that they would have paid more than the rates they were currently being charged. Thus, the survey biased the results on willingness to pay toward the current hotel rates.

A more sophisticated form of consumer survey is **conjoint analysis**, which has been used in the pricing and design of products ranging from computer hardware and software to hotels, clothing, automobiles, and information services. This technique is used in a more controlled research environment compared with interviews, which are more unstructured. In this approach, a consumer is faced with an

Conjoint analysis
An approach to analyzing consumer behavior that asks consumers to rank and choose among different product attributes, including price, to reveal their valuation of these characteristics.

---

[6]An application of a similar approach and an extensive discussion of the pricing of services are found in Stowe Shoemaker and Anna S. Mattila, "Pricing in Services," in *Handbook of Pricing Research in Marketing*, ed. Vithala R. Rao (Cheltenham, UK: Edward Elgar, 2009), 535–56.
[7]This example is drawn from Monroe, *Pricing: Making Profitable Decisions*, 107–8.

array of products that have different attributes and prices and is asked to rank and choose among them. The analysis allows the marketer to determine the relative importance of each attribute to the consumer. Conjoint analysis does not directly measure stated purchase intentions, but it focuses on the preferences that underlie those intentions. This technique allows marketers to identify consumer segments for which consumers have a different willingness to pay and varying price elasticities. It also gives researchers the ability to check to see if consumers' responses are at least consistent. Computer interviewing has become a standard procedure for conjoint analysis.[8]

The advantage of conjoint analysis is that it presents the consumer with a realistic set of choices among both product characteristics and prices. For example, in the case of a new automobile, managers might develop an analysis that focuses on attributes such as brand, engine power, fuel consumption, environmental performance, and price. Different levels of each of the attributes are presented to the consumer. Comparisons are set up where the consumer has to make a trade-off between different characteristics. Thus, his or her choices reveal information about consumer preferences for the product characteristics.[9] Note that conjoint analysis employs an approach to consumer behavior that is similar to the economic indifference curve model described in the appendix to Chapter 3 of this text.

Test Marketing and Price Experiments

Test marketing and price experiments are particularly important for analyzing consumer reaction to new products. **Test marketing** allows companies to study how consumers handle, use, and repurchase a product, and it provides information on the potential size of the market. In *sales-wave research*, consumers who are initially offered the product at no cost are then reoffered the product at different prices to determine their responses. Simulated test marketing involves selecting shoppers who are questioned about brand familiarity, invited to screen commercials about well-known and new products, and then given money to purchase both the new and the existing products. Full-scale test marketing usually occurs over a period of a few months to a year in a number of cities and is accompanied by a complete advertising and promotion campaign. Marketers must determine the number and types of cities for the testing and the type of information to be collected. Information on consumer behavior in the test cities is gathered from store audits, consumer panels, and buyer surveys.

Price experiments to determine the effect of changes in prices may be conducted in test market cities or in a laboratory setting. Direct mail catalogs can also be used for these experiments, as prices can be varied in the catalogs shipped to different regions of the country without a high level of consumer awareness. Although testing in a laboratory situation helps to control for other factors influencing consumer behavior, the disadvantage of this approach is that it is not a natural shopping environment, so consumers may behave differently in the experimental environment. Doing an experiment in an actual test market may be more realistic, but it raises problems about controlling the influence on consumer behavior of variables other than price.[10]

Test marketing
An approach to analyzing consumer behavior that involves analyzing consumer response to products in real or simulated markets.

Price experiments
An approach to analyzing consumer behavior in which consumer reaction to different prices is analyzed in a laboratory situation or a test market environment.

---

[8]For an illustration of the use of conjoint analysis by a small sporting goods manufacturer, see Box 12-4, "A Conjoint Study: Power Powder Ski," in Nagle, Hogan, and Zale, *The Strategy and Tactics of Pricing*, 5th ed., 291–93.

[9]More details of this approach to analyzing consumer behavior are presented in Kotler, *Marketing Management: The Millennium Edition*, 339–40; Dolan and Simon, *Power Pricing: How Managing Price Transforms the Bottom Line*, 55–69; and Nagle, Hogan, and Zale, *The Strategy and Tactics of Pricing*, 269–304.

[10]Additional discussion of these approaches is provided by Kamel Jedidi and Sharan Jagpal, "Willingness to Pay: Measurement and Managerial Implications," in *Handbook of Pricing Research in Marketing*, ed. Vithala R. Rao (Cheltenham, UK: Edward Elgar, 2009), 37–60.

Analysis of Census and Other Historical Data

The most recent U.S. census is always a vital marketing tool, given the development of **targeted marketing**, which defines various market segments or groups of buyers for particular products based on the demographic, psychological, and behavioral characteristics of these individuals. For example, Sodexho Marriott Services, a provider of food services to universities and other institutions, analyzed census data to develop menu programs specifically designed for students on particular campuses. Starbucks Corporation has used complex software algorithms to analyze both census and historical sales data in order to obtain a positive or negative response to every address considered as a potential store site.[11]

Companies such as Claritas of San Diego have provided consulting services on how to use census data to develop marketing plans and analyze consumer behavior. Using census data on age, race, and median income and other survey lifestyle information, such as magazine and sports preferences, Claritas developed 62 clusters or consumer types for targeted marketing. Hyundai Corporation used these data and buyer profiles to determine which of its models will appeal to consumers in different parts of a community and to plan the locations of new dealerships. Hyundai also used cluster data to send test-drive offers to certain neighborhoods, instead of entire cities, and reported that it cut its cost per vehicle sold in half as a result of this targeting strategy.[12]

Many companies have used census and survey data to develop new marketing strategies focused on older customers, a population segment that has often been overlooked in the past.[13] A study by AARP, the advocacy group for people over 50, found that, for many products, the majority of people over 45 were not loyal to a single brand. Companies have begun to realize that this segment of the population is increasing in size, may have more discretionary income than younger groups, and may respond to appropriate advertising.

More companies are also using retail store scanner data that provide almost immediate information on the sales of different products. Scanner data are much less costly to obtain than panel data from research companies that collect data from panels of a few thousand households. Scanner data have become the major source of information on the price sensitivity of consumer-packaged goods.[14]

Targeted marketing
Selling that centers on defining different market segments or groups of buyers for particular products based on the demographic, psychological, and behavioral characteristics of the individuals.

Unconventional Methods

In May 2001, Procter & Gamble announced plans to send video crews with cameras into 80 households around the world to record the daily routines of the occupants.[15] The company anticipated that this approach would yield better and more useful data than the consumer research methods discussed above because consumer behavior would be directly observed in a household setting rather than in an experimental environment. This approach would also avoid the response bias that can be present in a consumer survey. More recently, Procter & Gamble began partnering with Google Inc. to develop strategies appealing to online customers. The company invited "mommy bloggers"—women who run popular Web sites about child rearing—to tour the baby division to increase awareness and obtain feedback on Procter & Gamble products.[16]

---

[11]Amy Merrick, "New Population Data Will Help Marketers Pitch Their Products," *Wall Street Journal*, February 14, 2001.

[12]Ibid.

[13]Kelly Greene, "Marketing Surprise: Older Consumers Buy Stuff, Too," *Wall Street Journal*, April 6, 2004.

[14]Nagle, Hogan, and Zale, *The Strategy and Tactics of Pricing*, 271–76.

[15]Emily Nelson, "P & G Plans to Visit People's Homes to Record (Almost) All Their Habits," *Wall Street Journal*, May 17, 2001.

[16]Ellen Byron, "A New Odd Couple: Google, P&G Swap Workers to Spur Innovation," *Wall Street Journal*, November 19, 2008.

To try to halt a 30-year decline in the sales of white bread, Sara Lee Corp. used taste testers to try to determine the optimum amount of whole grains that could be introduced into white bread to provide additional health benefits without discouraging users of traditional white bread who preferred that taste and consistency to darker and grainier whole grain breads.[17] The result, a bread called Soft & Smooth with 70 calories and 2 grams of fiber per slice, became one of the best-selling brands in 2006 and encouraged other companies to produce similar breads.

Retailers have found that Western-style supermarkets with clean, wide aisles and well-stocked shelves do not work well in India, particularly for lower-middle-class shoppers who are more comfortable in tiny, cramped stores.[18] One retailer, Pantaloon Retail (India) Ltd., spent $50,000 in a store to replace long, wide aisles with narrow, crooked ones to make the store messier, noisier, and more cramped. Products were clustered on low shelves and in bins because customers were used to shopping from stalls and finding products such as wheat, rice, and lentils in open containers that they could handle and inspect. Pantaloon Retail (India) Ltd. eventually became India's largest retailer in 2007 with annual sales of $875 million.

The case that opened this chapter illustrated how companies are now using new technologies to obtain data from cable television subscribers and credit card users to gather ever more detailed information on consumer buying habits and to link online and real-world behavior.

Evaluating the Methods

All research on consumer behavior involves extrapolating from a sample of data to a larger population. When designing surveys and forming focus groups for interviews, marketers must be careful that participating individuals are representative of the larger population. For example, Procter & Gamble does 40 percent of its early exploratory studies of new products in its hometown of Cincinnati. Given the number of P&G employees and retirees in the area, the company needs to make certain that its focus group members do not have an undue positive bias toward the products or are not influenced by family connections with the company.[19]

As mentioned earlier, responses given in an experimental format may not reflect actual consumer behavior. Although economists have recently used more experimental techniques, for many years these researchers preferred to rely on market data that showed how consumers actually *behaved*, not how they *said* they would behave. Surveys and focus groups must also be designed to determine the independent effect of each of the demand function variables on product sales or quantity demanded. Finding simple correlations between market variables and product sales does not mean that these variables have the same effect with other variables held constant. Nagle et al. have argued that managerial judgment should always be used in combination with any of these measurement techniques. For example, if managers know that 80 percent of the company's consumers for a particular product are women who are employed full time, that information should be used to determine how any in-home survey or shopping center experiment is undertaken.[20]

---

[17]Steven Gray, "How Sara Lee Spun White, Grain into Gold," *Wall Street Journal*, April 25, 2006.

[18]Eric Bellman, "In India, a Retailer Finds Key to Success Is Clutter," *Wall Street Journal (Online)*, August 8, 2007.

[19]Emily Nelson, "P & G Keeps Focus Groupies of Cincinnati Busy as Guinea Pigs in Product Studies," *Wall Street Journal*, January 24, 2002.

[20]Nagle, Hogan, and Joseph, *The Strategy and Tactics of Pricing*, 294–300.

Managerial Rule of Thumb

Marketing Methods for Analyzing Consumer Behavior

When using expert opinion, consumer surveys, test marketing, and price experiments to analyze consumer behavior, managers must consider the following points:

1. Whether the participating groups are truly representative of the larger population?
2. Whether the answers given in these formats represent actual market behavior?
3. How to isolate the effects of different variables that influence demand? ∎

Consumer Demand and Behavior: Economic Approaches

As we mentioned in the introduction to this chapter, many companies hire business economists to develop quantitative estimates of the relationships among the variables influencing the demand for their products. Results of a survey of 538 companies employing 4 to over 380,000 employees published in the mid-1990s indicated that 37.4 percent of the companies had economics departments.[21]

Economists typically use the statistical technique of **multiple regression analysis** to estimate the effect of each relevant independent variable on the quantity demanded of a product, *while statistically holding constant the effects of all other independent variables*. This approach involves the analysis of historical data to develop relationships among the variables and to predict how changes in these variables will affect consumer demand.

In the physical sciences, many of these types of relationships can be tested experimentally in the laboratory. However, experiments in the social and policy sciences are often very expensive, time-consuming, and complex to perform. Although the use of experimental approaches has been increasing in different areas of economics,[22] most product demand research still relies on statistical or econometric techniques, such as multiple regression analysis, to examine the relationship between two variables, while statistically holding constant the effects of all other variables.

In the remainder of this section, we present an introduction to the use of multiple regression analysis and references for further study of the topic. We begin by focusing on a case involving one dependent and one independent variable, which we illustrate with a Microsoft Excel spreadsheet. We then move to an Excel case involving two independent variables to show how additional variables can modify the results of an analysis. Although both Excel examples are too simplistic for real-world market analysis, they illustrate the basic principles of the econometric approach to demand estimation. We next present a discussion of how regression analysis has been used to examine the factors influencing the demand for automobiles. In the last section of the chapter, we discuss the relationship between the consumer research data that managers and marketers use and the statistical analysis of consumer behavior that economists undertake.[23]

Multiple regression analysis
A statistical technique used to estimate the relationship between a dependent variable and an independent variable, *holding constant the effects of all other independent variables.*

---

[21]John J. Casson, "The Role of Business Economists in Business Planning," *Business Economics* 31 (July 1996): 45–50. Information about current jobs for business economists can be found at the National Association for Business Economics Career Center, http://nabe.com/careers/index.html.

[22]John A. List, "Why Economists Should Conduct Field Experiments and 14 Tips for Pulling One Off," *Journal of Economic Perspectives* 25 (Summer 2011): 3–16.

[23]Economists also use models to forecast the future values of economic variables based on trends in these values over time. We do not include these techniques in this book.

Relationship Between One Dependent and One Independent Variable: Simple Regression Analysis

Let's begin with a very simple hypothetical example of a demand function. Suppose that a manager has a sample of data on price and quantity demanded for oranges, shown in Figure 4.1 and in the bottom part of Table 4.1 [Actual Q (lbs.), Actual P (cents/lb.)].[24] These data could be either **cross-sectional data** or **time-series data**. If the data are cross-sectional data, they represent the behavior of different individuals facing different prices for oranges at a specific point in time. If the data are time-series data, they represent a set of observations on the same observational unit at a number of points in time, usually measured annually, quarterly, or monthly. Many recent studies use **panel data** sets, which are based on the same cross-sectional data observed at several points in time.[25]

If we want to estimate the relationship between quantity demanded and price, we can first just examine the data points in Figure 4.1 and Table 4.1. These data points show what appears to be a negative relationship between the variables—that is, as price decreases, quantity demanded increases, or as price increases, quantity demanded decreases.

Quantitative Measure   Most managers need more information about this relationship than can be inferred just by examining the raw data in Figure 4.1 and Table 4.1. Managers want a quantitative measure of the size of this relationship that shows how much quantity demanded will change as price either increases or decreases. One quantitative measure would be to draw the line that best reflects the relationship shown by the data points in Figure 4.1 and Table 4.1. We would like to draw a straight line indicating a linear relationship between the variables because a linear relationship is the easiest case to analyze. However, we can see in Figure 4.1 that all the data points will not fall on a single straight line. For example, at a price of 70 cents per pound, four individuals demand different quantities. Thus, there is variation in the data, which means that some data points will deviate from any line fitted to the data. We want to find the line that "best fits" the data.

As with any straight line, a linear demand relationship can be expressed in an equation, as shown in Equation 4.1.

4.1 $Q = a - bP$

where

Q = quantity demanded
a = vertical intercept
b = slope of the line = $\Delta Q/\Delta P$
P = price

Cross-sectional data
Data collected on a sample of individuals with different characteristics at a specific point in time.

Time-series data
Data collected on the same observational unit at a number of points in time.

Panel data
Cross-sectional data observed at several points in time.

FIGURE 4.1
Hypothetical Demand for Oranges
This figure plots the sample data of the demand for oranges showing price (cents per lb.) and quantity demanded (lbs.).

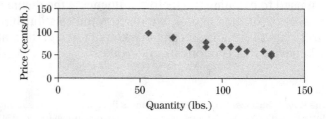

---

[24]This example is drawn from Jan Kmenta, *Elements of Econometrics* (New York: Macmillan, 1971). See that text for a complete derivation and discussion of the statistical procedures and results.
[25]William H. Greene, *Econometric Analysis*, 7th ed. (Upper Saddle River, NJ: Prentice Hall, 2012).

TABLE 4.1   Simple Regression Analysis Results

REGRESSION STATISTICS

Multiple R	0.943
R square	0.889
Adjusted R square	0.878
Standard error	8.360
Observations	12.000

ANALYSIS OF VARIANCE (ANOVA)

	Degrees of Freedom	Sum of Squares	Mean Square	F-statistic	Significance of F-statistic
Regression	1.000	5601.111	5601.111	80.143	0.000
Residual	10.000	698.889	69.889		
Total	11.000	6300.000			

	Coefficients	Standard Error	t-statistic	P-value	Lower 95 percent	Upper 95 percent
Intercept	210.444	12.571	16.741	0.00000001	182.435	238.454
Price	−1.578	0.176	−8.952	0.00000434	−1.970	−1.185

RESIDUAL OUTPUT

Observation	Predicted Q	Residuals	Actual Q (lbs.)	Actual P (cents/lb.)
1	52.667	2.333	55	100
2	68.444	1.556	70	90
3	84.222	5.778	90	80
4	100.000	0.000	100	70
5	100.000	−10.000	90	70
6	100.000	5.000	105	70
7	100.000	−20.000	80	70
8	107.889	2.111	110	65
9	115.778	9.222	125	60
10	115.778	−0.778	115	60
11	123.667	6.333	130	55
12	131.556	−1.556	130	50

The vertical intercept, a, represents the quantity demanded of the product as a result of other variables that influence behavior that are not analyzed in Equation 4.1. For example, the quantity demanded may be influenced by an individual's income or by the size of the firm's advertising budget. The slope parameter, b, shows the change in quantity demanded that results from a unit change in price. We have assumed that b is a negative number, given the usual inverse relationship between price and quantity demanded. Once we know the parameters, a and b, we know the specific relationship between price and quantity demanded shown in Table 4.1, and we know how quantity demanded changes as price changes.

Simple Regression Analysis   The relationship between price and quantity demanded can be estimated in this hypothetical example using **simple regression analysis**, as there is only one independent variable (P) and one dependent variable (Q). Regression analysis, as noted above, is a statistical technique that provides an equation for the line that "best fits" the data. "Best fit" means minimizing the sum of the squared deviations of the sample data points from their mean or average value.[26] Most of the actual data points will not lie on the estimated regression line due to the variation in consumer behavior and the influence of variables *not* included in Equation 4.1. However, the estimated line captures the relationship between the variables expressed in the sample data.

To estimate Equation 4.1, a manager needs to collect data on price and quantity demanded for a sample of individuals, as represented by the data points in Figure 4.1 and Table 4.1. The manager can then use any standard statistical software package to estimate the regression parameters, coefficients a and b in Equation 4.1, for that sample of data.[27] The computer program estimates the parameters of the equation and provides various summary statistics.

The results of such an estimation process, using the Excel regression feature, are shown in the middle rows of Table 4.1. The estimated value of the intercept term is 210.444, while the estimated value of the price coefficient is –1.578. The demand relationship is shown in Equation 4.2:

$$\textbf{4.2}\quad Q = 210.444 - 1.578P$$

The price coefficient, –1.578, shows that the quantity demanded of oranges decreases by 1.578 pounds for every one cent increase in price. However, both economists and managers are usually more interested in the price elasticity of demand than in the absolute changes in quantity and price. Because this is a linear demand curve, the price elasticity varies along the demand curve. Equation 4.3 shows the calculation of price elasticity at the average price (70 cents per pound) and average quantity demanded at that price (100 pounds), based on Equation 4.2.

$$\textbf{4.3}\quad e_P = \frac{(\Delta Q)(P)}{(\Delta P)(Q)} = \frac{(-1.578)(70)}{(100)} = -1.105$$

Equation 4.3 shows that the demand for oranges is slightly price elastic using the average values of the data in this sample. The percentage change in the quantity demanded of oranges is slightly greater than the percentage change in price.

Significance of the Coefficients and Goodness of Fit   There are numerous questions involving how well the regression line fits the sample data points in any regression analysis. Two important issues are:

1. Hypothesis testing for the significance of the estimated coefficients
2. The goodness of fit of the entire estimating equation

Because the estimated coefficients in Equation 4.2 are derived from a sample of data, there is always a chance that the sizes of the estimated coefficients are dependent on that particular sample of data and might differ if another sample

---

[26]The technical details of this process can be found in any standard econometrics textbook. See, for example, Robert S. Pindyck and Daniel L. Rubinfeld, *Econometric Models and Economic Forecasts*, 4th ed. (New York: McGraw-Hill, 1998); Jeffrey M. Wooldridge, *Econometric Analysis of Cross Section and Panel Data*, 2nd ed. (Cambridge, MA: The MIT Press, 2010), and the books by Greene and Kmenta noted above.
[27]Standard statistical packages include SAS, SPSS, and STATA. Spreadsheet software packages such as Excel also include regression analysis.

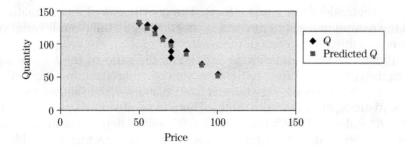

FIGURE 4.2
Simple Regression Analysis
Actual Versus Predicted Results
This figure plots the actual and predicted quantity demanded relative to price in the simple regression analysis of quantity and price.

was used. The coefficients might also not be different from zero in the larger population. This issue would be of particular concern with the small data sample in Table 4.1. Table 4.1 includes the predicted value of quantity demanded and the residual, or the difference between the actual and predicted values, for each observation. Figure 4.2 plots the predicted quantity demanded at each price with the actual quantity demanded. Although the actual and predicted values appear to be relatively similar, we need a quantitative measure of how well the data fit the estimated equation.

Regression analysis packages provide an estimate of the **standard error** of each estimated coefficient, a measure of how much the coefficient would vary in regressions based on different samples. A small standard error means that the coefficient would not vary substantially among these regressions. In Table 4.1, the standard error of the price coefficient is 0.176, while that of the constant term is 12.571. Managers can use a *t*-**test**, based on the ratio of the size of the coefficient to its standard error, to test for the significance of the coefficients of the independent variables in a regression analysis. The *t*-test is used to test the hypothesis that a coefficient is significantly different from zero (i.e., whether there is a high probability that, in repeated drawings of samples from the population, the coefficient will be a number different than zero or $H_1: B \neq 0$) versus the hypothesis that the coefficient is equal to zero ($H_0: B = 0$). This result is typically indicated by a *t*-statistic greater than 2.0, which means that a manager can be 95 percent certain that the coefficient is not zero in the larger population.

Large values of the *t*-statistic show statistically significant results because the standard error is small relative to the size of the estimated coefficient. In Table 4.1, the *t*-statistic for the price coefficient is –8.952, while that for the constant term is 16.741. Because both of these numbers are greater than 2 in absolute value, a manager can be at least 95 percent certain that the estimated coefficients are statistically significant and that the data support the hypothesis $H_1: B \neq 0$. The Excel program shows the actual degree of significance associated with the *t*-statistics. There is a 434 in 100,000,000 chance that the price coefficient is not statistically significant, while there is a 1 in 100,000,000 chance that the constant term is not statistically significant.

The Excel program also calculates **confidence intervals** around the estimated coefficients. These statistics show the range of values in which we can be confident that the true coefficient actually lies with a given degree of probability, usually 95 percent. Given the results in Table 4.1, a manager can be 95 percent confident that the true value of the price coefficient lies between –1.185 and –1.970 and that the constant term lies between 182.435 and 238.454.

The goodness of fit of the entire estimating equation to the data set is shown by the **coefficient of determination (R^2)**. The value of this coefficient ranges from 0 to 1, with the size of the coefficient indicating the fraction of the variation in the dependent variable that is explained statistically by the variables included in the estimating equation. In Table 4.1, the variation in quantity demanded is due partly to the variation in price (the regression effect) and partly to the effect of a random

Standard error
A measure of the precision of an estimated regression analysis coefficient that shows how much the coefficient would vary in regressions from different samples.

t-**test**
A test based on the size of the ratio of the estimated regression coefficient to its standard error that is used to determine the statistical significance of the coefficient.

Confidence interval
The range of values in which we can be confident that the true coefficient actually lies with a given degree of probability, usually 95 percent.

Coefficient of determination (R^2)
A measure of how the overall estimating equation fits the data, which shows the fraction of the variation in the dependent variable that is explained statistically by the variables included in the equation.

disturbance (the residual or error effect). The coefficient of determination tests how well the overall model fits the data by decomposing the overall variation into the variation resulting from each of these effects.

The coefficient of determination is defined as the ratio of the sum of squared errors from the regression effect to the total sum of squared errors (regression plus residual effect). In Table 4.1, this ratio is 5,601/6,300 = 0.889 (shown as the value of the R^2 statistic at the top of the table). There is no absolute cutoff point for the value of the R^2 statistic. The values of the coefficient of determination are typically higher for time-series data than for cross-sectional data, as many variables move together over time, which can explain the variation in the dependent variable. R^2 statistics for time-series analyses can exceed 0.9 in value, while those for cross-sectional studies are often in the range of 0.3–0.4.

When more variables are added to a regression equation, the R^2 statistic can never decrease in size. Thus, one method for obtaining a higher value of this statistic is to keep adding independent variables to the estimating equation. Because this procedure could give misleading results, managers can also use the **adjusted R^2 statistic**, which is defined in Equation 4.4.

Adjusted R^2 statistic
The coefficient of determination adjusted for the number of degrees of freedom in the estimating equation.

$$4.4 \quad \overline{R}^2 = 1 - (1 - R^2)\frac{(n - 1)}{(n - k)}$$

where

$\overline{R}^2 =$ adjusted R^2

$R^2 =$ coefficient of determination

$n =$ number of observations

$k =$ number of estimated coefficients

Degrees of freedom
The number of observations (n) minus the number of estimated coefficients (k) in a regression equation.

The number of observations (n) minus the number of estimated coefficients (k) is called the **degrees of freedom** in the estimating equation. You cannot have more estimated coefficients than observations in an equation. The estimated equation in Table 4.1 has 10 degrees of freedom because there are 12 observations and 2 estimated coefficients. The adjusted R^2 statistic is typically lower than the coefficient of determination because it adjusts for the number of degrees of freedom in the estimating equation, and the statistic could actually be negative. In Table 4.1, the value of the adjusted R^2 statistic is 0.878 compared to 0.889 for the coefficient of determination. There is only a small difference between the two statistics, given the 10 degrees of freedom in the equation.

F-statistic
An alternative measure of goodness of fit of an estimating equation that can be used to test for the joint influence of all the independent variables in the equation.

An alternative measure of goodness of fit is the **F-statistic**, which is the ratio of the sum of squared errors from the regression effect to the sum of squared errors from the residual effect, or the variation explained by the equation relative to the variation not explained.[28] A larger F-statistic means that more variation in the data is explained by the variables in the equation. The value of the F-statistic in Table 4.1 is 80.143, which is well beyond the 95 percent probability level.

The F-statistic can be used to test the significance of all coefficients jointly in equations that have multiple independent variables. It is similar in concept to the t-statistic for testing the significance of individual regression coefficients. It is possible that the t-statistics might indicate that the individual coefficients are not statistically significant, while the F-statistic is statistically significant. This result could occur if the independent variables in the equation are highly correlated with each other. Their individual influences on the dependent variable may be weak, while the joint effect is much stronger.

---

[28]These terms are adjusted for their degrees of freedom.

Relationship Between One Dependent and Multiple Independent Variables: Multiple Regression Analysis

We now extend the Excel example of simple regression analysis showing the relationship between price and quantity demanded of oranges in Table 4.1 to a multiple regression analysis, which adds advertising expenditure to the estimating equation in Table 4.2. Although we know that many other variables should also influence the

TABLE 4.2 Multiple Regression Analysis Results

REGRESSION STATISTICS

Multiple R	0.980
R square	0.961
Adjusted R square	0.952
Standard error	5.255
Observations	12.000

ANOVA

	Degrees of Freedom	Sum of Squares	Mean Square	F-statistic	Significance of F-statistic
Regression	2.000	6051.510	3025.755	109.589	0.000000481
Residual	9.000	248.490	27.610		
Total	11.000	6300.000			

	Coefficients	Standard Error	t-statistic	P-value	Lower 95 percent	Upper 95 percent
Intercept	116.157	24.646	4.713	0.001	60.404	171.909
Price	−1.308	0.129	−10.110	0.000	−1.601	−1.015
Advertising	11.246	2.784	4.039	0.003	4.947	17.545

RESIDUAL OUTPUT

Observation	Predicted Q	Residuals	Quantity (lbs.)	Price (cents/lb.)	Advertising Expenditure ($)
1	47.222	7.778	55	100	5.50
2	69.297	0.703	70	90	6.30
3	92.497	−2.497	90	80	7.20
4	103.327	−3.327	100	70	7.00
5	95.455	−5.455	90	70	6.30
6	107.263	−2.263	105	70	7.35
7	87.583	−7.583	80	70	5.60
8	111.553	−1.553	110	65	7.15
9	122.029	2.971	125	60	7.50
10	115.281	−0.281	115	60	6.90
11	124.632	5.368	130	55	7.15
12	123.861	6.139	130	50	6.50
Average			100	70	6.70

demand for oranges, we can illustrate multiple regression analysis by simply adding one more variable to the equation.

We use multiple regression analysis to estimate the demand function in Equation 4.5.

4.5 $Q = a - bP + cADV$

> *where*
> Q = quantity demanded
> a = constant term
> b = coefficient of price variable = $\Delta Q/\Delta P$, all else held constant
> P = price
> c = coefficient of advertising variable = $\Delta Q/\Delta ADV$, all else held constant
> ADV = advertising expenditure

As with the simple regression analysis example, we are estimating a linear relationship between the dependent variable, quantity demanded, and the two independent variables—price and advertising expenditure. The constant term, a, shows the effect on quantity demanded of other variables not included in the equation. The coefficients, b and c, show the effect on quantity demanded of a unit change in each of the independent variables. Each coefficient shows this effect while statistically holding constant the effect of the other variable. Thus, using multiple regression analysis to estimate demand relationships from behavioral data solves the "all else held constant" problem by statistically holding constant the effects of the other variables included in the estimating equation.

The demand relationship estimated in Table 4.2 is shown in Equation 4.6, using the variables defined in Equation 4.5.

4.6 $Q = 116.157 - 1.308P + 11.246ADV$

We can see that the coefficient of the price variable in Equation 4.6 is different from that in Equation 4.2 even though we use the same data in both equations. The difference arises from the fact that Equation 4.6 includes advertising expenditure, so that this equation shows the effect of price on quantity demanded, holding constant the level of advertising. Because no other variables are held constant in Equation 4.2, the price variable coefficient in that equation may pick up the effects of other variables not included in the equation that also influence the quantity demanded of oranges. This result is likely to occur if there are other excluded variables that are highly correlated with price. Thus, it is important to have a well-specified estimating equation based on the relevant economic theory.

The coefficients of the price and advertising variables in Equation 4.6 show the change in quantity demanded resulting from a unit change in each of these variables, all else held constant. As with the simple regression analysis example, these coefficients can be used to calculate the relevant elasticities. Using the average values of price, quantity demanded, and advertising expenditure, we calculate the price elasticity of demand in Equation 4.7 and the advertising elasticity in Equation 4.8.

$$4.7 \quad e_P = \frac{(\Delta Q)(P)}{(\Delta P)(Q)} = \frac{(-1.308)(70)}{(100)} = -0.9156$$

$$4.8 \quad e_{ADV} = \frac{(\Delta Q)(ADV)}{(\Delta ADV)(Q)} = \frac{(11.246)(6.70)}{(100)} = 0.7535$$

The price elasticity calculated in Equation 4.7 is smaller than that calculated in Equation 4.3. In fact, the estimated elasticity coefficient in Equation 4.7—derived from Equation 4.6, with the level of advertising expenditure held constant— indicates that demand is price inelastic, while the coefficient in Equation 4.3— derived from Equation 4.2, which does not include the level of advertising expenditure—indicates elastic demand. It appears that the price variable in Equation 4.2 is picking up some of the effect of advertising on demand because the latter variable is not included in that equation. Managers must realize that econometric results can vary with the specification of the demand equation. All relevant variables need to be included in these equations to derive the most accurate empirical results.

Table 4.2 also presents the summary statistics for the multiple regression analysis. We can see that the standard errors of the two independent variables and the constant term are all small relative to the size of the estimated coefficients, so that the t-statistics are larger than 2 in absolute value. The two independent variables and the constant term are statistically significant well beyond the 95 percent level of confidence. Table 4.2 also shows the confidence intervals for all of the terms.

Figure 4.3 shows the actual and predicted values of quantity demanded relative to price, while Figure 4.4 shows the same values relative to advertising expenditure. Regarding the goodness of fit measures, the value of the coefficient of determination (R^2) is 0.961, while that of the adjusted R^2 statistic is 0.952. Although the latter is smaller than the former as expected, both statistics increased in value from the simple regression analysis in Table 4.1, indicating the greater explanatory power of the multiple regression model. The F-statistic is also highly significant in Table 4.2.

Other Functional Forms

The linear demand functions, estimated in Equations 4.2 and 4.6, imply both that there is some maximum price that drives consumers' quantity demanded of the product back to zero and that there is some maximum quantity that people demand at a zero price. As we have seen, the price elasticity of demand also changes at different prices along a linear demand curve. These characteristics of a linear demand function may not always adequately represent the behavior of different groups of individuals or the demand for various products, particularly at the end points of the demand curve.

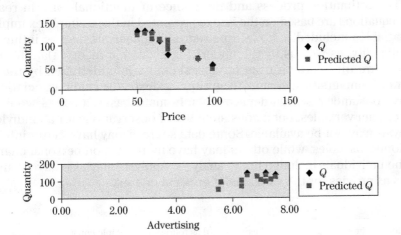

FIGURE 4.3

Multiple Regression Analysis, Fit of Price Variable

This figure plots the actual and predicted quantity demanded relative to price in the multiple regression analysis of quantity, price, and advertising expenditure.

FIGURE 4.4

Multiple Regression Analysis, Fit of Advertising Variable

This figure plots the actual and predicted quantity demanded relative to advertising expenditure in the multiple regression analysis of quantity, price, and advertising expenditure.

FIGURE 4.5
Log-Linear Demand Curve
A log-linear demand curve has a constant price elasticity everywhere along the curve.

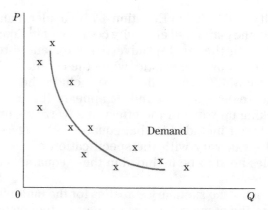

It is often hypothesized that a multiplicative nonlinear demand function of the form shown in Equation 4.9 (where the variables are defined as in Equation 4.5) better represents individuals' behavior:

4.9 $Q_X = (a)(P_X^b)(ADV^c)$

This function, illustrated in general in Figure 4.5, is called a log-linear demand function because it can be transformed into a linear function by taking the logarithms of all the variables in the equation. This function is also called a *constant-elasticity demand function* because the elasticities are constant for all values of the demand variables and are represented by the exponents, *b* and *c*, in Equation 4.9.[29] Thus, the price and advertising elasticities can be read directly from the statistical results if this type of function is used in the estimation process. No further calculations are needed to determine the elasticities. This function may also better represent consumer behavior in certain cases because it implies that as price increases, quantity demanded decreases, but does not go to zero.

Demand Estimation Issues

Demand functions estimated for actual products are obviously much more complex than the simple examples presented in Equations 4.2 and 4.6. Managers could not use the results of such simple equations for decision making. However, these examples provide a starting point for understanding the more complex analyses discussed below. The estimation process and the choice of functional form in real-world demand equations are based on the issues presented in these simple examples.

The variables included in a multiple regression analysis may be influenced by data availability, as well as by the underlying economic theory. Data for demand estimation are often drawn from large-scale surveys undertaken by the federal government, universities, nonprofit groups, industry or trade associations, and company consumer research departments. In many cases, analysts would like to include certain variables, but a consistent set of observations for all individuals in the analysis may not be available. Some data sources may have better information on economic variables, while others may have more data on personal characteristics of the individuals included in the analysis. Analysts may also have to use other variables as proxies for the variables of greatest interest.

---

[29]Using calculus, the price elasticity can be calculated as follows for a simple constant elasticity demand function:

$e_P = (dQ_X/dP_X)(P_X/Q_X)$

$Q_X = (a)(P_X^b)$

$e_P = [(a)(b)P_X^{b-1}][P_X/Q_X] = [(b)(a)P_X^b]/[(a)(P_X^b)] = b$

Similar calculations follow for other terms in such a function.

Every multiple regression analysis is influenced by the sample of data—time-series, cross-sectional, or panel—that is used. The analyst wants to estimate behavioral relationships that can be generalized beyond the sample of observations included in the analysis. Yet large-scale data collection can be very expensive and time-consuming. Thus, the analyst must be concerned that the estimated relationships may hold only for the sample of data analyzed, and not the larger population. As we discussed above, the analyst engages in hypothesis testing to determine how much confidence can be placed in the results of a particular analysis and whether these outcomes can be generalized to a larger population.

Managerial Rule of Thumb

Using Multiple Regression Analysis

In using multiple regression analysis to estimate consumer demand, a manager must decide which variables to include in the analysis. Various types of statistical problems can arise if relevant variables are excluded from the analysis or if irrelevant variables are included. The choice of variables is derived from economic theory, real-world experience, which is the problem under consideration, and common sense. ∎

Case Study of Statistical Estimation of Automobile Demand

We now discuss issues arising with the use of multiple regression analysis to estimate the demand for automobiles and the associated elasticities.[30] This discussion is drawn from a research study that clearly illustrates many of the methodological problems just presented.

Automobile demand studies have used both cross-sectional and time-series analysis with aggregate and disaggregated data. Studies have been undertaken for the entire market, market segments (domestic vs. foreign), and particular brands of automobiles. Thus, given the differences in data sets, the functional forms of the estimating equations, and the variables included, we would expect to find a range of elasticity estimates in these studies. Aggregate time-series studies generally estimate market automobile price elasticities to be less than 1 in absolute value and income elasticities to be greater than +2.00, indicating a lack of sensitivity to price for automobiles as a commodity, but a strong sensitivity in the demand for automobiles to changes in income. The disaggregated cross-sectional studies found price elasticities for particular vehicle types ranging from –0.51 to –6.13. The large elasticities at the upper end of the range should not be surprising, given the degree of substitution between different brands of cars.

Price elasticities have been found to be smaller for subcompact and compact vehicles compared to larger models and for two-vehicle households compared to one-vehicle households. The cross-section literature also found income elasticities greater than +1.00 and, in some cases, greater than +5.00. A 1985 study estimated an income elasticity of +1.96 for a Chevy Chevette and +7.49 for a Mercedes 280S, indicating a substantial consumer response for these models to changes in income. Automobile demand by households owning one vehicle tended to be less sensitive to changes in income than by two-vehicle households.

---

[30]This discussion is based on Patrick S. McCarthy, "Market Price and Income Elasticities of New Vehicle Demands," *Review of Economics and Statistics* 78 (August 1996): 543–47.

Automobile demand studies typically include price, income, credit availability, and automobile stocks as independent variables. One issue that has been debated in the literature is whether to include variables measuring automobile quality, which are typically derived from *Consumer Reports* and surveys by J.D. Power and Associates, a major marketing research firm. Thus, complex research studies often use data from sources that both managers and consumers read. Excluding quality variables from demand estimation studies could create econometric problems. The estimated price elasticity of demand coefficient would be biased downward if a model is estimated without including quality variables and if quality is positively associated with price and demand. Statistical and econometric problems can also arise if the independent variables in the model are highly correlated with each other. It may be difficult to separate out the effect of price from the other variables in this case. These issues again illustrate the problem of estimating the relationship between price and quantity demanded, "all else held constant."

In a 1996 study, Patrick S. McCarthy[31] estimated automobile demand based on data from the J.D. Power and Associates 1989 New Car Buyer Competitive Dynamics Survey of 33,284 households. This survey contained information on the vehicle purchased, household socioeconomic and demographic characteristics, and various activities associated with purchasing the vehicle. McCarthy's sample of 1,564 households, which was approximately 5 percent of the usable survey records, was randomly drawn from the larger survey to enable generalizations to be made to the larger population. The author supplemented the data from the J.D. Power survey with data on price, warranty, exterior and interior size, fuel economy, reliability, and safety from the *1989 Automotive News Market Data Book*, *Consumer Reports*, and the *1989 Car Book*. He obtained gasoline prices from the *Oil and Gas Journal* and population estimates from the U.S. Bureau of the Census.

Table 4.3 shows the independent variables, estimated coefficients, and summary statistics for McCarthy's study. The independent variables included measures of automobile costs (price and operating cost per mile), physical characteristics and vehicle style (horsepower, length, government crash test results, and vehicle type), quality (results of a consumer satisfaction index), manufacturer, consumer search activities (the number of first and second visits to different dealers and whether the consumer repurchased the same brand as previously), and household socioeconomic data. The study used multinomial logit analysis, a special form of regression analysis in which the dependent variable is a discrete variable (to purchase or not purchase a specific vehicle) rather than a continuous variable (the number of vehicles purchased).

McCarthy was satisfied with the precision of the estimating model in terms of the estimated signs of the variables, the *t*-statistics, and the coefficient of determination. Most of the signs of the variables were estimated as predicted, and the *t*-statistics indicated that the variables were statistically significant. The value of the coefficient of determination (0.26) was low, but comparable to those of other cross-sectional studies.[32]

The results in Table 4.3 show that both higher vehicle prices, relative to annual income, and higher vehicle operating costs lowered the quantity demanded of automobiles (the negative sign on those coefficients). Thus, the estimated demand curve is downward sloping. Vehicle safety, net horsepower, and overall vehicle

---

[31]Ibid.

[32]The coefficient of determination and other measures of goodness of fit are slightly different in this model than in the standard linear regression model, given the discrete nature of the dependent variable.

TABLE 4.3   The Demand for Automobiles

	INDEPENDENT VARIABLES	COEFFICIENT (*T*-STATISTIC)
Cost-related attributes	Vehicle price/annual income	−2.452 (−9.1)
	Operating cost per mile (cents)	−0.4498 (−5.8)
	Metropolitan population if >50,000	0.0000173 (1.4)
Vehicle style and physical attributes	Crash test variable	0.2409 (3.0)
	Net horsepower	0.00949 (6.0)
	Overall length (inches)	0.0166 (5.4)
	SUV, van, pickup truck	1.445 (4.8)
	Sports car segment	−1.277 (−4.7)
	Luxury segment—domestic	−0.4944 (−3.7)
Perceived quality	Consumer satisfaction index	0.0085 (3.5)
Vehicle search costs	1st dealer visit—domestic	3.034 (11.1)
	1st dealer visit—European	4.274 (15.2)
	1st dealer visit—Asian	3.726 (11.6)
	Subsequent dealer visits—Domestic	0.3136 (5.6)
	Subsequent dealer visits—European	0.7290 (5.7)
	Subsequent dealer visits—Asian	0.3337 (5.9)
	Repurchase same brand	2.320 (2.0)
Socioeconomic variables	Resident of Pacific Coast	−1.269 (−5.0)
	Age > 45 years old	0.9511 (4.8)
Manufacturing brand variables	Chrysler	1.007 (4.7)
	Ford, General Motors	1.721 (8.5)
	Honda, Nissan, Toyota	1.267 (9.1)
	Mazda	1.005 (5.5)
Summary statistics	R^2	0.26
	Number of observations	1564

Source: Patrick S. McCarthy, "Market Price and Income Elasticities of New Vehicle Demands," *Review of Economics and Statistics* 78 (August 1996): 543–47. © 1996 by the President and Fellows of Harvard College and the Massachusetts Institute of Technology.

length all had a significantly positive effect on automobile demand (as evidenced by the positive coefficients for these variables). Increased values of these variables would shift the demand curve to the right. Consumers in this sample exhibited a greater demand for vans, SUVs, and pickup trucks relative to automobiles and station wagons and a smaller demand for sports cars and domestic cars in the luxury segment.

We can also see that demand was positively related to increases in perceived quality (the positive coefficient on the consumer satisfaction index variable) and that search costs influenced vehicle demands. McCarthy argued that the positive coefficients on the dealer-visits variables indicated that the information benefits from an additional visit more than offset the additional search costs, but that the additional benefits declined with subsequent visits. The variable showing whether

TABLE 4.4 Automobile Demand Elasticities

	OWN-PRICE ELASTICITY	CROSS-PRICE ELASTICITY	INCOME ELASTICITY
Entire market	−0.87	0.82	1.70
Market segment			
Domestic	−0.78	0.28	1.62
European	−1.09	0.76	1.93
Asian	−0.81	0.61	1.65

Source: Patrick S. McCarthy, "Market Price and Income Elasticities of New Vehicle Demands," *Review of Economics and Statistics* 78 (August 1996): 543–47. © 1996 by the President and Fellows of Harvard College and the Massachusetts Institute of Technology.

a consumer repurchased the same vehicle brand also had a positive coefficient, indicating a positive effect on demand. Because repurchasing the same brand lowers search and transactions costs, this variable had the expected positive sign. These results indicate that consumers react not just to the monetary price of an automobile, but also to the full purchasing costs, including the costs of obtaining information and searching for the vehicle. The study also determined that younger consumers and those residing on the Pacific Coast had smaller demands for domestic vehicles than other age and geographic groups.

Table 4.4 shows McCarthy's estimated price and income elasticities for both the entire market and the domestic, European, and Asian segments. The estimated demand for automobiles in this study was generally price inelastic, although the elasticity estimate for European models was slightly greater than 1 in absolute value. The cross-price elasticities were estimated to be positive numbers, indicating substitute goods, as economic theory suggests. Sales of European and Asian automobiles responded more to changes in the prices of substitute brands than did sales of U.S. automobiles. All income elasticities were found to be greater than +1.00, indicating substantial sensitivity to income changes.

The McCarthy study is particularly useful for managers because it is short and well written, and it focuses on the issues relevant to managerial decision making. Although academic consumer demand studies do not always meet these criteria, they can be useful starting points for managers. While the results of academic research studies may sometimes be too general for managerial decision making, they can be suggestive of strategies that managers should pursue. For example, McCarthy found that vehicle characteristics, quality, and consumer search variables were important influences on automobile demand.

One other problem with academic studies is the time lag often involved in their publication. The McCarthy article was published in 1996, using data from 1989. This type of lag is typical for academic research because articles are peer reviewed and revised several times.[33] While this time lag may limit the usefulness of academic research for managerial decision making, it does not make these studies worthless. The peer review process increases the reliability of the research results. In many cases, these results are available online or in the form of working papers long before they are officially published. Studies of past market behavior can also give managers insights into future trends.

---

[33]The use of electronic communication has considerably reduced the time lags in the academic review process.

Many of these issues regarding the estimation of price and advertising elasticities have been raised in the marketing literature.[34] Elasticity studies, particularly of specific product brands, may produce biased estimates if they do not include variables measuring product quality, the distribution of the product, advertising expenditures, other promotion activities such as coupons and rebates, and lagged prices and sales. Thus, one of the major problems in statistical demand studies is to correctly specify the model being estimated and to locate data on all the variables that should be included in the model.

Managerial Rule of Thumb

Using Empirical Consumer Demand Studies

Empirical consumer demand studies are important to managers because they show the types of data available for analyzing the demand for different products. Many data sources, such as industry and consumer surveys that researchers discover, may not have been widely publicized. Demand studies also discuss previous analyses, and they indicate how researchers conceptualize the problem of estimating the demand for a particular product. ∎

Relationships Between Consumer Market Data and Econometric Demand Studies

In the 1998 book *Studies in Consumer Demand: Econometric Methods Applied to Market Data*, Jeffrey A. Dubin illustrated the relationships between consumer market data, which managers typically use, and formal econometric demand studies based on these data.[35] In many cases, researchers analyze market data to obtain insights on what variables to include in their econometric models of demand. Although Dubin employed advanced econometric methods to estimate the demand for various products, we focus on two selected cases—Carnation Coffee-mate and Carnation Evaporated Milk—to illustrate the relationships between consumer market data and econometric models of demand. We also discuss a recent study estimating the demand for cheese in the United States.

Case Study I: Carnation Coffee-mate

To estimate the value of intangible assets, such as brand names, Dubin used Carnation Coffee-mate as one of his examples. He began with consumer surveys drawn from Carnation's marketing files and interviews with key individuals who were marketing the products during the 1980s. Dubin used a Carnation Consumer Research Department survey to help define the market for the product. According

---

[34]Gerard J. Tellis, "The Price Elasticity of Selective Demand: A Meta-Analysis of Econometric Models of Sales," *Journal of Marketing Research* 25 (November 1988): 331–41; Raj Sethuraman and Gerard J. Tellis, "An Analysis of the Tradeoff Between Advertising and Price Discounting," *Journal of Marketing Research* 28 (May 1991): 160–74.

[35]Jeffrey A. Dubin, *Studies in Consumer Demand: Econometric Methods Applied to Market Data* (Boston: Kluwer Academic Publishers, 1998).

to this survey, 37 percent of all cups of coffee were whitened, with milk used in half of these cases and a nondairy powdered creamer in another 20 percent. Coffee-mate was the best-selling nondairy powdered creamer, with Cremora by Borden a major competitor. In addition to milk, other substitutes for Coffee-mate included cream, evaporated milk, and powdered milk.

Trends in coffee consumption also affected the demand for whiteners, given the complementary relationship between the two goods. A beverage industry survey showed that there had been a long-term decline in the per-capita daily consumption of coffee in the United States between 1962 and 1985. Although the average number of cups consumed by adults and the proportion of the population drinking coffee declined, these trends were offset by increases in the total U.S. population, so that the total amount of coffee consumed actually increased.

Marketing studies showed that coffee consumption differed by season, region, gender, and age. Socioeconomic status also played a role in consumption. A Carnation marketing study showed that Coffee-mate consumption was highest among coffee drinkers who had incomes under $10,000, had no more than a high school education, were employed in blue-collar occupations, lived in smaller cities or rural areas, and were African Americans. Studies also indicated that Coffee-mate had higher brand loyalty than its competitors and that Coffee-mate users were less likely to use coupons to purchase the product.

Carnation Coffee-mate Demand Model Variables and Elasticities

Dubin based his demand model for Coffee-mate on these survey results. He used a constant elasticity model, as illustrated in Equation 4.9 and Figure 4.5, so that his estimated coefficients were the various elasticities of demand. Dubin included the following variables in his analysis:

- The price of Coffee-mate
- The prices of substitute goods
- Variables accounting for trends over time and seasonality effects
- Real income (adjusted for price changes) per capita
- Frequency of coffee consumption
- The total volume of all commodity sales in the region
- Real advertising expenditure of branded creamers
- Retail support measures, including in-aisle displays, in-ad coupons, and special pricing

He focused on the 16-ounce size of Coffee-mate, which had the highest sales volume in the product line and was marketed primarily in the retail distribution channel.

Dubin estimated a price elasticity coefficient of –2.01 for the 16-ounce Coffee-mate, as well as positive cross-price elasticities with its competitor brands. In addition to the role of price, he found seasonal effects on the demand for Coffee-mate (increased consumption in February and March), resulting from the patterns of coffee consumption. Although the real income and coffee consumption variables were not significantly different from zero, the all-commodity sales variable was highly significant, indicating the impact of activity in larger markets on the demand for nondairy creamer. Of the retail support variables, only in-ad coupons and special prices showed positive effects on the demand for Coffee-mate. Displays of the product within the stores did not have an impact on consumer demand, according to the study results. Increased advertising for Coffee-mate also did not increase the demand for the product. However, increased advertising for Cremora actually increased the demand for Coffee-mate. Dubin attributed this result to the increased consumer awareness of creamers from advertising even if that advertising was not directed specifically to Coffee-mate. Thus, the study of Coffee-mate both confirmed the predictions of economic theory about price and cross-price elasticities and tested for the influence of other variables suggested by consumer research.

Case Study II: Carnation Evaporated Milk

Dubin also examined the market for evaporated milk, focusing on the leading brand, which was produced by Carnation as well. Marketing studies had shown that there were two distinct market segments—those individuals who used evaporated milk in coffee and everyday foods, such as soups, potatoes, and sauces, and those who used it for holidays and seasonal foods. These groups had different purchasing patterns, brand preferences, and demographic characteristics. A 1987 Carnation marketing study found that while only 13 percent of all evaporated milk consumers made five or more purchases per year, they represented 61 percent of the total category sales volume. In addition, 60 percent of evaporated milk consumers made only one purchase per year (representing 15 percent of sales volume). Compared to its competitors, Carnation sales were more concentrated among light users of evaporated milk. Much consumer research also indicated that Hispanics and African Americans tended to be heavy users of evaporated milk for both everyday and holiday foods unique to their cultures. This demographic trend created a geographic pattern of demand, with increased consumption in the South and Southwest, where many members of these groups live. Evaporated milk consumption was found to be greater in the fall and winter months, given the use of this product in coffee, baked goods, and soups, products more likely to be consumed during those months. Consumer research also indicated that younger, less affluent, and less educated households were more likely to purchase store label or generic evaporated milk than brand names.

Carnation Evaporated Milk Demand Model Variables and Elasticities
Given this background, Dubin estimated the demand for Carnation evaporated milk as a function of the following variables:

- The price of the Carnation product
- The price of substitute goods
- Variables accounting for trends over time, seasonality effects, and regional differences
- Real income level
- The percent of the population that is Hispanic
- Real advertising expenditures
- Retail support measures, including in-aisle displays, local advertising, and special pricing

Dubin found that Carnation evaporated milk had a price elasticity of –2.03, while its competitors had smaller elasticities of –0.88 (PET Evaporated Milk) and –1.22 (all other brands). He estimated the expected positive cross-price elasticities between these products. Dubin found a positive effect of retail support, particularly through displays and local advertising. He found that Carnation's advertising increased the overall demand for evaporated milk, while PET's advertising was not significant in influencing demand. Although real income was positively related to the demand for evaporated milk, the Hispanic population variable was not significant in the analysis. The latter result was surprising, given the emphasis placed on this subgroup in the consumer marketing studies. Either this variable was not important by itself, or it was correlated with other variables, and the statistical analysis was unable to determine its independent effect.

Case Study III: The Demand for Cheese in the United States

The demand for cheese in the United States has been influenced by numerous factors including an increased availability of cheese varieties, greater use of cheese by fast food and pizza restaurants, increased use of cheese by food manufacturers and individuals cooking at home, increased consumption of ethnic foods using large amounts of cheese, and changes in consumer demographics.[36] Cheese is also now sold in many forms including consumer-sized cuts, bagged shredded cheese, and processed cheese slices. Cheese production and sales have become key components of the U.S. dairy industry.

Davis et al. used 2006 Nielsen Homescan data containing demographic and food purchase information for a nationwide panel of representative households to estimate the demand for cheese in its different forms and the corresponding elasticities. Households in the panel had a handheld device to scan at home all food purchased at any retail outlet. Each purchase record contained data on product characteristics, quantity purchased, price paid with and without promotions, date of purchase, store, and brand information. Researchers also obtained information on the size and composition of each household, household income, and the origin, age, race, gender, education, and occupation of household members. Davis et al. based their econometric analysis on a Tobit demand system estimator that accounted for the fact that some households had zero purchases of cheese during the relevant time period.

Davis et al. found that all of their estimated own-price and cross-price elasticities were statistically significant and that all own-price elasticities were negative as expected. The largest own-price elasticities were for cottage cheese (–2.49), grated cheese (–2.07), and shredded cheese (–3.74), indicating sizeable changes in the quantity demanded of these cheeses in response to a 1 percent change in their prices. The cross-price elasticities for all cheese forms were positive, indicating that they were substitute goods. Consumers were likely to switch to other cheese forms if the price of their initial choice of cheese increased beyond a certain threshold. Demographic factors were not as important in the analysis as the price and income variables. However, household size and whether a female was the head of a household did impact the demand for cheese. Results of studies such as this can assist cheese manufacturers and marketers in making decisions on production changes and marketing strategies.

[36]This discussion is based on Christopher G. Davis, Donald Blayney, Diansheng Dong, Steven T. Yen, and Rachel J. Johnson, "Will Changing Demographics Affect U.S. Cheese Demand?" *Journal of Agricultural and Applied Economics* 43 (May 2011): 259–73.

Managerial Rule of Thumb

Using Consumer Market Data

Business economists and researchers use the consumer market data familiar to managers and marketers to estimate statistical/econometric models of demand and consumer behavior. These demand studies, in turn, can assist managers in developing competitive strategies by indicating the importance of the characteristics influencing the demand for different products and by showing what trade-offs consumers may be willing to make among those characteristics. ■

Summary

In this chapter, we illustrated two major approaches to gathering information about consumer behavior and demand for different products: (1) marketing and consumer research methods that include surveys, experiments, and test marketing; and (2) statistical and econometric approaches to formally estimating demand relationships. Managers tend to favor the former approach, while economists in business and academia use the latter.[37] Most of the data for econometric analyses, however, are derived from consumer research studies. We have suggested that managers be familiar with both approaches because each provides useful information on consumer behavior.

Managers need to realize that marketing analysis builds on the fundamental economic concepts of demand and elasticity. Marketers take these basic economic concepts and develop analyses of brand differentiation, market segmentation, and new product pricing. While some of the formal statistical approaches used by economists to estimate demand relationships may appear abstract and academic to managers and marketers, these approaches may do a better job of determining the effects of different variables on demand, while holding all else constant. This information is useful to both academic researchers attempting to improve the methods of demand estimation and managers needing to make decisions about advertising spending or how to counter the strategic moves of a competitor.

Key Terms

adjusted R^2 statistic, p. 98

coefficient of determination (R^2), p. 97

confidence interval, p. 97

conjoint analysis, p. 89

cross-sectional data, p. 94

degrees of freedom, p. 98

direct consumer surveys, p. 89

expert opinion, p. 88

F-statistic, p. 98

multiple regression analysis, p. 93

panel data, p. 94

price experiments, p. 90

simple regression analysis, p. 96

standard error, p. 97

targeted marketing, p. 91

test marketing, p. 90

time-series data, p. 94

t-test, p. 97

---

[37]Skouras et al. have suggested that these differences have arisen because improving business performance has been the primary purpose of marketing, while economics has been more focused on improving the organization of society. These researchers characterized marketing as a discipline concerned with business practice, while economics is a social science discipline. See Thanos Skouras, George J. Avlonitis, and Kostis A. Indounas, "Economics and Marketing on Pricing: How and Why Do They Differ?" *Journal of Product & Brand Management* 14 (2005): 362–74.

Exercises

Technical Questions

1. In each of the following examples, describe how the information given about consumer demand helped managers develop the appropriate strategies to increase profitability and how this information was obtained:

   a. Auto industry executives have begun to focus attention on their 20-, 30-, and 40-year-old customers, known as Generations X and Y, and away from the baby boomer generation. Recognizing that baby boomers are at least 60 years old, managers realize that their future depends on adapting to the tastes of younger generations. The auto industry is now offering more smartphone-driven multimedia systems and is considering increased use of autonomous driving capability. Luxury car producers are developing less-expensive models, and companies such as Toyota are redesigning their cars to be more compact, efficient, and sporty.[38]

   b. Companies such as Procter & Gamble Co., Unilever PLC, and Kimberly Clark Corp. are now using retina-tracking cameras to test consumer responses to new products. Kimberly Clark wanted to know which designs on its Viva paper towels were noticed in the first 10 seconds a customer looked at a shelf. This is the period when shoppers typically place items in their carts. Research has shown that what people want to do and what they say they want to do are often quite different. Companies are making increased use of this technology and three-dimensional computer simulations of product designs due to the lower costs of this technology.[39]

   c. Anheuser-Busch InBev NV and other beer producers are trying to win back customers who have switched to smaller brewers or to liquor. Anheuser launched Bud Light Platinum with a 6 percent alcohol content compared with 4.2 percent in Bud Light. Platinum is sweeter and sold in a cobalt blue bottle designed to be more popular in bars where much of this beer is sold. The company experiments with three new beers each day in its research brewery. Anheuser is also developing new products such as Bud Light Lime-a-Rita, which tastes like a margarita, and a tea-and-lemonade drink and a cider, each containing 4 percent alcohol. The company is using its Clydesdale horses to bring more free beer samples to festivals and fairs.[40]

2. The following figure plots the average farm prices of potatoes in the United States for the years 1989 to 1998 versus the annual per capita consumption. Each point represents the price and quantity data for a given year. Explain whether simply drawing the line that approximates the data points would give the demand curve for potatoes.

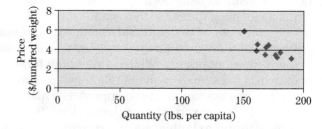

FIGURE 4.E1

Demand for Potatoes, 1989–1998

Source: Daniel B. Suits, "Agriculture," in *The Structure of American Industry,* ed. Walter Adams and James Brock, 10th ed. (Upper Saddle River, NJ: Prentice-Hall, 2001).

3. In multiple regression analysis, explain why the typical hypothesis that analysts want to test is whether a particular regression coefficient (B) is equal to zero ($H_0: B = 0$) versus whether that coefficient is not equal to zero ($H_1: B \neq 0$).

---

[38]Joseph B. White, "Auto Makers Look Past Baby Boomers," *Wall Street Journal (Online)*, January 16, 2013.

[39]Emily Glazer, "The Eyes Have It: Marketers Now Track Shoppers' Retinas," *Wall Street Journal (Online)*, July 12, 2012.

[40]Mike Esterl, "How to Build Buzz for Bud: More Alcohol, Lime-a-Rita," *Wall Street Journal (Online)*, March 29, 2012.

Application Questions

1. Find recent evidence in the *Wall Street Journal* and other business publications on how companies are expanding the use of the techniques described in the opening case to understand and impact consumer behavior.

2. "All else held constant" is the major problem facing all methods of estimating the demand for business products. Compare and contrast how the marketing and economic approaches deal with this problem.

3. Explain what types of biases arise in the different approaches to understanding consumer demand and behavior.

4. How does the empirical analysis of automobile demand presented in this chapter illustrate the fact that not only do consumers consider the monetary price of purchasing an automobile, but also they are sensitive to other costs (or the "full price") of the purchase?

5

Production and Cost Analysis in the Short Run

n this chapter, we analyze production and cost, the fundamental building blocks on the supply side of the market. Just as consumer behavior forms the basis for demand curves, producer behavior lies behind the supply curve. The prices of the inputs of production and the state of technology are two factors held constant when defining a market supply curve. Production processes (or "production functions," as economists call them) and the corresponding cost functions, which show how costs vary with the level of output produced, are also very important when we analyze the behavior and strategy of individual firms and industries.

We begin this chapter with a case that discusses efficiency and costs in the fast-food industry. Next we discuss short-run versus long-run production and costs and present a model of a short-run production function. We also examine economic data on the differences in productivity among firms and industries. We then present a model of short-run cost functions and discuss evidence on the shapes of these cost functions. We also distinguish between the types of costs measured by accountants and the cost concepts used by economists.

Case for Analysis

Production and Cost Analysis in the Fast-Food Industry

The fast-food industry in the United States has typically used drive-through windows to increase profitability. With 65 percent of fast-food revenue derived from drive-through windows, these windows have become the focal point for market share competition among fast-food outlets such as Wendy's, McDonald's, Burger King, Arby's, and Taco Bell. Even chains that did not use drive-through windows in the past, such as Starbucks and Dunkin' Donuts, have added them to their stores.[1]

Production technology changes have included the use of separate kitchens for the drive-through window, timers to monitor the seconds it takes a customer to move from the menu board to the pickup window, kitchen redesign to minimize unnecessary movement, and scanners that send customers a monthly bill rather than having them pay at each visit. Now, in an attempt to cut costs and increase speed even further, McDonald's franchises have tested remote order-taking.[2] It takes an average of 10 seconds for a new car to pull up to a drive-through menu after one car has moved forward. With a remote call center, an order-taker can answer a call from a different McDonald's where another customer has already pulled up. Thus, a call center worker in California may take orders from Honolulu, Gulfport, Miss., and Gillette, Wyo. This means that during peak periods, a worker can take up to 95 orders per hour. The trade-offs with this increased speed at the drive-through window are employee dissatisfaction with constant monitoring and the stress of the process, decreases in accuracy in filling orders, and possible breakdowns in communication over long distances. However, this technology may be expanded to allow stores, such as Home Depot, to equip carts with speakers that customers could use to wirelessly contact a call center for shopping assistance.

In Asia and other parts of the world where crowded cities and high real estate costs limit the construction of drive-throughs, McDonald's and KFC have added motorbike delivery as part of their growth strategy.[3] Fifteen hundred of the 8,800 restaurants in McDonald's Asia/Pacific, Middle East, and Africa division offer delivery, while half of the new restaurants KFC builds in China each year will offer delivery. The delivery option requires an area in the restaurant to assemble orders that are placed in battery-powered induction heating boxes. Along with cold items in insulated containers, all of the orders are placed on the back of yellow and red McDonald's branded motorbikes or electric scooters. Most McDonald's delivery orders are phoned in, but the company has started offering Internet-based ordering in Singapore and Turkey. The number of call centers may be reduced in the future as online ordering increases. Neither McDonald's nor KFC plan to use this technology in the United States, where McDonald's derives two-thirds of its sales from drive-through customers.

This case illustrates how firms can use production technology to influence their costs, revenues, and profits. Because firms in more competitive markets may not have much ability to influence the prices of their products, they may depend more on strategies to increase the number of customers and lower the costs of production. These strategies may involve changing the underlying production technology, lowering the prices paid for the inputs used, and changing the scale of operation.

To analyze these issues, we'll first discuss the nature of a firm's production process and the types of decisions that managers make regarding production. We'll then show how a firm's costs of production are related to the underlying production technology. Because the time frame affects a manager's decisions about production and cost, we distinguish between the short run and the long run and discuss the implications of these time frames for managerial decision making. This chapter focuses on short-run production and cost decisions, while we analyze production and cost in the long run later (Chapter 6).

[1]Jennifer Ordonez, "An Efficiency Drive: Fast-Food Lanes, Equipped with Timers, Get Even Faster," *Wall Street Journal*, May 18, 2000.

[2]Matt Richtel, "The Long-Distance Journey of a Fast-Food Order," *The New York Times (Online)*, April 11, 2006.

[3]Julie Jargon, "Asia Delivers for McDonald's," *Wall Street Journal (Online)*, December 13, 2011.

Defining the Production Function

To analyze a firm's production process, we first define a production function and distinguish between fixed and variable inputs and the short run versus the long run.

The Production Function

Production function
The relationship between a flow of inputs and the resulting flow of outputs in a production process during a given period of time.

A **production function** describes the relationship between a flow of inputs and the resulting flow of outputs in a production process during a given period of time. The production function describes the *physical relationship* between the inputs or factors of production and the resulting outputs of the production process. It is essentially an engineering concept, as it incorporates all of the technology or knowledge involved with the production process. The production function illustrates how inputs are combined to produce different levels of output and how different combinations of inputs may be used to produce any given level of output. It shows the maximum amount of output that can be produced with different combinations of inputs. This concept rules out any situations where inputs are redundant or wasted in production. The production function forms the basis for the economic decisions facing a firm regarding the choice of inputs and the level of outputs to produce.[4]

A production function can be expressed with the notation in Equation 5.1:

5.1 $Q = f(L, K, M \ldots)$

where
Q = quantity of output
L = quantity of labor input
K = quantity of capital input
M = quantity of materials input

As with demand relationships, Equation 5.1 is read "quantity of output is a function of the inputs listed inside the parentheses." The ellipsis in Equation 5.1 indicates that more inputs may be involved with a given production function. There may also be different types of labor and capital inputs, which we could denote by L_A, L_B, L_C and K_A, K_B, and K_C, respectively. Note that in a production function, capital (K) refers to *physical* capital, such as machines and buildings, not financial capital. The monetary or cost side of the production process (i.e., the financial capital needed to pay for workers and machines) is reflected in the functions that show how costs of production vary with different levels of output, which we'll derive later in the chapter.

A production function is defined in a very general sense and can apply to large-scale production processes, such as the fast-food outlets in this chapter's opening case analysis, or to small firms comprising only a few employees. The production function can also be applied to different sectors of the economy, including both goods and services. In this chapter, we use very simple production functions to illustrate the underlying theoretical concepts, while the examples focus on more complex, real-world production processes.

Fixed Inputs Versus Variable Inputs

Fixed input
An input whose quantity a manager cannot change during a given period of time.

Variable input
An input whose quantity a manager can change during a given period of time.

Managers use both fixed inputs and variable inputs in a production function. A **fixed input** is one whose quantity a manager cannot change during a given time period, while a **variable input** is one whose quantity a manager can change during a given

---

[4]The production function incorporates *engineering* knowledge about production technology and how inputs can be combined to produce the firm's output. Managers must make *economic* decisions about what combination of inputs and level of output are best for the firm.

time period. A factory, a given amount of office space, and a plot of land are fixed inputs in a production function. Automobiles or CD players can be produced in the factory, accounting services can be undertaken in the office, and crops can be grown on the land. However, once a manager decides on the size of the factory, the amount of office space, or the acreage of land, it is difficult, if not impossible, to change these inputs in a relatively short time period. The amount of automobiles, CD players, accounting services, or crops produced is a function of the manager's use of the variable inputs in combination with these fixed inputs. Automobile workers, steel and plastic, accountants, farm workers, seed, and fertilizer are all variable inputs in these production processes. The amount of output produced varies as managers make decisions regarding the quantities of these variable inputs to use, while holding constant the underlying size of the factory, office space, or plot of land.

Short-Run Versus Long-Run Production Functions

Two dimensions of time are used to describe production functions: the short run and the long run. These categories do not refer to specific calendar periods of time, such as a month or a year; they are defined in terms of the use of fixed and variable inputs.

A **short-run production function** involves the use of at least one fixed input. At any given point in time, managers operate in the short run because there is always at least one fixed input in the production process. Managers and administrators decide to produce beer in a brewery of a given size or educate students in a school with a certain number of square feet. The size of the factory or school is fixed in the short run either because the managers have entered into a contractual obligation, such as a rental agreement, or because it would be extremely costly to change the amount of that input during the time period.

In a **long-run production function**, all inputs are variable. There are no fixed inputs because the quantity of all inputs can be changed. In the long run, managers can choose to produce cars in larger automobile plants, and administrators can construct new schools and abandon existing buildings. Farmers can increase or decrease their acreage in another planting season, depending on this year's crop conditions and forecasts for the future. Thus, the calendar lengths of the short run and the long run depend on the particular production process, contractual agreements, and the time needed for input adjustment.

Short-run production function
A production process that uses at least one fixed input.

Long-run production function
A production process in which all inputs are variable.

Managerial Rule of Thumb

Short-Run Production and Long-Run Planning

Managers always operate in the short run, but they must also have a long-run planning horizon. Managers need to be aware that the current amount of fixed inputs, such as the size of a factory or amount of office space, may not be appropriate as market conditions change. Thus, there are more economic decisions for managers in the long run because all inputs can be changed in that time frame and inputs can be substituted for each other. ∎

Productivity and the Fast-Food Industry

The fast-food case that opened this chapter gave a good illustration of the differences between short- and long-run production functions. With a given technology and fixed inputs, as employees at the drive-through windows work faster to reduce turnaround time for a drive-through customer, the quality of the service begins to decline, and worker frustration and dissatisfaction increase. This situation represents the increased use of variable inputs relative to the fixed inputs in the short run. The management response to these problems has been to implement new technologies for the production process: placing an intercom at the end of the drive-through line to correct mistakes in orders; finding better ways for employees to perform multiple tasks in terms of kitchen arrangement; and, most recently, outsourcing the drive-through calls to remote call centers or offering delivery in certain countries. This situation represents the long run, in which all inputs can be changed.

Model of a Short-Run Production Function

In this section, we discuss the basic economic principles inherent in a short-run production function, illustrated in the fast-food example. To do so, we need to define three measures of productivity, or the relationship between inputs and output: total product, average product, and marginal product. We then examine how each measure changes as the level of the variable input changes.

Total Product

Total product
The total quantity of output produced with given quantities of fixed and variable inputs.

Total product is the total quantity of output produced with given quantities of fixed and variable inputs.[5] To illustrate this concept, we use a very simple production function with one fixed input, capital $(\overline{K})$, and one variable input, labor (L). This production function is illustrated in Equation 5.2.

$$5.2 \quad TP \text{ or } Q = f(L, \overline{K})$$

where

TP or Q = total product or total quantity of output produced
L = quantity of labor input (variable)
$\overline{K}$ = quantity of capital input (fixed)

Equation 5.2 presents the simplest type of short-run production function. It has only two inputs: one fixed $(\overline{K})$ and one variable (L). The bar over the K denotes the fixed input. In this production function, the amount of output (Q) or total product (TP) is directly related to the amount of the variable input (L), while holding constant the level of the fixed input $(\overline{K})$ and the technology embodied in the production function.

Average Product and Marginal Product

Average product
The amount of output per unit of variable input.

Marginal product
The additional output produced with an additional unit of variable input.

To analyze the production process, we need to define two other productivity measures: average product and marginal product. The **average product** is the amount of output per unit of variable input, and the **marginal product** is the additional output produced with an additional unit of variable input. These relationships are shown in Equations 5.3 and 5.4.

$$5.3 \quad AP = TP/L \text{ or } Q/L$$

where
AP = average product of labor

$$5.4 \quad MP = \Delta TP/\Delta L = \Delta Q/\Delta L$$

where
MP = marginal product of labor

---

[5]This variable is sometimes called total physical product to emphasize the fact that the production function shows the physical relationship between inputs and outputs. We use total product for simplicity.

TABLE 5.1   A Simple Production Function[a]

QUANTITY OF CAPITAL (K) (1)	QUANTITY OF LABOR (L) (2)	TOTAL PRODUCT (TP) (3)	AVERAGE PRODUCT (AP) (4)	MARGINAL PRODUCT (MP) ($\Delta TP/\Delta L$) (5)	MARGINAL PRODUCT (MP) (dTP/dL) (6)
10	1	14	14.0	14	18
10	2	35	17.5	21	24
10	3	62	20.7	27	28
10	4	91	22.8	29	30
10	4.5	106	23.6	30	30.25
10	5	121	24.2	30	30
10	6	150	25.0	29	28
10	6.75	170	25.1875	26.67	25.1875
10	7	175	25.0	25	24
10	8	197	24.6	22	18
10	9	212	23.6	15	10
10	10	217	21.7	5	0
10	11	211	19.2	−6	−12

[a]In this example, the underlying equations showing total, average, and marginal products as a function of the amount of labor, L (with the level of capital assumed constant), are

$TP = 10L + 4.5L^2 - 0.3333L^3$

$AP = 10 + 4.5L - 0.3333L^2$

$MP = dTP/dL = 10 + 9L - 1.0L^2$

Table 5.1 presents a numerical example of a simple production function based on the underlying equations shown in the table. Marginal product in Table 5.1 can be calculated either for discrete changes in labor input (Column 5) or for infinitesimal changes in labor input using the specific marginal product equation in the table (Column 6). Column 5 shows the marginal product between units of input (Column 2), whereas Column 6 shows the marginal product calculated precisely at a given unit of input. Column 6 gives the exact mathematical relationships discussed below.

Relationships Among Total, Average, and Marginal Product

Let's examine how the total, average, and marginal product change as we increase the amount of the variable input, labor, in this short-run production function, holding constant the amount of capital and the level of technology. We can see in Table 5.1 that the total product or total amount of output (Column 3) increases rapidly up to 4.5 units of labor. This result means that the marginal product, or the additional output produced with an additional unit of labor (Column 6), is increasing over this range of production. Between 4.5 and 10 units of labor, the total product (Column 3) is increasing, but the rate of increase, or the marginal product, is becoming smaller (Columns 5 and 6). Total product reaches its maximum amount of 217 units when 10 units of labor are used, but total product decreases if 11 units of labor are employed. The marginal product of labor is 5 as labor is increased from 9 to 10 units and −6 as labor is increased from 10 to 11 units (Column 5). Therefore, the marginal product is zero when the total product is precisely at its maximum value of 217 units (Column 6).

The average product of labor, or output per unit of input (Column 4), also increases in value as more units of labor are employed. It reaches a maximum value with 6.75 units of labor and then decreases as more labor is used in the production process. As you can see in Table 5.1, when the marginal product of labor is greater than the average product of labor (up to 6.75 units of labor), the average product value increases from 14 to 25.1875 units of output per input. When more units of labor are employed, the marginal product becomes less than the average product, and the average product decreases in value. Therefore, the marginal product must equal the average product when the average product is at its maximum value.[6]

Figures 5.1a and 5.1b show the typical shapes for graphs of the total, average, and marginal product curves. These graphs illustrate the relationships in Table 5.1, but are drawn more generally to move beyond this specific numerical example. Labor input is measured on the horizontal axis of both Figures 5.1a and 5.1b, with different quantities shown as L_1, L_2, and L_3. The total product is measured on the vertical axis of Figure 5.1a, while the average and marginal products are measured on the vertical axis of Figure 5.1b. The variables are measured on separate graphs because the sizes of the numbers are quite different, as was shown in Table 5.1.

FIGURE 5.1

The Short-Run Production Function

The short-run production function illustrates the law of diminishing returns where the marginal product, or the additional output produced with an additional unit of variable input, eventually decreases.

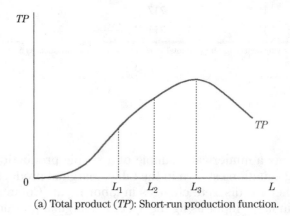

(a) Total product (*TP*): Short-run production function.

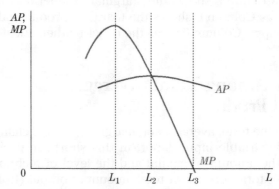

(b) Average product (*AP*) and marginal product (*MP*): Short-run production function.

---

[6]The maximum point of average product in Table 5.1 occurs at 6.75 units of labor, where both the average and the marginal products have the value of 25.1875 units of output per input. This relationship holds for any average and marginal variables. Suppose your average grade on two exams is 80. Your third exam is your marginal grade. If you receive a 90 on the third exam, your average grade increases to 83.3. However, if you receive a grade of 60 on your third exam, your average drops to 73.3. If the marginal variable is greater than the average variable, the average variable increases. If the marginal variable is less than the average variable, the average variable decreases.

As in Table 5.1, Figure 5.1a shows the total product (or level of output) first increasing very rapidly up to labor input level L_1 and then increasing at a slower rate as more labor input is added. The total product curve becomes flatter and flatter until it reaches a maximum output level at labor input level L_3. If more labor is added beyond level L_3, the total amount of output, or the total product, decreases. This total product curve implies that the marginal product of labor first increases rapidly, then decreases in size, and eventually becomes zero or even negative in value, as illustrated in Figure 5.1b.

We can also see in Figure 5.1b the typical relationship between the marginal product and average product curves. Between zero and L_2 units of labor, the marginal product curve lies above the average product curve, which causes the average product curve to increase. Beyond L_2 units of input, the marginal product curve lies below the average product curve, which causes the average product curve to decrease. Therefore, the marginal product curve must intersect the average product curve at the maximum point of the average product curve. Table 5.2 summarizes these relationships.

Economic Explanation of the Short-Run Production Function

Why do the graphs of total, average, and marginal products in Figures 5.1a and 5.1b typically have these shapes? To answer this question, we need to focus on the marginal product curve. In Figure 5.1b, the marginal product curve increases up to labor input level L_1. We call this the region of **increasing marginal returns**. Once we have employed L_1 units of labor, the marginal product of labor begins to decline and keeps decreasing until it becomes zero, when L_3 units of labor are utilized. This portion of the marginal product curve illustrates what is known as the **law of diminishing marginal returns** (or the **law of the diminishing marginal product**). All short-run marginal product curves will eventually have a downward sloping portion and exhibit this law. Beyond L_3 units of labor, the marginal product of labor is negative. This is the region of **negative marginal returns**.

The law of diminishing marginal returns occurs because the capital input and the state of technology are held constant when defining a short-run production function. As more units of labor input are added to the fixed capital input, the marginal product may increase at first (zero to L_1 units of labor in Figure 5.1b), but the curve will eventually decline and possibly reach zero or negative values (beyond L_3 units of labor in Figure 5.1b). The additional output generated by the additional units of the variable input (the marginal product) must decrease at some point because there are too many units of the variable input combined with the fixed input. (For

Increasing marginal returns
The results in that region of the marginal product curve where the curve is positive and increasing, so that total product increases at an increasing rate.

Law of diminishing marginal returns or law of the diminishing marginal product
The phenomenon illustrated by that region of the marginal product curve where the curve is positive, but decreasing, so that total product is increasing at a decreasing rate.

Negative marginal returns
The results in that region of the marginal product curve where the curve is negative and decreasing, so that total product is decreasing.

TABLE 5.2   Relationships Among Total Product (*TP*), Average Product (*AP*), and Marginal Product (*MP*) in Figures 5.1a and 5.1b

INPUT RANGE	EFFECT ON TOTAL AND/OR AVERAGE PRODUCT	EFFECT ON MARGINAL PRODUCT
Input values: zero to L_1	TP increases at increasing rate	MP is positive and increasing
Input values: L_1 to L_3	TP increases at decreasing rate	MP is positive and decreasing
Input values: beyond L_3	TP decreases	MP is negative and decreasing
Input values: L_3	TP is at a maximum	MP equals zero
Input values: zero to L_2	AP increases	MP is greater than AP
Input values: beyond L_2	AP decreases	MP is less than AP
Input values: L_2	AP is at a maximum	MP equals AP

example, there are too many automobile workers in the factory, too many accountants in the office space, or too many farmhands on the plot of land.) The production process becomes constrained by the amount of the fixed input, so that additional units of the variable input become redundant.

Although a firm is constrained by its scale of production (the amount of its fixed inputs) and by the state of technology embodied in the production function, the entire set of curves in Figures 5.1a and 5.1b can shift if the firm either changes the scale of production or adopts new technology. As we saw in the fast-food example, this was the managerial response to diminishing returns in the drive-through window.

Real-World Firm and Industry Productivity Issues

The model of a short-run production function is very important for the development of the theory of cost and profit maximization and for the analysis of firms in different market environments. Before proceeding with short-run cost theory, we'll discuss several other examples of productivity differences among firms and industries.

Other Examples of Diminishing Returns

The poultry industry has always faced the problem that chickens, unlike pigs and cattle, cannot be herded.[7] Chickens raised for meat are allowed to roam freely inside huge chicken houses, so that poultry farmers have traditionally had to rely on human catchers to run around inside the barns grabbing chickens by hand. Adding increased amounts of catchers to a chicken house would easily result in diminishing returns. Human catchers are typically expected to grab as many as 1,000 birds an hour. As with the drive-through fast-food windows, output quality deteriorates as birds are injured through the speed of the process. Bruised chickens cannot be sold at grocery meat counters.

After years of failure, manufacturers finally produced machines capable of catching and caging chickens, up to 150 birds per minute. A five-man crew with this mechanical harvester can do the work of eight men alone, with chicken injuries reduced by as much as 50 percent. This technological change would shift the previous set of marginal and average product curves upward, representing increased productivity.

Online retailers, which face increased demand during the holidays, have to decide whether it is more efficient to hire additional workers to fill the orders or to change technology by using robots.[8] Amazon.com has hired more workers who walk 18 to 20 miles per day down aisles lined with shelves to load carts with orders and bring them back to packing stations. The company holds weekly brainstorming sessions to prevent diminishing returns and increase productivity. Crate & Barrel employs robots who carry shelves with the company's products to workers who, without walking around the building, pick the items they need to fill orders. The choice between these approaches is influenced by the costs of hiring additional workers versus the costs of the robots, which may not be used in nonpeak seasons.

As hospitals treat increasing numbers of patients, concerns have arisen about how to reduce the number of medical errors and improve patient safety. Errors

---

[7]Scott Kilman, "Poultry in Motion: With Invention, Chicken Catching Goes High-Tech," *Wall Street Journal*, June 4, 2003.
[8]Geoffrey A. Fowler, "Holiday Help: People vs. Robots," *Wall Street Journal (Online)*, December 19, 2010.

and accidents are examples of diminishing returns in this production process. Although procedures related to human error, such as encouraging nurses to wash their hands more often and improving physicians' handwriting on prescriptions, have been instituted, changes in the nature of the capital inputs, the hospital buildings themselves, are now being undertaken. Technological innovations include the design of identical rooms so that doctors and nurses can find equipment easily, placing nurses' stations so that all patients are visible, and using filters and ultraviolet devices to trap and kill germs and improve the hospital airflow. These changes have reduced infection rates, injuries from falls, and medication errors, thus lowering patient length of stay, which, in turn, frees up beds and allows hospitals to serve more patients.[9]

Hospital emergency rooms have typically encountered diminishing returns where patients have to wait so long that they leave without treatment. The number of emergency departments has decreased by one-third over the past two decades while the number of patients seeking care has increased by 40 percent and, as a result, long waits have become common. Many patients, who leave without being seen, need medical care and/or hospitalization. Hospitals have attempted to offset diminishing returns by streamlining the method of triage from 10 minutes to three to five minutes, using less-costly nurse practitioners and physicians assistants, and reserving beds for only the sickest patients.[10]

In the luxury handbag industry, Louis Vuitton incurred diminishing returns and production shortages from the organization of its production process. Traditionally, each factory had approximately 250 employees with each worker specializing in one skill such as cutting leather and canvas, gluing and sewing, or making pockets. Specialists worked on only one batch of bags at a time, while half-completed purses waited on carts until someone wheeled them to the next section of the assembly line. Using techniques from the Japanese auto industry, Vuitton has now organized groups of 6 to 12 workers arranged in clusters of U-shaped workstations containing sewing machines on one side and assembly tables on the other. Workers pass their work around the cluster and are able to make more types of bags because each worker is less specialized.[11]

Productivity and the Agriculture Industry

New production methods for agricultural crops have led to large increases in productivity in this sector over time. A significant example is an experiment in China that resulted in a doubling of rice crop yields without the use of expensive chemical fungicides.[12] Instead of continuing the practice of planting a single type of rice, farmers planted a mixture of two different types of rice. This change greatly reduced the incidence of rice blast, the major disease of this crop, and, in turn, increased productivity and allowed farmers to abandon expensive chemical treatments of their crops.

Concerns still exist about diminishing returns in rice production as the increased demand for this food staple has caused farmers to increase fertilizer and water use, exhausting the soil and draining the water table. Many rice farmers have also begun planting two crops a year, which places further demands on the soil. Recent

---

[9]Gautam Naik, "To Reduce Errors, Hospitals Prescribe Innovative Designs," *Wall Street Journal*, May 8, 2006.

[10]Laura Landro, "ERs Move to Speed Care: Not Everyone Needs a Bed," *Wall Street Journal (Online)*, August 2, 2011.

[11]Christina Passariello, "Louis Vuitton Tries Modern Methods on Factory Lines," *Wall Street Journal*, October 9, 2006.

[12]Carol Kaesuk Yoon, "Simple Method Found to Vastly Increase Crop Yields," *New York Times*, August 22, 2000.

technological innovations that have attempted to offset these diminishing returns include developing seed varieties that can withstand droughts or floods, planting rice in dry soil rather than flooded paddies, altering the way rice plants perform photosynthesis, and developing hybrid varieties than can increase yields by as much as 20 percent.[13]

Productivity and the Automobile Industry

The automobile industry is an obvious example of an industry in which huge productivity increases have occurred over time, beginning with Henry Ford's use of the assembly line at the beginning of the twentieth century. However, Japan's use of improved production techniques in the 1970s and 1980s created major problems for the U.S. auto industry. The number of vehicles per worker had ranged between 8 and 15 for both domestic and foreign producers in 1960. Although productivity for General Motors, Ford, and Chrysler remained in that range in 1983, the number of vehicles per worker increased to 42 for Nissan and 58 for Honda in that year.[14]

The Japanese productivity advantage in the early 1980s did not result primarily from differences in technology or labor.[15] Approximately two-thirds of the cost advantage resulted from changes in management focusing on inventory systems, relations with suppliers, and plant layout. Japanese production was organized around a lean and coordinated system, with inventories delivered from nearby suppliers every few hours. Workers could stop the assembly line as soon as problems arose, which improved quality and eliminated the need for repair stations. The organization of the Japanese workforce with far fewer job classifications also gave Japanese plants greater flexibility and less downtime than U.S. plants.

In response to these productivity differences, the U.S. automobile industry has initiated drastic productivity and management changes over the past 20 years, including redesigned production operations, reorganized management procedures, and the closing of outdated plants. Between 1979 and 1998, assembly productivity increased 45 percent at Chrysler and 38 percent at General Motors and Ford. The relative disadvantage in productivity of the Big Three U.S. automakers in terms of total hours per vehicle produced relative to the Japanese decreased from 45 percent in 1995 to 14 percent in 2005. Some of the Big Three auto plants are among the most productive automotive facilities in North America. However, although the U.S. automakers are adapting their assembly lines to produce different models on the same line, they still lag behind the Japanese in this area.

A recent technological innovation is the use of the Internet to link companies with their auto parts suppliers to facilitate bidding on and executing contracts.[16] Traditionally, the supply process involved periodic contracts with thousands of suppliers for a variety of parts, components, and general supplies. Bids were evaluated through phone calls and exchange of paper. Ford and GM introduced online supply exchanges in 1999 for price quotes, bidding, and monitoring the physical movement of supplies. Separate exchanges have been replaced by Covisint, which

---

[13]Patrick Barta, "Feeding Billions, a Grain at a Time," *Wall Street Journal*, July 28, 2007.

[14]Michael A. Cusumano, *The Japanese Automobile Industry* (Cambridge, MA: Harvard University Press, 1985), 187–88.

[15]The discussion of productivity in the automobile industry is based on John E. Kwoka Jr., "Automobiles: Overtaking an Oligopoly," in *Industry Studies*, ed. Larry L. Duetsch, 2nd ed. (Armonk, NY: Sharpe, 1998), 3–27; James W. Brock, "Automobiles," in *The Structure of American Industry*, eds. Walter Adams and James W. Brock, 10th ed. (Upper Saddle River, NJ: Prentice Hall, 2001), 114–36; and James W. Brock, "The Automobile Industry," in *The Structure of American Industry*, ed. James W. Brock, 12th ed. (Upper Saddle River, NJ: Prentice Hall, 2009), 155–82.

[16]This discussion is based on: John E. Kwoka, Jr., "Automobiles: The Old Economy Collides with the New," *Review of Industrial Organization* 19 (2001): 55–69; and John Larkin, "Global Collaboration Easier, More Productive and Safer," *Automotive Industries* 186 (2) (Second Quarter 2007): 60–61.

served DaimlerChrysler, Renault S.A., and Nissan Motor Co., in addition to Ford and GM. In early 2007, General Motors announced that it was using Covisint to connect and integrate more than 18,000 production and nonproduction suppliers including firms in Europe, Asia, and Latin America. Cost savings of up to 15 percent of annual purchasing costs have been estimated from the use of this new technology.

Even with more advanced technologies, diminishing returns can still occur in the auto production process. Toyota Motor Corporation's goal of overtaking General Motors as the world's No. 1 auto maker and fast-paced expansion resulted in an increasing number of quality problems in North America, Japan, and elsewhere that threatened Toyota's image. Toyota began to rely more heavily on computer-aided design tools that shorten vehicle-development times by skipping steps such as making physical prototypes to test components. Computer-aided engineering tools also allow potential design flaws to slip through the production process. To overcome these problems, Toyota began adding as much as three to six more months to projects with a normal development lead time of two to three years.[17]

However, management pressure for rapid growth combined with the complexity of the company's products led to further quality problems in 2009 and 2010. A slipping floor mat that was believed to entrap the accelerator pedal led to an accident that killed a California state trooper and three of his passengers in August 2009. This malfunction of the floor mat led to a recall of 3.8 million vehicles in the United States. Toyota also dealt with the controversy over whether its electronic throttle-control system led to unintended acceleration. In 2010, Toyota created a new quality control group of 1,000 engineers in Japan, and the company formed rapid-response teams to address quality or safety problems around the world.[18]

Productivity Changes Across Industries

Productivity changes differ substantially across industries in the United States. While productivity for the overall economy increased 0.45 percent per year from 1958 to 1996, annual growth ranges varied from 1.98 percent in electronic and electric equipment to –0.52 percent in government enterprises.[19]

Data released in 2000 showed accelerating labor productivity in a range of industries, including the service sector and durable goods manufacturing. Many of these productivity gains can be attributed to the increased use of information technology (IT) in these industries.[20]

More recent analyses indicate that information technology accounted for almost 80 percent of the increase in productivity growth in the late 1990s. Each generation of new computer equipment greatly outperformed prior generations. Given large price declines for information technology investment, firms made massive investments in IT equipment and software and substituted IT assets for other productive inputs. The impact of IT on productivity growth declined in both a relative and absolute sense in the post-2000 period with IT investment accounting for about one-third of the productivity growth in this period. This was still a substantial impact, given that IT investment was less than 5 percent of aggregate output.[21]

[17]Norihiko Shirouzu, "Toyota May Delay New Models to Address Rising Quality Issues," *Wall Street Journal*, August 25, 2006.

[18]Mike Ramsey, "Corporate News: U.S. Ends Toyota Probe—Recall of Additional 2.17 Million Vehicles for Floor-Mat Problems Closes Case," *Wall Street Journal (Online)*, February 25, 2011; Robert E. Cole, "What Really Happened to Toyota?" *Sloan Management Review* 52 (4) (Summer 2011): 29–35.

[19]Dale W. Jorgenson and Kevin W. Stiroh, "U.S. Economic Growth at the Industry Level," *American Economic Review* 90 (2) (May 2000): 161–67.

[20]Martin Neil Bailey, "The New Economy: Post-Mortem or Second Wind?" *Journal of Economic Perspectives* 16 (2) (Spring 2002): 3–22.

[21]Dale W. Jorgensen, Mun S. Ho, and Kevin J. Stiroh, "A Retrospective Look at the U.S. Productivity Growth Resurgence," *Federal Reserve Bank of New York Staff Reports*, no. 277, February 2007.

A study of productivity growth over the entire period 1960 to 2007 found that the leaders in innovation among the IT-using sectors were wholesale and retail trade. Companies such as Wal-Mart and Cicso developed integrated supply chains around the world that linked electronic cash registers at retail outlets with business-to-business ordering systems. Two IT-producing sectors, semiconductors and computers, sustained very rapid growth throughout the period. Agriculture, broadcasting, and telecommunication services also contributed strongly to productivity growth.[22] Research has also shown that U.S. firms maintained a productivity advantage over European firms because they were better able to exploit the use of IT.[23]

Model of Short-Run Cost Functions

Cost function
A mathematical or graphic expression that shows the relationship between the cost of production and the level of output, all other factors held constant.

We now analyze how a firm's costs of production vary in the short run, where at least one input of production is fixed. We first discuss the economic definition of cost and then develop **cost functions** that show the relationship between the cost of production and the level of output, all other factors held constant.

Measuring Opportunity Cost: Explicit Versus Implicit Costs

Opportunity cost
The economic measure of cost that reflects the use of resources in one activity, such as a production process by one firm, in terms of the opportunities forgone in undertaking the next best alternative activity.

Explicit cost
A cost that is reflected in a payment to another individual, such as a wage paid to a worker, that is recorded in a firm's bookkeeping or accounting system.

Implicit cost
A cost that represents the value of using a resource that is not explicitly paid out and is often difficult to measure because it is typically not recorded in a firm's accounting system.

Economists have a very specific way of defining the costs of production that managers should, but do not always, consider. To correctly measure all the relevant costs of production, managers need to make certain they are measuring the opportunity costs of the resources they are using. **Opportunity costs** reflect the cost of using resources in one activity (production by one firm) in terms of the opportunities forgone in undertaking the next best alternative activity. In most cases, these costs are **explicit costs** because they are paid to other individuals and are found in a firm's bookkeeping or accounting system. However, even these bookkeeping costs may reflect an accounting definition rather than a true economic definition of opportunity cost. In other cases, these costs are **implicit costs**. This means that although they represent the opportunity cost of using a resource or input to produce a given product, they are not included in a firm's accounting system and may be difficult to measure.

In many cases, the prices that a firm actually pays for its inputs reflect the opportunity cost of using those inputs. For example, if the wages of construction workers are determined by the forces of demand and supply and if all workers who want to work are able to do so, the monetary or explicit cost paid to those workers accurately reflects their opportunity cost or their value in the next best alternative. If the workers are currently employed by Firm A, managers at Firm B must pay a wage at least equal to that paid by Firm A if they want to hire the workers away from Firm A. If a firm leases office space in a building or a farmer rents a plot of land, the explicit rental payments to the owners of these inputs reflect the opportunity cost of using those resources.

What happens if the firm already owns the building or the plot of land? In these cases, there may not be any budgetary or accounting cost recorded. Does this zero accounting cost mean that the opportunity cost of using those resources is also zero? The answer to this question is usually no, because the firm could rent or lease those resources to another producer. If Firm A could rent the office space it owns

---

[22]Dale W. Jorgenson, Mun S. Ho, and Jon D. Samuels, "Information Technology and U.S. Productivity Growth: Evidence from a Prototype Industry Production Account," *Journal of Productivity Analysis* 36 (2011): 159–75.

[23]Nicholas Bloom, Raffaella Sadun, and John Van Reenen, "Americans Do It Better: US Multinationals and the Productivity Miracle," *American Economic Review* 102 (1) (2012): 167–201.

to Firm B for $100,000 per year, then the opportunity cost to Firm A of using that space in its own production is $100,000 per year. This is an implicit cost if it is not actually included in the firm's accounting system.

If managers do not recognize the concept of opportunity cost, they may have too much investment tied up in the ownership of buildings, given the implicit rate of return on these assets compared with the return on other uses of these resources. For example, Reebok made the strategic decision to contract with other manufacturers around the world to produce its shoes rather than invest in plants and equipment itself. Its managers estimated that there was a greater rate of return from these activities than from investment in buildings.[24]

Another example of an implicit cost is the valuation of the owner's or family member's time in a family-operated business. In such businesses, family members may not explicitly be paid a salary, so the costs of their time may not be included as a cost of production. However, this practice overstates the firm's profitability. If the owner or family member could earn $40,000 per year by working in some other activity, that figure represents the opportunity cost of the individual's time in the family business, but this cost may be implicit and not be reflected in any existing financial statement. It does reflect a real cost of using those resources in a production process.

In certain cases, accounting costs may not accurately represent the true opportunity cost of using the resource, given the distinction between historical and opportunity cost. **Historical costs** reflect what the firm paid for an input when it was purchased. For machines and other capital equipment, this cost could have been incurred many years in the past. Firms have their own accounting systems to write off or depreciate this historical cost over the life of the capital equipment. In many cases, these depreciation guidelines are influenced by Internal Revenue Service regulations and other tax considerations. From an opportunity cost perspective, the issue is what that capital equipment could earn in its next best alternative use at the current time. This rate of return may bear little relationship to historical cost or an annual depreciation figure.

Historical cost
The amount of money a firm paid for an input when it was purchased, which for machines and capital equipment could have occurred many years in the past.

Accounting Profit Measures Versus Economic Profit Measures

The other important example of opportunity cost relates to the return on financial capital invested in a firm. If investors can earn 10 percent in an alternative investment of similar risk, this 10 percent return is an implicit cost of production. A firm must pay at least 10 percent on its invested capital to reflect the true opportunity cost of this resource and to prevent investors from placing their money elsewhere. A firm's **profit** is defined as the difference between its total revenue from sales and its total cost of production. Given the different approaches used by accountants and economists, we now distinguish between accounting and economic profit. **Accounting profit** measures typically focus only on the explicit costs of production, whereas **economic profit** measures include both the explicit and the implicit costs of production.

There are numerous problems involved in correctly calculating a firm's economic profit, many of which relate to the value of the capital costs of plant and equipment.[25] The appropriate capital cost measure is an annual rental fee or the price of renting the capital per time period, not the cost of the machine when it was purchased. The rental cost should be based on the replacement cost of the

Profit
The difference between the total revenue a firm receives from the sale of its output and the total cost of producing that output.

Accounting profit
The difference between total revenue and total cost where cost includes only the explicit costs of production.

Economic profit
The difference between total revenue and total cost where cost includes both the explicit and any implicit costs of production.

---

[24]This example is drawn from Shlomo Maital, *Executive Economics* (New York: Free Press, 1994), 30.
[25]This discussion is based on Dennis W. Carlton and Jeffrey M. Perloff, *Modern Industrial Organization*, 4th ed. (Boston: Pearson Addison-Wesley, 2005), 247–53.

equipment or the long-run cost of purchasing an asset of comparable quality. This rental rate should be calculated after economic depreciation is deducted on the equipment. Economic depreciation reflects the decline in economic value of the equipment, not just an accounting measure, such as straight-line depreciation. Advertising and research and development expenditures also create problems for the calculation of economic profit because, as with capital equipment, the benefits of these expenditures typically extend over a number of years. Economic profit should also be calculated on an after-tax basis and adjusted for different degrees of risk because investors generally dislike risk and must be compensated for it.

This distinction between accounting and economic profit has played an important role at the Coca-Cola Company.[26] Coca-Cola had long followed a strategy of obtaining its resources through equity financing—selling stock to shareholders—rather than debt financing—borrowing from banks. Thus, the company had very low explicit interest payments on its books. Realizing that shareholders could also invest elsewhere, former CEO Roberto Goizueta calculated that the opportunity cost of the shareholders' equity capital was a 16 percent rate of return. He then learned that all Coke's business activities except soft drinks and juices returned only 8 to 10 percent per year. Coca-Cola was essentially borrowing money from shareholders at 16 percent per year and paying them only an 8 percent return. These opportunity costs are difficult to detect because Coke's treasurer did not write an annual check for 16 percent of the company's equity capital. The cost was reflected in Coke's capital stock growing less rapidly than it could have grown.

Goizueta's response to this management problem was to turn an implicit cost into an explicit cost:[27]

> His solution was first to sell off those businesses whose capital made a lower return—i.e., less than 16 percent—than it cost, and second, introduce a system of accounting in which every operating division of Coca-Cola knew precisely its *economic profit*. What he meant by economic profit was sales revenue minus operating costs, including an opportunity-cost charge for capital. Those divisions earning a 16 percent return on their shareholder's capital were told that their *economic* profit was zero. And each division's operations were judged solely on the basis of the *economic* profit it earned. The results of doing so at Coca-Cola were not slow in coming. "When you start charging people for their capital," Goizueta said, "all sorts of things happen. All of a sudden, inventories get under control. You don't have three months' concentrate sitting around for an emergency. Or you figure out that you can save a lot of money by replacing stainless-steel containers with cardboard and plastic."

Managerial Rule of Thumb

The Importance of Opportunity Costs

Measuring true opportunity costs can be difficult for managers because accountants are trained to examine and measure costs explicitly paid out. Valuing implicit costs may seem like an imaginary exercise to accountants. However, as in the Coca-Cola example, managers must recognize the importance of these costs and devise strategies for turning implicit costs into explicit costs that can be used for strategic decision making. ■

---

[26]This example is drawn from Maital, *Executive Economics*, 23–25.
[27]Ibid., 24–25.

Definition of Short-Run Cost Functions

A **short-run cost function** shows the relationship between output and cost for a firm based on the underlying short-run production function we looked at earlier in the chapter. Thus, the shapes of the marginal and average product curves in Figure 5.1b influence the shapes of the short-run cost curves, or how costs change as production is increased or decreased. Given that the production function shows only the technology of how inputs are combined to produce outputs, we must introduce an additional piece of information, the prices of the inputs of production, to define cost functions. To continue with the example presented in Table 5.1, Equation 5.2, and Figures 5.1a and 5.1b, we define P_L as the price per unit of labor (the variable input) and P_K as the price per unit of capital (the fixed input). The former can be thought of as the wage rate per worker, while the latter can be considered the price per square foot of office space or the price per acre of land.

We use this information on production and input prices to define the family of short-run cost functions in Table 5.3. Even though we define some of the cost functions in Table 5.3 in terms of the inputs of production (labor and capital), we show numerical and graphical relationships between costs and the level of output (costs as a function of output). The underlying production function gives us the relationship between the level of labor input (L) and the resulting level of output (Q).

Fixed Costs Versus Variable Costs

Three categories of costs—total, average, and marginal, with further subdivisions between fixed and variable costs—are shown in Table 5.3. **Total fixed cost** is the cost of using the fixed input, $\overline{K}$. It is defined as the price per unit of capital times the quantity of capital (i.e., price per square foot of office space times the number of square feet). Because the quantity of capital does not change, total fixed cost remains constant regardless of the amount of output produced. **Total variable cost** is defined as the price per unit of labor (or wage rate) times the quantity of labor input. This cost does change when different levels of output are produced because it reflects the use of the variable input. **Total cost** is the sum of total fixed and total variable costs.

Each of the average costs listed in Table 5.3 is the respective total cost variable divided by the amount of output produced. **Average fixed cost** is the total fixed cost per unit of output, while **average variable cost** is the total variable cost per unit of output. As you can see in Table 5.3, **average total cost** is defined as total cost per unit of output, but it also equals average fixed cost plus average variable cost. This equivalence results from the fact that $TC = TFC + TVC$. Dividing each one of these terms by Q gives the relationship $ATC = AFC + AVC$.

Short-run cost function
A cost function for a short-run production process in which there is at least one fixed input of production.

Total fixed cost
The total cost of using the fixed input, which remains constant regardless of the amount of output produced.

Total variable cost
The total cost of using the variable input, which increases as more output is produced.

Total cost
The sum of the total fixed cost plus the total variable cost.

Average fixed cost
The total fixed cost per unit of output.

Average variable cost
The total variable cost per unit of output.

Average total cost
The total cost per unit of output, which also equals average fixed cost plus average variable cost.

TABLE 5.3   Short-Run Cost Functions (Based on the production function in Equation 5.2 and input prices P_L and P_K)

COST FUNCTION	DEFINITION
Total fixed cost	$TFC = (P_K)(\overline{K})$
Total variable cost	$TVC = (P_L)(L)$
Total cost	$TC = TFC + TVC$
Average fixed cost	$AFC = TFC/Q$
Average variable cost	$AVC = TVC/Q$
Average total cost	$ATC = TC/Q = AFC + AVC$
Marginal cost	$MC = \Delta TC/\Delta Q = \Delta TVC/\Delta Q$

TABLE 5.4   Short-Run Cost Functions (Based on the production function from Table 5.1 and input prices $P_K = \$50$ and $P_L = \$100$)

K (1)	L (2)	TP = Q (3)	TFC (4)	TVC (5)	TC (6)	AFC (7)	AVC (8)	ATC (9)	MC (10)
10	0	0	$500	$0	$500				
10	1	14	$500	$100	$600	$35.71	$7.14	$42.85	$7.14
10	2	35	$500	$200	$700	$14.29	$5.71	$20.00	$4.76
10	3	62	$500	$300	$800	$8.06	$4.84	$12.90	$3.70
10	4	91	$500	$400	$900	$5.49	$4.40	$9.89	$3.45
10	5	121	$500	$500	$1,000	$4.13	$4.13	$8.26	$3.33
10	6	150	$500	$600	$1,100	$3.33	$4.00	$7.33	$3.45
10	7	175	$500	$700	$1,200	$2.86	$4.00	$6.86	$4.00
10	8	197	$500	$800	$1,300	$2.54	$4.06	$6.60	$4.55
10	9	212	$500	$900	$1,400	$2.36	$4.25	$6.61	$6.67
10	10	217	$500	$1,000	$1,500	$2.30	$4.61	$6.91	$20.00

Marginal cost
The additional cost of producing an additional unit of output, which equals the change in total cost or the change in total variable cost as output changes.

Marginal cost is the additional cost of producing an additional unit of output. As you can see in Table 5.3, $MC = \Delta TC/\Delta Q = \Delta TVC/\Delta Q$. This equivalence results from the fact that marginal cost shows the changes in costs as output changes. Total variable costs change as the level of output varies, but total fixed costs are constant regardless of the level of output. Therefore, total fixed costs do *not* influence the marginal costs of production, and the above definition holds.

Table 5.4 presents short-run cost functions that are based on the production function from Table 5.1, a price per unit of capital of $50, and a price per unit of labor of $100.

Relationships Among Total, Average, and Marginal Costs

The first three columns of Table 5.4 show the production function drawn from Table 5.1. Total fixed cost (Column 4) shows the total cost of using the fixed input, which remains constant at $500 ($50 per unit times 10 units), regardless of the amount of output produced. Total variable cost in Column 5 ($100 times the number of units of labor used) increases as more output is produced. Total cost (Column 6) is the sum of total fixed and total variable costs.

Average fixed cost (Column 7) decreases continuously as more output is produced. This relationship follows from the definition of average fixed cost, which is total fixed cost per unit of output. Because total fixed cost is constant, average fixed cost must decline as output increases and spreads the total fixed cost over a larger number of units of output. Both average variable cost (Column 8) and average total cost (Column 9) first decrease and then increase. We can see that average total cost always equals average fixed cost plus average variable cost. Marginal cost (Column 10) also first decreases and then increases much more rapidly than either average variable cost or average total cost.

Figures 5.2a and 5.2b show the typical shapes for graphs of the total, average, and marginal cost curves. Although these graphs illustrate the relationships in Table 5.4, they are drawn to present the general case of these functions.

In Figure 5.2a, total fixed costs (*TFC*) are represented by a horizontal line, as these costs are constant regardless of the level of output produced. Note that these fixed costs are incurred *even at a zero level of output*. If land is rented or office

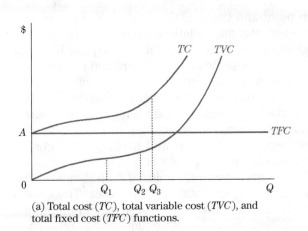

(a) Total cost (*TC*), total variable cost (*TVC*), and total fixed cost (*TFC*) functions.

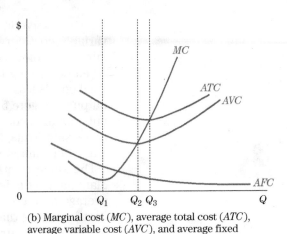

(b) Marginal cost (*MC*), average total cost (*ATC*), average variable cost (*AVC*), and average fixed cost (*AFC*) functions.

FIGURE 5.2
Short-Run Cost Functions
The short-run total cost functions in Figure 5.2a are related to the average and marginal cost functions in Figure 5.2b.

space is leased, these costs must be covered even if no output is produced with those fixed inputs. Total variable costs, on the other hand, are zero when no output is produced because the variable input is used only when there is a positive amount of output. Total variable costs are shown as increasing slowly at first and then more rapidly as output increases. The total cost curve has the same general shape as the total variable cost curve because the distance between the two curves is total fixed cost, which is constant ($TC = TFC + TVC \Rightarrow TFC = TC - TVC$). The total cost of producing zero units of output is represented by the distance $0A$, or the amount of the fixed costs. The total fixed cost is the vertical distance between the total cost and total variable cost curves at any level of output.[28]

In Figure 5.2b, the average fixed cost curve is declining throughout the range of production for the reasons discussed above. Both average variable cost and average total cost are drawn as U-shaped curves, showing that these average costs first decrease, reach a minimum point, and then increase. Average total cost lies above average variable cost at every unit of output, but the distance between the two curves decreases as output increases, as that distance represents average fixed cost, which is declining ($ATC = AFC + AVC \Rightarrow AFC = ATC - AVC$).

Marginal cost in Figure 5.2b is also a U-shaped curve, showing that marginal cost first decreases, reaches a minimum level, and then increases very rapidly as output increases. Why would a marginal cost curve typically have this shape? Look back at Figure 5.1b, which shows the short-run production function that underlies these cost functions. Note the range of diminishing returns or declining marginal product in Figure 5.1b. If the additional output obtained from using an additional unit of labor input is decreasing, then marginal cost, or the additional cost of producing another unit of output, must be increasing. Thus, the explanation for the upward sloping short-run marginal cost curve is the existence of diminishing returns in the short-run production function.

Likewise, the shape of the average variable cost curve in Figure 5.2b is determined by the shape of the underlying average product curve in Figure 5.1b. When average product increases, average variable cost decreases. If average product decreases, average variable cost increases.

---

[28]In Table 5.4 total variable cost and total cost may look as if they are increasing at a constant rate. When these costs are plotted against the level of output, not the level of input, they exhibit the shapes of the curves in Figure 5.2a.

Also observe in Figure 5.2b that the marginal cost curve intersects the average variable cost curve at its minimum point and the average total cost curve at its minimum point. This is the same average–marginal relationship that we discussed when describing the short-run production function earlier in the chapter. If marginal cost is less than average variable cost, as shown between zero and Q_2 units of output in Figure 5.2b, average variable cost is decreasing. Beyond Q_2 units of output, marginal cost is greater than average variable cost, so average variable cost is increasing. Thus, the marginal cost curve must intersect the average variable cost curve at its minimum point, or Q_2 units of output.

The same relationships hold between marginal cost and average total cost. Marginal cost is less than average total cost up to Q_3 units of output. This causes average total cost to decrease in this range. Beyond Q_3 units of output, marginal cost is greater than average total cost, so average total cost increases. Thus, the marginal cost curve must intersect the average total cost curve at its minimum point, or Q_3 units of output. The only difference in this marginal–average relationship between the production and cost functions is that the marginal cost curve intersects the average cost curves at their minimum points, whereas the marginal product curve intersects the average product curve at its maximum point. This intersection occurs at either a maximum or a minimum point of the average curves.

Relationship Between Short-Run Production and Cost

The relationships we've described in this chapter show the influence of the underlying production technology on the costs of production. These relationships, based on the production function defined in Equation 5.2 and graphed in Figures 5.1a and 5.1b, are explored further in Table 5.5. This table shows that marginal cost and marginal product are inversely related to each other, as are average variable cost and average product. The derivation in the right column of Table 5.5 uses the definitions of marginal cost and average variable cost to show the inverse relationship between these costs and marginal product and average product, respectively. These relationships are shown graphically in Figures 5.3a and 5.3b.

Figures 5.3a and 5.3b show the relationship between short-run production and cost functions. In these figures, labor input level L_1 is used to produce output level Q_1, while labor input L_2 is used to produce output level Q_2. The graphs clearly show the inverse relationship between the product and cost variables. The marginal product of labor increases up to L_1 input level, so the marginal cost of production decreases up to Q_1 units of output. The decreasing marginal product beyond L_1 units of labor (diminishing returns) causes the marginal cost curve to rise beyond Q_1 units of output. The average product curve increases, reaches its maximum at L_2 units of input, and then decreases. This causes the average variable cost curve to decrease, reach a minimum value at Q_2 units of output, and then increase.

TABLE 5.5 Short-Run Production and Cost Functions

COST/PRODUCTION RELATIONSHIP	DERIVATION
Relationship between marginal cost (MC) and marginal product of labor (MP_L)	$MC = \dfrac{\Delta TVC}{\Delta Q} = \dfrac{(P_L)(\Delta L)}{\Delta Q}$ $MC = \dfrac{P_L}{(\Delta Q/\Delta L)} = \dfrac{P_L}{MP_L}$
Relationship between average variable cost (AVC) and average product of labor (AP_L)	$AVC = \dfrac{TVC}{Q} = \dfrac{(P_L)(L)}{Q}$ $AVC = \dfrac{P_L}{(Q/L)} = \dfrac{P_L}{AP_L}$

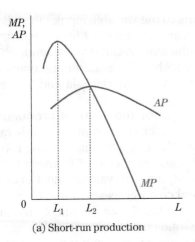

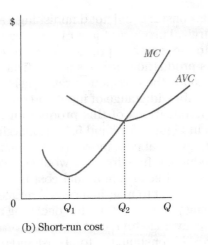

(a) Short-run production

(b) Short-run cost

Other Short-Run Production and Cost Functions

We have argued that the underlying production function determines the shapes of the short-run cost curves, and we have illustrated the standard case with a marginal product curve that first increases and then decreases, resulting in decreasing and then increasing marginal cost. These traditional-shaped curves result from diminishing returns in the production function as increased variable inputs are used relative to the amount of the fixed inputs.

Consider an alternative set of production and cost curves shown in Figures 5.4a, 5.4b, 5.4c, and 5.4d. Figure 5.4a shows a linear total product curve that results in the constant marginal product curve in Figure 5.4b. This production function

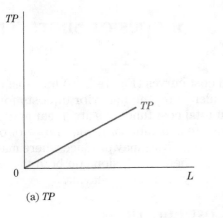

(a) *TP*

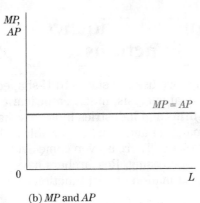

(b) *MP* and *AP*

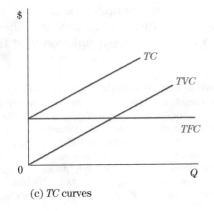

(c) *TC* curves

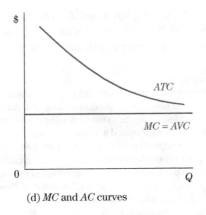

(d) *MC* and *AC* curves

exhibits constant, and not diminishing, returns to the variable input, labor. Because the marginal product of labor is constant, the average product is also constant and equal to the marginal product. Although diminishing returns will eventually set in for this production process as the firm approaches the maximum capacity of its fixed inputs, the production relationships shown in Figures 5.4a and 5.4b may be valid over a wide range of input and output.

The implications of this production function for the costs of production are shown in Figures 5.4c and 5.4d. If marginal product is constant over this range of output, marginal cost must also be constant. There are no diminishing returns in the production function that would cause the marginal cost of further production to increase. Because marginal cost is constant, average variable cost is also constant and equal to marginal cost. Average total cost decreases throughout because it is being pulled down by the declining average fixed cost. Marginal cost must be less than average total cost because average total cost is decreasing. Because marginal cost is constant, the total cost and total variable cost functions must be linear, with the difference between the two curves equal to total fixed cost.

Managerial Rule of Thumb

Understanding Your Costs

Managers need to understand how their firm's technology and prices paid for the inputs of production affect the firm's costs. They need to know the difference between costs that change with output (variable costs) and those that are unrelated to the output level (fixed costs). They also need to understand the difference between average cost (cost per unit of output) and marginal cost (the additional cost of producing an additional unit of output). ■

Empirical Evidence on the Shapes of Short-Run Cost Functions

Although we use the standard U-shaped cost curves (Figure 5.2b) for most of our theoretical analysis, much empirical evidence on the behavior of costs for real-world firms and industries indicates that total cost functions are linear and, therefore, marginal and average variable costs are constant for a wide range of output (Figure 5.4d). There is even some evidence that firms may produce where marginal cost is decreasing. Researchers have based their conclusions on both the econometric estimation of cost functions and surveys of firms' behavior.[29]

Econometric Estimation of Cost Functions

Much of the empirical estimation of cost functions was undertaken in the 1940s, 1950s, and 1960s.[30] Joel Dean's classic studies of a furniture factory, a leather belt shop, and a hosiery mill all showed that a linear total cost function best fit the

[29]A focus on the average total cost of production may predate modern economic theory. Between 1800 and 1805, German sheet music publisher Gottfried Christoph Hartel calculated the average total cost of printing sheet music using two different technologies: engraving and printing with movable type. His calculations for engraved music implied a linear total cost function with a fixed setup cost of 900 Pfennigs per sheet and a constant marginal cost of 5 Pfennigs per sheet. These calculations influenced his decision not to publish Ludwig van Beethoven's early works, for which sales volumes were uncertain and average total costs were high, but to publish a number of the composer's later works. See Frederic M. Scherer, "An Early Application of the Average Total Cost Concept," *Journal of Economic Literature* 39 (September 2001): 897–901.

[30]Jack Johnston, *Statistical Cost Analysis* (New York: McGraw-Hill, 1960); Joel Dean, *Statistical Cost Estimation* (Bloomington, IN: Indiana University Press, 1976).

data. These studies examined data sets where the plant, equipment, and technology were relatively constant over the data period analyzed. Jack Johnston estimated cost functions for British electric generating plants, road passenger transport, and a multiproduct food processing firm. From both his own estimation work and a comprehensive survey of existing studies, Johnston concluded that a constant marginal cost and declining average total cost best characterized the cost-output data for a wide variety of firms.

More recent studies have used much more sophisticated econometric techniques and have estimated cost structures in the context of larger decisions such as inventory management. Analyzing the food, tobacco, apparel, chemical, petroleum, and rubber industries from 1959 to 1984 and the automobile industry from 1966 to 1979, one researcher found evidence for declining marginal costs of production.[31] To determine whether these results were related to the use of industry-level data, this researcher reestimated cost equations for 10 divisions of the automobile industry and still found evidence of declining marginal costs. Other researchers[32] developed elaborate models of firm pricing behavior that are consistent with a constant marginal cost of production.

Survey Results on Cost Functions

Although some early work used a survey or questionnaire approach to make inferences about firms' cost functions, most of the more recent research studies have been econometric analyses. One notable exception is the survey by Alan Blinder and his colleagues at Princeton University in the early 1990s.[33] Blinder and his colleagues drew a sample of 333 firms in the private, unregulated, nonfarm, for-profit sector of the economy, 200 of which participated in the survey.

The researchers asked officials in these companies a series of structured questions designed to test alternative theories about why firms do not change prices regularly in response to changing economic conditions. Although the main goal of the survey was to test hypotheses about price stickiness, the researchers included a number of questions about the firms' cost structures.

Officials in firms responding to the survey reported on average that 44 percent of their costs were fixed and 56 percent were variable. If these results can be generalized to the entire economy, fixed costs appear to be more important to firms than is shown in the standard cost curves of economic theory (see Figure 5.2b). Fixed costs were less important in wholesale and retail trade (mean of 33 percent) and construction and mining (mean of 29 percent) and more important in transportation, communications, and utilities (mean of 53 percent) and services (mean of 56 percent). The researchers found that many executives did not think in terms of fixed versus variable costs. Eighteen executives, or 9 percent of the sample, did not answer the question.

The researchers also had difficulty asking whether marginal cost varied with production because many executives were not familiar with this concept. The researchers had to frame the question in terms of the "variable costs of producing additional units." The researchers often had to repeat, rephrase, or explain the question to executives who did not understand the concept. Even with this effort, 10 interviewees were unable to provide an answer. The responses to this question were quite surprising in light of standard economic theory.

[31]Valerie A. Ramey, "Nonconvex Costs and the Behavior of Inventories," *Journal of Political Economy* 99 (1991): 306–34.
[32]Robert E. Hall, "Market Structure and Macroeconomic Fluctuations," *Brookings Papers on Economic Activity* 2 (1986): 285–322; Robert E. Hall, "The Relation Between Price and Marginal Cost in U.S. Industry," *Journal of Political Economy* 96 (1988): 921–47.
[33]Alan S. Blinder, Elie R. D. Canetti, David E. Lebow, and Jeremy B. Rudd, *Asking About Prices: A New Approach to Understanding Price Stickiness* (New York: Sage, 1998).

Forty-eight percent of the respondents indicated that their marginal costs were constant, 41 percent said they were decreasing, and only 11 percent responded that their marginal costs were increasing. Although some, if not many, respondents may have confused marginal and average costs and may really have been reporting that their average costs were decreasing, this survey response indicates that business executives do not perceive the textbook U-shaped marginal cost curve to be relevant in many situations.

Constant Versus Rising Marginal Cost Curves

Some of this discrepancy between textbook U-shaped cost curves and real-world constant or declining marginal cost curves can be explained by the fact that economic theory shows the range of possibilities for the cost relationships, not what actually exists in different firms and industries. Econometric estimation based on real-world data and surveys of executives may show constant or declining marginal cost for the range of output that the firm is actually producing. Even if firms are currently producing with constant marginal cost, they will, at some point, reach the capacity of their fixed inputs, which will cause marginal cost to increase.

Another explanation for the discrepancy regarding the shapes of the cost curves relates to the differences between agricultural and manufacturing production.[34] The concept of diminishing returns and rising short-run marginal cost—with its emphasis on the fixed, indivisible factors of production, such as land, and on the variable, divisible factors, such as labor, which change in proportion to the use of the fixed factors—was derived from agricultural settings. That producers experience diminishing returns is very plausible when adding additional amounts of labor, capital equipment, seed, and fertilizer to a fixed amount of land. There is no need to distinguish between the *stock* of the fixed input, land, and the *flow* of services derived from it. The land provides services continuously and is not turned off at night.

However, this model may be less appropriate in manufacturing and industrial settings. Much research has indicated that inputs in these settings are likely to be used in fixed proportions up to the capacity of the plant. Although the stock of a fixed input is fixed, the flow of services from that stock may be varied and combined with the services of a variable input in fixed proportions. The size of a machine may be fixed, but the number of hours it is put in operation can be varied. Both capital and labor *services* are variable in the short run and can be changed together in fixed proportions, thus preventing diminishing returns and rising marginal costs from occurring in many manufacturing operations.

In manufacturing assembly operations, the normal work period of the plant is used to adjust the level of output in the short run. For example, automobile assembly plants use a relatively fixed number of employees per shift and a preset speed for the flow of materials and components through the line. Output can be adjusted by changing the length of existing shifts or adding additional shifts in the face of changing demand. Other assembly operations, such as a collection of sewing machines in clothing manufacturing, are organized around workstations rather than a rigid assembly line. Output is varied in these operations by changing the duration and intensity of the work period at the individual workstations.

---

[34]This discussion is based on Carol Corrado and John J. Mattey, "Capacity Utilization," *Journal of Economic Perspectives* 11 (1997): 151–67; Richard A. Miller, "Ten Cheaper Spades: Production Theory and Cost Curves in the Short Run," *Journal of Economic Education* 31 (Spring 2000): 119–30; and Richard A. Miller, "Firms' Cost Functions: A Reconstruction," *Review of Industrial Organization* 18 (2001): 183–200.

In continuous processing operations, such as oil refineries, steel mills, cement plants, and paper mills, plants operate nearly 24 hours per day, 7 days per week, given the large shutdown and start-up costs. Output is typically varied by shutting down part or all of the plant. In all of these cases, output is adjusted by increasing or decreasing the amount of capital and labor services in constant proportion so that diminishing returns do not occur and a constant marginal cost can be maintained.

There may be areas other than manufacturing where this type of production technology is applicable. For example, even though the size of a restaurant is fixed, managers may shut down part of the table space, given a lack of demand. Once again, the services of the fixed input are varied even though the stock is constant. These services can then be used in a fixed proportion with other variable inputs, such as labor, to avoid the problem of rising marginal cost.

Implications for Managers

Costs play an important role in determining an effective competitive strategy, particularly if a firm does not have much control over the price of its product. The distinction between fixed and variable costs is important, as is the concept of marginal cost. However, as noted in the survey by Blinder and his colleagues, many executives and managers are not familiar with these concepts. Cost accounting systems often focus more on management, control, and Internal Revenue Service considerations than on concepts useful for decision making. It may also be more difficult for managers to cut costs when firms are profitable than when they are not because it may be less obvious that competitors are catching up.[35]

Lack of knowledge about costs is not a recent phenomenon. Even though Henry Ford pioneered the use of mass production and the assembly line as a cost-cutting measure, he disliked bookkeepers and accountants. Shlomo Maital tells the following story:

> Once, walking into a room, Henry Ford asked an aide what the white-collar workers in the room do. Told they were accountants, he ordered, "I want them all fired. They're not productive, they don't do any real work." The result was chaos, as Arjay Miller (who later became president) discovered. Miller was asked to obtain a monthly estimate of Ford company profits. Doing so required estimates of revenues and costs. Sales projections were fairly straightforward. But Miller was amazed to learn that the Ford Motor Co. estimated its costs by dividing its bills into four piles (small, medium, large, extra-large), guessing at the average sum of the bills in each pile, *then measuring the height of each pile* and multiplying the height in inches by average bill size. The system was not unlike that used 20 years earlier; when piles of bills were not quite so unwieldy, the understaffed accountants had weighed them.[36]

Maital also relates how Akio Morita, the founder of Sony Corp., made a better strategic decision for his company based on his knowledge of the costs of production. In 1955, Morita was trying to market a small, cheap, practical transistor radio in the United States. Several buyers asked for price quotes on 5,000, 10,000, 30,000, 50,000, and 100,000 units. Because Sony's current capacity was less than 1,000 radios per month, Morita knew that the entire production process would have to be expanded to fill these large orders and that this would impact the costs of

---

[35]This insight is drawn from Maital, *Executive Economics*, 76.
[36]Ibid., 69.

production. Morita essentially drew the economist's U-shaped average cost curve showing that he would charge the regular price for 5,000 units and a discount for 10,000 units, but successively higher prices for 30,000, 50,000, and 100,000 units. These higher prices reflected increased short-run average and marginal costs of production.[37]

Summary

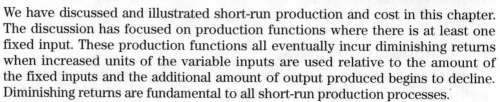

We have discussed and illustrated short-run production and cost in this chapter. The discussion has focused on production functions where there is at least one fixed input. These production functions all eventually incur diminishing returns when increased units of the variable inputs are used relative to the amount of the fixed inputs and the additional amount of output produced begins to decline. Diminishing returns are fundamental to all short-run production processes.

We then illustrated the impact of the production function on the costs of production. Diminishing returns in production cause short-run marginal cost to increase for a producer. We saw how the U-shaped cost curves of economic theory show the full range of outcomes in a production process, but that real-world cost curves may have different shapes. Marginal cost may be constant over a wide range of output as managers take steps to prevent diminishing returns from occurring immediately. We also discussed the concept of opportunity cost, which measures the value of any resource in terms of its next best alternative use. Economists use this concept when discussing cost, and managers should use it for correct decision making. The latter do not always do so, given the problems in correctly measuring opportunity costs.

Later we examine long-run production and cost, where all inputs in a production function are variable. This discussion focuses on input substitution and the shape of the long-run average cost curve. All of these issues are fundamental to the discussion of pricing and other competitive strategies.

Key Terms

accounting profit, p. 127

average fixed cost, p. 129

average product, p. 118

average total cost, p. 129

averaged variable cost, p. 129

cost function, p. 126

economic profit, p. 127

explicit cost, p. 126

fixed input, p. 116

historical cost, p. 127

implicit cost, p. 126

increasing marginal returns, p. 121

law of diminishing marginal returns or law of the diminishing marginal product, p. 121

long-run production function, p. 117

marginal cost, p. 130

marginal product, p. 118

negative marginal returns, p. 121

opportunity cost, p. 126

production function, p. 116

profit, p. 127

short-run cost function, p. 129

short-run production function, p. 117

total cost, p. 129

total fixed cost, p. 129

total product, p. 118

total variable cost, p. 129

variable input, p. 116

[37]Ibid., 66–68.

Exercises

Technical Questions

1. The following table shows data for a simple production function.

Capital (K)	Labor (L)	Total Product (TP)	Average Product (AP)	Marginal Product (MP)
10	0	0	—	—
10	1	5		
10	2	15		
10	3	30		
10	4	50		
10	5	75		
10	6	85		
10	7	90		
10	8	92		
10	9	92		
10	10	90		

   a. From the information in the table, calculate marginal and average products.
   b. Graph the three functions (put total product on one graph and marginal and average products on another).
   c. For what range of output does this function have diminishing marginal returns?
   d. At what output is average product maximized?

2. The following table shows data for a simple production function.

Capital (K)	Labor (L)	Total Product (TP)	Average Product (AP)	Marginal Product (MP)
10	0		—	—
10	1			25
10	2			75
10	3			120
10	4			83
10	5			54
10	6			35
10	7			22
10	8			10
10	9			4
10	10			1

   a. From the information in the table, calculate total and average products.
   b. Graph the three functions (put total product on one graph and marginal and average products on another).
   c. For what range of output does this function have diminishing marginal returns?
   d. At what output is average product maximized?

3. Jim is considering quitting his job and using his savings to start a small business. He expects that his costs will consist of a lease on the building, inventory, wages for two workers, electricity, and insurance.

   a. Identify which costs are explicit and which are opportunity (implicit) costs.
   b. Identify which costs are fixed and which are variable.

4. Jill resigns from her job, at which she was earning $50,000 per year, and uses her $100,000 savings, on which she was earning 5 percent interest, to start a business. In the first year, she earns revenue of $150,000, and her costs are as follows:

Rent	$25,000
Utilities	$12,000
Wages	$30,000
Materials	$20,000

   a. Calculate Jill's accounting profit.
   b. Calculate Jill's economic profit.

5. The following table shows data for the simple production function used in Question 1. Capital costs this firm $20 per unit, and labor costs $10 per worker.

K	L	TP	TFC	TVC	TC	AFC	AVC	ATC	MC
10	0	0							
10	1	5							
10	2	15							
10	3	30							
10	4	50							
10	5	75							
10	6	85							
10	7	90							
10	8	92							

   a. From the information in the table, calculate total fixed cost (TFC), total variable cost (TVC), total cost (TC), average fixed cost (AFC), average variable cost (AVC), average total cost (ATC), and marginal cost (MC).
   b. Graph your results, putting TFC, TVC, and TC on one graph and AFC, AVC, ATC, and MC on another.
   c. At what point is average total cost minimized? At what point is average variable cost minimized?

6. The following table shows data for the simple production function used in Question 2. Capital costs this firm $50 per unit, and labor costs $20 per worker.

K	L	MP	TFC	TVC	TC	AFC	AVC	ATC	MC
10	0	—			—				—
10	1	25							
10	2	75							
10	3	120							
10	4	83							
10	5	54							
10	6	35							
10	7	22							
10	8	10							
10	9	4							
10	10	1							

a. From the information in the table, calculate total fixed cost (*TFC*), total variable cost (*TVC*), total cost (*TC*), average fixed cost (*AFC*), average variable cost (*AVC*), average total cost (*ATC*), and marginal cost (*MC*). (Note that in this case, you are starting from *MP*, not *TP*, and, thus, you should calculate *TP* first if you didn't already do that in Question 2.)

b. Graph your results, putting *TFC*, *TVC*, and *TC* on one graph and *AVC*, *ATC*, and *MC* on another.

c. At what point is average total cost minimized? At what point is average variable cost minimized?

7. Consider the shape of the production and cost functions for two different firms.

a. For Firm 1, workers have constant marginal product. That is, each worker produces exactly the same amount as the previous worker. Use this information to graph the approximate shape of the firm's short-run product and cost curves.

b. For Firm 2, workers have diminishing marginal returns everywhere. That is, each worker always produces less than the previous worker. Use this information to graph the approximate shape of the firm's short-run product and cost curves.

8. How would an improvement in technology that increased the marginal productivity of labor change the firm's cost curves?

9. Suppose that a firm's only variable input is labor. When 50 workers are used, the average product of labor is 50, and the marginal product of the 50th worker is 75. The wage rate is $80, and the total cost of the fixed input is $500.

a. What is average variable cost? Show your calculations.

b. What is marginal cost? Show your calculations.

c. What is average total cost? Show your calculations.

d. Is each of the following statements true or false? Explain your answer.

1. Marginal cost is increasing.
2. Average variable cost is increasing.
3. Average total cost is decreasing.

Application Questions

1. In the fast-food industry case that opened this chapter, describe how diminishing returns set in for the production process and how management responded to this situation.

2. The following information is about pharmaceutical manufacturing.[38]

   The Food and Drug Administration (FDA) has concluded that the pharmaceutical industry needs to adopt manufacturing innovations, partly to raise quality standards. In other industries, manufacturers constantly change their production lines to find improvements. But FDA regulations leave drug-manufacturing processes virtually frozen in time. As part of the drug-approval process, a company's detailed manufacturing plan—and even the factory itself—must obtain FDA approval. After approval, even a tiny change in how a drug is produced requires another round of FDA review and authorization that involves time and paperwork.

   Quality testing is done by hand. Computerized equipment and robots are not used as commonly as in other high-tech industries. Most

[38]Leila Abboud and Scott Hensley, "New Prescription for Drug Makers: Update the Plants," *Wall Street Journal*, September 3, 2003.

pharmaceuticals are made according to recipes that involve many separate steps. Each step produces an intermediate batch of chemicals that must be stored, sometimes for long periods. Only then can the process move on to the next step. Gauging the dryness of a batch requires a technician to stop a dryer, break a vacuum seal, and pluck a sample by hand for testing in a specialized laboratory. Before the concoction can move on, a worker might have to wait hours for test results.

Under the old system for testing for bacterial contamination, a scientist looked for contamination by peering through a microscope to count colonies of organisms in a petri dish.

a. Describe how diminishing returns are likely to set in for the pharmaceutical production process.
b. Why do you think the FDA allowed firms to maintain these types of production processes?

3. The following discussion describes a new inventory system used by J. C. Penney[39]:

> In an industry where the goal is rapid turnaround of merchandise, J.C. Penney stores now hold almost no extra inventory of house-brand shirts.

Less than a decade ago, Penney would have stored thousands of them in warehouses across the U.S., tying up capital and slowly going out of style.

The entire program is designed and operated by TAL Apparel Ltd., a closely held Hong Kong shirt maker. TAL collects point-of-sale data for Penney's shirts directly from its stores in North America for analysis through a computer model it designed. The Hong Kong company then decides how many shirts to make, and in what styles, colors, and sizes. The manufacturer sends the shirts directly to each Penney store, bypassing the retailer's warehouses and corporate decision makers.

a. Discuss how this case illustrates the concept of the opportunity cost of capital.
b. How does this innovation also help in demand management?

4. Explain why a change in a firm's total fixed cost of production will shift its average total cost curve, but not its marginal cost curve.
5. Is it true that in a short-run production process, the marginal cost curve eventually slopes upward because firms have to pay workers a higher wage rate as they produce more output? Explain your answer.

---

[39]Gabriel Kahn, "Made to Measure: Invisible Supplier Has Penney's Shirts All Buttoned Up," *Wall Street Journal*, September 11, 2003.

6

Production and Cost Analysis in the Long Run

I n this chapter, we examine production and cost issues in the long run, where all inputs in a production process are variable. In doing so, we'll build on the short-run production and cost issues you have learned. As you'll learn in this chapter, a manager faces more decisions in the long run because it is possible to change the combination of all inputs used in the production process.

We begin this chapter with a case, the iPhone in China, which focuses on the long-run decisions made by Apple Inc., and on similar decisions by other manufacturing companies. This case is an example of a long-run production function, in which all inputs can be varied and possibly substituted for each other. We discuss both the feasibility of input substitution in technological terms and the possible incentives for input substitution in various sectors of the economy. We present an intuitive analysis of these issues in the chapter and include the formal model of long-run production, the isoquant model, in the chapter appendix.

We then define and examine long-run cost functions, focusing on a firm's long-run average cost. We show how this concept is derived in economic theory, and we then provide numerous illustrations of the shapes of long-run average cost curves for different firms and industries. We end the chapter by discussing implications of a firm's long-run average cost for a manager's competitive strategy.

Case for Analysis

The iPhone in China

At a dinner in February 2011, Steve Jobs of Apple Inc. reportedly responded to President Barack Obama's question about what it would take to make iPhones in the United States and bring those jobs home by saying that these jobs were not coming back.[1] Apple had made the long-run decision that its iPhones and iPads would be made overseas, given cheaper labor, large-scale foreign factories, and the flexibility, diligence, and industrial skills of foreign workers. Labor cost is actually a small component of total costs for most high-technology companies. More important is the expense of buying parts and managing supply chains that involve hundreds of companies.

These issues were illustrated in 2007 when Jobs demanded an iPhone glass screen that could not be scratched about a month before the phone was to appear in stores. Although Apple had already selected an American company, Corning Inc., to manufacture large panes of strengthened glass, the problem was how to cut the glass to fit an iPhone screen. A Chinese company, subsidized by the government, received the contract. iPhones are now being assembled in a complex known at Foxconn City that has 230,000 employees, many working six days a week, often for 12-hour days, and living in company barracks. Although Apple managers had estimated that it would take nine months to find 8,700 industrial engineers in the United States to oversee the assembly lines needed to produce iPhones, it reportedly took 15 days to find those engineers in China. Even though iPhone software and marketing campaigns were created in the United States, Apple made the decision to locate its manufacturing in China because it believed there were not enough U.S. workers with the needed skills or factories with sufficient resources.

The quest by Apple for long-run efficiency and cost cutting has not come without controversy.[2] It has been alleged that Chinese workers assembling iPhones and iPads work excessive overtime, live in crowded dorms, and may have to stand so long that their legs swell. There have been charges that these suppliers did not properly dispose of hazardous waste, falsified records, and disregarded workers' health. Workers have been killed by explosions in the plants and injured by the chemicals used to clean iPhone screens. Apple developed a code of conduct specifying that working conditions in its supply chain are safe, workers are treated with respect, and manufacturing processes will not harm the environment. The company's own audits found consistent violations of this code of conduct. In March 2012, the Fair Labor Association found, in an audit of 35,500 workers at three Foxconn facilities, at least 50 legal or code violations or policy gaps, including violation of 60-hour workweeks and other health- and safety-related problems, such as the lack of systems for protecting workers from excessive heat.[3]

Other manufacturing companies face long-run decisions similar to those of Apple Inc. The combination of inputs that firms use, as well as location decisions, depends upon the type of products manufactured and the costs of all the inputs of production. Standard Motor Products in North Carolina, which makes and distributes replacement auto parts, competes with Chinese firms.[4] Fuel injectors are made in the United States because they require current technology, strong quality assurance, and highly skilled workers. They are also likely to be made in small batches for different makes and models of cars. Many of Standard's customers, who see the company as a distributor rather than a manufacturer, expect the company to be able to deliver its products anywhere in the United States within 48 hours. These decisions led the company to increase its fuel injector production in the United States. Company managers continually re-evaluate the decision about whether to outsource, but argue that they would need to save at least 40 percent of U.S. costs to do so.

Several Canadian manufacturers and other companies have moved their facilities to the United States, citing more competitive wages, lower energy costs, and increased productivity.[5] In 2012, wages and benefits at a Caterpillar rail-equipment plant in Illinois were less than half of those at the company's locomotive-assembly plant in Ontario. Navistar International Corp. sought more flexible work rules and lower wage costs when it closed its plant in Ontario and relocated production to Ohio. Sweden's Electrolux AB planned to close its Quebec plant and manufacture its ovens, ranges, and cooktops in Memphis, Tennessee. Bridgestone Corp. had built industrial radial tires only in Japan, but decided in 2011 to build another plant in South Carolina to get increased productivity and to minimize transportation costs for many customers.

[1]This discussion is based on Charles Duhigg and Keith Bradsher, "How the U.S. Lost Out on iPhone Work," *The New York Times (Online)*, January 21, 2012.

[2]This discussion is based on Charles Duhigg and David Barboza, "In China, Human Costs are Built into an iPad," *The New York Times (Online)*, January 25, 2012.

[3]Jessica E. Vascellaro, "Audit Faults Apple Supplier," *Wall Street Journal (Online)*, March 30, 2012.

[4]Adam Davidson, "Making It in America," *The Atlantic (Online)*, January/February 2012.

[5]James R. Hagerty and Kate Linebaugh, "In U.S., a Cheaper Labor Pool," *Wall Street Journal (Online)*, January 6, 2012.

Model of a Long-Run Production Function

Long-run production function
A production function showing the relationship between a flow of inputs and the resulting flow of output, where all inputs are variable.

This case study illustrates **long-run production functions**, where all inputs in the production process are variable and inputs may be substituted for each other. The case also shows that the long run is a planning horizon. Managers at Apple Inc. and the other companies discussed in the case considered new technologies and changes in all of the inputs of production in their decisions.

A simplified long-run production function is presented in Equation 6.1:

6.1 $Q = f(L, K)$

> *where*
> Q = quantity of output
> L = quantity of labor input (variable)
> K = quantity of capital input (variable)

Unlike a short-run production function, both inputs in this production function can be varied. Thus, the amount of output that can be produced is related to the amount of both capital and labor used. In this section, we'll discuss how changes in the scale of production impact costs in the long run. But first let's look at the concept of input substitution, another important issue that arises when more than one input is variable.

Input Substitution

Labor-intensive method of production
A production process that uses large amounts of labor relative to the other inputs to produce the firm's output.

Capital-intensive method of production
A production process that uses large amounts of capital equipment relative to the other inputs to produce the firm's output.

Input substitution
The degree to which a firm can substitute one input for another in a production process.

Suppose that a firm has already decided that it wants to produce quantity Q_1 in the production function in Equation 6.1. With this production function, firms have still another economic choice to make. Because both inputs are variable, the firm must decide what combination of inputs to use in producing output level Q_1. The firm might use either a labor-intensive or a capital-intensive method of production. With a **labor-intensive method of production**, managers use large amounts of labor relative to other inputs to produce the firm's product. However, it might also be possible to use a production method that relies on large quantities of capital equipment and smaller amounts of labor; this is called a **capital-intensive method of production**. The number of methods that can be used depends on the degree of **input substitution**, or the feasibility of substituting one input for another in the production process.

A manager's choice of inputs will be influenced by:

- The technology of the production process
- The prices of the inputs of production
- The set of incentives facing the given producer[6]

---

[6]The formal rule to minimize the cost of using two variable inputs, labor (L) and capital (K), to produce a given level of output in a production process is to use quantities of each input such that $(MP_L/P_L) = (MP_K/P_K)$, where MP is the marginal product showing the additional output generated by an additional unit of each input, P_L is the price per unit of labor, and P_K is the price per unit of capital. The intuition of this rule is shown as follows. Assume that there is diminishing marginal productivity (diminishing returns) for both inputs and that the above ratio is 10/1 for labor and 5/1 for capital. If 1 more unit of labor and 1 less unit of capital are used in the production process, there is a gain of 10 units of output and a loss of 5 units, so it makes sense to reallocate the inputs. However, as more labor is used, its marginal product decreases, while the marginal product of capital increases as less of this input is used. Thus, eventually the ratios will equalize—say, at 8/1. No further reallocation of inputs will increase output for a given input cost or reduce cost for a given level of output. This rule, which is formally derived in Appendix 6A, *shows that managers minimize costs by considering both the technology of the production process, which influences productivity, and the prices of the inputs.*

The Technology of the Production Process   Production functions vary widely in the technological feasibility of input substitution. The development of the assembly line in the automobile industry is one of the best examples of changes in production technology and the substitution of capital for labor.[7] Before Henry Ford introduced the assembly line, it took 728 hours to assemble an automobile from a pile of parts located in one place. Initially, Ford installed a system in which a winch moved the auto-body frame 250 feet along the factory floor and workers picked up parts spaced along that distance and fitted them to the car. Longer assembly lines, more specialized workers, and automatic conveyer belts eventually resulted in tremendous reductions in the time necessary to make one automobile.

The fast-food industry is another example of a production process built around a capital-intensive assembly line in each franchise that includes conveyer belts and ovens resembling commercial laundry presses. High-technology capital-intensive production methods have also been developed to supply the inputs to these franchises. The Lamb Weston plant in American Falls, Idaho, one of the biggest french fry factories in the world, was founded in 1950 by F. Gilbert Lamb, inventor of the Lamb Water Gun Knife, a device that uses a high-pressure hose to shoot potatoes at a speed of 117 feet per second through a grid of sharpened steel blades to create perfect french fries.[8]

In 2007, airlines and airports considered adopting radio-frequency ID (RFID) baggage tags to replace existing bar code–printed tags. Industry studies had shown that the RFIDs, which transmit a bag's identifying number in a manner similar to a toll-road pass, could reduce lost luggage by 20 percent. The system was estimated to be 99 percent accurate in reading baggage tags, a significant improvement over the 80 to 90 percent accuracy of optical scanners reading bar-coded tags. U.S. airlines spent approximately $400 million on lost luggage in 2006 to reimburse passengers and deliver late bags to hotels and homes. This decision to change technology had been limited in the past by the cost of the RFIDs of approximately $1.00 per tag compared with 4 cents for a bar code–printed tag. However, the price of the RFID tags had begun to decrease to as low as 15 cents per tag.[9]

In the railroad industry, managers have begun to consider the use of plastic railroad ties made from old tires, grocery bags, milk cartons, and Styrofoam coffee cups as a replacement for wooden ties, which are vulnerable to rot, fungus, and termite infestation. Quality is a crucial issue in this decision because railroad ties, which are spaced 18 or 24 inches apart, must be stiff enough to support heavy-laden freight trains but flexible enough to bounce back from their tremendous impact. Plastic tie manufacturers claim their ties can last for at least 50 years, but these ties typically cost twice as much as wood ties.[10]

Mining companies are now using high-tech equipment to lower their costs of production by using fewer workers and by providing them increased protection.[11] Rio Tinto connected its Australian mines to satellite links so that workers could remotely drive drilling rigs, load cargo, and use robots to plant explosives. Robots can drill 1 million holes in the ground in a year, eliminating thousands of man-hours of work. BHP Billiton Ltd. and Caterpillar Inc. are designing driverless trucks, and Rio Tinto is studying how to use a train that does not need human operators for loading and delivery.

---

[7]This discussion is drawn from Shlomo Maital, *Executive Economics* (New York: Free Press, 1994), 94–95.
[8]For an extensive description of this production process, see Eric Schlosser, *Fast Food Nation* (Boston: Houghton Mifflin, 2001), 130–31.
[9]Scott McCartney, "A New Way to Prevent Lost Luggage," *Wall Street Journal*, February 27, 2007.
[10]Daniel Machalaba, "New Recyclables Market Emerges: Plastic Railroad Ties," *Wall Street Journal*, October 19, 2004.
[11]Robert Guy Matthews, "Miner Digs for Ore in the Outback with Remote-Controlled Robots," *Wall Street Journal (Online)*, March 1, 2010.

Changing technology affects all types of production. When AOL Inc. wanted to determine if it was getting the best use of its video library, it needed to measure which of its thousands of Web pages published daily contained videos. The company could have designed video-detecting software or hired temporary workers for the task. However, it decided to use crowdsourcing—breaking a project into small components and farming those tasks out to the general public by posting the requests on a Web site. The project was operating within a week and took only several months to complete. AOL estimated that the project cost as much as two temporary workers hired for the same time. Analysts have estimated that crowd-sourced labor can cost companies half as much as typical outsourcing. Some crowdsourced tasks take only a few seconds and pay a few cents per task, while more complex writing or transcription tasks may pay $10 or $20 per job.[12]

Other production processes may not be as conducive to substitution between inputs, particularly if they involve a series of complex processes and a highly trained labor force such as found in the pipe organ industry. At the Schantz Organ Co., the largest maker of pipe organs in the United States, each worker takes an average of 30 to 40 hours of hand labor to bend specially made sheets of soft metal into the 61 pipes comprising one of the shorter "ranks" or rows of pipes with the seam of each pipe hand-dabbed with solder. The number of ranks can range from 3 to 150 or more. It takes four to five years for a worker to become a good pipe maker, while the "voicers" who tune the pipes spend up to seven years as apprentices. Although some new technologies, such as computer-controlled routers, have been adopted, labor costs represent 57 percent of the $8 million sales revenue at Schantz. The average labor cost relative to shipments for all U.S. manufacturing is 17 percent, while it is as low as 2 percent in some highly automated sectors such as soybean processing.[13]

Economists have traditionally argued that input substitution may be less feasible in the provision of services, particularly in the public sector, than in the production of goods, a factor that has become increasingly important as the U.S. economy has become more service oriented.[14] In some service areas, this argument is being questioned as more input substitution occurs than might be expected. For example, hospitals are using an increasing number of robots to haul food trays, linens, trash, medical records, and medications from one area to another in the facility. Robots are also used to connect doctors with patients through videoconferencing and to enable doctors to obtain clinical information from remote monitors in real time.[15]

The process of syndicating corporate loans among banks has undergone rapid technological change. Until the late 1990s, syndicating a large corporate loan meant that a bank had to distribute an offering document, often totaling 200 pages, to 50 to 100 banks using overnight mail, fax machines, and hordes of messengers. That process, now largely handled through banking Web sites, may reduce the time to close a deal by 25 percent.[16]

The U.S. Postal Service has developed increasingly sophisticated equipment to detect illegible handwriting on envelopes. Computers have learned to interpret scrawls and squiggles, with some machines processing 36,000 letters per hour. However, the Postal Service still employs hundreds of workers at their Remote Encoding Centers to sit in silence day and night interpreting incomprehensible writing.[17]

Input substitution is occurring even in the fine arts. In November 2003, the Opera Company of Brooklyn announced that it would stage *The Marriage of Figaro*

[12]Rachel Emma Silverman, "Big Firms Try Crowdsourcing," *Wall Street Journal (Online)*, January 17, 2012.
[13]Timothy Aeppel, "Few Hands, Many Hours," *Wall Street Journal*, October 27, 2006.
[14]William Baumol, "Macroeconomics of Unbalanced Growth: The Anatomy of the Urban Crisis," *American Economic Review* 62 (June 1967): 415–26.
[15]Timothy Hay, "The Robots Are Coming to Hospitals," *Wall Street Journal (Online)*, March 15, 2012.
[16]Steve Lohr, "Computer Age Gains Respect of Economists," *New York Times*, April 14, 1999.
[17]Barry Newman, "Poor Penmanship Spells Job Security for Post Office's Scribble Specialists," *Wall Street Journal (Online)*, November 3, 2011.

with only 12 musicians and a technician overseeing a computer program that would play all the other parts.[18] The conductor, Paul Henry Smith, has developed the Fauxharmonic Orchestra, a computer program composed of over a million recorded notes played by top musicians. The latest software lets users choose from a large library of digitally stored sounds, adjust for texture and nuance, and assemble them into a complete symphony. A conductor's jacket, a cyclist's jersey embedded with a dozen sensors, has been developed to map conductors' movements and physiology and translate them to control a piece of music.[19]

Empirical studies have found that labor productivity growth in the service industries has proceeded at about the economy-wide rate since 1995. These increases are broad-based and not just found among a small number of large industries. Much of this growth is related to the increased use of information technology.[20]

The Prices of the Inputs of Production   As mentioned above in the case of the adoption of radio-frequency ID baggage tags and plastic railroad ties, the prices of the inputs of production also influence the degree of input substitution. To minimize their costs of production, firms want to substitute cheaper inputs for more expensive ones. How much substitution can occur in the face of high input prices depends on the technology of the production process and institutional factors.

As the movement toward electricity deregulation intensified in southern California and other parts of the country in the late 1990s and at the turn of the century, electricity prices fluctuated and in some cases increased dramatically as market forces swept into the formerly regulated industry. Companies responded to increased electricity prices through both input substitution and implementation of innovative contracts with their service providers. Because Intel Corporation used huge amounts of electricity to keep its automated, temperature- and humidity-sensitive semiconductor-fabrication operations running 24 hours a day, the company could not enter into interruptible supply contracts with electricity generators that would provide lower prices, but a nonconstant supply. Instead, Intel negotiated voluntary consumption restrictions through reduced lighting and air-conditioning levels, and it designed factory equipment that was less energy-intensive.[21]

Increased costs of gas, oil, and electricity have continued to influence managerial decisions about input use. Arla Foods, a farmer-owned cooperative based in Denmark and the world's fifth-largest dairy producer by revenue, cut energy use in response to Denmark's high taxes on energy consumption. Arla undertook about a dozen projects to save energy including changing the water chiller, replacing the absorption dryer in the cheese-aging room, and repairing leaks in compressed-air pipes.[22]

Law firms have begun using software that enables the discovery process—providing documents relevant to a lawsuit—to be done electronically rather than by using higher-priced lawyers and paralegals. Linguistic discovery technologies use specific search words to find and sort relevant documents, while other technologies use a sociological approach that mimics human deduction. This software mines documents for the activities and interactions of people and seeks to visualize chains of events. Some software can recognize the sentiment in an e-mail message or detect subtle differences in the style of a message.[23]

[18]Jon E. Hilsenrath, "Behind Surging Productivity: The Service Sector Delivers," *Wall Street Journal*, November 7, 2003.
[19]Jacob Hale Russell and John Jurgensen, "Fugue for Man & Machine," *Wall Street Journal*, May 5, 2007.
[20]Jack E. Triplett and Barry P. Bosworth, "'Baumol's Disease Has Been Cured: IT and Multifactor Productivity in U.S. Services Industries," in *The New Economy and Beyond: Past, Present, and Future*, ed., Dennis W. Jansen (Northampton, MA: Edward Elgar, 2006), 34–71.
[21]Jonathan Friedland, "Volatile Electricity Market Forces Firms to Find Ways to Cut Energy Expenses," *Wall Street Journal*, August 14, 2000.
[22]Leila Abboud and John Biers, "Business Goes on an Energy Diet," *Wall Street Journal*, August 27, 2007.
[23]John Markoff, "Armies of Expensive Lawyers, Replaced by Cheaper Software," *The New York Times (Online)*, March 4, 2011.

Managers have attempted to replace workers with machinery even in the fresh fruit industry where many products have traditionally been picked by hand to maintain quality. One company in the Florida citrus industry turned to canopy shakers to harvest half of the 40.5 million pounds of oranges grown annually from its 10,000 acres in southwestern Florida. In less than 15 minutes, these machines can shake loose 36,000 pounds of oranges from 100 trees, catch the fruit, and drop it into a storage car, a job that would have taken four pickers an entire day.[24]

Input substitution may also result from the scarcity of a particular input. In March 2012, an explosion at a German plant depleted supplies of a resin used to make automobile fuel and brake lines. Evonik Industries AG was the only integrated maker of the resin, nylon-12, which is a precise blend of chemicals that can resist reacting with gasoline and brake fluids. Concerned that the shortage would shut down auto assembly plants, chemical companies such as DuPont began searching for replacement materials. Evonik discussed with its customers whether another biologically based polymer might work as a replacement for some applications of nylon-12.[25]

The ability to change all inputs in the face of changing input prices has affected the development of numerous industries over time.[26] Supermarkets have become the dominant form of grocery store in the United States. Because these stores are a land-intensive form of organization—given their size and the need for parking lots around them—their development depends on the availability of large accessible plots of land at relatively low prices. In Germany, where less land is available and the population is more concentrated in central cities, small supermarkets or minimarkets have increased productivity by making bulk purchases at the firm level and by providing only a small variety of goods.

The ability to manufacture goods with cheaper labor abroad led to the decline of U.S. manufacturing from 20 percent of GDP in 1980 to 12 percent in 2006. However, even some types of manufacturing are better done closer to the customer. These include appliances and electronic equipment that are high-end, locally customized, delicate, very large, or have manufacturing processes that involve almost no labor, such as medical testing or automated electric-component, chemical, or metal-fabricating plants.[27] In 2011 Otis Elevator Co. moved production from its factory in Nogales, Mexico, to a new plant in South Carolina. Otis moved production to Mexico in 1998 to minimize costs, but logistics costs increased substantially since that time. The new plant will be closer to many of the company's customers who are on the East Coast of the United States. Savings will also be derived from having all of the company's white-collar workers associated with elevator design and production located at the new factory. The plant will also use more automation to reduce the need for production workers.[28]

The Incentives Facing a Given Producer   The third factor influencing input substitution is the set of incentives facing a given producer. Firms will substitute cheaper inputs of production for more expensive ones if they face major incentives to minimize their costs of production.

The Role of Competitive Environments   Input substitution will occur most often in a competitive market environment where firms are trying to maximize their profits or are operating under extreme conditions.

---

[24]Eduardo Porter, "In Florida Groves, Cheap Labor Means Machines," *New York Times*, March 22, 2004.
[25]Jeff Bennett and Jan Hromadko, "Nylon-12 Haunts Car Makers," *Wall Street Journal (Online)*, April 17, 2012; Jeff Bennett, "Search Begins for New Resin," *Wall Street Journal (Online)*, April 18, 2012.
[26]This discussion is based on Martin Neil Bailey and Robert M. Solow, "International Productivity Comparisons Built from the Firm Level," *Journal of Economic Perspectives* 15 (Summer 2001): 151–72.
[27]Mark Whitehouse, "For Some Manufacturers, There Are Benefits to Keeping Production at Home," *Wall Street Journal*, January 22, 2007.
[28]Timothy Aeppel, "Otis Shifts Work Closer to Home," *Wall Street Journal (Online)*, October 7, 2011.

The substitution of machinery for labor in the fresh-fruits industry discussed above was a response to increased global competition facing American farmers. In the early 1990s, Florida orange farmers had overplanted, and there were large bumper crops in Brazil where harvesting costs were about one-third as high as in Florida. These changes gave Florida growers the incentive to invest over $1 million per year into research in mechanical harvesting to reduce their costs. By the 1999–2000 harvest, this investment resulted in four different types of harvesting machines working commercially.[29]

The grocery industry, which is very competitive, has tried to cut costs through reduced bag usage. Supervalu Inc. expected to save millions of dollars each year through a bagging program that put more items in each bag or omitted the bag altogether. The company's rigorous program prohibited double bagging and the use of bags for large items with handles and also emphasized the use of plastic bags, which cost 2 cents per bag compared with 5 cents for a paper bag. Supervalu Inc., which convened a company-wide task force to study bag use in 2008, could encounter customer resistance from the use of plastic bags or complaints over the increased weight of the bags.[30]

U.S. airlines, operating under extreme competition and facing huge increases in the cost of fuel, are trying to gain control over the costs of plane parts either by searching for less expensive suppliers or by determining how to make the parts themselves at significantly lower costs. Continental Airlines estimates that it has saved almost $2 million per year by making its own parts such as tray tables and window shades.[31]

The airlines have also used new aviation software to help minimize their fuel costs and the overflight fees charged by countries for using their airspace. These fees, which cost the world's air carriers $20 billion per year, are usually based on takeoff weight and distance travelled. The software, which calculates multiple scenarios, balances the overflight fees with additional fuel costs if an alternative route is less direct. United Airlines expects that once the software system is fully installed for its 1,600 daily mainline flights, the company will save more than $20 million per year.[32]

United has also been using smaller jets with fewer cabin crew members to reduce costs on a growing number of long, trans-Atlantic routes to European cities that would not generate enough traffic to justify larger planes. However, strong headwinds have forced many flights to make unexpected stops in Canada and elsewhere to take on additional fuel. In December 2011, United's 757 flights had to stop 43 times out of 1,100 flights to refuel compared with only 12 unscheduled stops a year earlier. The resulting delays caused passengers to miss connections and required the airline to pay for hotels and other compensation.[33]

Firms that have some degree of market power may have fewer incentives to constantly search for the cost-minimizing combination of inputs. Economists have called this concept **X-inefficiency**.[34] Both statistical and case study evidence indicates that some degree of X-inefficiency exists in less-competitive industries where firms have greater market power.[35] Studies of manufacturing sector productivity

X-inefficiency
Inefficiency that may result in firms with market power that have fewer incentives to minimize the costs of production than more competitive firms.

---

[29]Porter, "In Florida Groves, Cheap Labor Means Machines."

[30]Ilan Brat, "At Supervalu, Cost Cuts Are in the Bag," *Wall Street Journal (Online)*, March 22, 2011.

[31]Melanie Trottman, "Nuts-and-Bolts Savings," *Wall Street Journal*, May 3, 2005.

[32]Susan Carey, "Calculating Costs in the Clouds," *Wall Street Journal*, March 6, 2007.

[33]Susan Carey and Andy Pasztor, "Nonstop Flights Stop for Fuel," *Wall Street Journal (Online)*, January 11, 2012.

[34]Harvey Leibenstein, "Allocative Inefficiency vs. X-Inefficiency," *American Economic Review* 56 (1966): 392–415.

[35]Frederic M. Scherer and David Ross, *Industrial Market Structure and Economic Performance*, 3rd ed. (Boston: Houghton Mifflin, 1990), 668–72.

Best practices
The production techniques adopted by the firms with the highest levels of productivity.

indicate that firms increase productivity when they are exposed to the world's **best practices**—the production techniques adopted by the firms with the highest levels of productivity.[36] A study of nine manufacturing industries in the United States, Germany, and Japan concluded that industries with the greatest exposure to the best practices used by the world's high-labor-productivity industries had relatively higher productivity themselves.[37]

In retail trade, Wal-Mart has played a central role in increasing overall productivity, given its large size and highly productive methods of operation related to logistics, distribution, and inventory control. By the late 1970s, all stores, distribution centers, and the company's headquarters were connected to a computer network. Wal-Mart installed bar code readers in all its distribution centers by the late 1980s, which reduced the labor cost of processing shipments by one-half. The company is currently one of the leaders in the use of radio-frequency identification to track shipments of its products.[38]

In 2012 Proctor & Gamble Co. announced plans to eliminate more than 4,000 jobs and cut $1 billion from its massive marketing budget. Investors and analysts had complained that the company operated on a higher cost base than many of its rivals, a particular problem in the face of weaker growth in developed markets in the United States and Europe. These changes were expected to save $10 billion by 2016.[39]

Lean production
An approach to production pioneered by Toyota Motor Corporation in which firms streamline the production process through strategies such as strict scheduling and small-batch production with low-cost flexible machines.

Labor Issues Proponents of cost-cutting strategies may run into resistance from individuals and organizations that feel threatened by these strategies. United States auto workers have in the past opposed **lean production**, a strategy U.S. automobile manufacturers adopted from Toyota Motor Corporation that includes strict scheduling and small-batch production with low-cost flexible machines, a major change from previous auto production methods.[40]

Worker and union attitudes at Ford have changed more recently as the company's future became more tenuous. In 2007, the company, which lost $12.7 billion the previous year, persuaded the United Auto Workers locals at 33 of its 41 plants to accept "competitive operating agreements" that loosened various complex and often costly work rules. Union members have agreed that some non-Ford workers earning half their pay could take certain jobs in a plant.[41]

In 2011 Volkswagen AG announced the opening of a new Tennessee auto plant that would pay starting workers $27 per hour in wages and benefits compared with $52 per hour at the Detroit Big Three auto makers. Some nonunion U.S. plants owned by Toyota Motor Corp., Honda Motor Co., Hyundai Motor Co., and Kia Motors Corp. also had plants in the South with labor costs similar to that of VW. Auto unions agreed to lower pay for new hires in the auto bailout restructuring of General Motors and Chrysler. Because only a small number of workers have come in at the lower levels, labor costs for these companies remain higher than for new plants in the South.[42]

On the U.S. west coast, the International Longshore and Warehouse Union (ILWU) has had a major influence on what wages dockworkers are paid and on how the production process is structured. In 2002, there was a dispute between the Pacific Maritime Association, which represents the operators of the terminals, and the ILWU over the introduction of electronic technology to automatically collect

---

[36]Bailey and Solow, "International Productivity Comparisons."
[37]Many companies have also adopted the Six Sigma management strategies to improve manufacturing processes and reduce costs. See Motorola University—What is Six Sigma? (http://www.motorola.com).
[38]Emek Basker, "The Causes and Consequences of Wal-Mart's Growth," *Journal of Economic Perspectives* 21 (3) (Summer 2007): 177–98.
[39]Emily Glazer and Paul Ziobro, "P&G to Cut Over 4,000 Jobs," *Wall Street Journal (Online)*, February 24, 2012.
[40]Norihiko Shirouzu, "Beyond the Tire Mess, Ford Has a Problem with Quality," *Wall Street Journal*, May 25, 2001.
[41]Jeffrey McCracken, "Desperate to Cut Costs, Ford Gets Union's Help," *Wall Street Journal*, March 2, 2007.
[42]Mike Ramsey, "VW Chops Labor Costs in U.S." *Wall Street Journal (Online)*, May 23, 2011.

cargo information that union clerks had been entering manually into computers.[43] This issue reached an impasse in October 2002, when management locked out the dockworkers.[44] Later that fall, an agreement was reached in which the union agreed to allow the installation and use of new information technology, such as software for designing how containers are filled and global-positioning-satellite-system technology for tracking cargo, in return for the protection of the jobs (until they retired) of registered dockworkers whose work was displaced by the technology.[45] Although the ILWU has great power to influence productivity and costs on the docks, this power is not unlimited, given increased competition from nonunion ports in certain U.S. states and other countries and pressure from large retailers, such as Wal-Mart, to cut costs in their supply systems.[46]

The limitations of lean production and streamlined supply chains were demonstrated after the earthquake and tsunami in Japan in March 2011, which led to parts shortages for auto makers and electronics manufacturers. However, building redundancies into a supply chain is difficult because the strategy is time consuming and does not pay off unless there is a disaster. Companies also face risks if governments collapse. The fall of Egypt's government in the wake of the Arab Spring movement led McCormick & Co. to stockpile various herbs it bought there and to find alternative sources. Supply chains may also be disrupted by U.S trade sanctions in various parts of the world.[47]

Nonprofit Organizations   Organizations that do not face strict profit-maximizing constraints may also have fewer incentives to minimize the costs of production. There is continuing controversy over whether nonprofit hospitals, whose typical goals are to serve the community and provide services that may not be profitable, achieve these goals or use their revenue to build expensive facilities and pay high executive salaries.[48] Past evidence indicated that hospital administrators engaged in "medical arms races," competing with each other on the purchase of costly high technology equipment and driving up overall health care costs.[49] These outcomes occurred before the widespread utilization of prospective payment systems by Medicare and other managed care organizations, whose goals are to cut costs and impose the discipline of the competitive market in the health care sector. Recent studies have shown that for-profit and nonprofit hospitals tend to act more similar when they are located in the same metropolitan areas and compete with each other.[50]

Wide variations have been reported in the prices hospitals paid for major medical devices such as defibrillators and hip replacements. The choice of these devices has often been determined by physicians, who may prefer a particular manufacturer regardless of price. These practices may change as hospitals employ more doctors directly, giving them incentives to cut costs for the organization.[51]

[43]Daniel Machalaba and Queena Sook Kim, "West Coast Docks Face a Duel with Union About Technology," *Wall Street Journal*, May 17, 2002.

[44]Jeanne Cummings and Carlos Tejada, "U.S. Judge Swiftly Orders End to Lockout at West Coast Ports," *Wall Street Journal*, October 19, 2002.

[45]Daniel Machalaba and Queena Sook Kim, "West Coast Ports, Dockworkers Set Tentative Deal on Key Issue," *Wall Street Journal*, November 4, 2002.

[46]Anne Marie Squeo, "How Longshoremen Keep Global Wind at Their Backs," *Wall Street Journal*, July 26, 2006.

[47]Maxwell Murphy, "Reinforcing the Supply Chain," *Wall Street Journal (Online)*, January 11, 2012.

[48]John Carreyrou and Barbara Martinez, "Nonprofit Hospitals, Once for the Poor, Strike It Rich," *Wall Street Journal*, April 4, 2008.

[49]Rexford E. Santerre and Stephen P. Neun, *Health Economics: Theories, Insights, and Industry Studies*, 4th. ed. (Mason, OH: Thomson South-Western, 2007), 401–03.

[50]Mark Schlesinger and Bradford H. Gray, "How Nonprofits Matter in American Medicine, and What to Do About It," *Health Affairs* (June 20, 2006): W287–W303.

[51]Christopher Weaver, "Study: Hospitals Overpay for Devices," *Wall Street Journal (Online)*, February 3, 2012.

Political and Legislative Influences   Political and legislative factors can also influence input combinations. In 1999, California became the first state to require hospitals to meet fixed nurse-to-patient ratios.[52] This legislation was a reaction to concerns about the quality of health care in light of the cost-cutting efforts of managed care systems.

Legislating input combinations can have unforeseen consequences.[53] In the nursing example, it is not clear what nurse–patient threshold is necessary for improved outcomes. Minimum nurse-to-patient ratios may also cause hospitals to focus too narrowly on staffing instead of other factors that might contribute to the quality of care. As an alternative to mandated ratios, some hospitals have begun redesigning medical-surgical units so that nurses can spend more time on direct patient care and using sophisticated computer software to help analyze staffing needs and nurse allocation.[54] A recent study concluded that registered nurse staffing increased considerably in California hospitals as a result of the mandate and that there was no evidence of a lower nursing skill mix. Better patient outcomes seemed to be associated with these changes, although the issue of increased costs has not been examined.[55]

Model of a Long-Run Cost Function

Long-run average cost (LRAC)

The minimum average or unit cost of producing any level of output *when all inputs are variable.*

Let's now discuss how costs vary in the long run by focusing on the concept of **long-run average cost (*LRAC*)**. This is defined as the minimum average or unit cost of producing any level of output *when all inputs are variable.* In this section, we'll derive the long-run average cost curve and show the range of possibilities for its shape. We'll then discuss the actual shapes of the *LRAC* curve for different firms and define the minimum efficient scale (*MES*) of operation. We'll conclude this section by discussing the implications of the shape of the *LRAC* curve for competitive strategy.

Derivation of the Long-Run Average Cost Curve

Short-run average total cost (SATC)

The cost per unit of output for a firm of a given size or scale of operation.

Figure 6.1 shows several **short-run average total cost (*SATC*)** curves drawn for different scales of operation. These curves represent the average total cost of production for firms with different-sized manufacturing plants or different amounts of the fixed input buildings. For simplicity, the curves are labeled $SATC_1$, $SATC_2$, $SATC_3$, and $SATC_4$ to show the short-run average total cost associated with the first scale of operation, the second scale of operation, and so on. These are the same short-run average total cost curves that you saw in Chapter 5, except that we are now showing curves representing different scales of production.

You can see in Figure 6.1 that the cheapest method of producing up to Q_1 units of output is to use the plant represented by $SATC_1$. The short-run average total cost for this plant size would first decrease and then begin to increase as diminishing returns set into the production function. If the firm decided that it wanted to produce a level of output greater than Q_1, it would minimize its cost by building a larger plant and switching to cost curve $SATC_2$, associated with that larger plant. Between Q_1 and Q_2 units of output, $SATC_2$ represents the optimal plant size with the lowest

[52]Todd S. Purdum, "California to Set Level of Staffing for Nursing Care," *New York Times*, October 12, 1999.
[53]Janet M. Coffman, Jean Ann Seago, and Joanne Spetz, "Minimum Nurse-to-Patient Ratios in Acute Care Hospitals in California," *Health Affairs* 21 (5) (September–October 2002): 53–64.
[54]Laura Landro, "Why Quota for Nurses Isn't Cure-All," *Wall Street Journal*, December 13, 2006.
[55]Matthew D. McHugh, Lesly A. Kelly, Douglas M. Sloane, and Linda H. Aiken, "Contradicting Fears, California's Nurse-to-Patient Mandate Did Not Reduce the Skill Level of the Nursing Workforce in Hospitals," *Health Affairs* 30 (July 2011): 1299–306.

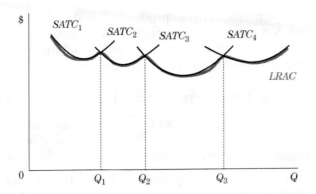

FIGURE 6.1
Derivation of the long-run average cost (LRAC) curve
The long-run average cost curve, which shows the minimum average cost of producing any level of output when all inputs are variable, is the envelope curve of the various short-run average total cost curves.

average cost of production. The firm would not want to use this $SATC_2$ plant to produce fewer than Q_1 units of output because the $SATC_2$ curve lies above the $SATC_1$ curve in that range of production. The plant with the $SATC_2$ curve has larger fixed costs of production than the $SATC_1$ plant, so its average total costs of production do not become lower until the fixed costs are spread over greater output.

The same arguments hold for still larger levels of output. The $SATC_3$ curve represents the lowest cost of production for output levels between Q_2 and Q_3, while $SATC_4$ minimizes cost for output levels larger than Q_3. The shaded long-run average cost (*LRAC*) curve in Figure 6.1 traces out the locus of points of minimum average cost. It is derived as an envelope curve of the respective short-run average cost curves and shows the minimum average cost of production *when all inputs are variable*.

Economies and Diseconomies of Scale

If we assume that plant size can be varied continuously, the *LRAC* curve in Figure 6.1 becomes the smooth, U-shaped curve in Figure 6.2. The downward sloping portion of this curve, up to output level Q_1 in Figure 6.2, is defined as the range of **economies of scale**. This means that the average costs of production are lowered as the firm produces larger output levels with an increased scale of production. Large-scale production is cheaper than small-scale production up to output level Q_1. Beyond output level Q_1, larger-sized plants result in a higher average cost of production, or **diseconomies of scale**. With a U-shaped *LRAC* curve, as shown in Figure 6.2, the size of plant represented by the $SATC_2$ curve represents the optimal scale of production. This plant size minimizes the overall average costs of production, assuming that the firm wants to produce output at or near level Q_1. The standard U-shaped *LRAC* in Figure 6.2 shows that larger-scale production first lowers

Economies of scale
Achieving lower unit costs of production by adopting a larger scale of production, represented by the downward sloping portion of a long-run average cost curve.

Diseconomies of scale
Incurring higher unit costs of production by adopting a larger scale of production, represented by the upward sloping portion of a long-run average cost curve.

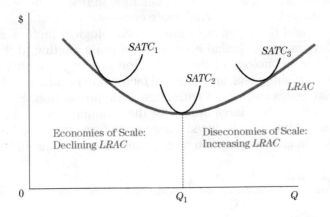

FIGURE 6.2
The Standard Long-Run Average Cost Curve (LRAC)
A firm can experience both economies of scale (decreasing LRAC) or diseconomies of scale (increasing LRAC) as it expands plant size. The size of the plant represented by the SATC$_2$ curve minimizes the overall average cost of production, assuming the firm wants to produce output at or near level Q$_1$.

and then increases the average cost of production. It also shows there is an optimal plant size in terms of minimizing the average costs of production. Note there is no distinction between fixed and variable costs when defining the long-run average cost curve because all costs are variable in the long run.

Factors Creating Economies and Diseconomies of Scale

Figure 6.2 shows a possible shape for an *LRAC* curve that encompasses both economies and diseconomies of scale. What factors would cause economies of scale to exist, and why might diseconomies of scale set in at large levels of output?

Factors Creating Economies of Scale The major factors creating economies of scale are as follows:

- Specialization and division of labor
- Technological factors
- The use of automation devices
- Quantity discounts
- The spreading of advertising costs
- Financial factors

As Adam Smith noted over 200 years ago in *The Wealth of Nations*, large-scale production allows for increased specialization and the division of labor among different tasks.[56] In the case of ball-bearing production, a skilled operator on a general-purpose lathe can customize a few bearings in five minutes to one hour. If a sizeable batch of bearings is needed, operators will use a more specialized automatic screw machine. However, it is not cost-effective to use this machine until at least 100 bearings are needed, and the costs decrease even more with 1,000 or 10,000 bearings. For very large quantities, such as 1,000,000 bearings per year, an automated, computer-guided production approach will be adopted. With this scale of production, unit costs may be 30 to 50 percent lower than with a medium-volume batch. However, the production line must be kept running two shifts per day without a changeover to realize these cost reductions.

Economies of scale can arise from expanding the size of individual processing units in chemical and metallurgical processing industries such as petroleum refining, iron ore reduction, and chemical synthesis. Due to the physical relationships between processing unit size and level of output, increases in capacity occur with a less-than-proportionate increase in equipment cost. The number of workers needed to operate a larger processing unit may barely exceed what is needed for a smaller unit.

"Economies of massed reserves" may also play a role in various types of industrial production. Plants may keep specialized machines in reserve to sustain production in case the machine currently operating breaks down. In a large plant with several machines, holding a single extra machine in reserve does not add proportionately to costs and, therefore, can create economies of scale.

Specialization and the division of labor, technological factors, and the use of automation devices are technical economies of scale relating to the combination of inputs and the technology of the production process. Quantity discounts, the spreading of advertising costs, and financial factors are pecuniary gains, as they represent financial issues associated with large-scale production. Firms may receive discounts when they place large orders for their inputs. Advertising costs per unit decrease as more output is produced. Large-scale firms may also be able to obtain loans and other financial support on more generous terms than smaller firms.

---

[56]The following examples of economies and diseconomies of scale are based on Scherer and Ross, 97–106.

Factors Creating Diseconomies of Scale   Diseconomies of scale are associated with the following:

- The inefficiencies of managing large-scale operations
- The increased transportation costs that result from concentrating production in a small number of very large plants

If the specialization and division of labor that create economies of scale are pushed too far, workers can become alienated by dull, routine jobs. Inefficiencies will set into the production process that will begin to raise costs. The long-run average cost curve will then slope upward, reflecting the higher costs of larger plants. Managers have responded to these types of problems with quality circles and job enrichment programs to try to limit the impact on costs.

Other factors also contribute to diseconomies of scale. If greater numbers of workers are needed for large-scale production, they may have to be drawn from a greater distance away or from other labor markets by paying higher wages, which increases the costs of production. Physical laws, such as the bursting point of large pipes, will eventually limit the size of the capital equipment in a production process. Perhaps the most important limitation to large-scale production is the management function. Plants can become too large to manage efficiently. Chief executive officers and other upper-level management can become too far removed from the day-to-day production and marketing operations, so that their ability to make sound decisions decreases.

General Motors (GM) is the classic example of a firm that tried to avoid the inefficiencies of managing a large enterprise through decentralization. Beginning in the 1920s, GM delegated much authority to operating divisions and established a set of managerial incentives related to performance objectives of these divisions. Tendencies toward centralization reappeared in the 1950s and continued through the 1970s. By the mid-1980s, GM found that it was not able to respond to the increased foreign competition and changing consumer preferences as easily as many of its smaller rivals.

Current evidence shows that there are definite limits to economies of scale in the automobile industry. The average capacity of GM, Ford, and Chrysler plants is between 190,000 and 270,000 vehicles per year, which suggests this may be the optimum-sized plant. The Big Three auto makers have also reduced their size by divesting large portions of their parts- and components-making operations. They are also increasingly outsourcing the production of entire modules—parts preassembled into complete units—to other suppliers. Industry experts estimate that these reductions may cut production costs by as much as 30 percent. Small, more flexible assembly plants also allow the auto makers to more quickly adapt to changing consumer fashions and preferences.[57]

Other Factors Influencing the Long-Run Average Cost Curve

Two other factors that can affect the shape or position of the long-run average cost curve are learning by doing and transportation costs.[58]

Learning by doing reflects the drop in unit costs as total cumulative production increases because workers become more efficient as they repeat their assigned tasks. This process was first observed in defense production during World War II. For the B-29 bomber, unit costs declined by 29.5 percent on

Learning by doing
The drop in unit costs as total cumulative production increases because workers become more efficient as they repeat their assigned tasks.

[57]James W. Brock, "The Automobile Industry," in *The Structure of American Industry*, ed. James W. Brock, 12th ed. (Upper Saddle River, NJ: Prentice-Hall, 2009), 155–82.
[58]This discussion is based on Scherer and Ross, 98–108.

average with each doubling of cumulative output. Large-scale integrated circuit production also exhibits the efficiencies of learning by doing, given the difficulty of learning to deposit the correct amount of material into various parts of the circuits. It has been estimated that costs can decrease by 25 to 30 percent with each doubling of cumulative output due to the learning process. The cost advantages from learning by doing affect the position, not the shape, of the long-run average cost curve because they are associated with the cumulative output produced by the firm, not the level of output at different scales of operation. Substantial cost savings from learning by doing would cause the *LRAC* curve to shift down.

Transportation costs can affect the shape of the long-run average cost curve for a firm, particularly the point of minimum average cost. If production is centralized in a small number of large plants, then the product has to be delivered over greater distances to the customers. Transportation costs are particularly important for heavy, bulky products such as bricks and ready-made concrete. If these transportation costs increase with large-scale production, the long-run average cost curve that includes these costs will have a lower optimum scale of operation than a curve without these costs. These levels of output could differ substantially depending on the shapes of, and relationship between, the transportation cost curve and the *LRAC* curve.

The Minimum Efficient Scale of Operation

Minimum efficient scale (MES)

That scale of operation at which the long-run average cost curve stops declining or at which economies of scale are exhausted.

An important concept that affects the structure of an industry and the resulting competitive strategy is the **minimum efficient scale (*MES*)** of operation in that industry. The *MES* is that scale of operation at which the long-run average cost curve stops declining or at which economies of scale are exhausted. At this scale, there are no further advantages to larger-scale production in terms of lowering production costs. The important point is the location of this minimum efficient scale relative to the total size of the market. Figure 6.3 shows the minimum efficient scales associated with four different *LRAC* curves and a market demand curve.

The four *LRAC* curves differ in terms of the location of their minimum efficient scales of operation and the gradient or slope of their cost curves—that is, how quickly costs change as output varies.[59] Firm A represents a firm that could operate in a competitive market with a large number of producers. It has a relatively small *MES* compared to the size of the market. Any scale economies are exhausted quickly. The cost curve also has a relatively steep gradient, indicating

FIGURE 6.3
Minimum Efficient Scale (MES) with Different LRAC Curves
For various firms, the minimum efficient scale (MES), where the LRAC stops decreasing, is reached at different points relative to total market demand.
Source: Adapted from Shepherd, William G., *The Economics of Industrial Organization*, 4th ed., Upper Saddle River, NJ: Prentice Hall, 1997.

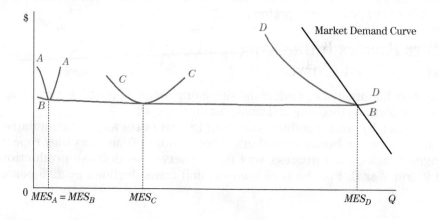

[59]This discussion is drawn from William G. Shepherd, *The Economics of Industrial Organization*, 4th ed. (Upper Saddle River, NJ: Prentice Hall, 1997), 169–71.

that producing output at a level much greater or less than MES_A will result in a rapid increase in costs. Thus, a competitive market could support a large number of these small A-type firms.

Firm B has the same minimum efficient scale of operation as Firm A. Unlike Firm A, its *LRAC* curve is relatively flat over a large range of output. This means that there is no optimal scale of operation for Firm B. Firms of many different sizes are consistent with this *LRAC* curve. Competition is viable because the *MES* is relatively small, but larger firms may exist because diseconomies of scale do not set in over the relevant range of the market. These larger firms may have enough market power to give them a competitive advantage even though their costs are not reduced by the larger-scale production.

Firm C has a cost structure that is more consistent with an oligopoly market structure. The minimum efficient scale is one-third of the market, so it is likely that only a few firms will emerge in the market. The gradient of the curve is relatively steep, so this scale of operation is optimal. Firm D represents a natural monopoly, where one large-scale firm will dominate the market. The minimum efficient scale of production comprises the entire market. Any smaller firms will have greatly increased costs of production.

Methods for Determining the Minimum Efficient Scale   What is the shape of the *LRAC* curve for different firms and industries, and what is the minimum efficient scale of operation? Researchers have obtained empirical estimates of long-run costs through the following techniques:

- Surveys of expert opinion (engineering estimates)
- Statistical cost estimation
- The survivor approach

Surveying expert opinion is a time-consuming process that relies on the judgments of those individuals closely connected with different industries. Reporting biases may obviously occur with this approach. With statistical cost estimation, researchers attempt to estimate the relationship between unit costs and output levels of firms of varying sizes *while holding constant all other factors influencing cost in addition to size.* This is usually done with multiple regression analysis in a manner similar to that for demand estimation (Chapter 4). With the survivor approach, the size distribution of firms is examined to determine the scale of operation at which most firms in the industry are concentrated. The underlying assumption is that this scale of operation is most efficient and has the lowest costs because this is where most firms have survived. Each of these approaches has its strengths and limitations.[60]

Most of this research has shown that *LRAC* curves typically look like the curve in Figure 6.4 rather than that in Figure 6.2. The curve in Figure 6.4 resembles the *B* curve in Figure 6.3. Economies of scale for many firms occur over a modest range of output, and then the *LRAC* curve becomes essentially flat, with neither further economies nor diseconomies in the relevant range of the market.

Empirical Estimates of the Minimum Efficient Scale   In general, research evidence shows that the minimum efficient scale for most industries is small relative to entire demand in the U.S. market and that the gradient of the *LRAC* curve—how quickly costs change as output increases—is not steep. When transportation costs are taken into account, these results are modified somewhat, as these costs lead to geographic markets that are considerably smaller than the national measures.[61]

---

[60]Scherer and Ross, 111–18; Shepherd, 179–85.
[61]Scherer and Ross, 117.

FIGURE 6.4
**Empirical Long-Run Average Cost
(LRAC) Curve**
*This figure shows the typical shape
for a firm's LRAC curve based on
empirical data.*

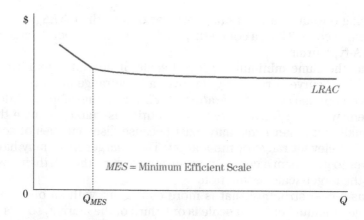

For the beer industry, there is a fairly large decrease in the long-run average cost curve up to a plant with a capacity of 4.0 million barrels per year, with smaller cost decreases up to a plant with an annual capacity of 12 million barrels. Survivor analysis has shown a decline in breweries with a capacity of less than 2 million barrels and a large increase in plants with a capacity of more than 5 million barrels. The 18 plants of Anheuser-Busch and Miller in 1998 had an average capacity slightly exceeding 8.6 million barrels.[62] In the 1970s, technological change occurred in the beer industry that favored large-scale firms and drove many small firms from the market. The *MES* was 1 million barrels during most of the 1960s, but this increased to 8 million in 1970, 16 million in 1980 and 1990, and 18 million in 2000. Between 1950 and 1991, no firms entered the industry, while 344 of 369 firms exited.[63] Even as this trend was occurring, there was a concurrent development of small microbreweries serving local markets. The number of breweries with 10,000- to 15,000-barrel capacity increased from around 50 in 1986 to more than 175 in 1998. However, the share of the market of all microbreweries was estimated to be only 0.16 percent in 1990.[64]

Widely cited empirical evidence on multiplant economies of scale that pertain to the entire firm, although dated, suggests that scale factors alone do not explain the large-scale production that exists in many sectors of the economy.[65] The cost gradient for multiplant economies is only slight to moderate for most industries. In beer brewing, petroleum refining, and refrigerators, the actual scale of operation appears to be driven by economies of scale. However, in fabric weaving, steel, and storage batteries, the average market share far exceeds the minimum necessary to achieve multiplant economies of scale.

More recent research indicates that aggregate concentration, or the share of private-sector economic activity attributed to the largest 100, 500, and 1,000 companies, declined during the 1980s and early 1990s, but increased again in the late 1990s.[66] Moderately large firms appear to have increased in relative importance, given the greater influence of sunk costs, such as advertising and promotion, to be spread over the output produced. Firm size also tended to increase due to the

---

[62]Kenneth G. Elzinga, "The Beer Industry," in *The Structure of American Industry*, ed. James W. Brock, 12th ed. (Upper Saddle River, NJ: Prentice Hall, 2009), 128–54.

[63]Joe R. Kerkvliet, William Nebesky, Carol Horton Tremblay, and Victor J. Tremblay, "Efficiency and Technological Change in the U.S. Brewing Industry," *Journal of Productivity Analysis* 10 (1998): 271–88; Victor J. Tremblay and Carol Horton Tremblay, *The U.S. Brewing Industry* (Cambridge, MA: The MIT Press, 2005), 30–34.

[64]Elzinga, 138–140; Kerkvliet et al., 271–88.

[65]Scherer and Ross, 140.

[66]This discussion is based on Lawrence J. White, "Trends in Aggregate Concentration in the United States," *Journal of Economic Perspectives* 16 (Fall 2002): 137–60.

rising importance of exports for the U.S. economy and the scale needed to compete abroad. Improved monitoring and managing technologies may have stimulated the growth of middle-range firms, but these technologies also allowed firms to monitor their partners in alliances and joint ventures more effectively, eliminating the need for extremely large-scale companies.

Long-Run Average Cost and Managerial Decision Making

In June 1999, Toyota Motor Corporation announced that it was planning to expand its North American capacity through either a new production line or a new factory in response to strong demand in the U.S. market for sport-utility vehicles.[67] This decision was driven by the strength of the American economy and the demand for Toyota automobiles at that time, which was much stronger than expected. The company, which had an annual production capacity in North America of approximately 1.2 million vehicles, sold 1.37 million vehicles in the United States and 130,000 vehicles in Canada in 1998. The company president stated, "We can't sit around and wait another five years to build new facilities." Industry analysts argued that it would be cheaper for Toyota to build a second line at an existing plant than to build an entirely new plant. They also noted that if the automobile demand driven by the strong economy was not sustained, the expansion decision could result in an excess supply of sport-utility vehicles. This example shows that cost factors are part of a manager's long-run strategic decision to expand capacity. Overall strategy depends on how well a manager relates production and cost decisions to changes in consumer demand.

Economies of scale can influence the production of services as well as goods. There has been much controversy over this issue in the hospital industry, particularly given the changes in the health care system over the past two decades. Early statistical studies found that economies of scale existed up to a hospital size of around 500 beds.[68] However, these studies may not have adequately controlled for the multiproduct nature of hospitals and for the possible lack of incentives for cost minimization discussed previously. Survivor analysis has indicated that from 1970 to 1996, the percentage of hospitals with under 100 beds decreased, while the percentage with 100 to 400 beds increased. It now appears that the minimum point of the long-run average cost curve for short-term community hospitals is reached at around 200 beds and that the cost curve is probably shallow. This means that hospitals of many different sizes can compete with each other. Some hospital administrators may be able to develop positions in niche or specialized markets that allow them to remain profitable even if they are not of optimal size.

Summary

In this chapter, we discussed the long-run decisions that managers must make regarding strategies to minimize the costs of production. We saw how issues were more complex in the long run than in the short run, given that the scale of operation is also variable in this time frame. Managers need to consider whether the current scale of operation is optimal, given estimates of long-run demand and market size. Costs may be decreased by changing the combination of inputs used in the

[67]Norihiko Shirouzu, "Toyota Plans an Expansion of Capacity Due to Demand," *Wall Street Journal*, June 29, 1999.
[68]This discussion is based on Santerre and Neun, 384–87.

production process, changing the entire scale of operation, or making decisions to produce in other countries where productivity may be higher or costs are lower.

The empirical evidence on economies of scale showed that the long-run average cost curve tends to be relatively flat for many firms when looking at both single-plant and multiplant operations. This means that there is no single optimal size firm in these industries in terms of minimizing the unit costs of production. We may expect to see firms of many different sizes in these industries. A manager's choice of firm size may be influenced by cost considerations, but it also depends on many other factors. We pull these factors together in our discussion of the four basic types of market structure—perfect competition, monopolistic competition, oligopoly, and monopoly (Chapters 7, 8, and 9).

Appendix 6A Isoquant Analysis

Economists have developed a model of long-run production decisions that incorporates output, the technology of production, and the prices and quantities of the inputs. We will use this model to illustrate input substitution, cost minimization, the derivation of short- and long-run cost curves, and technological change.[69]

Production Technology and Input Substitution

We begin our analysis with the long-run production function shown in Equation 6.A1:[70]

6.A1 $Q = f(L, K)$

where

Q = quantity of output

L = amount of the labor input (variable)

K = amount of the capital input (variable)

Both inputs are variable in this production function and can be changed when different levels of output are produced or substituted for each other in the production of a given level of output. We illustrate this input substitution with an *isoquant*, a theoretical construct based on the technology of production that shows alternative combinations of inputs a manager can use to produce a given level of output. *Isoquant* means equal quantity because any point on the curve represents the same amount of output. There are a whole series of isoquants for a given production process, with isoquants farther from the origin representing larger amounts of output.

Figure 6.A1 shows two typical production isoquants. Isoquant Q_1 shows the various combinations of labor and capital that can be used to produce output level Q_1. This level of output could be produced with a capital-intensive process at point A (L_1 amount of labor and K_1 amount of capital) or with a more labor-intensive process at point B (L_2 amount of labor and K_2 amount of capital). Based on the

---

[69]You will notice many similarities between the isoquant model in this appendix and the economic model of consumer choice (Chapter 3).

[70]This is the same function as Equation 6.1 in the text.

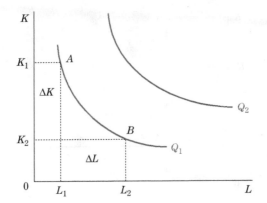

FIGURE 6.A1
A Production Isoquant
*An isoquant represents production
technology by showing the marginal
rate of technical substitution or
the rate at which one input can
be substituted for another while
maintaining the same level of output.*

technology embodied in the production function, either combination of inputs is feasible to use to produce output level Q_1. Point A involves more capital and less labor, while point B uses more labor and less capital. Thus, the two points illustrate input substitution in the production process.

Isoquant Q_2 shows alternative combinations of labor and capital that can be used to produce output level Q_2, where Q_2 is greater than Q_1. There are other isoquants (not pictured) farther from the origin that show even larger levels of output.

The shape of the isoquants shows the degree of input substitution that is possible in any production process. Comparing point B with point A on isoquant Q_1 in Figure 6.A1, we see that if the amount of capital is reduced from K_1 to K_2, or ΔK, the amount of labor must be increased from L_1 to L_2, or ΔL, to produce the same level of output, Q_1. The ratio, $\Delta K/\Delta L$, is called the *marginal rate of technical substitution* of labor for capital ($MRTS_{KL}$). It shows the rate at which one input can be substituted for another while still producing the same amount of output.

If this ratio is shown for very small changes in labor and capital, it is represented by the slope of a line tangent to the isoquant at different points on the curve. The isoquant in Figure 6.A1 exhibits a diminishing marginal rate of technical substitution, as the slope of a tangent to the isoquant at point B is flatter than the slope of the tangent at point A. Figure 6.A1 shows a production process in which the inputs are imperfect substitutes for each other because the marginal rate of technical substitution depends on the amounts of the inputs used.

There are two polar cases for the shapes of isoquants, shown in Figures 6.A2 and 6.A3. Figure 6.A2 illustrates the case where the two inputs are perfect substitutes for each other. There is a given marginal rate of technical substitution between the inputs that does not depend on the combination of inputs used. Thus, the isoquant is a straight line with a constant slope. In Figure 6.A3, the two inputs

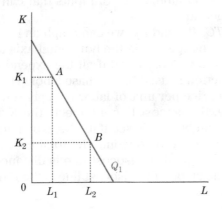

FIGURE 6.A2
Perfect Substitutes
*The inputs in this production function
are perfect substitutes for one
another.*

FIGURE 6.A3

Perfect Complements (Fixed Proportions)

The inputs in this production function can be used only in fixed proportions.

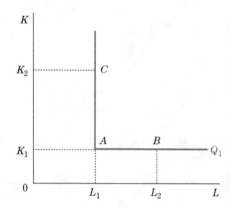

are perfect complements with each other. This isoquant is often called a fixed-proportions production function. It implies that there is only one combination of inputs (L_1, K_1, at point A) that can be used to produce output level Q_1 and that the inputs have to be used in this proportion. No input substitution is possible because moving along the isoquant in either direction (from point A to point B or from point A to point C) involves the greater use of one input and no smaller amount of the other input.

The Isocost Line

To show how a firm would minimize the costs of producing a given output level, we need the *isocost line*, which presents alternative combinations of inputs that result in a given total cost of production with a given set of input prices. Equation 6.A2 represents a given isocost (equal cost) line:

6.A2 $TC = P_L L + P_K K$

where

TC = total cost of production

P_L = price per unit of labor

L = quantity of labor input

P_K = price per unit of capital

K = quantity of capital input

Equation 6.A2 shows that the expenditure on the labor input (price per unit times quantity of labor) and on the capital input (price per unit times quantity of capital) equals a given expenditure on inputs, or the total cost of production. Thus, an isocost line shows alternative combinations of inputs that can be purchased with a given total cost of pro duction.

With a given value of TC, P_L, and P_K, we can graph an isocost line, as shown in Figure 6.A4. The isocost line intersects the horizontal axis at the maximum level of labor input (L_1) that can be purchased if all the expenditure representing the given total cost of production is used to purchase labor. The total cost of production (TC) divided by the price per unit of labor (P_L) gives this maximum amount of labor input. Likewise, the isocost line intersects the K-axis at the maximum level of capital (K_1) that can be purchased if all the expenditure is on capital. This amount of capital is determined by dividing the total cost (TC) by the price per unit of capital (P_K). The slope of the isocost line is distance $0K_1/0L_1 = (TC/P_K)/(TC/P_L) = P_L/P_K$. Thus, the slope of the isocost line is the ratio of the prices of the two inputs of production.

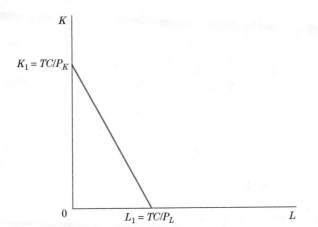

FIGURE 6.A4

The Isocost Line

The isocost line shows alternative combinations of the inputs (L, K) that can be purchased for a given total cost (TC) and with given input prices (P$_L$, P$_K$).

We illustrate a change in the total cost of production, holding input prices constant, in Figure 6.A5. Because the slope of the isocost line is the ratio of the prices of the two inputs of production and because prices are being held constant, a change in the total cost of production is represented by a parallel shift of the isocost line. If the total cost of production increases from TC_1 to TC_2, the isocost line shifts out from ISC_1 to ISC_2, as shown in Figure 6.A5. For a higher total cost of production, the firm can purchase more of both inputs, more of one input and no less of the other, or less of one input and a great amount more of the other.

We illustrate a decrease in the price of labor, holding constant the price of capital and the total cost of production, in Figure 6.A6. The isocost line swivels out, pivoting on the K-axis. Because the price of capital has not changed, the maximum quantity of K that can be purchased does not change either. However, the price of labor has decreased, so labor has become cheaper relative to capital. Isocost line ISC_2 has a flatter slope because the slope of the isocost line is the ratio of the prices of the two inputs, which has changed.

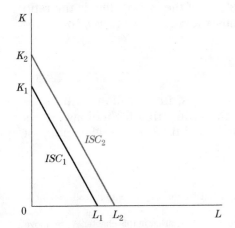

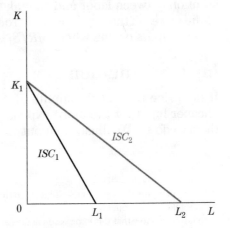

FIGURE 6.A5

Change (Increase) in the Total Cost of Production (Input Prices Constant)

An increase in the total cost of production, with input prices constant, is represented by a parallel outward shift of the isocost line.

FIGURE 6.A6

Change (Decrease) in the Price of Labor (All Else Constant)

A decrease in the price of labor, all else constant, is represented by an outward swiveling of the isocost line.

FIGURE 6.A7

Cost Minimization

The cost-minimizing combination of inputs (L_1, K_1) *is represented by point A, the tangency between the isoquant and the isocost line where the marginal rate of technical substitution equals the ratio of the input prices.*

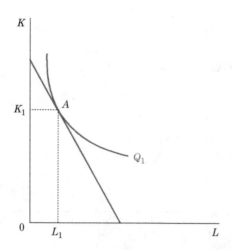

Cost Minimization

We now use isoquants and isocost lines to illustrate in Figure 6.A7 the combination of inputs that minimizes the cost of producing a given level of output. In Figure 6.A7, if managers have decided to produce output level Q_1, they must still determine what combination of inputs to use, as any point on Q_1 represents a feasible combination of inputs. Given the prices of the inputs of production whose ratio is reflected in the slope of the isocost line, the solution to this problem is to find the isocost line closest to the origin that is just tangent to the given isoquant, Q_1. This point of tangency occurs in Figure 6.A7 at point A, representing L_1 amount of labor input and K_1 amount of capital. Any other point on the isoquant represents a higher total cost of production, as these points lie on isocost lines farther from the origin. Any other point on the given isocost line represents a combination of labor and capital that is not sufficient to product output level Q_1. Thus, the combination of labor and capital at points A, L_1, and K_1 represents the cost-minimizing combination of inputs that can be used to produce output level Q_1.[71]

At this point of tangency (point A), the slope of the isoquant is equal to the slope of the isocost line. The slope of the isoquant is the marginal rate of technical substitution between labor and capital, while the slope of the isocost line is the ratio of the prices of the two inputs of production. Thus, the *cost-minimizing combination of inputs* occurs where $MRTS_{LK} = (P_L/P_K)$.[72]

Input Substitution

If the price ratio of the inputs of production changes, firms will substitute the cheaper input for the more expensive input if the production technology allows them to do so. We illustrate input substitution in Figure 6.A8. The original point of

---

[71]Point A in Figure 6.A7 is also the solution to the problem of maximizing the level of output produced for a given total cost of production.

[72]We now can show that this expression is the same rule that we presented earlier in this chapter. As we move along isoquant Q_1 in Figure 6.A1, the change in output is represented by the following equation: $\Delta Q = (MP_L)(\Delta L) + (MP_K)(\Delta K)$, where MP is the marginal product of each input. The change in the amount of output is a function of changes in the quantities of both inputs and their respective marginal productivity. Because the change in output along a given isoquant is zero by definition, the expression becomes $0 = (MP_L)(\Delta L) + (MP_K)(\Delta K)$. Rearranging terms, $-(MP_L)(\Delta L) = (MP_K)(\Delta K)$ and $(MP_L)/(MP_K) = -(\Delta K)/(\Delta L)$. The right side of the last equation is the $MRTS_{LK}$. Therefore, the cost-minimizing equation above in the text shows that $MRTS_{LK} = (MP_L)/(MP_K) = (P_L/P_K)$. Rearranging terms again gives the expression in footnote 6: $(MP_L/P_L) = (MP_K/P_K)$.

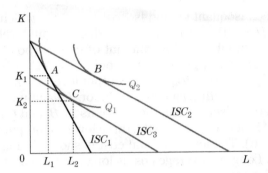

FIGURE 6.A8
Input Substitution
To minimize the costs of production, firms will substitute a cheaper input, labor, for a more expensive input, capital, when the price of labor decreases.

cost minimization to produce output level Q_1 is point A, with L_1 amount of labor and K_1 amount of capital. This point results from the tangency of isoquant Q_1 and isocost line ISC_1. If the price of labor decreases, the isocost line swivels from ISC_1 to ISC_2. This change means that, for the same total cost of production, the firm is now able to produce output level Q_2 with the combination of inputs represented by point B.

Suppose the firm only wants to produce output level Q_1. Even in this case, it will use more of the cheaper input, labor, and less of the relatively more expensive input, capital. This outcome is shown by point C in Figure 6.A8, the tangency between isocost line ISC_3 and isoquant Q_1. Isocost line ISC_3 is drawn parallel to isocost line ISC_2, so it represents the new lower price of labor inherent in the ISC_2 line. However, line ISC_3 is tangent to isoquant Q_1 and closer to the origin than isocost line ISC_2. Therefore, it now costs less to produce output level Q_1, given the lower price of labor. The firm will produce at point C, using L_2 amount of labor and K_2 amount of capital, instead of point A, with L_1 amount of labor and K_1 amount of capital. Thus, the firm substitutes labor for capital when the price of labor decreases relative to the price of capital.[73]

Changes in the Costs of Production

We now use the isoquant model to illustrate both short- and long-run costs of production, as shown in Figure 6.A9. In this figure, the original level of production is output level Q_1, with the input combination at point A (L_1, K_1). This point represents

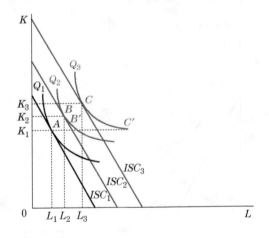

FIGURE 6.A9
Short- and Long-Run Costs of Production
To minimize the costs of production, firms choose a different combination of inputs in the long run, when all inputs are variable (points B and C), than in the short run, when the capital input is fixed (points B' and C').

---

[73]For the fixed-proportions production function of Figure 6.A3, the firm would not be able to substitute labor for capital. The total cost of production would still be reduced, given the decrease in the price of labor, but not as much as it would if input substitution were possible.

the tangency between isoquant Q_1 and isocost line ISC_1, which incorporates total cost of production TC_1. If the firm wants to produce output level Q_2 in the long run, it will use L_2 amount of labor and K_2 amount of capital (point B), as both inputs are variable. The total cost of production at point B is TC_2, which is incorporated in isocost curve ISC_2. Likewise, to produce output level Q_3, the firm in the long run should move to point C, with L_3 amount of labor, K_3 amount of capital, and TC_3 total cost of production (isocost line ISC_3). Points A, B, and C represent the least-cost combination of inputs to produce the three levels of output when all inputs are variable (the long run). The long-run total cost is shown in Figure 6.A9 with each of the isocost lines. Long-run average cost is long-run total cost divided by the corresponding level of output. Long-run marginal cost is the change in long-run total cost divided by the change in output.

Figure 6.A9 also shows the short-run costs of production if the capital input is fixed at level K_1. In the short run with fixed capital, the firm would move from point A to point B' in order to produce output level Q_2 and to point C' in order to produce output level Q_3. Point B' lies on an isocost line farther from the origin than point B (not shown), and point C' lies on an isocost line farther from the origin than point C (not shown). Thus, the cost of production rises faster in the short run when the level of capital is fixed at K_1 than when all inputs are allowed to vary (the long run). We saw earlier in this chapter that short-run average total cost rises more quickly for a given firm than does long-run average cost. This result occurs because the firm is unable to change to the cost-minimizing combination of inputs in the short run, given that some inputs (capital, in this case) are fixed.

Technological Change

Technological change in the production function is illustrated by a shift in the isoquants as in Figure 6.A10. The original point of production of output level Q_1 is at B, with L_2 amount of labor and K_2 amount of capital. Technological change typically increases productivity and decreases the costs of production. In Figure 6.A10, we represent this type of technological change by a shift of the Q_1 isoquant from Q_1 to Q_1'. The Q_1' isoquant is now tangent to an isocost line closer to the origin at point A, representing a lower total cost of production. Thus, productivity has now increased, as the firm is able to produce output level Q_1' using only L_1 amount of labor input and K_1 amount of capital input.

FIGURE 6.A10

Change in Technology

A change in technology is represented by a shifting of an isoquant showing the same level of output.

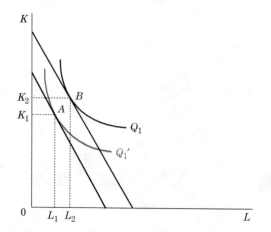

Key Terms

best practices, p. 150

capital-intensive method of
     production, p. 144

diseconomies of scale, p. 153

economies of scale, p. 153

input substitution, p. 144

labor-intensive method of
     production, p. 144

lean production, p. 150

learning by doing, p. 155

long-run average cost
     (*LRAC*), p. 152

long-run production function, p. 144

minimum efficient scale
     (*MES*), p. 156

short-run average total cost (*SATC*),
     p. 152

X-inefficiency, p. 149

Exercises

Technical Questions

1. A company operates plants in both the United States (where capital is relatively cheap and labor is relatively expensive) and Mexico (where labor is relatively cheap and capital is relatively expensive).

   a. Why is it unlikely that the cost-minimizing factor choice will be identical between the two plants? Explain.

   b. Under what circumstances will the input choice be relatively similar?

2. The following graph shows short-run average total cost (*SATC*) curves for three different scales of production. If these are the only plant sizes possible for this firm, what will the firm's long-run average cost curve be?

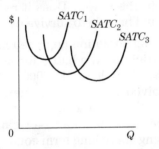

3. Industry studies often suggest that firms may have long-run average cost curves that show some output range over which there are economies of scale and a wide range of output over which long-run average cost is constant; finally, at very high output, there are diseconomies of scale.

   a. Draw a representative long-run average cost curve, and indicate the minimum efficient scale.

   b. Would you expect that firms in an industry like this would all produce about the same level of output? Why?

4. Each of the following statements describes a market structure. What would you expect the long-run average cost curve to look like for a representative firm in each industry? Graph the curve, and indicate the minimum efficient scale (*MES*).

   a. There are a few large firms in the industry.

   b. There are many firms in the industry, each small relative to the size of the market.

5. [Appendix Exercise] For each of the following technologies, graph a representative set of isoquants:

   a. Every worker requires exactly one machine to work with; no substitution is possible.

   b. Capital and labor are perfect substitutes.

   c. The firm is able to substitute capital for labor, but they are not perfect substitutes.

6. [Appendix Exercise] A firm pays $10 per unit of labor and $5 per unit of capital.

   a. Graph the isocost curves for *TC* = $100, *TC* = $200, and *TC* = $500.

   b. Suppose that the cost of capital increases to $10. Graph the new isocost curves.

7. [Appendix Exercise] The following graph shows the firm's cost-minimizing input choice at current factor prices.

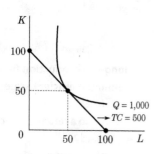

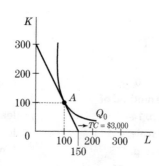

a. What are the current prices of capital and labor, based on the graph?

b. Suppose that the price of labor increases. If the firm wishes to continue to produce the current level of output, how will the firm's optimal input choice change (relative to its current choice)? Support your answer with a graph.

8. [Appendix Exercise] The following graph shows the firm's cost-minimizing input choice at current factor prices. The firm is currently employing 100 units of capital and 100 units of labor. The wage rate is $20, and the price per unit of capital is $10.

a. In the short run, the firm cannot change its level of capital. The price of labor rises to $25. If the firm wishes to continue to produce the current level of output, show the firm's short-run cost-minimizing input choice.

b. What will happen to the firm's short-run cost curves?

c. How will the firm's cost-minimizing input choice be different in the long run, when all factors of production are variable? Support your answer with a graph.

Application Questions

1. Discuss how the examples in the opening case show how the choices facing a firm making a long-run decision on plant location are much greater than those for a firm with a plant already in operation. Why is the long run considered to be a planning horizon?

2. In the current business news media, find and discuss two other examples of input substitution.

3. The following graph shows economies of scale in the beer brewing industry.[74]

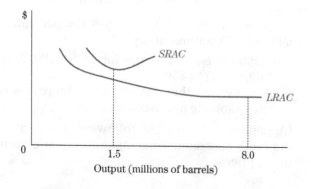

Output (millions of barrels)

a. What does this graph tell us about the nature of economies of scale in the beer brewing industry?

b. What are the particular problems associated with the firm represented by the SATC curve shown in the graph? Does it represent a firm that would be able to survive over time?

4. The following quotation appeared in a *Wall Street Journal* article on the battle for market share in the automobile industry in 2000: "The huge fixed costs involved in developing new vehicles and running big auto factories means auto makers feel compelled to maintain—or expand—market share. Losing share long term could mean shutting down factories, or running factories at unprofitable rates." Do these statements support economic theory and show that economies of scale do not benefit a firm if the output level is small? Explain.

5. A 1964 study of the broiler chicken processing industry showed that "processing costs decreased continually with output size, but after

---

[74]Elzinga, 95.

10 million birds per year the decrease was small." Researchers concluded from the study that "an output of 10 million birds per year, representing 0.33 percent of 1969 broiler production, captured most of the efficiencies." A more recent study concluded that "a technically efficient and cost-effective processing plant should process 8,400 birds per hour. Expanding this processing rate to an annual production volume results in an estimated *MES* [minimum efficient scale] value of 0.4 percent of the market."[75] Do these results show that competition among a large number of plants and firms in the broiler chicken industry is possible? Explain.

[75]Richard T. Rogers, "Broilers," in *Industry Studies*, ed. Larry L. Duetsch, 2nd ed. (Armonk, NY: Sharpe, 1998), 83.

7 Market Structure: Perfect Competition

n this chapter, we begin our discussion of market structure, or the environment in which firms operate. This discussion integrates demand and pricing material with production and cost issues (Chapters 3, 4, 5, and 6).

You have learned that there are four major forms of market structure: perfect competition, monopolistic competition, oligopoly, and monopoly. The perfectly competitive firm has no market power because it cannot influence the price of the product. On the other end of the spectrum is the monopoly firm that has market power because it can use price and other strategies to earn larger profits that typically persist over longer periods of time. Between these two benchmarks are the market structures of monopolistic competition and oligopoly. Firms have varying degrees of market power in these market structures that combine elements of both competitive and monopoly behavior.

Managers are always trying to devise strategies that will help their firms gain and maintain market power. If, and how, they can do this depends on the type of market structure in which their firms operate.

We begin this chapter with a case study that describes the operation of the potato industry, an industry that contains the essential elements of the model of perfect competition. We discuss reactions of different potato farmers to changes in industry prices, attempts by potato farmers to coordinate the amount of potatoes they produce, and legal challenges to this coordinated activity. We also describe how changes in tastes and preferences and government regulations have influenced the demand for potatoes and the fortunes of the industry. We then discuss the model of perfect competition in depth. We end the chapter with a discussion of managerial strategies in several additional highly competitive industries that shows how firms in all of these industries attempt to shield themselves from the volatility of the competitive market.

Case for Analysis

Competition and Cooperative Behavior in the Potato Industry

In 1996 there was a major increase in the supply of fresh potatoes, which drove potato prices from $8 per 100 pounds in 1995 to between $1.50 and $2 per 100 pounds in 1996, a price that was one-third the cost of production. Based on the substantial profits they had earned with their 1995 crops, farmers increased production in 1996, resulting in a 48.8-billion-pound crop, the largest in U.S. history.[1]

This was typical behavior in the potato industry where individual potato farmers let the market determine the price they obtained for their crops. High prices caused farmers to overproduce, which drove prices down below the costs of production for many farmers, making the industry unprofitable. Each farmer typically tried to gain market share under the assumption that other farmers would have a small crop due to weather, frosts, pests, or some other natural disaster. If growing conditions turned out favorable, the increased supply of potatoes pushed prices down, causing financial hardship.

Idaho farmers had some competitive advantage in the markets for bagged potatoes in supermarkets and for baked potatoes in restaurants. Their potatoes often sold for a premium price of $2 or more per 100 pounds as a result of brand name recognition. Thus, Idaho producers gained some market power in these segments by turning an undifferentiated product into an identifiable brand.[2]

In September 2004, Idaho potato farmers formed a cooperative, United Potato Farmers of America, to help manage supply in the potato industry to keep prices high and increase profits.[3] The group expanded nationally and recruited farmers from California, Oregon, Wisconsin, Colorado, Washington, and Texas. In 2005 United Potato helped take 6.8 million hundred-pound potato sacks off the U.S. and Canadian markets, which helped increase open-market returns 48.5 percent from the previous year. Each year United Potato's board of directors would meet before planting season to decide whether farmers were on track to overproduce and to set a target for acreage reduction based on reports from the field and input from analysts. The cooperative was successful in its first years of operation. However, some growers expressed concern about whether the cooperative could maintain its control over supply and whether most of the benefits of the organization flowed only to Idaho producers. Potato growers serve different customers. French fry producers typically have contracts with food companies that set production levels and prices, whereas many other farmers sell their product on the open market.

United Potato argued that its behavior was legal under the Capper-Volstead Act that exempted farmers from federal antitrust laws and permitted them to share prices and control supply. However, in 2010 plaintiffs representing consumers who bought fresh or processed potatoes filed suit against United Potato and other cooperatives charging that they violated the Capper-Volstead Act by operating as a price-fixing trade group rather than a legitimate cooperative.[4] The plaintiffs wanted compensatory and punitive damages, court costs, and a court order for defendants to surrender profits that resulted from their illegal conduct. In December 2011, a federal judge denied a motion to dismiss the antitrust conspiracy claims even though the cooperatives continued to argue that their behavior was permissible under the Capper-Volstead Act. The court issued an advisory opinion that the Capper-Volstead Act permitted concerted action after production but not coordinated action that reduced acreage for planting before production.

There have also been changes in the demand for potatoes that have caused problems for potato farmers. The U.S. Department of Agriculture reported that, after a decade of phenomenal growth, U.S. consumption of french fries was expected to decrease 1 percent in the fiscal year ending June 30, 2002.[5] Most of this decrease was anticipated to result from slower expansion of the fast-food industry due to market saturation and increased numbers of outlets, such as Subway restaurants, that do not sell french fries.

U.S. exports of fries have also slowed, given a saturated Japanese market and the difficulties U.S. firms face in entering the Chinese market. The U.S. Department of Agriculture has also developed a fry made from a rice flour mixture that absorbs 30 percent less oil when cooked and could become a substantial competitor to the traditional french fry in the future. Although the french-fry industry has fought back by introducing new

---

[1]Stephen Stuebner, "Anxious Days in Potatoland: Competitive Forces Threaten to Knock Idaho from Top," *New York Times*, April 12, 1997.

[2]Stuebner, "Anxious Days in Potatoland."

[3]Timothy W. Martin, "This Spud's Not for You," *Wall Street Journal (Online)*, September 26, 2006.

[4]Brad Carlson, "Federal Lawsuit Alleges Potato Price-Fixing: Idaho Federal District Court Hears Round of Claims to Dismiss," *The Idaho Business Review (Online)*, June 20, 2011; Gregory E. Heltzer and Nicole Castle, "Potato Price-Fixing Case Survives Motion to Dismiss Holds That Pre-Production Agricultural Output Restrictions Are Not Exempt Under Capper-Volstead," *Antitrust Alert*, December 8, 2011.

[5]This discussion is based on Jill Carroll and Shirley Leung, "U.S. Consumption of French Fries Is Sliding As Diners Opt for Healthy," *Wall Street Journal*, February 20, 2002.

products, including blue, chocolate, and cinnamon-and-sugar french fries, there are still severe consequences for potato producers from the decreased fry consumption.

Potato farmers and potato prices have also been affected by changes in consumers' eating habits, including the popularity of the low-carbohydrate Atkins diet. It has been estimated that consumption of fresh potatoes per head is 40 percent below the level of 40 years ago because Americans do less cooking at home.[6] In 2011, a Harvard nutrition study concluded that a four-year weight gain among the survey participants was most strongly associated with potato chips, followed by potatoes, sugared drinks, unprocessed red meats, and processed meats. Industry spokesmen indicated that this study might have an impact similar to that of the Atkins diet.[7]

There was also a controversy in 2011 when the U.S. Department of Agriculture (USDA) proposed to eliminate white potatoes from federally subsidized school breakfasts and to limit them sharply at lunch.[8] In response, the National Potato Council urged the entire potato industry to mobilize. After intense lobbying, the U.S. Senate in the November 2011 agricultural funding bill added language blocking the USDA from limiting potatoes and gave the agency flexibility to regulate the preparation of potatoes in its final version of school nutrition guidelines. Members of the potato industry and their Congressional supporters were still concerned that the potato was being slighted compared with other vegetables.

---

[6]"United States: Pass the Spuds: The Potato Industry," *The Economist* 378 (March 25, 2006): 62.
[7]Brad Carlson, "Idaho Potato Industry Hit by Harvard Nutrition Study," *The Idaho Business Review (Online)*, July 1, 2011.

[8]Jennifer Levitz and Betsy McKay, "Spuds, on the Verge of Being Expelled, Start a Food Fight in the Cafeteria," *Wall Street Journal (Online)*, May 17, 2011; Jen Lynds, "Lawmakers, Industry Decry 'Backdoor Approach' to Limiting Potatoes in Schools," *Bangor Daily News (Online)*, January 26, 2012.

The Model of Perfect Competition

The description of the potato industry in the chapter's opening case shows that this industry closely approximates a perfectly competitive industry. The actual model of perfect competition is hypothetical. Although no industry meets all the characteristics described here, the industries discussed in this chapter come close on many of them.

Characteristics of the Model of Perfect Competition

Perfect competition
A market structure characterized by a large number of firms in the market, an undifferentiated product, ease of entry into the market, and complete information available to all market participants.

As shown in Table 7.1, **perfect competition** is a market structure characterized by

1. A large number of firms in the market
2. An undifferentiated product
3. Ease of entry into the market or no barriers to entry
4. Complete information available to all market participants

In perfect competition, we distinguish between the behavior of an individual firm and the outcomes for the entire market or industry. The opening case discussed both the production decisions of individual farmers and the outcomes for the entire potato industry. The model of perfect competition is characterized by having so many firms in the industry that no single firm has any influence on the price of the product. Farmers make their own independent planting decisions and take the price that is established in the market by the overall forces of demand and supply. Because each farmer's individual output is small relative to the entire market, individual producers are **price-takers** who cannot influence the price of the product.

Price-taker
A characteristic of a perfectly competitive market in which the firm cannot influence the price of its product, but can sell any amount of its output at the price established by the market.

In a perfectly competitive market, products are undifferentiated. This market characteristic means that consumers do not care about the identity of the specific supplier of the product they purchase. Their purchase decision is based on price. In the potato industry, this characteristic holds in the french-fry market, where processors do not differentiate among the suppliers of potatoes except in terms of transportation costs. The case noted that this

TABLE 7.1   Market Structure

CHARACTERISTIC	PERFECT COMPETITION	MONOPOLISTIC COMPETITION	OLIGOPOLY	MONOPOLY
Number of firms competing with each other	Large number	Large number	Small number	Single firm
Nature of the product	Undifferentiated	Differentiated	Undifferentiated or differentiated	Unique differentiated product with no close substitutes
Entry into the market	No barriers to entry	Few barriers to entry	Many barriers to entry	Many barriers to entry, often including legal restrictions
Availability of information to market participants	Complete information available	Relatively good information available	Information likely to be protected by patents, copyrights, and trade secrets	Information likely to be protected by patents, copyrights, and trade secrets
Firm's control over price	None	Some	Some, but limited by interdependent behavior	Substantial

characteristic does not hold in the markets for restaurant baked potatoes and bagged potatoes, where the Idaho brand name carries a premium price.

The third characteristic of the perfectly competitive model is that entry into the industry by other firms is costless or that there are no barriers to entry. This characteristic is reasonably accurate in the potato industry, as the number of producers has increased around the world to satisfy the demands of french-fry processing plants in different countries.

The final characteristic of the perfectly competitive model is that complete information is available to all market participants. This means that all participants know which firms are earning the greatest profits and how they are doing so. Although this issue is not explicitly discussed in the opening case, it appears that information on the technology of growing potatoes is widespread and can be easily transferred around the world. Individual farmers typically have a good understanding of the costs of production and the relationship between prices and costs in the industry.

Model of the Industry or Market and the Firm

Let's examine the impact of these characteristics in the model of the perfectly competitive industry or market in Figure 7.1a and the individual firm in Figure 7.1b. Figure 7.1a presents the model of demand and supply that we have introduced (Chapter 2). The industry or market demand curve is a downward sloping demand curve showing the relationship between price and quantity demanded by the consumers in the market, holding all other factors constant. The industry supply curve shows the relationship between the price of the good and the quantity producers are willing to supply, all else held constant.

We now add a description of the individual firm in perfect competition to this model (see Figure 7.1b). Note first that the demand curve facing the individual firm is horizontal. The individual firm in perfect competition is a price-taker. It takes

FIGURE 7.1
The Model of Perfect Competition
The perfectly competitive firm takes the equilibrium price set by the market and maximizes profit by producing where price, which also equals marginal revenue, is equal to marginal cost. The level of profit earned depends on the relationship between price and average total cost.

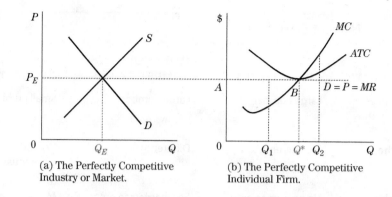

(a) The Perfectly Competitive Industry or Market.

(b) The Perfectly Competitive Individual Firm.

the price established in the market and must then decide what quantity of output to produce. Because the firm cannot affect the price of the product, it faces a perfectly or infinitely elastic demand curve for its product.

Determining the Profit-Maximizing Level of Output How much output will this individual firm want to produce? The answer to that question depends on the goal of the firm, which we assume is **profit maximization**, or earning the largest amount of profit possible. Our definition of profit is given in Equation 7.1.

Profit maximization
The assumed goal of firms, which is to develop strategies to earn the largest amount of profit possible. This can be accomplished by focusing on revenues or costs or both factors.

7.1 $\pi = TR - TC$

where
π = profit
TR = total revenue
TC = total cost

Profit is the difference between the total revenue the firm receives from selling its output and the total cost of producing that output. Because both total revenue and total cost vary with the level of output produced, profit also varies with output. Given the goal of profit maximization, the firm will find and produce that level of output at which profit is the maximum.[9]

To do so, the firm should follow the **profit-maximizing rule**, given in Equation 7.2.

Profit-maximizing rule
To maximize profits, a firm should produce the level of output where marginal revenue equals marginal cost.

7.2 Produce that level of output where $MR = MC$

where
MR = marginal revenue = $\Delta TR / \Delta Q$
MC = marginal cost = $\Delta TC / \Delta Q$

---

[9]Various organizations may pursue other goals. Niskanen (1971) proposed the goal of budget maximization for government bureaucracies. In this environment, managers receive rewards for the size of the bureaucracies they control, even if some employees are redundant. Newhouse (1970) and Weisbrod (1988) also proposed alternative goals for nonprofit organizations. Even profit-maximizing firms may not always choose the levels of inputs and output that maximize profits in the short run. There may also be the principal-agent problem where profit maximization might be the goal of a firm's shareholders but not necessarily of the managers or agents they hire to run the firm. See William A. Niskanen, *Bureaucracy and Representative Government* (Chicago: Aldine-Atherton, 1971); Joseph Newhouse, "Toward a Theory of Nonprofit Institutions: An Economic Model of a Hospital," *American Economic Review* 60 (March 1970): 64–74; Burton A. Weisbrod, *The Nonprofit Economy* (Cambridge, MA: Harvard University Press, 1988); and Paul Milgrom and John Roberts, *Economics, Organization, and Management* (Englewood Cliffs, NJ: Prentice-Hall, 1992).

Marginal revenue is the additional revenue earned by selling an additional unit of output, while marginal cost is the additional cost of producing an additional unit of output. If a firm produces the level of output at which marginal revenue equals marginal cost, it will earn a larger profit than by producing any other amount of output.

Although we can derive this rule mathematically,[10] Figure 7.1b presents an intuitive explanation for why output level Q^*, where marginal revenue equals marginal cost, maximizes profit for the perfectly competitive firm. In Figure 7.1b, we have drawn a short-run marginal cost curve, which has a long upward sloping portion due to the law of diminishing returns in production.

We have discussed the relationship between demand and marginal revenue for a firm facing a downward sloping demand curve (Chapter 3). The demand curve showing price was always greater than marginal revenue for all positive levels of output. However, the perfectly competitive firm faces a horizontal or perfectly elastic demand curve. In this case, *and only in this case*, the demand curve, which shows the price of the product, is also the firm's marginal revenue curve.

Price equals **marginal revenue for the perfectly competitive firm** because the firm cannot lower the price to sell more units of output, given that it cannot influence price in the market. If the price of the product is $20, the firm can sell the first unit of output at $20. The marginal revenue, or the additional revenue that the firm takes in from selling this first unit of output, is $20. The firm can then sell the next unit of output at $20, given the price-taking characteristic of perfect competition. Total revenue from selling two units of output is $40. The marginal revenue from selling the second unit of output is $40 – $20 or $20. Therefore, the marginal revenue the firm receives from selling the second unit is the same as that received from selling the first unit and is equal to the product price. This relationship holds for all units of output.

An intuitive argument for why the firm's profit-maximizing level of output (Q^* in Figure 7.1b) occurs where marginal revenue equals marginal cost is that producing any other level of output will result in a smaller profit. To understand this argument, let's examine output levels both larger and smaller than Q^*. Consider output level Q_2 in Figure 7.1b, where $MR < MC$. At this level of output, the additional revenue that the firm takes in is less than the additional cost of producing that unit. Thus, the firm could not be maximizing profits if it produced that unit of output. This same argument holds not only for output Q_2, but also for all units of output greater than Q^*. Now look at output Q_1. At this level of output, $MR > MC$. The firm makes a profit by producing and selling this unit because the additional revenue it receives is greater than the additional cost of producing the unit. However, if the firm stopped producing at output Q_1, it would forgo all the profit it could earn on the units of output between Q_1 and Q^*. Thus, stopping production at Q_1 or at any unit of output to the left of Q^* would not maximize the firm's profits. Therefore, Q^* has to be the profit-maximizing unit of output where the firm earns the greatest amount of profit possible.[11]

---

[10]Given $TR(Q)$ and $TC(Q)$,

$$\pi = TR(Q) - TC(Q)$$
$$d\pi/dQ = dTR/dQ - dTC/dQ = 0$$
$$dTR/dQ = dTC/dQ \text{ or } MR = MC$$

Differentiating the profit function with respect to output and setting the result equal to zero gives maximum profit, which occurs where marginal revenue equals marginal cost.

[11]A graph of profit versus output would resemble a hill where profit starts low, increases and reaches a maximum, and then decreases. The equality of marginal revenue and marginal cost gives the level of output (Q^* in Figure 7.1b) at which the top of the hill is located. One qualification is that the equality of marginal revenue and marginal cost must be achieved where marginal cost is upward sloping. Profit would be minimized if marginal revenue equaled marginal cost on the downward sloping portion of the marginal cost curve. In certain situations the profit-maximizing level of output may be the loss-minimizing level of output. If market conditions are so unfavorable that a firm is not able to earn a positive profit at any level of output, the level of output where marginal revenue equals marginal cost will be the level where the firm minimizes its losses. If it produced any other level of output, it would suffer greater losses.

Determining the Amount of Profit Earned   The next question we examine is what amount of profit the firm in Figure 7.1b will earn if it produces output level Q^*. Although producing where marginal revenue equals marginal cost tells us that the firm is maximizing its profits, this equality does not tell us the amount of profit earned. To know whether profits are positive, negative, or zero, we need to examine the relationship either between total revenue and total cost or between price and average total cost. This relationship is shown in Table 7.2.

If you know total revenue and total cost at the current level of output, you can quickly calculate the amount of profit earned. If you have total revenue and total cost function graphs showing how these variables change with the level of output produced, you can find the profit-maximizing level of output, where there is the greatest distance between the two curves, and calculate the profit at that point.[12]

Table 7.2 shows an alternative method of calculating profit that will be very useful in our market models. We can substitute $(P)(Q)$ for total revenue and $(ATC)(Q)$ for total cost in Table 7.2. Rearranging terms gives the expression $(P-ATC)(Q)$ for profit. Therefore, if we know, either numerically or graphically, the relationship between product price and the average total cost of production, we know whether profit is positive, negative, or zero.

We can see that the firm in Figure 7.1b is earning zero profit because it is producing the level of output Q^*, where the product price just equals the average total cost of production. Graphically, the product price is distance $0A$ and the product quantity is distance $0Q^*$, so total revenue (which equals price times quantity) is the area $0ABQ^*$. Average total cost is the distance Q^*B (which equals $0A$) and quantity is the distance $0Q^*$, so total cost (which equals average total cost times quantity) is also the area $0ABQ^*$. Therefore, total revenue equals total cost, and profits are zero.

The Shutdown Point for the Perfectly Competitive Firm   We show the zero profit point for the perfectly competitive firm again in Figure 7.2 as output level Q_2, where price P_2 equals average total cost. Suppose the price in the market falls to P_1. The goal of profit maximization means that the firm will now produce output Q_1 because that is the output level where the new price (P_1), which is equivalent to marginal revenue (MR_1), equals marginal cost. However, price P_1 is below

---

TABLE 7.2   Calculation of Profit

$$\pi = TR - TC$$
$$\pi = (P)(Q) - (ATC)(Q)$$
$$\pi = (P - ATC)(Q)$$
If $P > ATC, \pi > 0$
If $P < ATC, \pi < 0$
If $P = ATC, \pi = 0$

---

[12]In mathematical terms, profit is maximized at the output level where the slope of the total revenue curve (marginal revenue) equals the slope of the total cost curve (marginal cost). This is the level of output where there is the greatest distance between the two curves. Examining the values of total revenue and total cost gives you the amount of profit at that output level.

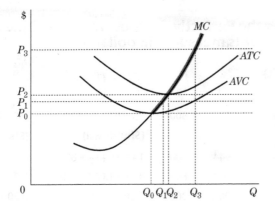

FIGURE 7.2
The Supply Curve for the
Perfectly Competitive Firm
The perfectly competitive firm
will shut down if the market price
falls below average variable cost.
The supply curve for the perfectly
competitive firm is that portion of its
marginal cost curve above minimum
average variable cost.

the average total cost at output level Q_1. Although the firm is earning negative economic profits or suffering losses by producing output level Q_1, it should continue to produce at this price because it is covering all of its variable costs ($P_1 > AVC$) and some of its fixed costs. Remember that fixed costs are shown as the vertical distance between AVC and ATC. The firm could not continue forever in this situation, as it needs to cover the costs of its fixed input at some point. However, it is rational in this case for managers of the firm to wait and see if the product price will increase.

If the price should fall still further to P_0 ($= MR_0$) and the firm produces output Q_0 (where $MR_0 = MC$), the firm is just covering its average variable cost ($P_0 = AVC$), but it is not covering any of its fixed costs. If the price falls below P_0 and is expected to remain there, managers would be better off shutting the firm down. By shutting down, the firm would lose only its fixed costs. If it continued to operate at a price below P_0, the firm would lose both its fixed costs and some of its variable costs, as price would be less than average variable cost. Thus, P_0, the price that equals the firm's minimum average variable cost, is the **shutdown point for the perfectly competitive firm**.

We illustrate these relationships among prices, costs, and profits for a specific set of cost and revenue functions in Table 7.3, Columns 1–8, where the alternative methods for calculating profit are shown in Columns 9 and 10. Columns 4 and 5 show that the firm is always following the profit-maximizing rule because it is producing where marginal revenue equals marginal cost. For the perfectly competitive firm, marginal revenue also equals price. The zero-profit level of output for the firm is 10 units, where total revenue equals total cost ($1,200) or price equals average total cost ($120). At a price of $204, the firm produces 12 units of output and earns a positive profit of $928.

If the price falls to $60, the firm produces 8 units of output and earns –$544 in profit. This price is less than average total cost ($128), but greater than average variable cost ($28). Thus, the firm is covering some of its fixed costs at this level of output. Total revenue of $480 exceeds total variable cost of $224 ($TC - TFC$), so that $256 is applied to the fixed costs. If the price falls to $24, the firm produces 6 units of output and suffers a loss of $800. This price is exactly equal to the minimum average variable cost, so the firm covers all of its variable costs, but loses the entire fixed cost of $800. If the price falls to $15 and the firm continues to produce, the best it could do would be to produce 5 units of output and suffer a loss of $850. Because this price is below the average variable cost, the firm would be better off shutting down and losing only the $800 of fixed costs. Thus, the actual level of output at a price of $15 would be zero, with a profit equal to –$800.

Shutdown point for the perfectly competitive firm
The price, which equals a firm's minimum average variable cost, below which it is more profitable for the perfectly competitive firm to shut down than to continue to produce.

TABLE 7.3   Numerical Example Illustrating the Perfectly Competitive Firm (Q measured in units; all costs, revenues, and profits measured in dollars)

Q (1)	AVC (2)	ATC (3)	MC (4)	$P = MR$ (5)	$TR = PQ$ (6)	TC (7)	TFC (8)	$\Pi = TR - TC$ (9)	$\Pi = (P - ATC)Q$ (10)
5	25	185	15	15	75	925	800	$75 - 925 = -850$ (Shutdown)	$(15 - 185)5 = -850$ (Shutdown)
6	24	157.33	24	24	144	944	800	$144 - 944 = -800$	$(24 - 157.33)6 = -800$
8	28	128	60	60	480	1,024	800	$480 - 1,024 = -544$	$(60 - 128)8 = -544$
10	40	120	120	120	1,200	1,200	800	$1,200 - 1,200 = 0$	$(120 - 120)10 = 0$
12	60	126.67	204	204	2,448	1,520	800	$2,448 - 1,520 = 928$	$(204 - 126.67)12 = 928$

Source: This example is based on the following cost functions derived and modified from Alpha C. Chiang, *Fundamental Methods of Mathematical Economics*, 3rd ed. (New York: McGraw-Hill, 1984). We have not analyzed specific mathematical cost functions in this text, but we have discussed general cost and revenue functions.

Total fixed cost: $TFC = 800$

Total variable cost: $TVC = Q^3 - 12Q^2 + 60Q$

Total cost: $TC = TFC + TVC = 800 + Q^3 - 12Q^2 + 60Q$

Average fixed cost: $AFC = 800/Q$

Average variable cost: $AVC = Q^2 - 12Q + 60$

Average total cost: $ATC = TC/Q = AFC + AVC = (800/Q) + Q^2 - 12Q + 60$

Marginal cost: $MC = dTC/dQ = 3Q^2 - 24Q + 60$

Supply curve for the perfectly competitive firm
The portion of a firm's marginal cost curve that lies above the minimum average variable cost.

Supply Curve for the Perfectly Competitive Firm Figure 7.2 shows that if the price determined in the market is P_0, the firm will produce output level Q_0 because that is the profit-maximizing level of output where $P = MR = MC$ and $P = AVC$. If the price increases to P_1, the firm will increase its output to Q_1. Similarly, if the price is P_2, the firm will produce output level Q_2, and it will increase output to level Q_3 if the price rises to P_3. This procedure traces the **supply curve for the perfectly competitive firm**. This supply curve, which shows a one-to-one relationship between the product price and the quantity of output the firm is willing to supply, is that portion of the firm's marginal cost curve above the minimum average variable cost. The firm will stop producing if the price falls below the average variable cost. This supply curve is upward sloping because the firm's marginal costs are increasing as the firm reaches the capacity of its fixed inputs.

Supply curve for the perfectly competitive industry
The curve that shows the output produced by all perfectly competitive firms in the industry at different prices.

Supply Curve for the Perfectly Competitive Industry In Figure 7.1a we drew the **supply curve for the perfectly competitive industry** as upward sloping. We can now see the rationale for the shape of this industry curve, given the shape of the firm's supply curve. The industry supply curve shows the quantity of output produced by all firms in the perfectly competitive industry at different prices. Because individual firms produce more output at higher prices, the industry supply curve will also be upward sloping.[13]

The industry supply curve would typically be flatter than the firm's supply curve because it reflects the output produced by all firms in the industry at each price. However, the slope of the industry supply curve could become steeper if the prices of any inputs in production increase as firms produce more output. If any inputs are in limited supply, firms might bid up their prices as they increase output. We typically assume that input prices are constant even with changes in production. Appendix 7.A discusses industry supply in more detail and presents several agricultural examples.

---

[13]This is the short-run supply curve for the perfectly competitive industry, as it assumes that the number of firms in the industry is constant.

The Short Run in Perfect Competition

Figure 7.2 presents the possible short-run outcomes for a firm in a perfectly competitive industry. The short run is a period of time in which the existing firms in the industry cannot change their scale of operation because at least one input is fixed for each firm. Firms also cannot enter or exit the industry during the short run.

The different prices facing the firm in Figure 7.2 are determined by the industry demand and supply curves (Figure 7.1a). Because the firm cannot influence these prices, it produces the profit-maximizing level of output (where $P = MR = MC$) and can earn positive, zero, or negative profit, depending on the relationship between the existing market price and the firm's average total cost. At price P_3, the firm earns positive profit; at price P_2, zero profit; and at prices P_1 and P_0, negative profit. If the price falls below P_0, the firm will consider shutting down.

Long-Run Adjustment in Perfect Competition: Entry and Exit

Both entry and exit by new and existing firms and changes in the scale of operation by all firms can occur in the long run. We analyze each of these factors in turn to illustrate the characteristics of the long-run equilibrium that occurs in perfect competition. Although we describe these two adjustments sequentially, they could also occur simultaneously.

Returning to Figure 7.2, we now argue that the zero-profit point at output level Q_2 and price P_2 represents an equilibrium situation for the firm in perfect competition. This outcome results from the method that economists use (and managers should use) to define costs. As you have learned, costs in economics are defined from the perspective of opportunity cost, which includes both explicit and implicit costs (Chapter 5). The costs measured by the ATC curve in Figure 7.2 include both the explicit costs and any implicit costs of production. Suppose that investors have a choice between investing in this firm and buying a government security paying 8 percent. Managers of the firm would have to pay at least 8 percent to attract financial investors to the firm. This 8 percent rate of return is included in the average total cost curve in Figure 7.2.[14] Thus, the firm in Figure 7.2 is earning a zero economic profit that includes a normal rate of return on the investment in the firm. Resources in this activity are doing as well as if they were invested elsewhere. Therefore, the zero economic profit point is an **equilibrium point for the perfectly competitive firm**.

We illustrate this concept by showing what happens if an equilibrium situation is disturbed in Figures 7.3a and 7.3b. Suppose that some factor causes the industry

Equilibrium point for the perfectly competitive firm The point where price equals average total cost because the firm earns zero economic profit at this point. Economic profit incorporates all implicit costs of production, including a normal rate of return on the firm's investment.

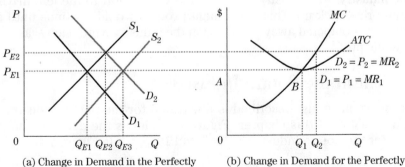

(a) Change in Demand in the Perfectly Competitive Industry or Market.

(b) Change in Demand for the Perfectly Competitive Individual Firm.

FIGURE 7.3

Long-Run Adjustment in Perfect Competition: Entry and Exit

An increase in industry demand will result in a positive economic profit for a perfectly competitive firm. However, this profit will be competed away by the entry of other firms into the market in the long run. The zero economic profit point or the point where price equals average total cost is the equilibrium point for the perfectly competitive firm.

---

[14]Former Coca-Cola CEO Robert Goizueta judged his managers in each operating division on the basis of their economic profit earned (Chapter 5).

demand curve to shift out from D_1 to D_2 in Figure 7.3a. This shift could result from a change in any of the factors held constant in demand curve D_1, including consumer tastes and preferences, consumer income, and the price of goods related in consumption (substitutes and complements). This increase in demand causes the equilibrium price in the market to rise from P_{E1} to P_{E2} and the equilibrium quantity to increase from Q_{E1} to Q_{E2}.

How does the perfectly competitive firm respond to this change in the market? The firm's reaction is shown in Figure 7.3b. Because the firm is a price-taker, it must accept the new equilibrium price and determine the level of output that maximizes profit at this new price. The firm faces a new horizontal demand curve, D_2, where the new price, P_2, equals the new marginal revenue, MR_2. To maximize profits, the firm must produce where MR_2 equals MC, or at output level Q_2. However, at this level of output, the firm is now earning positive economic profits because the price of the product, P_2, is greater than the average total cost of production at output Q_2. Firms in this industry are now doing better than firms in other areas of the economy. Given this situation, firms in other sectors of the economy will enter this industry in pursuit of these positive economic profits. All firms know of the existence of these positive economic profits, given the characteristic of perfect information in the model of perfect competition. Other firms are able to enter the industry, given the characteristic of perfect mobility or no barriers to entry.

Entry by new firms into the industry is shown by a rightward shift of the industry supply curve in Figure 7.3a from S_1 to S_2. As the supply curve shifts along demand curve D_2, the equilibrium price begins to fall. Thus, the price, marginal revenue, and demand line D_2 in Figure 7.3b start to shift down. The profit-maximizing level of output for the firm moves back toward Q_1, and the level of positive economic profit decreases because the price of the product is closer to the average total cost of production.

Entry continues until the industry supply curve has shifted to S_2. At this point, the firm is once again producing Q_1 level of output and earning zero economic profit (Figure 7.3b). Industry output is larger (Q_{E3}) because there are more firms in the industry (Figure 7.3a). However, because firms in the industry are once again earning zero economic profit, there is no incentive for further entry into the industry. Thus, the zero-economic-profit point is an equilibrium position for firms in a perfectly competitive industry.[15]

If, starting at the equilibrium position in Figure 7.3a, there was a decrease in industry demand, the return to equilibrium would occur, but in the opposite direction. The decrease in demand would result in a lower equilibrium price. A lower equilibrium price in the market would cause some firms to exit from the industry because they were earning negative economic profits or suffering losses. As firms exited the industry, the industry supply curve would shift to the left, driving the equilibrium price back up. This adjustment process would continue until all the losses had been competed away and firms in the industry were once again earning zero economic profit.

Adjustment in the Potato Industry

The process we have just described is illustrated for the potato industry in the opening discussion of this chapter. Figure 7.4a shows the demand and supply conditions for the potato industry in 1995 and 1996, while Figure 7.4b shows the

---

[15]Figure 7.3 illustrates the case of a constant-cost industry where the entry of other firms does not affect the cost curves of firms in the industry. If entry increased the demand for inputs, which increased their prices and caused firms' cost curves to shift up, the equality of price and average total cost would occur at a higher level of cost and this would be an increasing-cost industry. If the opposite should happen and costs were lower after entry, this would be a decreasing-cost industry.

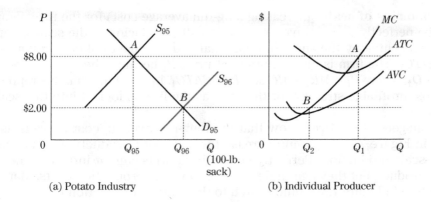

FIGURE 7.4
Adjustment in the Potato Industry
The original equilibrium at point A in Figures 7.4a and 7.4b shows the high price ($8.00 per 100-pound sack) and profits for potato farmers in 1995. In response to these profits, farmers planted more potatoes in 1996, shifting the supply curve from S_{95} to S_{96}. This increase in supply drove the price down to $2.00 per 100-pound sack (point B), less than the average total cost for many producers, leaving farmers with heavy debts.

profitability of individual farmers. The high price of $8.00 per 100-pound sack and the profits earned by individual farmers are shown at point A in both of the figures. In response to these prices and profits, farmers planted more potatoes in 1996, shifting the supply curve from S_{95} to S_{96}. Favorable weather and insect conditions helped increase this supply, which drove the price of potatoes down to $2.00 per 100-pound sack (point B in Figure 7.4a). This price was below the average total cost for many farmers, leaving them with significant debts (point B in Figure 7.4b).

Although not discussed, it is likely that many farmers produced fewer potatoes in 1997, shifting the supply curve to the left and driving price back up toward the zero-economic profit equilibrium, as the competitive model predicts. Further changes in the potato market would result from the subsequent decreased demand for french fries discussed in the case.

Long-Run Adjustment in Perfect Competition: The Optimal Scale of Production

We have just seen how entry and exit in a perfectly competitive industry result in the zero-economic profit equilibrium ($P = ATC$). That discussion focused on the role of entry and exit in response to positive or negative economic profits in achieving equilibrium. However, we illustrated the discussion in terms of a given scale of operation or a given set of short-run cost curves. Firms also must choose their optimal scale of operation. Let's now look at how a competitive market forces managers to choose the most profitable scale of operation for the firm and how entry and exit again result in a zero-economic profit equilibrium.

Figure 7.5 shows a U-shaped long-run average cost curve ($LRAC$). This curve incorporates both **economies of scale** (decreasing long-run average cost) and

Economies of scale
Achieving lower unit costs of production by adopting a larger scale of production, represented by the downward sloping portion of a long-run average cost curve.

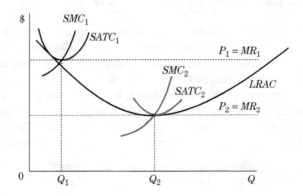

FIGURE 7.5
Long-Run Adjustment in Perfect Competition: The Optimal Scale of Operation
In the long run, the perfectly competitive firm has to choose the optimal scale of operation. This decision, combined with entry and exit, will force price to equal long-run average cost.

Diseconomies of scale
Incurring higher unit costs of production by adopting a larger scale of production, represented by the upward sloping portion of a long-run average cost curve.

diseconomies of scale (increasing long-run average cost) for the firm. Suppose that the perfectly competitive firm is originally producing at the scale of operation represented by the short-run marginal and average total cost curves SMC_1 and $SATC_1$. The firm is in equilibrium at price P_1 because the firm is producing output Q_1, where $P_1 = MR_1 = MC$ and $P_1 = SATC_1$. In the short run, this represents the most profitable strategy for the firm, as the firm is locked into this scale of production.

If managers of the firm know that the long-run average cost curve is as pictured in Figure 7.5, they can decrease their costs of production by moving to larger-scale production. Perfectly competitive firms cannot influence the price of the product, but they can find means of lowering production costs. Managers of the firm in Figure 7.5 should switch to the scale of production represented by the short-run marginal and average total cost curves SMC_2 and $SATC_2$. Price P_1 is significantly above the short-run average total cost represented by $SATC_2$, so that a firm of this size would earn positive economic profits.

Positive economic profits, however, will attract other firms to the industry, and entry will shift the industry supply curve (not pictured in Figure 7.5) to the right, lowering price. These new firms entering the industry will also build plants at the SMC_2 and $SATC_2$ scale of operation, as that size represents the scale of operation that minimizes a firm's costs. This process will continue until all economic profits have been competed away and price equals long-run average cost. Firms will produce at the scale of operation represented by SMC_2 and $SATC_2$ and will earn zero economic profit. This scale is at the minimum point of the long-run average cost curve, so that production costs are minimized. Figure 7.5 combines the two types of adjustments that are made to reach equilibrium ($P = LRAC$) in the long run:

1. The choice of the scale of operation that minimizes costs in the long run
2. Entry by firms, which lowers product price and competes away any positive economic profits

Managerial Rule of Thumb

Competition Means Little Control over Price

Managers in highly or perfectly competitive markets have little or no control over the price of their product. They typically compete on the basis of lowering the costs of production. Perfectly competitive firms will end up earning zero economic profit because entry by other firms will rapidly compete away any excess profit. ■

Other Illustrations of Competitive Markets

Most markets that people encounter on a day-to-day basis are not perfectly or even highly competitive because these markets do not meet the four characteristics discussed earlier in the chapter. We examine the agricultural sector in more detail to show how farming is one of the best examples of a perfectly competitive industry. Using the cases of broiler chickens, red meat, and milk, we then show how industries or sections of industries can become less competitive over time through mergers among producers and increased product differentiation. These factors represent violations of the first two characteristics in the competitive model:

1. A large number of price-taking firms in each industry
2. Production of an undifferentiated product

We then discuss how the trucking industry, although not perfectly competitive, illustrates many of the behaviors and outcomes of an extremely competitive industry.

In this discussion, we introduce the concept of **industry concentration**, which is a measure of how many firms produce the total output of an industry. The more concentrated the industry, the fewer the firms operating in the industry. By definition, a perfectly competitive industry is so unconcentrated that individual firms are price-takers and do not have any market power. We will discuss different measures of industry concentration when we describe the strategies and behaviors of managers in firms with market power.

Industry concentration
A measure of how many firms produce the total output of an industry. The more concentrated the industry, the fewer the firms operating in that industry.

Competition and the Agricultural Industry

Although the number of farms has decreased significantly over the past 70 years, there are still approximately 2 million farms in the United States today.[16] The average farm contains less than 440 acres, but large-scale farms dominate much of the market due to economies of scale. While only 5 percent of all farms contain 1,000 acres or more, these farms cover more than 40 percent of total farm acreage. Today corporate farms operate 12 percent of all U.S. farmland and sell 22 percent of the total value of farm crops.

Although farming has become an increasingly concentrated industry, the perfectly competitive model can still be used to characterize it. The largest 2 or 3 percent of the growers of any particular product are characterized by a large number of independent producers. For example, 2 percent of the largest farms grow half of all the grain in the United States. However, this 2 percent consists of 27,000 farms. In contrast, highly competitive manufacturing industries, such as men's work clothing and cotton-weaving mills, have 300 and 200 firms, respectively. There are nearly 100 times as many independent producers in farming as in most competitive manufacturing industries.

Demand for most farm crops is highly inelastic. People can only eat so much food, most commodities have few good substitutes, and these commodities constitute small shares of the total costs of the processed products to which they are converted. Products are typically grown and brought to market without individual farmers knowing exactly what price they will receive. If, as we discussed in the opening case of this chapter, farmers have responded to previous high prices and there are unusually good growing conditions, there may be large increases in supply, which drive down prices. A decrease in product price with inelastic demand results in a decrease in total revenue for producers because consumers do not increase quantity demanded in proportion to the price decrease.

This outcome results in what has been called the "farm problem" in the United States and most industrialized countries. Prices for farm products are extremely volatile. For example, from 1970 to 2006 the mean annual corn price received by Iowa farmers was $2.23 per bushel, but prices ranged from a low of $1.04 to a high of $3.20. Because farm incomes are subject to extreme changes not under the control of farmers, governments have often implemented farm price support programs and other methods to control production. These programs have caused imbalances between supply and demand in otherwise competitive markets, as support prices are higher than the equilibrium prices in these markets. The lack of control over prices has also led farmers to organize cooperatives, as discussed in the opening case.

---

[16]This discussion is based on Daniel B. Suits, "Agriculture," in *The Structure of American Industry*, eds. Walter Adams and James W. Brock, 11th ed. (Upper Saddle River, NJ: Prentice Hall, 2005), 1–22; Bruce W. Marion and James M. MacDonald, "The Agriculture Industry," in *The Structure of American Industry*, ed. James W. Brock, 12th ed. (Upper Saddle River, NJ: Prentice-Hall, 2009), 1–29.

Competition and the Broiler Chicken Industry

Broiler chickens present an interesting example of an industry that traditionally was unconcentrated and produced a relatively undifferentiated product, but that has changed significantly over time.[17] Broiler processing is a vertically integrated industry with the processors either owning or contracting each stage of the system from the breeder farms through the processing plants to the final products for market. Concentration in the broiler processing industry remained relatively low from 1954 until the mid-1970s. The four largest firms in the industry accounted for only 18 percent of the market over this period. Although this concentration increased throughout the 1980s, so that the four largest firms produced 40 percent of industry output by 1989, concentration in the broiler industry was still less than that found in other food manufacturing industries. Most of the increase in industry concentration during the 1980s resulted from mergers among the leading firms in the industry. Tyson Foods was the leading broiler processor, with a 22 percent market share, followed by Gold Kist and Perdue Farms, each with 8 percent, and ConAgra Poultry, with 6 percent. Many of the smaller broiler processors specialized in various regions of the country.

Integration reduced costs by coordinating production at each stage to avoid overproduction and shortages and by achieving economies of scale to purchase feed, medicine, and equipment at lower prices. In the 1930s, there were approximately 11,000 independent facilities hatching broiler chicks, each with an average capacity of 24,000 eggs. By 2001, the number of hatcheries had declined by 97 percent to only 323, each with an average incubator capacity of 2.7 million eggs. Integration increased quality control and allowed firms to complete the entire production process in one localized area. This change had an important effect on costs, given the high rate of bird death and weight loss during transport. Integration also helped in the diffusion of new technology given that off-farm firms had greater access to capital and credit opportunities that could be used for new investments in genetic research and feed development.[18]

Both real and subjective product differentiation exists among the different broiler processors. Early differentiation focused on differences in product quality, product form, and the level of services provided to the retailer. In the 1970s, Holly Farms was the first processor to develop tray-packed chicken ready for the meat case. Processors today often apply the retailer's own scanner pricing labels before shipment. Skin color became a differentiating characteristic, with Perdue Farms making its yellow color the first theme in its advertising campaign. This was followed by an emphasis on the fat content of the chickens. The amount of advertising in relation to product sales is a measure of product differentiation, as there is no need for individual suppliers to advertise an undifferentiated product in the perfectly competitive model. Broiler chicken advertising gained momentum with Frank Perdue of Perdue Farms, who was used in ads for his own product because he looked and sounded like a chicken. By 1990, the broiler industry was spending over $30 million on advertising, with Perdue Farms accounting for 41.6 percent of the total expenditure. Even with these increases, the advertising–sales ratio for broiler producers was just 0.2 percent in 1992 compared to an average for all food and tobacco industries of 2.0 percent.[19]

---

[17]This discussion is based primarily on Richard T. Rogers, "Broilers: Differentiating a Commodity," in *Industry Studies*, ed. Larry L. Duetsch, 2nd ed. (Armonk, NY: Sharpe, 1998), 65–100.

[18]Elanor Starmer, Aimee Witteman, and Timothy Wise, "Feeding the Factory Farm: Implicit Subsidies to the Broiler Chicken Industry." Medford, MA: Tufts University Global Development and Environmental Institute Working Paper No. 06-03, June 2006.

[19]Food industries with the highest ratios in 1992 included chewing gum (16 percent), breakfast cereals (11 percent), chocolate candy (13 percent), and instant coffee (10 percent). See Rogers, "Broilers," 79–88.

Competition among broiler processors depends on the marketing channel used and the extent of value-added processing involved. Food service and retail food stores are the two major marketing channels. Value-added processing ranges from unbranded fresh whole chickens to breaded nuggets and marinated prime parts. Firms tend to compete within these subcategories and to create barriers to entry in these submarkets. Other market niches are kosher chickens and free-range chickens, grown with fewer antibiotics and hormones. Consumer prices vary by these different subcategories.

We noted above that, for competitive firms, price = marginal revenue = marginal cost for profit maximization and price = average total cost in equilibrium. Analysts often use the **price-cost margin (*PCM*)** from the Census of Manufactures as a proxy for these relationships. As would be expected for a competitive industry, broiler processing has one of the lowest PCMs in the food system. In 1992, the PCM for broilers was 11.9 percent compared with an average of 30 percent for all food and tobacco product classes. For more concentrated and differentiated food industries, the PCM ranged as high as 67.2 percent for breakfast cereals, 56.7 percent for chewing gum, and 49.6 percent for beer.

In 2011, chicken farmers again confronted the issue of reducing supply, given increasing feed costs and weak demand.[20] Yet it appeared that none of the large producers, including Sanderson Farms, Inc., Tyson Foods Inc., and Pilgrim's Price Corp., wanted to be the first to cut back production. Eggs set in incubators, an indicator of future chicken supply, only started to level off. There were still expectations that consumers would switch from beef and pork to chicken, which gave companies an incentive to delay production cuts. Most uncertainty was related to the weather in the corn belt that would influence the price of corn used for chicken feed.

However, as in the opening case on the potato industry, chicken producers' behavior has also been subject to litigation.[21] In October 2011, a federal judge ruled that Pilgrim's Pride Corp. knowingly tried to manipulate chicken prices in 2009 and ordered the company to pay $26 million in damages to poultry growers in Arkansas. The judge concluded that a decision to close a chicken-processing plant in Arkansas was made to influence the price of chicken, and that the company violated the Packers and Stockyards Act of 1921, which prohibited livestock companies from unfair and deceptive practices.

Thus, although the broiler processing industry exhibits many characteristics of a highly competitive industry, there are forces leading toward increased industry concentration and less-competitive behavior. This is to be expected, as most managers want to gain control over their market environment and insulate themselves from the overall supply and demand changes of a competitive market.

Price-cost margin (*PCM*)
The relationship between price and costs for an industry, calculated by subtracting the total payroll and the cost of materials from the value of shipments and then dividing the results by the value of the shipments. The approach ignores taxes, corporate overhead, advertising and marketing, research, and interest expenses.

Competition and the Red-Meat Industry

Managers in the red-meat packing industry have recently followed the same strategies as those in the broiler chicken industry by introducing a campaign to turn what had been an undifferentiated product into one with brand names.[22] Hormel Foods, IBP, and Farmland Industries, along with the meatpacking divisions of

---

[20]Ian Berry, "Chicken Companies Wait in Vain for Industry Cutbacks," *Wall Street Journal (Online)*, May 20, 2011.

[21]Marshall Eckblad, "Pilgrim's Pride Manipulated Chicken Prices, Judge Rules," *Wall Street Journal (Online)*, October 4, 2011.

[22]This discussion is based on Scott Kilman, "Meat Industry Launches Campaign to Turn Products into Brand Names," *Wall Street Journal*, February 20, 2002.

Cargill and ConAgra Foods, now sell prepackaged meat, including steaks, chops, and roasts, under their brand names. According to the National Cattlemen's Beef Association, 474 of these new beef products were introduced in 2001 compared with 70 in 1997. This is an important trend in an industry with $60 billion in annual sales.

Branding represents a major shift in the red-meat industry, which traditionally labeled only its low-end products such as Spam. It also represents a strategy to combat the long-term decline in red-meat consumption in the United States, including the 41 percent decline in beef demand over the past 25 years. Much of this decline is related to health concerns regarding red-meat consumption. With both spouses working in many families, the time needed to cook roast beef is also a factor that has decreased beef demand. Managers in the red-meat industry were forced to develop and invest in new technology to produce roasts and chops that could be microwaved in less than 10 minutes. This involved cooking the beef at low temperatures for up to 12 hours and designing a plastic tough enough to hold the beef and its spices during this cooking process, consumer refrigeration, and microwaving.

Managers also faced the problem of acceptance of this new product by both consumers and retail stores. Hormel targeted women in their twenties, who were the first generation to grow up with microwave ovens and who might have less reluctance than older women to put red meat in the microwave. All producers focused their marketing campaigns on the convenience of the new products, which they contend allow women to prepare a home-cooked meal for a family dinner while having time to relax. The goal of IBP's marketing director, Jack Dunn, has been to "create an irrational loyalty to our product."[23]

While many grocery stores welcomed the Hormel and IBP products, Kroger, the largest chain in the country, developed its own brand of fresh beef, the Cattleman's Collection. Kroger managers followed the product differentiation strategy, but created a brand that consumers could not find elsewhere, which was more profitable for them than selling brands from other companies. All producers used coupons, product demonstrations, and extensive advertising budgets to promote the new products. These actions represent the behavior of managers in firms with market power (Chapter 8). Thus, the strategy of managers in competitive industries is to develop market power by creating brand identities for previously undifferentiated products. This process involves analyzing and changing consumer behavior and developing new technology and production processes.

The red-meat industry has also developed other strategies to influence demand. In 2009, the National Cattlemen's Beef Association launched the MBA (Masters of Beef Advocacy), a course that trained ranchers, feedlot operators, butchers, and chefs how to promote and defend red meat. MBA students listened to six online lectures on beef production and were assigned homework such as writing a pro-beef letter to a local newspaper. There was also in-person training on how to use social media to increase beef consumption.[24]

However, in 2012, there were two major issues that adversely affected the demand in the red-meat industry. The first was a report by the Harvard School of Medicine, which concluded that increased consumption of 3 ounces of red meat each day was associated with a 12 percent greater risk of premature death. Overall, that included a 16 percent greater risk of death due to heart disease and a 10 percent greater risk of death due to cancer. Increased risks from the consumption of processed

[23]Ibid.
[24]Stephanie Simon, "Beef Industry Carves a Course: Cattlemen's Group Promotes Red Meat, Trains Recruits to Win Over Consumers," *Wall Street Journal (Online)*, March 7, 2011.

meat, such as bacon, were even greater.[25] The second was the controversy over the addition of "pink slime," or lean finely textured beef to ground beef.[26] Although this additive had been used for nearly two decades, a huge backlash developed on social media after celebrity chef Jamie Oliver detailed its production on a television show. Most major grocery chains announced they would phase out carrying ground beef that used the filler. Beef Products Inc., a major producer of the additive, closed three plants that made the lean finely textured beef. However, the red-meat industry fought back by arguing that eliminating the filler would result in more cows being slaughtered and in ground beef with more fat. The additive also received support from the U.S. Department of Agriculture and governors of five beef-producing states.

Competition and the Milk Industry

We have noted throughout this chapter that managers in competitive industries form industry or trade associations to promote the overall product, even if the identity of specific producers is not enhanced. This is a strategy to increase industry demand, as illustrated in Figure 7.3a. The milk industry has followed this strategy with its "Got milk?" and milk mustache campaigns.[27] Milk consumption had been decreasing in the early 1990s before the initial "Got milk?" campaign was launched by Dairy Management Inc., representing dairy farmers, and the Milk Processor Education Program, sponsored by commercial milk producers. These organizations, with marketing budgets of $24 million in California and $180 million nationwide, are financed largely by industry members.

A study by the California Milk Processor Board in early 2001 indicated that milk consumption in California had stabilized at the precampaign levels instead of continuing to decrease at 3 percent per year. Nationwide annual milk consumption also increased from 6.35 billion gallons to 6.48 billion gallons from 1995 to 2000. Although this campaign has increased the overall demand for milk, major national brands have yet to develop because milk production and pricing vary and are regulated by geographic region. The milk industry has also had to confront changes in lifestyles that work against it. Fewer people in all age groups are eating dry cereal with milk, and more are purchasing breakfast bars in the morning. In an attempt to stop the declining consumption in the teenage market, milk producers are developing single-serve packages and introducing an increasing variety of milk flavors.

To enter Asian markets, New Zealand's Fonterra, one of the world's largest milk producers, has experimented with exotic flavors such as wheatgrass and the pandan leaf. Asia's $35 billion overall dairy market has been expanding at a rate of 4 percent annually compared with a 2 percent annual increase in the United States. Fonterra also arranged for teaching hospitals in Hong Kong and Malaysia to conduct clinical trials to demonstrate the effect of milk on bone density, and it placed two dozen bone scanners in supermarkets across Asia to show consumers that their bones were not as dense as recommended by health experts.[28] These moves represent the combined strategies of differentiating products and increasing overall demand in an industry that is still highly competitive.

[25]Nicholas Bakalar, "Risks: More Red Meat, More Mortality," *The New York Times (Online)*, March 12, 2012.
[26]Ian Berry, " 'Pink Slime' Fight Hurts Beef Demand, Tyson Says," *Wall Street Journal (Online)*, March 28, 2012; Bill Tomson and Mark Peters, " 'Pink Slime' Defense Rises," *Wall Street Journal (Online)*, March 29, 2012; John Bussey, "Cows: The Innocent Bystanders," *Wall Street Journal (Online)*, April 5, 2012.
[27]Bernard Stamler, "Got Sticking Power?" *New York Times*, July 30, 2001.
[28]Cris Prystay, "Milk Industry's Pitch in Asia: Try the Ginger or Rose Flavor," *Wall Street Journal*, August 9, 2005.

In 2004, the federal Dietary Guidelines Advisory Committee suggested that adults increase their milk consumption from two to three servings per day to "reduce the risk of low bone mass and contribute important amounts of many nutrients." The dairy industry campaigned intensely for this change, launching a "3-A-Day" advertising campaign supported by companies such as Kraft Foods Inc. and warning of a "calcium crisis." The National Dairy Council, funded by the country's dairy farmers, spent $4 to $5 million in 2003 on research concluding that calcium and other nutrients in dairy products had significant health benefits.[29] Political action is, therefore, another way to influence demand for a product.

Milk producers associations continued with these strategies in 2011 and 2012. In November 2011, the National Milk Producers Federation proposed an overhaul of federal dairy policy that the Federation argued would save the government money and would prevent steep declines in the price of milk.[30] The proposed program would force dairy farmers to cut production when milk prices fell toward unprofitable levels, a program similar to those that existed before the 1990s. Although the Federation argued that the program would reduce price volatility, many analysts estimated that consumer prices would rise substantially.

The Milk Processor Education Program announced an updated version of the National Milk Mustache "got milk?" campaign in February 2012.[31] The goal of this initiative, the Breakfast Project, was to promote milk drinking during breakfast and to use Salma Hayek, a bilingual spokesperson, in both English and Spanish advertisements. The project, aimed toward the Hispanic community, would use, "It's not breakfast without milk," as its tagline. Analysts estimated that the average American drank 21.3 gallons of milk in 2000 compared with 20.8 gallons in 2010.

Competition and the Trucking Industry

The trucking industry is another example of a highly, if not perfectly, competitive industry. There are more than 150,000 companies in the truckload segment of the industry, which delivers full trailer loads of freight.[32] Most of these companies operate six or fewer trucks, and many are family-run businesses that make just enough money to cover truck payments and living costs. The large number of trucking firms, each with little market power, means that these firms exhibit the price-taking behavior and face the horizontal demand curve of firms in the model of perfect competition.

As expected in a competitive industry, the changing forces of demand and supply can alter the profitability of trucking companies very quickly. In December 1999, trucking companies increased rates by 5 to 6 percent, given higher fuel prices and a shortage of truck drivers. Demand during this period was strong due to continued economic growth and greater reliance on trucking for freight transportation. However, the push from the cost side, combined with the limited ability to raise prices, meant that profits were still low for many trucking companies.

By the fourth quarter of 2000, trucking companies faced not only continued higher costs, but also adverse weather and an overall slowing in the economy.[33]

[29]Nicholas Zamiska, "How Milk Got a Major Boost by Food Panel," *Wall Street Journal*, August 30, 2004.
[30]Scott Kilman, "Dairy Farmers vs. Consumers," *Wall Street Journal (Online)*, November 25, 2011.
[31]Tanzina Vega, "Two Languages, but a Single Focus on Milk at Meals," *The New York Times (Online)*, February 22, 2012.
[32]Daniel Machalaba, "Trucking Firms Seek Rate Increase as Demand Rises, Fuel Costs Jump," *Wall Street Journal*, December 9, 1999.
[33]This section is based on the following articles: Sonoko Setaishi, "Truckers See Lackluster Results, Hurt by Higher Costs, Flat Rates," *Wall Street Journal*, January 15, 2001; Sonoko Setaishi, "Truckers Face Dismal 1Q Amid Softer Demand, Higher Costs," *Wall Street Journal*, April 5, 2001; Robert Johnson, "Small Trucking Firms Are Folding in Record Numbers Amid Slowdown," *Wall Street Journal*, June 25, 2001.

Snowstorms in the Midwest forced many companies' trucks to sit idle during the winter of 2000–2001. The slowing of consumer spending lowered sales of products that truckers haul. Business inventories began to increase, which made companies reluctant to ship more merchandise. Close to 4,000 trucking companies went out of business in 2000, and approximately 1,100 failed in the first quarter of 2001. As failed trucking companies left the industry, the remaining companies saw prices rise and became somewhat more profitable. Sale prices for used trucks decreased substantially due to the large number of trucking company bankruptcies. These bargains encouraged some truckers to reenter the business. Excess capacity continued to put downward competitive pressure on trucking rates, and rising costs for labor, fuel, and equipment continued to impact the trucking industry in 2006 and 2007. Increasing retirements among the nation's drivers combined with the stressful nature of the job reduced the supply of drivers, causing wages to increase. Diesel fuel costs represent 25 percent of operating costs in the industry resulting in truckers spending $103 billion on 53 billion gallons of fuel in 2006. Demand for hauling services was negatively influenced by the defaults in the subprime mortgage markets. In response, some companies reduced the number of company-owned trucks in their fleets and shifted business to other freight services.[34]

The trucking industry was severely impacted by the economic downturn in 2008 and 2009. More than 3,000 firms with fewer than five power units went bankrupt in 2008. Refrigerated carriers suffered the least because they carried food, but flatbed carriers that relied on the housing industry and commercial construction were impacted the most. The reduced capacity from the recession could allow truckers to raise rates as the economy rebounded in 2010 and 2011. However, drivers' wages, fuel costs, and high truck prices were likely to impact the recovery of the trucking industry.[35]

This discussion of the trucking industry illustrates the forces in the perfectly competitive model discussed in this chapter. Trucking firms have little power over price and are subject to the forces that change industry demand and supply. When demand declines and prices begin to decrease, some firms go out of business as price falls below their average variable costs. After firms exit the industry, prices begin to rise again, and the profitability of the remaining firms improves. Those firms still in the industry move back toward the zero-profit equilibrium point. Some individuals and companies may even see opportunities to earn greater than normal profits, which would cause new entry into the industry. Thus, there is a constant push toward the zero-economic profit equilibrium in a perfectly or highly competitive industry.

Managerial Rule of Thumb

Adopting Strategies to Gain Market Power in Competitive Industries

Managers in highly competitive industries can gain market power by merging with other competitive firms, differentiating products that consumers previously considered to be undifferentiated commodities, and forming producer associations that attempt to change consumer preferences and increase demand for output of the entire industry. ▪

[34]Ian Urbina, "Short on Drivers, Truckers Offer Perks," *New York Times*, February 28, 2006; Daniel P. Bearth, "Trucking Faced Economic, Regulatory Challenges," *Transport Topics*, December 24–31, 2007; Joan Garrett, "The Burden of Diesel Costs," *McClatchy-Tribune Business News*, January 11, 2008.
[35]Dave Willis, "Trucking—The Road to Recovery," *Rough Notes (Online)*, January, 2011; Jonathan Reiskin, "Trucking Is Doing Better Than U.S. Economy: Double-Dip Recession Unlikely, Experts Say," *Transport Topics*, October 24, 2011.

Summary

Perfect competition is a form of market structure in which individual firms have no control over product price, which is established by industry or market demand and supply. In the short run, perfectly competitive firms take the market price and produce the amount of output that maximizes their profits. Profits earned in the short run can be positive, zero, or negative. Perfectly competitive firms are not able to earn positive economic profits in the long run because these profits will be eroded by entry of other firms. Likewise, any losses will be removed by firms leaving the industry. To lower their costs, firms also seek to produce at the optimal scale of operation. However, this scale will be adopted by all firms in the long run, and entry will force prices to equal long-run average cost, the zero-economic profit equilibrium.

Managers of firms in perfectly or highly competitive environments often attempt to gain market power by merging with other firms, differentiating their products, and forming associations to increase the demand for the overall industry output. We discuss these strategies in more detail when we examine firms with market power.

Appendix 7A Industry Supply

Elasticity of Supply

The shape of the industry supply curve reflects the *elasticity of supply* within that industry. The elasticity of supply is a number showing the percentage change in the quantity of output supplied relative to the percentage change in product price. Because the quantity supplied usually increases with price, a supply elasticity is a positive number. As with demand elasticity, a supply elasticity number greater than 1 indicates *elastic supply*. The percentage change in quantity of output supplied is greater than the percentage change in price. *Inelastic supply* occurs when the percentage change in quantity supplied is less than the percentage change in price.[36]

A vertical supply curve represents *perfectly inelastic supply*, where there is a fixed quantity of the product supplied that is not influenced by the product price. In this case, the product price is determined entirely by changes in demand for the product as the demand curve moves up and down along a vertical supply curve. The best example of perfectly inelastic supply would be a painting, such as the Mona Lisa, by a deceased artist. There is only one of these paintings, and the supply will never be increased. The other polar case is *perfectly elastic supply*, illustrated by a horizontal supply curve. In this case, the industry is willing to supply any amount of product at the market price. Supply curves that are approaching being vertical are relatively more inelastic and show a smaller response of quantity supplied to changes in price, while flatter curves indicate a much larger (more elastic) supply response.

---

[36]William G. Tomek and Kenneth L. Robinson, *Agricultural Product Prices*, 3rd ed. (Ithaca, NY: Cornell University Press, 1990), 59–75.

Agricultural Supply Elasticities

Supply curves for various agricultural products are illustrated by an S-shaped curve, as shown in Figure 7.A1.[37] Changes in supply elasticity for a particular farm product are likely to occur at a price that just covers average variable costs or at a price at which the returns from alternative uses of resources are approximately equal. As we discussed earlier in the chapter, a price below the average variable cost means that a farmer will not offer any output for sale. At a price exceeding the average variable cost, supply may be elastic if more land is brought into production. Intermediate-level prices may cause supply elasticity to decrease if no additional land is available for cultivation or if equipment and labor are fully employed, whereas even higher prices may bring these resources into production and increase supply elasticity.

Supply elasticities are typically lower for major crops grown in areas where there are few alternative uses of land, such as dry-land wheat, than for minor crops and poultry products. Supply elasticities can also differ by the stage of production. For broiler chickens, for example, the supply price response is greater for the breeding flock that supplies chicks for the broiler industry than for the production of broilers.

The aggregate supply relationship for all farm output in most countries is very price inelastic in the short run. Resources committed to agriculture tend to remain in use, especially if alternative uses of these resources are limited. The land, labor, and equipment employed in agriculture often have few alternative uses elsewhere. And even with low product prices, farmers may produce other crops rather than seek employment off the farm. From 1929 to 1932, when farm prices fell by 50 percent, the aggregate amount of farm output remained relatively constant. The short-run price elasticity of aggregate farm output in the United States has been estimated to be no larger than 0.15.

The increased specialization in farm equipment and skills has made short-run supply response even more difficult over time. For livestock products, supply changes are limited by the availability of the female stock and the time required to produce a new generation. Time periods up to eight years or more are required for a complete quantity adjustment to changing prices for some tree crops. Crop yields are influenced by the availability of irrigation water, the amount of fertilizer applied, and the pest control programs employed. Irrigation water is, in turn, influenced by pumping costs and water allotment rights. The weather, of course, also has a major influence on agricultural supply. If the weather is unusually wet, farmers may not be able to plant the desired acreage of their most profitable crop and may be forced to plant an alternative crop with a shorter growing season.

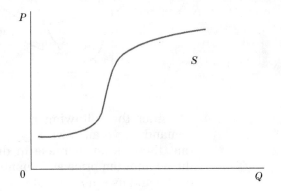

FIGURE 7.A1

Representative Supply Curve for a Farm Product

The elasticity of supply for a farm product will vary with the price of the product.

---

[37]The following discussion is based on Ibid., 59–61.

Key Terms

diseconomies of scale, p. 182

economies of scale, p. 181

equilibrium point for the perfectly
    competitive firm, p. 179

industry concentration, p. 183

marginal revenue for the perfectly
    competitive firm, p. 175

perfect competition, p. 172

price-cost margin (*PCM*), p. 185

price-taker, p. 172

profit maximization, p. 174

profit-maximizing rule, p. 174

shutdown point for the perfectly
    competitive firm, p. 177

supply curve for the perfectly
    competitive firm, p. 178

supply curve for the perfectly
    competitive industry, p. 178

Exercises

Technical Questions

1. For each of the following graphs, identify the firm's profit-maximizing (or loss-minimizing) output. Is each firm making a profit? If not, should the firm continue to produce in the short run?

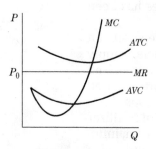

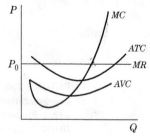

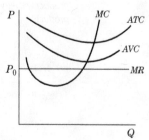

2. Consider a firm in a perfectly competitive industry. The firm has just built a plant that cost $15,000. Each unit of output requires $5 worth of materials. Each worker costs $3 per hour.

   a. Based on the information above, fill in the table on the following page.
   b. If the market price is $12.50, how many units of output will the firm produce?
   c. At that price, what is the firm's profit or loss? Will the firm continue to produce in the short run? Carefully explain your answer.
   d. Graph your results.

3. The following graph shows the cost curves for a perfectly competitive firm. Identify the shutdown point, the breakeven point, and the firm's short-run supply curve.

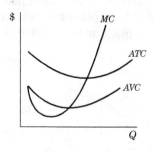

4. Consider the following graph, which shows a demand curve and two supply curves. Suppose that there is an increase in demand. Compare the equilibrium price and quantity change in both cases, and use those results to explain what you can infer about the elasticity of supply.

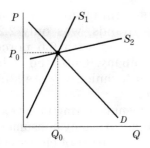

5. Draw graphs showing a perfectly competitive firm and industry in long-run equilibrium.

   a. How do you know that the industry is in long-run equilibrium?

   b. Suppose that there is an increase in demand for this product. Show and explain the short-run adjustment process for both the firm and the industry.

   c. Show and explain the long-run adjustment process for both the firm and the industry. What will happen to the number of firms in the new long-run equilibrium?

6. Draw graphs showing a perfectly competitive firm and industry in long-run equilibrium.

   a. Suppose that there is a decrease in demand for this product. Show and explain the short-run

   adjustment process for both the firm and the industry.

   b. Show and explain the long-run adjustment process for both the firm and the industry. What will happen to the number of firms in the new long-run equilibrium?

7. The following graph shows the long-run average cost curve for a firm in a perfectly competitive industry. Draw a set of *short-run* cost curves consistent with output Q_E and use them to explain

   a. Why the only output that a competitive firm will produce in the long run is Q_E

   b. Why it will be a profit-maximizing decision to produce more than Q_E in the short run if the price exceeds P_E

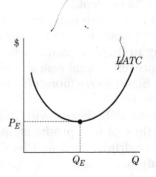

Number of Worker Hours	Output (Q)	Total Fixed Cost (TFC)	Total Variable Cost (TVC)	Total Cost (TC)	Marginal Cost (MC)	Average Variable Cost (AVC)	Average Total Cost (ATC)
0	0				—	—	—
25	100						
50	150						
75	175						
100	195						
125	205						
150	210						
175	212						

Application Questions

1. Discuss how the facts in the opening case study and the subsequent discussion of the potato industry illustrate the lack of control over prices by individual potato producers in a competitive market, the response to high prices predicted by the model of perfect competition, and the attempts by producers in a competitive market to gain control over price. Check recent business publications to find out how successful the United Potato Growers of America cooperative has been since the time of this chapter's case study.

2. Discuss the shifts in demand and supply and the impact on prices and the profitability of individual producers that occurred in the cranberry industry in 2006 and 2007 resulting from the following facts:[38]

   a. Cranberries are no longer relegated to a Thanksgiving side dish. They can now be found in more than 2,000 products from muffin mix to soap.

   b. Cranberries prefer cold winters and plenty of rain. So last year's unusually warm winter and a summer drought in many parts of the United States and Canada hurt the crop now being harvested. However, one producer says that although his crop is down 30 percent this year, the higher prices will result in a profit decline of only 10–15 percent.

   c. Research has shown that cranberries help prevent urinary tract infections. More studies are underway to help determine whether cranberries can prevent dental plaque and tooth decay and help blood move more effectively through blood vessels.

   d. Ocean Spray and other growers have unleashed a steady flow of new products, including new low-calorie drinks such as Diet Ocean Spray. The company has also introduced a line of "Grower's Reserve" 100 percent natural juices, including a "Super Antioxidant" variety with blueberry, pomegranate, and cranberry juices.

3. The following facts characterize the furniture industry in the United States:[39]

   a. The industry has been very fragmented, so that few companies have the financial backing to make heavy investments in new technology and equipment.

   b. In 1998, only three U.S. furniture manufacturers had annual sales exceeding $1 billion. These firms accounted for only 20 percent of the market share, with the remainder split among 1,000 other manufacturers.

   c. Capital spending at one manufacturer, Furniture Brands, was only 2.2 percent of sales compared with 6.6 percent at Ford Motor Company. Outdated, labor-intensive production techniques were still being used by many firms.

   d. Furniture manufacturing involves a huge number of options to satisfy consumer preferences, but this extensive set of choices slows production and raises costs.

   e. Small competitors can enter the industry because large manufacturers have not built up any overwhelming advantage in efficiency.

   f. The American Furniture Manufacturers Association has prepared a public relations campaign to "encourage consumers to part with more of their disposable income on furniture."

   g. In fall 2003, a group of 28 U.S. furniture manufacturers asked the U.S. government to impose antidumping trade duties on Chinese-made bedroom furniture, alleging unfair pricing.

   h. The globalization of the furniture industry since the 1980s has resulted from technological innovations, governmental implementation of economic development strategies and regulatory regimes that favor global investment and trade, and the emergence of furniture manufacturers and retailers with a capacity to develop global production and distribution networks. The development of global production networks using Chinese subcontractors has accelerated globalization in recent years.

   Discuss how these facts are consistent with the model of perfect competition.

4. Evaluate the following statement:
   In the short run, information about a perfectly competitive firm's fixed costs is needed to determine *both* the profit-maximizing level of output and the amount of profit earned when producing that level of output.

---

[38]Joseph Pereira and Betsy McKay, "Bounty of the Bog Gets Pricier," *Wall Street Journal*, November 21, 2007.

[39]James R. Hagerty and Robert Berner, "Ever Wondered Why Furniture Shopping Can Be Such a Pain?" *Wall Street Journal*, November 2, 1998; Dan Morse, "U.S. Furniture Makers Seek Tariffs on Chinese Imports," *Wall Street Journal*, November 3, 2003; and Mark H. Drayse, "Globalization and Regional Change in the U.S. Furniture Industry," *Growth and Change* 39 (June 2008): 252–82.

5. In a perfectly competitive industry, the market price is $25. A firm is currently producing 10,000 units of output, its average total cost is $28, its marginal cost is $20, and its average variable cost is $20. Given these facts, explain whether the following statements are true or false:

a. The firm is currently producing at the minimum average variable cost.

b. The firm should produce more output to maximize its profit.

c. Average total cost will be less than $28 at the level of output that maximizes the firm's profit.

Hint: You should assume normal U-shaped cost curves for this problem.

8

Market Structure: Monopoly and Monopolistic Competition

I n this chapter, we contrast perfectly and highly competitive markets with the market structures of monopoly and monopolistic competition. These markets, along with oligopoly markets, are called *imperfectly competitive markets* or *imperfect competition.* We show how managers of firms in these markets have varying degrees of *market power,* or the ability to influence product prices and develop other competitive strategies that enable their firms to earn positive economic profits. The degree of a firm's market power is related to the *barriers to entry* in a given market—the structural, legal, or regulatory characteristics of a firm and its market that keep other firms from producing the same or similar products at the same cost.

We begin this chapter with the case of Eastman Kodak Co., and we describe how the changing markets for cameras and film eroded the once-substantial market power of this well-known company. After discussing the case, we present the monopoly model and illustrate the differences between this model and the perfectly competitive model. We then describe the major sources and measures of market power, illustrating the strategies that managers use to maintain and increase market power in several different industries. We also discuss basic antitrust policies that the federal government employs to control market power and promote competition, and we illustrate how market power tends to disappear in the monopolistically competitive market structure.

Case for Analysis

Changing Market Power for Eastman Kodak Co.

Eastman Kodak Co., one of the most well-known and once-successful companies in the United States, filed for bankruptcy in January 2012.[1] This was a substantial change in direction for a company that once dominated its industry and had a near-monopoly on camera film, which earned it profits that it paid out to workers on "wage dividend days." The company invented the digital camera in 1975, but then did not develop the new technology. In the film market, Kodak lost market share to foreign companies in the 1980s and stopped making investments in film in 2003.[2]

Discussion of a possible Kodak bankruptcy appeared in the media in fall 2011.[3] After considering chemicals, bathroom cleaners, and medical testing devices in the 1980s and 1990s, the company struggled to rebuild its operations around commercial and consumer printing to offset the decline in film and photography gear sales. In August 2011, it began attempting to sell its portfolio of 1,100 digital patents to increase its cash position. Many potential buyers, however, were uncertain about buying patents from a company that might face bankruptcy. Kodak also sued companies such as Apple Inc. and HTC Corp. for patent infringement, alleging that these companies violated Kodak patents regarding the transmission of photos from mobile phones and tablets and image previewing by digital cameras. Kodak announced that it raised $3 billion between 2003 and 2010 from suits for patent infringement and

licensing deals that settled these cases. However, the company alleged that Apple and HTC Corp. took advantage of its weakened financial condition to drag out litigation over the patent violations. A large burden of retiree benefits, the weak economy since 2008, and moves by vendors to cut relationships with the company also contributed to the bankruptcy filing.

In early 2012 it was not clear whether the company would be able to emerge from bankruptcy in better financial condition and ready to survive in the consumer and commercial inkjet printing market dominated by rivals such as Hewlett-Packard Co. Kodak had to subsidize sales to build the market for its ink, and its workforce decreased from 64,000 in 2003 to 17,000 in 2011. In February 2012, the company announced that it would stop production of digital cameras, pocket video cameras, and digital picture frames, instead licensing its brand to other manufacturers.[4] This strategy removed the company from the camera business, which it had pursued since George Eastman introduced the first Kodak camera in 1888. The company's U.S. market share in digital cameras decreased from 16.6 percent in 2008 to 11.6 percent in 2011. The company had sustained the digital camera business because it helped win shelf space for its consumer inkjet printers. However, by early 2012 Kodak's goal was to build its consumer business around online and retail-based photo kiosks, desktop inkjet printing, and camera accessories and batteries.

[1]Mike Spector, Dana Mattioli, and Peg Brickley, "Can Bankruptcy Filing Save Kodak?" *Wall Street Journal (Online)*, January 20, 2012.

[2]Mike Spector and Dana Mattioli, "Kodak Teeters on the Brink," *Wall Street Journal (Online)*, January 5, 2012.

[3]The following discussion is based on Dana Mattioli, "Squeeze Tightens on Kodak," *Wall Street Journal (Online)*, November 4, 2011; Dana Mattioli and Mike Spector, "Kodaks Rescue Plans Hit Hurdles," *Wall Street Journal (Online)*, December 19, 2011; and Dana Mattioli, "Kodak Sues Apple, HTC, and Realigns," *Wall Street Journal (Online)*, January 10, 2012.

[4]Dana Mattioli, "Kokak Shutters Camera Business," *Wall Street Journal (Online)*, February 10, 2012.

Firms with Market Power

Market power
The ability of a firm to influence the prices of its products and develop other competitive strategies that enable it to earn large profits over longer periods of time.

The opening case illustrates how one firm, Eastman Kodak Co., gained **market power** by developing the camera business for the general public and controlling the production of film, only to see this power eroded by failing to keep up with new technology and market changes. Firms attempt to gain market power through their pricing strategies, cost reduction, and new product development. However, this market power can decrease over time as market conditions fluctuate and the strategies of competitors evolve. We discuss numerous strategies that firms use to gain and preserve market power after we present the monopoly model and contrast it with the model of perfect competition.

The Monopoly Model

Monopoly
A market structure characterized by a single firm producing a product with no close substitutes.

The *industry* or market demand curve in perfect competition is the standard downward sloping demand curve even though the perfectly competitive *firm* faces a horizontal demand curve. If we begin with our definition of a **monopoly** as a market structure characterized by a single firm producing a product with no close substitutes, we can see that a monopolist faces a downward sloping demand curve because the single firm produces the entire output of the industry. More generally, we argue that any firm in imperfect competition faces a downward sloping demand curve for its product. Firms in imperfect competition are therefore *not* price-takers; if managers want to sell more output, they must lower the price of their product. Raising the price means they will sell less output. Thus, firms in imperfect competition are **price-setters**. Managers of these firms must set the optimal price, which we define as the price that maximizes the firm's profits. This price depends on the firm's demand, marginal revenue, and marginal cost curves, but may also be determined through markup pricing methods.

Price-setter
A firm in imperfect competition that faces a downward sloping demand curve and must set the profit-maximizing price to charge for its product.

Figures 8.1a and 8.1b present the monopoly model. In these figures, the monopolist faces a downward sloping demand curve. A linear downward sloping demand curve has a marginal revenue (MR) curve that intersects the vertical axis at the same point as the demand curve and has a slope that is twice as steep as the demand curve. In Figures 8.1a and 8.1b, we have also included a marginal cost (MC) and average total cost (ATC) curve.

Given that the goal of the firm is to maximize profit, the firm in Figures 8.1a and 8.1b will produce output level Q_M where marginal revenue equals marginal cost. This is the standard rule for profit maximization from the model of perfect competition (Chapter 7). The difference here is that the marginal revenue curve is downward sloping and separate from the demand curve. The price (P_M) that the

FIGURE 8.1A
The Monopoly Model with Positive Economic Profit
The monopolist maximizes profits by producing where marginal revenue equals marginal cost and typically earns positive economic profit due to barriers to entry.

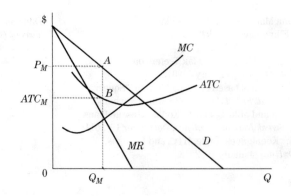

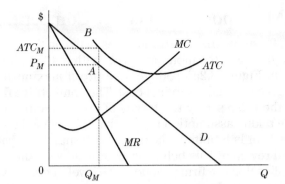

FIGURE 8.1B
The Monopoly Model with Negative Economic Profit or Losses
The monopolist could suffer losses if average total cost is greater than price at the profit-maximizing level of output.

monopolist can charge for output Q_M is read directly off the demand curve above that output level. As you may recall, a demand curve shows the price at which a given quantity is demanded, as well as the quantity demanded at any given price. We can see in Figures 8.1a and 8.1b that this price-quantity combination is the optimal combination for the firm, as there is no other price at which marginal revenue equals marginal cost.

We next examine whether the firm in Figure 8.1a is earning positive, negative, or zero economic profit. To do so, we look at the relationship between price and average total cost. As shown in Figure 8.1a, this firm is earning positive economic profit because price is greater than average total cost at output level Q_M. Total revenue is represented by the area $0P_MAQ_M$, while total cost equals the area $0(ATC_M)BQ_M$. Thus, economic profit is the area of the rectangle $P_MAB(ATC_M)$.

In the competitive model, we argued that positive economic profits would disappear through the entry of other firms into the industry, which would lower the product price until it was again equal to average total cost (Chapter 7). This outcome is less likely to happen in the monopoly model or for firms with market power due to the existence of barriers to entry that prevent other firms from producing the same or similar products at the same cost.

A monopolist does not necessarily earn an economic profit. If the average total cost curve is located above the demand curve, the firm earns negative economic profit or suffers losses, as in Figure 8.1b. Total revenue (area $0P_MAQ_M$) is now less than total cost (area $0(ATC_M)BQ_M$), so the loss to the firm is measured by the area $((ATC_M)BAP_M)$. If price is less than average variable cost, this firm can minimize its losses by shutting down for the same reasons as in the case of perfect competition. Given the existence of barriers to entry, these outcomes are less likely for the monopoly firm, but can still occur, as we discuss below.

The monopoly firm in Figures 8.1a and 8.1b does not have a supply curve. A supply curve is associated with the price-taking behavior of a firm in perfect competition (Chapters 2, 7). For a firm with market power, a demand shift will cause the profit-maximizing output and price to change because the marginal revenue curve shifts. If the costs of production change such that the marginal cost curve shifts, there will also be a different profit-maximizing level of output and price. Thus, unlike the perfectly competitive market, there is no one-to-one relationship between price and quantity supplied for any firm with market power.

We can also see in Figures 8.1a and 8.1b that product price P_M is greater than the marginal cost of production at the profit-maximizing level of output for the monopoly (Q_M). This outcome represents another difference with the perfectly competitive firm that produces where product price equals marginal cost. This inequality of price and marginal cost forms the basis for one of the measures of market power we'll discuss later in the chapter.

Comparing Monopoly and Perfect Competition

Figures 8.2a and 8.2b summarize the differences between the outcomes for the perfectly competitive *firm* and the monopoly *firm* with market power.[5] The perfectly competitive firm in Figure 8.2a produces the profit-maximizing level of output where marginal revenue equals marginal cost. The competitive firm is a price-taker that responds to the price set by the forces of demand and supply in the overall market. This price-taking assumption means that the demand curve facing the perfectly competitive firm is infinitely elastic or horizontal and that the price equals the firm's marginal revenue. This behavior, combined with the goal of profit maximization, also implies that the firm produces the level of output where price equals marginal cost and that the firm's supply curve is the upward sloping portion of its marginal cost curve above minimum average variable cost.

In long-run equilibrium, perfectly competitive firms produce where price equals average total cost and earn zero economic profit, given that any positive or negative profits will be competed away by entry into and exit from the market. In perfect competition, the equality of price and average total cost also occurs at the minimum point of the average total cost curve. Thus, firms are producing at the lowest point on their average total cost curve and, due to the forces of entry and exit, are charging consumers a price just equal to that average total cost. Managers of perfectly competitive firms would like to earn positive economic profits, but they are unable to do so in this market environment.

The monopoly firm in Figure 8.2b also produces where marginal revenue equals marginal cost, given the goal of profit maximization. However, this firm must set the optimal price, which depends on its demand and cost conditions. The firm with market power will produce a level of output at which price is greater than marginal cost, given the downward sloping demand and marginal revenue curves. Firms with market power typically produce where price is greater than average total cost and earn positive economic profit. However, the amount of this profit and how long it exists depend on the strength of the barriers to entry in this market.

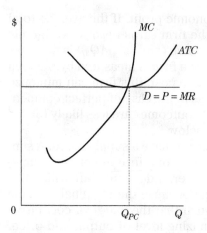

FIGURE 8.2A
The Perfectly Competitive Firm
At Q_{PC}:
MR = MC
  P = ATC
  P = MC
Minimum Point of ATC *Curve*
Price-Taker
Firm Has Supply Curve

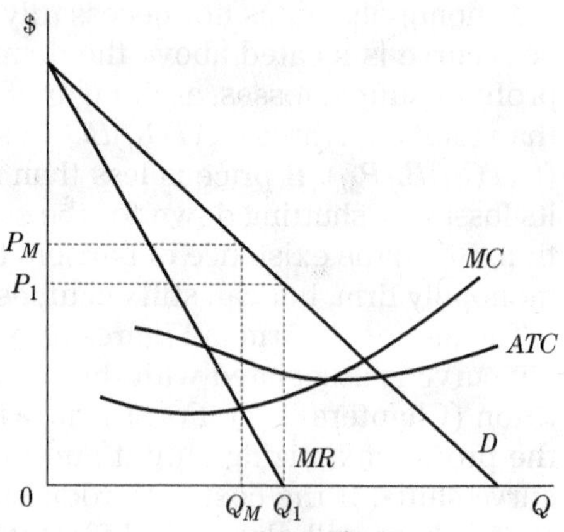

FIGURE 8.2B
The Monopoly Firm
At Q_M:
MR = MC
  P > ATC
  P > MC
Not at Minimum Point of ATC
Price-Searcher
Firm Has No Supply Curve

[5]The industry or market demand and supply curves are not illustrated here for the perfectly competitive firm.

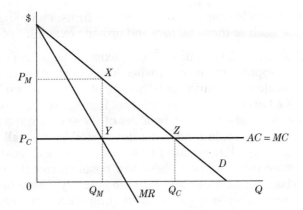

FIGURE 8.3
Comparing a Perfectly Competitive and a Monopolistic Industry
A monopolistic industry will produce a smaller amount of output and charge a higher price than a competitive industry with the same demand and cost conditions.

Firms with market power might also pursue other goals in the short run, such as sales or revenue maximization, to gain market share and increase profits over future periods. This outcome would occur in Figure 8.2b at output level Q_1, where marginal revenue equals zero.[6] The corresponding price, P_1, would be lower than the profit-maximizing price, P_M.

The differences in outcomes between *industries* in monopoly and perfect competition are shown in Figure 8.3, which presents the downward sloping demand and marginal revenue curves facing a monopolist. For simplicity, we assume that the monopolist's average cost is constant and, therefore, equal to its marginal cost. The monopolist produces output Q_M, where marginal revenue equals marginal cost, and charges price P_M. The output that is produced by a competitive industry with comparable demand and cost curves is Q_C. This is the level of output where price P_C equals marginal cost, the rule for profit maximization in the perfectly competitive model.[7] Because price P_C equals average cost, this outcome represents the zero-economic profit equilibrium in perfect competition.

We can see in Figure 8.3 that, with the same demand and cost conditions, the price will be higher and the output lower under monopoly than under perfect competition. The higher price results in the monopolist earning an economic profit represented by the area $P_M XYP_C$, compared with the zero-economic profit equilibrium of competition. Consumers value the units of output between Q_M and Q_C by the prices measured along segment XZ of the demand curve. Because these prices are higher than the corresponding marginal cost, consumers would have purchased these units of output if they had been produced by the monopolist. Therefore, monopoly results in a misallocation of resources compared with perfect competition. These conclusions are derived from the static model of perfect competition and monopoly presented in Figure 8.3. In the following sections, we will see that there are other factors to consider in comparing competitive firms and firms with market power.

Sources of Market Power: Barriers to Entry

The following are the major **barriers to entry** that help firms maintain market power and earn positive economic profits:

1. Economies of scale
2. Barriers created by government
3. Input barriers
4. Brand loyalties
5. Consumer lock-in and switching costs
6. Network externalities

Barriers to entry
The structural, legal, or regulatory characteristics of a firm and its market that keep other firms from producing the same or similar products at the same cost.

---

[6]Total revenue is maximized where marginal revenue equals zero (Chapter 3).
[7]Price equals marginal revenue in perfect competition, so that producing where marginal revenue equals marginal cost is equivalent to producing where price equals marginal cost (Chapter 7).

These factors apply to all imperfectly competitive firms, including oligopoly firms. We'll now describe each of these factors and provide examples of their effects.

Economies of Scale   Economies of scale exist when a firm's long-run average cost curve (*LRAC*) slopes downward or when lower costs of production are associated with a larger scale of operation at either the plant or the firm level. Economies of scale can act as a barrier to entry in different industries because only large-scale firms can achieve the cost-reduction benefits of these economies. Industries with significant economies of scale tend to be dominated by a small number of large firms. Even though these large-scale firms may have lower costs of production, there is no guarantee they will pass these low costs on to consumers in the form of lower prices, given the lack of entry into the industry. Therefore, managers may simply use economies of scale as part of their competitive strategy to earn positive economic profits. As we discuss later in this chapter, this trade-off between lower costs from large-scale production and the market power of these firms is one of the dilemmas of U.S. antitrust policy.

Mergers are one means of achieving the necessary size to realize economies of scale. From 1990 to 2005 there were nearly 3,800 bank mergers in the United States involving $3.6 trillion in assets. Several of the largest bank mergers in history occurred in 1998, including NationsBank–Bank of America, Banc One–First Chicago NBD, and Norwest–Wells Fargo.[8] Banks rely on extensive computer systems with substantial fixed costs and relatively small variable costs, so that total computing and maintenance costs increase relatively little as transactions volumes increase. Greater bank size can result in increased employee specialization and the spreading of advertising costs. Mergers can eliminate redundancies in many back-office functions. Mergers can also increase market power and the ability to hold loan interest rates and fees above competitive levels.

Banking industry studies have indicated that mergers have both increased market power and resulted in cost reductions.[9] Studies during the 1980s and 1990s found evidence of increased profit efficiency and better risk diversification but no evidence of significant cost efficiency gains. Several more recent studies found evidence of downward pressure on rates paid on deposits after mergers. However, there may be cost efficiency gains, particularly for larger banks. Some studies have also suggested there are efficiency gains at incumbent nonmerging banks who respond to the news of a merger by increasing their own efficiency to remain viable competitors.

In 2011 pharmacy-benefit manager Express Scripts Inc. paid $29.1 billion to acquire Medco Health Solutions Inc.[10] These companies, which typically work for employers and health plans, negotiate favorable prices with pharmaceutical companies and drugstores. Medco and Express claimed that the merger would reduce approximately $1 billion in costs. This merger is consistent with trends in the health care industry where medical providers and insurers have been merging both to reduce expenses and to gain market power.

At least 60 mergers in major law firms occurred in the United States and abroad in 2011. This was the highest level of mergers since 2008 and represented a 54 percent increase from 2010. Mergers offered firms, who had been unable to raise rates during the recession, the ability to lower costs through ready-made regional offices

---

[8]This discussion is based on Steven Pilloff, "The Banking Industry," in *The Structure of American Industry*, ed. James Brock, 12th ed. (Upper Saddle River, NJ: Prentice-Hall, 2009), 265–93.
[9]David Van Hoose, *The Industrial Organization of Banking* (Berlin: Springer-Verlag, 2010); Frederic Michael Scherer, "A Perplexed Economist Confronts 'Too Big to Fail,'" *The European Journal of Comparative Economics* 7 (2010): 267–84.
[10]Anna Wilde Mathews and Jonathan D. Rockoff, "Megadeal Unites Drug Rivals," *Wall Street Journal (Online)*, July 22, 2011.

and expanded law practices. Factors such as globalization, the rise of business in Asia, and consolidation among clients also led to the increase in merger activity.[11]

The increasing minimum efficient scale (MES) of production in the beer industry has been one of the factors leading to the large number of mergers in the industry. In 1950 there were 350 firms in the beer industry that could efficiently support 829 firms. By 1960, 175 brewers were forced to compete in a market that could efficiently support only 88 firms, and by 2000 there were 24 brewers in an industry that could support only 11. The large-scale production in the beer industry was also influenced by successful marketing campaigns and the use of television to market and advertise nationally. There is strong evidence suggesting that television advertising caused national brewers to increase their overall advertising, which then generated growth relative to regional and local brewers.[12]

These trends continued in late 2007 when London's SABMiller PLC announced its plans to combine its U.S. unit, Miller Brewing Co., with the U.S. division of Molson Coors Brewing Co., creating a joint venture called MillerCoors. A week later European brewers Heineken NV and Carlsberg AS announced they had formed a consortium to bid for the United Kingdom's best-selling brewer, Scottish & Newcastle PLC. These mergers were a reaction to sluggish beer sales growth in Western Europe and the United States, increasing competition from wine and spirits, and the rising cost of key input commodities such as grain, glass, and aluminum. Miller and Coors sought to become a stronger competitor to the long-dominant Anheuser-Busch Co.[13]

In November 2008, Anheuser-Busch merged with Belgian brewer InBev to become Anheuser-Busch InBev, the world's largest brewer. This helped the company increase the sales of Budweiser in countries such as Canada, Brazil, Russia, and China to offset the loss of market share in the United States. By 2012 both Molson Coors and Anheuser-Busch InBev launched iced tea-flavored beer to offset the competition from craft brewers and liquor companies that had been increasing their market share in North America.[14]

Consolidation has also been proposed in the mining industry. In November 2007, Anglo-Australian miner BHP Billiton announced a $125 billion proposal to merge with Anglo-Australian rival Rio Tinto. This merger would combine the world's No. 1 and No. 3 miners into a company worth at least $320 billion, bigger than every global oil company except ExxonMobil and Russia's OAO Gazprom. The merged mining company would be the world's largest producer of copper and aluminum, the second largest iron ore provider, and potentially the largest source of uranium.[15] However, in November 2008, BHP Billiton abruptly stopped its pursuit of Rio Tinto, given the inherent risk in the $68 billion deal from falling commodity prices and the slowing world economy. BHP feared that its debt would increase too much if the merger occurred.[16]

In 2012 Rio Tinto wrote down $18.2 billion or nearly half of the $38 billion purchase price of Alcan Inc. that it bought in 2007. The company overpaid for Alcan

---

[11]Jennifer Smith, "Stark Choice for Lawyers—Firms Must Merge or Die," *Wall Street Journal (Online)*, January 20, 2012.

[12]Victor J. Tremblay and Carol Horton Tremblay, *The U.S. Brewing Industry* (Cambridge, MA: The MIT Press, 2005), 45–8.

[13]Jason Singer and David Kesmodel, "Why Consolidation Storm Is Brewing in Beer Industry," *Wall Street Journal*, October 18, 2007.

[14]Mike Esterl, "Sudsy American Dream Sells Abroad," *Wall Street Journal (Online)*, March 8, 2012; Mike Esterl, "Introducing Iced-Tea Beer," *Wall Street Journal (Online)*, March 7, 2012.

[15]Patrick Barta and Robert Guy Matthews, "Mining Firms Bulk Up, Echoing Big Oil Mergers," *Wall Street Journal*, December 18, 2007; Dennis K. Berman, "Proposed Mining Megadeal Could Make the Earth Move," *Wall Street Journal*, February 12, 2008.

[16]Robert Guy Matthews, Dana Cimilluca, and Patrick Barta, "Death of a Megadeal: BHP Ends Its Pursuit of Rio," *Wall Street Journal*, November 26, 2008.

at what was the top of the market and when there was significant merger activity. Aluminum prices, which were just under $3,000 per ton in 2007, fell to under $1,500 per ton in 2009 before returning to around $2,000 per ton in 2012. Chinese production of aluminum increased from 12.5 million tons in 2007 to 17.8 million tons in 2011, a more significant increase than many firms in the industry expected.[17]

Significant mergers in the airline industry also occurred in the past decade, including US Airways and America West, Delta and Northwest, Southwest and Air Tran, Air France and KLM, and United and Continental. Delta also considered a merger with US Airways early in 2012. United promised Wall Street investors $1.2 billion in new revenue and cost savings from the merger with Continental. However, this merger involved decisions on everything such as how to board flights, what information to print on boarding passes, what shape the plastic cups should be for cold beverages, and what coffee to serve. In 2011 United, which had 33 teams working on integration, spent $170 in the fourth quarter alone on everything from technology training to repainting airplanes.[18]

Barriers Created by Government   Barriers to entry created by government include licenses, patents, and copyrights. Each of these regulations was created for various public policy purposes, but all have the potential to act as barriers to entry.

Licenses   Licensing of physicians and other professionals is usually justified on the basis of maintaining the quality of the individuals in these professions. However, because the licensure of physicians also restricts their numbers, it acts as a barrier to entry and can generate higher profits for those in the profession. Physicians have raised the quality argument in disputes over the range of medical services that other medical professionals, such as physicians' assistants and nurses' aides, can perform. Critics have charged that physicians are simply trying to maintain their incomes in the face of increased competition among medical service providers. The debate has also surfaced between psychiatrists and psychologists. For many years, the American Psychological Association lobbied for legislation that would allow psychologists to write prescriptions for their patients, a privilege that was given only to psychiatrists.[19] Psychiatrists argued that patients often have other medical problems that psychologists would not understand and, therefore, psychologists should not be able to write prescriptions. Yet there is also a potential loss of income for psychiatrists should this restriction be lifted. Proponents have also argued that this change would increase the availability of mental health services in underserved areas. In March 2002, New Mexico became the first state to grant limited prescribing privileges to psychologists. Louisiana and the U.S. territory of Guam also passed similar laws, while lobbying groups urged a similar change in Missouri's laws in 2008.[20]

Regulatory bodies are involved with attempts to both loosen and tighten licensing requirements. Under a 1994 state law, persons wanting to practice commercial interior design in Florida must be licensed, which involves completing six years of schooling and apprenticeships and passing a two-day exam.[21] In 2011 a bill was introduced in the legislature to deregulate this occupation and others, including

---

[17]John W. Miller, "Alcan Proves Costly to Rio Tinto," *Wall Street Journal (Online)*, February 10, 2012.

[18]Drake Bennett, "Making the World's Largest Airline Fly," *Bloomberg Businessweek (Online)*, February 2, 2012; Gina Chon, Anupreeta Das, and Susan Carey, "Delta Weighs a US Air Deal," *Wall Stret Journal (Online)*, January 28, 2012.

[19]Erica Goode, "Psychologists Get Prescription Pads and Furor Erupts," *New York Times*, March 26, 2002; Ellen Barry, "Psychiatrists Fight Blurring Line with Psychologists," *Boston Globe*, June 1, 2002.

[20]Rosemary Frei, "The Prescribing Psychologist," *Medical Post*, November 2, 2004; Anonymous, "Prescription Privileges Law for Missouri Psychologists Improves Patient Access to Quality Mental Health Care," *PR Newswire*, January 9, 2008.

[21]Arian-Campo Flores, "In Florida, Interior Decorators Have Designs on Deregulation: But Pros Say Scrapping Licensing Laws Won't Be Pretty: Flaming Carpets, Staph," *Wall Street Journal (Online)*, April 15, 2011.

yacht brokers and hair braiders. Opponents of deregulation argued that opening the profession to lesser-trained individuals would raise safety and building concerns, including the increased use of flammable carpets and porous countertops spreading bacteria. Supporters of the law argued that it would create jobs, foster competition, and lower prices for consumers.

Similar arguments occurred when the Connecticut State Dental Commission ruled that only licensed dentists could offer on-site teeth whitening and that violators would be subject to jail time.[22] Dentists asserted that teeth whitening could cause gum and tooth sensitivity and that tooth discoloration might be caused by underlying medical conditions that dentists would be better able to detect. After the Food and Drug Administration ruled that teeth-whitening products were cosmetics, drugstores began selling whitening strips, and both dentists and nondentists set up whitening treatments in malls and salons. Dentists typically charged between $300 and $700 for a whitening session, while nondentists charged between $100 and $150. Opponents of the ruling argued that dentists were simply trying to stifle competition.

Patents and Copyrights   Patents and copyrights give the producer of a new invention or printed work the right to the profits from that work for a number of years in order to encourage research, innovation, and the development of new products. These issues of research and new product development go beyond the static competitive and monopoly comparisons in Figure 8.3 that do not focus on dynamic changes in industries over time. Patents can help firms gain market power through innovation and then act as a barrier to entry, protecting that information and innovation for a given period of time. Economist Joseph Schumpeter first presented the argument that a market structure with monopoly power through patents might be more conducive to innovation than a more competitive market.[23] The public policy concern is that highly competitive markets may result in too few innovations if any positive economic profits from competitive firms are competed away too rapidly. Public policy makers believe that competitive markets will produce too few innovations and too little new information and are, therefore, willing to grant firms some degree of market power to stimulate innovation.

In some industries, patents may not be as important in maintaining a competitive advantage as factors such as secrecy, lead time, the lowering of costs through greater experience in production, and increased sales and service efforts. However, patents play an extremely important role in achieving and maintaining market power in the pharmaceutical industry. The role of patents in protecting the profits of pharmaceutical producers is illustrated by the steps these manufacturers are willing to take to prevent competition from generic drugs when their patents expire or are about to expire.[24] A generic drug has the same chemical content as the corresponding branded drug, but it cannot be sold until the patent on the branded drug expires. On average, a generic drug can decrease U.S. sales of a

---

[22]Jennifer Levitz, "Whitening Upstarts Make Dentists Gnash Teeth," *Wall Street Journal (Online)*, November 15, 2011.

[23]Joseph Schumpeter, *Capitalism, Socialism, and Democracy*, 3rd ed. (New York: Harper and Row, 1950). Evidence on this issue is mixed, particularly for the U.S. economy. See Dennis W. Carlton and Jeffrey M. Perloff, *Modern Industrial Organization*, 4th ed. (Boston, MA: Pearson Addison-Wesley, 2005), Chapter 16. Much of the discussion of patents in this text is drawn from the Carlton and Perloff book.

[24]Gardiner Harris and Chris Adams, "Drug Manufacturers Are Intensifying Courtroom Attacks That Slow Generics," *Wall Street Journal*, July 12, 2001; Gardiner Harris, "Why Drug Makers Are Failing in Quest for New Blockbusters," *Wall Street Journal*, April 18, 2002; Laurie McGinley and Scott Hensley, "Drug Industry Exhorts Companies to Avoid Coalition Pushing Generics," *Wall Street Journal*, May 3, 2002. See also Ernst E. Berndt, "Pharmaceuticals in U.S. Health Care: Determinants of Quantity and Price," *Journal of Economic Perspectives* 16 (Fall 2002): 45–66.

branded drug by approximately 50 percent during the first six months of competition. To prevent competition from generics, the major drug companies have often filed suits raising concerns about the safety of generic drugs and the procedures used to make these pharmaceuticals. In some instances, the drug companies have changed the dosage of medications to prevent generic substitution because the new drugs are no longer exactly equivalent to the branded drugs. Even if these strategies do not prevent the generics from being introduced, the strategies may delay the introduction of generics, which increases the sales of the branded drug during the delay period.

Competition from generics has been of particular importance to the drug companies since 2000, when patents on many of their major revenue-generating drugs began to expire.[25] The market power of the pharmaceutical industry has also been reduced because it has become much more difficult for these companies to develop new drugs that are significantly different from existing drugs and to raise prices on their existing drugs, given increased competition among the drug manufacturers and managed care's role in containing the costs of health care. Thus, protection of market power through patent disputes has been the major competitive strategy of the pharmaceutical industry.[26] Law practices have also developed that specialize in patent infringement.[27]

More recently pharmaceutical companies have often capitulated in patent dispute cases by agreeing to shorten the patent life of a drug, foregoing hundreds of millions of dollars in potential revenue, in return for the assurance that they can market the drug for a few years free from the threat of litigation by their generic rivals. For example, Cephalon Inc. settled with three of the four generic makers of its sleep-disorder drug, Provigil, by allowing the generic manufacturers to sell the medicine in 2011, three years before the disputed patent expired.[28] However, in 2008 Cephalon also sharply increased the price of Provigil in anticipation of launching a longer-acting version of the drug called Nuvigil, which would have a lower price. The company anticipated that users would switch to Nuvigil by the time the Provigil patent expired.[29]

In November 2011, Pfizer's blockbuster drug, Lipitor, went off patent.[30] Lipitor was the top-selling drug of all time, earning Pfizer more than $81 billion in sales since 1997. To counter the loss of revenue, Pfizer established contracts with drug benefit plans to provide patient discounts to encourage continued use of Lipitor. Pfizer offered cards that lowered the co-payment to $4 per month for a prescription. Pfizer also partnered with a Michigan pharmacy to mail Lipitor to patients who ordered the drug directly through the pharmacy. The company continued to market Lipitor heavily, spending $659 million in 2011, and it offered to sell Lipitor to health plans at generic prices for the first 180 days if the plans sold it instead of other versions. Pfizer also increased its marketing of Lipitor in fast-growing emerging markets, such as China, and it increased its efforts to develop new drugs for diseases such as Alzheimer's. Global Lipitor sales decreased 24 percent to $2 billion and U.S. sales fell 42 percent after the drug went off patent.

---

[25]Eli Lilly & Company's patent on the antidepressant Prozac and Merck & Company's patent on the ulcer drug Pepcid both expired in 2001.

[26]Harris and Adams, "Drug Manufacturers Are Intensifying."

[27]Ashby Jones, "When Lawyers Become 'Trolls,'" *Wall Street Journal (Online)*, January 23, 2012.

[28]Leila Abboud, "Branded Drugs Settling More Generic Suits," *Wall Street Journal*, January 17, 2006.

[29]Jonathan D. Rockoff, "How a Drug Maker Tries to Outwit Generics," *Wall Street Journal*, November 17, 2008.

[30]This discussion is based on Peter Loftus, "Forget Generics, Pfizer Has Plenty of 'Lipitor for You,'" *Wall Street Journal (Online)*, November 2, 2011; Jonathan D. Rockoff, "Helping Lipitor Live Longer," *Wall Street Journal (Online)*, November 22, 2011; and Peter Loftus, "Pfizer, Lilly Profits Fall as Drugs Lose Patents," *Wall Street Journal (Online)*, February 1, 2012.

Similar issues regarding patent infringement have arisen in the market for computer printer ink. Ink cartridges are a major source of revenue for Hewlett-Packard Co., which has a market share of 50 percent in the United States and more than 4,000 patents on its ink formulations and cartridge design. Because the company made more than 80 percent of its 2005 operating profit of $5.6 billion from ink and toner supplies, it sued other ink and cartridge manufacturers and stores with ink-cartridge refilling stations for patent infringements. The company employs chemists who analyze competitors' inks to determine whether H-P patents have been violated.[31]

In February 2012, Apple Inc. filed suit in a U.S. district court in California accusing Samsung Electronics Co. of violating four patents that were distinguishing features of the iPhone. These patents included the slide to unlock function of the phones, technology for searching multiple sources of information, and technology for correcting misspelled words. As with Eastman Kodak in the opening case, these patent infringement suits have become essential parts of companies' competitive strategies. In the fourth quarter of 2011, Apple barely beat out Samsung with 23.5 percent of global smartphone shipments compared with 22.8 percent for Samsung.[32]

Input Barriers Other barriers to entry include control over raw materials or other key inputs in a production process and barriers in financial capital markets. For example, the De Beers diamond cartel traditionally controlled the major sources of diamonds and, therefore, had a monopoly on diamond production.[33] Formed during the 1930s, De Beers and the companies with whom it contracted controlled 70 to 80 percent of the world's supply of rough diamonds and influenced almost every stage of diamond production from extraction to the distribution of rough diamonds. However, even this market power is constantly threatened by the development of new sources of diamonds, changing consumer preferences for less-than-perfect gems, and the increased competition by Internet sellers and retail chains such as Wal-Mart and Costco.

In the airlines industry, the major companies control the crucial inputs of airport gates and time slots for flying.[34] Dominant airlines effectively own their hub airports because they have long-term leases on the gates, which they can even leave unused. These airlines have veto rights over airport expansion that could increase competition, and they may even control ground-handling and baggage services.

In 1999, the *Wall Street Journal* reported on a particularly vivid example of this barrier to entry, the case of Spirit Airlines.[35] After seven years of operation, Spirit Airlines had been unable to acquire or sublease any gates at the Detroit airport, the major hub for Northwest Airlines. Thus, Spirit flew at the convenience of the major airlines because it had to negotiate the rental of gates for the specific departures and arrivals of its planes on a daily basis, often when planes were en route to Detroit. Spirit had to pay $250 to $400 per turn to rent spare gates for a total of $1.3 million per year, which the company claimed was more than twice the amortized cost of owning two gates with jetways.

[31]Christopher Lawton, "H-P Chemists Hunt Violators of Ink Patents," *Wall Street Journal*, August 29, 2006.
[32]Ian Sherr and Jessica E. Vascellaro, "Apple Hits Samsung Phone," *Wall Street Journal (Online)*, February 13, 2012.
[33]Donald G. McNeil, Jr., "A Diamond Cartel May Be Forever: The Hereditary Leader of De Beers Pursues Post-Apartheid Growth," *New York Times*, January 12, 1999; Anthony DePalma, "Diamonds in the Cold: New Canadian Mine Seeks Its Place in a De Beers World," *New York Times*, April 13, 1999; Leslie Kaufman, "Once a Luxury, Diamond Rings Now Overflow Bargain Tables," *New York Times*, February 13, 2002; Tracie Rozhon, "Competition Is Forever," *New York Times*, February 9, 2005.
[34]William G. Shepherd and James W. Brock, "The Airline Industry," in *The Structure of American Industry*, ed. James Brock, 12th ed. (Upper Saddle River, NJ: Prentice Hall, 2009), 235–64.
[35]Bruce Ingersoll, "Gateless in Detroit, Low-Fare Spirit Docks at Rivals' Convenience," *Wall Street Journal*, July 12, 1999.

Barriers to purchasing the inputs of production can also arise from lack of access to financial capital by small firms compared with larger firms. Research studies have shown that larger firms can enjoy up to a percentage point difference in terms of the interest cost of financing new investment. Small firms tend to have smaller security offerings, so that the fixed transactions costs are spread over fewer securities. Investors often perceive the offerings of small corporations as being more risky and, therefore, demand higher interest payments.[36]

Brand Loyalties   The creation of brand loyalties through advertising and other marketing efforts is a strategy that many managers use to create and maintain market power. The beer industry presents one of the best examples of this strategy.[37] Many blind taste tests have shown that consumers cannot distinguish between brands of beer. In one taste test sponsored by *Consumer Reports*, a panel of 17 knowledgeable tasters, ranging from brewmasters to brewing students, was asked to assess the qualities and defects of dozens of brands of beer.[38] The two top-ranked brands were among the least expensive, while the brands that were ranked the lowest were among the most expensive ones. The correlation coefficient between the prices of 16 beers and their taste-test quality ratings was 0.018, which was not significantly different from zero.

Because there are few real differences among many brands of beer, the major beer companies have focused their advertising and marketing efforts on creating perceived differences, many of which are associated with different prices—popular, premium, and super premium. Beer advertising also focuses on images of pleasure, belonging, and other psychological benefits of the product. Persuasive advertising is dominant in the beer industry because the product is a relatively inexpensive perishable good. Thus, consumers have few incentives to spend time and energy trying to collect objective information about the product. Beer companies have also used advertising to segment their brand images along white-collar and blue-collar lines.[39]

Brand loyalty is created in other industries by determining the proper amount to spend on customer service. In 2003, Starbucks Corp. made the decision to invest $40 million systemwide to add 20 hours of labor per week in each store to speed up service. Studies had shown that speed of service was critical to customers' satisfaction and that highly satisfied customers spent 9 percent more than those who were simply satisfied.[40] More recently as Starbucks began an expansion into juice bars, the company faced the challenge of entering new markets without diluting its traditional brand. The company unveiled a new logo that dropped the words, "Starbucks coffee," indicating a shift in its strategy.[41]

Lock-in and switching costs

A form of market power for a firm in which consumers become locked into purchasing certain types or brands of products because they would incur substantial costs if they switched to other products.

Consumer Lock-In and Switching Costs   Barriers to entry can also result if consumers become locked into certain types or brands of products and would incur substantial switching costs if they changed. Carl Shapiro and Hal R. Varian have outlined the major types of **lock-in and switching costs**.[42] Although these

---

[36]Frederic Michael Scherer and David Ross, *Industrial Market Structure and Economic Performance*, 3rd ed. (Boston: Houghton Mifflin, 1990), 126–30.

[37]This discussion is drawn from Douglas F. Greer, "Beer: Causes of Structural Change," in *Industry Studies*, ed. Larry L. Duetsch, 2nd ed. (Armonk, NY: Sharpe, 1998), 28–64. Individual brands of beer are not cited in this article.

[38]*Consumer Reports*, June 1996, 10–17, as reported in Greer, 42.

[39]Victor J. Tremblay and Carol Horton Tremblay, *The U.S. Brewing Industry* (Cambridge, MA: The MIT Press, 2005).

[40]Ryan Chittum, "Price Points," *Wall Street Journal*, October 30, 2006.

[41]Julie Jargon, "Latest Starbuck Concoction: Juice," *Wall Street Journal (Online)*, November 11, 2011.

[42]The discussion of lock-in, switching costs, and network externalities is based on Carl Shapiro and Hal R. Varian, *Information Rules: A Strategic Guide to the Network Economy* (Boston, MA: Harvard Business School Press, 1999), 103–225.

types of lock-in are dominant in the information industries, they represent managerial strategies that can be used elsewhere in the economy to gain and maintain market power.

Contractual Commitment   A contractual commitment to purchase from a specific supplier is the most explicit type of lock-in because it is a legal document. Some contracts force the buyer to purchase all requirements from a specific seller for a period of time, whereas others specify only a minimum order requirement.

Durable Purchases   In the 1980s, Bell Atlantic selected AT&T over Northern Telecom and Siemens for the purchase of its 5ESS digital switches to operate its telephone network, given the quality of the AT&T product. However, the company also submitted itself to extensive lock-in, as the switches utilized a proprietary operating system controlled by AT&T. AT&T also remained in control of a wide range of enhancements and upgrades to its switches. The market power to AT&T from this lock-in was particularly important because the switches had a useful life of 15 or more years and were costly to remove or reinstall. Customers may be able to circumvent some of this lock-in if they can lease rather than purchase the equipment.

Brand-Specific Training   Closely related to the durable equipment lock-in is the brand-specific training that may be required for the personnel who use the equipment. If employees become accustomed to a particular brand of software, switching will be much more difficult unless competing software is also easy to learn and use. For example, Microsoft Word provides technical assistance screens to former WordPerfect users to lower the switching costs to the Microsoft product.

Information and Databases   The costs of transferring information from one database to another or of switching from one technology to another can be substantial, particularly if the original database or technology has unique characteristics. There were typically large switching costs when consumers changed from phonograph records to CDs to DVDs. Tax preparation software, on the other hand, is often designed so that later versions are compatible with earlier versions and the company can attract and lock in a new group of consumers. In Apple's patent infringement suit against Samsung discussed previously, Apple argued that the first smartphones users buy have a major impact on future purchases because customers learn a given operating system and store data on a particular type of phone.[43]

Specialized Suppliers   Sellers of specialized equipment also use lock-in to gain market power. This specialization becomes a more powerful strategy for the seller if alternative firms are no longer in business after an initial purchase is made. The Department of Defense has long faced this problem, given the limited number of defense contractors supplying the Department.

Search Costs   Large search costs for alternative suppliers give existing firms a competitive advantage. Search costs involve the time and effort both for consumers to gather information about alternative products and for new suppliers to search out and attract new customers.

Loyalty Programs   Loyalty programs are another explicit strategy for increasing consumer lock-in. The best examples are the airlines' frequent-flyer programs. These programs create customer loyalty because frequent-flyer points may be

[43]Sherr and Vascellaro, "Apple Hits Samsung Phone."

forfeited if they are not used within a certain time period and many benefits, such as preferential service, are based on cumulative usage of the airline. Hotels, grocery stores, and local retailers have also implemented similar loyalty programs. The number of such programs is expected to increase as businesses gain better access to databases on consumer buying habits.

Switching Costs Example   Direct deposits of paychecks, Social Security, and pension checks and automatic payments of utility, phone, and insurance bills have increased the switching costs among bank checking account customers in recent years. These innovations have caused the 15 percent of customers who leave their bank every year to decline as more customers are locked in by the automated transactions to their accounts. In response, many banks have made increased efforts to lure customers from their competitors by offering to contact companies and employers for their customers to help change the automatic transactions from their old to their new accounts. These switching services may be used strategically as certain services may be available only to customers who purchase premium and more profitable services from the bank.[44]

Switching Costs and the Internet   In the late 1990s and early 2000s, many believed that e-commerce and the use of the Internet would lead to more intense price competition due to less product differentiation, lower search costs, and lower fixed costs.[45] The geographical dimension of product differentiation would be eliminated, price searches would be facilitated online, and Internet firms would likely have lower fixed costs leading to greater entry and more competition. However, research has shown that there is price dispersion online, and that online prices may not be much lower than offline prices. The amount of price dispersion in markets with "branded" Web sites is substantial, and price dispersion has been found in markets where consumers use price search engines.

These results mean that firms can develop market power even on the Internet. Amazon.com and Barnes & Noble online do not have the geographic differentiation that occurs in the offline world, but they compete on the basis of consumer preferences for service, atmosphere, and reputation. Search costs also may not be lower on the Internet because retailers can engage in strategies such as offering complicated menus of prices, bundling products, personalizing prices, or making the process of comparing prices complex. Because Internet firms such as Amazon.com offer multiple products, they may set prices lower today so that customers will not incur the real or psychic costs of trying out another bookstore and will continue to purchase from Amazon in the future. As in the offline world, Internet firms can also set low prices for low quality items on Pricewatch and then design their Web sites to persuade consumers who visit to purchase additional items or higher quality items at higher prices.[46]

---

[44]Jane J. Kim, "Banks Push Harder to Get You to Switch," *Wall Street Journal*, October 12, 2006.

[45]This discussion is based on Glenn Ellison and Sara Fisher Ellison, "Lessons About Markets from the Internet," *Journal of Economic Perspectives* 19 (Spring 2005): 139–58; and Erik Brynjolfsson, Astrid A. Dick, and Michael D. Smith, "A Nearly Perfect Market? Differentiation vs. Price in Consumer Choice," *Quantitative Marketing & Economics* 8 (2010): 1–33.

[46]Researchers have shown that the costs of switching from eBay, the largest single online marketplace, to an alternative Web site for an established seller with a strong reputation on eBay averages around 3 percent of the item's value. See Mikhail Melnik and James Alm, "Seller Reputation, Information Signals, and Prices for Heterogeneous Coins on eBay," *Southern Economic Journal* 72 (2005): 305–27; Mikhail Melnik and James Alm, "Does a Seller's eCommerce Reputation Matter? Evidence from eBay Auctions," *Journal of Industrial Economics* 50 (2002): 337–49. For a recent review of the economics of eBay, see Kevin Hasker and Robin Sickles, "eBay in the Economics Literature: Analysis of an Auction Marketplace," *Review of Industrial Organization* 37 (2010): 3–42.

Managerial Rule of Thumb

Using Lock-In as a Competitive Strategy

To best use lock-in as a competitive strategy, managers should be prepared to invest in a given base of customers by offering concessions and attractive terms to initially gain these customers. Being first to market is one of the best ways to obtain the initial advantage. Selling to influential buyers and attracting buyers with high switching costs are other strategies for building a consumer base. After attracting new customers, managers need to make them entrenched to increase their commitment to the products and technology. Loyalty programs and cumulative discounts are part of these entrenchment strategies. Leveraging a firm's established base of customers also involves selling complementary products to the customers and selling access to the customer base to other producers. ■

Network Externalities   **Network externalities** act as a barrier to entry because the value of a product to consumers depends on the number of customers using the product. Examples of such products include software networks, compatible fax machines and modems, e-mail software, ATMs, and particular computer brands such as Macintosh. Often one brand of a product becomes the industry standard, and its value increases when it does so.

Network externalities
A barrier to entry that exists because the value of a product to consumers depends on the number of consumers using the product.

Network externalities can be considered demand-side economies of scale, in contrast to the supply-side economies that we discussed earlier in this chapter. Microsoft's dominance in software results from these demand-side economies of scale. These economies are prominent in the information industry, and their power increases as the size of the network grows.

Changes in Market Power

Market power can be a very fluid and elusive concept. In this section, we look at several examples that illustrate how managers had to change their strategies to keep up with the dynamics of the marketplace and to avoid losing market power.

Shifting Demand for Kleenex   Kimberly-Clark Corp., maker of Kleenex, an 83-year-old brand, has been faced both with increased competition from cheap generic tissue and with pressure to add high-tech ingredients to basic paper products.[47] Kleenex, which has $1.6 billion in global sales, is part of the company's consumer tissue division, which produces more than a third of the company's annual sales. However, consumer tissue has the smallest profit margin of the company's three divisions, given the high prices of energy and wood pulp. Furthermore, the facial tissue category has been shrinking since 2001, with tissue sales suffering their largest decline in the past five years. Lower-priced private brands have gained market share, and consumers have often used substitute products, such as paper towels, toilet paper, and free napkins from fast-food restaurants. Advances in cold therapies, both prescription and over-the-counter, may also have decreased the demand for tissues.

Kimberly-Clark's response in 2004 was to develop Anti-Viral, a Kleenex laced with a mild pesticide to fight cold and flu viruses. In developing this new product, Kimberly-Clark needed to obtain approval from the Environmental Protection Agency to use a pesticide in the tissue. It had to re-think its marketing because it had always presented Kleenex with a soft touch, not as a killer of viruses. The company had tried a similar germ-fighting tissue in 1984 but had to pull the product

---

[47]This discussion is based on Ellen Byron, "Can a Re-Engineered Kleenex Cure a Brand's Sniffles?" *Wall Street Journal*, January 22, 2007.

after just a few months in five test markets. Consumers were resistant to the idea of a chemical-laced tissue in this period before widespread use of antibacterial soaps, fabrics, and hand wipes. The product also cost more than regular tissues.

By 1987 Procter & Gamble had launched Puffs Plus With Lotion, the first tissue treated with lotion. Kimberly-Clark developed its own similar product and found that customers would pay extra for these characteristics. These changes encouraged the company to develop the anti-virus tissue even though some health experts remain skeptical of Anti-Viral's health benefits. Kimberly-Clark did not want to promote the health benefits too aggressively so that the product did not become "the sick box." The Environmental Protection Agency required that Kleenex state on its label that the product had not been tested against bacteria, fungi, or other viruses, and it made certain that the box design did not appeal to children. By 2007, Anti-Viral held 4 percent of the U.S. market and had generated more than $140 million in global sales since it was launched in 2004.

Retailers Fight Showrooming and Phone Apps   Retailers such as Wal-Mart Inc., Best Buy Co., and Target Corp. have developed a variety of strategies to combat consumer use of phone apps to compare online and bricks-and-mortar prices. The goal is to prevent consumers from simply using physical stores as showrooms to gather information about products and then buy them online.[48] The use of smartphones has made it difficult for retailers to charge higher prices in stores than on their Web sites. Phone apps allow consumers to scan barcodes, take photos of products, and then search for lower prices online. Price comparison app, TheFind, estimated that it averaged between 18 million and 20 million price checks per month in 2011, while surveys showed that 40 percent of consumers have used an in-store shopping app or search engine.

In reaction to these trends, retailers began using the same technology to target customers inside competitors' stores. Best Buy partnered with TheFind to send personalized ads to shoppers when the program detected they were in stores such as Wal-Mart. Offers were sent to customers who allowed the program to use their phone's global positioning system to track their location. Retailers could also offer discounts on other products in their stores. They also began increasing the importance of exclusives and store-branded merchandise that prevented consumers from being able to compare items. Retailers are using technology, such as Scan It, that scans items as they are added to a shopping cart and keeps a running total of purchases. Scan It allows retailers to send coupons to customers while they are in the store. It may permit retailers to cut back on the number of their employees, or it may free up workers to provide more customer service. Target has specifically asked its suppliers to create special products that would set it apart from its competitors and to help match its rivals' prices.

Physical retailers face fundamental problems because online-only retailers have significantly lower labor costs and do not collect sales taxes in most states. Analysts have noted that Amazon has an entirely different business model from Wal-Mart and Target. Amazon uses its other profitable units, such as cloud data storage and Web site fees, to subsidize its consumer products and sell them at discounted prices.

Borders Bookstores' Online Strategy   Borders Group Inc. had traditionally focused on opening more stores rather than emphasizing online book sales.[49]

---

[48]This discussion is based on Miguel Bustillo and Ann Zimmerman, "Phone-Wielding Shoppers Strike Fear into Retailers," *Wall Street Journal (Online)*, December 16, 2010; Ann Zimmerman, "Check Out the Future of Shopping," *Wall Street Journal (Online)*, May 18, 2011; Dana Mattioli, "Retailers Try to Thwart Price Apps," *Wall Street Journal (Online)*, December 23, 2011; and Ann Zimmerman, "Showdown Over 'Showrooming,' " *Wall Street Journal (Online)*, January 23, 2012.

[49]This discussion is based on Jeffrey A. Trachtenberg, "Borders Business Plan Gets a Rewrite," *Wall Street Journal*, March 22, 2007; and Greta Guest, "Bookseller Will Innovate Beyond Online in Stores: New Solutions on Way for Retail Puzzle," *McClatchy-Tribune Business News*, October 14, 2007.

It increased the number of its U.S. superstores from 290 in 2000 to 499 in 2007, and the number of its overseas superstores from 22 in 2001 to 73 in 2007. Borders transferred its online business to Amazon.com in 2001. Amazon was to operate the Web site, keeping all revenue generated except for a commission paid to Borders. This strategy proved incorrect as sales at U.S. bookstores dropped 2.9 percent in 2006 while online book sales soared.

In March 2007, Borders announced that it would reopen its own branded Web site in early 2008, ending the alliance with Amazon.com, and that it would sell or franchise most of its 73 overseas Borders stores. The company also planned to close nearly half of its Waldenbooks outlets in the United States. These changes reflected the increased competition that book retailers faced from the sluggish book market and from Web-based and other discount booksellers such as Amazon.com and Costco Wholesale Corp. These outlets sold a variety of goods in addition to books, so they could offer the books at substantially reduced prices and make up the revenue on the other goods. Borders also designed new superstores that would include a digital center where customers could purchase a variety of digital products.

In March 2008 Borders put itself up for sale after surprising investors by disclosing a potential liquidity problem. The turmoil in the credit markets had closed off some of its usual sources of financing. At that time Barnes & Noble announced that it would look at the option of purchasing Borders. No sale occurred by fall 2008, and Borders still experienced credit and financial problems. In November 2008, the company posted a net loss of $175.4 million.[50] The company eventually filed for bankruptcy in February 2011 and raced, unsuccessfully, to find a buyer. Borders was liquidated, and its stores closed later in 2011. Although the company's original success 40 years earlier resulted from its huge assortment of books that rivals could not match, the store was unable to keep up with changing consumer preferences for books delivered to their door or downloaded to electronic devices.[51]

Measures of Market Power

Economists have developed several measures of market power, some of which are based on the models of market structure we discussed earlier in this chapter. Managers can use these measures to gain a better understanding of their markets and to anticipate any antitrust actions in their industry, as the Justice Department uses a number of these measures to determine whether antitrust actions are warranted in merger cases.

The Lerner Index   The **Lerner Index** focuses on the difference between a firm's product price and its marginal cost of production, which, as we discussed previously, exists for a firm with market power, but does not exist for a perfectly competitive firm. The Lerner Index is defined in Equation 8.1:

Lerner Index
A measure of market power that focuses on the difference between a firm's product price and its marginal cost of production.

$$8.1 \quad L = \frac{(P - MC)}{P}$$

where

L = value of the Lerner Index

P = product price

MC = marginal cost of production

---

[50]Jeffrey A. Trachtenberg and Karen Richardson, "At Borders Group, the Next Best Seller Might Be Itself," *Wall Street Journal*, March 21, 2008; Jeffrey A. Trachtenberg, "Barnes & Noble Studies Bid for Borders," *Wall Street Journal*, May 21, 2008; Jeffrey A. Trachtenberg and Sara Silver, "Borders's Loss Deepens," *Wall Street Journal*, November 26, 2008.
[51]Mike Spector and Jeffrey A. Trachtenberg, "Borders Succumbs to Digital Era in Books," *Wall Street Journal (Online)*, July 20, 2011.

Because profit-maximizing perfectly competitive firms produce where price equals marginal cost, the value of the Lerner Index is zero under perfect competition and increases as market power increases. The value of the index and market power vary inversely with the price elasticity of demand.

Although this measure of market power is derived directly from economic theory, it is often difficult to use in practice because data on marginal cost are scarce. Many managers are unable to answer questions about their firm's marginal cost because the concept is foreign to them (Chapter 5). Given these data problems, this ratio is often calculated as the difference between price and average variable cost or as sales revenue minus payroll and materials costs divided by sales. This approach typically ignores capital, research and development, and advertising costs. It may also be biased if average and marginal costs are not constant and equal to each other. The price-cost margin of 11.9 percent for the highly competitive broiler chicken industry is substantially different from the much higher margins in the more concentrated, differentiated food industries (Chapter 7).[52]

Marginal costs have been estimated for the airline industry, so that price/marginal cost ratios can be calculated for different market structures on various routes within the industry.[53] On average, price is slightly more than double marginal cost on all U.S. routes and market structures. However, price is 3.3 times marginal cost when one firm monopolizes a route and 3.1 times marginal cost when there is a dominant firm. This research shows that the amount by which price exceeds marginal cost depends more on whether there is a dominant firm or dominant pair than on the total number of firms in the market. Market power is clearly shown in cases where a single firm dominates a route. Even if two firms dominate, the excess of price over marginal cost is substantially lower than if a single firm dominates.

Cross-Price Elasticity of Demand   The cross-price elasticity of demand, or the percentage change in the quantity demanded of good X relative to the percentage change in the price of good Y, is another measure of market power. If two goods have a positive cross-price elasticity of demand, they are substitute goods. The higher the cross-price elasticity, the greater the potential substitution between the goods, and the smaller the market power possessed by the firms producing the two goods.

Concentration ratios
A measure of market power that focuses on the share of the market held by the X largest firms, where X typically equals four, six, or eight.

Concentration Ratios   **Concentration ratios** measure market power by focusing on the share of the market held by the X largest firms, where X typically equals four, six, or eight.[54] The assumption is that the larger the share of the market held by a small number of firms, the more market power those firms have. One problem with concentration ratios is that they describe only one point on the size distribution of firms in an industry. One industry could have four firms that each hold 20 percent of the market share, while another could have four firms that hold 60, 10, 5, and 5 percent shares. The four-firm concentration ratios would be equal for both industries, but most researchers and managers would argue that the degree of competition would be quite different in the industries.

---

[52]Richard T. Rogers, "Broilers: Differentiating a Commodity," in *Industry Studies*, ed. Larry L. Duetsch, 2nd ed. (Armonk, NY: Sharpe, 1998), 65–100.

[53]Jeffrey M. Perloff, Larry S. Karp, and Amos Golan, *Estimating Market Power and Strategies* (New York: Cambridge University Press, 2007), 28–30; Jesse C. Weiher, Robin C. Sickles, and Jeffrey M. Perloff, "Market Power in the U.S. Airline Industry," in *Measuring Market Power, Contributions to Economic Analysis*, vol. 255, ed. Daniel J. Slottje (Amsterdam: Elsevier, 2002), 309–23.

[54]The discussion of concentration ratios, the Herfindahl-Hirschman Index (*HHI*), and antitrust issues is based on the following sources: Carlton and Perloff, *Modern Industrial Organization*; W. Kip Viscusi, Joseph E. Harrington, Jr., and John M. Vernon, *Economics of Regulation and Antitrust*, 4th ed. (Cambridge, MA: MIT Press, 2005); John E. Kwoka, Jr. and Lawrence J. White (eds.), *The Antitrust Revolution: Economics, Competition, and Policy*, 5th ed. (New York: Oxford University Press, 2009).

Another problem with concentration ratios is that the market definitions used in their construction may be arbitrary. The economic definition of a market focuses on those goods that are close substitutes in both consumption and production. Substitutes in consumption would imply a high cross-price elasticity of demand, as noted above. Substitution in production would imply that a high price for good A would cause some firms to switch production in their facilities from good B to good A. The concentration ratios published by the U.S. Bureau of the Census do not generally conform to the economic definition of a market because the Census definitions were developed "to serve the general purposes of the census and other government statistics" and were "not designed to establish categories necessarily denoting coherent or relevant markets in the true competitive sense, or to provide a basis for measuring market power."[55] Thus, the Census definitions often include products that are not close substitutes in the same industry, and they may omit products that are close substitutes. If consumer demand indicates that plastic bottles compete with glass bottles, the concentration ratio for the glass bottle industry may not provide much information about the competitive nature of that industry.

Concentration ratios also are often based on national statistics and may not reflect differences in transportation costs among local markets that could result in substantial concentration at that level. In addition, concentration ratios ignore imports and exports, which for industries such as the domestic automobile producers could lead to a very biased view of market competition.

The Herfindahl-Hirschman Index   The **Herfindahl-Hirschman Index (HHI)** is a measure of market power that makes use of more information about the relative market shares of firms in the industry. The *HHI* is defined as the sum of the squares of the market share of each firm in the industry. The values of the *HHI* range from near zero for competitive firms to 10,000 if one firm monopolizes the entire market ($HHI = 100^2$). The *HHI* is also sensitive to unequal market shares of different firms. For example, if an industry has two firms with equal market shares, the *HHI* equals $(50)^2 + (50)^2 = 2,500 + 2,500 = 5,000$. If the market shares of the two firms are 90 and 10 percent, the value of the *HHI* equals $(90)^2 + (10)^2 = 8,100 + 100 = 8,200$.

The *HHI* is important because the Antitrust Guidelines of the Justice Department use the index to evaluate the competitive effects of mergers between firms in order to determine whether any antitrust action is appropriate. These Guidelines, which were updated in August 2010, classify markets as unconcentrated (*HHI* below 1,500), moderately concentrated (*HHI* between 1,500 and 2,500), and concentrated (*HHI* above 2,500).[56] Mergers involving an increase of the *HHI* of less than 100 points ordinarily require no further analysis. Increases in the *HHI* of more than 100 points in moderately concentrated markets and between 100 and 200 points in highly concentrated markets raise significant competitive concerns and often warrant scrutiny. Increases of more than 200 points in highly concentrated markets are presumed to be likely to increase market power but may be rebutted by persuasive evidence.

An *HHI* of 1,000 would result from a market with 10 equal-sized firms, each with a 10 percent market share, while an *HHI* of 1,800 would result from a market with five to six equal-sized firms. The two *HHI* decision points correspond roughly to four-firm concentration ratios of 50 and 70 percent, respectively.

Another way to use the *HHI* is to calculate the number of "effective competitors" by examining the inverse of the *HHI* when market shares are expressed as fractions

Herfindahl-Hirschman Index (*HHI*)
A measure of market power that is defined as the sum of the squares of the market share of each firm in an industry.

---

[55]Quoted in Viscusi, Harrington, and Vernon, 158–9.
[56]U.S. Department of Justice and the Federal Trade Commission, *Horizontal Merger Guidelines*, Issued August 19, 2010, http://www.justice.gov/atr/public/guidelines/hmg-2010.html.

TABLE 8.1   Measures of Market Power, Selected Manufacturing Industries (1997)

INDUSTRY	CR4	CR8	HHI (50 LARGEST COMPANIES)
Meat products	35	48	393
Breakfast cereal	83	94	2,446
Cigarettes	99	N/A	N/A
Sawmills	15	20	87
Book printing	32	45	364
Household refrigerators/freezers	82	97	2,025
Motor vehicles/car bodies	87	94	N/A
Computers	40	68	658

Source: U.S. Department of Commerce, 1997 Economic Census: Concentration Ratios in Manufacturing (2001, Table 2), http://www.census.gov/prod/ec97/m31s-cr.pdf.

rather than percentages.[57] This procedure may give a more intuitive meaning to values of the *HHI*. For example, in the above case of two firms with equal market shares, the number of effective competitors is $1/0.5 = 2.00$. In the case of two firms with market shares of 90 and 10 percent, the number of effective competitors is $1/0.82 = 1.22$. Thus, in the second case there is only slightly more than one effective competitor in the market.

Table 8.1 shows the four- and eight-firm concentration ratios and the *HHI* for several major manufacturing industries in the United States for 1997. For the four-firm concentration ratios of the 470 manufacturing industries in the *1997 Census of Manufactures*, the ratio is below 40 percent for more than half of the industries, between 41 and 70 percent in about a third of the industries, and over 70 percent in approximately 10 percent of the industries.[58]

Antitrust Issues

Antitrust laws
Legislation, beginning with the Sherman Act of 1890, that attempts to limit the market power of firms and to regulate how firms use their market power to compete with each other.

As we mentioned earlier, the U.S. government has developed **antitrust laws** to limit the market power of firms and to regulate how firms use market power to compete with each other. In this section, we present some of the basic issues of antitrust legislation that managers should know, and we relate these issues to the previous discussion of market power.

Three major pieces of legislation have shaped U.S. antitrust policy:

- The Sherman Act of 1890
- The Clayton Act of 1914
- The Federal Trade Commission Act of 1914

Section 1 of the Sherman Act prohibits contracts, combinations, and conspiracies in restraint of trade, while Section 2 prohibits monopolization, attempts to monopolize, and combinations or conspiracies to monopolize "any part of the trade or commerce among the several states, or with foreign nations." Section 1 targets price-fixing arrangements and prohibits explicit cartels. As interpreted, Section 2 does not prohibit monopoly, but focuses on the behavior of firms with market power.

---

[57]Steven A. Morrison, "Airline Service: The Evaluation of Competition Since Deregulation," in *Industry Studies*, ed. Larry L. Duetsch, 2nd ed. (Armonk, NY: Sharpe, 1998), 147–75.
[58]Carlton and Perloff, *Modern Industrial Organization*.

The Sherman Act was amended in 1914 by the Clayton Act and the Federal Trade Commission Act. The Clayton Act focused on four specific practices:

1. Price discrimination that lessens competition (amended in 1936 by the Robinson-Patman Act)
2. The use of tie-in sales, in which a consumer can purchase one good only if he or she purchases another as well; and exclusive dealings, where a manufacturer prohibits its distributors from selling competing brands that lessen competition
3. Mergers between firms that reduce competition (as amended by the Celler-Kefauver Act of 1950)
4. The creation of interlocking directorates (interrelated boards of directors) among competing firms

The Federal Trade Commission Act created the Federal Trade Commission (FTC) to enforce antitrust laws and resolve disputes under the laws. Section 5 of the FTC Act prohibits "unfair" competition.

These antitrust laws were written in very general terms, so their intent has been interpreted through court cases and litigation over the years. Although some cases of monopolization have been attacked directly, greater attention has been paid to anticompetitive practices that facilitate coordination among sellers, vertical structures and arrangements that increase market power where a firm participates in more than one successive stage of production and distribution, and mergers that increase concentration and the likelihood of coordinated behavior among firms.

Regarding mergers, the Justice Department and the FTC currently operate under the Horizontal Merger Guidelines, which were established in 1982 and revised in 1992, 1997, and 2010. The goal of the guidelines is to prevent harm to consumers enabled by the use of increased market power that might result from a merger. To do so, the guidelines focus on six major issues:

1. The definition of the relevant market
2. The level of seller competition in that market
3. The possibility that a merging firm might be able to unilaterally affect price and output
4. The nature and extent of entry into the market
5. Other characteristics of the market structure that would influence coordination among sellers
6. The extent to which any cost savings and efficiencies could offset any increase in market power

The 2010 Guidelines provided more clarity and transparency on how the Justice Department and the FTC make decisions on whether a merger would harm competition. The Guidelines stated that merger analysis does not use a single methodology but is a fact-based process using multiple tools. The Guidelines included a new section, "Evidence of Adverse Competitive Effects," that discussed categories and sources of evidence the agencies found informative in predicting the likely competitive effects of mergers, and presented the updated values of the *HHI* discussed previously.[59]

---

[59]For further discussion of the new guidelines and comparisons with earlier guidelines, see U.S. Federal Trade Commission, *Federal Trade Commission and U.S. Department of Justice Issue Revised Horizontal Merger Guidelines*, press release, August 19, 2010, http://www.ftc.gov/opa/2010/08/hmg.shtm; U.S. Department of Justice and the Federal Trade Commission, *Horizontal Merger Guidelines*; Carl Shapiro, "The 2010 Horizontal Merger Guidelines: From Hedgehog to Fox in Forty Years," *Antitrust Law Journal* 77 (2010): 49–107; Herbert Hovenkamp, "Harm to Competition Under the 2010 Horizontal Merger Guidelines," *Review of Industrial Organization* 39 (2011): 3–18; and Michael A. Salinger, "The 2010 Revised Merger Guidelines and Modern Industrial Economics," *Review of Industrial Organization* 39 (2011): 159–68.

Almost every merger case centers on the definition of the relevant market. Regarding the merger of Whirlpool and Maytag, the issue was whether front-loading washing machines were in the same market as top-loading machines. In the telecommunications industry, the question is whether cell phones are in the same market as landline phones. For movie theaters, the issue is how close together two movie theaters need to be in order to be considered in the same market.[60]

We illustrate these issues in the case of the proposed merger of Staples and Office Depot in 1997. This case shows the managerial strategies used to defend the firms' actions and how the litigation focused on the microeconomic issues developed in this text. We then briefly discuss the 2011 proposed merger of AT&T and T-Mobile and the reasons why this merger did not occur.

The Proposed Merger of Staples and Office Depot In September 1996, Office Depot and Staples, the two largest office superstores in the United States, announced an agreement to merge.[61] Staples, which introduced the superstore concept in 1986, operated 550 stores in 1997, while Office Depot owned approximately 500 stores. Although there had been 23 office superstores competing earlier in the 1990s, by the time of the proposed merger, only Office Max was a close rival to Staples and Office Depot. Over this time period, the superstore chains had driven thousands of small, independent office supply companies out of business because these smaller companies could not compete with the economies of scale and the market power of the 23,000- to 30,000-square-foot superstores stocking 5,000 to 6,000 items. Consumers had benefited from the low prices and the one-stop shopping for office supplies.

Seven months after the merger was proposed, the FTC voted to oppose the merger on the grounds that it would harm competition and lead to higher prices in the office superstore market. The FTC argued that the relevant market was the "sale of consumable office supplies through office superstores," not the entire market for office supplies. The FTC made this distinction because the superstores carry a broad range of office supplies and maintain a huge inventory that lets consumers do one-stop shopping at these stores. Neither small retailers nor mail-order suppliers could provide this range of services and, thus, the FTC claimed that the superstores operate in a separate market. The FTC presented company documents that showed that the superstores considered only other superstores as their main competitors and that the presence of nonsuperstore competitors had little effect on the prices charged by the superstores. Staples' documents also showed that the company anticipated having to lower prices or raise quality if the merger did not take place and that its retail margins would decline by 1.5 percentage points by 2000 if the merger was not approved.

The FTC thus claimed that the superstores were their own effective competition and that a merger between Staples and Office Depot would allow the new store to raise prices until it was eventually constrained by the nonsuperstore competition. Both Staples and Office Depot had significantly lower prices when they competed with each other in local markets. When all three superstores (Staples, Office Depot, and Office Max) were located in the same geographic area, their prices

[60]Dennis W. Carlton, "Does Antitrust Need to Be Modernized?" *Journal of Economic Perspectives* 21 (Spring 2007): 155–76. A related issue is whether markets are contestable with ease of entry and exit. Industries with only a few firms can be competitive if there is the threat of entry by other firms and if firms can also exit readily. See Carlton and Perloff, *Modern Industrial Organization.*
[61]This discussion is based on Serdar Dalkir and Frederick R. Warren-Boulton, "Prices, Market Definition, and the Effects of Merger: Staples–Office Depot (1997)," in *The Antitrust Revolution: Economics, Competition, and Policy*, eds. John E. Kwoka, Jr., and Lawrence J. White, 5th ed. (New York: Oxford University Press, 2009), 178–99. This case has been called a watershed event in the development of FTC thinking about merger review. See Salinger, "The 2010 Revised Merger Guidelines and Modern Industrial Economics."

were virtually the same, but they were lower than those of the nonsuperstores. The FTC developed a large-scale econometric analysis similar to those discussed in Chapter 4 that predicted that a merger between Staples and Office Depot would raise prices in markets where all three stores were present by 8.49 percent, exceeding the 5 percent rule in the guidelines.

The FTC also argued that the threat of entry by another superstore, such as Office Max, would not prevent the merged store from raising prices until the new entry actually occurred. The FTC claimed that economies of scale at both the store level and the chain level could act as a significant barrier to entry. Staples' strategy had already been to build a critical mass of stores in a given geographic region so that it would be cost-effective to advertise in the regional media.

Staples' and Office Depot's defense in this case was based on the following:

1. A claim that the FTC's definition of the relevant product market was incorrect
2. An argument that efficiencies from the merger, combined with ease of entry into the market and a history of a low pricing policy, made it unlikely that the merger would raise prices

Staples and Office Depot claimed that they were in competition with all other office suppliers, not just the superstores, and that the FTC had taken statements from their documents out of context. This argument meant that the two stores were part of a larger market and had only small market shares. They also claimed that there would be substantial economies of scale from the merger in terms of production, administrative, marketing, advertising, and distribution costs and that the merged firm would pass two-thirds of these cost reductions on to consumers. Staples and Office Depot claimed that entry into the office supply business was relatively easy because stores could be constructed within several months. They cited data on planned store openings by Office Max to justify this contention.

The judge in this case accepted the arguments by the FTC and granted a preliminary injunction blocking the merger, which was then dropped by the companies. He accepted the FTC's definition of the relevant market and found that a merger would have had anticompetitive effects. The premerger *HHI* in the least concentrated market was 3,600, while it was approximately 7,000 in the most concentrated market. The judge accepted the pricing evidence that showed that an office superstore was likely to raise prices when it faced less competition from similar firms. He also found that economies of scale were a significant barrier to entry, particularly because many markets were already saturated by existing office supply superstores.

The AT&T and T-Mobile Merger   In March 2011, AT&T Inc. announced that it was buying T-Mobile USA from Deutsche Telekom AG for $39 billion in cash and stock.[62] This move would merge the second- and fourth-largest U.S. mobile carriers to create the nation's largest wireless carrier. AT&T asserted that the merger would result in $40 billion in cost cuts, while giving the company an additional 130 million customers. AT&T argued that the merger would solve network congestion by combining two companies using the same technology and alleviate a spectrum shortage that would prevent T-Mobile from building a next-generation network. The company also argued that the move would bring better coverage to rural areas. AT&T arranged an 18-month commitment for a one-year bank loan from J. P. Morgan to finance the deal, and it agreed to pay Deutsche Telekom a $3 billion fee and give it additional spectrum if the deal was not closed. In anticipation of antitrust challenges, AT&T did a market-by-market analysis of where its

---

[62]Shayndi Raice and Anupreeta Das, "AT&T to Buy Rival in $39 Billion Deal," *Wall Street Journal (Online)*, March 20, 2011; Shayndi Raice, Amy Schatz, and Anupreeta Das, "AT&T Digs in for a D.C. Fight: With Deal to Buy Rival T-Mobile Sealed, Battle Now Moves to Washington," *Wall Street Journal (Online)*, March 21, 2011.

overlap with T-Mobile was the greatest and concluded that the antitrust risk was bearable. The carrier was willing to make substantial divestitures of some of its services to make the deal go through.

In the months following this announcement, opposition to the merger grew as competitors, state regulators, and elected officials voiced their concerns about the merger.[63] Although Sprint Nextel Corp., the third largest wireless carrier, was the most vocal opponent, Leap Wireless International joined the opposition arguing that the merger would overly concentrate the rights to use the airwaves. California and Louisiana regulators announced they would review the proposal. AT&T hired consultants who showed that the company and T-Mobile had different classes of customers that rarely overlapped. The consultants argued that T-Mobile customers bought cheap phones and no-frills services that did not compete with AT&T's high-end offerings including the iPhone.

On August 31, 2011, the U.S. Justice Department filed a civil antitrust lawsuit to block the proposed merger.[64] The Justice Department argued that the merger would substantially lessen competition for wireless services across the United States, resulting in higher prices, poorer quality services, fewer choices, and fewer innovative products. The suit noted that AT&T and T-Mobile were two of only four mobile wireless providers with nationwide networks and competitive practices associated with a national scale and presence. The government asserted that AT&T and T-Mobile competed head to head in at least 97 of the nation's top 100 Cellular Market Areas (CMAs), which included over half of the U.S. population. The merger would substantially lessen competition in all of these areas. The Justice Department argued that the Big Four carriers competed with each other nationally, and that the merger would reduce this competition and could result in increased coordination among the remaining carriers to the detriment of customers.

The Justice Department also claimed that in 96 of the largest CMAs, the post-merger *HHI* would exceed 2,500 and that the merger would increase the *HHI* by more than 200 points. The government estimated that in more than half of the CMAs, the combined company would have a greater than 40 percent market share, and that nationally the merger would result in an *HHI* of more than 3,100, an increase of nearly 700 points.

The government noted that the independent T-Mobile had developed strategies for aggressive pricing, value leadership, and innovation. The company viewed itself as "the No. 1 value challenger of the established big guys in the market and as well positioned in a consolidated 4-player national market." T-Mobile had been responsible for a number of innovative "firsts" in the wireless industry, which had exerted competitive pressure on AT&T. T-Mobile had developed "Disruptive Pricing" plans to attract future smartphone customers. The Justice Department argued that entry by any new competitors in response to the merger would be difficult, time-consuming, and expensive, and that AT&T could not demonstrate any merger-specific efficiencies that would offset the acquisition's anticompetitive effects. The government concluded that the presence of an independent, competitive T-Mobile and the competition between AT&T and T-Mobile resulted in lower prices for customers than otherwise would have existed.

In November 2011, the proposed merger was dealt a further setback as the Federal Communications Commission (FCC) issued a report stating that the merger would limit competition in virtually every U.S. city and lead to higher prices for consumers. The report found that the loss of an independent T-Mobile would

---

[63]Shayndi Raice and Thomas Catan, "AT&T's Critics on Deal Growing," *Wall Street Journal (Online)*, May 31, 2011.

[64]This discussion is drawn from the government's lawsuit: U.S. Department of Justice, Antitrust Division v. AT&T Inc. and Deutsche Telekom AG, Case: 1:11-cv-01560, August 31, 2011, http://www.justice.gov/opa/pr/2011/August/11-at-1118.html.

give AT&T a "unilateral incentive" to raise prices and that Verizon Wireless and Sprint would follow suit. The FCC argued that AT&T did not need the spectrum from T-Mobile to build its next-generation wireless network and that the merger would result in a net loss of direct jobs. AT&T responded that the FCC report was "an advocacy piece and not a considered analysis."[65]

As December 2011 progressed, AT&T came ever closer to abandoning the proposed merger.[66] The companies announced they were considering "whether and how to revise our current transaction." Deutsch Telekom was evaluating various alternative strategies, such as network-sharing deals, merging with another wireless carrier, or finding a private-equity cash infusion. The companies were discussing proposals with Leap Wireless International Inc. to divest assets worth more than 30 percent of the merger's value to handle the antitrust issues. However, the talks faltered as participants began to believe that even this deal was unlikely to appease the Justice Department. In mid-December, AT&T finally gave up the fight and withdrew it acquisition proposal because it believed it could not satisfy the Justice Department's concerns over the anticompetitive nature of the merger.

In January 2012, T-Mobile and AT&T filed a request with the FCC for approval of the transfer of $1 billion in wireless airwaves that AT&T promised if the merger collapsed. AT&T announced it would turn over the airwaves and $3 billion in cash to T-Mobile. In February 2012, it was reported that AT&T was analyzing new strategies to increase its access to the airwaves, including potential transactions with Leap Wireless International, Dish Network Corp. or MetroPC Communications Inc.[67]

Managerial Rule of Thumb

Understanding Antitrust Laws

Managers of firms with market power are in a constant struggle to preserve and increase this power. Their ability to do so is constrained by antitrust legislation and other regulations. Many of these laws were written in terms of general principles, so managers may not know whether their actions are illegal unless the government initiates litigation. ∎

Monopolistic Competition

We now turn to the model of **monopolistic competition**, a market structure characterized by a large number of small firms that have some market power from producing differentiated products. Because this model incorporates many of the concepts we developed in the first part of this chapter, this section presents only a brief discussion of monopolistic competition.

Monopolistic competition
A market structure characterized by a large number of small firms that have some market power from producing differentiated products. This market power can be competed away over time.

---

[65]Amy Schatz and Greg Bensinger, "FCC Blasts AT&T Deal," *Wall Street Journal (Online)*, November 30, 2011; Amy Schatz, "AT&T Slams FCC, Says Report on Deal Is Unfair," *Wall Street Journal (Online)*, December 2, 2011.

[66]Anton Troianovski, Anupreeta Das, and Thomas Catan, "Revisions Weighed for AT&T Deal," *Wall Street Journal (Online)*, December 13, 2011; Anupreeta Das, Gina Chon, and Anton Troianovski, "AT&T Talks to Sell T-Mobile Assets Go Cold," *Wall Street Journal (Online)*, December 19, 2011; Anton Troianovski, "AT&T Hangs Up on T-Mobile," *Wall Street Journal (Online)*, December 20, 2011; Thomas Catan and Brent Kendall, "AT&T Case Shows Antitrust Mettle," *Wall Street Journal (Online)*, December 21.2011.

[67]Greg Bensinger, "T-Mobile, AT&T Seek Approval of Spectrum Transfer," *Wall Street Journal (Online)*, January 24, 2012; Gina Chon, Anton Troianovski, and Anupreeta Das, "AT&T Hunts Spectrum," *Wall Street Journal (Online)*, February 16, 2012.

Characteristics of Monopolistic Competition

Monopolistic competition lies on one end of the competitive spectrum, close to the model of perfect competition. However, as the name implies, the model incorporates elements of both the perfectly competitive and the monopoly models.

The following are the major characteristics of the model of monopolistic competition:

1. Product differentiation exists among firms
2. There are a large number of firms in the product group
3. No interdependence exists among firms
4. Entry and exit by new firms is relatively easy

Monopolistic competition describes the operation of the small retail stores, restaurants, barber shops, beauty salons, and repair shops that most people encounter in their daily lives. These establishments offer differentiated products, so they do not fit under the model of perfect competition. All Chinese restaurants serve Chinese food, but the range and types of offerings differ among establishments. The location of these businesses also serves as another aspect of product differentiation. Customers may choose a restaurant or repair shop with higher prices that is close to home, even if cheaper products and services are available elsewhere. In monopolistic competition, there are a large number of firms producing the same or similar products. The term *product group* is often used to characterize monopolistically competitive firms in contrast to the industry of perfect competition, which includes all firms producing the same homogeneous product. Given the large number of firms in a product group, there is no interdependence in their behavior. Finally, entry and exit are relatively easy in a product group. There are no substantial barriers to entry, such as economies of scale, which would make firms unlikely to enter the product group if positive economic profits were being earned.

Short-Run and Long-Run Models of Monopolistic Competition

The short-run and long-run models of monopolistic competition are presented in Figures 8.4a and 8.4b, respectively. The short-run model in Figure 8.4a is the same as the monopoly model in Figure 8.1. The monopolistically competitive firm faces

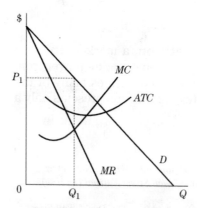

FIGURE 8.4A
Monopolistic Competition, Short Run
At Q_1:
MR = MC
  P > ATC
  P > MC
ATC *Not at Minimum Point*

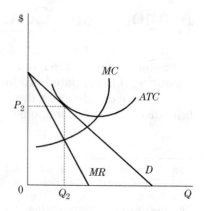

FIGURE 8.4B
Monopolistic Competition, Long Run
At Q_2:
MR = MC
  P = ATC
  P > MC
ATC *Not at Minimum Point*

a downward sloping demand curve, as do all firms in imperfect competition. At any given price, the demand curve for the monopolistically competitive firm may be more elastic than that for the monopolist, given the larger number of substitutes. The monopolistically competitive firm produces the profit-maximizing level of output, where marginal revenue equals marginal cost, and charges the price read off the demand curve. The firm typically earns positive economic profits ($P > ATC$) in the short run because factors such as product differentiation and geographic location give the firm market power. This is the monopolistic aspect of this model.

Given that entry is relatively easy in the long run, the short-run positive economic profits in Figure 8.4a cannot be sustained. Other firms will begin to produce the same or similar products. This will cause the demand curve in Figure 8.4a to shift back in toward the origin and become more elastic as other firms absorb some of the demand previously faced by this firm. The demand curve will shift back until it is tangent to the average total cost curve, resulting in zero economic profit. This position of long-run equilibrium is shown in Figure 8.4b. The firm earns zero economic profit ($P = ATC$) at the profit-maximizing level of output ($MR = MC$). Although this result is a "competitive" type of outcome due to entry into the product group, the equality of price and average total cost does not occur at the minimum point of the average total cost curve, as it does in the model of perfect competition. Monopolistically competitive firms do not have an incentive to produce at the lowest point of their average total cost curve. Because the monopolistically competitive firm has market power and faces a downward sloping demand curve, it also produces where price is greater than marginal cost. This result is different from the perfectly competitive outcome, where price equals marginal cost.

Any positive economic profits tend to disappear relatively quickly for a monopolistically competitive firm, given the lack of substantial barriers to entry. Managers in these firms must continually search for strategies, including product differentiation, market niches, geographic location, and advertising, that can give them at least temporary market power. The monopolistically competitive firm, unlike the perfectly competitive firm, does have an incentive to advertise.

Examples of Monopolistically Competitive Behavior

To illustrate how monopolistically competitive firms attempt to keep market power in the face of intense competition, we discuss the strategies that many of these firms have developed.

Drugstores   Small independent drugstores have been able to compete against the large chains by cutting prices down to cost on at least some of their drugs to match the lower prices chains have achieved through economies of scale. The independents have also developed innovative strategies such as providing more consultation time with the pharmacists, filling special orders on the same day, accepting IOUs from patients unable to pay, and finding products not carried by the chains, including homeopathic remedies. Even so, the number of independent drugstore outlets fell 24 percent to 20,641 between 1992 and 1998 as the number of chain sites increased 16 percent. The chains have responded to the strategies of these monopolistically competitive firms by offering a friendlier atmosphere and more individualized service in some of their outlets.[68]

---

[68]Laura Johannes, "Feisty Mom-and-Pops of Gotham Take Aim at Drugstore Chains," *Wall Street Journal*, March 20, 2000.

These trends have continued in recent years.[69] The National Community Pharmacists Association reported that the number of community pharmacies dropped 5 percent in 2006 and net operating income fell by 30 percent. Independent pharmacies face increased pressure on their costs and prices from pharmacy-benefit managers employed by the major private health insurance companies and from the Medicare and Medicaid programs. For customers with health insurance who may pay the same price for a prescription wherever they have it filled, customer service and convenience are critical to the success of individual pharmacies. Approximately half of the 23,000 independent pharmacies in the United States are in communities with fewer than 20,000 people, thus filling a niche that the large corporate chains may avoid. Independent pharmacies can also purchase services from other firms, such as Cardinal Health, which offers a claim management program, or PharmAccount, which developed a set of calculators providing detailed reports on true dispensing costs, the costs of providing services such as medication therapy management, and a calculator focused on a pharmacy's financial data. Community pharmacies are also increasing their emphasis on specialty drugs—those that are high-cost, injectable, infused, oral, or inhaled, and that generally require close supervision and monitoring.

Many independents have affiliated with networks such as AmerisourceBergen's Good Neighbor Pharmacy with more than 3,600 independents. The Good Neighbor Pharmacy provides retail coaching to independents and identifies key metrics these pharmacists should follow in their markets. The number of local ethnic drugstores has also increased, particularly in New York City, where multiple languages may be spoken in the stores. Independent drugstores have also ranked highly in consumer satisfaction surveys by Consumer Reports, which found that independents made fewer errors, offered swifter service, and were more likely to have medications ready for pickup when promised.[70]

Hardware Stores　Small independent hardware stores have followed similar strategies to compete with chains such as Home Depot and Lowe's by offering personal service and convenience and by selling items that require instructions and advice from knowledgeable salespersons.[71] Small hardware stores are usually located in neighborhoods close to their customers, which gives them geographic market power because the 112,000-square-foot chain warehouse stores are typically built in locations requiring customers to drive to the stores.

Many small hardware stores are also able to obtain some economies of scale because they are part of cooperatives such as Ace Hardware Corp. and TruServe Corp., which owns the True Value, ServiStar, and Coast to Coast trading names. The cooperatives buy goods in bulk on behalf of their members, who then can obtain merchandise 10 to 20 percent cheaper than if they purchased it on their own. The cooperatives also undertake research on store design and promotion, which the individual stores would not be able to afford, and they may manufacture exclusive lines of paint, tools, or other products.

---

[69]This discussion is based on Reid Paul, "Besieged? Here's a Helping Hand for Independents," *Drug Topics*, 151 (17), September 3, 2007, 14; Jack Minch, "Competing with the Giants Pepperell's Tracie Ezzio Bucks Industry Trend with Independent Pharmacy," *Knight Ridder Tribune Business News*, September 26, 2007; Brian C. Rittmeyer, "Independent Pharmacies Face More Competition from Chains," *McClatchy–Tribune Business News*, December 13, 2007; Leah Perry, "Specialty Pharmacy: Don't Miss the Boat," *Drug Topics*, 152 (1), January 14, 2008, 22.

[70]Michael Johnsen, "Independent Network Shows Value of Service," *Drug Store News* 5 (April 19, 2010): 34; Cara Trager, "Take 2 Aspirin, in Every Language," *Crain's New York Business* 12 (March 21, 2011): 13; and Anonymous, "Consumer Reports' Drugstore Ratings: 94% of Shoppers 'Highly Satisfied' with Independents: Some Irked by Long Waits at Big Box Stores," *PR Newswire*, April 5, 2011.

[71]Barnaby J. Feder, "In Hardware War, Cooperation May Mean Survival," *New York Times*, June 11, 1997; James R. Hagerty, "Home Depot Raises the Ante, Targeting Mom-and-Pop Rivals," *Wall Street Journal*, January 25, 1998.

In 2003 Ace Hardware began developing an increasing number of larger format stores with a wide selection of national brands while trying to maintain the personalized service of the small independent stores. In 2006 the cooperative had more than 4,600 members who earned an estimated $13 billion in retail sales in 2005. The cooperative has been experimenting with nontraditional marketing strategies as well as two national community outreach programs.[72]

Independent hardware stores have developed new operations such as full-service paint departments and formed small cooperatives to create their own brand of paint. They may also develop specialty services such as marine goods, or stock a much more extensive inventory of seasonal items than Home Depot. In many cases these independent hardware stores are family-owned businesses that are not burdened with rent or mortgage payments because the stores have been owned by the families for years.[73]

Bookstores   Small independent bookstores, such as Chapter 11 the Discount Bookstore in Atlanta, developed market power through steep discounts on books, aggressive marketing, and accessible locations in strip malls.[74] Although Chapter 11 could not match the amenities and selection of Barnes & Noble and Borders superstores, it could offer low prices because its stores were small (3,000 to 6,000 square feet compared with 20,000 for the chains). Chapter 11 stores had special events such as book signings, and each store was allowed to tailor its selections to the characteristics of its neighborhood. Overall selections were focused on mass-market titles as opposed to specialty markets.

Other independent booksellers have followed similar strategies. An owner in Peoria Heights, Illinois, learned each of her patrons' reading preferences to sell books one-on-one while encouraging the customers to post their favorite authors and books on a chalk board in the store. In Indiana, 97 of its 142 bookstores were independent in 2007 and were located in rural communities outside the greater Indianapolis area, which were not served by the national chains. Alaska, with many towns too small to attract a chain store, had half the population but a third more independent bookstores than Hawaii, where Borders was the dominant bookseller. These independent stores innovated by hosting workshops, book clubs, and book signings and by specializing in areas such as pop culture titles or New Age topics.[75]

In 2010 and 2011 independent bookstores were making a comeback in New York City by carefully choosing their locations and merchandise mix. Some of these stores drew only 75 percent of their revenue from books with the remainder from items such as $6 handcrafted greeting cards. Longtime independent stores have noted that they had to embrace new technology, focus on small neighborhood stores, and often locate near schools and colleges. Expert recommendations, personal attention, and innovations such as literary speed dating have helped many of these stores thrive.[76]

[72]Lisa Girard, "Ace Drafts Blueprint for Growth," *Home Channel News*, 32 (13), October 2, 2006, 13.
[73]Tom Meade, "Hardware Survivors," *Knight Ridder Tribune Business News*, February 27, 2007; Marc D. Allan, "Retailer Battles Big Boxes," *Indianapolis Business Journal*, 28 (25), August 27, 2007, A29.
[74]Jeffrey A. Tannenbaum, "Small Bookseller Beats the Giants at Their Own Game," *Wall Street Journal*, November 4, 1997.
[75]Claire Kirch, "Indies Find a Niche," *Publishers Weekly*, 254 (13), March 26, 2007, 28; Karen Holt, "All Bookselling Is Local," *Publishers Weekly*, 254 (52), December 31, 2007, 12.
[76]Matthew Flamm, "Indie Bookstores Stage Comeback," *New York Business*, 6 (February 7, 2011), 2; Judith Rosen, "Golden Oldies: Survival Tips from the Country's Ten Oldest Bookstores," *Publishers Weekly*, 31, August 1, 2011; Scott Gargan, "Expert Recommendations, Personal Attention Keeps Pages Turning at Independent Bookstores," *McClatchy–Tribune Business News*, January 19, 2012; and Jane Henderson, "A Year When Borders Closed—and Small Bookstores Grew," *McClatchy–Tribune Business News*, January 1, 2012.

However, as the model of monopolistic competition would suggest, not all of these stores survive. The independent stores' share of book sales dropped from about 30 to 10 percent between 1990 and 2002, while the roster of the American Booksellers Association, the trade association for independent stores, decreased from 4,000 members in the early 1990s to 1,800 in 2007. In some cases loyal customers have banded together to put up the financial backing to keep the stores open. However, even the Atlanta-based Chapter 11 bookstore filed for Chapter 11 bankruptcy protection in 2006.[77]

Managerial Rule of Thumb

Maintaining Market Power in Monopolistic Competition

Managers of monopolistically competitive firms must develop a variety of strategies to maintain their market power in the face of intense competition. These strategies include exploiting geographic advantages, offering improved customer service, becoming part of larger cooperatives to lower costs, and developing specialized niches in the market. ∎

Summary

In this chapter, we discussed the strategies of firms with market power using the models of monopoly and monopolistic competition. We first showed how the outcomes of the models differed from those of perfect competition. We then discussed the sources and measurement of market power, how market power is used by firms, and why market power can change over time. We also discussed how firms' strategies are constrained by government antitrust legislation and other regulations as well as market demand.

Key Terms

antitrust laws, p. 216

barriers to entry, p. 201

concentration ratios, p. 214

Herfindahl-Hirschman
    Index (*HHI*), p. 215

Lerner Index, p. 213

lock-in and switching costs,
    p. 208

market power, p. 198

monopolistic competition, p. 221

monopoly, p. 198

network externalities, p. 211

price-setter, p. 198

---

[77]Carolyn Shapiro, "Small Local Stores Bank on Personal Service and Unique Offerings," *McClatchy–Tribune Business News*, December 6, 2007; Nathaniel Popper, "Weekend Journal: Taste: Who's Buying the Bookstore?" *Wall Street Journal*, January 18, 2008; Judith Rosen, "Next Chapter for Chapter 11," *Publishers Weekly*, 253 (18), March 1, 2006, 12.

Exercises

Technical Questions

1. Given the demand curve in the following graph, find (and label) the monopolist's profit-maximizing output and price.

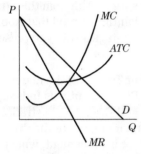

2. Show graphically an example of a monopolist that is producing the profit-maximizing output, but is *not* making a profit.

3. Suppose the demand curve for a monopolist is $Q_D = 500 - P$, and the marginal revenue function is $MR = 500 - 2Q$. The monopolist has a constant marginal and average total cost of $50 per unit.

   a. Find the monopolist's profit-maximizing output and price.
   b. Calculate the monopolist's profit.
   c. What is the Lerner Index for this industry?

4. Demonstrate graphically why persuasive advertising, which makes consumers more loyal to the advertised brand, is likely to increase a firm's market power (its ability to raise price above marginal cost). Will it necessarily increase profit as well?

5. The top four firms in Industry A have market shares of 30, 25, 10, and 5 percent, respectively. The top four firms in Industry B have market shares of 15, 12, 8, and 4 percent, respectively. Calculate the four-firm concentration ratios for the two industries. Which industry is more concentrated?

6. In both Industry C and Industry D, there are only four firms. Each of the four firms in Industry C has a 25 percent market share. The four firms in Industry B have market shares of 80, 10, 5, and 5 percent, respectively.

   a. Calculate the three- and four-firm concentration ratios for each industry.
   b. Calculate the Herfindahl-Hirschman Index for each industry.
   c. Are these industries equally concentrated? Explain your answer.

7. The following graph shows a firm in a monopolistically competitive industry.

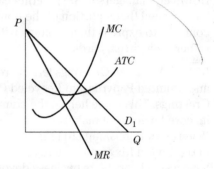

   a. Show the firm's short-run profit-maximizing quantity and price. Is the firm making a profit?
   b. Carefully explain what will happen in the industry over time, and draw a graph of a monopolistically competitive firm in long-run equilibrium.

8. Because products are typically differentiated in some way, there tends to be significant advertising in monopolistically competitive industries. How will advertising affect a typical firm in a monopolistically competitive industry? Explain, using a graph to support your answer.

Application Questions

1. Drawing on current business publications, discuss what has happened to Eastman Kodak Co. since the time this case was written. Has the company been able to develop strategies to regain market power?

2. The following discussion describes changes in the greeting card industry.[78]

   American Greetings Corp., which originated in the early 1900s, has been struggling in the face of a multiyear decline in industry-wide greeting-card

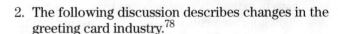

---

[78]Matt Jarzemsky, "Fewer Cards Could Damp Firm's Cheer," *Wall Street Journal (Online)*, December 19, 2011.

sales. Although the company is the second-largest greeting-card maker by sales, it achieved positive growth in the last two quarters of 2011, something it rarely accomplished in the previous two- and one-half years. The company increased revenue through the use of discounts to increase card sales and market share. However, it lowered its annual revenue growth projection from 5% to 3%.

The greeting card industry is facing increased competition from the use of e-cards and the rise of mobile phones to send messages. Many consumers are also replacing traditional holiday cards with photos uploaded to the Internet. Industry analysts have noted that greeting-card sales have declined steadily since 2005 with the trend expected to continue through 2015. However, managers in the greeting-card industry have argued that a portion of the population will continue to express their feelings with physical rather than virtual cards.

In 2009 American Greetings left the retail business and acquired Papyrus and Recycled Paper Greetings. This move helped the company focus on its core business of making cards. It also acquired Watermark Publishing Ltd to increase its presence in the United Kingdom. American Greetings does have a small part of its business devoted to selling e-cards and other digital offerings.

a. Discuss how the case of American Greetings Corp. relates to the market power issues described in the chapter.
b. How might American Greetings increase its market power in the future?

3. The following discussion describes a patent dispute in the pharmaceutical industry:[79]

In 2008, state and federal authorities were examining whether Abbott Laboratories violated antitrust laws in its efforts to prevent an Israeli company from successfully selling a generic version of its cholesterol medicine, TriCor. Although drug companies typically have 3 to 10 years of exclusive patent rights remaining when their products hit the market, they can often find ways to extend their monopolies by patenting slight improvements to those drugs. Twenty-five states and the District of Columbia filed suit in

federal court alleging that in addition to filing new patents on questionable improvements to TriCor, Abbott engaged in a practice known as "product switching." This strategy involved retiring an existing drug and replacing it with a modified version that was marketed as "new and improved," preventing pharmacists from substituting a generic for the branded drug when they filled prescriptions for it. Although this strategy is not illegal, the plaintiffs argued that Abbott employed it and other strategies solely to preserve its monopoly on TriCor.

One year after TriCor hit the market in 1999, Israeli Teva Pharmaceuticals Industries applied to the Food and Drug Administration (FDA) to market a similar version of the drug. Abbott sued Teva for patent infringement, which triggered a 30-month waiting period during which the generic drug could not be launched while patent challenges were being debated. During the waiting period, Abbott altered its product, lowering the dosage and changing it to a tablet from a capsule. It filed for a patent on this modified form of TriCor, bought back the remaining supplies of the capsules and replaced them with the lower-dose tablet. When the 30 months had elapsed, Teva could no longer launch its generic drug because it was no longer strictly bioequivalent to the modified TriCor.

This process was repeated again from 2002 to 2005. Teva filed a counter-suit alleging anti-trust law violation. The company argued that Abbott's strategy allowed pharmaceutical companies to protect their monopolies indefinitely. Abbott said it has the right to protect its innovations and denied switching formulations for the sole purpose of warding off generic competition. It said the two switches brought improvements for patients. Teva argued that the drug's active ingredient stayed the same and that the supposed improvements were smoke screens.

Describe the role of patents as barriers to entry in the pharmaceutical industry. In the current business media, follow up on this and other similar cases involving drug patents to determine the strategies that drug firms are currently employing to maintain their market power.

---

[79]Shirley S. Wang, "TriCor Case May Illuminate Patent Limits," *Wall Street Journal*, June 2, 2008.

4. The following discussion describes recent changes in the strategy of Parker Pen Co.[80]

   Although consumer interest in fine writing pens in the United States may seem equivalent to consumer response to Kodak film and cameras in the opening case of this chapter, Parker Pen Co., which is owned by Newell Rubbermaid Co., developed a strategy to build its presence in China where there is increased income and strong preferences for fine writing pens as part of China's gift-giving business culture. Executives in other parts of the world may have substituted smartphones and tablets for expensive pens, but Chinese professionals are often willing to pay thousands of dollars for them. In response, Parker Pen Co. has darkened its pens' ink to appeal to writers of Chinese characters and added a special Chinese character meaning prosperity and good luck to the pens' heads. These changes have increased sales from 30% to 50% in many of China's department stores.

   The number of Chinese earning a household income of more than one million yuan (approximately $156,000) increased 20% from 2010 to 2011. Pens are an affordable luxury, but also serve as a means for people to display their new wealth. Parker's pens sales had been declining in North America and Europe, so the company turned to China and adopted a higher pricing policy to emphasize the status of the pens. Parker does have competition for its expensive pens from Montblanc, which has opened stores to sell its pens and other products. However, Parker pens contribute "substantially" to overall sales growth for Newell Rubbermaid.

   a. Discuss the role of consumer demand in influencing Parker Pen's strategies.
   b. Do you think Parker will be able to maintain its market power in China? Explain.

5. Indicate whether each of the following statements is true or false, and explain your answer.

   a. If a monopolist is producing a level of output at which demand is inelastic, the firm is not maximizing profits, and increasing output will decrease total revenue.
   b. When a monopolist maximizes profits, the price is greater than the marginal cost of producing the output. This means that consumers are willing to pay more for additional units of the product than these additional units cost to produce. Thus, the monopolist should produce and sell additional units of output.
   c. A monopolistically competitive firm produces a level of output at which price equals $80, marginal revenue equals $40, average total cost equals $100, marginal cost equals $40, and average fixed cost equals $10. To maximize profit, the firm should produce a smaller output and sell it at a higher price.
   d. In a monopolistically competitive market, a firm has market power because it produces a differentiated product. This means that the firm earns positive economic profit in the long run.

---

[80]Cameron McWhirter and Laurie Burkitt, "In China, the Pen Is Mightier When It's Pricier," *Wall Street Journal (Online)*, November 2, 2011.

Market Structure: Oligopoly

I n this chapter, we examine the fourth market model, *oligopoly*. This model is close to the monopoly model and at the other end of the market structure spectrum from the model of perfect competition.

Oligopoly firms typically have market power derived from barriers to entry. However, the key characteristic of oligopoly is that there are a small number of firms competing with each other, so their behavior is mutually interdependent. This interdependence distinguishes oligopoly from all other market structures. In perfect competition and monopolistic competition, there are so many firms that each firm doesn't have to consider the actions of other firms. If a monopolist truly is a single firm producing a product with no close substitutes, it can also form its own independent strategies. However, when 4, 6, or 10 major firms compete with each other, behavior is interdependent. The strategies and decisions by managers of one firm affect managers of other firms, whose subsequent decisions then affect the first firm.

This chapter begins with the case of interdependent behavior in airline pricing. We'll then examine additional cases of oligopoly behavior drawn from the news media. Next we'll look at several models of oligopoly to see how economists have modeled both noncooperative and cooperative interdependent behavior. The goal is not to cover the huge number of oligopoly models that have been developed over the years, all of which attempt to illustrate different aspects of interdependent behavior. Instead, we'll present the insights of a few models and then illustrate these principles with descriptions of real-world oligopolistic behavior. We'll conclude by describing how government antitrust legislation and enforcement influence oligopoly behavior.

Case for Analysis

Oligopoly Behavior in the Airline Industry

Oligopolistic airline pricing behavior has occurred for many years. There are a small number of players in the airline industry, so that price changes by one airline affect the demand for flights of its competitors. As discussed later in this chapter, overt price fixing is illegal in this country and even tacit collusion can be dangerous for firms in terms of antitrust enforcement. Thus, the airlines often try to coordinate their strategies with one company taking a leadership role and then watching for the reactions of its competitors. Price changes are usually implemented on Thursdays or Fridays, so that the lead airline can watch the reaction over the weekend and then make adjustments by Monday. These reactions typically vary by the size and market power of the airline and may differ by the route flown. These behaviors have often been characterized as an intricate chess game.

In March 2002, American Airlines increased its three-day advanced purchase requirement on low-priced business tickets to seven days with the hope that competitors would follow this implicit price increase.[1] When the competitors refused to do so, American retaliated by offering deep discounts on business fares in several of the competitors' markets. In response, Northwest Airlines began offering $198 round-trip fares with connections on three-day advanced purchase tickets in 160 of American's nonstop markets, where the average unrestricted business fare was $1,600. American then offered $99 one-way fares in 10 markets each flown by Northwest, United, Delta, and US Airways. Only Continental Airlines' markets were excluded from these low fares, an outcome that probably resulted because Continental had matched American's original change in all markets.

In March 2004, Continental Airlines tried to raise its fares across the board to cover the rising cost of fuel. Low-cost rivals Southwest and JetBlue refused to follow because they had protected themselves against rising fuel costs with hedging agreements. Continental hedged fuel for 2003 but stopped buying the contracts when they became more expensive due to the rising oil prices. For an entire month, one airline or another tried to impose network-wide fare increases but had to back off because all of their rivals would not follow the increases except on certain routes.[2]

By spring 2005, the airlines had some greater pricing power, having achieved seven fare increases in the first five months of the year. Demand for airline seats had been increasing, particularly with the approach of summer. In May 2005, the price increase was led by American Airlines and was imposed even in markets where it competed with Southwest. As of the Friday afternoon when it was announced, Delta, Continental, Northwest, United, and US Airways had all matched the increase in varying combinations.[3]

By 2011 and 2012, high fuel prices forced most airlines to attempt to raise fares.[4] In February 2011, Delta led the increase and was quickly followed by American. However, given the impact of the slow recovery from the economic recession in 2008, both airlines backed off from the fare increases later in the week. These decisions were also influenced by the reaction of Southwest Airlines, the largest discount carrier in the United States, which did not raise prices. In early 2012, the airlines, which had quietly raised prices for the last half of 2011, continued to try to do so even before the summer 2012 travel season. It appeared that at this time even Southwest Airlines was more willing to accept the price increases than it had in the past.

---

[2]Elizabeth Souder, "Continental Attempts Fare Hike, But Rivals Won't Budge," *Wall Street Journal*, March 26, 2004.
[3]Melanie Trottman, "U.S. Airlines Attempt New Round of Fare Increases," *Wall Street Journal*, May 16, 2005.
[4]This discussion is based on Gulliver, "The Big Airlines Get Cold Feet," *The Economist (Online)*, February 20, 2011; and Kelly Yamanouchi, "Airlines Keep Adapting to High Fuel Costs," *Atlanta Journal Constitution (Online)*, March 4, 2012.

---

[1]Scott McCartney, "Airfare Wars Show Why Deals Arrive and Depart," *Wall Street Journal*, March 19, 2002.

Case Studies of Oligopoly Behavior

Oligopoly
A market structure characterized by competition among a small number of large firms that have market power, but that must take their rivals' actions into account when developing their own competitive strategies.

The behavior just described represents the interdependence of firms operating in an **oligopoly** market. This behavior has become more pervasive as oligopolies have come to dominate many industries in the United States, as shown in Table 9.1. We next discuss oligopoly behavior in several key industries.

The Airline Industry

In addition to the pricing strategies discussed in the opening case study, there are numerous other examples of oligopoly behavior in the airline industry. In the late 1990s, Frontier Airlines was the small upstart carrier trying to compete with United Airlines, particularly at the Denver airport. Frontier developed strategies to compete with its rival by "getting inside United's corporate head, anticipating its moves and countermoves, and chipping away as much business as it can get away with."[5] Frontier officials developed aggressive strategies on pricing and flight scheduling, but restrained these strategies enough to avoid provoking a substantial competitive response from United, which would have had a detrimental impact on Frontier.

Frontier learned from experience that United was likely to tolerate not more than two flights a day to one of its competitive cities and that timing Frontier's flights outside United's windows of connecting flights would make United unlikely to establish a new head-to-head competing flight. Frontier's managers also waited to announce the company's new flights from United's hub at Denver International Airport to Portland, Oregon, until United had loaded its summer schedule into the computer system. This tactic made it difficult for United to rearrange its published schedule of flights to compete against Frontier. Frontier's pricing strategy was to raise ticket prices enough to avoid a price-cutting response from United, but to keep prices low enough to appeal to customers and attract new business. Setting

TABLE 9.1 Oligopolistic Industries in the United States

INDUSTRY	NUMBER OF FIRMS	MARKET SHARE (PERCENT)
Carbonated soft drinks	3	80
Beer	3	80
Cigarettes	3	80
Recorded music	4	80
Railroad operations	4	100
Movies	6	85
Razors and razor blades	3	95
Cookies and crackers	2	80
Carpets	2	75
Breakfast cereals	4	80
Light bulbs	2	85
Consumer batteries	3	90

Source: Stephen G. Hannaford, *Market Domination! The Impact of Industry Consolidation on Competition, Innovation, and Consumer Choice* (Westport, CT: Praeger, 2007), 5. Reprinted by permission.

[5]Scott McCartney, "Upstart's Tactics Allow It to Fly in Friendly Skies of a Big Rival," *Wall Street Journal,* June 23, 1999.

prices far below those of United would have resulted in United not only lowering prices, but also scheduling many more flights to compete with Frontier. However, United's managers needed to make certain that their competitive strategies did not violate U.S. antitrust laws. The U.S. Justice Department had previously accused American Airlines of cutting prices and increasing capacity to stifle new competition in its Dallas–Fort Worth hub airport.

By the summer of 2003, there was a three-way struggle among United, which was now reorganizing its business in bankruptcy court; Frontier, the growing low-cost airline; and the city of Denver, which operated the city's airport, the hub for this competition.[6] Frontier claimed that while United's market share at the Denver airport had declined from 74 to 64 percent, the airport had increased the number of United's gates from 43 to 51. Frontier's market share had more than doubled, increasing from 5.6 to 13.3 percent, while the number of its gates increased from only 6 to 10. United also demanded that the city build a new $65 million regional jet terminal with an additional 38 gates. United wanted to hold its existing gates for future expansion, while Frontier argued that it could put many of those gates to more productive use. The city was caught between the demands of its dominant airline, which had less market power than before 1999, and those of the aggressive low-cost competitor.

Competition for amenities has been another aspect of oligopolistic strategies, particularly among international airlines. Lufthansa Airlines opened a first-class terminal in Frankfurt in 2005 where passengers could have a bubble bath, rest in a cigar room, and be driven to the plane in a Mercedes or Porsche. Middle Eastern carriers have installed lavish closed-door suites in the front of planes, while Virgin Atlantic opened a Clubhouse at London's Heathrow Airport with a beauty salon, cinema, and Jacuzzi.[7] In the fall of 2007, Singapore Airlines began the first commercial flight of the Airbus A380, the biggest passenger jet ever built, with 12 first-class passengers housed in fully enclosed cabins with expandable beds, while 60 seats in business class were 34 inches wide—twice the width of a typical economy seat.[8] Competition on lie-flat seating began in 1999 when Virgin Atlantic Airways introduced a flying bed for its Upper Class cabin that was slightly less than horizontal. British Airways responded by unveiling a fully horizontal business-class lie-flat seat in 2000. Virgin countered in 2003 with a bigger lie-flat seat angled to the aisle, herringbone style with seats arranged head to toe. Delta adopted the herringbone style, while Deutsche Lufthansa announced a Flying V style pattern in 2012 that paired seats with feet closer together than heads.[9]

By the spring of 2008, with the slow economy and oil prices exceeding $130 per barrel, all of the major U.S. airlines were adopting similar strategies to cut costs and raise prices. In June 2008, United Airlines followed the lead of American Airlines in charging passengers for the first checked bag. United had been the first airline to charge for the second checked bag in February 2008, and rivals soon followed. The airlines grounded planes and removed flights from schedules to limit the supply of seats and raise prices. They also searched for new ways to reduce costs, including installing winglets on jets to improve performance, eliminating magazines in cabins to reduce weight, carrying less fuel above required reserve levels, and washing jet engines with new machines that could deep clean while collecting and purifying the runoff.[10]

[6]Edward Wong, "Denver's Idle Gates Draw Covetous Eyes," *New York Times*, August 5, 2003.

[7]Scott McCartney, "A Bubble Bath and a Glass of Bubbly—at the Airport," *Wall Street Journal*, July 10, 2007.

[8]Bruce Stanley and Daniel Michaels, "Taking a Flier on Bedroom Suites," *Wall Street Journal*, October 24, 2007.

[9]Daniel Michaels, "Airlines Escalate Race in Lie-Flat Seating," *Wall Street Journal (Online)*, March 8, 2012.

[10]Scott McCartney, "As Airlines Cut Back, Who Gets Grounded?" *Wall Street Journal*, June 6, 2008; Scott McCartney, "Flying Stinks—Especially for the Airlines," *Wall Street Journal*, June 10, 2008; Jessica Lynn Lunsford, "Airlines Dip into Hot Water to Save Fuel," *Wall Street Journal*, June 11, 2008; Mike Barris, "United Matches American Airlines in Charging for First Checked Bag," *Wall Street Journal*, June 13, 2008.

The Soft Drink Industry

Although Coca-Cola Company and PepsiCo Inc. have long battled each other in the cola wars, their interdependent behavior has moved into the bottled water market with Coke's Dasani and Pepsi's Aquafina brands.[11] Although bottled water comprised less than 10 percent of each company's beverage sales in 2002, bottled water sales in the United States grew 30 percent in 2001 compared with 0.6 percent growth for soft drinks. The bottled water market in 2001 was dominated by a few large firms: Nestle's Perrier Group (37.4 percent market share), Pepsi (13.8 percent), Coca-Cola (12.0 percent), and Danone (11.8 percent). Coke and Pepsi tried to avoid the pricing wars in grocery stores that occurred with the colas, so they concentrated on selling single, cold bottles in convenience stores or vending machines. However, price discounting was already occurring in some grocery stores as more consumers bought water to take home. The rivals also focused on making the product readily available and packaging the water in convenient and attractive bottles. Pepsi launched its Aquafina in a new bottle with a transparent label, while Coke developed a Dasani bottle with a thin, easy-to-grip cap for sports enthusiasts.

The rivals have used different strategies to market goods that are virtually identical. Coke developed a combination of minerals to give Dasani a clean, fresh taste. The formula for this mix is kept as secret as the original Coke formula. Managers also paid much attention to developing the Dasani name, which was intended to convey crispness and freshness with a foreign ring. Pepsi claimed that Aquafina was purer because nothing was added to its exhaustively filtered water and focused its marketing activities around customers "wanting nothing." Both companies developed enhanced versions of their waters. Coke launched Dasani Nutriwater, with added nutrients and essences of pear and cucumber, in late 2002, while Pepsi introduced Aquafina Essentials, with vitamins, minerals, and fruit flavors, in the summer of 2002. In a joint venture with Group Danone, Coke also took over distribution of Dannon bottled water, which gave the company a low-priced brand that would complement the mid-priced Dasani.

By 2008 the two rivals were both managing a complex portfolio of drinks, given that U.S. consumers were buying fewer soft drinks and more beverages such as teas, waters, and energy drinks. From 2003 to 2008 noncarbonated beverages grew from one-quarter to one-third of the nonalcoholic beverage market. Pepsi diversified first by signing joint ventures with Lipton in 1991 and Starbucks in 1994 and acquiring SoBe in 2000 and Gatorade in 2001. These moves gave it the lead in teas, ready-to-drink coffees, and sports drinks. Coca-Cola countered by buying Glaceau enhanced waters and Fuze juice drinks and reaching agreements for Campbell's juice drinks and Caribou and Godiva bottled coffees. Coke and Pepsi continue to try to gain an advantage even in small markets by searching for nuances or trends to determine the best product mix.[12]

The cola wars heated up again in 2011 and 2012 when in March 2011 it was announced that Pepsi had fallen to No. 3 in U.S. soda sales, trailing both Coke and Diet Coke.[13] Coke had battled Pepsi ever since Coke's founding in 1886 and Pepsi's

[11]Betsy McKay, "Pepsi, Coke Take Opposite Tacks in Bottled Water Marketing Battle," *Wall Street Journal*, April 18, 2002; Scott Leith, "Beverage Titans Battle to Grow Water Business," *Atlanta Journal-Constitution*, October 31, 2002.
[12]Joe Guy Collier, "Cola Wars Aren't Just About Cola Any More," *Atlanta Journal-Constitution*, March 28, 2008.
[13]This discussion is based on Natalie Zmuda, "How Pepsi Blinked, Fell Behind Diet Coke: Rough Patches, Risky Moves Cost It Share: Will Return to Basics Be Enough to Get It Back in the Game?" and "Coke Vs. Pepsi: A Timeline," *Advertising Age (Online)*, 82 (March 21, 2011), 1; Mike Esterl and Valerie Bauerlein, "PepsiCo Wakes Up and Smells the Cola," *Wall Street Journal (Online)*, June 28, 2011; and Mike Esterl and Paul Ziobro, "PepsiCo Overhauls Strategy," *Wall Street Journal (Online)*, February 10, 2012.

founding in 1898. Pepsi was accused of changing its focus from cola to products that are "better for you" and engaging in activities such as the Refresh Project, which gave grants to consumers with "refreshing ideas that change the world," but may not have helped the company's profits. In 2010 and early 2011, the company set a goal of more than doubling revenue from its nutritious products by 2020 while developing a corporate image focusing on health and global responsibility. In response to the loss of market share, Pepsi announced in 2012 that it was cutting 8,700 jobs and increasing its marketing budget by $600 billion that year with most of this budget directed to five key brands: Pepsi, Mountain Dew, Gatorade, Tropicana, and Lipton. In February 2012, the company ran its first Super Bowl TV ad for Pepsi in three years.

The Doughnut Industry

In the summer of 2001, Krispy Kreme Doughnuts of Winston-Salem, North Carolina, announced its plans to open 39 outlets in Canada over the following six years to compete directly with Tim Hortons—an American-owned, but Canadian-operated chain that is considered to be somewhat of a national institution in Canada.[14] Canada is a profitable market because the country has more doughnut shops per capita than any other country. Tim Hortons was already the second-largest food service company in Canada, with 17 percent of quick-service restaurant sales. It drove out much of the competition through efficient service and aggressive tactics, such as opening identical drive-through outlets on opposite sides of the same street to attract customers traveling in either direction. Krispy Kreme is another large company, with $448.1 million in sales in 2001 and 192 stores across 32 states.

As Krispy Kreme managers made the decision to move north to Canada, Tim Hortons' managers were expanding south, focusing on U.S. border cities such as Detroit and Buffalo. The company had also invaded Krispy Kreme's territory by opening two stores in West Virginia and one in Kentucky. Both companies engaged in product differentiation, with Tim Hortons emphasizing its product diversity—soups and sandwiches as well as doughnuts—while Krispy Kreme focused on its signature product—hot doughnuts. Tim Hortons also relied on its Canadian roots to ward off the competition from its U.S. competitor by using "We never forget where we came from" as its advertising theme in Canada. The doughnut battle in Canada appears to be between these two oligopolistic competitors, who are directly countering each other's strategies. Dunkin' Donuts Inc., the world's largest doughnut chain, with 5,146 stores in 39 countries, has been in Canada since 1961, but owns only 6 percent of the Canadian doughnut/coffee shops.

Tim Hortons has continued its expansion in the United States, confronting both Krispy Kreme and Dunkin' Donuts. In 2007 most of its 340 stores in the United States were near the Canadian border in Michigan, Ohio, and upstate New York. By the end of 2008, the company had a goal of 500 U.S. stores, assuming it could establish a presence in New England, the home of Dunkin' Donuts. Although Hortons' style was more similar to Dunkin' than Starbucks, the company tried to differentiate itself from Dunkin' by offering more comfortable seats, china mugs, and cheaper coffee. Hortons has a strong association with coffee, although little name recognition in the United States. The company has encouraged its franchisees to get involved with local communities by sponsoring sports teams and summer camps.[15]

---

[14]Joel Baglole, "Krispy Kreme, Tim Hortons of Canada Square Off in Each Other's Territory," *Wall Street Journal*, August 23, 2001.

[15]Douglas Belkin, "A Canadian Icon Turns Its Glaze Southward," *Wall Street Journal*, May 15, 2007.

Dunkin' Donuts also tried to expand in the South, the West, and overseas by designing stores similar to coffeehouses and adding more sandwiches. This change in strategy came at a time when McDonald's had moved toward selling lattes and cappuccinos to the same type of customer. The challenge for Dunkin' was to decide how much style to add to its brand. Some of the new stores were painted in coffee-colored hues until long-time customers indicated they wanted more of the old bright pink and orange. A new hot sandwich was renamed a "stuffed melt" after customers complained that calling it a "panini" was too fancy. Research showed that Dunkin's customers were unpretentious and disliked the more stylized chains such as Starbucks. This research concluded that the Dunkin "tribe" members wanted to be part of the crowd, while members of the Starbucks tribe had a desire to stand out as individuals. Dunkin managers also decided to keep the goal of moving its customers through the cash register line in two minutes compared with Starbuck's goal of three minutes.[16]

When Dunkin' went public in 2011, it announced that it had experienced 45 consecutive quarters of positive comparable store-sales growth until the recession in 2008 and 2009.[17] The company had 206 net new store openings in 2010, planned to develop existing markets east of the Mississippi River, and also had international expansion plans, particularly in South Korea and the Middle East. Tim Horton's was still primarily focused in Ontario, Canada and had achieved only limited profitability with the stores it had opened in the northern U.S.

The Parcel and Express Delivery Industry

United Parcel Service (UPS) and Federal Express (FedEx) control approximately 80 percent of the U.S. parcel and express delivery services, with UPS having a 53 percent market share and FedEx a 27 percent share. Although these two firms are normally intense rivals, in early 2001 they formed an alliance to keep a third competitor, the German firm Deutsche Post AG, out of the U.S. market.[18] Both companies filed protests with the U.S. Department of Transportation, alleging that the German company was trying to get around U.S. laws to subsidize an expansion in the United States with profits from its mail monopoly in Germany. The U.S. companies contended that it was unfair for the German firm, which was partially owned by the German government, to compete in the United States because the U.S. Postal Service was not allowed to deliver packages in other countries. Deutsche Post AG owned a majority stake in Brussels-based DHL International Ltd., which had a stake in its U.S. affiliate, DHL Airways of Redwood City, California. UPS and FedEx contended that DHL International and Deutsche Post AG had essentially taken control of DHL Airways, placing that company in violation of federal laws prohibiting foreign ownership of more than 25 percent of a U.S. air carrier.

UPS and FedEx tried to block expansion of the German firm in the United States at the same time the U.S. companies tried to expand in Europe. That expansion was countered by Deutsche Post AG, as the German firm lowered its parcel-delivery prices in light of increased U.S. competition. UPS and FedEx

---

[16]Janet Adamy, "Dunkin' Donuts Tries to Go Upscale, But Not Too Far," *Wall Street Journal*, April 8, 2006; Janet Adamy, "Dunkin Donuts Whips Up a Recipe for Expansion," *Wall Street Journal*, May 3, 2007.

[17]This discussion is based on Lynn Cowan, "As Dunkin' Donuts Goes Public, It's Time to Question the Valuation," *Wall Street Journal (Online)*, July 26, 2011; John Jannarone, "Doughnut IPO a Slam-Dunk with Investors," *Wall Street Journal (Online)*, July 28, 2011; and Andrew Bary, "Dunkin' Brands Shares Look Too Pricey to Sample," *Wall Street Journal (Online)*, September 4, 2011.

[18]Rick Brooks, "FedEx, UPS Ask U.S. to Suspend DHL Flights, Freight Forwarding," *Wall Street Journal*, January 24, 2001; Rick Brooks, "FedEx, UPS Join Forces to Stave Off Foreign Push into U.S. Delivery Market," *Wall Street Journal*, February 1, 2001.

faced relatively weak competition in the U.S. delivery market and attempted through coordinated behavior to block entry by the German competitor.

DHL did enter the U.S. package delivery industry in 2003, although the company was still unprofitable in 2007. DHL captured 7 percent of the U.S. market by 2005 when it announced that it was "not setting out to create another UPS or FedEx." The company's reputation suffered from a difficult hub consolidation in 2005 that cost it customers and revenue. In the spring of 2008, DHL announced that it was planning to transfer its North American air-parcel deliveries to UPS and cut its U.S. network capacity on the ground by one-third. In November 2008, the company announced that it was ending its domestic U.S. deliveries by January 2009, while continuing delivery and pickup of international shipments. Blaming its cutbacks on both competition from UPS and FedEx and the declining economy, DHL planned to shut its 18 U.S. ground hubs, reduce the number of delivery stations from 412 to 103, and eliminate 9,500 jobs.[19]

By 2011, DHL rebuilt its U.S. operations around international shipments with sales of approximately $1 billion per year. The company had a daily volume of 115,000 international packages compared with a daily load of 1.2 million parcels before the 2008 pullback. The attempt to compete with UPS and FedEx cost DHL $9.6 billion in 2008 and was called a "disaster" by DHL managers. Analysts have stated that UPS and FedEx were "tickled pink" not to have DHL as a domestic rival because DHL had entered the United States with lower rates than the other two companies. UPS earned an average revenue per domestic package of $8.20 in 2004, which increased to $8.85 in 2010.[20]

Oligopoly Models

Economists have developed a variety of models to capture different aspects of the interdependent behavior inherent in oligopoly, although none of the models incorporates all elements of oligopolistic behavior.[21] The many models can be divided into two basic groups: noncooperative and cooperative models. In **noncooperative oligopoly models**, managers make business decisions based on the strategy they think their rivals will pursue. In many cases, managers assume that their rivals will pursue strategies that inflict maximum damage on competing firms. Managers must then develop strategies of their own that best respond to their competitors' strategies. The implication of many noncooperative models is that firms would be better off if they could cooperate or coordinate their actions with other firms.

This outcome leads to **cooperative oligopoly models**—models of interdependent oligopoly behavior that assume that firms explicitly or implicitly cooperate with each other to achieve outcomes that benefit all the firms. Although cooperation may benefit the firms involved, it can also set up incentives for cheating on the cooperative behavior, and it may be illegal. The above discussion of UPS and FedEx shows that oligopolists may engage in noncooperative behavior with each other and cooperative behavior to keep out further competition.

Noncooperative oligopoly models
Models of interdependent oligopoly behavior that assume that firms pursue profit-maximizing strategies based on assumptions about rivals' behavior and the impact of this behavior on the given firm's strategies.

Cooperative oligopoly models
Models of interdependent oligopoly behavior that assume that firms explicitly or implicitly cooperate with each other to achieve outcomes that benefit all the firms.

[19]Andrew Ward, "DHL Reins in Its Ambitions in U.S. Market," *Financial Times*, May 18, 2005; William Hoffman, "Debating DHL's Gains," *Traffic World*, May 21, 2007; Corey Dade, "FedEx Cuts Outlook as Conditions Worsen," *Wall Street Journal*, March 21, 2008; Mike Esterl and Corey Dade, "DHL Sends an SOS to UPS in $1 Billion Parcel Deal," *Wall Street Journal*, May 29, 2008; Corey Dade, Alex Roth, and Mike Esterl, "DHL Beats a Retreat from the U.S.," *Wall Street Journal*, November 8, 2008.

[20]Natalie Doss and Mary Jane Credeur, "With Overseas Delivery, DHL Rebuilds," *Transport Topics (Online)*, April 25, 2011.

[21]Many of these economic models are extremely mathematical. For a summary discussion, see Tonu Puu, *Oligopoly: Old Ends—New Means* (Berlin: Springer-Verlag, 2011).

Noncooperative Oligopoly Models

Let's now look at several models of noncooperative oligopoly behavior in which managers of competing firms make judgments and assumptions about the strategies that will be adopted by their rivals.

The Kinked Demand Curve Model

Kinked demand curve model

An oligopoly model based on two demand curves that assumes that other firms will not match a firm's price increases, but will match its price decreases.

One of the simplest models of oligopoly behavior that incorporates assumptions about the behavior of rival firms is the **kinked demand curve model**, shown in Figure 9.1. The kinked demand curve model assumes that a firm is faced with two demand curves: one that reflects demand for its product if all rival firms follow the given firm's price changes (D_1) and one that reflects demand if all other firms do not follow the given firm's price changes (D_2). Demand curve D_1 is relatively more inelastic than demand curve D_2 because D_1 shows the effect on the firm's quantity demanded if all firms follow its price change.

For example, if the firm considers raising the price above P_1, its quantity demanded will depend on the behavior of its rival firms. If other firms match the price increase, the firm will move along demand curve D_1 and have only a slight decrease in quantity demanded. However, if the rival firms do not match the price increase, the firm will move along demand curve D_2 and incur a much larger decrease in quantity demanded.

The same principle holds for price decreases. If the firm lowers its price below P_1 and other firms follow, the increase in quantity demanded will move along demand curve D_1. If other firms do not match the price decrease, the firm will have a much larger increase in quantity demanded, as it will move along the relatively more elastic demand curve, D_2.

The behavioral assumption for managers of the firm in this model is that other firms will behave so as to inflict maximum damage on this firm. This means that other firms will not follow price increases, so that only the given firm has raised the price, but other firms will match price decreases so as to not give this firm a competitive advantage. This assumption means that the portions of the two demand curves relevant for this firm are D_2 for prices above P_1 and D_1 for prices below P_1. Thus, the firm faces a kinked demand curve, with the kink occurring at price P_1.

The implications of this kinked demand curve model for profit maximization can be seen by noting the shape of the marginal revenue curve. The portion of MR_2 that is shown in Figure 9.1 is relevant for prices above P_1, whereas the illustrated portion of MR_1 is relevant for prices below P_1. These are the marginal revenue curves that correspond to demand curves D_2 and D_1 in those price ranges. The marginal

FIGURE 9.1
Kinked Demand Curve Model of Oligopoly
The kinked demand curve model of oligopoly incorporates assumptions about interdependent behavior and illustrates why oligopoly prices may not change in reaction to either demand or cost changes.

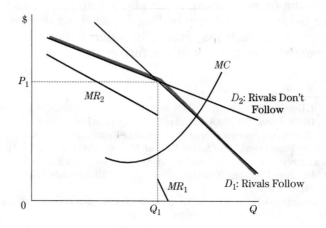

revenue curve is discontinuous at price P_1, where the kink occurs in the demand curve. Given the marginal cost curve shown in Figure 9.1, the profit-maximizing level of output is Q_1 and the optimal price is P_1.

As you can see in Figure 9.1, the marginal cost curve could shift up and down within the discontinuous portion of the marginal revenue curve and the profit-maximizing price and quantity would not change. This outcome is different from the standard model of a firm with market power where changes in demand and in either marginal revenue or marginal cost result in a new profit-maximizing price and quantity (Chapter 8).

Likewise, if the demand curves shift out, but the kink remains at the same price, the profit-maximizing price will not change. The kinked demand curve model of oligopoly implies that oligopoly prices tend to be "sticky" and do not change as much as they would in other market structures, given the assumptions that a firm is making about the behavior of its rival firms. Critics have charged that prices in oligopoly market structures are not more rigid than in other types of markets. The kinked demand curve model also does not explain why price P_1 exists initially. However, we saw examples of firms testing different price changes to determine the behavior of their rivals in the airlines examples. The kinked demand curve model is one illustration of that behavior.

Game Theory Models

Game theory incorporates a set of mathematical tools for analyzing situations in which players make various strategic moves and have different outcomes or payoffs associated with those moves. The tool has been applied to oligopoly behavior, given that the outcomes in this market, such as prices, quantities, and profits, are a function of the strategic behaviors adopted by the interdependent rival firms. Games can be represented by payoff tables, which show the strategies of the players and the outcomes associated with those strategies.

Game theory
A set of mathematical tools for analyzing situations in which players make various strategic moves and have different outcomes or payoffs associated with those moves.

Dominant Strategies and the Prisoner's Dilemma   The most well-known game theory example is the prisoner's dilemma, which is illustrated in Table 9.2. The example assumes that two outlaws, Bonnie and Clyde, have been captured after many years on a crime spree. They are both taken to jail and interrogated separately, with no communication allowed between them. Both Bonnie and Clyde are given the options outlined in the table, with Bonnie's options shown in bold. If neither one confesses to their crimes, there is only enough evidence to send each of them to prison for two years. However, if Bonnie confesses and Clyde does not, she will be given no prison term, while her evidence will be used to send Clyde to prison for 10 years. Clyde is made the same offer if he confesses and Bonnie does not. If both individuals confess, they will each receive a five-year prison term.

We assume that even though Bonnie and Clyde have been partners in crime, each one will make the decision that is in his or her own best interest. Bonnie's best strategy if Clyde does not confess is to confess, as she will not receive a prison

TABLE 9.2   The Prisoner's Dilemma

		CLYDE	
		DON'T CONFESS	**CONFESS**
Bonnie	**Don't Confess**	**2 years,** 2 years	**10 years,** 0 years
	Confess	**0 years,** 10 years	**5 years,** 5 years

term in that case. If Clyde does confess, Bonnie's best strategy is also to confess, as she will go to prison for only 5 years instead of the 10 years she would receive if she did not confess.

Clyde's reasoning will be exactly the same. If Bonnie does not confess, he should confess, as he will not go to prison. If Bonnie does confess, Clyde should also confess to minimize his prison sentence. Thus, both partners are led to confess, and they each end up with a prison term of five years. Both would have been better off if neither had confessed. However, in the given example, they were not able to communicate with each other, so neither one could be certain that the other partner would not confess, given the incentives of the example. Both Bonnie and Clyde would have been better off if they could have coordinated their actions or if they could have trusted each other enough not to confess.

Dominant strategy
A strategy that results in the best outcome or highest payoff to a given player no matter what action or choice the other player makes.

In game theory terms, both Bonnie and Clyde had a **dominant strategy**, a strategy that results in the best outcome or highest payoff to a given player no matter what action or choice the other player makes. If both players have dominant strategies, they will play them, and this will result in an equilibrium (both confessing, in the above example). The prisoner's dilemma occurs when all players choose their dominant strategies and end up worse off than if they had been able to coordinate their choice of strategy. All players are prisoners of their own strategies unless there is some way to change the rules of the game. Thus, one of the basic insights of game theory is that cooperation and coordination among the parties may result in better outcomes for all players. This leads to the cooperative models of oligopoly behavior that we'll discuss later in the chapter. The prisoner's dilemma results may also be less serious in repeated games as learning occurs, trust develops between the players of the game, or there are clear and certain punishments for cheating on any agreement.

A business example of the prisoner's dilemma focuses on the strategies of cigarette companies for advertising on television before the practice was banned in 1970.[22] The choice for competing firms was to advertise or not; the payoffs in profits in millions of dollars to each company are shown in Table 9.3.

The outcomes in Table 9.3 are similar to those in the Bonnie and Clyde example in Table 9.2. Each company has an incentive to advertise because it can increase its profits by 20 percent if it advertises and the other company does not. Advertising for both companies is a dominant strategy, so the equilibrium is that both companies will advertise. However, this outcome leaves each of them with profits of $27 million compared with profits of $50 million if neither company advertised. Simultaneous advertising tends to cancel out the effect on sales for each company while raising costs for both companies. Yet neither company would choose not to advertise, given the payoffs that the other company would obtain if only one company advertised. The companies were caught in a prisoner's dilemma.

TABLE 9.3   Cigarette Television Advertising

		COMPANY B	
		DO NOT ADVERTISE	**ADVERTISE**
Company A	**Do Not Advertise**	**50,** 50	**20,** 60
	Advertise	**60,** 20	**27,** 27

Source: Roy Gardner, *Games for Business and Economics* (New York: John Wiley, 1995), 51–53. Copyright © 1995. Reprinted by permission of John Wiley & Sons, Inc.

---

[22]This example is drawn from Roy Gardner, *Games for Business and Economics* (New York: John Wiley, 1995), 51–53.

In this case, the rules of the game were changed by the federal government. In 1970, the cigarette companies and the government reached an agreement that the companies would place a health warning label on cigarette packages and would stop advertising on television in exchange for immunity from lawsuits based on federal law. This outcome was beneficial for the cigarette industry because it removed the advertising strategy from Table 9.3 and let all companies engage in the more profitable strategy of not advertising on television.

Nash Equilibrium   Many games will not have dominant strategies, in which the players choose a strategy that is best for them regardless of what strategy their rival chooses. In these situations, managers should choose the strategy that is best for them, given the assumption that their rival is also choosing his or her best strategy. This is the concept of a **Nash equilibrium**, a set of strategies from which all players are choosing their best strategy, given the actions of the other players. This concept is useful when there is only one unique Nash equilibrium in the game. Unfortunately, in many games, there may be multiple Nash equilibria.

We illustrate a game with a unique Nash equilibrium in Table 9.4, where two firms are considering the effect on their profits of expanding their capacity.[23] Their choices are no expansion, a small capacity expansion, and a large capacity expansion. Expansion of capacity would allow a firm to obtain a larger market share, but it would also put downward pressure on prices, possibly reducing or eliminating economic profits. We assume that the decisions are made simultaneously with no communication between the firms and that the profits under each strategy (in millions of dollars) are shown in the table.

We can see in Table 9.4 that there isn't a dominant strategy for either firm. If Firm 2 does not expand or plans a small expansion, Firm 1 should plan a small expansion. However, if Firm 2 plans a large expansion, Firm 1 should not expand. The same results hold for Firm 2, given the strategies of Firm 1. Thus, there is not a single strategy that each firm should pursue regardless of the actions of the other firm. There is, however, a unique Nash equilibrium in Table 9.4: Both firms plan a small expansion. Once this equilibrium is reached, each firm would be worse off by changing its strategy.

However, as in the prisoner's dilemma, both firms would be better off if they could coordinate their decisions and choose not to expand plant capacity. In that situation, each firm would have a payoff of $18 million compared with the $16 million to each firm in the Nash equilibrium. However, that outcome is not a stable equilibrium. Each firm could increase its profits through a small expansion if it thought the other firm would not expand capacity. This strategy would lead both firms to plan a small capacity expansion, the Nash equilibrium. This example also shows the benefits of coordinated behavior among the firms.

Nash equilibrium
A set of strategies from which all players are choosing their best strategy, given the actions of the other players.

TABLE 9.4   Illustration of Unique Nash Equilibrium

		FIRM 2		
		DO NOT EXPAND	SMALL EXPANSION	LARGE EXPANSION
Firm 1	Do Not Expand	18, 18	15, 20	9, 18
	Small Expansion	20, 15	16, 16	8, 12
	Large Expansion	18, 9	12, 8	0, 0

Source: David Besanko, David Dranove, and Mark Shanley, *Economics of Strategy,* 2nd ed. (New York: John Wiley, 2000), 37–40. Copyright © 2000. Reprinted by permission of John Wiley & Sons, Inc.

[23]This example is drawn from David Besanko, David Dranove, and Mark Shanley, *Economics of Strategy,* 2nd ed. (New York: John Wiley, 2000), 37–40.

The above examples of the prisoner's dilemma and Nash equilibrium are cases of simultaneous decision making. Strategies and outcomes differ if the decision making is sequential, with one side making the first move. In this case, an unconditional move to a strategy that is not an equilibrium strategy in a simultaneous-move game can give the first mover an advantage as long as there is a credible commitment to that strategy.[24]

Strategic Entry Deterrence

Strategic entry deterrence

Strategic policies pursued by a firm that prevent other firms from entering the market.

Limit pricing

A policy of charging a price lower than the profit-maximizing price to keep other firms from entering the market.

Another way that managers in oligopoly firms can try to limit competition from rivals is to practice **strategic entry deterrence**, or to implement policies that prevent rivals from entering the market.[25] One such policy is **limit pricing**, or charging a price lower than the profit-maximizing price in order to keep other firms out of the market. Figure 9.2 shows a simple model of limit pricing.

Figure 9.2 shows the graphs for an established firm and for a potential entrant into the industry. The existing firm is assumed to have lower costs, given a factor such as economies of scale. The profit-maximizing level of output for the established firm is Q_M, where marginal revenue equals marginal cost. The price is P_M, and the profit earned is represented by the rectangle $(P_M)AB(ATC_M)$. Because the established firm earns positive economic profit by producing at the profit-maximizing price (P_M), this profit will attract other firms into the industry. Price P_M lies above the minimum point on the average total cost curve of the potential entrant (ATC_{EN}). Thus, the positive economic profit shown in Figure 9.2 is not sustainable for the established firm over time due to entry.

To thwart entry, the established firm can charge the limit price, P_L, or a lower price, rather than the profit-maximizing price P_M. The potential entrant would not find it profitable to enter at this price. The established firm could charge a price down to the point where its average total cost curve intersects its demand curve and still make positive or at least zero economic profit. The profit for the established firm at Q_L, which is represented by the rectangle $(P_L)CF(ATC_L)$, is lower than the profit at Q_M, but it is more sustainable over time.

FIGURE 9.2

Limit Pricing Model

With limit pricing, an established firm may set a price lower than the profit-maximizing price to limit the profit incentives for potential entrants to the industry.

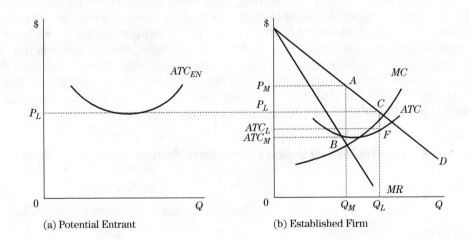

(a) Potential Entrant   (b) Established Firm

---

[24]A complete discussion of these issues in nonmathematical terms is found in Avinash K. Dixit and Barry J. Nalebuff, *Thinking Strategically: The Competitive Edge in Business, Politics, and Everyday Life* (New York: Norton, 1991). For a discussion of cooperative and noncooperative strategies, see Adam M. Brandenburger and Barry J. Nalebuff, *Co-opetition* (New York: Currency Doubleday, 1996).
[25]This discussion is based on Frederic Michael Scherer and David Ross, *Industrial Market Structure and Economic Performance*, 3rd ed. (Boston: Houghton Mifflin, 1990), 356–71.

However, these strategies must be credible, in that rivals must be convinced that the established firm will continue its policy of low prices. Even profits that exist at these prices may attract entry, particularly if potential entrants are able to adopt lower-cost technologies. Thus, many dominant oligopolists lose market share over time due to entry. The established firm loses the least amount of market share when it has a high market share, when economies of scale are important, and when the minimum efficient scale of production can satisfy a large fraction of industry demand.

When it introduced the Xerox 914 copier in 1959, the Xerox Corporation recognized that different degrees of competition and entry existed in the copier market based on volume of copies demanded. In the low-volume market, the company had no substantial cost advantage over competitors, so prices were set close to the profit-maximizing level with the expectation that market share would be lost to competitors. Twenty-nine firms entered this market between 1961 and 1967. In the medium- to high-volume market, Xerox had a modest to substantial cost advantage, so prices were set below the profit-maximizing level, but above the entry-deterring level. Entry by other firms was much less frequent in this market than in the low-volume market. By 1967, there were only 10 firms in the medium-volume market and 4 firms in the high-volume market. In the very high-volume market, Xerox enjoyed a substantial cost advantage protected by patents. In this market, the company was able to charge prices substantially exceeding costs for nearly a decade without attracting much entry.

Predatory Pricing

While limit pricing is used to try to prevent entry into the industry, **predatory pricing** is a strategy of lowering prices to drive firms out of the industry and scare off potential entrants. This strategy is not as widespread as often believed because the firm practicing predation must lower its price below cost and therefore incur losses itself with the expectation that these losses will be offset by future profits. The predatory firm must also convince other firms that it will leave the price below cost until the other firms leave the market. If the other firms leave and the predatory firm raises prices again, it may attract new entry. If all firms have equal costs, the predatory firm may incur larger losses than rival firms. The legal standard for predatory pricing is often considered to be pricing below marginal cost, which is typically approximated as pricing below average variable cost, given the lack of data on marginal cost.

The Case of Matsushita Versus Zenith   The basic issues of predatory pricing are illustrated in Figure 9.3.[26] This figure can be used to illustrate the issues in *Matsushita versus Zenith*, a court case in which the National Union Electric Corporation and Zenith Radio Corporation filed suit against Matsushita and six other Japanese electronic firms, accusing them of charging monopoly prices for televisions in Japan and then using those profits to subsidize below-cost television exports to the United States. In Figure 9.3, assume that P_C is the pre-predation competitive price for televisions in the United States and that it is equal to a constant long-run average and marginal cost. Quantity demanded at this price is Q_C. Suppose that the predatory price of the Japanese sellers is P_P and that in response to this price U.S. firms leave the market and cut back output, so that the total output produced by U.S. sellers is Q_{US}. Assume also that demand remains unchanged.

Predatory pricing
A strategy of lowering prices below cost to drive firms out of the industry and scare off potential entrants.

[26]This diagram and the discussion of *Matsushita v. Zenith* are based on Kenneth G. Elzinga, "Collusive Predation: Matsushita v. Zenith (1986)," in *The Antitrust Revolution: Economics, Competition, and Policy*, ed. John E. Kwoka, Jr., and Lawrence J. White, 3rd ed. (New York: Oxford University Press, 1999), 220–38.

FIGURE 9.3

Predatory Pricing

Predation:

Japanese share of

market = $Q_P - Q_{US}$ = NM = RG

Loss per unit to Japanese

firms = $P_C - P_P$ = NR

Total loss to Japanese firms = NRGM

Postpredation:

U.S. price = P_{US}

Japanese price = P_J

Japanese share of

market = $Q_{PP} - Q_{US}$

Japanese profits = RTLS

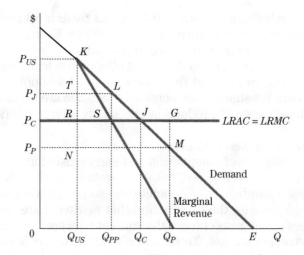

The total quantity demanded at the predatory price of P_P is Q_P, of which Q_{US} is supplied by U.S. firms. The Japanese firms must produce the remaining output, $Q_P - Q_{US}$. The loss to the Japanese firms is $P_C - P_P$ (= NR) per unit of output, which is the difference between the predatory price and long-run average cost. Thus, the total losses to the Japanese firms are represented by the area *NRGM*.

Assume that after predation is over, the U.S. firms are beaten back and continue to produce only output Q_{US}, which is sold at price P_{US}. The Japanese now face only the "residual" demand curve, which is *KE* on the demand curve. The marginal revenue curve associated with this residual demand curve intersects the long-run marginal cost curve at point *S*, so the Japanese will charge price P_J and produce output level $Q_{PP} - Q_{US}$. They will earn profits represented by the rectangle *RTLS*. These profits after recoupment (*RTLS*) must be greater than the losses suffered during predation (*NRGM*) for predatory pricing to be a successful policy. Although this outcome does not appear to be the case in Figure 9.3, this figure represents profits and losses for only one period. Actual benefits and costs must be measured over time, which may be a substantial number of years.[27]

In the court case of *Matsushita versus Zenith*, the economic analysis indicated that the Japanese firms could never have earned profits sufficient to recoup their losses from the alleged predatory pricing, and, therefore, the court ruled for the Japanese firms. The success of a predatory pricing policy depends on

• How far the predatory price is below cost
• The period of time during which the predatory price is in effect
• The rate of return used for judging the investment in predatory pricing
• How many rivals enter the industry after predation ends
• The length of time over which recoupment of profits occurs

For both color and black-and-white televisions, an economic analysis showed that the Japanese firms would not be able to recoup their profits, given the size of the loss from the predatory pricing below cost and the relatively modest price increases possible during the recoupment period. However, even in the face of losses, predatory pricing in one market might still be rational if a firm achieves the reputation of being aggressive. This reputation can spill over and deter entry in other markets.

---

[27]This process involves calculating the time value of money or the present value of the benefits and costs occurring at different points in time. These concepts are typically covered in finance courses.

The Case of Spirit Airlines Versus Northwest Airlines   In 1996, Spirit and Northwest Airlines became involved in a price war on two domestic routes that each airline served: Detroit–Philadelphia and Detroit–Boston.[28] In 2000, Spirit filed an antitrust suit against Northwest alleging that it engaged in predatory pricing to drive Spirit from the market, so that it could raise prices to monopoly levels. Northwest argued that this strategy represented head-to-head competition and that consumers benefited from the low prices.

As in the above discussion, the case revolved around market definition and whether Northwest could exercise monopoly power in the absence of Spirit Airlines and whether Northwest's prices were below an appropriate measure of its costs. The market definition-dispute centered on whether the appropriate product market was only local passengers on the two routes or whether it also included connecting passengers. There was also disagreement about whether there were substantial barriers to entry that allowed Northwest to acquire and keep monopoly power. Arguments over costs focused on the use of marginal versus average variable costs and the definition of fixed versus variable costs.

In 2005, the district court found the case in favor of Northwest Airlines and concluded that it did not engage in below-cost pricing during the period of the alleged predation. However, the U.S. Sixth Circuit Court of Appeals reversed the district court's holding in December 2005. As part of its ruling, the Sixth Circuit Court cited studies of how low-cost carriers increased competition and lowered prices. The Court noted that Northwest had previously referred to the Detroit airport as a "unique strategic asset," which required protection "at almost all costs." Northwest executives had also made statements in the past that the company would match or beat potential entrants' lowest fares, so that passengers would not have an incentive to fly with the new entrant.

Cooperative Oligopoly Models

The second set of oligopoly models focuses on cooperative behavior among rivals. Our examples of both the prisoner's dilemma and the Nash equilibrium showed that the pursuit of individual strategies, while making assumptions about a rival's behavior, could leave both firms worse off than if they had been able to collaborate or coordinate their actions.

Cartels

The most explicit form of cooperative behavior is a **cartel**, an organization of firms that agree to coordinate their behavior regarding pricing and output decisions in order to maximize profits for the organization. Figure 9.4 illustrates this concept of cartel **joint profit maximization**. It also illustrates why cartel members have an incentive to cheat on cartel agreements. The potential to cheat exists because what is optimal for the cartel organization may not be optimal for the individual cartel members.

Model of Joint Profit Maximization   For simplicity, Figure 9.4 illustrates the joint profit maximization problem for a cartel composed of two members. We have assumed that both firms have linear upward sloping marginal cost curves, but that these curves are not identical. At every level of output, Firm 1's marginal

Cartel
An organization of firms that agree to coordinate their behavior regarding pricing and output decisions in order to maximize profits for the organization.

Joint profit maximization
A strategy that maximizes profits for a cartel, but that may create incentives for individual members to cheat.

---

[28]This discussion is based on Kenneth G. Elzinga and David E. Mills, "Predatory Pricing in the Airline Industry: Spirit Airlines v. Northwest Airlines (2005)," in *The Antitrust Revolution: Economics, Competition, and Policy*, ed. John E. Kwoka, Jr., and Lawrence J. White, 5th ed. (New York: Oxford University Press, 2009), 219–47; and Kimberly L. Herb, "The Predatory Pricing Puzzle: Piecing Together a Unitary Standard," *Washington and Lee Law Review* 64 (Fall 2007): 1571–617.

FIGURE 9.4

Cartel Joint Profit Maximization
A cartel maximizes the profits of its members by producing where marginal revenue equals marginal cost for the cartel and then allocating output among its members so that the marginal cost of production is equal for each member. This procedure can give cartel members the incentive to cheat on the cartel agreement.

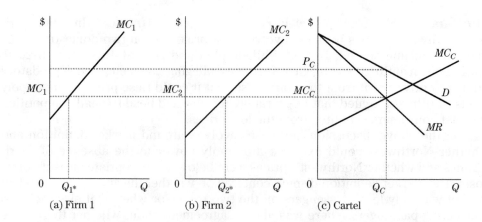

(a) Firm 1   (b) Firm 2   (c) Cartel

cost is higher than Firm 2's marginal cost. The costs of production do typically vary among cartel members, which is a major cause of the cheating problem discussed later in the chapter. The marginal cost curve for the cartel (MC_C) is derived

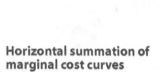

Horizontal summation of marginal cost curves
For every level of marginal cost, add the amount of output produced by each firm to determine the overall level of output produced at each level of marginal cost.

from the summation of the individual firms' marginal cost curves, or the **horizontal summation of marginal cost curves.**[29] For every level of marginal cost measured on the vertical axis, we add the amount of output Firm 1 would produce at that marginal cost to the amount of output Firm 2 would produce at the same marginal cost to determine the cartel output at that cost. Repeating this process for various levels of marginal cost traces out the cartel marginal cost curve (MC_C).

For joint profit maximization, the cartel must determine what overall level of output to produce, what price to charge, and how to allocate the output among the cartel members. The demand and marginal revenue curves facing the cartel are shown in Figure 9.4c. The profit-maximizing level of output (Q_C) is determined by equating marginal revenue with the cartel's marginal cost. The profit-maximizing price is, therefore, P_C.

Allocating Output Among Cartel Members   The cartel must then decide how to allocate this total output, Q_C, among the two cartel members. The optimal allocation that minimizes the costs of production is achieved by having each firm produce output levels such that their marginal costs of production are equal. The intuition of this rule can be seen in Table 9.5 In this table, Firm 1's marginal cost is always double that of Firm 2. If the goal is to produce 20 units of output overall and each firm produces 10 units, $MC_1 = \$40$, $MC_2 = \$20$, and $TC_1 + TC_2 = \$300$.

TABLE 9.5   Equating Marginal Cost to Minimize Total Cost

FIRM 1			FIRM 2		
Q	MC ($)	TC ($)	Q	MC ($)	TC ($)
5	20	50	5	10	25
10	40	200	10	20	100
15	60	450	15	30	225
20	80	800	20	40	400

This simple example is based on the following equations and the assumption of zero fixed costs: $TC_1 = 2Q^2$, $MC_1 = 4Q$, $TC_2 = Q^2$, and $MC_2 = 2Q$.
To find the cost-minimizing method of producing a total of 20 units of output, solve the equations $MC_1 = MC_2$ and $Q_1 + Q_2 = 20$. The solution is $Q_1 = 6.67$, $MC_1 = \$26.68$, $TC_1 = \$88.98$, $Q_2 = 13.33$, $MC_2 = \$26.66$, and $TC_2 = \$177.69$. $TC_1 + TC_2 = \$266.67$.

---

[29]This process is similar to the derivation of the market demand curve from individual firms' demand curves (Chapter 2).

Firm 1 should produce less output, as it has the higher marginal cost, and Firm 2 should produce more output, as it has the lower marginal cost. As Firm 2 produces more output, its marginal cost increases, while Firm 1's marginal cost decreases as it produces less output. As shown in Table 9.5, the cost-minimizing allocation of output between the firms is $Q_1 = 6.67$ and $Q_2 = 13.33$, with $TC_1 + TC_2 = \$266.67$.

Applying this rule to Figure 9.4, we see that Firm 1 should produce output level Q_{1*} and Firm 2 should produce output level Q_{2*} so that their marginal costs of production are equal to each other and to the cartel's marginal cost. The optimal outputs for Firms 1 and 2 are equal to the total cartel output ($Q_{1*} + Q_{2*} = Q_C$), as shown by the construction of the cartel marginal cost curve. This allocation rule for joint profit maximization is summarized in Equation 9.1:

9.1 $MC_1 = MC_2 = MC_C$

> *where*
> $MC_1 =$ Firm 1's marginal cost
> $MC_2 =$ Firm 2's marginal cost
> $MC_C =$ cartel's marginal cost (derived from horizontal summation of the firm's marginal cost curves)

Cheating in Cartels By solving the cartel joint profit-maximization problem, we can see the incentive for cheating in cartels. In Figure 9.4, the optimal level of output for Firm 1 is much less than the level of output for Firm 2. If Firm 1's marginal cost curve had intersected the axis above the value MC_C, its optimal allocation of output would have been zero. Joint profit maximization when firms have unequal costs of production implies that these firms' output shares will be unequal. If they are expected to sell this output at the cartel profit-maximizing price, the profits of the two firms will be quite different. Both firms have an incentive to expand output to the point where the cartel price (P_C) equals their marginal cost of production because this would be the best strategy for profit maximization by each individual firm.

Cartel Success A cartel is likely to be the most successful when

1. It can raise the market price without inducing significant competition from noncartel members.
2. The expected punishment for forming the cartel is low relative to the expected gains.
3. The costs of establishing and enforcing the agreement are low relative to the gains.[30]

If a cartel controls only a small share of the market, it can expect significant competition from noncartel members. The existence of positive economic profits from the cartel pricing policy is also likely to attract more competition. In the United States, price- and output-fixing agreements were made illegal by the Sherman Antitrust Act of 1890. Germany, Japan, and the United Kingdom once permitted the formation of cartels that their governments thought would increase efficiency.

More recently, countries in the European Union have adopted antitrust laws similar to those in the United States. In these cases, with the expected punishment

---

[30]This discussion is based on Dennis W. Carlton and Jeffrey M. Perloff, *Modern Industrial Organization*, 4th ed. (Boston: Pearson Addison-Wesley, 2005), 122–56. For an extensive discussion with numerous examples on how cartels are organized, see Herbert Hovenkamp and Christopher R. Leslie, "The Firm as Cartel Manager," *Vanderbilt Law Review* 64 (April 2011): 811–73.

for explicit agreements very severe, firms must consider the expected costs and benefits of less formal behavior, to be discussed below. The costs of organizing a cartel will be lower if there are few firms involved, the market is highly concentrated, the firms are producing nearly identical products, and a trade association exists.

All of these factors lower the costs of negotiating and bargaining among the cartel members. Cartels try to prevent cheating by dividing the market into specific buyers and geographic areas or by agreeing to fix market shares. Contracts may include agreements to a buyer that the seller is not selling at a lower price to another buyer. Cartel agreements may also include a trigger price. If the market price drops below this trigger price, firms can expand output to their precartel levels or abandon the cartel agreement.

Well-Known Cartels: OPEC   Perhaps the most well-known cartel is OPEC—the Organization of Petroleum Exporting Countries—founded by Saudi Arabia, Iran, Iraq, Kuwait, and Venezuela in 1960 to counter the market power of the major international oil companies.[31] During the early 1970s, world oil demand was at an all-time high, while the supply was increasingly concentrated in the low-production-cost countries of the Middle East. There was also a fringe of non-OPEC suppliers, but these countries faced substantially higher development and operating costs. In response to Western support for Israel during the Egyptian–Israeli War of 1973, OPEC instituted production cutbacks and an oil embargo against the West. The price of oil rose from less than $10 a barrel to over $30 per barrel as a result of this action. Another oil price increase occurred after the fall of the Shah of Iran in 1979. Oil demand in the United States declined sharply after the second price shock, and energy use in the European Union and Japan also began to decline. At the same time, oil output of OPEC member Venezuela and non-OPEC producers increased. The pricing behavior of the cartel resulted in the entry of new oil producers and changed consumer behavior, substantially weakening the cartel.

Saudi Arabia is the dominant player in the cartel, given its vast reserves of oil and its cost advantage in production. Thus, there are different incentives facing cartel members, as well as the competitive supply from non-OPEC members. OPEC members Saudi Arabia, Kuwait, and the United Arab Emirates have vast oil reserves, small populations, and large economies, so they are more conservative about selling oil for revenues than are poorer countries with large populations, such as Indonesia, Nigeria, and Algeria. OPEC's market share fell to 30 percent by 1985, largely due to production cutbacks by Saudi Arabia. Internal dissension about quotas occurred among OPEC members from the late 1980s to the 1990s. The major Arab oil producers expanded their output following the Gulf War in 1991, as bargaining power within OPEC seemed to be related to production capacity. Member quotas were raised in 1997 in anticipation of increased world demand. This did not materialize, so prices fell that year.

Since 2000, a similar pattern has continued, with OPEC members trying to enforce quotas, but with substantial competition from non-OPEC producers severely limiting the strength of the cartel.[32] In fall 2001, OPEC producers predicted that oil prices could fall to $10 per barrel. They argued that such a price drop might be the only way to make non-OPEC producers limit their output, which they had refused

---

[31]This discussion is based on Stephen Martin, "Petroleum," in *The Structure of American Industry*, eds. Walter Adams and James Brock, 10th ed. (Upper Saddle River, NJ: Prentice Hall, 2001), 28–56.
[32]"Non-OPEC Output Rose in November Weakening OPEC's Role in Oil Market," *Dow Jones Newswires*, December 13, 2001; "Russia Says It Will Phase Out Restrictions on Oil Exports," *Wall Street Journal*, May 19, 2002; Jim Efstathiou, "OPEC Members Wary of Looming Higher Non-OPEC Oil Supply," *Wall Street Journal*, May 20, 2002.

to do previously. OPEC members, excluding Iraq, had cut oil production by 290,000 barrels per day, but non-OPEC countries, such as Russia, Angola, and Kazakhstan, had increased output by 630,000 barrels per day. OPEC members reduced production in early 2002, but also pressured non-OPEC countries to do the same. Russia, Norway, Mexico, Oman, and Angola responded, but several months later Russia announced that it was planning to increase exports again. These actions on the part of both OPEC and non-OPEC members illustrate how difficult it is to maintain cartel behavior.

In fall 2006, there was again downward pressure on oil prices. OPEC had to decide what price to defend with a total limit on production and how to allocate quotas among members. OPEC officials publicly contradicted themselves over what type of system they were discussing. Many oil ministers suggested $55 per barrel of U.S. benchmark crude as the price the group would defend, although some wanted a price closer to $60. At this point OPEC had split into two camps. One group of countries, including Kuwait, Algeria, and Libya, were able to greatly exceed the individual production quotas OPEC had assigned each member. Other countries, such as Venezuela, Iran, and Indonesia, struggled to meet their quotas. Saudi Arabia had already been quietly trimming its output in the previous several months.[33]

By the fall of 2007, world demand drove oil prices to the $70 range in September and close to $100 per barrel by November. This created a different set of problems for the cartel. In September 2007, the cartel raised its output limits so that it would not appear to be benefiting while many of the world's economies slowed. Saudi Arabia, with its large reserves, again took the lead in increasing output. Many of the other countries were already pumping oil to the limit. At the OPEC meeting in November 2007, there was discussion about whether the current high prices were justified. The Saudi oil minister, the cartel's de facto leader, suggested he would prefer to see prices come down as did officials from the United Arab Emirates. However, Venezuela and Iran both defended the prices as fair. Venezuelan President Hugo Chavez also called for a return of the 1970s-style "revolutionary OPEC," although this view was not accepted by the Saudis.[34]

These divisions among OPEC members continued in recent years.[35] At an acrimonious meeting in June 2011, a group led by Saudi Arabia, Kuwait, Qatar, and the United Arab Emirates pushed for an increase in oil production of 1.5 million barrels a day, which would have brought OPEC's total production to 30.3 million barrels per day or approximately one-third of world supplies. The Saudis were blocked by six members, including Iran, Algeria, Angola, Venezuela, Ecuador, and Libya, who argued that the demand for oil would remain soft. Analysts noted that this was a split between the "haves" and "have-nots" in the cartel and reflected underlying political divisions over the Arab Spring democracy movement. Some analysts noted that Saudi Arabia might unilaterally increase its own production despite its stated quota. In February 2012, OPEC cut its demand-growth projections for 2012 by one-third, given the slowing of Asian economies. However, the cartel was still producing almost a million barrels per day above a target established in December 2011. Analysts expected this trend could increase strife among the cartel members.

---

[33]Bhushan Bahree, "A Slippery Debate Stirs in OPEC," *Wall Street Journal*, September 22, 2006; Chip Cummins, "Oil-Price Drop Challenges OPEC Unity," *Wall Street Journal*, October 19, 2006.

[34]Peter Fritsch and Oliver Klaus, "OPEC Seeks Soft Landing for Oil," *Wall Street Journal*, September 12, 2007; Neil King, Jr., "OPEC's Divisions Rise to Surface," *Wall Street Journal*, November 19, 2007.

[35]This discussion is based on Summer Said, Hassan Hafidh, and Benoit Faucon, "Meeting Casts Doubt on OPEC's Influence," *Wall Street Journal (Online)*, June 8, 2011; and Benoit Faucon, "OPEC Cuts Oil Demand View but Still Pumps More," *Wall Street Journal (Online)*, February 9, 2012.

The Diamond Cartel The international diamond cartel, which organizes the production side of the diamond market, may be the most successful and enduring cartel in the world.[36] DeBeers, the dominant company in the industry, was founded in 1880 and has been controlled by a single South African family, the Oppenheimers, since 1925. Eight countries—Botswana, Russia, Canada, South Africa, Angola, Democratic Republic of Congo, Namibia, and Australia—produce most of the world's gem diamonds under a system with an explicit set of rules. These countries adjust production to meet expected demand, stockpile excess diamonds, and sell most of their output to the Diamond Trading Company in London, which is owned by DeBeers.

Cecil Rhodes, the founder of DeBeers, realized from the start that the company needed to control the supply of diamonds to maintain their scarcity and perceived value and that the South African individual miners would be unable to control production. The solution was to organize a vertically integrated organization to manage the flow of diamonds from South Africa. Rhodes organized the Diamond Syndicate under which distributors would buy diamonds from him and sell them in agreed-upon numbers and at agreed-upon prices. This organization was taken over by the Oppenheimers, who, over the years, took new diamond producers into the fold. Demand was managed through the introduction of the slogan, "A diamond is forever," in 1948, which implicitly told customers that the product was too valuable ever to be resold and that diamonds equal love.

Even the controversy over "blood" or "conflict" diamonds benefited the cartel. Around the year 2000, activists began arguing that warlords in Sierra Leone, Liberia, the Congo, and elsewhere funded their brutal activities by the sale of diamonds and that these diamonds should be boycotted, a move that would have had a major impact on DeBeers. The end result of this controversy was the Kimberly Process, an international program begun in 2002 and supported by the producing countries, importing countries, nongovernmental organizations, the jewelry trade, and the United Nations. This program included a complex certification system for all diamonds regarding their origin and a commitment by all participants to adhere to the rules of the system. DeBeers wholeheartedly supported this program because the end result was to keep excess supplies off the market and prevent entry by new suppliers. Warlords and other small suppliers were kept out of the market, and the additional costs of tagging, monitoring, and auditing made entry more difficult for new and smaller players. Both DeBeers and the Canadian producers were the major beneficiaries of this program.

By the fall of 2011, there were further changes in the diamond cartel.[37] The Oppenheimers sold their remaining 40 percent stake in DeBeers to the mining giant Anglo American for over $5 billion. The family was concerned that too much of its fortune was tied up in one commodity, so there was a constant risk of a market crash. An increased number of diamond suppliers had fragmented old partnerships over many years. Many analysts saw the diamond industry consolidating, similar to the mining industry in general, with major players, such as Anglo American and Rio Tinto, spending billions to gain control of their mineral assets. Demand was expected to remain strong in the West and to increase in China, India, and the Middle East.

---

[36]This discussion is based on Debora L. Spar, "Continuity and Change in the International Diamond Market," *Journal of Economic Perspectives* 20 (Spring 2006): 195–208. For a further analysis, see Peter A. Stanwick, "DeBeers and the Diamond Industry: Squeezing Blood Out of a Precious Stone," *International Journal of Case Studies in Management* 9 (November 2011): 1–29.

[37]This discussion is based on Sugata Ghosh and Ram Sahgal, "Diamond Houses Keep Fingers Crossed After Change of Guard at DeBeers," *The Economic Times (Online)*, December 13, 2011; and Richard Warnica, "Diamonds Aren't Forever," *Maclean's*, January 16, 2012.

Tacit Collusion

Because cartels are illegal in the United States due to the antitrust laws, firms may engage in **tacit collusion**, coordinated behavior that is achieved without a formal agreement. Practices that facilitate tacit collusion include

Tacit collusion
Coordinated behavior among oligopoly firms that is achieved without a formal agreement.

1. Uniform prices
2. A penalty for price discounts
3. Advance notice of price changes
4. Information exchanges
5. Swaps and exchanges[38]

However, managers must be aware that many of these practices have been examined by the Justice Department and the Federal Trade Commission (FTC) to determine whether they have anticompetitive effects. Cases are often ambiguous because these practices can also increase efficiency within the industry.

Charging uniform prices to all customers of a firm makes it difficult to offer discounts to customers of a rival firm. This policy may be combined with policies that require that any decreases in prices be passed on to previous customers in a certain time period, as well as to current customers. This strategy decreases the incentives for a firm to lower prices. Price changes always cause problems for collusive behavior, as the firm that initiates the change never knows whether its rivals will follow.

In some cases, there is formal **price leadership**, in which one firm, the acknowledged leader in the industry, will institute price increases and wait to see if they are followed. This practice was once very common in the steel industry. However, price leadership can impose substantial costs on the leader if other firms do not follow. A less costly method is to post advance notices of price changes, which allows other firms to make a decision about changing their prices before the announced price increase actually goes into effect. We will discuss this practice in more detail below.

Price leadership
An oligopoly strategy in which one firm in the industry institutes price increases and waits to see if they are followed by rival firms.

Collusive behavior may also be strengthened by information exchanges, as when firms identify new customers and the prices and terms offered to them. This policy can help managers avoid price wars with rival firms. However, in the *Hardwood Case* (1921), lumber producers, who ran the American Hardwood Manufacturers Association, collected and disseminated pricing and production information. Although the industry was quite competitive, with 9,000 mills in 20 states and only 465 mills participating in the association, the Supreme Court ruled that the behavior violated the Sherman Antitrust Act, and the information exchange was ended.

Firms may also engage in swaps and exchanges in which a firm in one location sells output to local customers of a second firm in another location in return for the reciprocal service from the second firm. This practice occurs in the chemical, gasoline, and paper industries, where the products are relatively homogeneous and transportation costs are significant. These swaps can allow firms to communicate, divide the market, and prevent competition from occurring.

The Ethyl Case   In the *Ethyl Case* (1984), the FTC focused on several facilitating practices that it claimed resulted in anticompetitive behavior among the four producers of lead-based antiknock compounds used in the refining of gasoline—the Ethyl Corporation, DuPont, PPG Industries, and Nalco Chemical Company.[39]

---

[38]This discussion is based on Carlton and Perloff, *Modern Industrial Organization*, 379–87.
[39]George A. Hay, "Facilitating Practices: The Ethyl Case (1984)," in *The Antitrust Revolution: Economics, Competition, and Policy*, ed. John E. Kwoka, Jr., and Lawrence J. White, 3rd ed. (New York: Oxford University Press, 1999), 182–201.

The practices included advance notices of price changes, press notices, uniform delivered pricing, and most-favored-customer clauses. All four firms gave their customers notices of price increases at least 30 days in advance of the effective date. Thus, other firms could respond to the first increase before it was implemented.

Until 1977, the firms issued press notices about the price increases, which provided information to their rivals. All firms quoted prices on the basis of a delivered price that included transportation, and the same delivered price was quoted regardless of a customer's location. This delivered pricing strategy removed transportation costs from the pricing structure and simplified each producer's pricing format, making it easier to have a uniform pricing policy among the firms. The firms also used most-favored-customer clauses, in which any discount off the uniform delivered list price given to a single customer would have to be extended to all customers of that seller.

The effect of these clauses was to prevent firms from stealing rivals' customers by lowering prices to certain customers. This could easily happen in the antiknock compound industry because sales were made privately to each of the industrial customers and might not be easily detected by rivals. These clauses meant that the uncertainty about rivals' prices and pricing decisions was reduced. In this case, the FTC ruled against the industry, but the court of appeals overruled this decision. Much of the appellate court's decision was based on the fact that many of these practices were instituted by the Ethyl Corporation before it faced competition from the other rivals, and, therefore, the court concluded the purpose of these practices was not to reduce competition.

Airline Tariff Publishing Case Similar issues regarding communication of advanced pricing information arose in the *Airline Tariff Publishing Case* (1994).[40] In December 1992, the Justice Department filed suit against the Airline Tariff Publishing Company (ATPCO) and eight major airlines, asserting that they had colluded to raise prices and restrict competition. The Justice Department charged that the airlines had used ATPCO, the system that disseminates fare information to the airlines and travel agency computers, to carry on negotiations over price increases in advance of the actual changes. The system allowed the airlines to announce a fare increase to take effect some number of weeks in the future.

Often the airlines iterated back and forth until they were all announcing the same fare increase to take effect on the same date. The Justice Department alleged that the airlines used fare basis codes and footnote designators to communicate with other airlines about future prices. The airlines argued that they were engaging in normal competitive behavior that would also benefit consumers, who were often outraged when the price of a ticket increased between the time they made the reservation and the time they purchased the ticket. The Justice Department believed that any benefits of these policies were small compared with the ability of the airlines to coordinate price increases.

Under the settlement of the case, the airlines cannot use fare basis codes or footnote designators to convey anything but very basic information; they cannot link different fares with special codes; and they cannot pre-announce price increases except in special circumstances. The settlement does not restrict what fares an airline can offer or when specific fares can be implemented or ended. Since this antitrust dispute, the airlines have engaged in pricing practices discussed in the opening case—that is, posting an increase on a Friday afternoon, waiting to see if the rivals respond, and then either leaving the increase in place or abandoning it by Monday morning.

[40]Severin Borenstein, "Rapid Price Communication and Coordination: The Airline Tariff Publishing Case (1994)," in *The Antitrust Revolution: Economics, Competition, and Policy*, eds. John E. Kwoka, Jr., and Lawrence J. White, 3rd ed. (New York: Oxford University Press, 1999), 310–26.

Managerial Rule of Thumb

Coordinated Actions

Managers in oligopoly firms have an incentive to coordinate their actions, given the uncertainties inherent in noncooperative behavior. Their ability to coordinate, however, is constrained by a country's antitrust legislation, such as the prohibition on explicit cartels and the limits placed on many types of tacit collusion in the United States. There are also incentives for cheating in coordinated behavior. It is often the case that any type of behavior that moderates the competition among oligopoly firms is likely to be of benefit to them even if formal agreements are not reached. However, oligopolists, like all firms with market power, must remember that this power can be very fleeting, given the dynamic and competitive nature of the market environment. ■

Summary

In this chapter, we have focused on the interdependent behavior of oligopoly firms that arises from the small number of participants in these markets. Managers in these firms develop strategies based on their judgments about the strategies of their rivals and then adjust their own strategies in light of their rivals' actions. Because this type of noncooperative behavior can leave all firms worse off than if they coordinated their actions, there are incentives for either explicit or tacit collusion in oligopoly markets. Explicit collusive agreements may be illegal and are always difficult to enforce. Many oligopolists turn to forms of tacit collusion, but managers of these firms must be aware that their actions may come under scrutiny from governmental legal and regulatory agencies.

Key Terms

cartel, p. 245

cooperative oligopoly models, p. 237

dominant strategy, p. 240

game theory, p. 239

horizontal summation of marginal cost
  curves, p. 246

joint profit maximization, p. 245

kinked demand curve model, p. 238

limit pricing, p. 242

Nash equilibrium, p. 241

noncooperative oligopoly models,
  p. 237

oligopoly, p. 232

predatory pricing, p. 243

price leadership, p. 251

strategic entry deterrence, p. 242

tacit collusion, p. 251

Exercises

Technical Questions

1. The following graph shows a firm with a kinked demand curve.

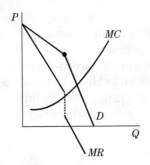

a. What assumption lies behind the shape of this demand curve?
b. Identify the firm's profit-maximizing output and price.
c. Use the graph to explain why the firm's price is likely to remain the same, even if marginal costs change.

2. The following matrix shows strategies and payoffs for two firms that must decide how to price.

		Firm 2	
		PRICE HIGH	PRICE LOW
FIRM 1	PRICE HIGH	**400**, 400	**–50**, 700
	PRICE LOW	**700**, –50	**100**, 100

a. Does either firm have a dominant strategy, and if so, what is it?

b. What is the Nash equilibrium of this game?

c. Why would this be called a prisoner's dilemma game?

3. Some games of strategy are cooperative. One example is deciding which side of the road to drive on. It doesn't matter which side it is, as long as everyone chooses the same side. Otherwise, everyone may get hurt.

		Driver 2	
		LEFT	RIGHT
DRIVER 1	LEFT	0, 0	−1000, −1000
	RIGHT	−1000, −1000	0, 0

a. Does either player have a dominant strategy?

b. Is there a Nash equilibrium in this game? Explain.

c. Why is this called a cooperative game?

4. A game that everyone knows is coin flipping. Suppose that Player 1 flips the coin (and is so skilled that he is able to flip it whichever way he wants) and Player 2 calls heads or tails. The winner gets $10 from the loser.

		Player 2 (call)	
		HEADS	TAILS
PLAYER 1 (FLIP)	HEADS	−10, 10	10, −10
	TAILS	10, −10	−10, 10

a. Does either player have a dominant strategy?

b. Is there a Nash equilibrium in this game? Explain.

c. Games like this are called *zero-sum games*. Can you explain why?

5. A monopolist has a constant marginal and average cost of $10 and faces a demand curve of $Q_D = 1000 − 10P$. Marginal revenue is given by $MR = 100 − 1/5Q$.

a. Calculate the monopolist's profit-maximizing quantity, price, and profit.

b. Now suppose that the monopolist fears entry, but thinks that other firms could produce the product at a cost of $15 per unit (constant marginal and average cost) and that many firms could potentially enter. How could the monopolist attempt to deter entry, and what would the monopolist's quantity and profit be now?

c. Should the monopolist try to deter entry by setting a limit price?

6. Consider a market with a monopolist and a firm that is considering entry. The new firm knows that if the monopolist "fights" (i.e., sets a low price after the entrant comes in), the new firm will lose money. If the monopolist accommodates (continues to charge a high price), the new firm will make a profit.

		Entrant	
		ENTER	DON'T ENTER
MONOPOLIST	PRICE HIGH	20, 10	50, 0
	PRICE LOW	5, −10	10, 0

a. Is the monopolist's threat to charge a low price credible? That is, if the entrant has come in, would it make sense for the monopolist to charge a low price? Explain.

b. What is the Nash equilibrium of this game?

c. How could the monopolist make the threat to fight credible?

7. The following graphs show a monopolist and a potential entrant.

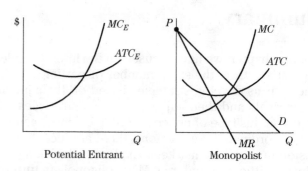

Potential Entrant   Monopolist

a. Label the monopolist's profit-maximizing price and quantity.

b. Identify a limit price that the monopolist could set to prevent entry.

c. How much does the monopolist lose by setting a limit price rather than the profit-maximizing price? Does that mean that this would be a bad strategy?

8. The following graphs show marginal cost curves for two firms that would like to form a cartel in the market in which they are selling.

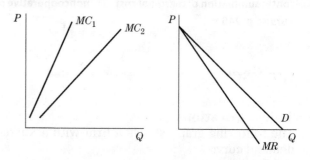

a. Use the two marginal cost curves to construct a combined marginal cost curve, and plot that on the market graph.

b. Label the cartel's profit-maximizing output and price, as well as the output of each firm.

c. Use your graphs to explain why each cartel member has an incentive to cheat on the agreement.

Application Questions

1. In current business publications, find examples of the continued oligopolistic behavior among the airlines similar to what we discussed in this chapter.

2. The following paragraphs provide a description of the competition between Home Depot and Lowe's on selling flowering plants:[41]

> In the spring Home Depot and Lowe's engage in an annual arms race to engineer and develop new scientifically altered versions of common flowering plants that are designed to bloom brighter or withstand neglect longer. The goal in particular is "to sell something the other guy doesn't."
>
> Home Depot is the world's largest home-improvement chain with $68 billion in annual revenue, while Lowe's is the second-largest with $49 billion in annual revenue. Although spring is the peak selling season for all merchandise, plants and trees are used to entice consumers into the stores. Analysts estimate that for every dollar customers spend on plants, they spend $3 on accessories such as hoses, shovels, and gloves. Both companies employ weather forecasters to advise them on when plants should appear in stores in different parts of the country.
>
> Lowe's uses a team of Ph.D. horticulturalists to choose among a thousand possible blooms developed by breeders around the world. After determining how the plants grow in different climates, the growers test mass production of hundreds and then thousands of plants. Both retailers try to secure exclusive rights to popular new varieties, although sometimes they are exclusive in name only.
>
> Lowe's uses a greenhouse complex in Huntersville, NC to grow plants and conduct consumer focus groups where customers can identify the flower varieties they most admire. Home Depot uses another greenhouse complex in Mills River, NC, two hours west, for the same purpose.

Discuss how the oligopoly models presented in this chapter apply to the behavior of Home Depot and Lowe's.

3. The following describes the ice cream industry in summer 2003:[42]

> Given the Federal Trade Commission's approval of Nestle's acquisition of Dreyer's Grand Ice Cream Inc., two multinationals, Nestle SA and Unilever, prepared to engage in ice cream wars. Unilever, which controlled the Good Humor, Ben & Jerry's, and Breyer's brands, held 17 percent of the U.S. market, while Nestle, owner of the Haagen-Dazs and Drumstick brands, would control a similar share after buying Dreyer's.
>
> Ice cream has long been produced by small local dairies, given the problems with distribution. Most Americans eat ice cream in restaurants and stores, although 80 percent of the consumption of the big national brands occurs at home. Both Unilever and Nestle want to move into the away-from-home market by focusing on convenience stores, gas stations, video shops, and vending machines, a strategy the rivals have already undertaken in Europe.
>
> Five national brands—Haagen-Dazs, Nestle, Ben & Jerry's, Breyer's, and Dreyer's— have developed new products and flavors, focusing on single-serving products that carry profit margins 15 to 25 percent higher than the tubs of ice cream in supermarkets. The higher profit margins can open new distribution outlets. Although traditional freezer space is very costly, Unilever, Nestle, and Dreyer's have pushed for logo-covered freezer cabinets in stores, given the higher profit margins.
>
> Under the FTC settlement, Nestle will be allowed to keep Dreyer's distribution network, which delivers ice cream directly to more than 85 percent of U.S. grocers. Unilever must use middlemen to deliver most of its Good Humor and Breyer's products. Nestle can expand from Dreyer's supermarket base to cinemas and gas stations with little extra cost. The supermarket ties may also help Nestle enter grocers' competitive prepared-foods section, so that consumers can easily purchase ice cream along with their deli and hot foods. Nestle agreed to sell a number of Dreyer's secondary brands as part of the FTC

---

[41]Miguel Bustillo, "The Garden Gloves Come Off—Big Box Retailers Battle to Engineer Prettier, Sturdier, Longer-Lasting Blooms," *Wall Street Journal (Online)* April 27, 2011.

[42]Deborah Ball, "Ice Cream Rivals Prepare to Wage a New Cold War," *Wall Street Journal*, June 26, 2003.

approval. However, Nestle-Dreyer's will be able to sign more licensing agreements with the wider distribution network, and the combined company will be able to turn more of Nestle's candies into Dreyer's ice cream.

a. Describe how the ice cream industry fits the oligopoly model.
b. How does the government influence oligopolistic behavior?
c. Do oligopolists always compete on the basis of price? Explain.

4. The following describes the competition between Google and Amazon for fast delivery of customer products.[43]

In 2011, Google, Inc. began to challenge Amazon's e-commerce dominance by engaging in discussions with major retailers and shippers about creating a service that would let customers shop online and receive their orders within a day for a low fee. This was a direct challenge to the Amazon Prime program that, for $79 per year, offered customers fast shipping at no additional charge for many items on the company's website. Amazon Prime increased the company's sales by 42% in the first nine months of 2011.

Google did not plan to sell products directly to consumers. The goal was to meld its search engine's product-search feature with a new quick-shipping service that Google would control. Both Google and Amazon had been moving toward similar strategies. Amazon had become a destination for product searches and a big seller of online advertising, encroaching on Google's territory. Google responded by moving into the online retail industry, dominated by Amazon, that was expected to grow 12% to $197 billion in 2011.

Analysts noted that same-day shipping was a costly and complex business. However, Google expected that the quick-shipping service would attract more consumers to its product-search service. Google had increased the quality of its product-search service by adding user ratings and reviews and helping customers determine where merchandise was available for pickup. Google's

new strategy would also put it in competition with eBay and Shoprunner Inc., both of which had fast-shipping programs.

Describe the strategies used by these oligopolists to fight the fast-shipping wars.

5. The following describes the relationship between two major shipping companies hauling liquid chemicals:[44]

Documents indicated that two shipping companies, Stolt-Nielsen SA and Odfjell ASA, colluded to divide up the market for transporting liquid chemicals across the sea. The companies discussed which shipping business each would bid for, route by route, even exchanging information on bid prices. Stolt officials also developed tables showing the increase in revenues from cooperation compared to all-out competition. The companies are unknown to most consumers, but they carry the chemicals that are used to make a variety of everyday products.

Carriers are allowed to cooperate in certain ways. They may pool their capacity if they both carry chemicals for a given producer on the same route. They may form joint ventures to bid for a piece of business. However, cooperation to divide markets or set prices would fall outside these areas.

The alleged collusion was in response to the Southeast Asian financial crisis of 1997, which depressed the volume of shipping, and a glut of new ships that decreased freight rates. Chemical company mergers also increased the producers' bargaining power, particularly the merger between Dow Chemical and Union Carbide in 2001. Each of the shipping companies had important pieces of business with each of the chemical companies that were merging. After the merger, either Stolt or Odfjell could be dislodged and price wars could break out. Documents indicated that officials of the two shipping companies held talks on dividing the pie, reviewing contracts around the world, trade lane by trade lane. Documents also indicated that the cooperation would keep freight rates 5 to 25 percent higher than otherwise. Stolt officials compared the economic costs of "going to war" with cooperation. On certain trade lanes, Stolt

---

[43]Amir Efrati and Stu Woo, "Google Targets Amazon's 'Prime' with 1-Day Delivery," *Wall Street Journal (Online)*, December 2, 2011.
[44]James Bandler, "Seagoing Chemical Haulers May Have Colluded on Rates," *Wall Street Journal*, February 20, 2003; Mark H. Anderson, "Shipper Stolt-Nielsen Is Indicted in U.S. Price-Fixing, Cartel Case," *Wall Street Journal*, September 6, 2006.

might benefit from individual action, but lower rates overall would result if the cooperation was abandoned.

Journals of company officials indicated that by April 2001, both companies were threatening price wars if the agreements could not be maintained. The journals are also filled with notations such as "no written agreements" or "no paper." Memos included the phrase, "Don't be seen as doing something together."

In September 2006, Stolt was indicted by a federal grand jury in Philadelphia on charges of price fixing and other illegal cartel activities. Stolt-Nielsen was initially granted amnesty as part of a Justice Department's investigation into the chemical-shipping industry, but department officials revoked it in 2004 after determining the company wasn't meeting the terms of the deal. The indictment cited company activity between August 1998 and November 2002. If convicted, corporate officials could face up to three years of imprisonment, $350,000 individual fines, and $10 million in corporate fines.

Explain how the discussion of cartel behavior in this chapter relates to this shipping company case.

6. In April 2011, the European Commission fined Procter & Gamble and Unilever PLC $450 million for operating a laundry–detergent cartel that fixed prices in eight European countries from 2002 to 2005. In December 2011, French anti-trust authorities fined Procter & Gamble, Henkel AG, and Colgate-Palmolive Co. for price-fixing in France from 1997 to 2004. Henkel was not fined in April because it alerted the commission to the cartel and received immunity. This move caused Unilever to cooperate with French authorities so that it received immunity and was not fined in December.[45]

The French authorities revealed that the companies met as far back as the 1980s to share price information and the companies used aliases to mask their identity at the meetings. The companies wanted "to limit the intensity of the competition between them and clean up the market." Managers took turns choosing spots for the secret meetings called "Store Checks," took documents home with them, and expensed restaurant bills under different names.

Initially the group rarely broke the rules of the agreements. However, monitoring special offers proved to be a complex process resulting in chaotic meetings. The price-fixing scheme began to dissolve by 2004 when the companies could not come to an agreement on price increases and promotions. Unilever broke the accord first followed by Procter & Gamble and Henkel.

Discuss the reasons why oligopoly theory would predict the above results for this price-fixing scheme.

---

[45]This case is based on Paul Sonne and Laurence Norman, "EU Fines Unilever, P&G Over Pricing," *Wall Street Journal (Online)*, April 14, 2011; and Max Colchester and Christina Passariello, "Dirty Secret in Soap Prices," *Wall Street Journal (Online)*, December 9, 2011.

10

Pricing Strategies for the Firm

I n this chapter, we analyze how differences in demand and elasticity lead managers to develop various pricing strategies. We show how knowledge of price elasticity among different groups of customers or for various products enables managers to price discriminate, or charge different prices to these groups. Such a strategy can increase the firm's level of profit above that achieved by charging a single price for all units of a good. To increase revenue and profit, managers have also increased the use of fees to charge for services that were previously included with other services or products.

We also discuss how a common managerial pricing strategy, markup or cost-plus pricing, can be consistent with our models of profit maximization based on the equality of marginal revenue and marginal cost, and we show how both of these pricing policies are related to the marketing literature.[1] We then examine why managers may not change prices immediately in response to changing demand and cost conditions, an issue that is also significant for macroeconomic analysis.

We begin this chapter with a case discussing airline pricing strategies. We then discuss the theory of markup pricing and price discrimination and give numerous examples of how managers can use these techniques.

---

[1]Philip Kotler, *Marketing Management: The Millennium Edition* (Upper Saddle River, NJ: Prentice Hall, 2000); Robert J. Dolan and Hermann Simon, *Power Pricing: How Managing Price Transforms the Bottom Line* (New York: Free Press, 1996); Vithala R. Rao (ed.), *Handbook of Pricing Research in Marketing* (Cheltenham, UK: Edward Elgar, 2009); Thomas T. Nagle, John E. Hogan, and Joseph Zale, *The Strategy and Tactics of Pricing*, 5th ed. (Upper Saddle River, NJ: Prentice Hall, 2011).

Case for Analysis

Airline Pricing Strategies: Will They Start Charging for the Use of the Lavatories?

The airlines have typically been the leaders in the use of differential pricing for essentially the same product, an airline seat from one destination to another. Although British Overseas Airways Corporation (now British Airways) began offering "Earlybird" discounts to increase demand for otherwise empty seats in 1972, the use of what has been called "revenue or yield management" was pioneered by American Airlines, whose managers realized in the mid-1970s that their excess capacity was more a revenue problem than a cost problem. In 1977 American began offering "Super Saver Fares," which were determined by seating capacity and required an advanced purchase. American increased the use of yield management techniques during the 1980s, particularly in response to the competitive threat from low-cost, low-fare airlines that emerged under airline deregulation. During the 1980s and 1990s other airlines increasingly adopted these same techniques, which today are an integral part of the operation of all airlines globally.[2]

Revenue or yield management creates different products through the design of usage rules and purchase restrictions for which consumers have varying degrees of willingness to pay.[3] Fewer rules and restrictions create a product which can command a higher price. The most important restrictions are advance purchase restrictions, minimum/maximum length of stay, weekend stay, and flexibility regarding ticket exchange, refunding, and time to ticketing. All of these restrictions differentiate higher-yield passengers from those who are more price-conscious and have greater price elasticity of demand. Fare products are grouped together into booking classes that vary either by fare type or value. Revenue management systems treat booking classes as independent consumer segments and then determine which booking classes should be made available for sale at any particular time. The systems estimate expected demand for booking classes in each market and then determine an optimal usage for the existing capacity that maximizes fare revenue. This optimization process includes probabilities of customer no-shows and cancellations based on passenger name record attributes.

These policies typically result in airline ticket prices that are highest on weekends and lowest on Tuesdays and Wednesdays.[4] Many fare sales, which may discount prices by 15 to 25 percent, are launched on a Monday night. Competitors often match those prices on Tuesday morning, and the sales expire by Thursday or Friday. Fare increases are often implemented on a Thursday night as the airline watches over the weekend to see if competitors match the price. If not, the fares can be rolled back by Monday morning. Airlines typically do not manage their inventory as actively on weekends, so that prices may automatically increase if cheaper seats are sold out. This weekly pricing schedule originated when sales were announced in newspaper ads and when most customers bought tickets from travel agents who were open Monday through Friday. Much of this pattern still remains in place even though customers now buy most tickets on the Internet. These patterns may change in the future with increased use of social media outlets, such as Facebook and Twitter, which enable airlines to send out sale prices directly to customers at any time. Consumers who use Web sites, such as Expedia, Travelocity, Kayak, and Mobissimo, to find the lowest fare may still have difficulty doing so, given that each of these Web sites uses its own technology to sort through airline schedules, fares, rules, and inventory. Although the airlines file prices for every conceivable route with the Airline Tariff Publishing Co., each route may have 20 different prices from each airline and 50 to 60 different rules.[5]

Since 2008 airline pricing strategies have evolved so that fees are now being charged for checked bags, snacks, pillows, and other items, which brought in an estimated $22 billion, or 5 percent, of global industry revenue in 2010.[6] In the United States, two low-fare carriers, Spirit and Allegiant Travel Co., have led the way by charging for almost everything except lavatory access and by marketing travel packages with the airfares. Spirit, which derives 27 percent of its revenues from fees, charges for a second carry-on bag and advance seat assignments. American and United Airlines charge their

---

[2]Robert G. Cross, Jon A. Higbie, and Zachary N. Cross, "Milestones in the Application of Analytical Pricing and Revenue Management," *Journal of Revenue and Pricing Management* 10 (2011): 8–18.

[3]This discussion is based on Dieter Westermann and John Lancaster, "Improved Pricing and Integration with Revenue Management—the Next Step toward Improved Revenues," *Journal of Revenue and Pricing Management* 10 (2011): 199–210.

[4]This discussion is based on Scott McCartney, "The Middle Seat: Whatever You Do, Don't Buy an Airline Ticket On…," *Wall Street Journal (Online)*, January 27, 2011.

[5]Scott McCartney, "Who's the Fairest Fare of All?" *Wall Street Journal (Online)*, January 12, 2012.

[6]Susan Carey, "Airlines to Load on More Fees: After Checked Bags, Carriers Seek to Charge for Early Boarding, Fancier Foods, and Reclining Seats," *Wall Street Journal (Online)*, March 7, 2011.

nonelite frequent fliers a fee for early boarding. Customers are willing to pay for this service as there is more competition for limited overhead bin space as passengers use more carry-on bags to avoid the checked bags fees. The major carriers have also discovered that passengers will pay for better seats in coach, and they are experimenting with charging for improved food options. The CEO of the European carrier Ryanair has considered charging for lavatories on short flights, arguing that removing two of the three toilets on a 737 would allow the addition of six revenue-generating extra seats.[7]

Many airlines charge passengers seat fees for a reserved seat other than one assigned by the airlines, which could be a middle seat or one not located next to family members. Carriers are blocking more seats from advance-seat selection, particularly for low-fare passengers, thus increasing the pressure for

passengers to pay a fee and reserve a seat rather than settle for an assigned one. One-third of all seats require extra fees or higher fares to reserve in advance on some Frontier Airlines flights. American Airlines has expanded its "preferred seat" program where the airline blocks seats for full-fare and elite-level customers and then opens them up for sale 24 hours before a flight.[8]

This case shows how the concepts of willingness to pay and price elasticity of demand are used by the airlines to develop pricing strategies that increase revenues. We will present more examples of these strategies later in the chapter. We first discuss how the commonly used strategy of markup pricing relates to willingness to pay and elasticity issues, and we present the theory of price discrimination that underlies the airline pricing strategies.

---

[7]Nagle et al., *The Strategy and Tactics of Pricing*, 10.

[8]Scott McCartney, "Now, Even the Cheap Seats on Airplanes Come with a Fee," *Wall Street Journal (Online)*, November 3, 2011.

The Role of Markup Pricing

Markup pricing

Calculating the price of a product by determining the average cost of producing the product and then setting the price a given percentage above that cost.

Markup pricing, also called cost-plus pricing, is a long-established business practice for determining product prices.[9] Under this procedure, firms estimate their costs of production and then apply a markup to the average cost to determine price. In some cases, the size of the markup is based on industry tradition, managers' experiences, or rules of thumb. For example, the rule of thumb in an electronics journal is that products sell for two and one-half times their production cost.[10] From a manager's perspective, markup pricing is considered a means of dealing with uncertainty in demand estimation, a method that is "fair" to both customers and firms, and a simplified approach to the pricing of large numbers of products, as the procedure involves only determining a product's average cost of production and then applying a percentage markup to that cost to determine the product price.

There has been much discussion about whether using a simplified rule of thumb, such as markup pricing, is consistent with the firm's goal of profit maximization (Chapter 7). Applying a *uniform* markup to all products would not be a profit-maximizing pricing strategy for a firm because this approach considers only the cost of production and does not incorporate information on demand and consumer preferences. However, many studies of managerial pricing decisions have shown that firms do not use a uniform markup for all products. According to Philip Kotler, common markups in supermarkets are 9 percent on baby foods, 14 percent on tobacco products, 20 percent on bakery products, 27 percent on dried foods and vegetables,

---

[9]Markup pricing was first analyzed by Hall and Hitch in 1939 and then studied more extensively in the 1950s and 1960s. See Robert L. Hall and Charles J. Hitch, "Price Theory and Business Behavior," *Oxford Economic Papers* 2 (May 1939): 12–45; A. D. H. Kaplan, Joel B. Dirlam, and Robert F. Lanzillotti, *Pricing in Big Business: A Case Approach* (Washington, DC: Brookings Institution, 1958); Robert F. Lanzillotti, "Pricing Objectives in Large Companies," *American Economic Review* 48 (December 1958): 921–40; Bjarke Fog, *Pricing in Theory and Practice* (Copenhagen: Handelshojskolens Forlag, 1994); the literature cited in Frederic Michael Scherer and David Ross, *Industrial Market Structure and Economic Performance*, 3rd ed. (Boston: Houghton Mifflin, 1990), chap. 7; Rao, *Handbook of Pricing Research in Marketing*; Nagle et al., *The Strategy and Tactics of Pricing*.

[10]Dolan and Simon, *Power Pricing*, 37.

37 percent on spices and extracts, and 50 percent on greeting cards.[11] Markup dispersion can also exist within categories of goods. For example, Kotler found markups ranging from 19 to 57 percent within the spices and extracts category. In many of these cases, it appears that the size of the markup is related to what managers believe the market will bear, or, in economic terms, the price elasticity of demand.

In the following discussion, we show why a policy of applying larger markups to products that have less elastic demand helps firms maximize their profits. This discussion will proceed in three steps:

1. We establish a mathematical relationship between marginal revenue and the price elasticity of demand.
2. We review the profit-maximizing rule of equating marginal revenue and marginal cost (Chapter 7).
3. We show how marking up a price above the average cost of production, where the markup is inversely related to the price elasticity of demand, is equivalent to pricing according to the profit-maximizing rule from economic theory (marginal revenue equals marginal cost). Thus, even though markup pricing is often considered a rule of thumb, applying it as described here is a profit-maximizing strategy for managers.

Marginal Revenue and the Price Elasticity of Demand

Equations 10.1 to 10.7 present a derivation of the relationship between marginal revenue—the change in total revenue from producing an additional unit of output—and the price elasticity of demand.

$$10.1 \quad MR = \frac{(\Delta TR)}{\Delta Q}$$

$$10.2 \quad \Delta TR = (P)*(\Delta Q) + (Q)*(\Delta P)$$

$$10.3 \quad MR = P*\frac{\Delta Q}{\Delta Q} + Q*\frac{\Delta P}{\Delta Q}$$

$$10.4 \quad MR = P + Q*\frac{\Delta P}{\Delta Q}$$

$$10.5 \quad MR = \left[P + Q*\left(\frac{\Delta P}{\Delta Q} \right)\left(\frac{P}{P} \right) \right]$$

$$10.6 \quad MR = P\left(1 + \frac{\Delta P}{\Delta Q}*\frac{Q}{P} \right)$$

$$10.7 \quad MR = P\left(1 + \frac{1}{e_p} \right)$$

Equation 10.1 is simply the definition of marginal revenue (*MR*)—the change in total revenue (*TR*) divided by the change in output or quantity (ΔQ) (Chapter 3). Equation 10.2 describes the change in total revenue, which is the numerator of Equation 10.1. When lowering price and moving down a demand curve, total

---

[11]Philip Kotler, *Marketing Management: Analysis, Planning, Implementation, and Control*, 8th ed. (Englewood Cliffs, NJ: Prentice Hall, 1994), 498–500; Kotler, *Marketing Management: The Millennium Edition*, 465–66.

TABLE 10.1   Marginal Revenue and Price Elasticity of Demand

$$MR = P\left(1 + \frac{1}{e_p}\right)$$

VALUE OF ELASTICITY	VALUE OF MARGINAL REVENUE	NUMERICAL EXAMPLE
$\lvert e_p \rvert > 1$ Elastic	$MR > 0$	$e_p = -2; MR = P\left(1 + \frac{1}{-2}\right) = \frac{1}{2}P > 0$
$\lvert e_p \rvert < 1$ Inelastic	$MR < 0$	$e_p = -1/2; MR = P\left(1 + \frac{1}{-1/2}\right) = -P < 0$
$\lvert e_p \rvert = 1$ Unit elastic	$MR = 0$	$e_p = -1; MR = P\left(1 + \frac{1}{-1}\right) = 0$

---

revenue changes because additional units of output are now sold at the lower price. This change in revenue is represented by the first right-hand term in Equation 10.2, $(P)*(\Delta Q)$. Total revenue also changes because the previous quantity demanded is now sold at a lower price. This change is represented by the second right-hand term in Equation 10.2, $(Q)*(\Delta P)$. Thus, Equation 10.2 is simply expressing the change in total revenue as price is lowered along a demand curve.

Equation 10.3 again presents the full definition of marginal revenue, using the definition of change in total revenue (ΔTR) from Equation 10.2. Equation 10.4 is a simplified version of Equation 10.3. In Equation 10.5, the last term of Equation 10.4 is multiplied by the term (P/P). Because this term equals 1, the value of the equation is not changed. Equation 10.6 simplifies Equation 10.5 by taking the price term outside the brackets and rearranging the other terms. The last term in Equation 10.6 is the inverse of the price elasticity of demand. This is expressed in Equation 10.7, which shows the formal relationship between marginal revenue and price elasticity: $MR = P[1 + (1/e_P)]$.

The implications of this relationship are shown in Table 10.1. When demand is elastic, marginal revenue is positive; when demand is inelastic, marginal revenue is negative; and when demand is unit elastic, marginal revenue is zero. The numerical examples in Table 10.1 illustrate this relationship for different elasticity values.

The Profit-Maximizing Rule

The second step in our discussion of price elasticity and optimal pricing is to review the rule for profit maximization used in all of our market structure models. To maximize profit, a firm needs to produce that level of output at which marginal revenue equals marginal cost. We now show how this rule, derived from economic theory and the mathematics of optimization, is consistent with the commonly used managerial technique of markup pricing, *when the size of the markup is inversely related to the price elasticity of demand.*

Profit Maximization and Markup Pricing

We begin the discussion relating markup pricing to the profit-maximizing rule by reprinting Equation 10.7 and adding the profit-maximizing rule in Equation 10.8.

$$10.7 \quad MR = P\left(1 + \frac{1}{e_p}\right)$$

$$10.8 \quad MR = MC$$

We now substitute the definition of marginal revenue from Equation 10.7 into Equation 10.8 and rearrange terms, as shown in Equations 10.9 to 10.11.

10.9 $P\left(1 + \dfrac{1}{e_p}\right) = MC$

10.10 $P = \dfrac{MC}{\left(1 + \dfrac{1}{e_p}\right)} = \dfrac{MC}{\dfrac{(e_p + 1)}{e_p}}$

10.11 $P = \left(\dfrac{e_p}{1 + e_p}\right)MC$

Equation 10.11 shows that the optimal price, which maximizes profits for the firm, depends on marginal cost and price elasticity of demand. Holding the marginal cost constant, the optimal price is *inversely* related to the price elasticity of demand. Firms usually base the price markups for their products on the average variable cost (variable cost per unit of output), not the marginal cost (the additional cost of producing an additional unit of output). Marginal cost equals average variable cost if average variable cost is constant, which may be the case over a given range of output for many firms.[12] Given this assumption and drawing on Equation 10.11, we derive the formula for the optimal markup, m, in Equations 10.12 and 10.13 by substituting average variable cost for marginal cost in Equation 10.11; defining m, the markup procedure, in Equation 10.12; and solving for m in terms of the price elasticity of demand by relating Equations 10.11 and 10.12. The end result is presented in Equation 10.13. The implications of the formula in Equation 10.13 are shown in Table 10.2.

10.12 $P = $ *average variable cost* $+ (m)($*average variable cost*$)$
$= (1 + m)$ *average variable cost*

10.13 $(1 + m) = \dfrac{e_p}{(1 + e_p)}$ or $m = \dfrac{-1}{(1 + e_p)}$

Table 10.2 shows that as the price elasticity of demand increases in absolute value, the optimal markup, which maximizes profit for the firm, decreases in size. If the price elasticity of demand is –2.0, the optimal markup of price above cost is 100 percent, whereas it is only 10 percent if the price elasticity of demand is –11.0. A large price elasticity typically occurs when there are many substitutes for a given product, so the producer of that product is constrained in terms of how much price can be raised above cost without losing a substantial number of customers.

TABLE 10.2 The Optimal Markup

$$m = \frac{-1}{(1 + e_p)}$$

ELASTICITY (e_p)	CALCULATION	MARKUP (PERCENT)
–2.0	$m = -[1/(1 - 2)] = +1.00$	1.00 or 100
–5.0	$m = -[1/(1 - 5)] = +0.25$	0.25 or 25
–11.0	$m = -[1/(1 - 11)] = +0.10$	0.10 or 10
∞	$m = -[1/(1 - \infty] = 0$	0.00 (no markup)

[12] If average variable cost is not constant, marginal cost may still not differ significantly from average cost in many cases. Firms may also mark up prices on the basis of long-run average cost, which is often constant and equal to long-run marginal cost.

The upper limit for the size of price elasticity is infinitely or perfectly elastic demand, which, as shown in Table 10.2, results in no markup above the average cost of production. This is the case of the perfectly competitive firm that faces the horizontal or perfectly elastic demand curve. Perfectly competitive firms are price-takers, which cannot influence the price of the product (Chapter 7). Therefore, perfectly competitive firms have no ability to mark up the price above cost.

You should also note that no values of elasticity less than 1 in absolute value are included in Table 10.2. Recall from Table 10.1 that these values of inelastic demand occur where marginal revenue is negative. Because profit maximization is achieved where $MR = MC$, the profit-maximizing level of output never occurs where marginal revenue is negative. This theoretical result is consistent with empirical price elasticity estimates (Chapter 3). Elasticity estimates for individual producers are greater than 1 in absolute value (elastic), even though estimates for the entire product category might be less than 1 (inelastic).

Business Pricing Strategies and Profit Maximization

In the 1950s and 1960s, the observed use of markup pricing by many companies generated an extensive debate about whether firms really pursued the goal of profit maximization. Doubts about this maximizing strategy were raised, particularly if firms simply used a given markup set by tradition or if they set prices to generate a given target rate of return that did not depend on market conditions.[13] The 1958 Lanzillotti study on the issue, which was based on interviews with officials in 20 large corporations, including Alcoa, A&P, General Electric, General Motors, Sears, and U.S. Steel, concluded that the goal of these companies was to earn a predetermined target rate of return on their investment. Prices were considered to be "administered" to achieve this goal. The implication was that major U.S. corporations selected a level of output to produce and priced it at a margin above cost that would earn a target rate of return on investment selected by the company.

In 1988, Kenneth Elzinga updated the Lanzillotti study to determine whether the firms included in the original research continued to target the same rates of return in subsequent years (1960 to 1984) as in the earlier period (1947 to 1955), and whether firms that specifically designated a target rate of return as the basis for their pricing policies had been able to achieve that return.[14] Elzinga found that most of the 20 original firms earned a lower rate of return in subsequent years compared with the original study period. He also found that companies that specifically stated a target rate of return typically did not meet that goal in the 1960 to 1984 period. In fact, several of the original companies either filed for bankruptcy or underwent reorganization in that latter period. Elzinga argued that firms responded to market forces in their price-setting behavior. He noted:[15]

> For a corporation to fail to meet an objective and then to settle for less also is consistent with the hypothesis that prices and profits are so powerfully influenced by market forces that firms cannot always systematically determine their own fate... The differences in interfirm behavior Lanzillotti recorded in his sample reveal not so much differences in objectives or goals as variations in adaptive behavior to differing market circumstances.

[13]This debate is summarized in the following literature: Kaplan, Dirlam, and Lanzillotti, *Pricing in Big Business*; Lanzillotti, "Pricing Objectives in Large Companies"; Morris A. Adelman, "Pricing Objectives in Large Companies: Comment," *American Economic Review* 49 (September 1959): 669–70; Alfred E. Kahn, "Pricing Objectives in Large Companies: Comment," *American Economic Review* 49 (September 1959): 670–78; Kenneth G. Elzinga, "Pricing Achievements in Large Companies," in *Public Policy Toward Corporations*, ed. Arnold A. Hegestad (Gainesville: University of Florida Press, 1988), 166–79; Fog, *Pricing in Theory and Practice*; Vithala R. Rao and Benjamin Kartono, "Pricing Objectives and Strategies: A Cross-Country Survey," in *Handbook of Pricing Research in Marketing*, ed. Vithala R. Rao (Cheltenham, UK: Edward Elgar, 2009), 9–36.
[14]Elzinga, "Pricing Achievements in Large Companies."
[15]Ibid., 171, 176.

Economist Bjarke Fog noted that prices can be determined along a continuum from complete reliance on costs only (a rigid markup or full cost approach) to the other extreme of reliance on demand only, with no reference to costs.[16] The inverse elasticity rule lies between these two extremes. Fog argued that there are examples of real-world pricing policies across this entire continuum. Thus, the profit-maximizing rule based on marginal analysis may be too complex to always apply in a world of imperfect information and uncertainty.

In a 2004 survey of 73 firms in the United States, 54 firms in Singapore, and 72 firms in India, researchers found that the most frequently used strategy was markup pricing (47.2 percent of firms) with a mean percentage importance of 37.8 percent.[17] This was followed by price signaling where firms use price to signal the quality of their products (37.7 percent of firms, mean importance of 22.6 percent), perceived value pricing where the price of the product is based on customers' perceptions of the product's value (34.2 percent of firms, mean importance of 33.1 percent), and parity pricing where firms match the price set by the overall market or the price leader (31.7 percent of firms, mean importance of 36.9 percent). Less than 5 percent of the firms in the sample used only one pricing strategy, and more than half the firms used at least four different pricing strategies. The most important objectives of the firms were to increase or maintain market share and increase or maintain sales volume. It appears that firms were trying to find the optimal balance between markup pricing and other methods that take into account factors in addition to costs. The study did not ask firms how they calculated the markup or whether it varied by product.

Markup Pricing Examples

Restaurant Industry   The divergence between the prices restaurants charge and the costs of producing the menu items goes far beyond the traditional view that the markup on liquor is much greater than the markup on food items. Markups on mussels can reach 650 percent, while those on salmon can exceed 900 percent.[18]

Restaurant owners typically aim for a price that is a 300 percent markup above the cost of the raw ingredients for their meals. However, various items on restaurant menus—such as gourmet seafood and certain cuts of beef—are so expensive that customers would not tolerate a 300 percent markup on those foods. Because restaurant owners cannot mark up these items by the desired amount, given the customers' price elasticity of demand, the owners must use even larger markups on less expensive items, including other meats, salmon, lettuce, and pasta. Restaurants have developed computer programs that allow owners to calculate the exact price of each ingredient in a dish and the overall cost of a single serving. Restaurant owners use these markup procedures based on price elasticity of demand because they see themselves operating in a very competitive industry with low profit margins.

Psychological factors also affect restaurant pricing. Pricing an item too low compared with other offerings might make customers think something is wrong with the item. Pricing an item too high simply means that people will not be willing to pay that price because it seems out of line compared with the rest of the items on the menu. Many people will not choose the least expensive item on the menu, so markups are often high on the next two or three higher-priced items.

Fixed-price meals also give restaurant owners greater pricing power. One Dallas, Texas, restaurant was able to mark up the price of its $90 prix fixe meal by 75 percent compared with a 66 percent markup on its a la carte menu.[19] This larger markup is based on customers' willingness to pay for the chef's key dishes

[16]Fog, *Pricing in Theory and Practice*, 73–81.

[17]Rao and Kartono, "Pricing Objectives and Strategies: A Cross-Country Survey," 16–29.

[18]Eileen Daspin, "What Do Restaurants Really Pay for Meals?" *Wall Street Journal*, March 10, 2000.

[19]Mike Spector, "The Prix Fixe Is in," *Wall Street Journal*, October 7, 2006.

and on cost advantages. Chefs can use fewer ingredients and purchase them in bulk for the more limited menus. The kitchens require a smaller staff and fewer stations, and the meals provide the opportunity to use food that might otherwise be thrown out.

Pricing in Professional Sports   We noted earlier in the chapter that the markup pricing formula and the profit-maximizing rule imply that firms will never price where demand is inelastic. This rule may be modified when firms offer multiple products that are complementary. Although the ticket price for a Major League Baseball (MLB) game more than doubled between 1991 and 2002 and subjected team owners to criticism in the popular press, many studies have shown that tickets to sporting events are regularly priced in the inelastic range of demand. MLB ticket price elasticities range from –0.06 to –0.93.[20]

Several explanations have been offered for this behavior. As with the 1950s business discussion above, some have questioned whether the goal of team owners is to maximize profits. Owners may receive satisfaction from controlling a professional sports team and may not be concerned with setting profit-maximizing prices. It is also possible that owners keep prices low in exchange for special political considerations from local governments, particularly regarding the public funding of stadiums. In the National Football League, there is some evidence suggesting a trade-off between ticket prices and stadium subsidies. Lower prices in the short run may also be necessary to maximize profits over a longer time period by creating fan loyalty.

It has also been suggested that inelastic ticket pricing may be explained by recognizing that team owners do not derive revenue simply from ticket sales. If complementary sources of revenue can more than offset the lost revenue from selling tickets at lower prices, these pricing policies may be optimal. One important complementary source of revenue is that derived from concession stands. High prices of hot dogs and other baseball favorites may more than compensate for the lower revenue from ticket sales.

Price elasticity estimates depend on the empirical method used in the estimation process. Although most studies have found the demand for major league baseball tickets to be inelastic, a study by Hakes and colleagues found a point estimate of –0.83 for multigame ticket packages, but confidence intervals that extended above –1.0, indicating possible elastic demand. This study was based on the analysis of one team, the Atlanta Braves, and a methodology that used differences in travel costs to attend games as a measure of the variation in price.[21]

Managerial Rule of Thumb

Markup Pricing

Managers may use a simple cost-based pricing method to achieve an acceptable outcome, even if they do not earn the maximum amount of profits. However, most managers appear to explicitly or implicitly use some type of inverse price elasticity rule, which involves both demand and cost factors, in calculating their markups. This strategy will bring them closer to earning the maximum amount of profit possible. ■

[20]This discussion is based on Anthony C. Krautmann and David J. Berri, "Can We Find It at the Concessions? Understanding Price Elasticity in Professional Sports," *Journal of Sports Economics* 8 (April 2007): 183–91.
[21]Jahn K. Hakes, Chad Turner, and Kyle Hutmaker, "I Don't Care If I Never Get Back? Time, Travel Costs, and the Estimation of Baseball Season Ticket Demand," *International Journal of Sport Finance* 6 (2011): 119–37.

Price Discrimination

We now discuss price discrimination, a pricing strategy closely related to markup pricing and one that is also dependent on the price elasticity of demand. We first illustrate the concept with several theoretical models, and we then discuss numerous managerial applications of this technique.

Definition of Price Discrimination

Price discrimination is the practice of charging different prices to various groups of customers that are not based on differences in the costs of production. This can entail charging different prices to different groups when the costs of production do not vary or charging the same price to different groups when there are differences in the costs of production.

> **Price discrimination**
> The practice of charging different prices to various groups of customers that are not based on differences in the costs of production.

The following are three basic requirements for successful price discrimination:

1. Firms must possess some degree of monopoly or market power that enables them to charge a price in excess of the costs of production. Thus, price discrimination can be used by firms in all the market structures discussed in Chapter 1 *except* perfect competition, where the individual firm has no influence on price. Successful price discrimination results when competitors cannot undersell the price-discriminating firm in its high-priced market.
2. Firms must be able to separate customers into different groups that have varying price elasticities of demand. The costs of segmenting and policing the individual markets must not exceed the additional revenue earned from price discrimination.
3. Firms must be able to prevent resale among the different groups of customers. Otherwise, consumers who are charged a low price could resell their product to customers who are charged a much higher price. Price discrimination also should not generate substantial consumer resentment at the differential prices or be illegal.[22]

These requirements are typically met in the airline industry. A small number of large airlines dominate the U.S. market, ensuring that these firms have market power. As noted previously, airline business and pleasure travelers have different elasticities of demand because pleasure travelers typically have much more flexibility in their schedules and are more price sensitive. Finally, resale can be prevented by requiring a specific name on the ticket, which will be monitored when the customer checks in for the flight, and by placing restrictions, such as a Saturday night stay, on the cheaper tickets. Price discrimination is always easier to implement for nondurable goods, such as an airline seat on a particular flight at a given time. Once the flight leaves, that good no longer exists and cannot be resold.

The airlines have made substantial investments in "yield management" computer software, which enables them to calculate how much different customers or groups of customers are willing to pay for their airline seats. Current yield management systems evaluate thousands of possible connections for each flight. Continental Airlines estimated that it increased its revenue by 0.5 to 0.7 percent, or around $50 million in 1999, using these systems.[23] The systems allowed Continental's pricing experts to open more seats to frequent flyer rewards or to post a special rate on the Internet to fill seats in a slow-selling market without having to offer an

---

[22]Kotler, *Marketing Management. The Millennium Edition.*
[23]Scott McCartney, "Bag of High-Tech Tricks Helps to Keep Airlines Financially Afloat," *Wall Street Journal,* January 20, 2000.

across-the-board fare reduction that would reduce profits in all markets. However, these systems can also make mistakes. In the spring of 1999, United Airlines' system overestimated demand for full-fare tickets and rejected reservations for less-expensive seats, resulting in a second-quarter revenue loss of at least $22 million.[24]

As noted in the third point for successful price discrimination, the power of the airlines to discriminate is not unlimited. Many businesses have started balking at the prices they have to pay for employee travel and are limiting travel, searching for discount fares that apply, or using substitutes for travel such as videoconferencing. In response, some airlines have begun offering discounts on full-fare coach seats aimed at business travelers. Test marketing has indicated that business travelers have become more price sensitive over time.[25]

By 2004 the difference between the average fare charged to business travelers and to leisure passengers had decreased dramatically. On the highly travelled New York to Los Angeles route, 15 percent of the passengers booked by the reservation company Sabre Holdings Corp. paid between $2,000 and $2,400 on average in June 2001, while only 3 percent paid that much in June 2004. Fifty-five percent paid between $200 and $400, up from 28 percent three years earlier. These changes resulted from both the increased use of discounted fares by business travelers and from greater competition among the airlines on these popular routes. The rise of low-cost carriers such as JetBlue Airways helped increase seat capacity 14 percent between 2001 and 2004 on the New York–Los Angeles route.[26]

We discussed current uses of airline price discrimination strategies in the opening case of this chapter. Numerous examples of these yield management techniques can be found in previously cited articles in the *Journal of Revenue and Pricing Management*.[27] One article by airline managers and consultants discusses the use of a metric, the Price Balance Statistic, to evaluate the quality of a given pricing strategy and to develop an optimal set of strategies. The Price Balance Statistic, defined as the change in revenue due to a unit change in fare price, is simply a modification of the economic concept of marginal revenue that we have shown is fundamental to the concept of profit maximization.[28]

Theoretical Models of Price Discrimination

Economists focus on three models of price discrimination—first-, second-, and third-degree—that illustrate the relationship of this strategy with demand and price elasticity. Before discussing each of these models and their implications, we describe how a demand curve illustrates consumer willingness to pay for a product and provides a rationale for price discrimination. Later in the chapter, we discuss other managerial applications of price discrimination, and we relate these approaches to strategies typically discussed in marketing courses.

Demand and Willingness to Pay   The standard assumption with a demand curve is that *all* units of a good are sold at whatever price exists in the market. In Figure 10.1, suppose that P_1 is the price of the good and Q_1 is the quantity demanded

[24]Ibid.

[25]Nicole Harris and Kortney Stringer, "Breaking a Taboo, Airlines Slash Traditionally Full Business Fares," *Wall Street Journal*, August 8, 2002; Scott McCartney, "Airlines Try Business-Fare Cuts, Find They Don't Lose Revenue," *Wall Street Journal*, November 22, 2002.

[26]Melanie Trottman, "Equalizing Air Fares," *Wall Street Journal*, August 17, 2004.

[27]Cross et al., "Milestones in the Application of Analytical Pricing and Revenue Management"; Westermann and Lancaster, "Improved Pricing and Integration with Revenue Management—the Next Step toward Improved Revenues."

[28]Timothy L. Jacobs, Richard Ratliff, and Barry C. Smith, "Understanding the Relationship Between Price, Revenue Management Controls and Scheduled Capacity—a Price Balance Statistic for Optimizing Pricing Strategies," *Journal of Revenue and Pricing Management* 9 (2010): 356–73.

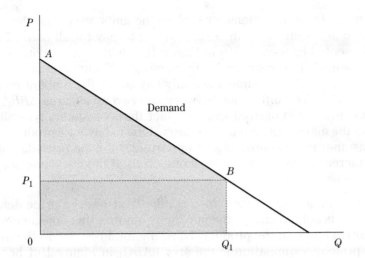

FIGURE 10.1
Demand, Willingness to Pay, and First-Degree Price Discrimination
The total amount consumers are willing to pay for Q_1 units of output is the area $0ABQ_1$, whereas the amount they actually pay at price P_1 is the area $0P_1BQ_1$. The difference is consumer surplus or area ABP_1. Under first-degree price discrimination firms are able to turn this consumer surplus into revenue.

at that price. The amount of money spent on the good is price times quantity, or the area $0P_1BQ_1$. However, this area does *not* represent the total amount that consumers would be willing to pay for the good rather than go without it. That total willingness to pay is represented by the area underneath the demand curve up to quantity Q_1, or area $0ABQ_1$. This difference between the amount actually paid when purchasing all units at price P_1 and the total amount consumers would be willing to pay results from the fact that the prices measured along a demand curve represent consumers' **marginal benefit** or valuation, the dollar value they attach to each additional unit of the product, as we show in the following example.

Marginal benefit
The valuation that a consumer places on each additional unit of a product, which is measured by the price of that product.

Table 10.3 shows a hypothetical demand schedule for oranges. If I observe you buying four oranges when the price of oranges is 25 cents, I can infer that you did not buy the fifth orange because it was worth less than 25 cents to you. (This argument assumes that you had more than a dollar in your pocket to spend on oranges.) If the price of oranges is 50 cents per orange and you buy only three oranges, I can infer that the third orange is worth at least 50 cents, but the fourth orange is worth less than 50 cents, but at least 25 cents because you bought the fourth orange when the price was 25 cents per orange. For simplicity, let's assume that the valuation of the fourth orange is exactly 25 cents and the third orange, 50 cents. With the same reasoning, the second orange is worth $0.75, and the first orange is worth $1.00. Thus, a market price reflects a consumer's marginal valuation or benefit, the amount of money he or she is willing to pay for the last or marginal unit consumed.[29]

TABLE 10.3   Individual Demand for Oranges (Hypothetical)

PRICE	QUANTITY DEMANDED
$0.25	4
$0.50	3
$0.75	2
$1.00	1

---

[29]Oranges were chosen in this example to illustrate the marginal benefit concept because income, for most people, is not a factor constraining their demand for oranges. It can be safely argued that the reason the consumer did not purchase the fifth orange, when oranges were priced at 25 cents per orange, is that the consumer did not value the fifth orange at 25 cents, *not* that the individual did not have the income to purchase the fifth orange. Oranges also illustrate the marginal concept because they are a small product about which the consumer would typically think in marginal terms and consider purchasing one more or one less orange.

Total benefit
The total amount of money consumers are willing to pay for a product rather than go without the product.

Consumer surplus
The difference between the total amount of money consumers are willing to pay for a product rather than do without and the amount they actually have to pay when a single price is charged for all units of the product.

First-degree price discrimination
A pricing strategy under which firms with market power are able to charge individuals the maximum amount they are willing to pay for each unit of the product.

If we add up all these valuations for each of the units, we obtain the total valuation, or the total amount consumers are willing to pay for all units. This dollar amount, represented by area $0ABQ_1$ in Figure 10.1, is the total willingness to pay, or the **total benefit** to consumers of that amount of output. If all units of output are sold at price P_1, consumers actually pay the dollar amount represented by the area $0P_1BQ_1$. The difference between the two areas, area ABP_1, is called **consumer surplus**. It is derived from the fact that consumers typically do not have to spend the maximum amount they are willing to pay for a product. The existence of consumer surplus provides an opportunity for the price-discriminating manager to increase profits by turning some or all of the consumer surplus into revenue for the firm.

First-Degree Price Discrimination   Under **first-degree price discrimination**, a manager is able to charge the maximum amount that consumers are willing to pay for each unit of the product. Thus, the total revenue to the firm under first-degree price discrimination is the area $0ABQ_1$ in Figure 10.1 because the consumer surplus, area ABP_1, is turned into revenue for the firm. In the numerical example of Table 10.3, at a common price of $0.25 per orange, the consumer demands four oranges and the producer receives $1.00 in revenue. Under first-degree price discrimination (if it were possible), the firm charges $1.00 for the first orange, $0.75 for the second, $0.50 for the third, and $0.25 for the fourth, for a total revenue of $2.50. The consumer surplus, valued at $1.50, is turned into revenue for the firm.

We now illustrate the differences in a firm's revenue and profit that result when charging a single profit-maximizing price and engaging in first-degree price discrimination, using a numerical demand example (Chapter 3). We continue with this example to show different types of price discrimination throughout the remainder of the chapter.

Figure 10.2 shows the demand function $Q = 12 - P$ or $P = 12 - Q$, drawn from Chapter 3. It also shows the marginal revenue function $MR = 12 - 2Q$. We now assume that marginal cost (MC) is constant at $2 and, therefore, equal to average cost. Table 10.4 shows the calculation of the profit-maximizing quantity and price, total revenue, total cost, and profit, assuming both a single profit-maximizing price and first-degree price discrimination. We can see that first-degree price discrimination increases total revenue from $35 to $47.50 and profit from $25 to $37.50.

First-degree price discrimination is a largely hypothetical case because firms are not usually able to charge the maximum price consumers are willing to pay for each unit of a product. A close example of first-degree price discrimination might be an old country doctor who knew all his patients and their income levels

FIGURE 10.2
Profit Maximization and First-Degree Price Discrimination
Profit maximization where MR = MC results in P = $7, Q = 5, TR = 35, TC = $10, and π = $25. Under first-degree price discrimination, the consumer surplus or the area of the triangle under the demand curve above a price of $7 is turned into revenue for the firm. This adds $12.50 to revenue and profit.

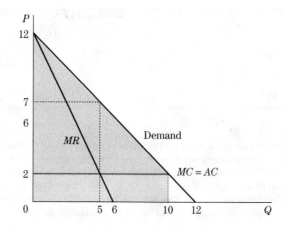

TABLE 10.4 Numerical Example of Profit Maximization with a Single Price and First- and Second-Degree Price Discrimination

PROFIT MAXIMIZATION WITH A SINGLE PRICE	PROFIT MAXIMIZATION WITH FIRST-DEGREE PRICE DISCRIMINATION
$Q = 12 - P$ or $P = 12 - Q$	The firm turns the consumer surplus in the triangle at the top of Figure 10.2 into revenue:
$MR = 12 - 2Q$	Consumer surplus $= (1/2)(5)(12 - 7)$
$MC = AC = 2$	$= (1/2)(5)(5) = \$12.50$
$MR = MC$	New $TR = \$35.00 + \$12.50 = \$47.50$
$12 - 2Q = 2$	New $\pi = \$47.50 - \$10.00 = \$37.50$
$2Q = 10$	**PROFIT MAXIMIZATION WITH SECOND-DEGREE PRICE DISCRIMINATION**
$Q = 5$	
$P = \$7$	
$TR = (P)(Q) = (\$7)(5) = \$35$	First 3 units: $P = \$9, Q = 3, TR = \$27$
$TC = (AC)(Q) = (\$2)(5) = \$10$	Second 2 units: $P = \$7, Q = 2, TR = \$14$
$\pi = TR - TC = \$35 - \$10 = \$25$	New $TR = \$27 + \$14 = \$41$
	New $\pi = \$41 - \$10 = \$31$

and charged different prices for the same services provided to each patient or a psychologist who uses a sliding fee scale for different clients. Haggling over the price of a new or used car at an auto dealership is another example of a firm trying to get each customer to pay the maximum amount he or she is willing to spend on the automobile. This is accomplished by the salesperson taking a personal interest in the customer, "asking what the customer does for a living (ability to pay), how long he has lived in the area (knowledge of the market), what kinds of cars she has bought before (loyalty to a particular brand), where she lives (value placed on the dealer's location), and whether she has looked at, or is planning to look at, other cars (awareness of alternatives)."[30] We discuss below how new technologies, including the Internet, are assisting firms in more closely approximating first-degree price discrimination.

Second-Degree Price Discrimination **Second-degree price discrimination** involves firms charging the maximum price consumers are willing to pay for different blocks of output. It is often called *nonlinear pricing* because prices depend on the number of units bought instead of varying by customer. Each customer faces the same price schedule, but customers pay different prices depending on the quantity purchased. Quantity discounts are an example of second-degree price discrimination. This strategy is illustrated in Figure 10.3. If all Q_1 units in the figure are sold at price P_1, the revenue to the firm is the area $0P_1BQ_1$ (price times quantity). However, if the firm can sell the first block of units, $0Q_3$, at price P_3 and the second block of units, Q_3Q_2, at price P_2 and the third block of units, Q_2Q_1, at price P_1, the total revenue to the firm is the area $0P_3CQ_3$ plus the area Q_3EDQ_2 plus the area Q_2FBQ_1, or the area of the three blocks underneath the demand curve. This area, which results from second-degree price discrimination, is larger than the area $0P_1BQ_1$, the revenue obtained by charging a single price for all units, but less than area $0ABQ_1$, the revenue from first-degree price discrimination. Electric utilities have used this form of price discrimination by charging different rates for various blocks of kilowatt hours of electricity.

Second-degree price discrimination
A pricing strategy under which firms with market power charge different prices for different blocks of output.

[30]Thomas T. Nagle and John E. Hogan, *The Strategy and Tactics of Pricing: A Guide to Growing More Profitably*, 4th ed. (Upper Saddle River, NJ: Pearson Prentice Hall, 2006), 65.

FIGURE 10.3

Second-Degree Price Discrimination

Under second-degree price discrimination, firms charge the maximum price consumers are willing to pay for different blocks of output. Revenue to the firm equals area $0P_3CQ_3$ plus area Q_3EDQ_2 plus area Q_2FBQ_1.

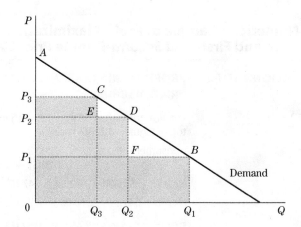

Figure 10.4 and Table 10.4 show the numerical example of second-degree price discrimination. The profit-maximizing quantity with a single price is five units in Table 10.4. Assume now that the first three units can be sold at a price of $9 and the remaining two units at a price of $7. Total revenue is $27 for the first three units and $14 for the last two units, or a total of $41. Profit is now $31. Revenue and profit are greater than when a single price is charged, but less than under first-degree price discrimination.

For second-degree price discrimination to be successful, firms must prevent consumers from combining their demand in order to take advantage of lower prices that could be offered for quantity sales. In Europe, neighboring households often form a purchasing alliance to obtain quantity discounts for the purchase of home heating oil. They then convince the driver to unofficially deliver the oil to their individual homes, a strategy that has saved up to 9 percent on their heating bills. Even after including a tip for the driver's cooperation, this strategy can save consumers money and thwart the intended price discrimination.[31]

Third-degree price discrimination

A pricing strategy under which firms with market power separate markets according to the price elasticity of demand and charge a higher price (relative to cost) in the market with the more inelastic demand.

Third-Degree Price Discrimination   **Third-degree price discrimination** is the most common form of price discrimination, in which firms separate markets according to the price elasticity of demand and charge a higher price

FIGURE 10.4

Profit Maximization and Second-Degree Price Discrimination

Under second-degree price discrimination, the first three units are sold at a price of $9, while the second two units are sold at a price of $7. Total revenue is $41. This strategy adds $6 to revenue and profit compared to charging a single price.

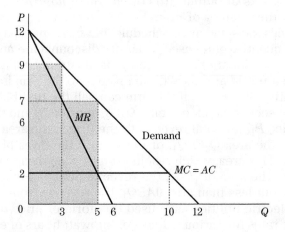

[31]Dolan and Simon, *Power Pricing*, 184–88.

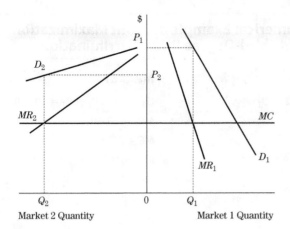

FIGURE 10.5
Third-Degree Price Discrimination
Under third-degree price discrimination, firms separate markets according to the price elasticity of demand and charge a higher price (relative to cost) in the market with the more inelastic demand.

(relative to cost) in the market with the most inelastic demand. There are different prices in different markets, but each consumer in a given market pays a constant amount for each unit purchased. This is the case of the airlines discussed above. We illustrate third-degree price discrimination with two markets in Figure 10.5, assuming that marginal cost is constant and equal in both markets and that demand is relatively more inelastic in Market 1 and more elastic in Market 2.

As we discussed with regard to Equation 10.8, profit maximization in each market is achieved where marginal revenue equals marginal cost in that market. Figure 10.5 shows a relatively inelastic demand curve, D_1, with its marginal revenue curve, MR_1, and a relatively more elastic demand curve, D_2, with its marginal revenue curve, MR_2. Quantity Q_1 maximizes profits for Market 1, while Q_2 maximizes profits for Market 2, as $MR = MC$ in each market at these output levels. The optimal price in each market is that price on the demand curve that corresponds to the profit-maximizing level of output, P_1 in Market 1 and P_2 in Market 2. As you see in Figure 10.5, the optimal price in Market 1, P_1, is higher than the optimal price in Market 2, P_2. Third-degree price discrimination results in a higher price being charged in the market with the relatively more inelastic demand. Charging the same price in both markets would result in lower profit because marginal revenue would not equal marginal cost in both markets at the levels of output corresponding to that common price.

Figure 10.6 and Table 10.5 illustrate the numerical example of third-degree price discrimination. In this case, the firm is able to separate its customers into two markets, the first with demand curve $Q_1 = 12 - P_1$ or $P_1 = 12 - Q_1$ and the second with demand curve $Q_2 = 20 - 2P_2$ or $P_2 = 10 - 0.5Q_2$. Marginal cost is again assumed to be constant, equal to 2, and equal to average cost. The calculation of maximum profit in each market is shown in Table 10.5.

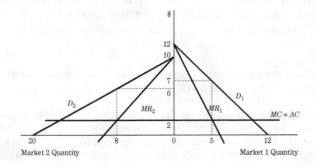

FIGURE 10.6
Profit Maximization and Third-Degree Price Discrimination
The firm will charge a higher price of $7 in Market 1, where demand is relatively more inelastic, and a lower price of $6 in Market 2, where demand is relatively more elastic.

TABLE 10.5 **Numerical Example of Profit Maximization and Third-Degree Price Discrimination**

MARKET 1	MARKET 2
$Q_1 = 12 - P_1$ or $P_1 = 12 - Q_1$	$Q_2 = 20 - 2P_2$ or $P_2 = 10 - 0.5Q_2$
$MR_1 = 12 - 2Q_1$	$MR_2 = 10 - Q_2$
$MC = AC = 2$	$MC = AC = 2$
$MR_1 = MC$	$MR_2 = MC$
$12 - 2Q_1 = 2$	$10 - Q_2 = 2$
$Q_1 = 5$	$Q_2 = 8$
$P_1 = \$7$	$P_2 = \$6$
$TR_1 = (P_1)(Q_1) = (\$7)(5) = \$35$	$TR_2 = (P_2)(Q_2) = (\$6)(8) = \$48$
$TC_1 = (AC)(Q_1) = (\$2)(5) = \$10$	$TC_2 = (AC)(Q_2) = (\$2)(8) = \$16$
$\pi_1 = TR_1 - TC_1 = \$25$	$\pi_2 = TR_2 - TC_2 = \$32$
If $P_1 = \$6, Q_1 = 6$	If $P_2 = \$7, Q_2 = 6$
$TR_1 = (\$6)(6) = \$36$	$TR_2 = (\$7)(6) = \$42$
$TC_1 = (\$2)(6) = \$12$	$TC_2 = (\$2)(6) = \$12$
$\pi_1 = \$36 - \$12 = \$24$	$\pi_2 = \$42 - \$12 = \$30$

Third-degree price discrimination results in a price of $7 being charged in Market 1 and a price of $6 being charged in Market 2. Market 1 has the relatively more inelastic demand curve, while the demand curve in Market 2 is relatively more elastic.[32] Thus, third-degree price discrimination results in a higher price being charged in the market with relatively more inelastic demand. If the same price was charged in both markets, overall profit would decrease. Table 10.5 shows that charging a price of $6 in Market 1 would lower profit from $25 to $24, while charging a price of $7 in Market 2 would lower profit from $32 to $30.

Price Discrimination and Managerial Decision Making

There are numerous examples of real-world price-discrimination strategies that are based on the theoretical models presented in the previous section. The goal of these strategies is to earn more revenue for the firm than would be possible by charging the same price to all customers or for all units of the product. In many cases, this result is achieved by turning the consumer surplus the customer receives from a single-price policy into revenue for the firm through the price-discrimination strategy.

Personalized pricing
Another name for first-degree price discrimination, in which the strategy is to determine how much each individual customer is willing to pay for the product and to charge him or her accordingly.

Personalized Pricing First-degree price discrimination has been called **personalized pricing** because the goal of the strategy is to determine how much each individual customer is willing to pay for the product and to charge him or her accordingly.[33] For example, Lexis-Nexis, the online database provider, is able

---

[32]Picking a common price of $6 for both markets and using the point price elasticity of demand formula, the price elasticity in Market 1 is $[P/(P - a)] = [6/(6 - 12)] = -1.0$. In Market 2, the price elasticity is $[6/(6 - 10)] = -1.5$. Price elasticity is greater in Market 2 than in Market 1.

[33]Much of the following discussion is based on Carl Shapiro and Hal R. Varian, *Information Rules: A Strategic Guide to the Network Economy* (Boston: Harvard Business School Press, 1999). Personalized pricing, group pricing, and versioning are all terms developed by Shapiro and Varian. These issues have been updated in Hal R. Varian, Joseph Farrell, and Carl Shapiro, *The Economics of Information Technology, An Introduction* (Cambridge, MA: Cambridge University Press, 2004).

to charge customers different prices based on the type and size of the subscribing organization, what databases are accessed and when, how much they are used, and whether information is printed or just viewed on the screen. Scanner technologies combined with the use of frequent-shopper cards allow grocery stores to monitor the buying habits and price sensitivity of individual customers for all the products they purchase. Automatic coupons, which lower the price for that customer, can be printed with the sales receipt for either the product purchased or relevant substitute or complementary goods. Grocery-industry veteran analyst Patrick Kiernan notes that "pricing is moving from the product to the store to the individual consumer." He argues that soon the only people paying the posted or "insult price" at the grocery store will be newcomers to the store or individuals who value their privacy so highly that they will not use a frequent-shopper card to take advantage of the selective price reductions.[34]

The Internet offers many opportunities for personalized pricing. Amazon.com tracks the purchases of its customers, adjusts prices, and recommends additional related books in subsequent sessions. Computer companies use e-mail to announce special promotions for certain customers. Online pricing can reduce the costs of reprinting catalogs to adjust the prices of items in oversupply for given customers.

Analysts have estimated that up to 50 percent of online retailers are also using some type of sophisticated promotional targeting. Overstock.com has been displaying several thousand different promotions ranging from free shipping offers to discounted products to different visitors based on 40 attributes related to the shopper's session, including time of day as well as the shopper's presumed gender. eBay Inc. displays different home pages to shoppers based on their previous viewing habits, while other customers are targeted by geography. Companies have examined keywords used on search engines such as Yahoo or Google to try to determine what offers are likely to be popular. Discounts that are targeted to first-time buyers mean that repeat customers may end up paying higher prices.[35]

Although many thought that the Internet might change the entire nature of retailing, there is some evidence that online retailing may be evolving into a competitive industry with low profit margins, similar to traditional offline retailing. In September 2000, Amazon.com faced a hostile consumer reaction when its customers learned through online chat boards that they were paying different prices for the same DVD movies. This policy was the result of a direct market test to gauge consumer price sensitivity. Amazon.com was forced to announce it would refund the difference between the highest and lowest prices offered in the market test. Even though this type of experimentation is undertaken on a regular basis in the real economy through differential catalog pricing, offline consumers are much less likely to be aware of these traditional retailing tactics.[36] Still, the Internet does present online retailers with a number of opportunities to generate market power and gain some control over prices (Chapter 8).

Group Pricing   Third-degree price discrimination can be termed **group pricing** because it is based on the underlying differences in price elasticities among different groups of consumers. Dell Computer Corporation has made extensive use of this pricing strategy. In June 2001, its Latitude L400 ultralight laptop was listed at $2,307 on the company's Web page directed to small businesses, at $2,228 for sales to health care companies, and at $2,072 for sales to state and

Group pricing
Another name for third-degree price discrimination, in which different prices are charged to different groups of customers based on their underlying price elasticity of demand.

---

[34]David Wessel, "How Technology Tailors Price Tags," *Wall Street Journal*, June 21, 2001.

[35]Jessica E. Vascellaro, "Online Retailers Are Watching You," *Wall Street Journal*, November 28, 2006.

[36]David P. Hamilton, "The Price Isn't Right," *Wall Street Journal*, February 12, 2001.

local governments.[37] Dell sales personnel continually canvassed their customers about their buying plans, their willingness to pay for new technology, and the options the customers were considering with Dell's rivals.

The company's price-discriminating strategy was aided by the company's close control over its costs of production at this time. Dell expected its suppliers to pass any cost reductions on to the company so that the reductions could be incorporated into Dell's pricing strategy.

Refinery officials have followed a similar strategy of using information on demand and elasticity to develop what the industry calls "zone pricing" for gasoline.[38] With this strategy, refineries charge dealers in different areas varying wholesale prices based on secret formulas that involve location, affluence of the customers in the area, and an estimate of what the local market will bear. The use of zone pricing can result in differential prices for gas stations that are located only a few miles apart. These stations may pay different prices even though they are supplied by the same refinery. It is estimated that Shell Oil has more than 120 zones in the state of Maryland alone. The price differences can change rapidly in response to changes in market conditions. Gasoline industry analysts have argued that there are three categories of gasoline consumers: "pricers, who will switch for a penny difference; switchers, who will do the same for two to three cents difference; and loyalists who follow the same patterns and may not even look at price."[39] Consumer behavior also varies by grade of gasoline. Price elasticity estimates of –6.0, –4.5, and –3.0 have been calculated for regular, mid-grade, and premium gasoline, respectively.[40]

Differential pricing on the basis of location is used in a variety of industries.[41] Health care professionals may have multiple offices in various parts of a city with varying fee schedules. Grocery chains often classify their stores by intensity of competition and use lower markups in those areas with more intense competition. Ski resorts near Denver typically use purchase location to segment the sales of lift tickets. Tickets purchased slope-side are the most expensive because they are typically purchased by more affluent customers staying in the slope-side hotels and condos. Tickets cost approximately 10 percent less in the nearby town of Dillon, where there are cheaper accommodations. In Denver itself tickets can be purchased at grocery stores and self-serve gas stations for 20 percent discounts. These are attractive to area residents who know the market and are more price-sensitive.

Pricing by location is also used by local governments to solve the problem of the lack of parking spaces in densely populated areas.[42] Seattle has abolished free street parking in a neighborhood just north of downtown, while London has meters that charge as much as $10 per hour. San Francisco has installed hundreds of street sensors to record the "parking events" across 200 parking spots. This technology would allow the city to charge the same rates as private lots for spaces near the stadium during a Giants game. The city has installed new kiosks that take credit cards as well as cash and increased the flat meter rate of $2 per hour to a four-hour rolling rate. This policy applies to areas with highly inelastic

---

[37]Gary McWilliams, "Dell Fine-Tunes Its PC Pricing to Gain Edge in Slow Market," *Wall Street Journal*, June 8, 2001.
[38]Alexei Barrionuevo, "Secret Formulas Set Prices for Gasoline," *Wall Street Journal*, March 20, 2000.
[39]Keith Reid, "The Pricing Equation: Which Price Is Right?" *National Petroleum News* 92 (February 2000): 17.
[40]Ibid., 17.
[41]This discussion is based on Nagle et al., *The Strategy and Tactics of Pricing*. For a discussion of the application of these principles to the pricing of services, see Stowe Shoemaker and Anna S. Mattila, "Pricing in Services," in *Handbook of Pricing Research in Marketing*, ed. Vithala R. Rao (Cheltenham, UK: Edward Elgar, 2009): 535–56.
[42]Conor Dougherty, "The Parking Fix," *Wall Street Journal*, February 3, 2007.

demand for parking spaces, while parking is likely to remain free and unrestricted in low-density areas and many residential neighborhoods.

Officials who manage the Eurotunnel, which allows customers to drive between Folkestone, England, and Calais, France, for a flat price, also use price discrimination. Prices that allow a customer to travel at any time of day are twice as high as those during the off-peak evening and night periods. Rates increase with the time elapsed between the outbound and return trips on the assumption that customers are willing to pay more to have their car with them on longer stays in the other country.[43]

This peak-load pricing, which has long been used by electric power companies with tiered prices to discourage heavy consumption, has been extended with the development of smart meters that can transmit data on how much power is being used at any given time, allowing companies to change prices throughout the day.[44] Smoothing demand leads to the more efficient use of power plants and reduced emissions. However, power companies still have to focus on potential consumer backlash and societal concerns over low-income customers' ability to pay higher prices.

The yield management techniques developed by the airlines and discussed in the opening case have been applied to numerous other industries.[45] Marriott International learned about yield management from the airlines in the mid-1980s and developed its revenue management systems that provided daily forecasts of demand and inventory for each of its rooms at its Marriott, Courtyard, and Residence Inns. Its demand forecasting system was built to forecast guest booking patterns and optimize room availability by price and length of stay. Rental car firms followed with the same type of techniques. United Parcel Service (UPS) originally set its prices on a cost-plus basis by filing tariffs with the federal government. Cost control, including decisions about how many steps the deliverymen should take from the truck to the door and in what order the keys should go on the drivers' rings, helped keep rates low. However, the development of FedEx and other competitors forced UPS to re-analyze its pricing strategies. Rather than focus on a discrete event, such as the purchase of an airline seat or hotel room, UPS negotiated annual rates for large-volume customers using a variety of services over the course of a year. In the 1990s Ford Motor Company moved from pricing its vehicles and options packages on the basis of annual volume estimates and profitability projections to the use of revenue management systems that increased the company's ability to make money without making more vehicles.

Faced with decreasing revenues, the Atlanta Symphony Orchestra first tried to promote convenience packages that enabled customers to select a series of concerts at a discounted rate.[46] However, customers who bought convenience packages did not want to invest more in terms of donations or additional single tickets. This problem led to an alternative approach of increasing revenue by re-pricing seats to reflect the experience of attending the performance. Pricing strategies were developed to reflect two segments of customers—those who were location sensitive and those who were price sensitive. Seat prices were increased for prime locations, such as the left side of the stage near the piano, which almost always

---

[43]Nagle et al., *The Strategy and Tactics of Pricing*.

[44]Rebecca Smith, "Electricity: The New Math: 'Smart' Meters Know When You're Running the Air-Con. 'Half an Hour to Go!' " *Wall Street Journal (Online)*, May 18, 2010.

[45]This discussion is based on Cross et al., "Milestones in the Application of Analytical Pricing and Revenue Management."

[46]This discussion is based on Laurie Garrow, Mark Ferguson, Pinar Keskinocak, and Julie Swann, "Expert Opinions: Current Pricing and Revenue Management Practice Across U.S. Industries," *Journal of Revenue and Pricing Management* 5 (2006): 237–47.

sold out, and prices changed dynamically based on booking pace versus booking availability. Pricing metrics focused less on sales volume and more on increasing revenue and attracting new customers.

Further Rationale for Group Pricing

Two other reasons for managers to use group pricing to attract additional customers are consumer **lock-in** and **network externalities**. Newspapers such as the *Wall Street Journal* offer reduced-rate student subscriptions to attract readers early in their careers, build loyalty, and make at least the psychological costs of switching to other news media relatively high. This is an example of consumer lock-in. Airline frequent flyer programs are another example of group price discrimination that may attract the customers, while the frequent flyer points raise the cost of switching to another airline. Network externalities arise when the value that an individual places on a good is a function of how many other people also use that good. Computer software is one of the best examples of this concept, given that businesses can function much more efficiently if everyone is using the same software. Selling the software at reduced prices to different groups or even giving it away may be a sound price-discrimination strategy if it enables that software to become the industry standard that all firms desire to use.

Versioning

Versioning is a price-discrimination strategy that has become much more widespread with the emergence of the information economy. Under this strategy, different versions of a product are offered to different groups of customers at various prices, each designed to meet the needs of the specific groups. The advantage of this strategy is that consumers reveal their willingness to pay for the different versions of the product through the choices they make. Managers are able to learn about their customers without getting involved with detailed consumer surveys or directs test marketing (Chapter 4).

Book publishers have long used versioning when they publish a hardcover edition of a book and then wait a number of months before the cheaper paperback edition is released. Those customers who must read the latest novel as soon as it is published will pay more to purchase the hardcover edition, while others with less intense preferences will wait and read the softcover edition. The same approach applies to first- and second-run movie theaters and the home video market.

Offering different versions of a product to casual versus more experienced users is a strategy used by Intuit for its Quicken financial software. When Basic Quicken was offered for approximately $20, Quicken Deluxe sold for approximately $60. Product versions may also differ by their speed of operation, flexibility of use, and product capability and by the technical support offered for the product. Selling both online and offline versions of books and other publications is another variant of this strategy. In many cases, the online version is free, but is less convenient to use. Companies offer the online version to stimulate sales of the offline product.[47]

Bundling

Bundling is a variant of product versioning in which the products are sold separately, but also as a bundle, where the price of the bundle is less than the sum of the prices of the individual products. Microsoft Office bundles its products together, but also sells them separately. If two products are bundled, such as a word processing package and a spreadsheet, the strategy is to get consumers to purchase both products because the incremental price for the second product is less than what it would be if they purchased the products separately. The firm attracts sales that it might not otherwise obtain with the

---

Lock-in
Achieving brand loyalty and a stable consumer base for a product by making it expensive for consumers to switch to a substitute product.

Network externalities
These result when the value an individual places on a good is a function of how many other people also use that good.

Versioning
Offering different versions of a product to different groups of customers at various prices, with the versions designed to meet the needs of the specific groups.

Bundling
Selling multiple products as a bundle where the price of the bundle is less than the sum of the prices of the individual products or where the bundle reduces the dispersion in willingness to pay.

---

[47]For a detailed discussion of all these strategies, see Shapiro and Varian, *Information Rules*, 37–80.

TABLE 10.6   Bundling

CUSTOMER	COMPUTER	PRINTER
1	$1,000	$250
2	$800	$300

individual pricing of the products because some customers will pay the small incremental price, but not the full price of the additional product.

Bundling is also a profitable strategy if it reduces the dispersion in the willingness to pay for the products, particularly if the dispersion is less for the bundle than for the individual components of the bundle. We illustrate this case in Table 10.6.

Table 10.6 shows the maximum price two customers are willing to pay for a computer and a printer. If the firm sells the components separately, it should charge a price of $800 for the computer and $250 for the printer. In this case, both consumers will buy both the computer and the printer, and the firm will earn revenue totaling $2,100 [($800 × 2) + ($250 × 2)]. Charging a higher price for either component means that only one customer will purchase each component. However, if the firm bundled the components and sold the bundle for $1,100, each customer would purchase the bundle, and the firm would receive $2,200 in revenue. Bundling reduces the dispersion in willingness to pay. If the firm could price discriminate between the two customers and charge each a different price, total revenue would increase to $2,350. Bundling becomes an optimal strategy if the firm must charge all customers the same price.

Bundling has been used in the music entertainment industry where tickets for headline and more cutting-edge performers are bundled together. Customers for headline entertainers often have less willingness to pay for cutting-edge performers, whereas the audience for the latter, often composed of students and musicians, is more price-sensitive to ticket prices of headline performers. Bundles that include a specific number of concerts of each type can generate more revenue than single ticket pricing only.[48]

Coupons and Sales: Promotional Pricing   The use of coupons and sales, or **promotional pricing**, is another example of price discrimination. These are effective pricing strategies because they not only focus on different price elasticities of demand, but also impose costs on consumers. Those individuals who clip coupons or watch newspaper advertisements for sales are more price sensitive than consumers who do not engage in these activities, and they are also willing to pay the additional costs of the time and inconvenience of clipping the coupons and monitoring the sale periods. This strategy is beneficial for the firm because it does not have to lower the price of its products for all customers and lose additional revenue.

Firms have become much more adept at using sales or markdowns to clear out excess inventory by using software designed to determine the size, number, and timing of the optimal markdowns of the price. This issue has always been a dilemma for retail firms, who do not want to sacrifice revenues by lowering the price too soon, but who do not want to be left with excess inventory that may never

Promotional pricing
Using coupons and sales to lower the price of the product for those customers willing to incur the costs of using these devices as opposed to lowering the price of the product for all customers.

---

[48]Nagle et al., *The Strategy and Tactics of Pricing*, 50–55. For a more technical discussion of bundling, see R. Venkatesh and Vijay Mahajan, "The Design and Pricing of Bundles: A Review of Normative Guidelines and Practical Approaches," in *Handbook of Pricing Research in Marketing*, ed. Vithala R. Rao (Cheltenham, UK: Edward Elgar, 2009): 232–57.

sell at the end of the season. Marked-down goods accounted for only 8 percent of department store sales in the 1970s, but increased to around 20 percent by 2001. The software programs used by retail firms are similar to the yield management programs that the airlines use for price discrimination on airline seats.

For example, ShopKo Stores, a discount chain system similar to Target Corporation, has used the Markdown Optimizer software to test the markdown strategy for 300 of its products. The company ended up using fewer markdowns than it had previously, but increased its sales of the test products by 14 percent compared with a year earlier. The gross profit margin for this merchandise increased by 24 percent, and the company sold 13 percent more of each product at the regular price than it had previously. Predicted markdowns ranged from 25.7 percent at high-volume superstores to 46.3 percent in the lowest-volume stores. Use of the program not only took advantage of differing price elasticities of demand, but also saved labor costs by having fewer markdowns. ShopKo estimated that it cost 18 cents to change the price on a single garment tag and 24 cents to change a shelf label.[49]

Two-part pricing

Charging consumers a fixed fee for the right to purchase a product and then a variable fee that is a function of the number of units purchased.

Two-Part Pricing   Another price-discrimination strategy that managers can use to increase their profits is **two-part pricing**. With this strategy, consumers are charged a fixed fee for the right to purchase the product and then a variable fee that is a function of the number of units purchased. This is a pricing strategy used by buyers clubs, athletic facilities, and travel resorts where customers pay a membership or admission fee and then a per-unit charge for the various products, services, or activities as members.

This strategy can be more profitable for a firm than simply charging the profit-maximizing price for all units of the product or service. To demonstrate this outcome, we draw again on the numerical example presented earlier in Table 10.4 and Figure 10.2. In that example, which we now show in Figure 10.7, we determined that $25 is the maximum profit that can be earned when all five units of output are sold at the profit-maximizing price of $7.

FIGURE 10.7

Profit Maximization and Two-Part Pricing

With two-part pricing, firms charge consumers a fixed fee for the right to purchase a product and then a variable fee that is a function of the number of units purchased.

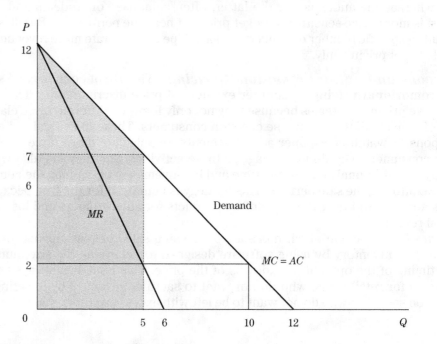

[49]Amy Merrick, "Retailers Try to Get Leg Up on Markdowns with New Software," *Wall Street Journal*, August 7, 2001.

Suppose instead that the firm sets the price equal to the marginal and average cost of $2. The consumer now demands 10 units of the product. The total revenue of $20 just equals total cost, so the firm earns no profit on these units. However, the amount of consumer surplus at a price of $2 is the triangular area underneath the demand curve, but above the price line. The numerical value of the consumer surplus in this triangular area is $(0.5)(10)(12 - 2) = \$50$ (the area of the triangle). This represents the difference between the consumer's total willingness to pay for the 10 units and the amount actually paid. Thus, the firm can charge a fixed fee of up to $50 for the right to purchase the product at a price of $2 per unit. As long as this fee is greater than $25 (the maximum profit earned under the single-price strategy), the firm's profits are greater with the two-part pricing strategy than with the single-price strategy. As with first-degree price discrimination or personalized pricing, this strategy attempts to turn consumer surplus into revenue for the firm. However, with any price-discrimination strategy, managers must also evaluate the administrative costs of that strategy compared with the single-price approach.

Price Discrimination Summary   Table 10.7 summarizes the types of price discrimination we have just discussed.

Unsuccessful Price Discrimination   Price discrimination may not be successful if the strategy causes substantial consumer resentment or a negative reaction from competitors. Coca-Cola Company's testing in 1999 of a vending machine that would automatically raise prices for its drinks in periods of increased and more inelastic demand, such as extremely hot weather, is such an example.[50] This price discrimination would have been achieved through the use of a temperature sensor and a computer chip. The process could also work in the opposite direction, thus lowering the price of a can of soda during periods of slow demand. Coke officials proposed this strategy because vending machines had become an increasingly important source of profits for both Coke and its competitor, Pepsico.

As might be expected, the proposed strategy drew many negative comments about its fairness and appropriateness. One beverage analyst commented, "What next? A machine that X-rays people's pockets to find out how much change they have

TABLE 10.7   Types of Price Discrimination

TYPE	DESCRIPTION
First-degree or personalized pricing	Charging each individual the maximum amount he or she is willing to pay for each unit of the product.
Second-degree	Charging the maximum price consumers are willing to pay for different blocks of output.
Third-degree or group pricing	Separating the markets into different groups of consumers and charging a higher price (relative to cost) in the market with the more inelastic demand. Sometimes called zone pricing.
Versioning	Offering different versions of a product to different groups of customers at various prices, each designed to meet the needs of the specific groups.
Bundling	Selling products separately, but also as a bundle, where the price of the bundle is less than the sum of the prices of the individual products.
Promotional pricing	Using coupons and sales to lower the price to customers with more elastic demands, but also imposing costs on these customers.
Two-part pricing	Charging consumers a fixed fee for the right to purchase a product and then a variable fee that is a function of the number of units purchased.

[50]Constance L. Hayes, "Variable-Price Coke Machine Being Tested," *New York Times*, October 28, 1999.

and raises the price accordingly?" Pepsi officials also took advantage of this move to develop a counter strategy: "We believe that machines that raise prices in hot weather exploit consumers who live in warm climates… At Pepsi, we are focused on innovations that make it easier for consumers to buy a soft drink, not harder."[51]

Price discrimination based on observation may also be counterproductive. Hotel managers often believe they can segment the market by being responsive to those customers who complain about the price. This strategy would involve offering a regular room rate first, then going to a small discount such as one based on an AAA membership if the customer resists, and finally, if there is excess capacity, finding a special block of discounted rooms. However, customers who complain are rarely the most pricesensitive. Business travelers love to negotiate and brag to each other about the great deals they obtain. Customers who do not complain are more likely to be leisure travelers who are more price sensitive, but who do not know the game of bargaining. They will simply hang up the phone and call an economy motel.[52]

Marketing and Price Discrimination

Numerous examples of price discrimination strategies also exist in the marketing literature, although they may be called by different names. For example, in *Marketing Management*, Philip Kotler discusses discriminatory pricing as presented above, but then devotes other sections of his pricing chapter to geographical pricing, price discounts, promotional pricing, two-part pricing, and product-bundling pricing, all of which are examples of price discrimination.[53] Other marketing texts and articles have similar coverage.[54] Market researchers Dolan and Simon cite the case of the differential price elasticities of large versus small customers purchasing industrial air-pollution test equipment.[55] Large customers, those who purchased over 1,000 units, were estimated to have a price elasticity of –2.20, while small buyers, those who purchased less than 100 units, had an elasticity of –1.54. These differences in elasticities resulted in firms charging medium-sized customers 24 percent less and large customers 36 percent less than small customers. Dolan and Simon note that firms have to be careful when using price-discrimination strategies, as they may be pricing very close to the maximum price that consumers are willing to pay.

A marketing analysis can often build on the economics of markup pricing and price discrimination to develop more effective competitive strategies and avoid either forgone profits or noncompetitive prices.[56] For example, when Glaxo introduced Zantac ulcer medication in 1983 to compete with SmithKline Beecham's Tagamet, the number one ulcer medicine and the best-selling drug in the world, conventional markup pricing above cost suggested a lower price for Zantac than Tagamet. However, a marketing analysis of the perceived value to the consumer resulted in a price 50 percent higher than for Tagamet. Zantac had a superior product performance with an easier schedule of doses, fewer side effects, and fewer reactions with other drugs. This analysis proved correct, as Zantac became the market leader within four years.

---

[51]Ibid.

[52]Nagle et al., *The Strategy and Tactics of Pricing.*

[53]Kotler, *Marketing Management: The Millennium Edition*, 471–78.

[54]See Kent B. Monroe, *Pricing: Making Profitable Decisions*, 2nd ed. (New York: McGraw-Hill, 1990); and Gerard J. Tellis, "Beyond the Many Faces of Price: An Integration of Pricing Strategies," *Journal of Marketing* 50 (October 1986): 146–60. More theoretical and conceptual discussions of these issues are found in Gary L. Lilien, Philip Kotler, and K. Sridhar Moorthy, *Marketing Models* (Englewood Cliffs, NJ: Prentice Hall, 1992); and Timothy M. Devinney, *Issues in Pricing: Theory and Research* (Lexington, MA: Lexington Books, 1988). Marketing examples are also found in the following previously-cited sources; Nagle et al., *The Strategy and Tactics of Pricing*; and Rao, *Handbook of Pricing Research in Marketing.*

[55]Dolan and Simon, *Power Pricing*, 174–75.

[56]The following examples are drawn from Robert J. Dolan, "How Do You Know When the Price Is Right?" *Harvard Business Review* (September–October 1995): 174–83.

In a second case, Northern Telecom believed its Norstar telephone system was superior to the competition, but could not be sold at the higher price that a conventional markup would dictate. The Norstar system was priced comparably to its competitors, and the company then examined its costs to determine how to make a profit. As Northern's competitors lowered their prices, Northern was able to decrease its costs so that both its profit margins and its share of the market increased.

Macroeconomics and Pricing Policies

The ability of different firms to mark up price above cost based on the price elasticity of demand is also influenced by overall macroeconomic conditions. The long-run economic expansion in the late 1990s made consumers less cost conscious and more value and status conscious. Thus, their demand for many products became more price inelastic. In May 2000, the Federal Reserve policy of higher interest rates to slow the economy was influenced by the perception that firms were beginning to be able to raise prices and maintain them. The economy appeared to be heating up enough to start another round of inflation.

In 1999, Johns Manville Corporation attempted to raise prices on its insulation and roofing products, but was unable to do so because customers threatened to switch suppliers. A year later, as economic growth was sustained, the company raised prices by as much as 5 percent on many products. UCB Chemical Corporation of Smyrna, Georgia, was also able to raise the prices of its inputs for inks, packaging, and fiber optics in spring 2000 for the first time since 1997. While some of these price increases resulted from passing higher costs of production along to consumers, the firms' increased ability to raise prices from greater and more inelastic demand also played a major role.[57]

This ability to raise prices, however, differed significantly among sectors of the economy. During this period of time, Eastman Kodak Company and Sears, Roebuck either tried to raise prices that could not be maintained or did not attempt to increase prices. Delta Airlines also found itself in this situation, given the availability of information on the Internet about prices of competitor airlines. Demand for other products became more inelastic because there had been decreases in the number of producers in several industries. Consolidation in the paper industry allowed P. H. Glatfelter Company of York, Pennsylvania, to raise prices 15 percent after five years of no increases.

With the slowing economy in 2007 and 2008, firms were again faced with a decreased ability to raise prices and with the possibility of having to offer discounts even if they cut into profit margins. The chief economist of the International Council of Shopping Centers noted that retailers "need to think about promoting more heavily to try to drive traffic." High-end shoppers were also focusing more on bargains. Although Saks Inc. reported a 4.1 percent increase in same-store sales in January 2008, the company noted that customers were shifting more of their spending to sales events. Discount chains and warehouse clubs performed relatively better during this period than did department stores and specialty-apparel chains.[58]

As the weak economic recovery continued into 2010 and 2011, the prices of goods rose more quickly than those for services. Increasing commodities prices pushed up the prices of goods 2.2 percent in 2011 compared with a year earlier, whereas the prices of services increased by only 1.2 percent. The weak housing

---

[57]Jacob M. Schlesinger and Yochi J. Dreazen, "Producers Start to Raise Prices, Stirring Fear in Inflation Fighters," *Wall Street Journal*, May 16, 2000.

[58]Amy Merrick and Kevin Kingsbury, "Retail Squeeze Felt Far Beyond Malls," *Wall Street Journal*, February 8, 2008.

market and continuing unemployment influenced consumer willingness to pay for services, which resulted in these smaller price increases.[59]

Even during this period, perceived elasticity of demand influenced managers' ability to raise prices. In January 2012, Starbucks Corp. announced brewed-coffee price increases averaging 1 percent in the Northeast and Sunbelt regions. Company officials believed that its high-end consumer base was less sensitive to prices than some of its rivals, particularly fast-food restaurants. However, Starbucks did not raise prices for packaged coffee sold at its cafes or grocery stores, even though coffee represented a larger portion of the cost of its packaged goods than of brewed coffee.[60]

The ability of firms to raise prices in the face of demand and cost changes has been a key issue in our microeconomic models of market structure. The models of imperfect competition imply that firms would change their prices as either demand or cost conditions changed. Much empirical data question this result.

A survey of firms' pricing and cost behavior by Alan Blinder and his colleagues indicated that the median number of price changes for a typical product in a given year is only 1.4 and that half of all price changes occur no more than once a year (Chapter 5).[61] Price changes typically lag about three months behind changes in either demand or cost.

In the survey, the most important reason firms gave for price rigidity was the fear that other firms would not follow price increases by a given firm. This is the behavior of oligopoly firms. Firms also found other ways to clear the market in response to changing demand and cost conditions, such as varying delivery lags, sales effort, product quality, and quality of service. These forms of nonprice competition, which act as substitutes for price changes, were important in most sectors of the economy surveyed by Blinder and his colleagues. Firms may also have tacit or implicit contracts with their customers not to raise prices when markets are tight. These implicit contracts may be intended to reduce consumers' search and shopping costs, or they may result from a concern for "fairness" in the pricing process.

More-recent studies of pricing changes in both the United States and Europe have found that prices of many goods and services do not respond immediately to changing demand and supply conditions.[62] Prices seem to change far less frequently in some European countries (Austria, Belgium, Finland, France, Germany, Italy, Luxembourg, the Netherlands, Portugal, and Spain) than in the United States, with the average duration of a price spell ranging from four to five quarters in Europe, twice as long as in the United States. The frequency of price changes varies substantially across products. Energy products and unprocessed food have frequent price changes, while processed food, nonenergy industrial

[59]Jon Hilsenrath and Justin Lahart, "Split in Economy Keeps Lid on Prices," *Wall Street Journal (Online)*, February 18, 2011.

[60]Annie Gasparro, "Starbucks to Raise Prices," *Wall Street Journal (Online)*, January 4, 2012.

[61]Alan S. Blinder, Elie R. D. Canetti, David E. Lebow, and Jeremy B. Rudd, *Asking About Prices: A New Approach to Understanding Price Stickiness* (New York: Russell Sage Foundation, 1998), 84–105.

[62]Emmanuel Dhyne, Luis J. Alvarez, Herve Le Bihan, Giovanni Veronese, Daniel Dias, Johannes Hoffmann, Nicole Jonker, Patrick Lunnemann, Fabio Rumler, and Jouko Vilmunen, "Price Changes in the Euro Area and the United States: Some Facts from Individual Consumer Price Data," *Journal of Economic Perspectives* 20 (Spring 2006): 171–92; Luis J. Alvarez, Emmanuel Dhyne, Marco Hoeberichts, Claudia Kwapil, Herve Le Bihan, Patrick Lunnemann, Fernando Martins, Roberto Sabbatini, Harald Stahl, Philip Vermeulen, and Jouko Vilmunen, "Sticky Prices in the Euro Area: A Summary of New Micro-Evidence," *Journal of the European Economic Association* 4 (April–May 2006): 575–84; Campbell Leith and Jim Malley, "A Sectoral Analysis of Price-Setting Behavior in U.S. Manufacturing Industries," *The Review of Economics and Statistics* 89 (May 2007): 335–42.

goods, and services have infrequent changes. Goods with relatively large inputs of labor are subject to less frequent price adjustments. There is no evidence of general downward price rigidity, although price decreases are less common in services. Price changes are generally not synchronized across products, even within the same country. These studies found that the use of implicit contracts was the most important reason preventing a rapid adjustment of prices. Firms tried not to jeopardize their customer relationships. Other explanations for the lack of price adjustments included explicit contracts that were costly to renegotiate, marginal costs that did not vary significantly, and the desire of firms not to change prices unless their competitors did so. These behaviors that result in price rigidity, or sticky prices, have implications for the macroeconomic analysis of the economy.[63]

Summary

In this chapter, we analyzed how knowledge of the price elasticity of demand for different products or among different groups of customers is fundamental to developing optimal pricing strategies. We illustrated the role of price elasticity in two common pricing strategies: markup pricing and price discrimination. We also highlighted the linkages between the economics of pricing and the role of marketing in developing competitive strategies.

We reviewed cost and profit maximization concepts in this chapter because average and marginal costs form the basis for markup pricing, price discrimination, and profit determination. Managers may have to look at the cost side of their operation to improve profits if they have little ability or are unable to change prices. We also noted that there are a number of reasons why managers may not immediately change their prices in response to changes in demand and cost conditions.

Key Terms

bundling, p. 278

consumer surplus, p. 270

first-degree price
    discrimination, p. 270

group pricing, p. 275

lock-in, p. 278

marginal benefit, p. 269

markup pricing, p. 260

network externalities, p. 278

personalized pricing, p. 274

price discrimination, p. 267

promotional pricing, p. 279

second-degree price
    discrimination, p. 271

third-degree price discrimination, p. 272

total benefit, p. 270

two-part pricing, p. 280

versioning, p. 278

---

[63]The increase in online commerce may change these results. In a study comparing online pricing behavior with that of brick-and-mortar stores selling books and CDs that are easily identified by their ISBN codes, the authors found that online menu costs are considerably smaller and therefore price changes are more frequent and in smaller amounts. See Erik Brynjolfsson and Michael Smith, "Frictionless Commerce: A Comparison of Internet and Conventional Retailers," *Management Science* 46 (2000): 563–85.

Exercises

Technical Questions

1. Given each of the following price elasticities, determine whether marginal revenue is positive, negative, or zero.

   a. -5

   b. -1

   c. -0.5

2. Given each of the following price elasticities, calculate the optimal markup.

   a. -15

   b. -8

   c. -3

3. Suppose a firm has a constant marginal cost of $10. The current price of the product is $25, and at that price, it is estimated that the price elasticity of demand is -3.0.

   a. Is the firm charging the optimal price for the product? Demonstrate how you know.

   b. Should the price be changed? If so, how?

4. The individual demand for a slice of pizza at Sam's Pizza is given by $Q_D = 6 - P$. Assume the marginal cost of a slice is constant at $1.00 and the marginal revenue (MR) function is $6 - 2Q$.

   a. What is the profit-maximizing price and quantity if Sam's sells all slices at a single price? What profit per customer will be earned?

   b. Suppose that Sam's decides to sell pizza at cost and charge a fixed price for this option. What quantity will a customer demand at the market price? What is the maximum fixed price Sam's can charge for this option?

5. Suppose that individual demand for a product is given by $Q_D = 1000 - 5P$. Marginal revenue is $MR = 200 - 0.4Q$, and marginal cost is constant at $20. There are no fixed costs.

   a. The firm is considering a quantity discount. The first 400 units can be purchased at a price of $120, and further units can be purchased at a price of $80. How many units will the consumer buy in total?

   b. Show that this second-degree price-discrimination scheme is more profitable than a single monopoly price.

6. An airline estimates that the price elasticity of demand for business travelers (who travel on weekdays) is -2, while the price elasticity of demand for vacation travelers (who travel on weekends) is -5. If the airline price discriminates (and costs are the same), what will be the ratio of weekday to weekend prices?

7. A monopolist sells in two geographically divided markets, the East and the West. Marginal cost is constant at $50 in both markets. Demand and marginal revenue in each market are as follows:

$$Q_E = 900 - 2P_E$$
$$MR_E = 450 - Q_E$$
$$Q_W = 700 - P_W$$
$$MR_W = 700 - 2Q_W$$

   a. Find the profit-maximizing price and quantity in each market.

   b. In which market is demand more elastic?

8. A cable company offers two basic packages: sports and kids, and a combined package. There are three different types of users: parents, sports fans, and generalists. The following table shows the maximum price that each type of consumer is willing to pay for each package.

	Sports Package	Kids Package
Parents	10	50
Sports Fans	50	10
Generalists	40	40

   a. If the cable company offers any one package for $50 or the combined bundled package for $70, who will buy each package?

   b. Explain why the company will make a higher profit with this method than if the bundled package option were not offered.

Application Questions

1. In the current business media, find examples of firms that changed from pricing based on cost to strategies that also incorporated information on the price elasticity of demand.

2. The following discussion focuses on the change in production and selling strategies of Timken Co., the Canton, Ohio, firm that is a major producer of bearings:[64]

   > To counter the low prices of imports, Timken Co. in 2003 began bundling its bearings with other parts to provide industrial business customers with products specifically designed for their needs. Timken had begun bundling prelubricated, preassembled bearing packages for automobile manufacturers in the early 1990s. Evidence indicated that companies that sold integrated systems rather than discrete parts to the automobile manufacturers increased their sales. Other industrial customers put the same pressure on Timken in the late 1990s to lower prices, customize, or lose their business to lower-priced foreign suppliers. Manufacturers are increasingly combining a standard part with casings, pins, lubrication, and electronic sensors. Installation, maintenance, and engineering services may also be included.

   > Suppliers, such as Timken, saw this as a means of increasing profits and making themselves more indispensable to the manufacturers. The strategy also required suppliers to remain in proximity with their customers, another advantage over foreign imports. This type of bundling does require significant research and development and flexible factories to devise new methods of transforming core parts into smart assemblies. The repackaging is more difficult for industrial than automobile customers because the volumes of production are smaller for the former. Timken also had to educate its customers on the variety of new products available.

   > Timken has an 11 percent share of the world market for bearings. However, imports into the United States doubled to $1.4 billion in 2002 compared with $660 million in 1997. Timken believes that the uniqueness of its product helps protect it from foreign competition. However, the company still lobbied the Bush administration to stop what it calls the dumping of bearings at low prices by foreign producers in Japan, Romania, and Hungary.

   a. What factors in the economic environment, in addition to foreign imports, contributed to Timken's new strategy in 2002 and 2003?

   b. How does this strategy relate to the discussion of bundling presented in the chapter? What additional factors are presented in this case?

3. The following discussion pertains to the pricing policies of Linear Technology Corp.:[65]

   > The semiconductor industry Linear Technology Corp. has maintained strong profitability by operating at the fringes where competition is low and margins are high. This midsize company makes 7,500 arcane, unglamorous products that solve real-world problems for a long list of customers, including analog chips that are too cheap for customers to haggle over, but perform chores too important to ignore. Many of Linear's chips cost less than 50 cents to build and sell for three to four times as much, but customers seldom complain about the markup.

---

[64]Carlos Tejada, "The Allure of Bundling," *Wall Street Journal*, October 7, 2003.
[65]George Anders, "In a Tech Backwater, a Profit Fortress Rises," *Wall Street Journal*, July 10, 2007.

Linear made a 39% profit on its $1.1 billion sales in 2006, more than five times the average for U.S. industrial companies. However, other bigger chip makers, including Texas Instruments Inc., Richtek Technology Corp. of Taiwan, and Freescale Semiconductor Inc. of Austin, Texas, are now moving into the market and others may follow suit. Unlike in the digital chip world, in which a single winning design bought by a few big customers can yield huge profits, Linear would rather see its order book packed with small to midsize orders from companies too busy to haggle over prices. Intermec Inc., which makes mobile data scanners, uses Linear chips to obtain extra life from its devices' batteries. The chips' total cost is less than 5% of the materials budget. Performance is crucial for this company; price is not.

Traditionally the dozen or so major analog chip companies have tiptoed around one another's product lines, helping keep profit margins high. Each company established its strength decades ago, making it easy to extend existing product families and deepen relations with longtime customers. "We chip away a little at each others' specialties," says Jerald Fishman, chief executive of Analog Devices. "But there isn't a lot of direct competition."

Discuss how price elasticity of demand influences the pricing strategies of Linear Technology Corp. What market model best describes this industry? Explain.

4. Discuss how the following strategies relate to the price-discrimination principles presented in this chapter.[66]

Wildeck, Inc. began manufacturing storage-rack protectors used to keep forklifts from damaging the corners of racks on factory floors about five years ago. However, a competitor began producing a similar product made from lighter steel that was priced 15 percent lower. Instead of lowering its price, Wildeck introduced a "lite" version of its protectors that sold for less than the competitor's product. Customers who inquired about the lite version were told the advantages of the heavier-duty product and often ended up buying the original. This strategy helped Wildeck hold its market share and institute a 5 percent price increase.

The Union Pacific railroad developed its "blue streak" service in September 2001 that promised to get shipments from Los Angeles to Atlanta in five days. This strategy allowed the railroad to compete more directly with truckers and charge up to a 40 percent premium over regular rail service. However, the service costs increased only slightly for Union Pacific.

5. Publishers have traditionally sold textbooks at different prices in different areas of the world. For example, a textbook that sells for $70 in the United States might sell for $5 in India.[67] Although the Indian version might be printed on cheaper paper and lack color illustrations, it provides essentially the same information. Indian customers typically cannot afford to pay the U.S. price.

a. Use the theories of price discrimination presented in this chapter to explain this strategy.

b. If the publisher decides to sell this textbook online, what problems will this present for the pricing strategy? How might the publisher respond?

6. Tolls on approximately one-third of the 5,000 miles of highway, bridges, and tunnels in the United States increased in 2005.[68] Tolls went from $2.00 to $3.00 on seven bridges in the San Francisco Bay Area. The Pennsylvania Turnpike increased the average fare by 43 percent, while the New York State Thruway increased its tolls by 25 percent for cars and 35 percent for trucks. Tolls on the Thruway were supposed to be removed a decade

[66]Timothy Aeppel, "Amid Weak Inflation, Firms Turn Creative to Boost Prices," *Wall Street Journal*, September 18, 2002.
[67]This example is drawn from Shapiro and Varian, *Information Rules*, 44–45.
[68]Daniel Machalaba, "Steep Increases Set for Toll Roads," *Wall Street Journal*, April 12, 2005.

ago when the bonds that financed the construction of the highway were paid off. However, these plans were changed when state officials decided they wanted the Thruway to finance another highway that is toll-free. For people who want to avoid toll roads, the costs are not insignificant. Alternatives may be less-direct routes that go through densely packed downtowns or sprawling suburbs. The number of cars using the Pennsylvania Turnpike decreased by less than 1 percent after the toll increase. Road officials need to use toll revenue

for repairs and maintenance. They are trying to soften the impact of higher tolls with smaller increases for drivers that pay electronically using a transponder mounted on the car windshield that deducts tolls from a customer's prepaid account.

a. Why are tolls a popular source of revenue from the viewpoint of road officials?
b. What is the impact of maintaining tolls on the New York State Thruway?
c. What is the price elasticity of demand for use of the Pennsylvania Turnpike?

11 Measuring Macroeconomic Activity

I n this chapter we change our focus from the microeconomic factors influencing managers—prices, costs, and market structure—to factors arising in the larger *macroeconomic* environment, such as the overall level of income and output produced in the economy, the price level, and the level of employment and unemployment. The latter factors are affected by the spending decisions of individuals and organizations throughout the economy. Thus, macroeconomic analysis focuses on the aggregate behavior of different sectors of the economy. However, changes in the macro environment affect individual firms and industries through the microeconomic factors of demand, production, cost, and profitability.

We begin this chapter with a case that describes measures of U.S. economic activity in spring 2012. We also discuss how firms in different industries responded to this economic data.

We then describe the framework used to measure overall economic activity or *gross domestic product* (GDP). We use this framework to develop the aggregate macroeconomic model (Chapters 11–15). Next we describe commonly used measures of the price level and the level of output and employment in the economy and relate these concepts to the major issues facing policy makers. Although managers cannot influence the macroeconomic environment, they need to understand the policies that change that environment to determine whether they need to modify their competitive strategies.

Case for Analysis

Measuring Changes in Macroeconomic Activity: Implications for Managers

At the end of May 2012, the government reported that the U.S. GDP grew in the first quarter of 2012 at an annualized rate of 1.9 percent, which was less than the 2.2 percent growth rate previously estimated. These and other data reflected a view of an economy that was slowly recovering from the recession that officially began in December 2007 and ended in June 2009. The government reported that the number of workers applying for jobless benefits increased by 10,000 in the previous week, while a regional manufacturing report for the Midwest showed slower growth in the previous month. First-quarter growth was decreased by less inventory building by companies than originally estimated, which meant that companies might replenish their stockpiles in the second quarter. Corporate profits increased $11.4 billion before taxes in the first quarter of 2012 following gains of $32.5 billion and $16.8 billion in the third and fourth quarters of 2011.[1]

The next day the government reported that employers added only 69,000 jobs (seasonally adjusted) in May 2012, the smallest increase in a year, while estimates for the two previous months were also decreased from their previous values. Governments continued to reduce payrolls by 13,000 jobs in May, while the number of long-term unemployed, those out of work for six months or longer, grew from 5.1 to 5.4 million. The unemployment rate increased from 8.1 percent in April to 8.2 percent in May 2012. A separate report showed that U.S. manufacturing growth slowed in May with decreases in both production and exports. The Institute for Supply Management reported that its purchasing managers' index decreased 1.3 points in May to 53.5, with a reading above 50 indicating that the sector is expanding.[2]

This slow recovery in economic activity had a substantial impact on all types of firms. Managers at H. J. Heinz Co., which makes ketchup and packaged foods, spent more on marketing to target increasing numbers of cost-conscious customers. The company planned to expand its presence in convenience stores, clubs, and drugstores, given slower sales in supermarkets. The company also tested smaller and cheaper package sizes to appeal to customers with reduced incomes. Joy Global Inc., a U.S. mining-equipment maker, said that the economic uncertainty could keep American mining companies from completing expansion projects and that international companies might not develop new operations.[3] Armstrong World Industries, a flooring manufacturer in Lancaster, PA, reported that it would hire more factory workers but only when home sales increased and nonresidential business stopped cutting back. The company was hurt by both cuts in school funding in the United States and weaker sales in Europe.[4]

In mid-June 2012, a measure of consumer sentiment from the University of Michigan and Thomson-Reuters decreased for the first time in 10 months and hit its lowest level since December 2011. The owner of an upscale spa and salon in Arlington, Texas reported that his customers were wary even when the economic news was good, given the mixed signals on the economy over the previous years. The chief executive of Harting Inc., an Illinois-based manufacturer of industrial connectors, noted a drop in demand for makers of machine tools used in factories around the world. U.S. business was slowing, while business in China and Europe was considered to be "non-existent." The recessions in many European countries and the possible fiscal cliff in the United States—tax increases and government spending cuts that might occur automatically as a result of the 2011 budget agreement—contributed to overall uncertainty. One economist noted that the U.S. economy was in "low-altitude orbit but threatened by uncontrolled meteors of euro crises and fiscal cliff that might knock it out of orbit."[5]

---

[1]Neil Shah and Kate Linebaugh, "First-Period U.S. Growth Was Slower Than Thought," *Wall Street Journal (Online)*, May 31, 2012.

[2]Josh Mitchell, "Grim Jobs Data Upend Debate at Fed, in Campaign," *Wall Street Journal (Online)*, June 1, 2012.

[3]Shah and Linebaugh, "First-Period U.S. Growth Was Slower Than Thought."

[4]Michell, "Grim Jobs Data Upend Debate at Fed, in Campaign."

[5]Ben Casselman and Phil Izzo, "Recovery Slows as Global Risks Rise," *Wall Street Journal (Online)*, June 15, 2012.

Measuring Gross Domestic Product (GDP)

Gross domestic product
The comprehensive measure of the market value of all currently produced final goods and services within a country in a given period of time by domestic and foreign-supplied resources.

Circular flow
The framework for the aggregate macroeconomic model, which portrays the level of economic activity as a flow of expenditure from consumers to firms or producers as consumers purchase goods and services produced by these firms. This flow then returns to consumers as income received from the production process.

Just as we have the framework of demand, supply, and markets to understand the impact of microeconomic variables on managers' competitive strategies, we need a framework to understand the variables influencing the overall level of economic activity. The most closely watched measure of economic activity is **gross domestic product (GDP)**, the market value of all currently produced final goods and services within a country in a given period of time by domestic and foreign-supplied resources. The framework underlying GDP is the **circular flow**, which is derived from market transactions. All of these transactions are exchanges of income for goods and services between demanders (consumers or households) and suppliers (producers or firms). In market transactions, consumers use a certain amount of their income to pay producers an amount equal to the market price of the goods and services times the quantity purchased, and the consumers receive the goods and services in return. Thus, there is a flow of expenditure from consumers to producers and a flow of goods and services in the opposite direction, from producers to consumers. Producers then use this revenue from the sale of the products to pay for the inputs used in producing the goods and services. Thus, there is a flow of income from firms to households who own these inputs and a flow of real resources from households to firms. Households use this income to again purchase other goods and services—hence, the name *circular flow*.[6]

The Circular Flow in a Mixed, Open Economy

Mixed economy
An economy that has both a private (household and firm) sector and a public (government) sector.

Open economy
An economy that has both domestic and foreign sectors.

Figure 11.1 illustrates the circular flow in a mixed, open economy. A **mixed economy** has both a private (household and firm) sector and a public (government) sector, whereas a private economy has only the household and firm sector. An **open economy** has domestic and foreign sectors, whereas a closed economy has only a domestic sector.

Figure 11.1 shows the household and firm sectors of the economy. Firms sell currently produced goods and services in the domestic markets in the top part of the figure, and households use part of their income on consumption expenditures (C) for these products. These expenditures by households become revenue for the firms. This revenue is used to pay the firms' expenses of production. These transactions occur in the resource markets in the bottom part of Figure 11.1, where firms purchase all of the inputs (labor, machinery, land, and so on) used to produce their goods and services. These payments to the factors of production occur as wages, rent, interest, and profits, which then become income (Y) to the household sector. This income is used to finance further consumption in another round of the circular flow. We show only the flow of income and expenditure in Figure 11.1, not the flow of goods, services, and resources, which occurs in the opposite direction of the arrows in the figure.

Figure 11.1 also incorporates investment expenditure (I) by the firm sector, spending by all levels of government (G), and the foreign sector (export spending,

---

[6]Income and expenditure are flows that occur over a period of time. This flow concept differs from the stock of wealth or debt that may result from this process. If consumers save some of their income, this action adds to their stock of wealth or the amount of financial assets they have at a point in time. If consumers' expenditure exceeds their income, they have to borrow the difference, and their stock of debt increases. Stocks (wealth and debt) are measured at a point in time, whereas flows (income, expenditure, and saving) are measured over time.

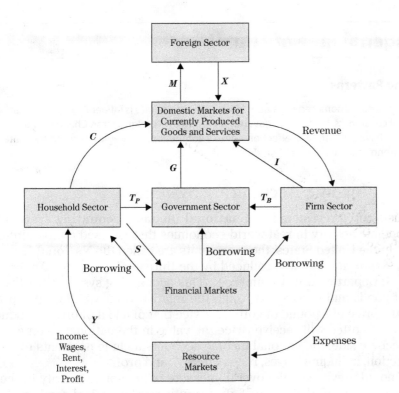

FIGURE 11.1
GDP and the Circular Flow
The circular flow is the framework that forms the basis for the aggregate macroeconomic model of the economy.
C = consumption spending
I = investment spending
G = government spending
X = export spending
M = import spending
Y = household income
S = household saving
T_P = personal taxes
T_B = business taxes

X, by foreign residents on domestically produced goods and services and import spending, M, by domestic residents on foreign goods and services). We are measuring GDP using the **expenditure or output approach** when we add consumption (C), investment (I), government (G), and net export expenditure (F)—which is export spending (X) minus import spending (M)—as shown in the top half of Figure 11.1. These components equal the **aggregate expenditure** (E) on the output produced in the economy, or $E = C + I + G + X - M$.

The economic activity in Figure 11.1 can also be measured by the **earnings or income approach**, which focuses on the flow of income in the bottom half of the figure. Given the circular flow, aggregate expenditure (E) on the output in the economy must equal the income (Y) earned from producing this output, or $E = Y$. Thus, throughout the remainder of this text, we use the terms *aggregate expenditure, output,* and *income* interchangeably.

Figure 11.1 also shows the three major uses that households make of their income. They first pay personal taxes (T_P) to support government activities. This leaves them with disposable income (Y_d), which they either spend on consumption goods and services (C) or save (S). The amount of income that is saved typically flows to the financial markets (banks, stock and bond markets, and other financial institutions), where it forms a pool of assets that can be borrowed by either firms or governments to finance investment expenditure (I) or government expenditure (G). Thus, government expenditure (G) is financed through personal taxes on households (T_P), business taxes on firms (T_B), and borrowing. Households may also borrow from the financial markets to finance consumption expenditure (C). However, households, on balance, are net savers. Analyzing the factors that affect all of the variables in Figure 11.1 and determining their impact on managers' strategies are the major goals of the remaining macroeconomic chapters in this text.

Expenditure or output approach
Measuring overall economic activity by adding the expenditure on the output produced in the economy.

Aggregate expenditure
The sum of consumption, investment, government, and net export spending on the total amount of real output produced in an economy in a given period of time, which equals the income generated from producing and selling that output.

Earnings or income approach
Measuring overall economic activity by adding the earnings or income generated by selling the output produced in the economy.

Managerial Rule of Thumb

Spending Patterns

The overall macroeconomic environment in which firms operate is influenced by aggregate spending decisions of consumers, businesses, governments, and the foreign sector. Changes in these spending patterns can have a substantial effect on a firm's competitive strategies because they alter the economic environment in which that firm does business. ■

National Income Accounting Systems

National income accounting system

A system of accounts developed for each country, based on the circular flow, whose purpose is to measure the level of economic activity in that country.

National Income and Product Accounts

The U.S. national income accounting system, operated by the Bureau of Economic Analysis (BEA) in the U.S. Department of Commerce.

Economists and forecasters use a **national income accounting system** to measure economic activity in real-world economies that is based on the circular flow concept. In the United States, these accounts are called the **National Income and Product Accounts** and are produced by the Bureau of Economic Analysis (BEA) in the U.S. Department of Commerce.[7] This accounting system uses the market prices of goods and services to weigh the relative value of all output produced. Thus, if the price of a pound of coffee is twice that of a loaf of bread, production of the pound of coffee will receive twice the value in the national income accounts. On the income side, the national income accounts include payments to all factors of production, including wages, rents, interest, and profit.

As we noted previously, the overall measure of economic activity in the United States, GDP, is the market value of all currently produced final goods and services over a period of time within the borders of the United States, whether produced by American or foreign-supplied resources.[8] GDP estimates are prepared quarterly by the BEA and published on its Web site (www.bea.gov) and in its monthly journal, the *Survey of Current Business*. The estimates are based on data gathered from surveys of households, businesses, and governments and from tax and regulatory reports submitted to various government agencies. These data may be collected weekly, monthly, quarterly, or annually.

Because there is a need to get the GDP estimates published as soon as possible, the initial or advanced estimate, which is published at the beginning of each quarter during the year for the quarter just completed, is followed by a series of revisions in the two subsequent months based on data not originally available. These preliminary and final estimates are followed by annual revisions in the three succeeding years and a benchmark revision on a periodic five-year schedule. The five-year benchmark revisions are made consistent with a data series carried back to 1929.[9]

---

[7]For a comprehensive discussion of the National Income and Product Accounts, see J. Steven Landefeld, Eugene P. Seskin, and Barbara M. Fraumeni, "Taking the Pulse of the Economy: Measuring GDP," *Journal of Economic Perspectives* 22 (Spring 2008): 193–216.

[8]GDP differs slightly from the measure used previously in the National Income and Product Accounts, gross national product (GNP), which is the value of all currently produced final goods and services over a period of time using resources of U.S. residents, no matter where produced. GNP includes and GDP excludes the income of U.S. residents and corporations earned abroad (interest, dividends, and reinvested profits) minus the earnings of foreign residents on their investments in the United States. The National Income and Product Accounts assume that these net earnings measure the net contribution of U.S.-owned investments abroad to the production of goods and services in other countries. GDP, therefore, is the value of goods and services produced within the United States, while GNP is the value of goods and services produced by residents of the United States. The United States switched to the GDP accounting system in 1992 to make the National Income and Product Accounts consistent with the national income accounting systems of other industrialized countries. The difference between the two measures is extremely small, approximately one-half of 1 percent of GDP in 2001. Throughout this text, we will use the current GDP accounting system.

[9]This discussion of the National Income and Product Accounts is based primarily on U.S. Department of Commerce, Bureau of Economic Analysis, *Concepts and Methods of the U.S. National Income and Product Accounts (Chapters 1–9)*, November 2011. Available at http://www.bea.gov/methodologies/index.htm#na.

Characteristics of GDP

GDP is the value of economic activity—a *monetary* measure of economic activity that includes only *final* goods and services and excludes market transactions that do not relate to the *current* production of goods and services. In the United States, GDP is calculated in dollar terms, whereas local currencies are used for other countries. As we noted above, market prices are used to weight the different goods and services included in GDP, so the value of GDP is a function of both the prices and the quantities of the goods produced in a given time period.

GDP includes the **final goods and services** (sold to end-users), but not any **intermediate goods and services** (used in the production of other goods and services). Although it might be possible to count all final goods and services produced in a given time period, it would be difficult to determine which goods and services are consumed by their end-users and which are used in the further production of other goods and services. Thus, to calculate GDP, government statisticians use the **value-added approach**. In this approach, only the value added in each stage of production (raw materials to semifinished goods to final products) is counted for inclusion in GDP. If the value of all intermediate and final goods was included in the GDP, there would be substantial double-counting of the nation's output.

For example, suppose that you buy a cup of coffee at Dunkin' Donuts for $1.00. Suppose also that Dunkin' Donuts pays $.60 for the coffee beans. The cost of the cup, the labor to serve the customer, and the profit to the company constitute the other $.40. Does GDP increase by $1.00 or $2.00 ($0.60 + $0.40 + $1.00) when this cup of coffee is produced and sold? The correct answer is $1.00 because that is the value of the final good purchased by the customer. This amount can be calculated by the value-added approach: $.60 is the value added by all other businesses to get the coffee beans to Dunkin' Donuts, and then an additional $.40 is added by Dunkin' Donuts when it turns the raw coffee beans into a cup of coffee. Counting both the intermediate good (raw coffee beans) and the final product (a cup of coffee) would overstate the contribution to GDP.

GDP for any time period includes only those goods and services currently produced in that period. Therefore, any secondhand sales are excluded. For example, even though there are many market transactions for used cars each year, these transactions are not included in the current year's GDP. To include them would result in double-counting because these automobiles were already counted in the year in which they were produced.[10] GDP also does not include any financial security transactions, such as the buying and selling of stocks and bonds. These financial transactions represent changes in the claims of ownership of existing assets, not the production of new goods and services. These transactions also cancel each other out because when you purchase the asset, someone else sells it.

GDP does not include most nonmarket activities that are not recorded in output or input market transactions. These activities include legal activities, such as unpaid housework done by a spouse, and illegal activities, such as prostitution and the sale of drugs. The latter activities are considered part of the **underground economy**, or those economic transactions that cannot be easily measured because they are not reported on income tax returns and other government economic surveys. Researchers have made a variety of attempts to measure the size of the underground economy. They have employed both direct methods—including studies of the compliance with income tax laws in reporting business incomes—and indirect methods—using information suggesting attempts to hide income, such as using cash rather than checks for transactions, as there is no paper or electronic

Final goods and services
Goods and services that are sold to their end-users.

Intermediate goods and services
Goods and services that are used in the production of other goods and services.

Value-added approach
A process of calculating the value of the final output in an economy by summing the value added in each stage of production (i.e., raw materials to semifinished goods to final products).

Underground economy
Economic transactions that cannot be easily measured because they are not reported on income tax returns or other government economic surveys.

---

[10]Although the production of the used automobile is not included in current GDP, any services performed by the salesperson or any repairs to the car represent value added by a used car dealer and are included in current GDP.

Imputed value
An estimated value for nonmarket transactions, such as the rental value of owner-occupied housing, included in GDP.

Transfer payments
Payments that represent the transfer of income among individuals in the economy, but do not reflect the production of new goods and services.

trail with cash transactions. Estimates of the effect of underreporting of the underground economy on the national income accounts have ranged from 1 to 33 percent of the GDP. Measuring the underground economy is a continuing problem for government statisticians and other researchers.[11]

The Bureau of Economic Analysis does calculate an **imputed value** for certain expenditures for which there are no market transactions. For example, if an individual rents a house, there is an explicit market transaction in which rent is paid to the landlord in return for the housing services. Individuals who own their homes also receive these housing services, but pay no explicit rent. The BEA *imputes* a rental value for these housing services and includes that figure in personal consumption expenditures, which are part of the GDP.

Transfer payments are also not included in the calculation of GDP. Transfer payments represent the transfer of income among individuals in the economy, but do not reflect the production of new goods and services. Transfer payments can be both public (Social Security, welfare, and veterans' payments) and private (transfers among members of a family). Public transfer payments are recorded in government budgets, but they are excluded from GDP because they do not represent payment for newly produced goods and services.

Real Versus Nominal GDP

Because GDP is a monetary measure that weights currently produced goods and services according to their market prices, it can increase from year to year because

1. The prices of goods and services produced increase, while quantities are held constant.
2. The quantities of goods and services increase, while the prices are held constant.
3. Both prices and quantities increase, the typical case.

Nominal GDP
The value of currently produced final goods and services measured in current year prices.

Real GDP
The value of currently produced final goods and services measured in constant prices, or nominal GDP adjusted for price level changes.

GDP deflator
A measure of price changes in the economy that compares the price of each year's output of goods and services to the price of that same output in a base year.

These factors create a difference between nominal GDP and real GDP. **Nominal GDP** is the value of goods and services measured in current year prices, whereas **real GDP** is the value of goods and services measured in constant prices. Real GDP is nominal GDP adjusted for price level changes.[12]

Table 11.1 illustrates the difference between nominal GDP and real GDP with BEA data for 2005 and 2006. These years were chosen for this example because the BEA defined 2005 as the base year, making real GDP and nominal GDP equal at $12,623.0 billion. In 2006, nominal GDP increased to $13,377.2 billion, or 5.97 percent, while real GDP increased to only $12,958.5 billion, or 2.66 percent. The **GDP deflator**, which is defined as (nominal GDP/real GDP) × 100, compares the price of each year's output of goods and services to the price of that same output in a base year (2005, in this case). From 2005 to 2006, the price level, or the GDP deflator, increased by 3.23 percent. We can see in Table 11.1 that the percentage increase in nominal GDP is approximately equal to the percentage increase in the price level plus the percentage increase in real GDP, or the amount of real goods and services.[13]

---

[11]Richard J. Cebula and Edgar L. Feige, "America's Unreported Economy: Measuring the Size, Growth and Determinants of Income Tax Evasion in the U.S." *Crime, Law and Social Change* 57 (2012): 265–85.

[12]For example, a 6 percent increase in nominal GDP could consist of a 6 percent increase in real goods and services and a 0 percent increase in prices, a 0 percent increase in real goods and services and a 6 percent increase in prices, or a 3 percent increase in real goods and services and a 3 percent increase in prices.

[13]Real GDP measures the increase in goods and services produced over time, while holding prices constant at the level of a base year. The BEA used to change the base year every three to four years. It now uses a chain-type price index in calculating the change in real GDP from year to year, which incorporates the average price of the goods in both years. The prices of both years are "chained" or multiplied together and averaged with a geometric mean. The continual updating of the base years with this approach reduces the problems regarding the distortion that changes in relative prices and quantities can cause in calculating real GDP.

TABLE 11.1   Nominal Versus Real GDP

VARIABLE	2005	2006
Nominal GDP	$12,623.0 billion	$13,377.2 billion
Percent change		5.97
Real GDP	$12,623.0 billion	$12,958.5 billion
Percent change		2.66
GDP deflator (price changes)	100	103.23
Percent change		3.23

Real GDP is considered a better measure of economic well-being than nominal GDP because increases in real GDP represent larger amounts of goods and services available for the individuals in that economy. Nominal GDP could increase solely from an increase in the price level, without any increase in goods and services. Individuals are not better off if they have no more goods and services, but have to pay higher prices for them. Figure 11.2 shows U.S. nominal GDP and real GDP for 1990 to 2011, with 2005 as the base year (as in Table 11.1). Nominal GDP is greater than real GDP after 2005, but it is less than real GDP before the base year.

Figures 11.3a and 11.3b compare nominal GDP and per capita GDP for selected countries for 2010. The dollar value of GDP in Figure 11.3a is closely related to the size of the country. However, the per capita GDP graph in Figure 11.3b better represents average output across countries. The United States has a large GDP in both absolute and per capita terms. Canada, the United Kingdom, and Sweden have a relatively small absolute GDP, but much higher values in per capita terms. Countries such as South Africa, Brazil, Nigeria, China, and India rank low in both absolute and per capita terms.

Real GDP is used to measure **business cycles**, the periodic increases and decreases in overall economic activity reflected in production, employment, profits, and prices. These business cycles are primarily associated with advanced industrialized nations with highly developed product and financial sectors. Analysts usually refer to the rising phase of a business cycle as an **expansion** and the falling phase as a **recession**. The Cambridge, Massachusetts–based National Bureau of Economic Research (NBER) is the private, nonprofit research organization that officially designates when a recession occurs.

Business cycles
The periodic increases and decreases in overall economic activity reflected in production, employment, profits, and prices.

Expansion
The rising phase of a business cycle, in which the direction of a series of economic indicators turns upward.

Recession
The falling phase of a business cycle, in which the direction of a series of economic indicators turns downward.

FIGURE 11.2
U.S. Nominal vs. Real GDP (2005 = 100)
The difference between nominal GDP measured in current year prices and real GDP measured in constant prices. Source: www.bea.gov, NIPA tables.

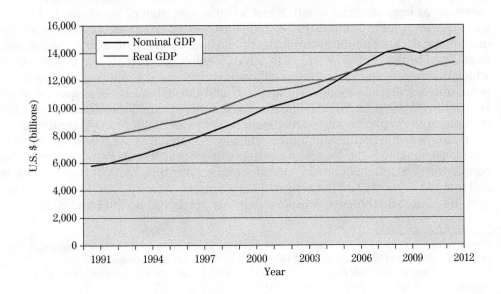

FIGURE 11.3A
2010 Nominal Gross Domestic Product (GDP) for Selected Countries
The differences in nominal GDP for selected countries.
Source: http://data.worldbank.org. Reprinted by permission of World Bank via Copyright Clearance Center.

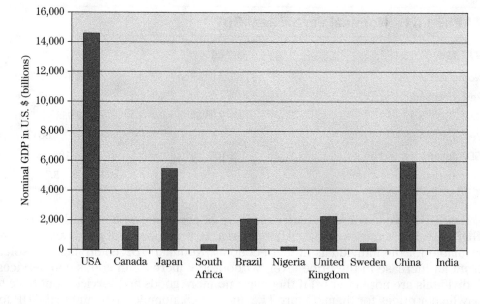

FIGURE 11.3B
2010 Nominal Gross Domestic Product (GDP) per Capita for Selected Countries
The differences in GDP per capita for selected countries.
Source: http://data.worldbank.org. Reprinted by permission of World Bank via Copyright Clearance Center.

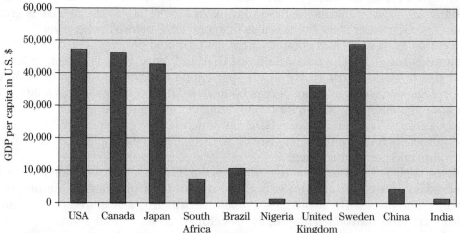

Figure 11.4 shows real GDP and the officially designated recessions from 1955 to 2011. Although the popular definition of a recession is a decline in real GDP for two quarters in a row, the NBER Business Cycle Dating Committee designates a recession as beginning the month when a broad spectrum of economic indicators turns downward. These indicators include business sales, industrial production, the unemployment rate, nonfarm employment and hours worked, and personal income, in addition to the trends in real GDP. An expansion is designated in the month in which the overall direction of these indicators turns upward. Although slowing U.S. economic activity was evident in late 2007 and throughout 2008, it was not until November 2008 that the NBER Business Cycle Dating Committee officially declared the date of the beginning of the recession as December 2007.[14] In September 2010, the Business Cycle Dating Committee officially declared that the recession ended in June 2009, making it the longest recession since World War II. In its statement the committee noted that economic conditions since that time had not been favorable and that the economy had not returned to its normal capacity.[15] As discussed in the opening case of this chapter, this slow recovery persisted into 2011 and 2012.

---

[14]National Bureau of Economic Research Business Cycle Dating Committee. "Determination of the December 2007 Peak in Economic Activity," December 11, 2008. Available at www.nber.org.
[15]National Bureau of Economic Research Business Cycle Dating Committee, "Statement," September 20, 2010. Available at www.nber.org/cycles/sept2010.html.

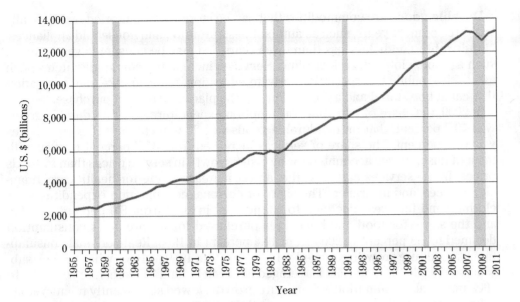

FIGURE 11.4
U.S. Real GDP and Recessions
*The relationship between real GDP
and recessions, the falling phase of a
business cycle in which the direction
of a series of economic indicators turn
downward.*
Source: www.bea.gov; www.nber.org

Alternative Measures of GDP

As we discussed earlier and illustrated in Figure 11.1, the level of economic activity or GDP can be calculated by either the expenditure/output approach (the top half of Figure 11.1) or the earnings/income approach (the bottom half of Figure 11.1). Let's examine both measures in turn for the U.S. economy.

The Expenditure or Output Approach   The expenditure or output approach focuses on spending on currently produced goods and services by four major sectors of the economy:

1. Personal consumption expenditures, or consumption (C)
2. Gross private domestic investment, or investment (I)
3. Government consumption expenditures and gross investment, or government (G)
4. Net export spending (F), which equals export spending (X) minus import spending (M)

Personal Consumption Expenditures[16]   **Personal consumption expenditures** are the largest component of GDP, typically averaging around two-thirds of the total. These consumption expenditures are subdivided into three categories:[17]

*   Durable goods
*   Nondurable goods
*   Services

Personal consumption expenditures
The total amount of spending by consumers on durable goods, nondurable goods, and services in a given period of time.

---

[16]The discussion of the components of GDP is based largely on U.S. Bureau of Economic Analysis, *Concepts and Methods of the U.S. National Income and Product Accounts*; and Clinton P. McCully, "Trends in Consumer Spending and Personal Saving, 1959–2009," *Survey of Current Business* 91 (June 2011): 14–23.

[17]Personal consumption expenditures represent purchases by persons—households and nonprofit institutions serving households (NPISHs). Final consumption expenditures by NPISHs are measured as the portion of personal consumption expenditures that represent services provided to households by NPISHs without explicit charge, such as the value of educational services provided by a nonprofit college or university above the tuition and other costs paid by or for the student's household. These services are typically not sold at market prices, so their value is measured by the cost of producing them. See *Concepts and Methods of the U.S. National Income and Product Accounts*.

Durable goods
Commodities that typically last three or more years, such as automobiles, furniture, and household appliances.

Nondurable goods
Commodities that last less than three years and may be consumed very quickly, such as food, clothing, and gasoline.

Services
Noncommodity items, such as utilities, public transportation, private education, medical care, and recreation.

Durable goods are commodities that can be stored or inventoried that typically last three or more years, such as automobiles, furniture, and household appliances. **Nondurable goods** last less than three years and may be consumed very quickly, such as food, clothing, and gasoline. **Services** include noncommodity items such as utilities, public transportation, private education, medical care, and recreation that cannot be stored and are consumed at the place and time of purchase.

In 2009, the share of personal consumption expenditure spent on durable goods was 10.3 percent, that on nondurable goods was 22 percent, and that on services was 67.7 percent. The share of services increased from 45.7 percent in 1959 with most of this increase accounted for by faster growth in service prices than in goods prices. In the services category, the largest increases were for health care, financial services, and insurance. The share of personal consumption expenditures for clothing and footwear declined to 3.2 percent in 2009 from 8.0 percent in 1959, and the share for food and beverages purchased for off-premises consumption declined to 7.8 percent in 2009 from 19.4 percent in 1959. Real personal consumption expenditure growth averaged 4.4 percent from 1959 to 1969, while in each subsequent decade through 1999 it averaged between 3.3 and 3.5 percent. From 1999 to 2009 personal consumption expenditure growth slowed significantly to an average 2.4 percent, largely due to slower growth in disposable personal income and an increase in the personal saving rate.[18]

The percent changes in real personal consumption expenditures have been more moderate in each of the recessions since 1960 than the overall changes in gross domestic purchases. Real personal consumption expenditures have decreased less than gross domestic purchases in five of those recessions, and the consumption expenditures increased in the other three recessions. These trends have been explained by the consumption expenditures on services, which increased in six of the recessions and decreased less than 0.5 percent in the other two recessions. Expenditures for durable goods decreased in all but two of the recessions, and expenditures for nondurable goods decreased in four of the recessions. In the 2007–2009 recession, the decline in real personal consumption expenditures lasted for 16 months, longer than in any recession back to 1960, and the 2.6 percent decrease was larger than in all but one of those recessions.[19]

Gross private domestic investment spending
The total amount of spending on nonresidential structures, equipment, and software; residential structures; and business inventories in a given period of time.

Gross Private Domestic Investment Spending **Gross private domestic investment spending**, a second component of GDP expenditure, has a very specific meaning in the National Income and Product Accounts. It includes

1. Business or nonresidential fixed investment (i.e., the purchase of structures, equipment, and software by firms)
2. Residential fixed investment (i.e., the purchase of new housing by households and landlords)
3. Changes in business inventories, goods that are produced, but not sold in a given year

Although individuals often say they are making an "investment" when they place some of their income in a savings account or mutual fund, these financial transactions are only portfolio allocations and are not considered to be investment in the national income accounts.

Business fixed investment
Spending on the structures, equipment, and software that provide the industrial capacity to produce goods and services for all sectors of the economy.

Business fixed investment encompasses the spending on structures, equipment, and software that provide the industrial capacity to produce goods and services for all sectors of the economy. This investment spending includes all

[18]McCully, "Trends in Consumer Spending and Personal Saving, 1959–2009."
[19]Ibid. Gross domestic purchases are calculated as the sum of personal consumption expenditures, gross private domestic investment, and government consumption expenditures and gross investment. Gross domestic purchases include imports of goods and services but exclude exports of goods and services.

privately owned buildings (factories, offices, and stores); nonbuilding structures (roads, power plants, telephone lines, and oil and gas wells); and machinery, computers, and other equipment lasting two or more years. These structures and equipment are used in new businesses and also replace and modernize existing capital facilities, as these facilities depreciate or wear out over time. Business fixed investment spending ranged from 14 to 17 percent of GDP from 1980 to 2008, with structures accounting for 3 to 5 percent and equipment for 7 to 9 percent.[20]

In 1999, the Bureau of Economic Analysis began counting software as part of nonresidential fixed investment, given that the average service life of software is three to five years. Previously, embedded or bundled software was included in investment, but not software purchases by business and government. Three types of software are now treated as business investment: prepackaged software sold in standard form and intended for nonspecialized uses; custom software specifically designed for a business enterprise or government unit; and own-account software, consisting of in-house expenditures for new or enhanced software created by a business or government for its own use.[21]

Residential fixed investment includes the spending on new construction of privately owned single-family and multifamily permanent housing units, mobile homes, nonhousekeeping dormitories, and fraternity and sorority houses, as well as improvements such as additions to, alterations of, and major replacements to existing residential structures. This category of spending also includes brokers' commissions on the sale of new and existing housing. Residential investment spending is dominated by the construction of new housing units.[22]

Changes in business inventories are typically the smallest component of gross private domestic investment, but one of its most volatile elements. Inventories represent goods that have been produced in a given period of time, but not sold. If an automobile is added to a firm's inventory during a given year, the BEA treats this transaction as though the firm has purchased the good. This "purchase" has a positive effect on GDP in that year, as it reflects current production. If the automobile is sold to a consumer the following year, there is negative business inventory investment. This sale is subtracted from GDP because it does not represent the production of current goods and services.[23]

Some business inventory changes are planned, as when a firm wants to maintain a relatively constant rate of output so as not to shut down a production line even though demand for the product may be seasonal. However, other inventory changes are unplanned. Firms may anticipate a certain rate of sales that fails to materialize because consumers decided to spend less than anticipated. Unplanned inventory adjustment plays a major role in our model of the macro economy.

> **Residential fixed investment**
> Spending on newly constructed housing units, major alterations of and replacements to existing structures, and brokers' commissions.

> **Changes in business inventories**
> Changes in the amount of goods produced, but not sold in a given year.

---

[20]U.S. Bureau of Economic Analysis, Table 1.1.10, Percentage Shares of Gross Domestic Product. Available at www.bea.gov.

[21]Brent R. Moulton, Robert P. Parker, and Eugene P. Seskin, "A Preview of the 1999 Comprehensive Revision of the National Income and Product Accounts," *Survey of Current Business* (August 1999), 7–20; *Recognition of Business and Government Expenditures for Software as Investment: Methodology and Quantitative Impacts, 1959–98* (May 2000). Available at www.bea.gov.

[22]Investment spending on structures (nonresidential and residential) typically accounted for about half of total private investment and about 10 percent of GDP. This share began decreasing in 2006. See Paul R. Lally, "How BEA Accounts for Investment in Private Structures," *Survey of Current Business* 89 (February 2009): 9–15.

[23]Personal consumption expenditures do include the net purchase—purchase less sales—of used goods from the business and government sectors. Negative changes in business inventories cancel these transactions, so that GDP includes only currently produced goods and services. See U.S. Department of Commerce, Bureau of Economic Analysis, *Personal Consumption Expenditures*, Methodology Paper Series, no. MP-6 (Washington, DC: U.S. Government Printing Office, June 1990).

Government Consumption Expenditures and Gross Investment   **Government consumption expenditures and gross investment** include federal, state, and local government purchases of finished products plus all direct purchases of resources. Government expenditures are divided into two categories:

1. Consumption: Current outlays for goods and services and depreciation charges on existing structures and equipment
2. Investment: Capital outlays for newly acquired structures and equipment

Government spending includes purchases of goods and services from private industry, the wages paid to public-sector workers, and depreciation charges on structures and equipment. The wages of government workers, such as police officers and firefighters, are used as a proxy for the value of the output they produce because that output is not bought and sold in the marketplace.

Although this category of spending includes all three levels of government—federal, state, and local—the level of expenditure included in the National Income and Product Accounts is smaller than that included in the budgets of these organizations. Given the definition of GDP, only expenditures related to the current production of goods and services are included in the national income accounts. Thus, as noted earlier in the chapter, all transfer payments are excluded from government expenditure in the national income accounts. These transfers include payments to individuals for Social Security, unemployment compensation, and income maintenance; federal grants to state and local governments and state grants to local governments; interest on government debt; foreign aid; and government loans less repayments.

In 2001, federal government expenditures measured by the national income accounts encompassed approximately 25 percent of the expenditures included in the federal budget.[24] Thus, the GDP measure of government consumption and investment expenditures substantially understates the impact of government on the economy. Items excluded from government spending do typically reappear in subsequent years' GDP expenditure figures. The transfer income from Social Security and other income maintenance programs becomes part of personal consumption expenditure. Grants to state and local governments appear as part of their consumption and investment expenditures. Foreign aid may become part of net export spending, while interest payments will be translated into domestic and foreign spending on goods and services.

Net Export Spending   The final category of GDP measured from the expenditure or output approach is **net export spending**, which is the difference between spending by other countries on domestically produced goods and services (**export spending**) and spending by domestic residents on goods and services produced in the rest of the world (**import spending**). Export spending is added to U.S. GDP because it represents spending on goods and services currently produced in this country by individuals in the rest of the world. However, import spending is subtracted from GDP because it represents spending by U.S. citizens on goods and services produced in the rest of the world. Net export spending represents the net expenditure from abroad for domestically produced goods and services, which provides income for domestic producers.

Net export spending can be either positive or negative depending on the balance between exports and imports. Net export spending can be a relatively small figure, even if the export and import flows are relatively large, as long as the two spending categories are relatively the same size. Foreign trade in goods includes agricultural, mineral, and manufactured items, while services include travel, transportation, royalties and licensing fees, insurance, telecommunications, and business services.

[24]U.S. Congressional Budget Office, *The Budget and Economic Outlook: Fiscal Years 2003–2012* (Washington, DC: U.S. Government Printing Office, January 2002).

This spending category also includes U.S. military sales contracts, direct defense expenditures, and miscellaneous U.S. government services.

Table 11.2 shows U.S. GDP for the year 2011 measured by the expenditure or output approach.[25] In this table, we can see that consumption spending was 71.1 percent of GDP. Changes in business inventories were positive and accounted for approximately 2.4 percent of gross private domestic investment. Given the definition of federal government spending used in the National Income and Product Accounts, state and local government spending was 1.5 times the amount of federal spending. Imports exceeded exports by $579 billion, resulting in a negative balance of trade.

TABLE 11.2   Gross Domestic Product and Its Components, 2011 Expenditure or Output Measurement

COMPONENT	VALUE IN BILLIONS OF DOLLARS (PERCENT OF GDP)
GROSS DOMESTIC PRODUCT (GDP)	**15,094.0**
PERSONAL CONSUMPTION EXPENDITURES (C)	**10,726.0 (71.1)**
Durable goods	1,162.9
Nondurable goods	2,483.7
Services	7,079.4
GROSS PRIVATE DOMESTIC INVESTMENT (I)	**1,916.2 (13.0)**
Fixed investment	1,870.0
Nonresidential	1,532.5
Structures	409.5
Equipment and software	1,123.0
Residential	337.5
Change in inventories	46.3
GOVERNMENT CONSUMPTION EXPENDITURES AND GROSS INVESTMENT (G)	**3,030.6 (20.1)**
Federal	1,232.9
National defense	824.9
Nondefense	407.9
State and local	1,797.7
NET EXPORTS OF GOODS AND SERVICES (F)	**−578.7 (−3.8)**
Exports (X)	2,085.5 (13.8)
Goods	1,473.4
Services	612.1
Imports (M)	2,664.2 (17.7)
Goods	2,237.9
Services	426.3

Source: U.S. Department of Commerce, Bureau of Economic Analysis, *National Income and Product Account Tables,* Table 1.1.5, Gross Domestic Product. Available at www.bea.gov/bea/national.

[25]This table shows nominal GDP or GDP measured in 2011 dollars to get a consistent set of measures with GDP measured from the earnings or income approach in Table 11.3.

FIGURE 11.5

Real GDP Growth—2000 to 2012.1 (annual growth rates in percent)

Value of newly produced final goods and services adjusted for changes in the price level (base year 2005). Real GDP data are important measures of the rate of change in percentage terms of the quantity of economic output over quarters and years.
Source: Federal Reserve Economic Data (FRED II), Economic Research, Federal Reserve Bank of St. Louis, http://research.stlouisfed.org/fred2/.

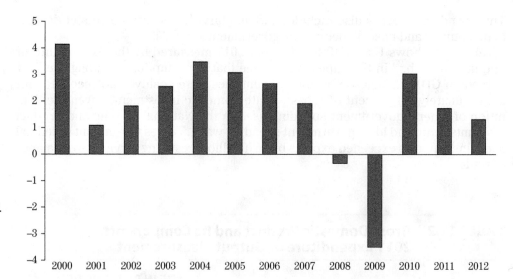

Although Table 11.2 provides a good description of the composition of GDP, analysts and managers are most interested in the rate of growth of real GDP and its components because these changes may alter a firm's competitive strategy in the future. Figure 11.5 shows the annual growth rate percentages for real GDP from 2000 to the first quarter of 2012 (2012.1). This figure clearly shows the effects of the recession in 2001, the gradual recovery in 2002 and 2003, the recession from 2007 to 2009, and the slow recovery since that time.

Figure 11.6 presents average annual growth rates for the components of real GDP for the same time period as that for Figure 11.5. This figure shows that consumer spending on nondurable good and services remained relatively constant over the period 2000 to 2007, whereas investment spending was extremely volatile. The major cause of the 2001 recession was the drop in investment spending, particularly on structures and equipment and software. Residential construction spending held up in the first part of the decade. However, the negative growth rates for investment and particularly residential investment from 2007 to 2009 show the impact of the collapse of the housing market and the effect of the turmoil in credit markets during this period. The figure also illustrates the negative growth rates for

FIGURE 11.6

Average Growth of Real GDP Components—2000 to 2012.1 (annual growth rates in percent)

The large differences in the percentage annual growth rates of the components of real GDP.
Source: Federal Reserve Economic Data (FRED II), Economic Research, Federal Reserve Bank of St. Louis, http://research.stlouisfed.org/fred2/.

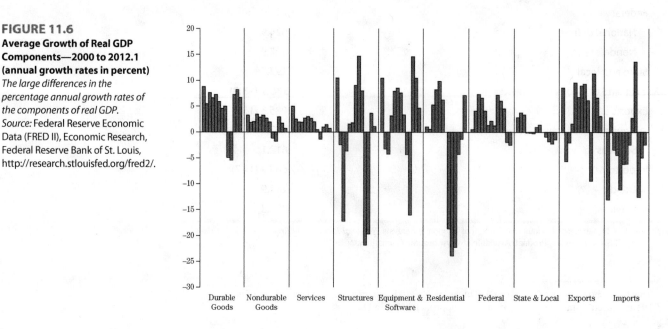

consumer spending in 2008 and 2009 and the major changes in export and import spending that can occur over relatively short periods of time.

The Income or Earnings Approach   We stated earlier in the chapter that GDP measured using the expenditure or output approach must equal GDP measured using the income or earnings approach, or $E = Y$. **National income** is the income generated from the sale of the goods and services produced in the economy and paid to the individuals and businesses who supply the inputs or factors of production. This amount, shown in the bottom half of Figure 11.1 and in Table 11.3, is composed of the following categories:

1. **Compensation of employees**: The wages and salaries, the Social Security payments made by employers, and the employer contributions for fringe benefits such as health insurance, and pensions. Employee compensation is the largest component of national income, typically around 60 to 70 percent of the total.
2. **Proprietors' income**: The income of unincorporated businesses, such as medical practices, law firms, small farms, and retail stores.
3. **Rental income**: The income households receive from the rental of their property.
4. **Corporate profits**: The excess of revenues over costs for the incorporated business sector of the economy.
5. **Net interest**: The interest private businesses pay to households for lending money to the firms minus the interest the businesses receive plus interest earned from foreigners.

National income
Income that is generated from the sale of the goods and services that are produced in the economy and that is paid to the individuals and businesses who supply the inputs or factors of production.

Compensation of employees
The wages and salaries and the fringe benefits paid by employers to employees.

Proprietors' income
The income of unincorporated businesses, such as medical practices, law firms, small farms, and retail stores.

Rental income
The income households receive from the rental of their property.

Corporate profits
The excess of revenues over costs for the incorporated business sector of the economy.

Net interest
The interest private businesses pay to households for lending money to the firms minus the interest businesses receive plus interest earned from foreigners.

TABLE 11.3 Gross Domestic Product and Its Components, 2011 Earnings or Income Measurement

COMPONENT	VALUE IN BILLIONS OF DOLLARS (PERCENT OF NATIONAL INCOME)
GROSS DOMESTIC PRODUCT	**15,094.0**
Less: Depreciation expenditures	1608.8
Less: Statistical discrepancy	−47.9
EQUALS: NATIONAL INCOME	**13,437.3**
Compensation of employees	8,292.7 (61.7)
Proprietor's income	1,108.9 (8.3)
Rental income	403.9 (3.0)
Corporate profits	1,942.8 (14.5)
Net interest	535.1 (4.0)
Less: Income earned, but not received	4,558.2
Plus: Income received, but not earned	4,126.2
EQUALS: PERSONAL INCOME	**13,005.3**
Less: Personal taxes	1,400.3
EQUALS: DISPOSABLE INCOME	**11,604.9**
Personal consumption expenditure ($10,726.0)	
plus other outlays ($329.1)	11,055.1
Personal saving	549.8

Source: U.S. Department of Commerce, Bureau of Economic Analysis, *National Income and Product Account Tables*, Table 1.7.5, Relation of Gross Domestic Product, Gross National Product, Net National Product, National Income, and Personal Income; Table 1.12, National Income by Type of Income; Table 2.1, Personal Income and Its Disposition. Available at www.bea.gov/national.

We can see in Table 11.3 that GDP does not equal national income until depreciation expenditures to replace existing capital equipment are subtracted and a statistical adjustment is made for the discrepancy that arises from the use of different data sources to calculate GDP from the expenditure approach and from the income approach.[26]

Personal income

Income received by households that forms the basis for personal consumption expenditures.

Table 11.3 also shows **personal income**, an important component of macroeconomic analysis, because it forms the basis for the personal consumption expenditures of the household sector. To derive personal income from national income, we must subtract income that is earned, but not received by households and add income that is received, but not currently earned by the households.[27]

Disposable income

Personal household income after all taxes have been paid.

Personal income can be further reduced to **disposable income**, which is current household income after all personal taxes have been paid (see Figure 11.1). The most important personal taxes affecting disposable income are income taxes, particularly the federal income tax. We express this relationship in Equation 11.1.

11.1 $Y_d = Y - T_P$

where

Y_d = disposable income

Y = personal income

T_P = personal taxes, primarily the federal income tax

Saving

That portion of households' disposable income that is not spent on consumption goods and services.

Households then divide their disposable income between personal consumption expenditures (C) and **saving** (S). Saving is that portion of their disposable income that is not currently spent.[28] This relationship is shown in Equation 11.2:

11.2 $Y_d = C + S$

where

Y_d = disposable income

C = personal consumption expenditures

S = saving

Personal income and taxes, disposable income, personal consumption expenditures, and saving for 2011 are all shown in Table 11.3. Changes in disposable income and consumption expenditures are particularly important for managers because spending on durable goods, nondurable goods, and services represents revenue to the business firms in the economy. Changes in these variables helped various industries recover from the 2001 recession and were crucial in determining how much the economy slowed down in 2007 and 2008.

---

[26]Depreciation expenditures are included in the expenditure side of GDP, but they are not paid out as income, so they must be subtracted to derive national income from GDP on the income side. There are also minor adjustments for business transfer payments, net subsidies for government enterprises, and net foreign factor income.

[27]Income that is earned but not received includes taxes on production and imports, undistributed corporate profits (or retained earnings), business contributions to social insurance programs such as Social Security, and any wages that have been accrued but not yet paid. Income that is received but not currently earned includes government transfer payments that were excluded from the expenditure side of GDP, but that are part of personal income; business transfer payments; and interest paid to households from nonbusiness sources. Government transfer payments include Social Security payments, unemployment insurance, food stamps, Medicare, Medicaid, and other income maintenance programs.

[28]Remember that saving is a flow concept because it represents that portion of a flow of current income that is not spent on durables, nondurables, and services (consumption expenditure). This is contrasted with wealth or the stocks of assets that households have at a given period of time.

Other Important Macroeconomic Variables

Two other variables are important in our discussion of the macroeconomic environment and its effects on managerial decisions: measures of the absolute price level and the labor force. From the labor force, we can derive the level of employment or unemployment in the economy.

Price Level Measures

Microeconomics focuses on relative prices, whereas macroeconomics focuses on the absolute price level. **Relative prices** show the price of one good in relation to the price of another good. Demand, supply, production, and cost in different market structures all involve relative prices. The **absolute price level** is a measure of the overall price level in the economy. Various indices are used to measure the prices of all goods and services and how these prices change over time—that is, the rate of **inflation**, a sustained increase in the price level over time, or **deflation**, a sustained decrease in the price level over time. In this chapter, we focus on three major indices: the GDP deflator, the Consumer Price Index, and the Producer Price Index.

The GDP Deflator   We defined the GDP deflator in our earlier discussion of real versus nominal GDP (see Table 11.1). The GDP deflator, illustrated in Figure 11.7, compares the price of each year's output of real goods and services to the price of that same output in a base year. It is a broad measure of price changes because it reflects the changes in consumption patterns over time included in GDP. The GDP deflator incorporates shifts in tastes and spending patterns as consumers substitute between new and older products and react to relative price changes of various products.

Table 11.4 shows the different rates of price increases among the components of GDP from 2005 to 2011 with 2005 as the base year. Of particular importance is the personal consumption price deflator because this is the primary index that the Federal Reserve analyzes in deciding how to influence interest rates.[29] Note,

Relative prices
The price of one good in relation to the price of another good.

Absolute price level
A measure of the overall level of prices in the economy using various indices to measure the prices of all goods and services.

Inflation
A sustained increase in the price level over time.

Deflation
A sustained decrease in the price level over time.

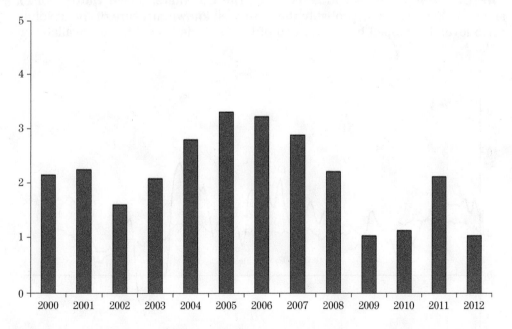

FIGURE 11.7
Annual Percentage Change in the GDP Deflator (ratio of current $ to chained 2005 $ = 100)
Nominal GDP/Real GDP—The deflator reflects continuing shifts in tastes and spending patterns because it accounts for actual spending as new or substitute products replace old ones and as consumers choose between higher- and lower-priced products or between items with slow or rapid price increases.
Source: Federal Reserve Economic Data (FRED II), Economic Research, Federal Reserve Bank of St. Louis, http://research.stlouisfed.org/fred2/.

---

[29]For example, see the section "Prices," in Board of Governors of the Federal Reserve System, *Monetary Policy Report to the Congress*, February 29, 2012.

TABLE 11.4   Price Deflators for GDP and Its Components, 2005–2011

	2005	2006	2007	2008	2009	2010	2011
GDP	100	103.23	106.23	108.58	109.73	110.99	113.36
Personal consumption expenditures	100	102.72	105.50	108.94	109.17	111.11	113.85
Durable goods	100	98.36	96.43	94.63	92.90	91.35	90.46
Nondurable goods	100	103.23	106.49	112.57	109.30	112.75	119.65
Services	100	103.42	106.98	110.58	112.35	114.47	116.51
Gross private domestic investment	100	104.27	106.29	107.62	106.37	104.68	106.62
Nonresidential	100	103.43	105.65	107.72	107.11	105.37	106.76
Residential	100	106.08	107.61	106.30	102.64	102.21	103.41
Government consumption expenditures and gross investment	100	104.84	109.86	115.25	114.88	117.45	121.09
Federal	100	104.11	107.75	111.23	111.00	113.65	116.86
State and local	100	105.28	111.11	117.67	117.21	119.70	123.66
Exports	100	103.44	106.90	111.98	105.96	110.62	117.55
Imports	100	104.13	107.79	119.24	106.57	113.03	121.78

Source: U.S. Department of Commerce, Bureau of Economic Analysis, National Income and Product Accounts Tables, Table 1.1.9, Implicit Price Deflators for Gross Domestic Product. Available at www.bea.gov.

however, the divergence in the rate of price increases among the components of personal consumption expenditures. The price index for durable goods fell over this period, while the index for services increased faster than GDP. The price index for nonresidental fixed investment increased and then decreased, while that for residential fixed investment decreased for most of the period. The price level for state and local governments increased more rapidly than that for the federal government.

Consumer Price Index (CPI)
A measure of the combined price consumers pay for a fixed market basket of goods and services in a given period relative to the combined price of an identical basket of goods and services in a base period.

The Consumer Price Index (CPI)   The **Consumer Price Index (CPI),** shown in Figure 11.8, is probably the most well-known measure of the absolute price level. Developed by the Bureau of Labor Statistics (BLS) and available at

FIGURE 11.8
Trends in Consumer Inflation Rates (annual percentage changes of monthly data using the CPI)
Consumer Inflation—The Consumer Price Index (CPI) is a measure of the average change over time in the prices paid by urban consumers for a market basket of consumer goods and services.
Source: Federal Reserve Economic Data (FRED II), Economic Research, Federal Reserve Bank of St. Louis, http://research.stlouisfed.org/fred2/.

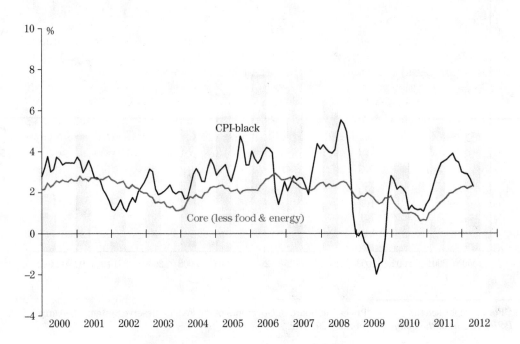

www.bls.gov/cpi/, the CPI measures the combined price consumers pay for a fixed market basket of goods and services in a given period relative to the combined price of an identical group of goods and services in a base period. The CPI uses a fixed market basket of goods that reflects the consumption patterns of a "typical" consumer in the base year. The base period is defined either as a single year or as a period of years, and the base period index is set equal to 100. All movements of the indicator indicate percentage changes from the base period. The formula for calculating the percentage change between two periods is

$$11.3 \quad \frac{\text{Period 2}}{\text{Period 1}} - 1.0 \times 100$$

The base period for the CPI is 1982 to 1984 = 100. A three-year base period is used by the BLS so that unusual consumer purchase patterns in any given year do not distort the index. The prices recorded are the actual transaction prices of the items in the fixed market basket of goods, including sales taxes, premiums on and discounts from listed prices, and import duties. The proportions for the various items in this fixed market basket, or the weights for each category of spending, are based on the dollar sales volume of each item in the base period and are derived from surveys of households in various geographic areas around the country. Prices for the goods and services included in the CPI are collected from 50,000 housing units and 23,000 retail and service establishments in 87 urban areas located throughout the country. Prices of fuels and some other items are obtained every month in all 87 locations. Prices of most commodities and services are collected every month in the three largest geographic areas and every other month in most areas. Data, which are obtained through personal visits and phone calls by BLS representatives, are presented both seasonally adjusted and unadjusted. Seasonally adjusted data are usually preferred because they eliminate the effect of changes, such as price movements from varying weather conditions, production cycles, model revisions, holidays, and sales that normally occur at the same time and in about the same magnitude every year.[30]

Although the weights are updated periodically, the fixed market basket procedure creates a number of problems in the CPI over time. One problem is substitution bias. Consumers will demand various quantities of goods and services in response to changes in their relative prices. Thus, consumers are likely to adjust their purchases more quickly than what is reflected in the relative weights of the expenditure categories in the CPI. This outcome means that the CPI may not reflect the actual price increases faced by consumers over time. The BLS has estimated that this lag in the index raises the annual CPI inflation rate 0.15 percentage point higher than would occur if the weights were updated every year.[31]

A second problem is that the CPI may not adjust adequately for changes in the quality of goods over time and for the introduction of new goods. If the quality of goods in the market basket improves over time and their prices increase, the index may not recognize that the price increase actually resulted from an increase in the quality of the product. A fixed market basket of goods also does not allow for the introduction of new goods until that market basket is revised at some point in the future.

Analysts and policy makers sometimes focus on the **core rate of inflation**, a measure of absolute price changes that excludes changes in energy and food prices (Figure 11.8). This core rate of inflation may more accurately reflect the underlying forces causing price increases rather than the special factors influencing food and energy prices. For example, food prices may fluctuate due to changes in the weather

Core rate of inflation
A measure of absolute price changes that excludes changes in energy and food prices.

---

[30]Bureau of Labor Statistics, "Consumer Price Index Overview," available at www.bls.gov/cpi.
[31]The GDP deflator incorporates the changes in consumption patterns over time that are included in GDP and does not use the fixed weights of the CPI approach.

TABLE 11.5   Percent Change in Expenditure Category, May 2011–May 2012 (Unadjusted)

EXPENDITURE CATEGORY	PERCENT CHANGE
Food	2.8
Pork	−0.3
Fresh fruits and vegetables	−2.1
Tomatoes	−19.7
Peanut butter	39.0
Gasoline (all types)	−4.0
Major appliances	6.9
Men and boys' apparel	5.5
Jewelry	−0.7
Televisions	−17.7
Personal computers and peripheral equipment	−10.6
Medical care services	3.9
Health insurance	13.0
College tuition and fees	5.3
Wireless telephone services	−0.6

Source: U.S. Bureau of Labor Statistics, "Table 2, Consumer Price Index for All Urban Consumers (CPI-U): U.S. City Average, by Detailed Expenditure Category, May 2012," *News Release, Consumer Price Index—May 2012*, June 14, 2012. Available at www.bls.gov.

and other natural conditions, including floods and hurricanes, while energy prices are influenced by how well the Organization of Petroleum Exporting Countries maintains control over oil pricing behavior by its members and nonmembers.

There can be significant changes in the component categories of the CPI that can be masked by focusing only on the changes in the overall index. Table 11.5 presents the categories of the CPI that have experienced large price decreases and increases from May 2011 to May 2012. The table shows that there are large variations in price changes within expenditure categories. The percentage change for food was 2.8, while there was a 0.3 percent decrease for pork. The decrease for tomatoes was much larger than for all fresh fruits and vegetables. Services such as health insurance and college tuition and fees had large price increases, while electronics such as televisions and personal computers had significant price decreases. Thus, a variety of changes in relative prices can occur at the industry and firm (micro) level, while the CPI is used to measure the overall trend in absolute prices at the macro level.

Producer Price Index (PPI)
A measure of the prices firms pay for crude materials; intermediate materials, supplies, and components; and finished goods.

The Producer Price Index (PPI)   The **Producer Price Index (PPI)**, illustrated in Figure 11.9, shows the rate of price increases at an earlier stage in the production process than the CPI and is a measure of the prices firms pay for intermediate goods and services. The PPI focuses on price changes of domestically produced goods and excludes services, construction, and imported goods. There are actually three indices reflecting different stages of production:

1. Crude materials for further processing (including corn, soybeans, cattle, crude petroleum, and timber)
2. Intermediate materials, supplies, and components (such as textiles, electric power, paper, glass, motor vehicle parts, and medical and surgical devices)
3. Finished goods (including fruits, meat, apparel, furniture, appliances, automobiles, and machinery)

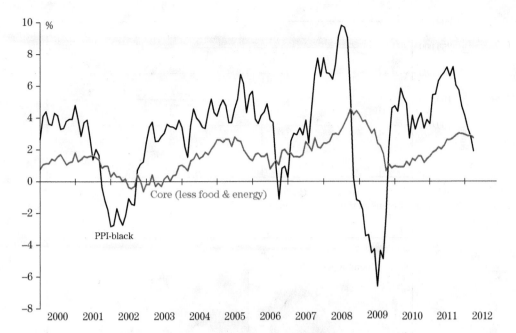

FIGURE 11.9
Trends in Wholesale Inflation Rates (annual percent changes of monthly data using the PPI)
Wholesale Inflation—The Producer Price Index (PPI) for finished goods measures the average change over time in the selling prices received by domestic producers of goods and services. PPIs measure price change from the perspective of the seller.
Source: Federal Reserve Economic Data (FRED II), Economic Research, Federal Reserve Bank of St. Louis, http://research.stlouisfed.org/fred2/.

Measures of Employment and Unemployment

Economists, policy makers, and managers are also concerned about the levels of employment and unemployment in an economy. The BLS has developed a specific set of statistics for categorizing the employment status of the population, as shown in Figure 11.10.[32]

The BLS obtains employment information from a monthly survey of a sample of approximately 60,000 households called the Current Population Survey (CPS). One-fourth of the households in the sample are changed each month. People are not asked directly whether they are employed or unemployed, but are asked a series of questions intended to determine their employment status.

The basic framework for calculating the number of employed and unemployed persons begins with the number of noninstitutionalized persons in the United States who are 16 years of age or older and who are not members of the U.S. armed forces. This definition excludes those persons who are confined to institutions, such as nursing homes or jails; those who are too young to work; and those who are in the armed forces. The BLS then subtracts those who are not actively seeking work, such as students, homemakers, and retirees, from this noninstitutionalized population. These individuals are not counted in the labor force.

The remaining group is defined as the **labor force**, which is divided into the employed and the unemployed. **Employed** persons are those who at the time of the survey were engaged in any work at all as paid employees; persons working in their own business, profession, or farm; persons working at nonpaid jobs in a family business or farm for at least 15 hours a week; and persons temporarily absent from their jobs due to illness, vacation, or other reasons. Persons with more than one job are counted only once, in their primary job. **Unemployed** persons are defined as those who were not working during the survey week, were available to work except for temporary illness, and had actively looked for work during the four-week period preceding the survey week. Actively seeking work means having

Labor force
Those individuals 16 years of age and over who are working in a job or actively seeking employment.

Employed
Persons 16 years of age and over who, in the survey week, did any work as an employee; worked in their own business, profession, or farm; or worked without pay at least 15 hours in a family business or farm.

Unemployed
Persons 16 years of age and over who do not currently have a job, but who are actively seeking employment.

---

[32]U.S. Department of Labor, Bureau of Labor Statistics, "How the Government Measures Unemployment," available at www.bls.gov/cps.

FIGURE 11.10
Labor Force Characteristics, 2011
The civilian labor force is composed of those individuals 16 years of age and over who are working in a job (employed) or who are actively seeking employment (unemployed).
Source: Bureau of Labor Statistics, http://www.bls.gov/cps/tables.htm.

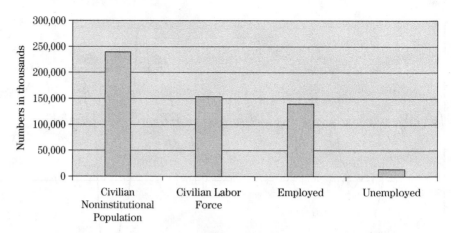

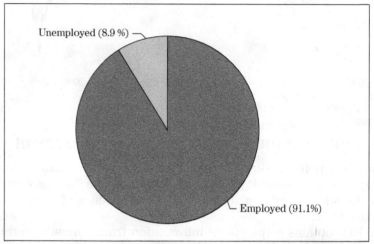

a job interview, contacting an employer about an interview, sending out resumes, placing or answering job advertisements, or consulting job registers.

In 2011, there were 239.6 million persons in the civilian noninstitutional population, of which 153.6 million, or 64.1 percent, were in the labor force. Of these, 139.9 million were employed and 13.7 million were unemployed.

The unemployment rate is calculated as follows:

$$11.4 \quad \textbf{Unemployment rate} = \frac{\textbf{number of unemployed}}{\textbf{labor force}} \times \textbf{100}$$

Thus, for 2011 the unemployment rate was 13.7 million / 153.6 million, or 8.9 percent.

Because the labor force includes both the employed and the unemployed, the unemployment rate is influenced by the number of individuals who are seeking, but cannot find work and by the size of the labor force. Persons 16 years of age or over who have looked for work in the past 12 months, but who are not currently seeking work because they believe that jobs are unavailable in their area or line of work or because they believe they would not qualify for existing job openings are considered to be **discouraged workers** who are not in the labor force. Discouraged workers are not considered unemployed because they are not actively seeking employment, but they are of concern to macroeconomic policy makers. The BLS estimated that there were 830,000 discouraged workers in May 2012, approximately the same as a year earlier.[33]

Discouraged workers
Persons 16 years of age and over who are not currently seeking work because they believe that jobs in their area or line of work are unavailable or that they would not qualify for existing job openings.

---

[33]U.S. Department of Labor, Bureau of Labor Statistics, *News Release: The Employment Situation—May 2012.* Available at www.bls.gov.

Over the course of a year, seasonal events, such as changes in weather, increased or decreased production, harvests, major holidays, and the opening and closing of schools, can cause significant changes in the nation's labor force, employment, and unemployment. These data can be seasonally adjusted for these events so that other nonseasonal factors, such as declines in overall economic activity and changes in the labor force participation of various groups, can be identified more easily. Seasonally adjusted data are more appropriate for the analysis of overall economic activity.[34]

One goal of macroeconomic policy is to promote full employment of the country's labor force. However, this policy does not seek to obtain a zero unemployment rate. Some unemployment will always exist as workers change jobs and move in and out of the labor force. Policy makers are also concerned with expanding output and employment but without exerting pressure on the price level. They often target the **natural rate of unemployment**, or the minimum level of unemployment that can be achieved without causing inflation to accelerate.[35] Estimates of the natural rate of unemployment have changed over time, given differences in economic conditions and labor market institutions. Estimates rose from 3 to 4 percent in the 1960s to 6 to 7 percent in the 1970s. By the mid-1990s, estimates had declined to between 5.2 and 6.3 percent. In the late 1990s and in 2000 and 2001, there was extensive debate about whether this rate was even lower. Researchers estimated that the rate increased during the pre-recession of 2007–2009 from a pre-recession rate of 5.0 percent to a value between 5.4 and 6.4 percent. Changes in the natural rate of unemployment are related to changes in the composition of the labor force and to increases in the productivity of the economy over time.[36]

Natural rate of unemployment
The minimum level of unemployment that can be achieved with current institutions without causing inflation to accelerate.

Managerial Rule of Thumb

Price Level and Unemployment

Managers need to be aware of how both the price level and the level of unemployment are changing. Changes in these variables can affect the demand and customer base for their products and production costs. Large changes in these variables are also likely to result in policy changes that influence the overall macroeconomic environment. ∎

Major Macroeconomic Policy Issues

We end this chapter by discussing the major macroeconomic policy issues that are of concern to economists and policy makers. We then discuss the implications of these issues for managers and their firms.

---

[34]U.S. Department of Labor, Bureau of Labor Statistics, "How the Government Measures Unemployment."
[35]The natural rate of unemployment is also called the nonaccelerating inflation rate of unemployment (NAIRU).
[36]Thomas B. King and James Morley, "In Search of the Natural Rate of Unemployment," *Journal of Monetary Economics*, 54 (March 2007): 550–64; Monica Dobrescu, Claudia Paicu, and Silvia Iacob, "The Natural Rate of Unemployment and Its Implications for Economic Policy," *Theoretical and Applied Economics* 18 (2011): 181–94; and Mary Daly, Bart Hobijn, Aysegul Sahin, and Rob Valletta, "A Rising Natural Rate of Unemployment: Transitory or Permanent?" *Federal Reserve Bank of San Francisco Working Paper #2011-05*, September 2011. Available at www.frbsf.org/publications/economics/papers/2011/wp11-05bk.pdf.

What Factors Influence the Spending Behavior of the Different Sectors of the Economy?

Spending decisions by the four major sectors of the economy are the primary determinants of the overall level of GDP:

1. Household personal consumption expenditure or, for simplification, consumption (C)
2. Business gross private domestic investment expenditure, or investment (I)
3. Government consumption expenditure and gross investment, or government (G)
4. Net exports of goods and services (F), or export expenditure (X) minus import expenditure (M)

Economists and policy makers are concerned about the factors that influence the spending behavior of the individuals or organizations in these different sectors. The interaction between these factors, such as lack of consumer confidence and decreases in government employment, influenced the slow economic recovery discussed in the opening case of this chapter. There are various indicators of economic activity in each of these sectors, such as the Institute for Supply Management purchasing managers' index, not all of which move in the same direction. This divergence makes it difficult for both policy makers and managers to determine exactly where the economy is headed and can lead to differences in forecasts of future economic activity.

How Do Behavior Changes in These Sectors Influence the Level of Output and Income in the Economy?

Equilibrium level of output and income
The level of aggregate output and income where there is a balance between spending and production decisions and where the economy will stay unless acted on by other forces.

Once we understand the factors influencing the spending patterns of the different sectors of the economy and the data used to measure these factors, we can determine the resulting level of output and income. We call this outcome the **equilibrium level of output and income**, the level toward which the economy is moving and at which it will stay unless a shock causes the economy to deviate from equilibrium.

Equilibrium implies a balance between the spending and production decisions in the economy. For example, in December 2008, Chrysler LLC confirmed that it would suspend all manufacturing operations for at least a month "in an effort to align production and inventory with U.S. market demand."[37] This behavior itself can change the equilibrium level of output and income in the economy. Thus, we need to know what factors determine equilibrium and how the economy moves from a disequilibrium situation to one of equilibrium.[38]

Can Policy Makers Maintain Stable Prices, Full Employment, and Adequate Economic Growth over Time?

Policy makers are concerned with keeping the country's resources fully employed while maintaining an environment with relatively stable prices and avoiding either inflation or deflation. The economy tends to experience increases and decreases

---

[37]Lauren Pollock and Neal E. Boudette, "Chrysler to Close Manufacturing Plants for a Month Starting Friday," *Wall Street Journal*, December 17, 2008.

[38]Although the variables and level of analysis are quite different, the process we follow to understand these factors is similar to that needed to understand the forces of demand, supply, and equilibrium in individual markets.

in activity, given the interactions among the spending decisions of individuals in the various sectors. One of the specific goals of policy makers is to keep the economy as close to full employment as possible without setting off a period of inflation as output and employment move close to the capacity of the economy. In the short run, there is often a trade-off between the level of unemployment and a stable price level. As the economy moves closer to full employment, there will be upward pressure on both wages and prices, which can cause the price level to increase.

The policy goals of full employment and stable prices have been established for both Congress and the Federal Reserve System by the Employment Act of 1946 and the Full Employment and Balanced Growth Act of 1978 (the Humphrey-Hawkins Act). The 1946 legislation requires government institutions to promote "maximum employment, production, and purchasing power." The 1978 act requires the chairman of the Federal Reserve System to appear before Congress twice a year to present the central bank's forecast for the economy and to discuss its future policies.

Both high unemployment and high inflation impose costs on the economy. High unemployment results in lost output. For individuals, unemployment means lost income, a deterioration in skills if the unemployment is prolonged, and a loss of self-worth. These factors can cause social unrest if the unemployment rate is substantial, as in the Great Depression of the 1930s, and they can result in increased crime and other antisocial behaviors during recessions.

Inflation and deflation also impose costs on the economy in terms of planning for the future and the establishment of contracts. Inflation can redistribute income between those who can raise their prices and wages and those who are unable to do so. Individuals living on fixed incomes from pensions or investments will be worse off if these sources of income do not increase with the inflation rate. Borrowers gain and lenders lose with inflation because the payments on loans, such as home mortgages, may not increase with inflation. Inflation results in uncertainty about what the real purchasing power of money will be in the future. It creates difficulties in writing contracts for future payments, and high inflation may even undermine individuals' faith in their government and economic system. Inflation reduces managerial efficiency, as managers are forced to spend time and resources to protect their firms against inflation.

Although the U.S. economy has not experienced a period of prolonged deflation since the Great Depression of the 1930s, falling prices can cause business profits to decrease and employees to be laid off if the price decreases result from a lack of spending in the economy. Borrowers lose and lenders gain in a deflationary environment. Firms may not be able to pay off their debts and may go into bankruptcy, further cutting wages and employment.[39]

Over longer periods of time, policy makers are concerned with the amount of economic growth or increase in real GDP, as this growth has a substantial impact on the well-being of individuals in the economy. In the short run, over several years in the future, the main focus of economic policy makers is on influencing expenditures (the demand side of the economy) to promote full employment with low inflation. Over longer periods of time, policy interest focuses more on the capacity of the economy to produce more goods and services (the supply side of the economy). These issues relate to increasing the quality, quantity, and productivity of the inputs of production.

---

[39]Greg Ip, "Inside the Fed, Deflation Is Drawing a Closer Look," *Wall Street Journal*, November 6, 2002; Daniel Gross, "Deflation Nation: What's So Bad About Falling Prices?" *Newsweek*, July 12, 2010; and Alex Monro, "The Dangers of Deflation," *Credit*, July/August 2010, 44–46.

How Do Fiscal, Monetary, and Balance of Payments Policies Influence the Economy?

Fiscal policy
Changes in taxes and spending by the executive and legislative branches of a country's national government that can be used to either stimulate or restrain the economy.

Monetary policy
Policies adopted by a country's central bank that influence interest rates and credit conditions, which, in turn, influence consumer and business spending.

Balance of payments issues
Issues related to the relative value of different countries' currencies and the flow of goods, services, and financial assets among countries.

Currency exchange rate
The rate at which one country's currency can be exchanged for that of another.

Trade balance
The relationship between a country's exports and imports, which may be either positive (exports exceed imports) or negative (imports exceed exports).

Capital flows
The buying and selling of existing real and financial assets among countries.

Given these policy goals, managers need to understand how spending in each of the sectors of the economy and the overall level of economic activity are affected by **fiscal policy**, or changes in taxes and government spending by the executive and legislative branches of government; **monetary policy**, or changes in the money supply and interest rates by the Federal Reserve, the country's central bank; and **balance of payments issues**, or changes in the rate at which different countries' currencies can be exchanged for each other and in the flow of goods and services and financial assets among countries.

Policy makers in a country's legislative and executive institutions use taxes and government expenditures as tools to influence the growth of GDP, among other goals. These tools include policies that influence aggregate expenditure (the demand side of the economy) and policies that affect incentives to work, save, and invest (the supply side of the economy). The central bank, which is independent from the government in the United States, uses its control over the money supply to change interest rates and credit conditions in order to influence consumer and business spending. All of these institutions must respond to changes in a country's **currency exchange rate**, the rate at which one country's currency can be exchanged for that of another; the **trade balance**, the relationship between a country's exports and imports; and **capital flows**, the buying and selling of existing real and financial assets among countries.

What Impact Do These Macro Changes Have on Different Firms and Industries?

As we have noted throughout this chapter, managers have little influence over the macro environment, but their competitive strategies and the profitability of their firms are influenced by macroeconomic events. Some of these events are the outcomes of specific monetary and fiscal policies, while others result from changes in the behavior of individuals, both domestically and around the world.

Managers need to understand and anticipate changes in the macro environment. They may do so by purchasing the services of various economic forecasting firms or by developing their own in-house forecasting capacity. In either case, they will focus on the variables described in this chapter and the remainder of the text. Managers also need to realize that their firms will be affected differentially by macroeconomic changes. The opening case gave examples of firms that were influenced by the slow economic activity either in the United States or the rest of the world. Firms that sell in international markets will be more influenced by factors such as fluctuating currency exchange rates than are those firms operating only in domestic markets. Some firms and industries are more sensitive to changes in interest rates than others. However, all firms will be affected by changes in the overall level of economic activity or GDP. Managers must be prepared to revise their competitive strategies in light of changing conditions in the macroeconomic environment.

Managerial Rule of Thumb

Competitive Strategies and the Macro Environment

The impact of the macro environment on competitive strategies may vary substantially among firms and industries. Managers need to develop the ability to forecast and anticipate changes in the macro environment by either purchasing services from forecasting firms or developing their own in-house forecasting capacity. ■

Summary

Managers need to understand the impact of the macroeconomic environment on their firms' and industries' competitive strategies. We illustrated how firms respond to changes in this environment in the opening case of this chapter. We then described the circular flow of economic activity that forms the basis for the analysis of the macroeconomic environment in which managers operate. We discussed the equality between aggregate expenditure on the output produced in an economy and aggregate income generated from the sale of that output, and we noted that economic activity could be measured by focusing on either expenditure or income.

We then analyzed the national income accounting system used in the United States to measure gross domestic product and its components. We also discussed measures of the price level and the level of employment and unemployment. We then related these variables to the major macroeconomic goals of policy makers, and we discussed how changes in macro events influence managerial strategies.

We now must begin our analysis of the aggregate macroeconomic model that will help managers understand the spending decisions of individuals in different sectors of the economy, how these decisions lead to an equilibrium level of aggregate output and income, and why that equilibrium changes over time.

Key Terms

absolute price level, p. 307
aggregate expenditure, p. 293
balance of payments issues, p. 316
business cycles, p. 297
business fixed investment, p. 300
capital flows, p. 316
changes in business inventories, p. 301
circular flow, p. 292
compensation of employees, p. 305
Consumer Price Index (CPI), p. 308
core rate of inflation, p. 309
corporate profits, p. 305
currency exchange rate, p. 316
deflation, p. 307
discouraged workers, p. 312
disposable income, p. 306
durable goods, p. 300
earnings or income approach, p. 293
employed, p. 311
equilibrium level of output and income, p. 314
expansion, p. 297
expenditure or output approach, p. 293

export spending, p. 302
final goods and services, p. 295
fiscal policy, p. 316
GDP deflator, p. 296
government consumption expenditures and gross investment, p. 302
gross domestic product (GDP), p. 292
gross private domestic investment spending, p. 300
import spending, p. 302
imputed value, p. 296
inflation, p. 307
intermediate goods and services, p. 295
labor force, p. 311
mixed economy, p. 292
monetary policy, p. 316
national income, p. 305
national income accounting system, p. 294
National Income and Product Accounts, p. 294

natural rate of unemployment, p. 313
net export spending, p. 302
net interest, p. 305
nominal GDP, p. 296
nondurable goods, p. 300
open economy, p. 292
personal consumption expenditures, p. 299
personal income, p. 306
Producer Price Index (PPI), p. 310
proprietors' income, p. 305
real GDP, p. 296
recession, p. 297
relative prices, p. 307
rental income, p. 305
residential fixed investment, p. 301
saving, p. 306
services, p. 300
trade balance, p. 316
transfer payments, p. 296
underground economy, p. 295
unemployed, p. 311
value-added approach, p. 295

Exercises

Technical Questions

1. Do government statisticians calculate GDP by simply adding up the total sales of all business firms in one year? Explain.

2. Evaluate whether *all* of the following are considered to be investment (*I*) in calculating GDP.

   a. The purchase of a new automobile for private, nonbusiness use
   b. The purchase of a new house
   c. The purchase of corporate bonds

3. Explain whether transfer payments, such as Social Security and unemployment compensation, are counted as government spending in calculating GDP.

4. Is it true that the value of U.S. imports is added to exports when calculating U.S. GDP because imports reflect spending by Americans? Explain.

5. Is real GDP defined as "the value of aggregate output produced when the economy is operating at full employment"? Explain.

6. Suppose an economy produces only two goods, cups of coffee and gallons of milk, as shown in Table 11.E1:

   a. Calculate the expenditure on each good and the nominal and real GDP for 2010, the base year.
   b. Repeat this exercise for each of the three alternative cases (1, 2, and 3).
   c. Explain the differences between nominal GDP and real GDP in each of these cases.

7. Adding to Table 11.1, if in 2007 real GDP was $13,206.4 billion and nominal GDP was $14,028.7 billion, calculate the percentage change from 2006 to 2007 in nominal GDP, real GDP, and the price level. What is the value of the GDP deflator in 2007?

TABLE 11.E1   Nominal Versus Real GDP

YEAR	COFFEE (CUPS)		MILK (GALLONS)		GDP (NOMINAL, REAL)
2010	Price	Quantity	Price	Quantity	
(The base year)	$1.00	10	$2.00	20	
Expenditure					
2011 (Case 1)	Price	Quantity	Price	Quantity	
	$1.50	10	$4.00	20	
Expenditure					
2011 (Case 2)	Price	Quantity	Price	Quantity	
	$1.00	15	$2.00	40	
Expenditure					
2011 (Case 3)	Price	Quantity	Price	Quantity	
	$1.50	15	$4.00	40	
Expenditure					

Application Questions

1. Drawing on current business publications and using the opening case of the chapter as a guide, discuss how the slow economic recovery in 2011 and 2012 has affected the current strategies of firms other than those mentioned in the case.

2. From the Bureau of Economic Analysis Web page (www.bea.gov), compare real GDP for 1970, 1980, 1990, 2000, and 2010. Show the percentage change in real GDP over each of those decades. Do the percentages of GDP spent on consumption (C), investment (I), government (G), exports (X), and imports (M) differ significantly among those years? Are there changes in the balance of trade over the period? Explain.

3. From the Bureau of Economic Analysis Web page (www.bea.gov), construct a table showing the annual percentage change in real GDP, gross private domestic investment (I), nonresidential fixed investment, and residential fixed investment from 2002 to 2011. Which component of investment had the greatest impact on the recession of 2007 to 2009?

4. Find an article in a current business publication that discusses revisions in the GDP data. How significant were these revisions for your example?

5. From the Bureau of Labor Statistics Web page (www.bls.gov/cpi), find the answers to the following questions:

   a. How is the CPI used?
   b. How is the CPI market basket determined?
   c. What goods and services does the CPI cover?
   d. How are CPI prices collected and reviewed?

6. From the Bureau of Labor Statistics Web page (www.bls.gov/cps), find the annual averages of the employment status of the civilian noninstitutional population from 1940 to date. Construct a table and chart showing the size of the civilian noninstitutional population, the civilian labor force, the number of employed, the number of unemployed, and the unemployment rates for 1969, 1982, 1992, 2000, 2003, 2007, and 2011. Discuss how these variables differed in those time periods.

7. From the National Bureau of Economic Research Web site (www.nber.org), find the official beginning and ending dates of the recessions that have occurred since 1965. Which recession was the longest and which was the shortest?

8. Drawing on current business publications, find an article in which either fiscal or monetary policy makers were describing their goals of maintaining stable prices, full employment, and adequate economic growth over time. Which goal was the most important at the time your article was written?

Spending by Individuals, Firms, and Governments on Real Goods and Services

I n this chapter, we begin to develop the aggregate macroeconomic model that will help managers understand the macroeconomy and answer the following:

- What factors influence the spending behavior of the different sectors of the economy?
- How do the behavior changes in these sectors influence the level of output and income in the economy?
- Can policy makers maintain stable prices, full employment, and adequate economic growth over time?
- How do fiscal, monetary, and balance of payments policies influence the economy?
- What impact do these macro changes have on different firms and industries?

We turn our attention to building the aggregate macroeconomic model that *explains* the spending decisions of the different sectors of the economy: personal consumption expenditure, investment expenditure, government expenditure, and net export expenditure. We begin this chapter with a case, "Mixed Signals on the U.S. Economy in Summer 2012."

Case for Analysis

Mixed Signals on the U.S. Economy in Summer 2012

In his testimony to Congress on July 17, 2012, Ben Bernanke, Chairman of the Board of Governors of the Federal Reserve System, summarized the conflicting data on the slow recovery of the U.S. economy from the recession of 2007–2009.[1] Chairman Bernanke noted that real gross domestic product (GDP) had increased at a 2 percent rate in the first quarter of 2012, down from 2.5 percent in the second half of 2011. Household spending increased but at a slower rate in the second quarter with households still having a relatively low level of confidence, given concerns about their income and employment prospects. Increases in manufacturing production and real business spending on equipment and software also slowed in early 2012 compared with the second half of 2011. Economic stresses in Europe combined with the slowing economies of other U.S. trading partners were restraining the demand for U.S. exports.

Federal Reserve projections for growth in real GDP ranged from 1.9 percent to 2.4 percent for 2012 and from 2.2 to 2.8 percent for 2013, lower than those made in January 2012. Bernanke argued that the U.S. economy was being held back by headwinds that included still-tight borrowing conditions for some businesses and households and the restraining effects of fiscal policy and fiscal uncertainty. Europe's financial markets and economies remained under significant stress, creating spillover effects for the rest of the world. The U.S. recovery was also endangered by the confluence of tax increases and spending reductions scheduled to take place early in 2013 if Congress did not take action by then.

The Monetary Policy Report to the Congress, released at the time of Bernanke's testimony, noted that activity in the housing sector was slightly stronger in 2012, but that the overall level was still low and continued to be held down by tight mortgage credit.[2] The strained budgets for state and local governments combined with the potentially more restrictive federal fiscal policy were also negative influences on real GDP growth. Gains in private payroll employment increased from 165,000 jobs per month in the second half of 2011 to 225,000 per month in the first quarter of 2012, but then decreased in the second quarter to 90,000 per month. The unemployment rate had decreased from 9 percent in Summer 2011, but was still 8.2 percent in June 2012.

These mixed signals put additional pressure on the Federal Reserve to take steps to boost growth through the use of its policy tools. The chief economist at the Manufacturers Alliance for Productivity and Innovation noted that the United States appeared to be trapped in a relatively modestly growing economy. Weakness in the housing market meant that the wealth effect from housing, where consumers spend based on the value of their homes, was still negative. Consumer confidence in July 2012 fell to its lowest level since December 2011.[3]

[1]Statement by Ben S. Bernanke, Chairman, *Board of Governors of the Federal Reserve System, before the Committee on Banking, Housing, and Urban Affairs, U.S. Senate*, July 17, 2012. Available at www.federalreserve.gov.

[2]Board of Governors of the Federal Reserve System, *Monetary Policy Report to the Congress*, July 17, 2012. Available at www. federalreserve.gov.

[3]Neil Shah, Jie Jenny Zou, and Nick Timiraos, "Housing Stirs, but Economy Slows," *Wall Street Journal (Online)*, July 18, 2012.

Framework for Macroeconomic Analysis

The aggregate model we use in macroeconomic analysis provides a framework for managers to examine changes in the macro environment, such as those discussed in the opening case. This model helps managers interpret the vast amount of macroeconomic data released by the government and other sources that reflect changes in behavior of the individuals and institutions in the different sectors of the economy.

Focus on the Short Run

Our analysis begins by distinguishing between short-run and long-run macroeconomic models. In the short run, a period of up to several years into the future, macroeconomic policy focuses primarily on the demand or expenditure side of the economy. **Potential GDP**, or the maximum amount of output that can be produced, varies little, if at all, over this period of time. Potential GDP depends on the size of the labor force, the number of structures and the amount of equipment in the economy, and the state of technology, factors that do not change rapidly over the short run. Thus, the short-run macroeconomic policy goal is managing aggregate expenditure to keep the economy close to its potential output and the labor force fully employed without setting off an increase in the price level or an inflationary spiral. As the economy approaches full employment and potential GDP, there is a tendency for prices and wages to rise. Because the goal of policy makers is to maintain both stable prices and high employment and output, short-run macroeconomic policy focuses on minimizing fluctuations around potential GDP. To achieve this goal, policy makers emphasize the demand side of the economy, using monetary and fiscal policies to either stimulate or reduce aggregate expenditures around a relatively fixed target.

Over a longer-run period, macroeconomic policy focuses more on potential GDP, or the supply side of the economy. Potential GDP can change over time because the size of the labor force, the number of structures and the amount of equipment, and the state of technology change. The standard of living of a society over long periods of time depends on increases in potential real GDP. Therefore, long-run macroeconomic policies concentrate on incentives for increasing productivity and the potential output of the economy. These policies include education and training programs to increase the quality of the labor force and tax incentives for businesses to increase investment and for workers to increase their participation in the labor force and their hours worked.

Some of these policies may have both demand- and supply-side effects. For example, tax incentives to stimulate business investment spending influence aggregate expenditure in the short run. The incentives should also increase the capacity of the economy to produce over the long run, as investment spending focuses on structures and equipment that can be used to produce goods and services in the future. Thus, investment spending plays a dual role, influencing both the demand and the supply sides of the economy. Much debate over macroeconomic investment expenditure policies centers on the size of the short-run (demand) versus long-run (supply) effects of these policies. In 2011 and 2012 there was also extensive political and policy debate over the long-run role of federal government expenditure, taxes, and the amount of deficit spending.[4]

Potential GDP
The maximum amount of GDP that can be produced at any point in time, which depends on the size of the labor force, the number of structures and the amount of equipment in the economy, and the state of technology.

[4]Congressional Budget Office, *The Budget and Economic Outlook; Fiscal Years 2012 to 2022,* January 2012. Available at www.cbo.gov.

This text focuses primarily on *short-run macroeconomic models* because managers and their firms are most affected by short-run factors. Managers' competitive strategies are influenced by changes in the macroeconomic environment over the next few months, quarters, and years, and not in the more distant future, because most business planning horizons are in the three- to five-year range. Managers need to be able to understand how changes in monetary and fiscal policies or international events affect the environment in which they operate and may create opportunities or impediments for their current competitive strategies.[5]

Analysis in Real Versus Nominal Terms

Changes in aggregate expenditure and gross domestic product can be measured in either **real terms** or **nominal terms**, depending on whether the price level is assumed to be constant or allowed to vary (Chapter 11). As we build the aggregate model, we assume in this chapter that the price level is constant. Thus, any changes in aggregate expenditure represent changes in real income and output (more or fewer real goods, services, and income). Although inflation (a general increase in the price level) represents a major policy problem for most industrialized countries, we will not discuss this problem until we fully develop the concepts of aggregate demand and aggregate supply (Chapter 14). This simplification of assuming that prices are constant allows us to focus on the behavioral factors influencing real spending in the various sectors of the economy (this chapter and Chapter 13).

Real terms
Measuring expenditures and income with the price level held constant, so that any changes in these values represent changes in the actual amount of goods, services, and income.

Nominal terms
Measuring expenditures and income with the price level allowed to vary, so that changes in these values represent changes in the actual amount of goods, services, and income; changes in the price level; or a combination of both factors.

Treatment of the Foreign Sector

Because export and import spending on currently produced goods and services is included in gross domestic product or aggregate expenditure, we incorporate this aspect of the foreign sector in this chapter. However, later we will discuss other international issues, such as the flows of financial assets among countries and currency exchange rate determination (Chapter 15).

Outline for Macroeconomic Analysis

Figure 12.1 presents a framework for developing the short-run aggregate macroeconomic model. We begin this chapter by analyzing the factors influencing real aggregate expenditure and defining the equilibrium level of expenditure and income. We then analyze the money market and the factors influencing the demand for and supply of money (Chapter 13). We show that monetary policy influences the interest rate, which is the crucial link between the real and monetary sides of the economy. We then relax the fixed price assumption to derive the aggregate demand curve, and we develop the concept of aggregate supply, which incorporates variables determining the size of potential GDP. Combining aggregate demand with aggregate supply allows us to fully develop the short-run aggregate macroeconomic model that incorporates all the factors influencing both the level of real income and output (real GDP) and the price level (Chapter 14).

[5]For a complete discussion of both short- and long-run macroeconomic models, see Robert J. Gordon, *Macroeconomics*, 12th ed. (New York: Addison-Wesley, 2012); Olivier Blanchard, *Macroeconomics*, 5th ed. updated (Upper Saddle River, N.J.: Prentice Hall, 2011); Richard T. Froyen, *Macroeconomics: Theories and Policies*, 10th ed. (Upper Saddle River, N.J.: Prentice Hall, 2013); and Andrew B. Abel, Ben S. Bernanke, and Dean Croushore, *Macroeconomics*, 7th ed. (Boston, MA: Addison-Wesley, 2011).

FIGURE 12.1
The Aggregate Macroeconomic Model
The components of the aggregate macroeconomic model.

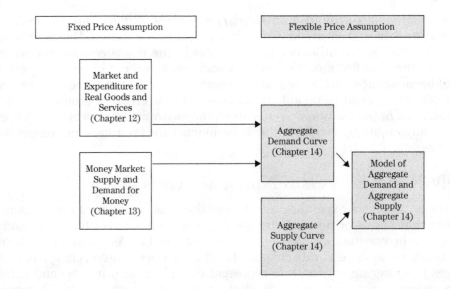

The Components of Aggregate Expenditure

Aggregate expenditure
The sum of personal consumption expenditure, investment expenditure, government expenditure, and net export expenditure in a given period of time.

Let's look at the components of **aggregate expenditure** as established by the U.S. Bureau of Economic Analysis (BEA): personal consumption expenditure (C), investment expenditure (I), government expenditure (G), and net export expenditure (F), or export spending (X) minus import spending (M).

Personal Consumption Expenditure

Personal consumption expenditure
The amount of spending by households on durable goods, nondurable goods, and services in a given period of time.

Personal consumption expenditure is the amount of spending by households on durable goods, nondurable goods, and services in a given period of time. It is influenced by the level of real income in the economy and by a number of other factors, such as weakness in the housing market, as noted in the opening case of this chapter.

Consumption function
The fundamental relationship in macroeconomics that assumes that household consumption spending depends primarily on the level of disposable income (net of taxes) in the economy, all other variables held constant.

The Relationship Between Personal Consumption Expenditure and Income   Personal consumption expenditure (C) on currently produced goods and services is determined primarily by the level of disposable income, or income net of personal taxes ($Y_d = Y - T_P$, where Y_d is disposable income, Y is personal income, and T_P represents personal taxes).[6] This concept, called the **consumption function**, was introduced by John Maynard Keynes, the father of modern macroeconomics, in his 1936 book *The General Theory of Employment, Interest, and Money.* The theory of the consumption function also assumes that as disposable income increases, consumption spending increases by a smaller amount. This assumption means that the **marginal propensity to consume (*MPC*)**, which is defined as $\Delta C/\Delta Y_d$ or $\Delta C/\Delta(Y - T_P)$, is less than 1. All other variables that affect consumption expenditure are assumed to be constant when defining the consumption function. In 2002, economists at Wells Fargo & Company attributed 75 percent of consumer spending to income, while those at the Conference Board used a 90 percent figure.[7]

Marginal propensity to consume (*MPC*)
The additional consumption spending generated by an additional amount of real income, assumed to take a value less than 1.

---

[6]Households receive some income in the form of transfer payments, income that results from transfers among individuals or governments and not from the production of goods and services (Chapter 11). The variable T_P is actually personal taxes net of any transfer income. For simplicity, we assume that transfers are zero in the model and refer to T_P as taxes. We also assume that taxes are lump sum and do not depend on the level of income.

[7]Bernard Wysocki, Jr., "Forget the Wealth Effect: Income Drives Spending," *Wall Street Journal*, August 12, 2002.

The impact of changes in overall real income on individual firms' and managers' strategies depends on the factors that affect the demand for that firm's product and on firms' reactions to changes in income such as occurred during the recession of 2007–2009. For example, in spring 2012 there was evidence that larger firms had survived the recession better than smaller firms. A survey of 468 companies included in Standard & Poor's 500-stock index indicated that these companies had done substantial cost cutting during the recession that allowed their sales, profits, and employment in 2011 to exceed that of 2007 before the economic downturn began. Starbucks Corp. and McDonald's Corp. suffered declines in 2009 but increased profit margins by adding menu items, closing unprofitable locations during the recession, and relying on strong sales outside the United States. However, revenues of home builders were less than half the peak of the last decade. Boston Scientific Corp., a medical-device maker, cut 3,000 jobs since 2007, but its revenue continued to decline and the company continued to report losses in 2012.[8]

Household **saving (S)** is the amount of disposable income that households do *not* spend on the consumption of goods and services (Chapter 11). Therefore, $S = Y_d - C$ or $C + S = Y_d$. The **marginal propensity to save (MPS)**, which is defined as $\Delta S/\Delta Y_d$ or $\Delta S/\Delta(Y - T_P)$, equals $1 - MPC$.

Saving (S)
The amount of disposable income that households do *not* spend on the consumption of goods and services.

Marginal propensity to save (MPS)
The additional household saving generated by an additional amount of real income, which equals $1 - MPC$.

The Level of Personal Taxes   As just noted, consumption depends on disposable income, or personal income less personal taxes. Therefore, any increases or decreases in taxes will influence consumption spending. For example, Congress passed the Economic Growth and Tax Relief Reconciliation Act of 2001 in June 2001 to help offset the effects of the economic downturn that occurred early that year. To speed up the effects of this tax cut on personal consumption expenditure, $300 and $600 rebate checks were mailed to households in the summer of 2001.[9]

In May 2003, Congress passed another tax cut designed to further stimulate the economy. This legislation affected personal taxes by cutting tax rates across the board, increasing the child care credit, and reducing the tax penalty on married couples. A number of provisions in the bill were scheduled to expire after several years.[10]

In February 2008, Congress passed and President Bush signed a $168 billion economic-stimulus bill designed to slow the decline in economic activity. Taxpayers received up to $600 for individuals or $1,200 for married couples, amounts that phased out at higher income levels. Millions of individuals who did not pay income taxes but who had incomes of at least $3,000 received smaller rebates.[11]

The effect of a tax cut on consumption expenditures depends on whether the cut is temporary or permanent and on who receives the cut. Temporary tax changes are likely to be much less effective than permanent changes in influencing consumption spending because individuals may not change their spending behavior in response to a temporary change in taxes. Economists have estimated that over a one-year time frame, a temporary tax change will have only a little more than half the impact of a permanent change of equal size and a tax rebate will have only 38 percent as

---

[8]Scott Thurm, "For Big Companies, Life is Good," *Wall Street Journal (Online)*, April 9, 2012.

[9]U.S. Congressional Budget Office, *The Budget and Economic Outlook: Fiscal Years 2003–2012* (Washington, DC: U.S. Government Printing Office, January 2002).

[10]Shailagh Murray, "House, Senate Hammer Out $350 Billion Tax-Relief Deal," *Wall Street Journal*, May 23, 2003; Greg Ip and John D. McKinnon, "Tax Plan Would Boost Growth, But Would Also Widen Deficits," *Wall Street Journal*, May 23, 2003.

[11]Sarah Lueck, "Congress Approves Economic-Stimulus Bill," *Wall Street Journal*, February 8, 2008.

much impact.[12] Lower- and middle-income households, who are likely to have constraints on their borrowing, are likely to have a larger marginal propensity to consume out of the income from a tax cut than nonconstrained households.[13]

By fall 2008, economists estimated that the February 2008 tax cut had only a small impact on the economy because consumers saved the rebates or used them to pay off debt rather than spending them, given the temporary nature of the program. A University of Michigan survey showed that only one-fifth of the respondents said that the rebates would lead them to increase spending. Survey estimates implied that the marginal propensity to consume was about one-third.[14] The economic-stimulus bill offset the declining economy only slightly in the second and third quarters of 2008.[15]

The 2001 rebate was part of a longer-lasting tax cut, while the 2008 rebate was a one-time event. However, the 2001 rebate went to all income groups, while the 2008 rebate was limited to low- and middle-income households. Because the first difference should have raised the MPC out of the 2001 rebate relative to 2008 and the second difference reduced it, the estimated MPCs were not significantly different for the two tax cuts.[16]

The Real Interest Rate   We argue later in the chapter that the real interest rate is a primary determinant of business investment spending. However, changes in interest rates can also influence consumer spending, particularly for durable goods such as automobiles and large appliances, for which consumers may have to borrow. For example, automobile dealers' zero percent financing and other incentives largely drove the 6.1 percent increase in consumer spending in the fourth quarter of 2001 that helped the economy come out of recession.[17]

When the Fed began its extensive interest rate cutting in September 2007 to try to offset problems in the housing market, rates on home-equity lines of credit, automobile loans, and credit cards all decreased. Home equity loan rates dropped from 8.25 to 6.27 percent between September 2007 and March 2008, although some companies, such as Countrywide Financial Corp. and Washington Mutual Inc., reduced or froze the amount of credit available to certain borrowers to protect themselves against falling home values and rising delinquencies. Credit card rates fell from 13.97 to 12.36 percent in this period, although some consumers began encountering their floor rates, predetermined points below which the rates charged would not decrease regardless of what happened to other interest rates in the economy. Automobile loan rates decreased from 7.72 to only 7.22 percent, a reflection of the heavy manufacturer incentives already being offered.[18]

---

[12]Shailagh Murray and John D. McKinnon, "Instant Tax Cuts to Stimulate Economy Have Fizzled, Even Backfired in Past," *Wall Street Journal*, April 4, 2001. Consumer behavior can be different than anticipated. When President George H.W. Bush announced in January 1992 that he was reducing the amount of tax withheld from paychecks, few economists expected that this change would stimulate consumption spending. A research study later showed that 43 percent of those who responded to a telephone survey said they would spend most of the increase in take-home pay and that this program would have a moderate effect in stimulating the economy. See Matthew D. Shapiro and Joel Slemrod, "Consumer Response to the Timing of Income: Evidence from a Change in Withholding," *American Economic Review* 85 (March 1995): 274–83.

[13]Alan J. Auerbach and William G. Gale, "Activist Fiscal Policy to Stabilize Economic Activity," Paper presented at the Federal Reserve Bank of Kansas City conference on Financial Stability and Macroeconomic Policy, held August 20–22, 2009. Available at www.kc.frb.org/publicat/sympos/2009/papers/auerbach-gale.09.30.09.pdf.

[14]Matthew D. Shapiro and Joel Slemrod, "Did the 2008 Tax Rebates Stimulate Spending?" *American Economic Review: Papers and Proceedings* 99 (May 2009): 374–79.

[15]Sudeep Reddy, "Congress Postpones Stimulus Plan to '09," *Wall Street Journal*, November 21, 2008; John B. Taylor, "Why Permanent Tax Cuts Are the Best Stimulus," *Wall Street Journal*, November 25, 2008.

[16]Auerbach and Gale, "Activist Fiscal Policy to Stabilize Economic Activity."

[17]"Economy Surged 5.8% in 1st Quarter as Businesses Slowed Inventory Cuts," *Wall Street Journal*, April 26, 2002.

[18]Jeff D. Opdyke and Jane J. Kim, "Why Only Some See Benefit from Fed's Cuts," *Wall Street Journal*, March 19, 2008.

It is the **real interest rate**, or the **nominal interest rate** adjusted for expected inflation, that influences both consumers' and firms' spending decisions. This is another application of real versus nominal variables and the influence of a constant versus a changing price level (Chapter 11). Lenders will charge borrowers a nominal interest rate (i), which is based on the real interest rate (r) and the expected rate of inflation. The real interest rate, which is necessary to induce them to make the loan and give up the use of their funds, would exist even if prices were stable. However, in times of inflation, lenders will add a premium to the real interest rate to compensate them for the fact that they will be paid back in dollars that have less purchasing power.

For example, in 1978, nominal interest rates averaged 8 percent, but the rate of inflation was 9 percent. Although nominal interest rates were high, the real interest rate was actually negative 1 percent. In early 1999, nominal rates were approximately 4.75 percent, while the inflation rate was 2 percent. Thus, the real interest rate in 1999 was 2.75 percent. The real rate was actually higher in the period of low inflation than in the period of high inflation.[19]

Consumer Confidence   Consumer confidence also affects consumer spending decisions such that decreases in confidence might make consumers restrain their spending, endangering the recovery from a recession or helping one to occur. There are two measures of consumer confidence: the **Consumer Sentiment Index (CSI)**, prepared by the University of Michigan and Thomson Reuters, and the **Consumer Confidence Index (CCI)**, prepared by the Conference Board, a nonprofit, nonpartisan research organization that monitors consumer confidence and business expectations about the future.[20] The CSI is published monthly and combines households' attitudes in the following three areas into one index:

1. Expected business conditions in the national economy for one and five years ahead
2. Personal financial conditions compared with the previous year and the next year
3. Consumer confidence regarding the purchase of furniture and major household appliances

The CCI, on the other hand, includes households' perceptions of general business conditions, available jobs in the households' local area, and expected personal family income in the coming six months. The CCI samples 5,000 households with a mail survey, whereas the CSI uses a telephone survey of 500 households. The CSI includes the purchase of big-ticket items, while the CCI asks about employment conditions. These differences mean that the two surveys do not necessarily show the same performance month to month. The CCI tends to be more erratic because the Conference Board interviews an entirely new group of people every month, while the University of Michigan interviews about 40 percent of its consumers a second time.[21] Figure 12.2 shows the CSI and the unemployment rate for the period 2000–2012.

Both of these measures decreased in mid-2012. The CSI decreased from 79.3 in May to 74.1 in June, the lowest level in 2012. The index had averaged 62.4 during the 2007–2009 recession and 89 in the five years prior to the recession. The CCI had

Real interest rate
The nominal interest rate adjusted for expected inflation, which is the rate that influences firms' investment decisions.

Nominal interest rate
The real interest rate plus the expected rate of inflation, which may differ substantially from the real interest rate during periods of inflation.

Consumer Sentiment Index (CSI)
An index, based on a telephone survey of 500 households conducted by the University of Michigan, that measures households' attitudes regarding expected business conditions, personal financial conditions, and consumer confidence about purchasing furniture and major household appliances.

Consumer Confidence Index (CCI)
An index, based on a mail survey of 5,000 households conducted by the Conference Board, that measures households' perceptions of general business conditions, available jobs in the households' local area, and expected personal family income in the coming six months.

[19]Federal Reserve Bank of San Francisco, *U.S. Monetary Policy: An Introduction.* Available at www.frbsf.org/publications/federalreserve/monetary/index.htm.
[20]Norman Frumkin, *Tracking America's Economy*, 4th ed. (Armonk, NY: M.E. Sharpe, 2004); Bernard Baumohl, *The Secrets of Economic Indicators*, 3rd ed. (Upper Saddle River, NJ: FT Press, 2013); The Conference Board, *Consumer Confidence Survey Technical Note*, February 2011. Available at http://www.conference-board.org.
[21]Baumohl, *The Secrets of Economic Indicators*, 3rd ed., 112–119.

FIGURE 12.2

Consumer Sentiment and the Unemployment Rate

The University of Michigan's Consumer Sentiment Index is an indicator of major turning points in the business cycle.

The unemployment rate is the percent of the labor force not employed and actively seeking work; the labor force includes adult (16 years of age and older), noninstitutional, civilian workers.

Source: Federal Reserve Economic Data (FRED II), Economic Research, Federal Reserve Bank of St. Louis, http://research.stlouisfed.org/fred2/.

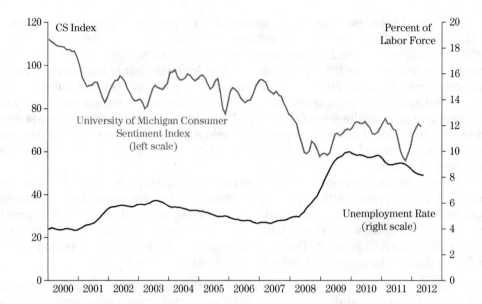

declined in May and then fell further in June from 64.4–62.0.[22] The Federal Reserve noted that both of these measures were above their lows during the summer of 2011, but that they had not yet returned to pre-recession levels.[23]

There is continuing debate about how well these confidence indices actually predict changes in consumer spending. Most economists argue that broad changes in the indices over time are related to changes in consumption spending, but that the indices will not provide an exact prediction of consumer spending changes, particularly on a month-to-month basis. One study, which compared simple statistical models with and without the consumer confidence and sentiment indexes, found that including these indexes provided only a slight improvement in the forecasts.[24]

Consumer confidence was of particular concern to managers and analysts in the period following the terrorist attacks of September 2001 and at the time of the Iraq war in March 2003.[25] Consumer demand in the hotel, travel, and tourism industries decreased substantially in the days following the terrorist attacks. This was the period when the automobile industry responded by offering zero percent financing initiatives to offset the lack of demand resulting from the ongoing recession and the attacks. The opening days of the Iraq war in March 2003 did not appear to have a major impact on consumer confidence and spending behavior. Research on the confidence and sentiment indexes has suggested that consumers did not view the 1993 World Trade Center bombing and the 1995 Oklahoma City bombing as significantly affecting the overall economy, but the Persian Gulf War lowered the indexes by 14 and 8 points, respectively. The September 11th terrorist attacks did not appear to have an effect separate from that of the ongoing recession at that time.[26]

---

[22]"United States: U.S. Consumer Sentiment Hits a 6-month Low Amid Sluggish Job Growth," *Asia News Monitor,* June 19, 2012; "The Conference Board Consumer Confidence Index Declines Again," June 26, 2012. Available at www.conference-board.org.

[23]Board of Governors of the Federal Reserve System, *Monetary Policy Report to the Congress,* July 17, 2012.

[24]Frumkin, *Tracking America's Economy,* 4th ed.; "Consumer Spending: A Sentimental Journey?" *Wall Street Journal,* April 8, 2002.

[25]"Terrorist Attacks Briefly Stalled Economy, Federal Reserve Says," *Wall Street Journal,* October 24, 2001; "Despite the War in Iraq, Consumers Keep Buying," *Wall Street Journal,* March 24, 2003.

[26]C. Alan Garner, "Consumer Confidence after September 11," as reported in Frumkin, *Tracking America's Economy,* 4th ed., 140–41.

Wealth   Households can also finance consumption expenditures out of their existing stock of wealth.[27] The wealth effect of the stock market during the economic expansion of the late 1990s had a significant impact on household spending.[28] From 1989 to 1999, the real value of tangible assets increased 14 percent, the real value of financial assets other than stocks increased 38 percent, but the real value of stocks increased 262 percent. This wealth effect often means that consumers spend more in the current period due to the increase in the value of their retirement accounts, not because they are actually drawing down on these retirement accounts.

The decline in stock market wealth was a restraining influence on consumption spending in 2001.[29] The turmoil in the financial and credit markets also affected stock prices in the recession of 2007–2009. Figure 12.3 shows the annual percentage change in the Standard & Poors stock index from 2000 to 2012.

Several studies have reported that there is a greater wealth effect on consumer expenditure from the capital gains in housing than from the stock market. On average a dollar increase in housing wealth increases consumption spending by seven cents while the effect for financial wealth is approximately three cents.[30] This wealth effect became a particular issue in 2007 and 2008 with the upheaval in the housing and mortgage markets and the decline in the stock market in the fall of 2008. In December 2008, the Federal Reserve reported that U.S. household net worth fell 4.7 percent to $56.5 trillion in the third quarter of 2008, the fourth straight

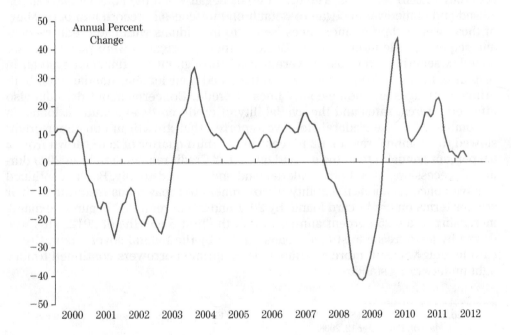

FIGURE 12.3
Stock Market Returns
The decline in stock market wealth was a restraining influence on consumption spending in the recession of 2001 and the recession of 2007–2009.
Source: Federal Reserve Economic Data (FRED II), Economic Research, Federal Reserve Bank of St. Louis. http://research.stlouisfed.org/fred2/

---

[27]Saving is the amount of a flow of income that is not spent by consumers in a given period of time (Chapter 11). This process of saving results in changes in the amount of consumer wealth, which may take the form of savings accounts, money market funds, and/or financial investments in stocks, bonds, other securities, and real estate.

[28]Yochi J. Dreazen, "Stocks Make Up Almost a Third of Household Wealth in the U.S.," *Wall Street Journal*, March 14, 2000; James M. Poterba, "Stock Market Wealth and Consumption," *Journal of Economic Perspectives* 14 (Spring 2000): 99–118.

[29]Board of Governors of the Federal Reserve System, *Monetary Policy Report to Congress* (Washington, DC: Federal Reserve System, February 27, 2002).

[30]Frumkin, *Tracking America's Economy*, 4th ed.; N. Kundan Kishor, "Does Consumption Respond More to Housing Wealth Than to Financial Market Wealth? If So, Why?" *Journal of Real Estate Finance and Economics*, 35 (2007): 427–48.

quarterly decline. Household net worth was 11 percent lower than a year earlier.[31] In 2012 the Federal Reserve noted that the ratio of household wealth to income had been on a slow upward trend since 2009. Although this ratio was far below that for the years leading up to the recession, it was approximately equal to the average level over the previous 20 years. Wealth losses were proportionately larger for the middle portion of the wealth distribution, given the importance of housing assets to that group.[32]

Consumer Credit   The availability of consumer credit also influences personal consumption spending. If an item is purchased on credit, the entire cost of the item is counted as a personal consumption expenditure at the time the purchase is made. The Federal Reserve Board monitors the use of consumer credit (a flow variable), or loans to households by banks, credit companies, and retail stores that cover items such as automobiles, credit cards, home improvements, education, vacations, and recreational vehicles.[33] From 1960 to 1996, there was a positive relationship between the percentage change in consumer credit outstanding and consumer expenditures. However, there was also substantial year-to-year variation in this relationship between the use of consumer credit and consumption spending, suggesting that other factors, such as household income and consumer confidence, play a larger role in influencing personal consumption expenditures.[34]

The availability of consumer credit was a major factor in the slowing of the U.S. economy in 2007 and 2008. The credit crisis began when the housing market collapsed and homeowners began to default on mortgages in record numbers. Many of these were subprime mortgages issued to individuals with bad credit records and requiring little money down. Because these mortgages were packaged into complex securities, the losses were spread throughout the financial system. In response, banks and other institutions tightened their lending standards on both prime mortgages and home-equity lines of credit. Concerns about defaults also affected interest rates and the availability of credit cards and student loans. In December 2008, the Federal Reserve reported that growth in consumer credit slowed to an annual rate of 1.2 percent in the third quarter of 2008, down from a 3.9 percent annual rate in the second quarter.[35] Credit remained tight in 2009 during the recession, given both weak demand and reduced supply. Banks continued to have concerns about the ability of consumers to repay loans resulting in their stricter terms on credit card loans. By 2011 and 2012 credit had begun to expand, increasing to a 6.25 percent annual rate in the first 5 months of 2012. This was driven by an increase in student loans funded by the federal government. Credit card lending was still more restrained as nonprime borrowers continued to face tight underwriting standards.[36]

---

[31]Phil Izzo, Brenda Cronin, and Sudeep Reddy, "Debt Shows First Drop as Slump Squeezes Consumers," *Wall Street Journal*, December 12, 2008.

[32]Board of Governors of the Federal Reserve System, *Monetary Policy Report to the Congress*, July 17, 2012.

[33]Jon Hilsenrath, "Consumer Credit Rose by $7.3 Billion in May," *Wall Street Journal*, July 9, 2003; Baumohl, *The Secrets of Economic Indicators*, 3rd ed., 107–11.

[34]Frumkin, *Tracking America's Economy*, 4th ed.

[35]Scott Patterson, "How the Credit Mess Squeezes You," *Wall Street Journal*, March 2, 2008; Daniel Gross, "Borrowers Are Out in the Cold; It's No Longer Just People with Bad Credit Who Are Feeling the Squeeze. Americans with Good Credit at All Income Levels Are Now Caught in a Full-Blown Credit Crunch," *Newsweek*, March 3, 2008; Board of Governors of the Federal Reserve System, *Monetary Report to Congress*, February 27, 2008; Izzo et al. "Debt Shows First Drop as Slump Squeezes Consumers," December 12, 2008.

[36]Board of Governors of the Federal Reserve System, *Monetary Policy Report to Congress*, February 24, 2010, July 17, 2012.

Level of Debt Increased use of consumer credit creates a larger stock of consumer debt outstanding, which may have a restraining influence on future consumption spending. The burden of this debt is measured as the ratio of consumer installment credit outstanding to disposable income. When this ratio increases, consumers will eventually become reluctant to add to their debt burden, and banks and other lenders will become stricter in their lending practices. However, it is unclear exactly where this turning point lies. Household spending decisions are influenced more by changes in income and expected income than by debt burden.[37]

In December 2008, the Federal Reserve reported that U.S. households decreased the amount of their debt at a 0.8 percent annual rate, the first drop in debt since the central bank started collecting this information in 1952. Although this change might be a positive long-run trend, it had a negative impact on consumer spending at that time.[38] Total household debt continued to decline in 2009. By 2012 household debt was still decreasing, but the continued contraction in mortgage debt was almost offset by a solid expansion in consumer credit.[39]

The Consumption Function This discussion of all the factors influencing personal consumption expenditure can be summarized in the generalized consumption function shown in Equation 12.1:

12.1 $C = f(Y, T_p, r, CC, W, CR, D)$
$(+)(-)(-)(+) \ (+) \ (+)(-)$

where

C = personal consumption expenditure
Y = personal income
T_P = personal taxes
r = real interest rate
CC = consumer confidence
W = consumer wealth
CR = available consumer credit
D = consumer debt

In this notation, consumption expenditure is expressed as a function of income, holding constant the other variables in the consumption function. The relationship between C and Y will determine the slope of the consumption function, while changes in the other variables will cause a shift in the consumption function.[40] The plus sign under the income variable shows that the consumption function will have a positive slope. The signs under the other variables show how the consumption function will shift when those variables change. A plus sign indicates a positive or upward shift of the function, whereas a negative sign indicates a negative or downward shift. This notation will be used throughout the macroeconomic portion of this text.

---

[37]Frumkin, *Tracking America's Economy*, 4th ed.
[38]Izzo et al. "Debt Shows First Drop as Slump Squeezes Consumers," December 12, 2008.
[39]Board of Governors of the Federal Reserve System, *Monetary Policy Report to the Congress*, February 24, 2010, July 17, 2012.
[40]This is the same notation we used for demand and supply analysis (Chapter 2). The f symbol means the variable on the left side of the equation "is a function of" or depends on the variables on the right side of the equation.

Equation 12.2 shows a linear consumption function:

12.2 $\quad C = C_0 + c_1Y$

where

$C_0 =$ autonomous consumption expenditures

$c_1 =$ marginal propensity to consume

$Y =$ personal income

Autonomous consumption expenditures
Consumption expenditures that are determined by factors other than the level of real income in the economy.

Equation 12.2 is the form of the consumption function we will use throughout our macroeconomic analysis. The constant term, C_0, represents **autonomous consumption expenditures**, or those consumption expenditures that are determined by the factors in Equation 12.1 other than income. The effects of all of these factors in Equation 12.1, which we discussed above, are combined to form the constant term in Equation 12.2. The variable c_1 in Equation 12.2 is the slope term that represents the marginal propensity to consume, or the proportion of the increase in real income households will spend on durables, nondurables, and services. These expenditures are **induced consumption expenditures**, as they result from changes in real income in the economy. This distinction between autonomous and induced expenditures also applies to the other components of aggregate expenditure we discuss later in the chapter.[41]

Induced consumption expenditures
Consumption expenditures that result from changes in the level of real income in the economy.

The linear consumption function is illustrated in Figure 12.4a. Autonomous consumption expenditures are represented by the vertical distance, C_0. The slope, c_1, is $\Delta C/\Delta Y$, or the marginal propensity to consume. Changes in any of the other variables in Equation 12.1 will cause the consumption function to shift in the direction indicated in that equation. The marginal propensity to consume for this type of consumption function has been estimated to be approximately 0.75.[42]

Gross Private Domestic Investment Expenditure

Gross private domestic investment
The total amount of spending on nonresidential structures, equipment, and software; residential structures; and business inventories in a given period of time.

As we discussed in the previous chapter, **gross private domestic investment** includes spending on business structures, equipment, and software; residential housing; and changes in business inventories. Firms invest in structures, equipment, and software to provide the capacity to produce increased amounts of goods and services as the economy grows, to replace capital goods that have worn out or become obsolete, to adopt new cost-saving production methods, or to produce new, higher-quality products. Residential housing spending is related to the level of income and interest rates in the economy, while inventory spending is largely a function of the overall level of economic activity. Thus, a variety of factors influence gross private domestic investment spending.

Business Investment Spending and Real Income Investment spending on structures and equipment is related to the level of real income and output in

---

[41]In Equation 12.2, personal taxes (T_P) are combined in the C_0 term because we are assuming that taxes do not depend on the level of income.

[42]Consumption functions estimated over longer periods of time have marginal propensities to consume closer to 0.90 and a zero vertical intercept. Economists have argued that these long-run consumption functions result from the upward shift of short-run consumption functions over time. Economists have also developed theories of consumer behavior that incorporate more sophisticated and realistic behavior than that implied by the Keynesian consumption function. See David C. Colander and Edward M. Gamber, *Macroeconomics* (Upper Saddle River, NJ: Prentice Hall, 2002), 341–54; Gordon, *Macroeconomics*, 12th ed., 481–512.

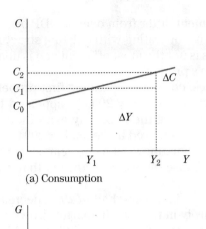

(a) Consumption

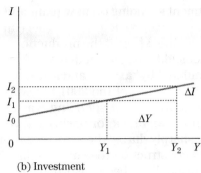

(b) Investment

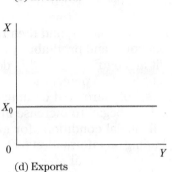

(c) Government

(d) Exports

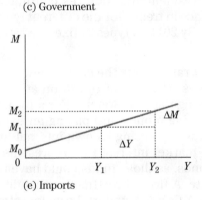

(e) Imports

FIGURE 12.4
The Components of Aggregate Expenditure
Consumption, investment, and import spending are all assumed to be a function of the level of real income. Government spending and export spending are assumed to be determined by factors other than the level of real income.

the economy.[43] The portion of investment spending related to the replacement of existing capital facilities tends to be relatively stable over time. However, additions to the capital stock can be much more volatile because firms want new facilities to meet expected sales, but they do not want excess capacity. If businesses are expecting a certain constant rate of growth of real income or GDP, they plan a rate of investment expenditure corresponding to this growth rate. However, if the economy's growth rate slows, business investment expenditures may actually decline, even though the economy's growth rate has only slowed and not actually declined.

Likewise, business investment can accelerate very rapidly if the growth rate of the economy increases, making business investment more volatile than overall economic growth. Business spending on structures and equipment expanded more rapidly than GDP in five of the six economic expansions between the 1960s and the 1990s, and it declined more rapidly than GDP in five of the six recessions during that time period. Between 1980 and 2001, investment spending rose more than GDP in three of the five upturns, and it declined in all four downturns. Trends in

[43]The discussion of investment spending is based on Charles L. Schultze, *Memos to the President: A Guide Through Macroeconomics for the Busy Policymaker* (Washington, DC: Brookings Institution, 1992); Frumkin, *Tracking America's Economy;* Barry P. Bosworth, *Tax Incentives and Economic Growth* (Washington, DC: Brookings Institution, 1984); and Gordon, *Macroeconomics.*

investment spending on new plant and equipment differ from overall GDP because investment can be deferred. Firms can continue operating with existing structures and equipment even if the production process is not the most efficient and is unable to meet sudden surges in demand for the firm's products.

Stimulated by tax cuts and low interest rates, consumer spending first propelled the economy out of the 2001 recession. However, by early 2005, it appeared that business investment spending was also stimulating the economy even though a temporary tax break for business investment had expired in December 2004. After falling sharply during the 2001 recession and stagnating for several years, business-related construction rose in 2004 and 2005 because the excess capacity that previously existed had been absorbed.[44]

Real fixed business investment had small gains in the first half of 2008, decreased slightly in the third quarter, and then fell sharply in the fourth quarter. Downturns in sales, production, and profitability as well as the reduced availability and higher cost of credit all contributed to this decrease. Investment in information technology equipment fell 12.5 percent in the second half of the year as business demand for computers, software, and communications equipment dropped substantially. Fixed investment began to increase in the second half of 2009 as sales, corporate profits, and financial conditions for many businesses improved. Firms started to increase spending on information technology capital to replace older, less-efficient equipment. However, real spending on nonresidential structures continued to decline steeply throughout 2009. This divergence in trends for the different types of fixed investment spending continued in 2010. By 2011 all types of fixed investment spending had begun to increase.[45]

The Real Interest Rate   The real interest rate affects the cost of new capital goods and spending on new residential homes. The rate of return on an investment must be greater than the cost of financing that investment. For a firm, this principle holds whether it is actually borrowing money and paying an explicit interest rate for the use of the funds or whether it is using its own internal funds or retained earnings. In the latter case, the market interest rate represents the opportunity cost of the firm using its own funds, as those funds could have been invested elsewhere at the market interest rate. A firm's investment expenditures are inversely related to market interest rates. A firm will undertake an investment with a 5 percent expected rate of return if the market interest rate is 4 percent, but not if it is 8 percent.[46]

The response to interest rate changes differs between consumption and the various components of investment. Simulations have shown that an unanticipated tightening in monetary policy that raises interest rates first impacts final demand, which falls relatively quickly after a change in policy. Production then starts to decrease, implying that inventories first rise and then fall, contributing to a decrease in overall GDP. Residential investment experiences the earliest and sharpest declines, with spending on both durable and nondurable consumer goods following closely behind. A monetary tightening eventually causes fixed business investment to decline, but this decrease lags behind the changes in housing and consumer durable spending.[47]

---

[44]Timothy Aeppel and Kemba Dunham, "Business Shows Stronger Role in Driving Growth," *Wall Street Journal*, March 7, 2005.

[45]Board of Governors of the Federal Reserve System, *Monetary Policy Report to the Congress*, February 24, 2009, February 24, 2010, March 1, 2011, and July 17, 2012.

[46]As we discussed with consumption spending, the real interest rate will differ from the nominal interest rate in periods of inflation.

[47]Ben S. Bernanke and Mark Gertler, "Inside the Black Box: The Credit Channel of Monetary Policy Transmission," *Journal of Economic Perspectives* 9 (Fall 1995): 27–48.

Businesses whose products require customer borrowing are very sensitive to interest rate changes. For example, the Wisconsin-based Manitowoc Company produces construction cranes whose prices range from $500,000 to $6 million, so most purchases require financing. During the recession of 2001, the company was forced to build cranes in 50–60 days instead of the 120 days that had been typical in the past because their customers were placing orders only after a contract was signed for a construction job instead of six months in advance in anticipation of the signing.[48]

Business Taxes   Business taxes also affect the cost of capital investment for firms. Taxes levied on a firm's earnings, such as the corporate income tax, raise the effective cost of funds. If a firm has to pay some of its return on investment to the government, this return must be higher to justify making the investment.

The government also uses policies such as investment tax credits to stimulate business investment. The effects of these policies on business investment are typically modest and occur over a long period of time. One study estimated that a 10 percent decrease in the cost of capital from an investment tax credit would increase gross investment in GDP by 0.5 percentage point during the five-year period subsequent to the change.[49] This result implies that the increase in annual investment is approximately equal to the loss in tax revenues from the tax credit. The effect of taxes on investment decisions depends on whether these decisions are influenced more by expected sales and income or by the cost of capital and the interest rate. The role of the cost of capital is influenced by the degree to which firms can substitute capital for other inputs of production. **Relative prices**—here, the cost of capital versus the cost of other inputs—play a greater role the more firms are technologically able to substitute capital for other inputs.

The 2003 tax cut we discussed previously affected businesses as well as households. The tax bill included a reduction in the top tax rate on stock dividends from 38.6 to 15 percent, as well as a reduction in the tax rate on capital gains, the increased value of assets that are sold, from 20 to 15 percent. Businesses were also allowed to write off investment expenses more quickly, giving them greater incentives for investment spending.[50]

Although most of the economic-stimulus package passed by Congress in February 2008 was designed to stimulate consumer spending, tax incentives to allow businesses to write off equipment purchases made in 2008 more quickly and to give small firms greater ability to write off their expenses were included in the bill. These incentives were only temporary, which would limit their impact, and might also simply cause a shift in investment spending plans from 2009 to 2008. Other business tax breaks, such as renewable-energy incentives and a provision allowing companies including home builders to obtain tax refunds from previous years when they were profitable, were debated but not included in the final bill.[51]

Modeling the behavior of business investment decisions is more difficult than modeling consumption, and there have been fewer business tax changes designed for stimulus effects. A series of studies has shown that the mix of investment spending is responsive to changes in the user cost of capital. One study indicated that the depreciation incentives in 2002–2004 caused firms to shift from nonqualifying to qualifying investment. Research has also shown that there are different investment

Relative prices
The price of one good in relation to the price of another good.

---

[48]Louis Uchitelle, "Thriving or Hurting, U.S. Manufacturers Brace for the Worst," *New York Times*, March 2, 2001.

[49]Bosworth, *Tax Incentives and Economic Growth*, 109–10.

[50]Greg Ip and John D. McKinnon, "Tax Plan Would Boost Growth, But Would Also Widen Deficits," *Wall Street Journal*, May 23, 2003.

[51]Sarah Lueck, "Congress Approves Economic-Stimulus Bill," *Wall Street Journal*, February 8, 2008; Patrice Hill, "Stimulus Package Seen as Cushion," *McClatchy-Tribune Business News*, February 14, 2008.

spending responses to temporary tax cuts during a recession than would occur in response to long-run tax reforms adopted under more normal circumstances.[52]

Expected Profits and Business Confidence   Firms make capital investments with the expectation that these investments will contribute to future profits. Thus, decisions about adding to capacity are influenced by expectations about the profits that can be obtained from these investments. Expectations about future profits are affected by judgments about whether past rates of profits can be sustained in the future. Rising profits and expanding markets stimulate business confidence and expectations that capital investments will pay off in the future. Increased profits also provide more internal funds to finance capital investments and are a major factor in lenders' and investors' decisions to provide external funds to the firm.

Expectations of large profits helped fuel economic growth during the late 1990s, but resulted in overcapacity in many industries, including computers, chemicals, autos, aircraft, and plastics. Although the recession of 2001 was relatively mild in terms of its effect on GDP, corporate profits declined by 15.9 percent during the year, one of the largest declines since World War II. These changes influenced many business investment decisions.[53]

The terrorist attacks in September 2001 further impacted business confidence and profit expectations. Responding to a survey in October 2001, more than a quarter of the 669 finance officers polled indicated they were postponing capital expenditures as a result of the attacks.[54] Even by April 2002, executives were still wary about future profits and were focusing more on cost-cutting measures than on plant expansion.[55]

Forecasters monitor executives' statements about their expected future profits as an indicator of where the economy is headed.[56] For example, the Conference Board measures business as well as consumer confidence through quarterly surveys of more than 100 chief executives in a wide variety of U.S. industries. This survey asks executives to assess both current economic conditions and conditions in their own industry versus those six months ago and to give their expectations for both the economy and their industry for the following six months.[57]

In January 2008, when the slowdown in the U.S. economy was becoming widely apparent, the Conference Board reported that its Measure of CEO Confidence fell to 39 in the final quarter of 2007 after declining to 44 in the third quarter. The last time the measure fell below 40 was in the final quarter of 2000. This decrease in business confidence was attributed to the trouble in the housing and credit markets, the volatility in the financial markets, and increases in energy prices. In 2008, the measure remained at 39 in the second quarter and 40 in the third quarter, levels associated with recession.[58] Four years later during the slow recovery from the recession, the measure fell from a value of 63 during the first quarter of 2012 to 47 during the second quarter. However, 64 percent of the CEOs surveyed expected profits to increase during the following 12 months, driven primarily by market demand growth.[59]

[52]Auerbach and Gale, "Activist Fiscal Policy to Stabilize Economic Activity."

[53]Louis Uchitelle, "Wary Spending by Executives Cools Economy," *New York Times*, May 14, 2001.

[54]Joann S. Lublin, "Businesses Delay Projects in Wake of Terror Attacks," *Wall Street Journal*, November 13, 2001.

[55]Jon E. Hilsenrath, "Businesses Sing Bottom-Line Blues As Profit Crunch Haunts Recovery," *Wall Street Journal*, April 1, 2002.

[56]Greg Ip, "A Few Economic Cues Should Show When Current Recession Will End," *Wall Street Journal*, January 4, 2002.

[57]The Conference Board, "The Conference Board Measure of CEO Confidence." Available at www .conference-board.org.

[58]The Conference Board, "CEO Confidence Declines Again, The Conference Board Reports," January 15, 2008; "CEOs Still Lacking Confidence, The Conference Board Reports," October 16, 2008. Available at www .conference-board.org.

[59]The Conference Board, "CEO Confidence Declines," July 5, 2012. Available at www.conference-board.org.

In the summer of 2012, businesses also reported cancelling new investments due to the uncertainty created by Congress regarding the impending tax increases and budget cuts in 2013. Given this uncertainty, Hubbell Inc., an electrical products manufacturer, announced that it had cancelled several million dollars' worth of equipment orders and delayed long-planned factory upgrades. The chief executive of Eaton, an Ohio maker of industrial equipment, called the situation "economic purgatory."[60]

Capacity Utilization Business investment in new structures and equipment also depends on the stock of capital goods on hand and how much they are utilized. **Capacity utilization rates (*CURs*)** are prepared monthly by the Federal Reserve Board for the manufacturing, mining, and electric and gas utilities industries. The CUR is the ratio of production (the numerator) to capacity (the denominator). For example, if a factory can produce 1,000 automobiles per month and is currently producing 750, its utilization rate is 75 percent. Higher CURs give firms the incentive to expand capacity through investment in new structures and equipment. Forecasters often estimate that there is a CUR threshold level at about 83 to 85 percent. Above this threshold, businesses increase investment in structures and equipment in order to expand capacity to meet anticipated demand for their products. Below this threshold, businesses are assumed to cut back on capital spending and concentrate on replacing inefficient and outmoded facilities. The Federal Reserve also looks at this threshold as an indicator of inflationary pressure in the economy, as firms are utilizing most of their existing capacity. The newer just-in-time inventory management methods used by many firms may change the role of capacity utilization in influencing business investment because fewer structures are needed to hold inventories. Capacity is considered to be "normal" operating time for each industry. The measure is also based only on U.S. operations, and may be influenced by mergers and acquisitions.[61] Figure 12.5 shows CURs for 2000 to 2012.

Capacity utilization rates (*CURs*)
The ratio of production to capacity calculated monthly for the manufacturing, mining, and electric and gas utilities industries and used as an indicator of business investment spending on structures and equipment.

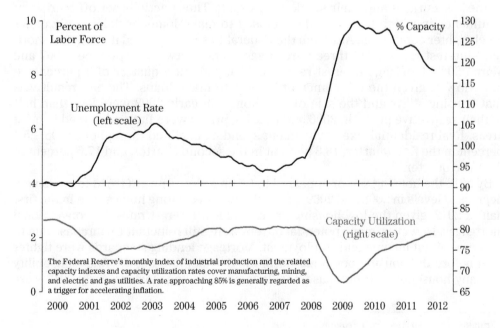

The Federal Reserve's monthly index of industrial production and the related capacity indexes and capacity utilization rates cover manufacturing, mining, and electric and gas utilities. A rate approaching 85% is generally regarded as a trigger for accelerating inflation.

FIGURE 12.5
Resource Utilization and Constraints
The Federal Reserve's monthly index of industrial production and the related capacity indexes and capacity utilization rates cover manufacturing, mining, and electric and gas utilities. The industrial sector, together with construction, accounts for the bulk of the variation in national output over the course of the business cycle. A capacity utilization rate approaching 85 percent is generally regarded as a trigger for accelerating inflation.
Source: Federal Reserve Economic Data (FRED II), Economic Research, Federal Reserve Bank of St. Louis, http://research.stlouisfed.org/fred2/.

---

[60]Nelson D. Schwartz, "Fearing an Impasse in Congress, Industry Cuts Spending," *The New York Times (Online)*, August 5, 2012.
[61]Baumohl, *The Secrets of Economic Indicators*, 3rd. ed., 170–80.

Residential Investment Spending   Spending on new residential construction is included as investment even though most of this spending is done by households and is part of household wealth. Similar to business fixed investment, residential investment is in long-lived structures that depreciate over time. BEA statisticians also consider that households are in the business of owning a home.

Both long- and short-term factors affect residential investment spending.[62] Demographic variables, such as trends in population, migration, and household formulation, are the major factors influencing new housing construction over the long run. Household formation is affected by marriage and divorce rates, adult children moving in or out of their parents' homes, and the sharing of structures by unrelated individuals. Other factors influencing long-run housing construction include the replacement of houses lost from the existing inventory and the demand for second homes. Short-term factors include the effects of business cycle expansions and recessions on employment, interest rates, and inflation. The housing market is particularly sensitive to changes in mortgage interest rates. Thus, income and the real interest rate are important influences on the residential construction component of gross private domestic investment.

The residential housing market was the crucial sector regarding the recession of 2007–2009. Beginning in the early years of the decade, both private lenders and government agencies, such as Freddie Mac and Fannie Mae, began promoting mortgages to subprime borrowers with poor credit records to buy homes with little or no money down. It is estimated that the percentage of subprime borrowers who did not fully document their income and assets increased from about 17 percent in early 2000 to 44 percent in 2006. Repayment of these loans was based on the premise that housing prices would continue to increase. These loans were also packaged into complex securities that were bought and sold throughout the financial system. When housing prices deflated in 2007, borrowers defaulted on their loans and financial institutions were left holding securities of uncertain value. Major investment banks took huge losses as they wrote down the value of these securities and their stock prices sank. These actions set off a crisis of confidence in which lenders either refused to make loans or did so only under much tighter conditions. Although the Federal Reserve lowered its targeted short-term interest rates a full three percentage points between September 2007 and March 2008, mortgage interest rates were only about a quarter of a percentage point lower, given the reluctance of lenders to make loans. The end result was that housing starts and the sale of new homes in early 2008 were less than half of their respective peaks in 2006 and housing prices were flat or declined in most areas. Real residential fixed investment spending declined throughout 2008: 25.1 percent in the first quarter, 13.3 percent in the second quarter, and 17.6 percent in the third quarter.[63]

By 2012 the housing sector appeared to be on a slow upward trend from its very depressed levels in 2008 and 2009. Sales of new and existing homes rose in the first half of 2012, given the low housing prices and low interest rates for conventional mortgages. However, many potential buyers were still reluctant to purchase due to concerns about income and employment. Mortgage lending standards were tighter than before the housing boom earlier in the decade, limiting the financing ability of many households to purchase. Single-family housing starts in early 2012 were

[62]Frumkin, *Tracking America's Economy*, 4th ed.
[63]Greg Ip, James R. Hagerty, and Jonathan Karp, "Housing Bust Fuels Blame Game," *Wall Street Journal*, February 27, 2008; Patterson, "How the Credit Mess Squeezes You."; Opdyke and Kim, "Why Only Some See Benefit from Fed's Cuts."; Testimony, Chairman Ben S. Bernanke, *Semiannual Monetary Report to the Congress*. Before the Committee on Financial Services, U.S. House of Representatives, February 27, 2008; U.S. Bureau of Economic Analysis News Release, November 25, 2008.

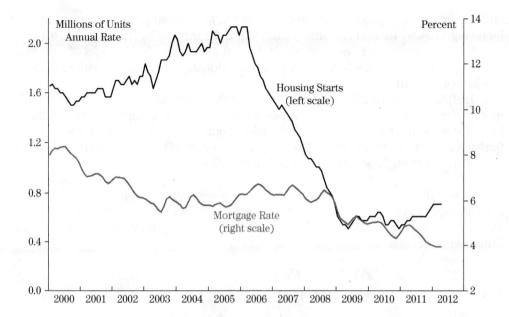

FIGURE 12.6
Housing Starts and Mortgage Rates
Residential investment spending is strongly influenced by mortgage interest rates.
Source: Federal Reserve Economic Data (FRED II), Economic Research, Federal Reserve Bank of St. Louis, http://research.stlouisfed.org/fred2/.

still less than half of the average pace of the previous 50 years.[64] Figure 12.6 shows housing starts and mortgage rates for the period 2000 to 2012.[65]

Inventory Investment   Inventory investment is more volatile than other forms of investment spending because inventories can be increased and decreased relatively quickly. Mistakes in inventory holdings can be reversed with less cost than incorrect decisions regarding the construction of new structures. Similar to nonresidential business investment, inventories are closely related to sales and the level of income in the economy. Although inventory spending is typically only approximately 1 percent of GDP, since World War II, changes in inventory investment have contributed more than twice as much to fluctuations in GDP than any other single component.[66] A decrease in inventory investment has accounted for 87 percent of the drop in GDP during the average postwar recession in the United States.[67]

The concern at the end of 2007 was housing inventories. The Federal Reserve chairman testified in February 2008 that homebuilders, "still faced with abnormally high inventories of unsold homes, are likely to cut the pace of their building activity further, which will subtract from overall growth and reduce employment in residential construction and closely related industries."[68] In December 2008, he noted that inventories of unsold new homes were still close to their record high, suggesting that residential construction was likely to "remain soft in the near term."[69]

At the end of 2008, inventories of unsold automobiles were also a major problem. Chrysler LLC announced that it would stop all manufacturing operations for at least a month, while General Motors Corp., Toyota Motor Corp., and Honda Motor Co.

---

[64]Board of Governors of the Federal Reserve System, *Monetary Policy Report to the Congress*, July 17, 2012.

[65]Different indicators of the state of the housing market are discussed by Baumohl, *The Secrets of Economic Indicators*, 3rd. ed., 204–31.

[66]Schultze, *Memos to the President*, 78–79.

[67]Alan S. Blinder and Louis J. Maccini, "Taking Stock: A Critical Assessment of Recent Research on Inventories," *Journal of Economic Perspectives* 5 (Winter 1991): 73–96.

[68]Testimony, Chairman Ben S. Bernanke, February 27, 2008.

[69]Board of Governors of the Federal Reserve System, Speech, Chairman Ben S. Bernanke at the Federal Reserve System Conference on Housing and Mortgage Markets, Washington, DC, December 4, 2008.

all announced steep production cuts. Toyota had already shut one of the two manufacturing lines at its San Antonio plant.[70] In February 2009, the Federal Reserve noted that the collapse in auto sales in fall 2008 pushed dealers' stocks of cars and light trucks to 100 days, which was well above industry norms and resulted in large production cuts in 2009.[71]

In the first quarter of 2012 motor vehicle inventories surged as automakers rebuilt inventories following the natural disasters disrupting global supply chains in 2011. Inventory-to-sales ratios for most industries suggested that stocks of goods were fairly well aligned with the rate of sales. A general rule of thumb is to have this ratio around 1.5 or enough inventory to provide for 1.5 months of sales.[72]

Investment spending function

The functional relationship between investment spending and income, holding all other variables that influence investment spending constant.

Investment Spending Function   The **investment spending function**—the functional relationship between investment spending and income, holding all other variables that influence investment spending constant—is shown in Equation 12.3:

$$\textbf{12.3} \quad I = f(Y, r, T_B, PR, CU)$$
$$(+)(-)(-)(+)(+)$$

where

I = investment spending
Y = real income
r = real interest rate
T_B = business taxes
PR = expected profits and business confidence
CU = capacity utilization

A linear relationship between investment spending and income is shown in Figure 12.4b and Equation 12.4.

$$\textbf{12.4} \quad I = I_0 + i_1 Y$$

where

I_0 = autonomous investment expenditure
i_1 = marginal propensity to invest
Y = real income

The slope of the investment function, i_1 in Equation 12.4, shows how investment spending changes with changes in income, or the marginal propensity to invest. These are induced investment expenditures. The vertical intercept, I_0, shows autonomous investment expenditures determined by the other factors in Equation 12.3 that are unrelated to income. The effects of all of these factors from Equation 12.3, discussed above, are combined to form the constant term, I_0, in Equation 12.4.[73]

---

[70]Lauren Pollock and Neal E. Boudette, "Chrysler to Close Manufacturing Plants for a Month Starting Friday," *Wall Street Journal*, December 17, 2008; Yoshio Takahashi and Kate Linebaugh, "Toyota Sees First Loss in 70 Years," *Wall Street Journal*, December 23, 2008.

[71]Board of Governors of the Federal Reserve System, *Monetary Policy Report to the Congress*, February 24, 2009.

[72]Board of Governors of the Federal Reserve System, *Monetary Policy Report to the Congress*, July 17, 2012; Baumohl, *The Secrets of Economic Indicators*, 3rd.ed., 162–69.

[73]Different combinations of these factors affect the three components of investment spending as noted in the discussion above.

Government Expenditure

Government expenditure in the national income accounts includes both consumption and investment expenditures by all levels of government—federal, state, and local—but does not include transfer payments from government to government or from government to individuals. For modeling purposes, we assume that all government expenditure is autonomous or determined by factors other than the level of real income in the economy. Government expenditure policy is determined by the legislative and executive institutions at all levels of government. The interplay of these institutions, political agendas, and unexpected events, such as the terrorist attacks in September 2001, influences the level of government spending as recorded in the national income accounts.

Federal government spending is used as an instrument of **fiscal policy**—changes in taxes and government expenditure designed to pursue the macroeconomic goals of full employment and low inflation. These spending changes can still be considered as autonomous—the result of policy decisions and not the level of real income.[74] The impact of fiscal policy and many political debates regarding the amount and types of government spending depend on the relationship between government revenue and expenditure or whether there is a **budget surplus** (revenue greater than expenditure) **or deficit** (revenue less than expenditure).

Figure 12.7 shows the relationship between federal government revenue and expenditure for the period 2000 to 2011. The Congressional Budget Office estimated that the budget deficit in fiscal year 2011 was $1.3 trillion or 8.7 percent of GDP. Revenues grew by $140 billion (6 percent) from 2010 to 2011, while federal spending grew by 4 percent to $3.6 trillion. Mandatory programs, governed by statutory criteria and not controlled by the annual appropriations process, accounted

Government expenditure
The total amount of spending by federal, state, and local governments on consumption outlays for goods and services, depreciation charges for existing structures and equipment, and investment capital outlays for newly acquired structures and equipment in a given period of time.

Fiscal policy
The use of expenditure and taxation policies by the federal government to pursue the macroeconomic goals of full employment and low inflation.

Budget surplus/deficit
The relationship between federal government revenue and expenditure with a surplus indicating revenue greater than expenditure and a deficit indicating revenue less than expenditure.

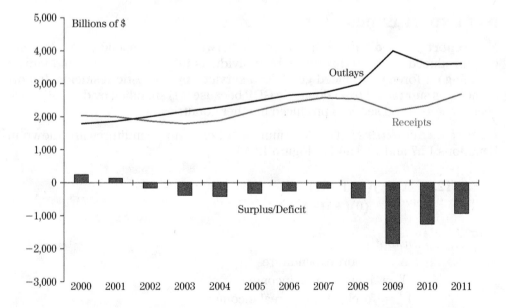

FIGURE 12.7
Federal Government Budget
The relationship between federal government revenue and expenditure determines whether there is a budget surplus or deficit.
Source: Federal Reserve Economic Data (FRED II), Economic Research, Federal Reserve Bank of St. Louis, http://research.stlouisfed.org/fred2/.

---

[74]This is a simplifying assumption used in the model. Some government expenditures, such as unemployment compensation, act as automatic stabilizers because they rise when real income falls and vice versa. Income taxes also act as automatic stabilizers. See Alan J. Auerbach and Daniel Feenberg, "The Significance of Federal Taxes as Automatic Stabilizers," *Journal of Economic Perspectives* 14 (Summer 2000): 37–56; and Darrel Cohen and Glenn Follette, "The Automatic Fiscal Stabilizers: Quietly Doing Their Thing," *FRBNY Economic Policy Review*, April 2000, 35–68.

for most of the change in expenditure in 2011. Total discretionary budget authority, authority provided in appropriation acts to incur financial obligations resulting in immediate or future outlays, decreased by $42 billion in fiscal year 2011.[75] Real federal government expenditure on consumption and gross investment, the part of federal spending included in the calculation of GDP, fell at an annual rate of 6 percent in the first quarter of 2012.[76]

The assumptions about government spending are incorporated in the government spending function in Equations 12.5 and 12.6 and in Figure 12.4c:

$$12.5 \quad G = f(Y, Policy)$$
$$ (0) \ (+)$$

where

G = government spending

Y = real income

Policy = institutional policy decisions at all levels of government

$$12.6 \quad G = G_0$$

where

G = government expenditure

G_0 = autonomous government expenditure

Both the equations and the figure show that government spending is assumed to be determined only by policy decisions and not by the level of real income in the economy. Autonomous government spending, G_0, is represented by the horizontal line in Figure 12.4c.

Net Export Expenditure

Net export expenditure
The difference between export spending on domestically produced goods and services by individuals in other countries and import spending on foreign-produced goods and services by domestic residents in a given period of time.

Net export expenditure is the difference between export spending on domestically produced goods and services by individuals in other countries and import spending on foreign-produced goods and services by domestic residents. Import spending is subtracted from domestic GDP because it is spending by domestic residents on goods and services produced in other countries.

Export Expenditure The determinants of export expenditures are shown in Equations 12.7 and 12.8 and in Figure 12.4d.

$$12.7 \quad X = f(Y, Y^*, R)$$
$$ (0)(+)(-)$$

where

X = export expenditure

Y = domestic real income

Y^* = foreign GDP or real income

R = currency exchange rate

---

[75]Congressional Budget Office, *The Budget and Economic Outlook: Fiscal Years 2012 to 2022*. Available at www.cbo.gov.

[76]Board of Governors of the Federal Reserve System, *Monetary Policy Report to the Congress*, July 17, 2012. Available at www.federalreserve.gov.

12.8 $X = X_0$

where

X = export spending

X_0 = autonomous export spending

We assume that export expenditures are unaffected by the level of domestic GDP or real income, but are positively influenced by the level of real income or GDP in the rest of the world. As economic activity in foreign economies increases, those individuals will spend some of that income on United States domestically produced goods and services. Thus, U.S. export spending is not affected by U.S. real income, but is influenced by the economic activity of its major trading partners, such as Japan and the European Union.

Export spending is also influenced by the **currency exchange rate**, or the rate at which one nation's currency can be exchanged for that of another, which is determined in foreign exchange markets. In this text, we define the exchange rate, R, as the number of units of foreign currency per U.S. dollar. As R increases, the dollar appreciates, and more units of foreign currency can be purchased for a dollar. If R decreases, the dollar depreciates, and fewer units of foreign currency can be purchased for a dollar. If the dollar appreciates against a foreign currency such as the Japanese yen, the yen depreciates against the dollar. Fewer dollars can be purchased for a given number of yen.

Tables 12.1 and 12.2 show the effects of both the depreciation and the appreciation of the dollar on U.S. exports and imports. Table 12.1 shows the depreciation of the U.S. dollar against the Japanese yen that occurred between January 2008 and January 2009. This change made U.S. exports less expensive and imports more expensive, so that exports increased and imports decreased. The opposite case held for the U.S. dollar and the yen between January 2009 and June 2009 in Table 12.2. The dollar appreciated against the yen, so that U.S. exports became more expensive and imports less expensive, which caused exports to decrease and imports to increase. Thus, export spending is inversely related to the currency exchange rate in Equation 12.7.

Equation 12.8 and Figure 12.4d show the level of export spending as autonomous or represented by a horizontal line. The level of this spending is determined by the level of foreign income and the exchange rate, not by the level of domestic real income.

Currency exchange rate
The rate at which one nation's currency can be exchanged for that of another, which is determined in foreign exchange markets.

TABLE 12.1   Effect of Dollar Depreciation on Exports and Imports

R = ¥/$	DOMESTIC PRICE	JAN 08: R = 108	JAN 09: R = 90	EFFECT
U.S. exports—computers	$10,000	¥1,080,000	¥900,000	X increases
U.S. imports—Japanese cars	¥2,000,0000	≈ $18,500	≈ $22,200	M decreases

TABLE 12.2   Effect of Dollar Appreciation on Exports and Imports

R = ¥/$	DOMESTIC PRICE	JAN 09: R = 90	JUNE 09: R = 97	EFFECT
U.S. exports—computers	$10,000	¥900,000	¥970,000	X decreases
U.S. imports—Japanese cars	¥2,000,000	$22,200	$20,600	M increases

Import Expenditure   The determinants of import expenditures are shown in Equations 12.9 and 12.10 and in Figure 12.4e.

$$12.9 \quad M = f(Y, R)$$
$$(+)(+)$$

where

M = import spending
Y = domestic real income
R = currency exchange rate

$$12.10 \quad M = M_0 + m_1 Y$$

where

M = import spending
M_0 = autonomous import spending
m_1 = marginal propensity to import
Y = domestic real income

The level of U.S. import spending is affected by the level of domestic real income, as U.S. residents will spend part of any increase in their income on goods and services produced by countries in the rest of the world.[77] Thus, the import spending line in Figure 12.4e has a positive slope, which is the marginal propensity to import (m_1) in Equation 12.10. Autonomous import spending, M_0, is influenced by the currency exchange rate, R. For example, as R increases or the U.S. currency appreciates against the yen, the level of spending on imports from Japan will increase because U.S. residents can purchase more yen for every dollar. This change causes M_0 to increase in both Equation 12.10 and Figure 12.4e.

Net Exports   In the second half of 2011 U.S. net exports rose at an annual rate of 4.75 percent strengthened by continued growth in overall foreign economic activity and delayed effects of the decline in the exchange rate of the dollar earlier in the year. The increase in exports was concentrated in the emerging market economies, while exports to the Euro area declined at the end of the year. The moderate growth in U.S. economic activity meant that import spending decreased from a 5 percent to a 3 percent annual rate. Net exports contributed about 0.25 percent to real U.S. GDP growth in the second half of 2011.[78]

The biggest concern in the first half of 2012 was the potential global economic slowdown. In May, the Organization for Economic Cooperation and Development cut its 2012 forecast for growth in developed economies, while the International Monetary Fund projected the global economy would grow more slowly than the 3.9 percent rate in 2011. Valspar, a global paint supplier, noted that almost all of its business in China had weakened. Hewlett-Packard worried whether conditions in Europe would be worse than expected.[79]

---

[77]All sectors of the economy import goods and services. BEA statisticians aggregate these import expenditures into one number, which is then subtracted from total export spending.

[78]Board of Governors of the Federal Reserve System, *Monetary Policy Report to the Congress*, February 29, 2012.

[79]Jon Hilsenrath and Joshua Mitchell, "New Signs of Global Slowdown," *Wall Street Journal (Online)*, May 25, 2012.

In the summer of 2012 Europe's crisis cut into the profits of U.S. companies, ranging from Ford Motor Co. to Apple, Inc., because Europe accounted for approximately one-fifth of all U.S. exports. Many Standard & Poor's 500 companies cited European economic conditions as a factor influencing their lower-than-expected revenue in the second quarter. Companies were concerned that austerity measures in Europe would continue to decrease sales in 2013. The strong dollar also had a negative effect on profits of U.S. companies. Colgate-Palmolive Co. reported that currency issues cut its profits by 9 percent during the second quarter, while Coca-Cola Co. expected exchange rates to decrease its profits by 8 percent to 9 percent in the third quarter. The strong dollar resulted from the weakness in the European economy and from inflows of foreign investment to the United States.[80]

Aggregate Expenditure and Equilibrium Income and Output

We now combine the components discussed above to define aggregate expenditure and the equilibrium level of income and output.

Aggregate Expenditure

Aggregate expenditure (E) represents the planned spending on currently produced goods and services by all sectors of the economy, as shown in Equation 12.11:

12.11 $E = C + I + G + X - M$

where

E = aggregate expenditure
C = consumption expenditure
I = investment expenditure
G = government expenditure
X = export spending
M = import spending

The general form of the **aggregate expenditure function**, which is the relationship between aggregate expenditure and income, holding all other variables constant, is shown in Equation 12.12:

12.12 $E = f(Y, T_P, r, CC, W, CR, D, T_B, PR, CU, G, Y^*, R)$
$(+)(-)(-)(+)(+)(+)(-)(-)(+)(+)(+)(+)(-)$

Aggregate expenditure function
The relationship between aggregate expenditure and income, holding all other variables constant.

where

E = aggregate expenditure
Y = real income
T_P = personal taxes
r = real interest rate
CC = consumer confidence

[80]Sam Schechner and Kate Linebaugh, "Europe's Crisis Hits Profits," *Wall Street Journal (Online)*, July 26, 2012; Chana R. Schoenberger and Nicole Hong, "Dollar's Surprising Strength Eats Into the Bottom Line," *Wall Street Journal (Online)*, July 29, 2012.

$$W = \text{consumer wealth}$$
$$CR = \text{consumer credit}$$
$$D = \text{consumer debt}$$
$$T_B = \text{business taxes}$$
$$PR = \text{expected profits}$$
$$CU = \text{capacity utilization}$$
$$G = \text{government spending}$$
$$Y^* = \text{foreign GDP or real income}$$
$$R = \text{currency exchange rate}$$

Equation 12.12 includes all the variables affecting each component of aggregate expenditure drawn from Equations 12.1, 12.3, 12.5, 12.7, and 12.9. Aggregate expenditure is a function of real income, holding constant all the other variables in Equation 12.12. A change in any of these variables would cause a shift in the expenditure function.

Equation 12.13 is the linear version of the aggregate expenditure function in Equation 12.12.[81]

12.13 $E = E_0 + (c_1 + i_1 - m_1)Y$

where

$$E = \text{aggregate expenditure}$$
$$E_0 = \text{sum of all autonomous expenditure components}$$
$$c_1 = \text{marginal propensity to consume}$$
$$i_1 = \text{marginal propensity to invest}$$
$$m_1 = \text{marginal propensity to import}$$
$$Y = \text{real income}$$

Figure 12.8 shows a graph of Equation 12.13. The vertical intercept in Figure 12.8 is autonomous aggregate expenditure, E_0, from Equation 12.13. A change in any of the variables other than real income (Y) in Equation 12.12 will cause E_0 in Equation 12.13 to change and the aggregate expenditure function in Figure 12.8 to shift. For example, an increase in consumer confidence, all else assumed constant, will shift the aggregate expenditure function up (higher aggregate expenditure at

FIGURE 12.8

Aggregate Expenditure Function
The vertical intercept, E_0, represents autonomous aggregate expenditure that is determined by factors other than real income. The slope of the function shows how various expenditures are induced by increases in real income.

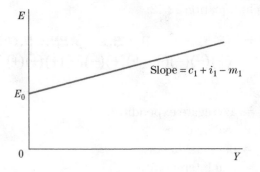

$^{81}E = C + I + G + X - M$
$E = C_0 + c_1Y + I_0 + i_1Y + G_0 + X_0 - M_0 - m_1Y$
$E = C_0 + I_0 + G_0 + X_0 - M_0 + c_1Y + i_1Y - m_1Y$
$E = E_0 + (c_1 + i_1 - m_1)Y, \textit{ where } E_0 = C_0 + I_0 + G_0 + X_0 - M_0$

every level of income), while an increase in personal taxes will shift the aggregate expenditure line down (lower aggregate expenditure at every level of income).[82]

The slope of the aggregate expenditure function in Equation 12.13 and Figure 12.8 is the sum of the marginal propensities to consume, invest, and import. The slope shows how various expenditures are induced by increases in real income. Higher marginal propensities to consume and invest out of income make the slope of the line steeper. A larger marginal propensity to import makes the aggregate expenditure function flatter because imports are subtracted from domestic GDP.

Equilibrium Level of Income and Output

We now use the aggregate expenditure function to define the equilibrium level of income and output. We first show why this equilibrium level exists and how income and output levels will change if the economy is in a disequilibrium state. We then discuss and illustrate changes in equilibrium levels of income and output.[83]

Definition of Equilibrium   The **equilibrium level of income and output** is that level of income at which the desired spending by all sectors of the economy just equals the value of the aggregate output produced and the income received from that production. At any other level of income, desired spending either exceeds the value of the output produced or is insufficient to purchase all of that output. In symbolic terms, equilibrium is shown in Equation 12.14:

12.14 $E = Y$

We can also use the definition in Equation 12.14 to define equilibrium in terms of injections into and leakages from the circular flow of economic activity. An **injection** is any supplement to consumer spending, the main component of the circular flow, that increases domestic aggregate output and income. Injections include business investment spending, government spending, and spending by foreigners on domestic exports, which represent additions to the circular flow of economic activity. **Leakages** are any uses of current income for purposes other than purchasing current domestically produced goods and services. Leakages, which include saving, tax payments (both personal and business), and spending on imports, represent withdrawals from the circular flow of economic activity.

In equilibrium, injections must equal leakages in the economy. There will be no tendency for income to either increase or decrease if this condition holds. The alternative definitions of equilibrium are shown in Table 12.3 for our model of an open, mixed economy.

Equilibrium level of income and output
The level of income or, equivalently, the aggregate output where the desired spending by all sectors of the economy just equals the value of the aggregate output produced and the income received from that production.

Injections
Any supplement to consumer spending that increases domestic aggregate output and income.

Leakages
Any uses of current income for purposes other than purchasing currently produced domestic goods and services.

TABLE 12.3   Equilibrium in the Open, Mixed Economy Model

$E = Y$	INJECTIONS = LEAKAGES
$C + I + G + X - M = C + S + T$	$I + G + X = S + T + M$

Note: Total taxes equal personal plus business taxes or $T = T_P + T_B$.

[82]In this example, we have assumed that personal taxes, T_P, are not a function of the level of real income. Given the importance of the federal income tax in the U.S. economy, this assumption is unrealistic. If taxes are both autonomous and a function of income ($T_P = T_0 + tY$, where T_0 represents autonomous personal taxes and t is the tax rate applied to income), both the slope and the vertical intercept of the aggregate expenditure function are affected by taxes. This change does not affect the underlying analysis developed here.
[83]This analysis was developed by John Maynard Keynes and is usually called the Keynesian model.

Simplified Illustration of Equilibrium Income and Output   We first illustrate equilibrium income with the following simplified aggregate expenditure function, Equation 12.15, which is based on Equation 12.13:

12.15 $E = E_0 + c_1Y$

where

E = aggregate expenditure
E_0 = sum of all autonomous expenditure components
c_1 = marginal propensity to consume
Y = real income

In Equation 12.15, we assume that all investment and import expenditures are autonomous and, therefore, not dependent on income, so that the i_1 and m_1 terms in Equation 12.13 equal zero. We also assume that taxes are lump sum or not a function of the level of income. All autonomous expenditures in Equation 12.15 are included in E_0, while c_1 equals the marginal propensity to consume.

We illustrate equilibrium in Figure 12.9, where E_I is an aggregate expenditure function with autonomous expenditure E_0 and a slope equal to the marginal propensity to consume (c_1). The aggregate expenditure function is a behavioral relationship that shows planned or desired expenditure by all sectors of the economy as a function of real income. The other line in the graph is a 45-degree line drawn from the origin, a theoretical construct that enables us to define equilibrium. At all points on the 45-degree line, aggregate expenditure (E) equals real income (Y) by definition. Equilibrium is defined as that level of income (Y_E) where the aggregate expenditure line crosses the 45-degree line (point A in Figure 12.9). Only at this level of income and output is the desired expenditure equal to the value of output produced and income generated.[84]

Adjustment Toward Equilibrium   It may be easiest to understand the concept of equilibrium if we examine what happens when the economy moves from one equilibrium to another. In Figure 12.10, suppose the starting equilibrium is at point A. This equilibrium level of income will change when any of the factors affecting autonomous expenditures in Equation 12.12 change. Changes in these factors will cause a shift in the aggregate expenditure function, as illustrated in Figure 12.10. In this figure, an increase in autonomous aggregate expenditures from E_0 to E_1 shifts the aggregate expenditure function from E_I to E_{II}. The original equilibrium, point A on E_I, is no longer an equilibrium because the desired spending (point C) is now greater than income and output at income level YE_1. At this level of real

FIGURE 12.9

Equilibrium Level of Income

Equilibrium is that level of real income, Y_E, where the aggregate expenditure line, E_I, crosses the 45° line. Only at this level of income and output is desired expenditure just equal to the value of the output produced and income generated.

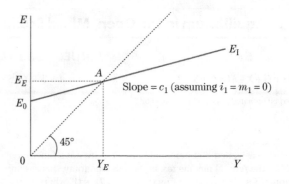

---

[84]Figure 12.9 is often called the Keynesian cross.

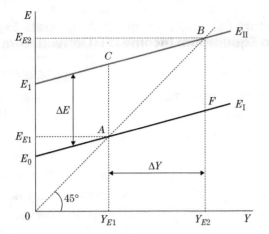

FIGURE 12.10
Changes in Equilibrium
*An increase in autonomous
aggregate expenditure from E_0 to
E_1 shifts the aggregate expenditure
line from E_I to E_{II}, resulting in an
increase in the equilibrium level of
income from Y_{E1} to Y_{E2}. The change
in income is greater than the change
in expenditure due to the multiplier
effect.*

income, individuals and governments now want to purchase more real goods and services than are currently produced. To meet this desired spending, firms have to draw down on their existing inventories of goods. This spending on inventories, or **unplanned inventory decrease**, represented by the distance CA in Figure 12.10, gives firms the incentive to increase production, which generates more real income and results in more aggregate expenditure or a movement along E_{II}. This incentive to increase production exists until reaching point B on aggregate expenditure function E_{II}, where the desired spending equals the amount of real output produced and income generated.

> **Unplanned inventory decrease**
> An unexpected decrease in inventories that occurs when desired aggregate expenditure exceeds the level of output currently produced.

The opposite situation exists if we begin our analysis at point B on aggregate expenditure function E_{II} with equilibrium income Y_{E2}. Suppose that autonomous expenditures decrease from E_1 to E_0, so that the aggregate expenditure function shifts down from E_{II} to E_I. Desired or planned expenditure at income level Y_{E2} is now represented by point F, a point below the 45-degree line. At point F, desired aggregate expenditure is less than the amount of currently produced goods and services. Firms cannot sell all of their goods, so there is an **unplanned inventory increase**, represented by the distance BF. This value of goods is put into firms' inventory. This situation then gives firms the incentive to decrease production, which generates lower real output and income and less aggregate expenditure (a movement along E_I). Firms have the incentive to continue decreasing production until desired expenditure just equals output and real income (point A). Thus, point A represents the new equilibrium level of income and output.

> **Unplanned inventory increase**
> An unexpected increase in inventories that occurs when desired aggregate expenditure is insufficient to purchase the level of output currently produced.

Numerous examples of inventory adjustment to a new equilibrium are reported in the *Wall Street Journal* and other business publications.[85] In describing the conditions *leading to the* recession in 2001, the *Wall Street Journal* reported:

> Manufacturers were largely blindsided by the dramatic drop in demand for their products and left holding too much inventory. To compensate, they slashed production faster than demand was falling. It happened with far greater speed and determination than in past slowdowns, especially among industrial manufacturers in the Midwest.[86]

---

[85]Remember that changes in inventories are counted as investment spending (I) in the national income accounts.
[86]Clare Ansberry, "Manufacturers Are Showing Some Faint Signs of Recovery," *Wall Street Journal*, December 6, 2001.

TABLE 12.4   Factors Causing Changes in Aggregate Expenditure (*E*) and Equilibrium Income (*Y*) (Derived from Equation 12.12)

	INCREASE IN *E, Y*		DECREASE IN *E, Y*	
FACTOR	IMPACT ON EXPENDITURE COMPONENT	FACTOR	IMPACT ON EXPENDITURE COMPONENT	
Decrease T_P	Increase *C*	Increase T_P	Decrease *C*	
Decrease *r*	Increase *C, I*	Increase *r*	Decrease *C, I*	
Increase *CC*	Increase *C*	Decrease *CC*	Decrease *C*	
Increase *W*	Increase *C*	Decrease *W*	Decrease *C*	
Increase *CR*	Increase *C*	Decrease *CR*	Decrease *C*	
Decrease *D*	Increase *C*	Increase *D*	Decrease *C*	
Decrease T_B	Increase *I*	Increase T_B	Decrease *I*	
Increase *PR*	Increase *I*	Decrease *PR*	Decrease *I*	
Increase *CU*	Increase *I*	Decrease *CU*	Decrease *I*	
Increase *G*	Increase *G*	Decrease *G*	Decrease *G*	
Increase *Y**	Increase *X*	Decrease *Y**	Decrease *X*	
Decrease *R*	Increase *X*, Decrease *M*	Increase *R*	Decrease *X*, Increase *M*	

Inventories are then drawn down before production is increased again. In the fourth quarter of 2001, James Glassman of J.P. Morgan Chase estimated that inventories were falling at a rate of 7 to 8 percent. CNW Marketing Research estimated that at least 70,000 automobile sales did not occur in December 2001 because dealers did not have the cars in inventory. In January 2001 18 of Ford Motor Company's 22 North American plants were idle, but by January 2002, all were in operation again to begin production for current sales and to replenish inventories.[87]

In early 2008 industry analysts estimated that light vehicle sales for the coming year would be 15.4 million or 2.5 percent less than anticipated. To minimize unintended inventory accumulation, Chrysler announced that it would broaden its traditional two-week shutdown in summer 2008 to include the entire company. Toyota Motor Corp. stated that it would cut production of big pickup trucks and sport-utility vehicles at two of its U.S. plants.[88]

The factors that can cause changes in aggregate expenditure and equilibrium income are summarized in Table 12.4. A change in any of these variables will cause the aggregate expenditure line, E_I, in Figure 12.10 to shift.

The Multiplier   You can see in Figure 12.10 that the increase in equilibrium income from Y_{E1} to Y_{E2} (ΔY) is greater than the increase in autonomous expenditure (ΔE) when aggregate expenditure increases from E_0 to E_1. This is the multiplier effect of a change in autonomous expenditure.

We illustrate the multiplier by substituting the aggregate expenditure function, Equation 12.15, into the equilibrium Equation 12.14, and solving for *Y* in Equations 12.16 through 12.19:

---

[87]Greg Ip, "A Few Economic Cues."

[88]John D. Stoll and Josee Valcourt, "Woes Continue to Thwart Auto Makers," *Wall Street Journal*, March 14, 2008.

12.16 $Y = E_0 + c_1 Y$

12.17 $Y - c_1 Y = E_0$

12.18 $Y(1 - c_1) = E_0$

12.19 $Y = \dfrac{E_0}{(1 - c_1)}$

Equation 12.19 shows that the equilibrium level of income is the level of autonomous expenditures multiplied by the term $1/(1 - c_1)$, where c_1 is the marginal propensity to consume. This term is called the **multiplier** because it shows the multiplied change in real income and output resulting from a change in autonomous expenditure. With $i_1 = m_1 = 0$, the size of the multiplier depends on the size of the marginal propensity to consume. Thus, if the marginal propensity to consume is 0.75, the multiplier is 4. Any increase in autonomous expenditure will generate an increase in equilibrium income four times as large.

The multiplier effect results from the fact that an increase in autonomous expenditure represents an injection of new spending into the circular flow of economic activity. For example, if the injection is an increase in government spending, an equal increase in income will be generated. If the marginal propensity to consume is 0.75, consumers will spend 75 percent of that increase in income. This will generate a further increase in income, of which consumers will spend 75 percent. This process will continue, with the increase in consumer spending becoming smaller in each round. The end result is a multiple increase in income determined by the size of the marginal propensity to consume and the term $1/(1 - MPC)$.[89]

In the complete model of Equation 12.13, where investment and import spending are also a function of income, the size of the multiplier is shown by Equation 12.20.

> **Multiplier**
> The multiple change in income and output that results from a change in autonomous expenditure.

12.20 $m = \dfrac{1}{1 - (c_1 + i_1 - m_1)} = \dfrac{1}{1 - c_1 - i_1 + m_1}$

where
   m = multiplier
   c_1 = marginal propensity to consume
   i_1 = marginal propensity to invest
   m_1 = marginal propensity to import

The size of the multiplier increases if the marginal propensity to invest, i_1, is greater than zero, as there is an additional injection into the circular flow from induced investment spending. If the marginal propensity to import, m_1, is greater than zero, the multiplier is decreased because induced import spending represents a leakage from the circular flow.

To compare this result with the simple multiplier ($c_1 = 0.75$, $m = 4$), assume that $c_1 = 0.75$, $i_1 = 0.1$, and $m_1 = 0.25$. In this case, the multiplier, $m = 1/[1 - (0.75 + 0.1 - 0.25)] = 1/0.4 = 2.5$. The simple multiplier is increased with the injection of induced investment spending, but reduced with the leakage of import spending.[90]

Appendix 12A presents a simple numerical example illustrating the equilibrium level of income, changes in that equilibrium, and the multiplier in a mixed, open economy.

---

[89]The increase in income, $\Delta Y = [\Delta G + (MPC)\Delta G + (MPC)^2\Delta G + (MPC)^3\Delta G +...] = [1 + (MPC) + (MPC)^2 + (MPC)^3 +...]\Delta G$. The multiplier, $\Delta Y/\Delta G = [1 + (MPC) + (MPC)^2 + (MPC)^3 +...]$. The latter is an infinite geometric series that reduces to $1/(1 - MPC)$. If $\Delta G = 20$ and $MPC = 0.75$, $\Delta Y = [20 + (.75)(20) + (.75)^2(20) + (.75)^3(20) +...] = [20 + 15 + 11.25 + 8.4375 +...] = 80$.

[90]If taxes (T) also depend on the level of income, the multiplier is reduced by this further leakage from the circular flow.

Effect of the Interest Rate on Aggregate Expenditures

Interest-related expenditure (*IRE*) function
The function that shows the inverse relationship between planned consumption and investment spending and the real interest rate, all else held constant.

Although all the variables influencing aggregate expenditure in Equation 12.12 and Table 12.4 are important, we want to extend our discussion of the role of the real interest rate, given that this variable is influenced by the monetary policy of a country's central bank. Changes in monetary policy have an impact on real variables in the economy in the short-run framework we are examining in this text through interest rate changes. This is why managers must pay attention to Federal Reserve policy and the statements that are made by the Federal Reserve chair and the presidents of the Federal Reserve banks.

Recall from our discussion of aggregate expenditure that some components of both consumption and investment spending are influenced by the real interest rate. Figure 12.11a introduces the **interest-related expenditure (IRE) function**, which shows planned consumption and investment spending as a function of the real interest rate, all else held constant. We have drawn this function as linear, although it could also be curved. The important point is that it is a downward sloping function showing an inverse relationship between the interest rate and planned consumption and investment expenditure, as both households and businesses will undertake less interest-related spending at a higher interest rate.[91]

We use the interest-related expenditure function in Figure 12.11a to show the impact of changes in the interest rate on the aggregate expenditure equilibrium in Figure 12.11b. Start with interest rate r_1, which generates planned interest-related spending IRE_1 in Figure 12.11a. This planned consumption and investment spending is included in the aggregate expenditure function $E(r_1)$ in Figure 12.11b. Equilibrium with this aggregate expenditure function occurs at point A and income level Y_1, as this is the point where the expenditure function crosses the 45-degree line in Figure 12.11b.

We can repeat this process for a lower interest rate, r_2, in Figure 12.11a. This lower interest rate results in larger planned interest-related spending, IRE_2 (point B). In Figure 12.11b, this autonomous change in investment spending shifts the aggregate expenditure line up from $E(r_1)$ to $E(r_2)$, resulting in a new equilibrium

FIGURE 12.11
Interest-Related Expenditure and Equilibrium in the Real Goods Market
Interest-related consumption and investment spending are determined in Figure 12.11a by changes in the real interest rate. This spending then influences the equilibrium level of real income in Figure 12.11b.

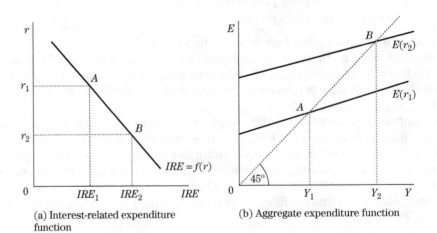

(a) Interest-related expenditure function

(b) Aggregate expenditure function

---

[91]Although household consumption expenditure and the components of business investment spending may be affected differentially by changes in the real interest rate, the *IRE* function shows the total amount of this interest-related spending at any given interest rate.

level of income, Y_2, at point B. This derivation shows that lower interest rates are consistent with higher equilibrium levels of income due to the increased consumption and investment spending that is generated by the lower rate.

All of the variables in Equation 12.12 and Table 12.4 cause the aggregate expenditure function to shift as shown in Figure 12.10. However, the real interest rate is the one variable that is the continuing focus of the monetary policy of a country's central bank.

Summary

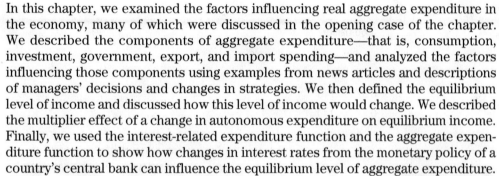

In this chapter, we examined the factors influencing real aggregate expenditure in the economy, many of which were discussed in the opening case of the chapter. We described the components of aggregate expenditure—that is, consumption, investment, government, export, and import spending—and analyzed the factors influencing those components using examples from news articles and descriptions of managers' decisions and changes in strategies. We then defined the equilibrium level of income and discussed how this level of income would change. We described the multiplier effect of a change in autonomous expenditure on equilibrium income. Finally, we used the interest-related expenditure function and the aggregate expenditure function to show how changes in interest rates from the monetary policy of a country's central bank can influence the equilibrium level of aggregate expenditure.

We now examine the monetary side of the economy to determine how changes in money supply and demand affect the interest rate (Chapter 13). We then integrate the real and monetary sides of the economy to develop the full aggregate model that managers can use to determine how macro changes influence their firms and industries (Chapter 14).

Appendix 12A Numerical Example of Equilibrium and the Multiplier

Table 12.A1 shows the autonomous spending components in the model (C_0, I_0, G_0, X_0, M_0) and the marginal propensities (c_1, i_1, m_1) that determine induced consumption, investment, and import spending. The equilibrium level of income ($350 billion) is calculated in the equations and illustrated in the middle part of the table. Only at this level of income is desired or planned spending by all sectors of the economy ($C + I + G + X - M$) equal to the level of income and output produced. At income levels less than $350 billion, desired spending is greater than the level of income and output produced, so there are unplanned inventory decreases and a tendency for income and output to increase. At income levels above $350 billion, desired spending is less than the level of income and output. There are unplanned inventory increases, and the tendency is for income and output to decrease.

We also illustrate the injection-leakage approach to equilibrium in the bottom part of Table 12.A1. In a mixed, open economy, the injections of investment, government, and export spending ($I + G + X$) must equal the leakages of saving, taxes, and import spending ($S + T + M$) in equilibrium. This condition holds only at the equilibrium level of income of $350 billion in Table 12.A1, where investment plus government plus export spending ($60 + $25 + $40 = $125 billion) equals saving plus taxes plus import spending ($−12.5 + 0 + $137.5 = $125 billion). At any other

TABLE 12.A1   Equilibrium in a Mixed, Open Economy (billions $)

SPENDING COMPONENTS

$$C_0 = 100, I_0 = 25, G_0 = 25, X_0 = 40, M_0 = 50, T = 0$$

MARGINAL PROPENSITIES

$$c_1 = 0.75, i_1 = 0.10, m_1 = 0.25$$

AGGREGATE EXPENDITURE

$$E = C_0 + c_1Y + I_0 + i_1Y + G_0 + X_0 + M_0 - m_1Y$$

$$E = C_0 + I_0 + G_0 + X_0 - M_0 + (c_1 + i_1 - m_1)Y$$

$$E = 100 + 25 + 25 + 40 - 50 + (0.75 + 0.10 - 0.25)Y$$

$$E = 140 + 0.6Y$$

EQUILIBRIUM

$$Y = E$$

$$Y = 140 + 0.6Y$$

$$Y - 0.6Y = 140$$

$$0.4Y = 140$$

$$Y_E = 350$$

Y	C = 100 + 0.75Y	S = Y - C = - 100 + 0.25Y	I = 25 + 0.1Y	G₀ = 25	X₀ = 40	M = 50 + 0.25Y	C + I + G + X - M	UNPLANNED INVENTORY ADJUSTMENT	CHANGE IN INCOME AND OUTPUT
250	287.5	-37.5	50	25	40	112.5	290	-40	Increase
300	325	-25	55	25	40	125	320	-20	Increase
350	**362.5**	**-12.5**	**60**	**25**	**40**	**137.5**	**350**	**0**	**None**
400	400	0	65	25	40	150	380	+20	Decrease
450	437.5	12.5	70	25	40	162.5	410	+40	Decrease

Y	I	G	X	TOTAL INJECTIONS	S	T	M	TOTAL LEAKAGES	INJECTION LEAKAGE BALANCE
250	50	25	40	115	-37.5	0	112.5	75	INJ > LK
300	55	25	40	120	-25	0	125	100	INJ > LK
350	**60**	**25**	**40**	**125**	**-12.5**	**0**	**137.5**	**125**	**INJ = LK**
400	65	25	40	130	0	0	150	150	INJ < LK
450	70	25	40	135	12.5	0	162.5	175	INJ < LK

level of income, there will be a tendency for output and income to either increase or decrease, given the imbalance between injections and leakages.

Note that the concept of equilibrium refers to planned or desired investment spending. As we discussed in Chapter 11, from the viewpoint of national income accounting, aggregate expenditure must equal income, given the definition of the circular flow. This accounting identity holds even when the economy is not in equilibrium, as inventory changes are counted as part of investment spending. For example, when income is $250 billion in Table 12.A1, aggregate planned expenditure $(C + I + G + X - M)$ is $290 billion, so the economy is not in equilibrium. Planned or desired spending is greater than the value of currently produced goods and services. However, actual expenditure equals actual income generated because

TABLE 12.A2   Changes in Aggregate Expenditure and Equilibrium Income and Output in a Mixed, Open Economy (Based on Model in Table 12.A1—billions $)

INCREASE GOVERNMENT EXPENDITURE BY $60 BILLION
SPENDING COMPONENTS

$$C_0 = 100, I_0 = 25, G_0 = 85, X_0 = 40, M_0 = 50, T = 0$$

MARGINAL PROPENSITIES

$$c_1 = 0.75, i_1 = 0.10, m_1 = 0.25$$

AGGREGATE EXPENDITURE

$$E = C_0 + c_1 Y + I_0 + i_1 Y + G_0 + X_0 - M_0 - m_1 Y$$
$$E = C_0 + I_0 + G_0 + X_0 - M_0 + (c_1 + i_1 - m_1)Y$$
$$E = 100 + 25 + 85 + 40 - 50 + (0.75 + 0.10 - 0.25)Y$$
$$E = 200 + 0.6Y$$

EQUILIBRIUM

$$Y = E$$
$$Y = 200 + 0.6Y$$
$$Y - 0.6Y = 200$$
$$0.4Y = 200$$
$$Y_E = 500$$

MULTIPLIER

$$\Delta Y = 500 - 350 = 150$$
$$\Delta G = 85 - 25 = 60$$
$$\Delta Y/\Delta G = 150/60 = 2.5$$
$$m = 1/[1 - (0.75 + 0.10 - 0.25)] = 1/[1 - 0.6] = 1/0.4 = 2.5$$

the $40 billion decrease in inventories is counted as part of investment spending. This $40 billion represents investment spending on goods that were produced in previous years, so it must be subtracted from current GDP. Measured aggregate expenditure ($290 billion minus $40 billion) equals income of $250 billion. This example illustrates the difference between the accounting identity of $E = Y$ and the behavioral relationship inherent in the equilibrium concept of $E = Y$.

Changes in aggregate expenditure and equilibrium income are illustrated in Table 12.A2, in which we assume that government expenditure has increased by $60 billion. This change has caused aggregate expenditure to increase, so that the new equilibrium level of income is $500 billion. The $60 billion increase in government expenditure resulted in a $150 billion increase in equilibrium income, or a multiplier of 2.5. Calculating the multiplier with Equation 12.20 also results in a value of 2.5.

Appendix 12B Algebraic Derivation of the Aggregate Expenditure Function

We use the linear spending equation from each sector of the economy to develop an algebraic aggregate expenditure function.

Consumption Spending (C)

12.B1 $C = c_0 + c_1(Y - T_P) - c_2r + c_3CC + c_4W + c_5CR - c_6D$

where

C = personal consumption expenditure
c_0 = other factors influencing consumption
Y = personal income
T_P = personal taxes
r = real interest rate
CC = consumer confidence
W = consumer wealth
CR = available consumer credit
D = consumer debt
c_1 to c_6 = coefficients for the relevant variables

12.B2 $C = C_0 + c_1Y$

where

$C_0 = [c_0 - c_1T_P - c_2r + c_3CC + c_4W + c_5CR - c_6D]$
c_1 = marginal propensity to consume

Investment Spending (I)

12.B3 $I = i_0 + i_1Y - i_2r - i_3T_B + i_4PR + i_5CU$

where

I = investment spending
i_0 = other factors influencing investment spending
Y = real income
r = real interest rate
T_B = business taxes
PR = expected profits and business confidence
CU = capacity utilization
i_1 to i_5 = coefficients for the relevant variables

12.B4 $I = I_0 + i_1Y$

where

$I_0 = [i_0 - i_2r - i_3T_B + i_4PR + i_5CU]$
i_1 = marginal propensity to invest

Government Spending (G)

12.B5 $G = G_0$

where

G = government expenditure
G_0 = autonomous government expenditure

Export Spending (X)

12.B6 $X = x_0 + x_1 Y^* - x_2 R$

where

X = export expenditure
x_0 = other factors influencing export expenditure
Y^* = foreign GDP or real income
R = currency exchangerate
x_1, x_2 = coefficients of the relevant variables

12.B7 $X = X_0$

where

$X_0 = [x_0 + x_1 Y^* - x_2 R]$

Import Spending (M)

12.B8 $M = m_0 + m_1 Y + m_2 R$

where

M = import spending
m_0 = other factors influencing import spending
Y = domestic real income
R = currency exchange rate
m_1, m_2 = coefficients of the relevant variables

12.B9 $M = M_0 + m_1 Y$

where

$M_0 = [m_0 + m_2 R]$
m_1 = marginal propensity to import

Aggregate Expenditure (E)

12.B10 $E = C + I + G + X - M$

12.B11 $E = C_0 + c_1 Y + I_0 + i_1 Y + G_0 + X_0 - M_0 - m_1 Y$

where

E = aggregate expenditure
Y = real income
C_0 = autonomous consumption expenditure
I_0 = autonomous investment expenditure
G_0 = autonomous government expenditure
X_0 = autonomous export expenditure
M_0 = autonomous import expenditure
c_1 = marginal propensity to consume
i_1 = marginal propensity to invest
m_1 = marginal propensity to import

$$12.B12 \quad E = C_0 + I_0 + G_0 + X_0 - M_0 + c_1 Y + i_1 Y - m_1 Y$$

$$12.B13 \quad E = E_0 + (c_1 + i_1 - m_1) Y$$

where

$$E_0 = [C_0 + I_0 + G_0 + X_0 - M_0]$$
$$c_1 = \text{marginal propensity to consume}$$
$$i_1 = \text{marginal propensity to invest}$$
$$m_1 = \text{marginal propensity to import}$$

Key Terms

aggregate expenditure, p. 324

aggregate expenditure function, p. 345

autonomous consumption
   expenditures, p. 332

budget surplus/deficit, p. 341

capacity utilization rates (*CURs*), p. 337

Consumer Confidence Index (*CCI*), p. 327

Consumer Sentiment Index (*CSI*), p. 327

consumption function, p. 324

currency exchange rate, p. 343

equilibrium level of income and
   output, p. 347

fiscal policy, p. 341

government expenditure, p. 341

gross private domestic investment,
   p. 332

induced consumption expenditures,
   p. 332

injections, p. 347

interest-related expenditure (*IRE*)
   function, p. 352

investment spending function, p. 340

leakages, p. 347

marginal propensity to consume
   (*MPC*), p. 324

marginal propensity to save (*MPS*),
   p. 325

Multiplier, p. 351

net export expenditure, p. 342

nominal interest rate, p. 327

nominal terms, p. 323

personal consumption expenditure,
   p. 324

potential GDP, p. 322

real interest rate, p. 327

real terms, p. 323

relative prices, p. 335

saving (*S*), p. 325

unplanned inventory decrease,
   p. 349

unplanned inventory increase,
   p. 349

Exercises

Technical Questions

1. Describe the difference between autonomous expenditure and induced expenditure. Which sectors of the economy are assumed to have both types of spending and which are not? Explain your answer.
2. Describe the effect of the currency exchange rate on export and import spending.
3. Explain how the aggregate expenditure function shifts in response to changes in each of the following variables:

   a. The real interest rate increases.
   b. Consumer confidence decreases.
   c. Higher taxes are imposed on business profits.
   d. The economies of many countries in the rest of the world go into recessions.

4. Evaluate the following statements as to whether they are true or false:

   a. The multiplier means that changes in wealth have a larger effect on consumption spending than changes in consumer confidence.
   b. Both an increase in government spending (G) and an increase in personal taxes (T_P) will shift the aggregate expenditure function in the same direction.
   c. The national income accounts show that real income (Y) *always* equals real expenditure (E), *given the definition of the circular flow of economic activity*. Thus, the economy must *always* be in equilibrium because that is *also* where $Y = E$.

5. Given the following variables in the open economy aggregate expenditure model, autonomous consumption (C_0) = 200, autonomous investment (I_0) = 200, government spending (G_0) = 100, export spending (X_0) = 100, autonomous import spending (M_0) = 100, taxes (T_P) = 0, marginal propensity to consume (c_1) = 0.8, marginal propensity to invest (i_1) = 0.1, and marginal propensity to import (m_1) = 0.15,

   a. Calculate the equilibrium level of income for the open economy aggregate expenditure model.
   b. If there is an increase in autonomous import expenditure from 100 to 200 resulting from an increase in the currency exchange rate, calculate the new equilibrium level of income and the value of the multiplier.
   c. Compared with the original equilibrium in part a, if the government decides to impose taxes (T_P) of 100, calculate the new equilibrium level of income.

   Hint: Remember that consumption has an autonomous component and is a function of disposable income, Y_d, where $Y_d = Y - T_P$.

6. In the aggregate expenditure model, assume that the consumption function is given by $C = 800 + 0.8(Y - T_P)$, that planned investment (I) equals 200, and that government purchases (G) and taxes (T_P) each equal 200. Assume that there is no import or export spending.

   a. Calculate the equilibrium level of income.
   b. If government purchases (G) increase by 100 (all else held constant), calculate the new equilibrium level of income and the value of the multiplier.
   c. Compared with the original equilibrium, if both government expenditure (G) and taxes (T_P) increase by 100, so that the government budget remains balanced, does the equilibrium level of income remain unchanged? Explain your answer.

Application Questions

1. Use the aggregate expenditure model developed in this chapter to explain the following statements:

   a. Coming amid continued turmoil in the financial and credit markets, the report sent stocks lower, with the Dow Jones Industrial Average falling 146.70 points Friday to close at 11,893.69.
   b. Administration officials said they were confident conditions would improve as tax rebates that are part of the recent $152 billion economic-stimulus package begin to reach consumers.
   c. The Fed is expected to cut interest rates again to prop up the economy.

2. Redraw Figures 12.11a and 12.11b to illustrate the effects on the resulting equilibrium level of income from *each* of the following changes:

   a. A greater sensitivity of interest-related consumption and investment expenditure to changes in the interest rate.
   b. A larger multiplier in the aggregate expenditure model.

3. Go to the Web site of the Conference Board (www.conference-board.org) and find the latest release of the Consumer Confidence Index. How has the index changed since its last release? What is the expected impact of this change on the economy?

4. A number of articles in the *Wall Street Journal* reported that the strong dollar, combined with the recession of 2001, forced many U.S. manufacturers to develop better methods to produce and sell their products. Use the discussion of the macro model in this chapter to explain why businesses would have implemented such changes in strategies.

5. What were the key provisions of the American Recovery and Reinvestment Act passed by Congress in February 2009? How has the impact of the Act been evaluated?

6. Compare and contrast current U.S. economic activity with that described in the opening case of this chapter.

13

The Role of Money in the Macro Economy

We have discussed the factors influencing aggregate spending on real goods and services in the different sectors of the economy (consumption + investment + government + export – import spending or $C + I + G + X - M$) (Chapter 12). This expenditure is based on the circular flow concept outlined previously (Chapter 11). In this chapter, we discuss how money and the monetary policy of a country's central bank influence interest rates. This discussion focuses on financial markets where various financial assets (i.e., stocks, bonds, Treasury securities) are bought and sold. We then integrate the real and monetary sides of the economy to show how monetary policy influences interest rates, which affects spending on real goods and services and the competitive strategies of firms producing those products (Chapter 14).

We begin this chapter with the case, "The Chairman's Quandary." This case discusses the dilemma facing Federal Reserve Chairman Ben Bernanke in the summer of 2012 as Federal Reserve policy makers tried to decide what future actions should be taken to stimulate the economy in a period in which many already thought that the Fed's actions were very limited. After discussing this case, we define the term *money* and show how the supply of money in the economy is influenced by both depository institutions and the Federal Reserve. We describe the various tools the Federal Reserve uses to change the money supply and interest rates, and we discuss the new tools the Federal Reserve has used since the recession of 2007–2009. Treating money as a commodity, we develop a model of the money market that includes the supply and demand for money, and we examine the resulting equilibrium price or interest rate in this market. We then show how changes in money demand and/or supply cause changes in this interest rate.

Case for Analysis

The Chairman's Quandary

In the spring and summer of 2012, the Federal Reserve appeared to be moving closer to taking additional action to use monetary policy to stimulate the economy. At the meeting of the Federal Open Market Committee (FOMC) in April, Federal Reserve officials reaffirmed their plans to keep short-term interest rates near zero until 2014. However, some officials predicted that economic growth might increase more than expected, warranting an increase in interest rates by the end of 2014. Federal Reserve Chairman Ben Bernanke declared that it was "a little premature to declare victory." He indicated support for a policy of keeping interest rates low and even launching new programs to stimulate economic growth. Although the unemployment rate dropped to 8.2 percent in March 2012 from 9.1 percent in August 2011, momentum in the labor market was still uncertain and inflation had picked up slightly.[1]

At its June 2012 meeting, the FOMC announced that it would extend a program known as "Operation Twist" through the end of 2012. With this program, the Federal Reserve sold short-term securities and used the revenues to buy longer-term securities to drive down long-term interest rates to stimulate business and household borrowing. Chairman Bernanke also announced that officials were ready to take additional steps to bring down unemployment if the economy did not recover on its own. This policy stance appeared to be a change from April, when Federal Reserve officials seemed to be more comfortable with the economy's progress. Under Operation Twist, the Federal Reserve would buy an additional $267 billion in long-term Treasury bonds and notes in exchange for an equivalent amount of short-term securities, expanding the total amount of the program to $667 billion. These policy changes were added to the strategy of holding short-term interest rates to near zero, which had been in effect since late 2008, assuring the financial community that these rates would not increase until late 2014, and purchasing more than $2.5 trillion worth of Treasury and mortgage securities.[2]

Over the course of the summer the Federal Reserve moved closer to taking further action.[3] In speeches and testimony, official made it clear that they were not satisfied with the current state of the economy. Chairman Bernanke noted that the economy appeared to be "stuck in the mud." Even members of the FOMC, who traditionally worried more about inflation and opposed more action to stimulate the economy, appeared to have shifted their stance. Yet many observers of the Fed still questioned what it would take for the Federal Reserve to act and what would be the impact of these actions.

In a press release following the July 31/August 1, 2012 meeting of the FOMC, officials again reaffirmed that they would keep short-term interest rates low through late 2014 and that they would "closely monitor incoming information on economic and financial developments and will provide additional accommodation as needed to promote a stronger economic recovery."[4] Observers noted that Chairman Bernanke was building a case to stimulate the economy and arguing that the Federal Reserve could achieve its goals without causing other problems. A former Federal Reserve vice-chairman said that the phrase "closely monitor" had been used to signal "a readiness to action that was more than the usual readiness to action."[5] Even so, critics still argued that Federal Reserve actions could do little to help the economy, might generate inflation, and would punish savers who were receiving little return on their bond investments.

---

[1]Jon Hilsenrath and Kristina Peterson, "Fed Holds Rates Steady, but Outlook Shifts," *Wall Street Journal (Online)*, April 26, 2012.

[2]Kristina Peterson and Jon Hilsenrath, "Fed Warns of Risk to Economy," *Wall Street Journal (Online)*, June 21, 2012.

[3]Jon Hilsenrath, "Fed Moves Closer to Action," *Wall Street Journal (Online)*, July 25, 2012; Sudeep Reddy, "Gauging the Triggers to Fed Action," *Wall Street Journal (Online)*, August 1, 2012.

[4]Board of Governors of the Federal Reserve System, *Press Release*, August 1, 2012. Available at www.federalreserve.gov.

[5]Jon Hilsenrath and Kristina Peterson, "Wary Fed Is Poised to Act," *Wall Street Journal (Online)*, August 2, 2012.

Money and the U.S. Financial System

Before discussing monetary policy and the U.S. financial system, let's define the commodity that we call money.

Definition of Money

Money
The stock of financial assets that can easily be used to make market transactions and that serves as a medium of exchange, a unit of account, and a store of value.

Money is the stock of financial assets that can be easily used as the medium of exchange for market transactions. It helps facilitate the buying and selling of goods and services, actions that are the essence of a market economy. Money can be defined most clearly in terms of the functions it performs because it serves as a medium of exchange, a unit of account, and a store of value.

Money as a Medium of Exchange   As just noted, money functions as a medium of exchange because it simplifies market transactions. In a **barter system**, goods and services are exchanged directly without a common unit of account. The problem with this system is that each individual has to find another person who wants to exchange the needed commodities, a task that would be very difficult in a modern industrialized economy with large numbers of individuals and commodities. An individual might directly exchange yard work for automobile repair with his or her neighbor without the use of money, but lawn maintenance services and automobile repair shops would not be able to serve all their customers if they did not use money as a medium of exchange.

Barter system
A system in which goods and services are exchanged directly without a common unit of account.

Money as a Unit of Account   As a unit of account, money provides the terms in which the prices of goods and services are quoted and debts are recorded. In the United States, the current price of a gallon of milk is approximately $3.00, while the price of a pound of margarine is around $1.00. Dollars are the unit of account in which we measure the relative prices of different goods and services. If we used something else as the unit of account, such as loaves of bread, all prices would be quoted in terms of loaves.

Money as a Store of Value   Money also functions as a store of value that can be used for future market purchases. Bread would not serve this purpose well over long periods of time because it would become stale and moldy and would be bulky to maintain. Even with paper currency, countries must make certain that their money actually does hold its value over time in terms of its purchasing power. In times of rapid inflation, individuals can lose faith in the value of their money.

Measures of the Money Supply

Liquidity
The ability of a financial asset to be used to immediately make market transactions.

Given that money is defined in terms of its functions and its ability to facilitate market transactions, there are various measures of the money supply. Table 13.1 illustrates these measures, which are often called *monetary aggregates*, for the United States.

These measures of the money supply differ in terms of their **liquidity**, or their ability to be used immediately to make market transactions. M1 is the most used definition of the money supply because it includes the most components. Coins and paper money are almost always accepted for transactions, while checks and travelers' checks are accepted in many situations.[6] Checking accounts are called **demand deposits**

Demand deposits
Another name for checking accounts or checkable deposits, one of the major components of the M1 measure of the money supply.

---

[6]As stated in the Coinage Act of 1965, "All coins and currencies of the United States (including Federal Reserve notes and circulating notes of Federal Reserve banks and national banking associations)…shall be legal-tender for all debts, public and private, public charges, taxes, duties and dues." However, there is no federal law mandating that individuals or organizations must accept currency or coins as payment for goods and services. A bus system may refuse to accept payment for fares in pennies or dollars. Gas stations and convenience stores may not accept bills larger than $20. These restrictions are legal as long as a notice is posted and a transaction has not already begun. See Federal Reserve Board, *Frequently Asked Questions (FAQs)* (available at www.federalreserve.gov/faq.htm).

TABLE 13.1   Measures of the U.S. Money Supply

MEASURE	DESCRIPTION	VALUE (JUNE 2012) SEASONALLY ADJUSTED (BILLIONS $)
C: CURRENCY	Coins held outside the Treasury, the Federal Reserve banks, and depository institutions, as well as paper money—Federal Reserve notes	1,045.2
M1: C PLUS:		
Checkable deposits	Deposits in checking accounts (demand deposits)	784.6
Travelers' checks	Checks that can be used as cash issued by nondepository institutions such as American Express	4.0
Other checkable deposits	Negotiable orders of withdrawal (NOWs) and automatic transfer service (ATS) account balances	422.3
Total M1		*2,256.1*
M2: M1 PLUS:		
Money market mutual fund shares	Shares of funds that invest in short-term financial assets and have check-writing privileges	640.9
Savings accounts	Interest-bearing accounts with no checking privileges	6,347.8
Small time deposits	Accounts of less than $100,000, such as certificates of deposit, that have fixed maturities and penalties for early withdrawal	699.7
Total M2		*9,944.5*

Sources: Board of Governors of the Federal Reserve System. *The Federal Reserve System: Purposes and Functions*, 9th ed. (Washington, DC: Board of Governors, 2005). Available at www.federalreserve.gov; Federal Reserve Statistical Release, Tables 1, 3, and 4, Money Stock Measures, H.6 (508), available at www.federalreserve.gov.

because they can be withdrawn on demand. Money market mutual fund shares and savings accounts are less liquid because these assets must typically be converted to cash or checking account deposits to be used for market transactions. Check-writing privileges from these additional M2 components are generally either restricted or limited to larger transactions. Time deposits in M2 are typically not immediately available for transactions without withdrawal penalties being imposed. Table 13.1 shows the substantial differences in the sizes of the different monetary aggregates.[7]

The most liquid components of the money supply best satisfy the medium of exchange function of money. The less liquid components and other financial instruments may act better as a store of value because they pay interest or higher rates of interest on the principal amount of the asset. We'll discuss later in the chapter how individuals make decisions on the amount of their assets to hold in the form of money versus other financial instruments.

Depository Institutions and the Fractional Reserve Banking System

Depository and other financial institutions act as intermediaries to channel income that is saved in the circular flow process to funds that are available for business investment spending and to finance government expenditure and household

Depository institutions
Institutions that accept deposits from individuals and organizations, against which depositors can write checks on demand for their market transactions and that use these deposits to make loans.

---

[7]Until March 2006, there was an M3 component of the money supply which consisted of M2 plus time deposits exceeding $100,000, institutional money funds, repurchase agreements, and eurodollars (one-day dollar-denominated deposits in foreign depository institutions and in foreign branches of American depository institutions). The Board of Governors stopped reporting this monetary aggregate in March 2006 due to data collection costs and to the fact that M3 did not prove essential for policy making and monetary analysis. See Edward Nelson, "Goodbye to M3," *Monetary Trends*, Federal Reserve Bank of St. Louis, April 2006.

Federal Deposit Insurance Corporation (FDIC)
The government regulatory institution that supervises the activities of depository institutions in the United States and provides depositors with accounts up to a certain amount (currently $250,000) with a guarantee that they will receive their funds even in the event of a bank failure.

Fractional reserve system
A banking system in which banks are required to keep only a fraction of their deposits as reserves.

Reserve requirement
Required reserves kept in banks' vaults or as deposits at the Federal Reserve divided by demand deposits or the fraction of deposits banks are required to keep as reserves.

borrowing (Chapter 11, Figure 11.1). Although a wide variety of institutions serve this role, the approximately 8,000 depository institutions in the United States play a special role regarding the money supply. Depository institutions accept deposits, backed by the **Federal Deposit Insurance Corporation (FDIC)**, from individuals and organizations against which the depositors can write checks on demand for their market transactions. The FDIC is the government regulatory institution that supervises the activities of depository institutions in the United States and provides depositors with accounts up to a certain amount (increased from $100,000 to $250,000 in October 2008) with a guarantee that they will receive their funds even in the event of a bank failure.[8]

Banks earn income by loaning out these deposits and charging interest for the loans. However, banks need to keep some of their deposits in reserve as depositors write checks and make withdrawals from their accounts. Banks in the United States operate in a **fractional reserve system**, in which the central bank or the Federal Reserve requires them to keep only a fraction of their deposits as reserves, either as cash in their vaults or as noninterest-bearing deposits at the Federal Reserve. This fraction is the **reserve requirement**, rr, or required reserves divided by demand deposits. Banks have the incentive to loan out excess reserves because they earn revenue by charging interest on these loans. Moreover, by using their excess reserves to make loans, banks actually create more money in the financial system.

If banks operated under a 100 percent reserve system, they would not be able to create any further money. For example, in Case 1 Table 13.2, Bank One would have to hold a $100 deposit in its entirety as reserves against withdrawals of that $100. Suppose that under a fractional reserve system, banks are required to hold only 10 percent of their deposits as reserves. This means that in Case 2 in Table 13.2, Bank One can loan out $90 of the original $100 and keep only $10 in reserve. If that $90 is deposited by the borrower in another bank in the system (Bank Two), only 10 percent or $9 needs to be held as reserves. Bank Two can loan out an additional $81. Thus, subsequent loans can be made with the declining amount of excess reserves left after each round of required reserves. The end result of this process is

---

TABLE 13.2 The Fractional Reserve Banking System

CASE 1: 100 PERCENT RESERVE REQUIREMENT		CASE 2: 10 PERCENT RESERVE REQUIREMENT	
BANK ONE BALANCE SHEET		**BANK ONE BALANCE SHEET**	
ASSETS	**LIABILITIES**	**ASSETS**	**LIABILITIES**
Reserves: $100	Deposits: $100	Reserves: $10	Deposits: $100
		Loans: $90	
		BANK TWO BALANCE SHEET	
		ASSETS	**LIABILITIES**
		Reserves: $9	Deposits: $90
		Loans: $81	

---

[8]Depository institutions include commercial banks, savings banks, savings and loan associations, and credit unions as well as U.S. branches and agencies of foreign banks and other domestic banking entities that engage in international transactions. For ease of explanation, we will call these institutions *banks*. See Board of Governors of the Federal Reserve System. *The Federal Reserve System: Purposes and Functions*, 9th ed. (Washington, DC: Board of Governors, 2005); Federal Deposit Insurance Corporation, "Deposit Insurance Summary." Available at www.fdic.gov.

to increase the money supply by a **simple deposit multiplier** that is based on the size of the reserve requirement (rr), as shown in Equation 13.1.

$$13.1 \quad d = [(1-rr) + (1-rr)^2 + (1-rr)^3 + \ldots] = [(1/rr)]$$

where

d = simple deposit multiplier

rr = reserve requirement

In the example above, $rr = 0.10$, so the simple deposit multiplier is 10. The original $100 deposit is converted to $1,000 of new money.

The actual money multiplier (mm) differs from the simple deposit multiplier (d), given the possible decisions by banks to hold reserves in excess of those required and by individuals to hold assets in cash rather than bank deposits, as shown in Table 13.3. In this table, the **money supply** is defined as currency plus demand deposits, or M1 from Table 13.1. The **monetary base** is defined as currency plus reserves. Some of these reserves are required by the central bank (which we discuss in more detail below), so the monetary base is a policy variable of the central bank. Banks may also choose to hold reserves in excess of what is required if they see a greater level of withdrawals or if they are reluctant to make loans, given unease over future economic conditions or the creditworthiness of current borrowers.

The **money multiplier** (mm) reflects the fact that money creation will be less if banks choose to hold reserves in excess of what is required or if individuals choose to hold some of their assets in cash rather than deposit them in a bank where they can be expanded through the money creation process.[9]

Table 13.4 shows the differences between the simple deposit multiplier and the money multiplier. With $rr = 0.1$, the simple money multiplier is 10. However, if individuals hold 10 percent of their assets as cash, the money multiplier is reduced to 5.5. In addition, if banks hold an additional 10 percent in excess reserves, the money multiplier is reduced to 3.667.

Simple deposit multiplier
The amount by which the money supply can be increased in a fractional reserve banking system, which equals (1/rr), where rr is the reserve requirement.

Money supply
Currency plus checkable accounts or demand deposits (M1).

Monetary base
Currency plus reserves (both required and excess), a variable controlled by central bank policy.

Money multiplier
The money multiplier, mm—which is usually smaller than the simple deposit multiplier, d—reflects individuals' decisions to hold some of their assets in cash rather than deposit them in a checking account and banks' decisions to hold excess reserves.

TABLE 13.3 The Money Multiplier

Money supply (M) = currency (CU) + demand deposits (DD)

Monetary base (B) = currency (CU) + required reserves (RR) + excess reserves (ER)

Money multiplier (mm) $= \dfrac{\text{Money supply}(M)}{\text{Monetary base}(B)} = \dfrac{CU + DD}{CU + RR + ER}$

Divide the numerator and denominator by DD:

Money multiplier (mm) $= \dfrac{(CU/DD) + (DD/DD)}{(CU/DD) + (RR/DD) + (ER/DD)} = \dfrac{c+1}{c+rr+e}$

where

c = currency/deposit ratio

rr = reserve requirement

e = excess reserve ratio

[9]In Table 13.2, if Bank One holds an extra 10 percent of its deposits as additional reserves, then it has only $80 to make loans that will create further money. Alternatively, if the customers receiving the original $90 in loans keep 10 percent or $9 in currency and deposit only $81 in Bank Two, that bank keeps $8.10 in reserves and it has only $72.90 to loan out to other customers.

TABLE 13.4   Differences Between the Simple Deposit Multiplier and the Money Multiplier

SIMPLE DEPOSIT MULTIPLIER, $d = 1/rr$	MONEY MULTIPLIER, $mm = (1 + c)/(c + rr + e)$
where	*where*
rr = reserve requirement	c = currency deposit ratio
$rr = 0.1$	rr = reserve requirement
$d = 1/0.1 = 10$	e = excess reserve ratio
	EXAMPLE 1
	$c = 0.1; rr = 0.1; e = 0$
	$mm = (1 + 0.1)/(0.1 + 0.1 + 0) = (1.1)/(0.2) = 5.5$
	EXAMPLE 2
	$c = 0.1; rr = 0.1; e = 0.1$
	$mm = (1 + 0.1)/(0.1 + 0.1 + 0.1) = (1.1)/(0.3) = 3.667$

Figure 13.1 shows the relationship between the monetary base (currency plus required reserves plus excess reserves), the policy tool of the central bank, and the money supply (currency plus demand deposits). As shown in the figure, currency is transmitted dollar for dollar from the monetary base to the money supply. However, excess reserves in the monetary base can be used to expand demand deposits and the money supply through the money multiplier. Any central bank policy that changes reserves will change the money supply.

FIGURE 13.1
The Monetary Base and the Money Supply
The monetary base (currency, required and excess reserves), a policy tool of the central bank, influences the money supply through the money multiplier.

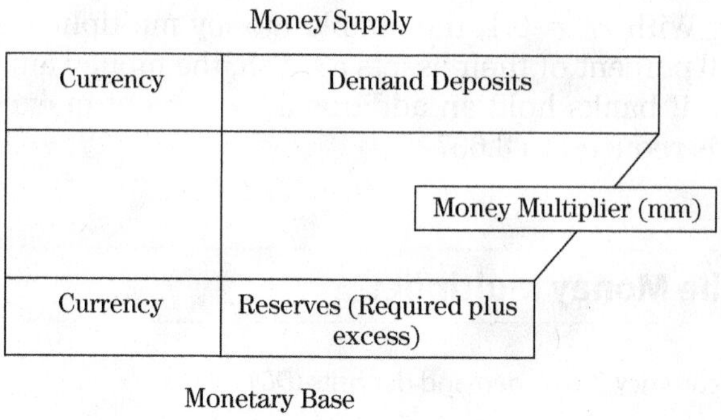

Money Supply

Currency	Demand Deposits
	Money Multiplier (mm)
Currency	Reserves (Required plus excess)

Monetary Base

Federal Reserve System (Fed)
The central bank in the United States that implements monetary policy and helps regulate and operate the country's financial system.

The Central Bank (Federal Reserve)

The **Federal Reserve System**, or just the Fed, is the central bank in the United States.[10] It was created in 1913 to help provide stability to the country's financial system. The Fed both implements monetary policy and helps regulate and operate the country's financial system. The system consists of the seven members of the

---

[10]This discussion is based on *The Federal Reserve System: Purposes and Functions* (Washington, DC: Board of Governors of the Federal Reserve System, 2005) (available at www.federalreserve.gov); Federal Reserve Bank of San Francisco, *U.S. Monetary Policy: An Introduction* (available at www.frbst.org/publications/ federalreserve/monetary); Alan S. Blinder, "How Central Should the Central Bank Be?" *Journal of Economic Literature* 48 (2010): 123–33; and Martin Feldstein, "What Powers for the Federal Reserve?" *Journal of Economic Literature* 48 (2010); 134–45. For a succinct overview of the Federal Reserve System and monetary policy presented in a series of lectures at George Washington University, see Board of Governors of the Federal Reserve System, *The Federal Reserve and the Financial Crisis: Chairman Bernanke's College Lecture Series*. Available at www.federalreserve.gov/newsevents/lectures/about.htm.

Board of Governors located in Washington, D.C., 12 Federal Reserve District Banks in major cities across the country, and approximately 2,900 member banks.[11] The members of the Board of Governors are appointed by the president and confirmed by the Senate. They are appointed for nonrenewable 14-year terms, with their appointments staggered so that one term expires on January 31 of each even-numbered year. The chairman and vice chairman of the Board are also appointed by the president and confirmed by the Senate for four-year terms.

The 12 Federal Reserve District Banks and their 25 branches undertake a variety of functions, including operating a nationwide payments system, regulating and supervising member banks, distributing currency and coins for the country, and serving as bankers for the U.S. Treasury. Each district bank has a board of directors chosen from both the public and the commercial banks that are part of the Federal Reserve System. The district banks provide economic information from across the country to the Federal Reserve System. This information is summarized in the **Beige Book**, which is published eight times a year and includes information on current economic conditions gathered from the banks' staff and interviews with business contacts, economists, market experts, and other sources. Topics in the Beige Book include consumer spending, services and tourism, construction and real estate, manufacturing, banking and finance, labor markets and prices, and agriculture and natural resources.

Banks that are members of the Federal Reserve System include all national banks chartered by the federal government through the Office of the Comptroller of the Currency in the Department of the Treasury and state banks that elect to become members of the system if they meet the standards set by the Board of Governors. Member banks must subscribe to stock in their regional Federal Reserve Bank, and they vote for some of the directors of their Federal Reserve Bank.

The Federal Reserve System was structured to be independent within the government. Although the Fed is accountable to Congress, it is insulated from day-to-day political pressures through the long, staggered terms of the Board of Governors, which extend beyond the term of any individual U.S. president. District bank presidents are appointed to five-year terms by the board of directors of each bank and not through the political process. The Federal Reserve System derives most of its income from interest on U.S. government securities that it acquires through open market operations, which we discuss later in the chapter. It also derives income from foreign currency investments, interest on loans to depository institutions, and fees for services provided to depository institutions. The Fed returns any earnings net of expenses to the U.S. Treasury. In 2011, this payment totaled $76.9 billion.[12] This financing arrangement makes the Fed independent of the political process by which Congress funds federal government agencies.

The Fed is, however, ultimately accountable to Congress and comes under government audit and review. The Fed chairman and other members of the system meet regularly with administration officials and report to Congress on monetary and regulatory issues.

The **Federal Open Market Committee (FOMC)** has the primary responsibility for conducting monetary policy. The FOMC has 12 members: the seven members of the Board of Governors, the president of the Federal Reserve Bank of New York, and four other Federal Reserve Bank presidents who serve one-year terms on a rotating basis. The remaining district bank presidents participate in the FOMC meetings, which are held eight times a year in Washington, DC, but do not vote on policy decisions.

Beige Book
A publication of the Federal Reserve System that includes information on current economic conditions gathered from the Federal Reserve banks' staff and interviews with business contacts, economists, market experts, and other sources.

Federal Open Market Committee (FOMC)
The Federal Reserve body that has the primary responsibility for conducting monetary policy.

---

[11]The Federal Reserve District Banks are located in the following cities: 1st District—Boston; 2nd District—New York; 3rd District—Philadelphia; 4th District—Cleveland; 5th District—Richmond; 6th District—Atlanta; 7th District—Chicago; 8th District—St. Louis; 9th District—Minneapolis; 10th District—Kansas City; 11th District—Dallas, and 12th District—San Francisco.

[12]Board of Governors of the Federal Reserve System, "Press Release: Reserve Bank income and expense data and transfers to the Treasury," January 10, 2012. Available at www.federalreserve.gov.

Tools of Monetary Policy

The Federal Reserve cannot influence income, output, and inflation directly. Instead, it engages in policy actions that influence the level of interest rates in the economy. Changes in interest rates influence real spending and output through the mechanisms we have previously discussed (Chapter 12). Fed policy focuses either on changing interest rates directly or on changing bank reserves, which then affects interest rates. The Federal Reserve uses three main tools for monetary policy changes: open market operations, the discount rate, and reserve requirements. We will discuss these tools first and then describe the nontraditional approaches the Fed developed to deal with the recession of 2007–2009.

Open market operations

The major tool of Fed monetary policy that involves the buying and selling of government securities on the open market in order to change the money supply and influence interest rates.

Open Market Operations   **Open market operations**, the major tool of Fed policy, involve the buying and selling of government securities on the open market (not on an organized stock exchange) by the Federal Reserve Bank of New York under the direction of the FOMC. The Fed engages in open market operations to influence the amount of reserves held by commercial banks, which, in turn, influences the **federal funds rate**, the rate banks charge each other for loans of reserves to meet their minimum reserve requirements. Banks are required to hold between 3 and 10 percent of their demand deposits as reserves, whether as cash in their vaults or as noninterest-bearing deposits with the Fed. They may also hold additional or excess reserves for clearing overnight checks or other purposes.

Federal funds rate

The interest rate that commercial banks charge each other for loans of reserves to meet their minimum reserve requirements.

If a bank needs additional reserves, it can borrow them at the federal funds rate from other banks in a private financial market called the **federal funds market**. Most loans in this market mature within one or two days, some within only a few hours. If increased reserves are supplied to this market, the federal funds rate will fall, making it easier for banks to borrow additional reserves and continue making loans. Changes in the federal funds rate are also reflected in other interest rates that influence real spending.

Federal funds market

The private financial market where banks borrow and loan reserves to meet the minimum reserve requirements.

If the Fed engages in **expansionary monetary policy**, its goal is to stimulate the economy and increase the rate of growth of real GDP. This goal is achieved by increasing the amount of bank reserves in the system and lowering the federal funds rate, which also tends to lower other interest rates in the economy. If the Fed wants the federal funds rate to fall, it will buy government securities from a bank. It pays for these securities with a check drawn on itself. When the selling bank presents the check for payment, the Fed increases the reserves in the account of the bank, and, thus, the total reserves in the banking system increase. This action differs from banks' purchases and sales of securities to each other because the Fed action represents a net addition of reserves to the banking system rather than a redistribution of existing reserves among the banks.

Expansionary monetary policy

Federal Reserve policy to increase the rate of growth of real GDP by increasing the amount of bank reserves in the system and lowering the federal funds and other interest rates.

Interest rates in the rest of the economy will tend to fall along with the federal funds rate. The Fed's purchase of government securities or bonds tends to drive up the price of bonds, which lowers their rate of interest (r) or current yield. Bonds are debt securities sold by governments, municipalities, corporations, and federal agencies to finance their activities. Households and institutions purchase them as a financial asset that pays interest income. The interest payment or coupon rate of the bond is typically fixed as a percent of the price or face value of the bond.

However, bonds are resold in competitive secondary markets, where their prices fluctuate according to the forces of demand and supply. If you purchase a new bond for $1,000 that pays $50 per year, the rate of return, or interest rate, is $50/$1,000, or 5 percent. If the price of that $1,000 bond increases in the secondary markets to $1,250 due to an increase in the demand for bonds, the current yield is lowered to 4 percent ($50/$1,250). Likewise, if the price of the bond should fall to $800, the interest rate yield is 6.25 percent ($50/$800). Thus, even though the Fed's actions have the greatest direct impact in the federal funds market, the impact on interest rates spills over into other financial markets.

Contractionary monetary policy

Federal Reserve policy to decrease the rate of growth of real GDP by decreasing the amount of bank reserves in the system and raising the federal funds and other interest rates.

Contractionary monetary policy has the opposite effect, slowing the rate of growth of real GDP by decreasing the amount of reserves in the banking system and raising the federal funds and other interest rates. When the Fed wants the funds rate to increase, it sells government securities. Banks pay the Fed for these securities with their reserves, which leaves fewer reserves in the banking system and causes the federal funds rate to rise. It is this dollar-for-dollar exchange of reserves for government securities that makes open market operations the most powerful and flexible tool of Fed monetary policy.

Table 13.5 shows the *intended* federal funds rate and changes in these rates from 2003 to 2012. These are the targeted federal funds rates set on the various meeting

TABLE 13.5   Intended or Targeted Federal Funds Rates

DATE	INCREASE (BASIS POINTS)	DECREASE (BASIS POINTS)	LEVEL (PERCENT)
2008			
December 16		75–100	0.00–0.25
October 29		50	1.00
October 8		50	1.50
April 30		25	2.00
March 18		75	2.25
January 30		50	3.00
January 22		75	3.50
2007			
December 11		25	4.25
October 31		25	4.50
September 18		50	4.75
2006			
June 29	25		5.25
May 10	25		5.00
March 28	25		4.75
January 31	25		4.50
2005			
December 13	25		4.25
November 1	25		4.00
September 20	25		3.75
August 9	25		3.50
June 30	25		3.25
May 3	25		3.00
March 22	25		2.75
February 2	25		2.50
2004			
December 14	25		2.25
November 10	25		2.00
September 21	25		1.75
August 10	25		1.50
June 30	25		1.25
2003			
June 25		25	1.00

Source: Board of Governors of the Federal Reserve System, Open Market Operations, *Intended Federal Funds Rate, Change (basis points) and Level.* Available at www.federalreserve.gov/monetary policy/openmarket.htm.

dates of the FOMC indicated in the table. The table shows that these targeted rates are typically changed gradually in response to varying economic conditions that reflect business and managerial decisions across the country.

In January 2001, in response to the slowing economy, the Fed began a series of rate cuts from the 6.50 percent targeted rate that had been in place since May 2000. The targeted rate was gradually lowered throughout 2001 and 2002 to 1.0 percent in June 2003, given the continued uncertainty about the economic recovery.

One year later in June 2004, the Fed began a series of steady quarter-point increases in the federal funds rate that lasted until a target rate of 5.25 percent was reached in June 2006. This policy recognized that the 1.0 percent rate was too stimulating once the economy began to grow on its own and was far below that needed for long-term price stability. The Fed maintained the 5.25 percent rate throughout the first half of 2007, even in the face of the developing problems in the housing and subprime mortgage markets. The impact of these factors on economic growth became apparent by the summer of 2007, and the Fed began a series of rapid cuts in the federal funds rate in September 2007 that lasted into 2008, including some that occurred before the regularly scheduled meetings of the FOMC.

By March 2008, the targeted rate was a full 2.5 points below the rate in September 2007. At this time there was still concern that lower rates might cause inflationary pressures. By fall 2008, inflationary expectations had receded as the consumer price index fell 1 percent from September to October, while credit markets were still frozen and economic activity continued to slow. The FOMC lowered the targeted rate to 1 percent in October 2008, a step that included an unprecedented coordinated rate cut by six major central banks. In December 2008, the FOMC cut the targeted rate to historic lows between zero and one-quarter point.[13]

This low targeted rate was maintained through the writing of this chapter in the summer of 2012. In its Monetary Policy Reports of 2009 and 2010, the FOMC indicated that economic conditions were "likely to warrant exceptionally low levels of the federal funds rate for some time [or an extended period]."[14] In its February 2012 Report, the FOMC was even more specific, noting that the exceptionally low levels of the federal funds rate would likely be kept through mid-2013. At this time the FOMC, reaffirming its commitment to pursuing its congressional mandate of promoting maximum employment, stable prices, and moderate long-term interest rates, stated that a 2 percent annual rate of inflation, as measured by the annual change in the personal consumption expenditure price index, was consistent over the longer run with the Fed's mandate.[15] In its July 2012 Report, the FOMC noted that the low federal funds rate would be maintained at least through late 2014.[16]

The FOMC also undertakes the buying and selling of government securities to counteract other influences on the banking system's reserves that are unrelated to monetary policy. These **technical factors** include changes in the amount of currency in circulation and in the size of U.S. Treasury balances at the Federal Reserve Banks. For example, individuals hold more currency during the holiday shopping season, so commercial banks must replenish their vault cash during these periods to maintain their reserves. The amount of U.S. Treasury reserves at the Fed can also change in response to individual and corporate income tax receipt dates and

Technical factors
Other influences on the commercial banking system's reserves that are unrelated to Fed monetary policy.

[13]Jon Hilsenrath and Kelly Evans, "Prices Post Rare Fall; A New Test for the Fed," *Wall Street Journal*, November 19, 2008; Jon Hilsenrath and Sudeep Reddy, "Fed Signals More Action as Slump Drags On," *Wall Street Journal*, December 2, 2008; Jon Hilsenrath, "Fed Cuts Rates Near Zero to Battle Slump," *Wall Street Journal*, December 17, 2008.

[14]Board of Governors of the Federal Reserve System, *Monetary Policy Report to the Congress*, February 24, 2009; February 24, 2010. Available at www.federalreserve.gov.

[15]Board of Governors of the Federal Reserve System, *Monetary Policy Report to the Congress*, February 29, 2012. Available at www.federalreserve.gov.

[16]Board of Governors of the Federal Reserve System, *Monetary Policy Report to the Congress*, July 17, 2012. Available at www.federalreserve.gov.

scheduled Social Security payments. Changes in reserves in response to these technical factors may either support or offset overall Fed monetary policy.

The Fed buys and sells securities outright through auctions in which securities dealers submit bids to buy or sell securities of the type and maturity that the Fed has stipulated. Orders are arranged by price, and the Fed purchases or sells as many securities as are needed for the particular policy action. The Fed may also engage in actions that only temporarily affect the supply of reserves in the banking system.[17]

The FOMC engages in securities transactions almost daily after analysis of economic conditions by the staff of the Board of Governors and the Federal Reserve Bank of New York. Once a policy is established, staff members at the Open Market Trading Desk of the New York Federal Reserve Bank contact some of the approximately three dozen securities dealers (called primary dealers) that work with the bank to execute the transactions that either credit or debit the dealers' banks and change the amount of reserves in the banking system. Short-term temporary operations are much more common than outright transactions due to daily fluctuations in the factors influencing the demand for reserve balances.

The FOMC reports its actions in the minutes of its meetings, which are published on the Federal Reserve Web page, and in press releases. For example, the press release for the July 31/August 1, 2012 meeting noted that:[18]

> Information received since the Federal Open Market Committee met in June suggests that economic activity decelerated somewhat over the first half of this year. Growth in employment has been slow in recent months, and the unemployment rate remains elevated. Business fixed investment has continued to advance. Household spending has been rising at a somewhat slower pace than earlier in the year. Despite further signs of improvement, the housing sector remains depressed. Inflation has declined since earlier this year, mainly reflecting lower prices of crude oil and gasoline, and longer-term inflation expectations have remained stable…
>
> The Committee expects economic growth to remain moderate over coming quarters and then to pick up very gradually. Consequently, the Committee anticipates that the unemployment rate will decline only slowly toward levels that it judges to be consistent with its dual mandate. Furthermore, strains in global financial markets continue to pose significant downside risks to the economic outlook…
>
> …the Committee expects to maintain a highly accommodative stance for monetary policy. In particular, the Committee decided today to keep the target range for the federal funds rate at 0 to ¼ percent and currently anticipates that economic conditions—including low rates of resource utilization and a subdued outlook for inflation over the medium run—are likely to warrant exceptionally low levels for the federal funds rate at least through late 2014…
>
> The Committee will closely monitor incoming information on economic and financial developments and will provide additional accommodation as needed to promote a stronger economic recovery and sustained improvement in labor market conditions in a context of price stability.

---

[17]If a temporary addition is needed, the Fed engages in short-term repurchase agreements, in which it buys securities from dealers who agree to repurchase them at a specified date and price. Most repurchase agreements mature within seven days, while some are completed overnight. To absorb reserves temporarily, the Fed engages in matched-sale purchase transactions, in which there is a contract for an immediate sale to, and a matching contract for future repurchase from, all securities dealers. These agreements also usually do not exceed seven days in length.

[18]Board of Governors of the Federal Reserve System, *Press Release*, August 1, 2012. Available at www.federalreserve.gov. When it publishes each FOMC press release, the online *Wall Street Journal* also includes a feature, "Parsing the Fed," in which analysts make a detailed comparison of the language in the current press release with the previous one. Many financial market participants perform the same type of analysis as they try to determine the future course of Fed policy.

The FOMC has made its decision process more transparent over time, almost turning the monetary stance announced in these briefings into another policy tool. In 1994, the FOMC began releasing a statement when it changed its targeted interest rate and, in 1998, it began announcing major shifts in its policy "bias" to raise or lower interest rates. In January 2000, these statements about policy bias were replaced by an assessment of the "balance of risks" affecting the economic policy goals of price stability and stable economic growth. The FOMC publishes a press release immediately after each of its meetings and the minutes of the meetings three weeks after they have occurred. In March 2011, the Fed also announced that Chairman Bernanke would hold press briefings four times per year to present the FOMC's current economic projections and to provide additional context for its policy decisions.[19]

Prime rate

The interest rate that banks charge on loans to their best customers.

Figure 13.2 shows the federal funds rate and the **prime rate**, which is the rate banks charge on loans to their best customers, from 2000 to 2012. The prime rate is shown as a step function, as banks set their prime rate on the basis of the rate established by the Fed. These are announced rates that remain in effect until they are changed by the Fed and the commercial banks. The federal funds rate, shown by the solid line in the table, is the *actual* federal funds rate, as opposed to the *intended or targeted* rate in Table 13.5. The Federal Reserve does not set the federal funds rate, which is determined by market forces in the federal funds market, but it uses its monetary tools to influence that rate in the direction set by the FOMC.

A decrease in the targeted federal funds rate (expansionary monetary policy) results in the lowering of other short-term interest rates, particularly those for automobile loans, home-equity lines of credit, adjustable-rate mortgages, and some credit cards. For example, the Federal Reserve's targeted funds rate cut in November 2002 made it easier for automobile companies to extend the zero percent financing that had been prevalent since the terrorist attacks in September 2001. The rate on most home-equity lines of credit follows the prime rate. Some

FIGURE 13.2

Selected Interest Rates

The prime rate, which banks charge their best customers, is set by commercial banks, whereas the federal funds rate is determined by market forces but influenced by the FOMC.

Source: Federal Reserve Economic Data (FRED II), Economic Research, Federal Reserve Bank of St. Louis, http://research.stlouisfed.org.fred2/.

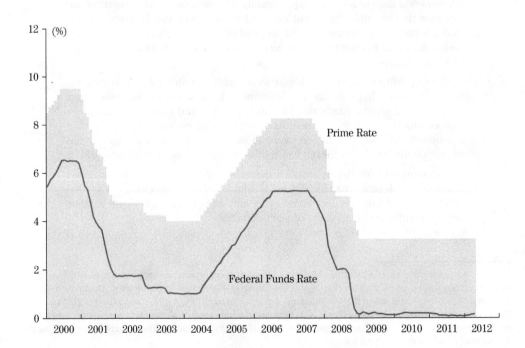

[19]Board of Governors of the Federal Reserve System, *Press Release*, March 24, 2011. Available at www.federalreserve.gov.

credit card rates decrease with expansionary policy, although many cards have fixed interest rates or floors under their adjustable rates. Long-term fixed mortgage rates typically do not respond directly to changes in the federal funds rate, as new mortgage rates tend to follow movements in the rates on long-term securities such as 10-year Treasury notes.[20]

The Discount Rate

The **discount rate** is the interest rate the Fed charges banks that borrow reserves at the Fed's discount window. An increase in this rate indicates contractionary monetary policy, making it more expensive for banks to borrow reserves, whereas lowering the discount rate signals expansionary policy. In the 1920s, the discount rate was the primary tool for Fed monetary policy. However, as financial markets became more developed and sophisticated, open market operations became the main policy tool. Currently, changes in the discount rate have a largely symbolic or announcement effect, indicating the direction of change in Fed policy. Because there is only a relatively small amount of borrowing at the discount window, any changes in this rate have only modest effects on the funding costs of depository institutions. Banks have been reluctant to borrow at the discount window, given that Fed discount officers routinely monitor their requests and the securities market also pays close attention to the volume of window borrowing. For loans extended after July 21, 2010, the Fed publicly discloses, after a two-year delay, details about the identity of the borrowing institution, the amount of the loan, and the interest rate.[21]

On January 9, 2003, the Fed instituted a new dual discount rate policy, under which a lower rate is charged on primary credit for banks in sound fiscal condition, while a higher rate is charged on secondary credit for banks that do not qualify for primary credit. The primary rate is typically set 1 percentage point above the funds rate targeted by the FOMC, while the secondary rate is set 50 basis points above the primary rate. Under this new system, called a Lombard facility, financially sound banks do not have to exhaust other sources of funds in order to obtain a discount window loan. In most cases Federal Reserve Banks do not require depository institutions to justify their requests for very short-term primary credit, while loans under the secondary credit program entail a higher level of Reserve Bank administration and oversight. This change has had little impact on monetary policy, which continues to be determined primarily by Fed open market operations.[22] In March 2008, the Fed also opened its discount window to investment banks to help ease the credit crisis that was occurring in the financial markets.

Table 13.6 lists the discount rates for several time periods. The discount rate is set by the Federal Reserve, as opposed to the federal funds rate, which is influenced by Fed actions. The concurrent changes in the discount rate and the targeted federal funds rate from 2004 to the present can be seen in Table 13.6. By fall 2008, the primary credit program was temporarily changed to allow primary credit loans for periods up to 90 days instead of just overnight or for very short periods. The spread of the discount rate over the federal funds rate was reduced to 25 basis points, and the Fed developed a program, the Term Auction Facility, under

Discount rate
The interest rate the Federal Reserve charges banks that borrow reserves at the Fed's discount window.

---

[20]Ruth Simon, "Will the Fed's Rate Cut Pay Off for Consumers?" *Wall Street Journal*, November 7, 2002; Ruth Simon and Zachery Kouwe, "Why a Rate Cut Might Hurt You," *Wall Street Journal*, June 25, 2003.
[21]Federal Reserve Discount Window/Payment System Risk. "Frequently Asked Questions—Discount Window Lending Programs." Available at www.frbdiscountwindow.org.
[22]See Deborah LaGomarsino, "Fed Approves Major Shift in How It Lends to Banks," *Wall Street Journal*, November 1, 2002; "The Fed Is Set to Roll Out a Revamped Lending Plan," *Wall Street Journal*, January 7, 2003; Federal Reserve Discount Window/Payment System Risk. "Frequently Asked Questions—Discount Window Lending Programs." Available at http://www.frbdiscountwindow.org.; Federal Reserve Bank of New York, "The Discount Window" (available at http://www.newyorkfed.org/aboutthefed); *The Federal Reserve System Purposes & Functions*, 2005.

TABLE 13.6   Discount Rates in Selected Periods

PERIOD IN EFFECT	PERCENT PER ANNUM
2/19/10 –	0.75[a]
12/16/08 to 2/18/10	0.50[a]
10/29/08 to 12/15/08	1.25[a]
10/08/08 to 10/28/08	1.75[a]
4/30/08 to 10/07/08	2.25[a]
03/18/08 to 4/30/08	2.50[a]
01/22/08 to 01/30/08	4.00[a]
11/01/07 to 12/12/07	5.00[a]
08/17/07 to 09/18/07	5.75[a]
06/29/06 to 08/17/07	6.25[a]
06/26/03 to 6/30/04	2.00[a]
01/09/03 to 06/25/03	2.25[a]
11/07/02 to 01/08/03	0.75
12/13/01 to 11/06/02	1.25
09/17/01 to 10/02/01	2.50
08/22/01 to 09/16/01	3.00
12/19/90 to 01/31/91	6.50
02/24/89 to 12/18/90	7.00
10/13/81 to 11/01/81	14.0
12/05/80 to 05/04/81	13.0

[a]These are the primary rates under the new dual discount rate policy established on January 9, 2003; they have been above the federal funds target rate. The policy was designed to improve the operation of the discount window for implementing monetary policy and providing a backup source of funds for depository institutions.

Source: Federal Reserve Discount Window/Payment System Risk. "Historical Discount Rates." Available at http://www.frbdiscountwindow.org.

which predetermined amounts of credit were auctioned to depository institutions for terms of up to 84 days. These Federal Reserve actions were designed to help increase liquidity in the financial markets and ease the ongoing credit crisis.[23]

Reserve Requirements   The Depository Institutions Deregulation and Monetary Control Act of 1980 made all depository institutions—commercial banks, savings banks, savings and loan associations, credit unions, and U.S. agencies and branches of foreign banks—subject to the Fed's reserve requirements, whether or not they were Federal Reserve member banks. As we discussed above, these requirements regulate the fraction of deposits that these banks and other institutions must hold either as cash in their vaults or as deposits at the Federal Reserve. Raising the reserve requirements has a contractionary effect on the economy, because banks will be able to make fewer loans and the money supply will either contract or expand less rapidly. As of December 29, 2011, the first $11.5 million of deposits are not subject to reserve requirements, deposits

[23]Board of Governors of the Federal Reserve System, *Monetary Policy Report to the Congress*, February 24, 2009. Available at www.federalreserve.gov.

up to $71.0 million have a 3 percent requirement, and deposits above that amount have a 10 percent requirement.[24] Thus, the requirements are structured to have less impact on small financial institutions. The use of reserve requirements as an active tool of monetary policy was more prevalent in the 1960s and 1970s than at present. Because even small changes in reserve requirements can have a major effect on the amount of reserves required, this tool is not appropriate for day-to-day changes in monetary policy.

Banks typically have an incentive to minimize their reserve levels because reserves held as either cash or deposits in an account with the Fed have traditionally not earned interest. The reserve requirements are typically higher than the level banks would impose on themselves for liquidity reasons, although there is some recent evidence that the reserve requirements may have become less binding as computer technology has allowed banks to temporarily "sweep" deposits from one type of account to another, which reduces the required reserve levels.[25] In October 2008, the Fed announced a new policy of paying interest on required reserve balances and excess balances. This policy was designed to help the FOMC target the federal funds rate by decreasing the incentives for institutions to trade balances in the market at rates much below that paid on the excess balances.[26] However, in summer 2012, there were calls for the Fed to lower the interest rate paid on excess reserves to zero or even charge banks a fee for holding their reserves at the Fed (a negative interest rate). This lack of return or imposition of a fee would give banks the incentive to loan these funds to consumers and businesses rather than hold them at the Fed.[27]

Appendix 13A presents a graphical discussion of the effect of the Fed's monetary instruments on the federal funds rate and the market for bank reserves.

Nontraditional Approaches   In response to the financial crisis and recession from 2007 to 2009, the Federal Reserve also developed an unprecedented set of lending programs and initiatives.[28] The financial crisis began after the boom in U.S. housing prices peaked around 2005. As housing prices declined, financial institutions holding large amount of mortgage-backed securities began to experience large losses, estimated to be approximately $500 billion in early 2008. This began a series of runs on the shadow banking system, institutions other than regulated depository institutions that channeled savings into investments. These institutions had short-term liabilities that were backed by longer-term assets

---

[24]Board of Governors of the Federal Reserve System, "Reserve Requirements." Available at www .federalreserve.gov/monetarypolicy/ reservereq.htm.

[25]Paul Bennett and Stavros Peristian, "Are U.S. Reserve Requirements Still Binding?" *FRBNY Economic Policy Review*, May 2002, 53–68; *The Federal Reserve System Purposes & Functions*, 2005.

[26]Board of Governors of the Federal Reserve System, "Reserve Requirements." Available at www .federalreserve.gov/monetarypolicy/reservereq. htm; Board of Governors of the Federal Reserve System, "Interest on Required Balances and Excess Balances." Available at www.federalreserve.gov/monetarypolicy/ reqresbalances.htm; Federal Reserve Bank of New York, "FAQs about Interest on Reserves and the Implementation of Monetary Policy." Available at www.newyorkfed.org/markets/ior_faq.html.

[27]Alan S. Blinder, "How Bernanke Can Get Banks Lending Again," *Wall Street Journal (Online)*, July 22, 2012.

[28]This discussion is based on Board of Governors of the Federal Reserve System, "Recent Financial and Economic Developments" and "Appendix: Federal Reserve Initiatives to Address Financial Strains," *Monetary Policy Report to the Congress*, February 24, 2009. Available at www.federalreserve.gov; Statement by Ben S. Bernanke, Chairman, Board of Governors of the Federal Reserve System, before the Financial Crisis Inquiry Commission, Washington, DC, September 2, 2010. Available at www. federalreserve.gov; and Frederic S. Mishkin, "Over the Cliff: From the Subprime to the Global Financial Crisis," *Journal of Economic Perspectives* 25 (Winter 2011): 49–70. For further discussion, see also Vincent Reinhart, "A Year of Living Dangerously: The Management of the Financial Crisis in 2008," *Journal of Economic Perspectives* 25 (Winter 2011): 71–90; and Gary Gorton and Andrew Metrick, "Getting Up to Speed on the Financial Crisis: A One-Weekend-Reader's Guide," *Journal of Economic Literature* 50 (2012): 128–50.

such as mortgage-based securities. As the value of these securities decreased and lowered the value of the collateral, these institutions had to sell off assets and restrict borrowing. Short-term financing for the investment bank Bear Stearns collapsed in March 2008. Because the bank could not sell off its long-term assets quickly enough, the Fed brokered a deal with JP Morgan Chase to purchase Bear Stearns, and the Fed took $30 billion of the bank's assets on its books. As noted previously in this chapter, the Fed also opened its discount window to investment banks at this time.

In September 2008, Lehman Brothers, the fourth-largest investment bank by asset size, filed for bankruptcy after suffering losses in the subprime mortgage market. This was followed by the collapse of American International Group (AIG), which had written over $400 billion in insurance contracts (credit default swaps) that had to be paid when subprime mortgage securities suffered losses. The Fed loaned AIG $85 billion to keep it solvent, with total loans from the Fed and the U.S. government eventually rising to over $170 billion. At the same time the Reserve Primary Fund, a large money market fund that held securities from Lehman Brothers, could no longer afford to redeem its shares at the par value of $1.00 ("breaking the buck"). This caused a run on money market funds that spilled over into the banking system.

Runs on the shadow banking system increased after September 2008, banks began to hoard cash and were unwilling to lend to each other, and the situation turned into a global financial crisis. The decreased lending and widening spread between interest rates on Treasury securities and more risky assets impacted the real economy with U.S. real GDP declining at annual rates of 5.4 percent and 6.4 percent in the fourth quarter of 2008 and first quarter of 2009, respectively. The unemployment rate then increased to over 10 percent by October 2009.

In response to this situation, the Fed turned to two major nonconventional policy measures—liquidity provision and asset purchases. To increase liquidity, the Fed established the temporary Term Auction Facility (TAF) that enabled banks to borrow anonymously at a rate determined through a competitive auction. The Fed increased its lending to investment banks, which promoted the purchase of commercial paper and mortgage-backed securities, and it increased liquidity through swap lines with foreign central banks. The Fed also engaged in outright asset purchases with the intent of raising the prices of particular classes of bonds and lowering interest rates for consumers and businesses. A larger asset purchase program, quantitative easing, began in November 2008 and extended through 2010 with the purchase of $1.25 trillion of mortgage-backed securities and $300 billion of Treasury issues and debt issued by Fannie Mae and Freddie Mac with the goal of reducing residential mortgage rates. In a second round of quantitative easing, the Fed bought $600 billion of Treasury securities in 2010 and 2011.[29]

As discussed in the opening case, the Fed also engaged in the Maturity Extension Program or "Operation Twist," a program in which the Fed sold short-term securities and used the revenues to buy longer-term securities with the goal of driving down long-term interest rates to stimulate business and household borrowing. The FOMC announced a $400 billion program in September 2011 and extended the program in June 2012 with the goal of purchasing an additional $267 billion in Treasury securities by the end of the year.[30]

---

[29]Jon Hilsenrath, "Fed Moves Closer to Action."

[30]Kristina Peterson and Jon Hilsenrath, "Fed Warns of Risk to Economy;" Board of Governors of the Federal Reserve System, "Maturity Extension Program and Reinvestment Policy, Frequently Asked Questions." Available at www.federalreserve.gov.

Managerial Rule of Thumb

Federal Reserve Policy

Managers must watch Federal Reserve policy statements and actions to judge where the economy is headed and how monetary policy will influence economic activity. The actions of the FOMC regarding the federal funds rate are the best guides to the direction of overall monetary policy. ■

Equilibrium in the Money Market

Now that we have presented the fundamentals of the banking system and the functioning of the Federal Reserve, we will use this background to develop a model of the money market, which we use to analyze the supply of money, the demand for money, and equilibrium in the money market.

The Supply of Money

Our discussion in the previous section focused on the Federal Reserve System's control over the money supply. An increase in the money supply, primarily through the open market buying of government securities, has the effect of lowering the federal funds rate, given the increased reserves in the banking system. This effect also causes other interest rates, such as the prime rate and rates on automobile and home-equity loans, to fall. For now, we assume that the Fed has perfect control over the money supply and can cause it to change a given amount with certainty. This assumption is a simplification we use for our model building. Later we discuss the problems involved with the real-world implementation of monetary policy (Chapter 14).

Real Versus Nominal Money Supply   We also note that the Fed controls the **nominal money supply (M_S)**, which is the dollar value of the M1 measure of the money supply shown in Table 13.1. The Fed influences the money supply through the open market operations that we discussed above. However, it is the **real money supply**, which is the nominal money supply divided by the price level (P), or M_S/P, that influences the economic behavior of individuals in an economy, as we show in the following simplified example.

We can illustrate the difference between the nominal and real money supplies in terms of a simple example involving one good, a can of soda, and the money carried in your pocket, your nominal money supply. Suppose that you normally drink 2 cans of soda per day and the price per can is $1.00. If you carry $2.00 in your pocket (the nominal money supply or M_S), your real money supply is (M_S/P_S) = ($2.00/$1.00) = 2 cans of soda. This real money supply, defined in terms of goods rather than dollars, is what influences behavior. If a friend gives you an extra $2.00 tomorrow, your nominal money supply increases to $4.00, and your real money supply increases to 4 cans of soda, assuming the price of soda is constant. You may consider this to be an excess supply of money if you consume only 2 cans of soda per day, and you may put that extra $2.00 into another form of financial asset. Thus, an increase in the nominal money supply results in an increase in the real money supply if the price level is constant.

In a second example, suppose that tomorrow you have only $2.00 in your pocket, but that the price of a can of soda falls to $0.50. In this case, your real money supply is also 4 cans of soda. Your real money supply has increased to 4 cans of soda even though your nominal money supply has remained constant at $2.00. Thus,

Nominal money supply (M_S)
The money supply (M1), controlled by the Federal Reserve, which is defined in dollar terms.

Real money supply (M_S/P)
The nominal money supply divided by the price level, which expresses the money supply in terms of real goods and services and which influences behavior.

an increase in the real money supply also occurs if the nominal money supply is constant, but the price level decreases. You again have an excess supply of money because you now need to carry only $1.00 in your pocket to buy 2 cans of soda.

Our analysis of money supply and demand will be undertaken in real terms or in terms of the goods and services that can be purchased with a given nominal money supply and price level. Our models focus on the nominal money supply (M1) controlled by the Federal Reserve and a measure of the absolute price level (P) for the entire economy (Chapter 11). However, the principles in these models are the same as those in the above one-good, one-price, and personal money supply examples.

Real Money Supply Function   The real money supply function is shown in Equations 13.2 and 13.3

$$\textbf{13.2}\quad \textbf{\textit{RLMS}} = \textbf{\textit{M}}_S/\textbf{\textit{P}}$$

> *where*
> $RLMS$ = real money supply
> M_S = nominal money supply
> P = price level

$$\textbf{13.3}\quad \textbf{\textit{RLMS}} = \textbf{\textit{M}}_S/\textbf{\textit{P}} = f(r, M_S, P)$$
$$(0)(+)(-)$$

> *where*
> $RLMS$ = real money supply
> r = real interest rate
> M_S = nominal money supply (controlled by Federal Reserve policy)
> P = price level

Equation 13.2 is the definition of the real money supply, whereas Equation 13.3 shows the general relationship among the real money supply, the real interest rate, the nominal money supply, and the price level. As with our notation throughout this text, the symbol f means that the variable on the left side of the equation is a function of, or depends on, the variables on the right side of the equation. The first variable on the right-hand side of Equation 13.3 determines the slope or shape of the curve, while the other variables cause the curve to shift. Equation 13.3 states that the real money supply does not depend on the interest rate. It is determined only by the price level and Federal Reserve policy regarding the nominal money supply. If the Federal Reserve engages in expansionary open market operations (or decreases the discount rate or the reserve requirement) and the price level is constant, the increase in the nominal money supply causes the real money supply to increase. If the price level decreases, all else held constant, the real money also increases, as in the soda example presented above.

Figure 13.3 illustrates two real money supply functions on a graph showing the real interest rate (r) and real money balances (M/P). Both money supply curves are vertical, indicating that the money supply is not a function of the interest rate. The initial money supply curve, $RLMS_1$, is determined by Federal Reserve policy. An increase in the real money supply is shown by a shift of the curve from $RLMS_1$ to $RLMS_2$, as real money balances increase from $(M_S/P)_1$ to $(M_S/P)_2$. This increase in real money balances could result from either an increase in the nominal money supply (M_S) by the Federal Reserve or a decrease in the price level (P).

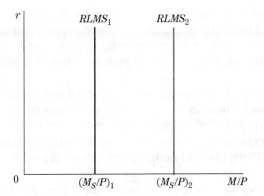

FIGURE 13.3
Real Money Supply Functions
Either an increase in the nominal money supply (M$_S$) by the Federal Reserve or a decrease in the price level (P) will cause the real money supply function to shift from RLMS$_1$ to RLMS$_2$.

The Demand for Money

Equation 13.4 shows a generalized **real money demand** function.[31]

$$13.4 \quad RLMD = M_D/P = f(r, Y)$$
$$(-)(+)$$

where

$$RLMD = \text{real money demand}$$
$$M_D = \text{nominal money demand}$$
$$P = \text{price level}$$
$$r = \text{real interest rate}$$
$$Y = \text{real income}$$

Real money demand
The demand for money in real terms, which is a function of the real interest rate and the level of real income.

The demand for money in real terms focuses on the portfolio decision that individuals make in terms of holding assets in the form of money versus other types of securities. To illustrate this portfolio allocation decision, we assume, for simplicity, that there are two assets that individuals can hold. The first is a liquid asset, money (currency and checkable or demand deposits), which pays them no interest. The second asset is illiquid and represents all other financial assets. For simplicity, we term this asset a government bond, which pays a positive interest rate, r.[32] Individuals hold money because it is liquid and enables them to engage in market transactions. Bonds are less liquid because they cannot immediately be used for market transactions, but they pay a positive rate of return. Thus, the interest rate represents the opportunity cost of holding assets in the form of money.[33] At higher interest rates, individuals will hold fewer assets in the form of money or

---

[31]The demand for money balances is expressed in real terms, as with the previous discussion of the money supply and the soda example. We assume people are aware of price level changes and demand nominal money balances (M_D) in order to maintain their real purchasing power (M_D/P). If you drink 2 cans of soda per day and the price of a can increases from $1.00 to $2.00, your nominal money demand increases from $2.00 to $4.00. However, your real money demand is the same in both cases ($2.00/$1.00 equals 2 cans of soda, or $4.00/$2.00 equals 2 cans of soda). Real money demand depends on the real interest rate and real income, but not the price level.

[32]Although checking accounts may pay some interest on the amount deposited, this interest rate is typically lower than what can be earned on other financial investments, such as money market funds and mutual funds. Thus, it is reasonable to characterize the asset allocation choice as between an asset with zero interest (money) and one with a positive rate of interest (bond).

[33]Technically, it is the nominal interest rate, i, that influences the demand for money and the real interest rate, r, that influences investment and consumption spending. If the rate of inflation is very low, these two rates are approximately equal.

will demand a smaller quantity of money because they do not want to sacrifice the interest they could earn on the bonds. At lower interest rates, the opportunity cost of holding money is less, so a larger quantity of money will be demanded. Thus, as shown in Equation 13.4, the quantity of money demanded and the interest rate are inversely related.

Real money demand also depends on the level of real income (Y) in the economy. As income increases, there is a larger level of output produced and more expenditure on that output. Individuals demand more money to finance the increased amount of market transactions associated with the higher levels of income, output, and expenditure. Thus, the real demand for money is positively related to the level of real income in the economy.

Figure 13.4 shows two money demand functions, $RLMD_1$ and $RLMD_2$. Each money demand function in Figure 13.4 is downward sloping, showing the inverse relationship between the quantity of money demanded and the interest rate. Thus, for demand function $RLMD_1$, real money balances demanded at interest rate r_1 are $(M/P)_1$, while a larger quantity of real balances, $(M/P)_2$, is demanded at the lower interest rate, r_2. The demand functions are drawn as straight lines, although they could be curved. Demand function $RLMD_1$ corresponds to real income level Y_1. If real income increases from Y_1 to Y_2, the money demand function shifts out to $RLMD_2$. There is a larger demand for money, $(M/P)_3$, at any given interest rate (r_2) with money demand function $RLMD_2$, given the larger number of transactions associated with the higher level of income.

Although income and the interest rate are the two major determinants of the demand for money, other autonomous factors can also shift the money demand curve.[34] For example, financial innovations, such as the use of ATMs and electronic banking, have caused a decrease in the demand for money and a leftward shift of the money demand curve at any given interest rate and level of income. In the past, individuals had to travel to a bank or other financial institution to transfer money from a mutual fund or savings account into their checking account or make a withdrawal from an account. Now this can be done electronically or with an ATM. This means that individuals demand less money at any given interest rate and level of income because they can easily transfer funds into their checking accounts from other securities that pay interest.

FIGURE 13.4

Real Money Demand Functions
A change in the interest rate, all else held constant, causes a movement along a given money demand curve (RLMD₁). A change in income or other autonomous factors influencing money demand shifts the curve from RLMD₁ to RLMD₂.

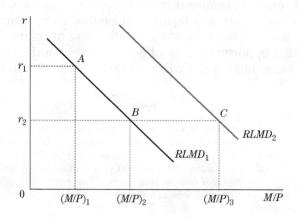

Equilibrium in the Money Market

As with all markets, equilibrium in the money market occurs at that interest rate where the quantity of money demanded equals the quantity of money supplied. At any other rate, there will be market disequilibrium, where the imbalance between quantity demanded and quantity supplied will set forces into motion that bring the market back to equilibrium.[35]

Change in the Supply of Money

We illustrate the process of restoring equilibrium in the money market by showing an increase in the real money supply in Figure 13.5. This change could result from either an increase in the nominal money supply by the Federal Reserve or a decrease in the price level. The original equilibrium in the money market in Figure 13.5 is at point A and interest rate r_1. Suppose there is an increase in the nominal money supply by the Fed, assuming a constant price level. This policy change shifts the money supply curve from $RLMS_1$ to $RLMS_2$. Point A' represents the point where there is an excess supply of money at interest rate r_1.

To understand individual behavior in reaction to this excess supply of money, we assume that an individual is faced with the choice of holding bonds that pay a positive rate of interest or holding money that pays no interest.[36] Also remember, as we discussed previously in the chapter, that the price of a bond is inversely related to its interest rate or current yield. At point A' and interest rate r_1 in Figure 13.5, individuals demand less money than the amount supplied. They want to hold more bonds and less money, so they will buy bonds with their excess supply of money, which drives up the price of bonds. This, in turn, drives down the current yield or interest rate. However, at a lower interest rate, individuals desire to hold more of their assets in the form of money, given the lower opportunity cost, so that their quantity demanded of money increases. The market is pushed toward a new equilibrium at point B and interest rate r_2 as individuals move down the money demand curve.[37]

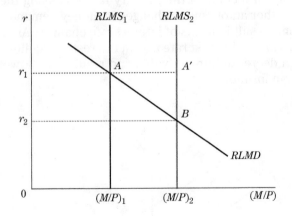

FIGURE 13.5

Increase in the Real Money Supply

Beginning at the original equilibrium (point A), an increase in the real money supply from RLMS₁ to RLMS₂ causes the interest rate to fall from r₁ to r₂ to restore equilibrium in the money market (point B).

---

[35]The equilibrium price in the money market is the interest rate. Also, the Federal Reserve is the monopoly supplier of money in this market.

[36]As noted above, we are using bonds to represent all types of financial instruments that individuals and organizations may purchase.

[37]Review the soda and personal money supply examples again if you need help in understanding this process.

The effect of the increase in the money supply is to lower the interest rate from r_1 to r_2. Likewise, a decrease in the money supply from $RLMS_2$ to $RLMS_1$ shifts the curve in the opposite direction, from point B and interest rate r_2 to point A and a higher equilibrium interest rate, r_1. Figure 13.5, therefore, can be used to illustrate the effect of a monetary policy change by the Federal Reserve.

The increase in the real money supply in Figure 13.5 could also result from a decrease in the price level, with the nominal money supply held constant. As illustrated in the soda examples, a decrease in the price level increases the purchasing power of the money supply. We portray this change with the shift of the real money supply curve from $RLMS_1$ to $RLMS_2$ in Figure 13.5. The end result is also a decrease in the interest rate from r_1 to r_2.

Change in the Demand for Money

Equilibrium in the money market can change if the demand for money shifts. Figure 13.6 illustrates an increase in the demand for money resulting from a change in income. The initial equilibrium in Figure 13.6 is with money demand curve $RLMD_1$ at point A and interest rate r_1. This money demand curve corresponds to income level Y_1. If income increases from Y_1 to Y_2, there is an increased demand for money, or a shift in the money demand curve to $RLMD_2$ in order to finance the additional transactions associated with the higher level of income. After the increase in the demand for money, point A is no longer an equilibrium point, as there is now excess demand for money at interest rate r_1 (point A'). At point A', individuals want to hold more of their assets as money than they currently do at this interest rate. To satisfy this excess demand for money, individuals sell bonds to obtain money. This increased supply of bonds drives down the price of bonds in the bond market. The decrease in the price of bonds means that the current yield or the effective interest rate on the bonds increases. However, with higher interest rates, individuals will desire to hold less of their assets as cash, given the increased opportunity cost. The quantity demanded of money will decrease as individuals move up money demand curve $RLMD_2$ in Figure 13.6 toward a new equilibrium at point B and interest rate r_2.

Although a change in income is the primary factor causing the money demand curve to shift, any other autonomous changes in money demand will also shift the curve, with the same result in terms of interest rate changes. An increase in money demand results in a higher interest rate in order to restore equilibrium in the money market, whereas a decrease in money demand results in a lower interest rate in order to restore equilibrium.

FIGURE 13.6

Change in the Demand for Money
Beginning at the original equilibrium at point A, an increase in the demand for money due to an increase in real income from Y₁ to Y₂ results in an increase in the interest rate from r₁ to r₂ to restore equilibrium at point B.

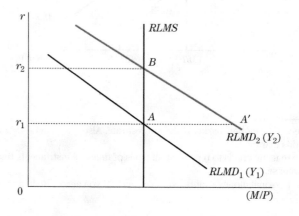

Overall Money Market Changes

Shifts in the demand for and/or supply of money change equilibrium interest rates in the money market. These interest rate changes then affect managerial and consumer spending decisions and the equilibrium level of income through the interest-related expenditure and aggregate expenditure functions (Chapter 12). The opening case of this chapter focused on the Fed's actions to further stimulate the economy in light of the extremely low federal funds rate-policy that had been in effect since 2008. We will examine all of these issues in more detail later in the text (Chapter 14).

Summary

In this chapter, we have examined the effects of money and monetary policy on the economy. We first analyzed the role of money in the banking system. We then discussed the role of the Federal Reserve and its tools for implementing monetary policy. Next we developed a model of the money market, analyzing both the demand and the supply of money. We showed how an equilibrium interest rate resulted in the money market and how that rate could change. Changes in interest rates affect managerial decisions because they influence the cost of borrowing for the firm and they change consumer spending patterns.

We are now ready to develop the overall aggregate macroeconomic model that integrates the real and monetary sides of the economy and helps managers understand how changes in the macro environment affect their competitive strategies (Chapter 14).

Appendix 13A Monetary Tools and the Market for Bank Reserves

Figure 13.A1 summarizes the effect of the monetary instruments of the Federal Reserve on the federal funds rate and the market for bank reserves. Figure 13.A1a shows the demand and supply for bank reserves and equilibrium in the market, which determines the federal funds rate (FFR). Banks are required to hold the quantity of reserves indicated by Q_{RR}. If the cost of borrowing or the interest rate decreases, they will have an incentive to borrow more reserves to guard against unforeseen contingencies. Thus, the demand curve for bank reserves slopes downward. The supply of reserves is established by Fed open market operations (Q_{OMO}). Banks with excess reserves will supply more reserves to the federal funds market as the interest rate increases. Thus, the supply curve for reserves is upward sloping.

Equilibrium in the reserves market is determined by the forces of demand and supply, which are influenced by the Fed's monetary instruments. Figure 13.A1b shows an increase in the supply of reserves, represented by the shift of the supply curve from S_{RES1} to S_{RES2}, which lowers the federal funds rate from FFR_1 (point A) to FFR_2 (point B). This shift in the supply curve results from open market operations that increase reserves from Q_{OMO1} to Q_{OMO2}. Figure 13.A1c illustrates a decrease in the reserve requirement, which lowers the amount of reserves that banks must maintain from Q_{RR1} to Q_{RR2}. This change shifts the demand curve for reserves to the left, as fewer reserves are required at any interest rate. The changes illustrated in Figures 13.A1b and 13.A1c result in a lower federal funds rate, which has an expansionary effect on the economy.

FIGURE 13.A1

Effect of Monetary Tools in the Market for Bank Reserves

FFR = *federal funds rate*

Q_{OMO} = *quantity of reserves established by open market operations*

D_{RES} = *demand for bank reserves*

S_{RES} = *supply of bank reserves*

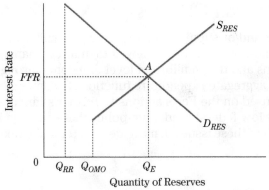

(a) Equilibrium in the market for reserves

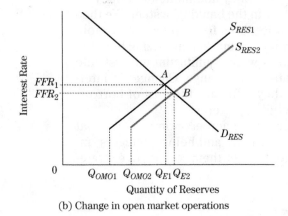

(b) Change in open market operations

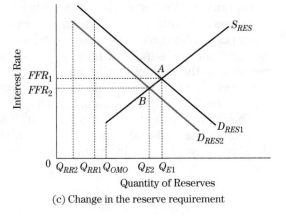

(c) Change in the reserve requirement

Key Terms

barter system, p. 362

Beige Book, p. 367

contractionary monetary policy, p. 368

demand deposits, p. 362

depository institutions, p. 363

discount rate, p. 373

expansionary monetary policy, p. 368

Federal Deposit Insurance Corporation (FDIC), p. 364

federal funds market, p. 368

federal funds rate, p. 368

Federal Open Market Committee (FOMC), p. 367

Federal Reserve System (Fed), p. 366

fractional reserve system, p. 364

liquidity, p. 362

monetary base, p. 365

money, p. 362

money multiplier, p. 365

money supply, p. 365

nominal money supply (M_S), p. 377

open market operations, p. 368

prime rate, p. 372

real money demand, p. 379

real money supply (M_S/P), p. 377

reserve requirement, p. 364

simple deposit multiplier, p. 365

technical factors, p. 370

Exercises

Technical Questions

1. Explain which of the following are counted as part of the money supply (M1):

   a. Checking account deposits
   b. Stocks
   c. Savings account deposits
   d. Government bonds

2. What is a fractional reserve banking system? What is its role in the monetary side of the economy?

3. If the reserve requirement (rr) is 0.2, what is the simple deposit multiplier? If, in addition, the currency deposit ratio (c) is 0.05 and the excess reserve ratio (e) is 0.15, what is the money multiplier? Explain why the money multiplier differs from the simple deposit multiplier.

4. What are the three tools the Federal Reserve uses to change the money supply and interest rates in the economy? Which of these tools is most important and why?

5. Explain which of these interest rates the Federal Reserve sets:

   a. The discount rate
   b. The federal funds rate
   c. The prime rate

6. In each of the following cases, explain whether the statements are true or false:

   a. If the real money demand is greater than the real money supply, interest rates must rise to reach equilibrium in the money market as people sell bonds to obtain more money.
   b. The federal government's control of the money supply, which influences interest rates, is the primary tool that policy makers use to impact the macro economy.
   c. A decrease in the reserve requirement decreases the money supply because banks have fewer reserves.
   d. The real money demand curve shows how households and businesses change their spending in response to changes in the interest rate.
   e. Both an increase in the nominal money supply by the Federal Reserve and an increase in the price level will cause the real money supply curve to shift to the right.

Application Questions

1. In current business publications or on the Federal Reserve Web site (www.federalreserve.gov), find the press release from the most recent meeting of the FOMC. What is the targeted federal funds rate? How does the FOMC evaluate the balance of risks between its goals of price stability and sustainable economic growth?

2. Drawing on articles in the *Wall Street Journal* and other business publications, evaluate the following statement: "What the FOMC says is becoming as important as what it does regarding monetary policy implementation." Find the "Parsing the Fed" feature in the online *Wall Street Journal* for the most recent FOMC press release. Does this feature support the statement in quotes?

3. On the Federal Reserve Web site (www.federalreserve.gov), find the version of the Beige Book that summarizes economic conditions in your Federal Reserve district. Summarize those conditions and relate them to current FOMC policy.

4. On the Federal Reserve Web site (www.federalreserve.gov), find the minutes of the most recent FOMC meeting. (Minutes of a given meeting are published after the next scheduled meeting, so they lag behind the press releases of the most recent meeting.) Summarize the factors that led to the decision regarding the federal funds rate at that meeting.

5. Building on Figures 13.5 and 13.6, show how equilibrium in the money market would change:

   a. If money demand is less sensitive to the interest rate or
   b. If there is a greater responsiveness of money demand to changes in income

14

The Aggregate Model of the Macro Economy

We have already discussed spending on real goods and services by individuals, firms, and governments and the influence of money and Federal Reserve monetary policy on the economy (Chapters 12 and 13). All of this discussion was in real terms because we assumed that prices were constant in this framework. In real-world economies, the price level changes, and inflation can be a serious policy problem. In addition, our framework has focused solely on the expenditure or demand side of the economy (Chapters 12 and 13). The price level and potential output in the economy are also influenced by supply-side factors. We need to develop the full model of aggregate demand and supply to address these problems, so that managers have a framework for analyzing the entire range of macroeconomic factors that influence their firms and industries.

We begin this chapter with the case, "What Role for Inflation?" We'll use the aggregate model we develop in the chapter to analyze the issues raised in this case by developing an aggregate demand curve based on our earlier framework and introducing the concept of aggregate supply to examine the constraints on expenditure imposed by the supply side of the economy.

Case for Analysis

What Role for Inflation?

We have noted that the goals of economic policy makers, including the Federal Reserve, are to maintain full employment, stable prices, and adequate economic growth over time. The major concern for the Federal Reserve in the spring/summer of 2012 was whether the U.S. economy was growing too slowly to bring down unemployment. As the Federal Open Market Committee (FOMC) moved toward a decision regarding further stimulus of the economy, several committee members, usually termed the "hawks," continued to voice concerns that additional stimulus in the short run could result in increased inflation in the long run. These members also argued that further bond buying or quantitative easing would have minimal long-term benefit to the economy.[1]

Debates over changes in the general price level had existed since the financial crisis in 2008.[2] Some analysts and FOMC members argued that deflation could result, given the depth of the recession and the high unemployment. With the existing slack in the economy, workers and businesses might accept lower wages and prices to generate demand for their products. Others argued that the extensive monetary stimulus through the use of the many unconventional tools, including the provision of liquidity and purchase of financial assets, would result in inflation. Some critics of the Fed argued that low interest rates earlier in the decade had actually fuelled the credit and housing price bubbles that led to the financial crisis. There was also concern early in 2012 that rising oil prices could derail the weak economic recovery, given the impact of oil on virtually every sector of the U.S. economy. Many analysts attributed an unexpected drop in consumer confidence in February to the higher gasoline prices.

Analysts continued to focus much attention on commodity prices, which had fallen for decades but then began rising around the year 2000. These increases were attributed to increased demand from China, India, and other emerging markets and from speculation in financial markets. Energy prices had increased 163 percent over the previous four decades. However, metal prices adjusted for inflation were approximately the same as in 1973, while food prices had decreased over the past few decades.[3]

In each of its *Monetary Policy Reports to the Congress* the Fed discussed trends in consumer prices. In July 2012, it noted that price inflation moved down, on net, during the first half of the year. The oil price increases that occurred in the first three months of the year were more than reversed during the second quarter. The overall personal consumption expenditure price index increased at an annual rate of 1.5 percent between December 2011 and May 2012 compared with an increase of 2.5 percent over 2011. The Fed argued that, in addition to the oil price decreases, the low inflation resulted from a decrease in non-oil import prices, low labor costs associated with the weak labor market, and stable inflation expectations.[4]

At its January 2012 meeting, the FOMC released a statement of its longer-run goals and policy strategy to increase the transparency of its actions. The statement emphasized the Fed's commitment to its Congressional mandate to promote maximum employment, stable prices, and moderate long-term interest rates. The FOMC also noted that an annual inflation rate of 2 percent as measured by the personal consumption expenditure price index was most consistent over the longer run with the Fed's statutory mandate. The statement indicated that the FOMC members' estimates of the longer-run normal rate of unemployment were between 5.2 and 6.0 percent and that the Fed would follow a balanced approach to returning both inflation and unemployment to levels consistent with its mandate.[5]

All of these data led analysts to believe that the FOMC would take additional steps to stimulate the economy in the fall of 2012, given that inflation did not appear to be a substantial problem at that time.

[1] Jon Hilsenrath, "Fed 'Hawks' Weigh In Against More Action," *Wall Street Journal (Online)*, August 17, 2012.

[2] This discussion is based on Jon Hilsenrath, "Fed Pondering Why Inflation and Deflation Threats Ebbed," *Wall Street Journal (Online)*, May 21, 2012; Jon Hilsenrath, Luca Di Leo, and Michael S. Derby, "Little Alarm shown at Fed At Dawn of Housing Bust," *Wall Street Journal (Online)*, January 13, 2012; and Ben Casselman and Conor Dougherty, "Oil Rise Imperils Budding Recovery," *Wall Street Journal (Online)*, February 16, 2012.

[3] David Wessel, "Hot Commodity: Research on Prices," *Wall Street Journal (Online)*, April 25, 2012.

[4] Board of Governors of the Federal Reserve System, *Monetary Policy Report to the Congress*, July 17, 2012. Available at www.federalreserve.gov.

[5] Ibid.

The Model of Aggregate Demand and Supply

As noted earlier in this chapter, policy makers are concerned with the macro goals we have described previously: maintaining stable prices, full employment, and a sustainable rate of economic growth over time (Chapter 11). In the summer of 2002, the Fed's focus was on stimulating the economy as it emerged from the 2001 recession, even though Fed policy makers knew that the targeted federal funds rate at that time was not consistent with maintaining low inflation in the long run. Given the weak recovery from the recession of 2007–2009, the concern from 2008 to 2012 was how much could the economy be stimulated without increasing inflationary pressures. Much of this discussion focused on the use of the Fed's nontraditional tools, such as the purchase of securities or quantitative easing.

To fully analyze these and other policy issues, we need the complete macroeconomic model of aggregate demand (*AD*) and aggregate supply (*AS*), which allows us to consider the impact of changes in real spending and monetary policy on both the level of real output and the price level. We first derive the aggregate demand curve and show how it shifts. After discussing the concept of aggregate supply and potential output, we integrate both concepts into the complete macroeconomic model of the economy.

The Aggregate Demand Curve

Aggregate demand curve
The curve that shows alternative combinations of the price level (*P*) and real income (*Y*) that result in simultaneous equilibrium in both the real goods and the money markets.

The **aggregate demand curve** shows alternative combinations of the absolute price level (*P*) and real income (*Y*) or GDP that result in simultaneous equilibrium in both the real goods and the money markets. We have established the concept of equilibrium in the real goods market and in the money market (Chapters 12 and 13). By itself, the aggregate demand curve does not show where the economy will actually operate. The aggregate demand curve gives the total amount of real goods and services (real GDP) that will be demanded by all sectors of the economy (household, business, government, and foreign) at different price levels.

Deriving the Aggregate Demand Curve   As background for deriving the aggregate demand curve, let's review the impact on the money market of a change in the price level. We have noted that a change in the real money supply results from either a change in the nominal money supply by the Federal Reserve or a change in the price level (Chapter 13). In Figure 14.1, we illustrate the effect of a decrease in the price level from P_1 to P_2, holding the nominal money supply constant. The initial equilibrium in the money market is at interest rate r_1, or point *A*. The decrease in the price level causes the real money supply to increase from $RLMS_1$ to $RLMS_2$. The interest rate must fall to r_2, or point *B*, to restore equilibrium in the money market. Thus, a decrease in the price level, holding the

FIGURE 14.1

Change in the Price Level and the Effect on the Money Market
A decrease in the price level from P$_1$ to P$_2$ causes the real money supply to increase from RLMS$_1$ to RLMS$_2$. Equilibrium moves from point A to point B, and the interest rate falls from r$_1$ to r$_2$.

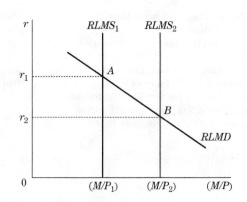

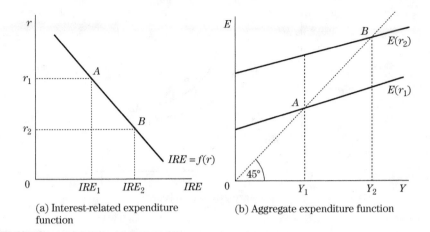

FIGURE 14.2

Interest-Related Expenditure and Equilibrium Income

A decrease in the interest rate from r_1 to r_2 increases interest-related consumption and investment expenditure from IRE₁ to IRE₂ and equilibrium income from Y₁ to Y₂.

(a) Interest-related expenditure function

(b) Aggregate expenditure function

nominal money supply constant, causes the real money supply to increase and the interest rate to fall, whereas an increase in the price level, all else held constant, causes the real money supply to decrease and the interest rate to rise.

Figure 14.2 presents the interest-related expenditure function and the aggregate expenditure function that we have discussed (Chapter 12, Figure 12.11). These functions show that at interest rate r_1, there is interest-related consumption and investment expenditure IRE_1, which results in an equilibrium level of income Y_1 (point A in these figures). If the interest rate decreases to r_2, interest-related consumption and investment expenditure increases to IRE_2, which results in a higher equilibrium level of income Y_2 (point B in these figures).

Figure 14.3 uses these concepts to derive the aggregate demand curve. The axes of this graph are the price level (P) and the level of real income (Y). Point A in Figure 14.3 corresponds to equilibrium point A in the money market in Figure 14.1 with interest rate r_1 and price level P_1 and to equilibrium point A in the real goods market in Figure 14.2 with interest-related expenditure IRE_1 and level of real income Y_1. Thus, point A in Figure 14.3 shows a price level P_1 and a level of real income Y_1 such that there is simultaneous equilibrium in both the real goods market and the money market.

Point B in Figure 14.3 shows a lower price level P_2 and a larger level of real income Y_1. The decrease in the price level has caused the real money supply curve in Figure 14.1 to shift to the right, which has resulted in a lower interest rate r_2 to restore equilibrium in the money market (point B). This lower interest rate r_2 has stimulated more interest-related consumption and investment expenditure IRE_2 in Figure 14.2, which has increased the equilibrium level of real income to Y_2

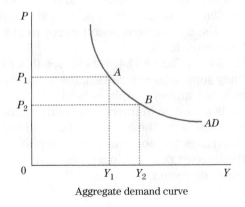

Aggregate demand curve

FIGURE 14.3

Deriving the Aggregate Demand Curve

If the price level decreases from P₁ to P₂ with the nominal money supply, M₅₁, constant, the real money supply increases, which lowers the interest rate and increases equilibrium income. Equilibrium moves from point A (price level P₁ and real income level Y₁) to point B (price level P₂ and real income level Y₂). The AD curve traces out these alternative points of equilibrium.

FIGURE 14.4

Expansionary Monetary and Fiscal Policy and the Aggregate Demand Curve

An increase in the nominal money supply by the Federal Reserve from M_{S1} to M_{S2} (assuming a constant price level, P_1) lowers the interest rate and increases the equilibrium level of income. Since the new equilibrium point B is at the same price level (P_1) as point A, but represents a larger level of income, point B must lie on a separate aggregate demand curve. Thus, an increase in the money supply causes the AD curve to shift to the right. Expansionary fiscal policy also results in a higher equilibrium level of income at the same price level and is represented by a rightward shift in the AD curve.

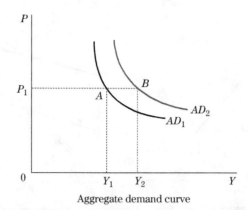

Aggregate demand curve

(point B). Thus, point B in Figure 14.3 shows another combination of the price level and real income level such that there is simultaneous equilibrium in the real goods and money markets. Points A and B therefore represent points on an aggregate demand curve, AD. This curve slopes downward, indicating that a larger level of real income is consistent with a lower price level and a smaller level of real income is consistent with a higher price level.

Shifting the Aggregate Demand Curve   The aggregate demand curve can shift as a result of deliberate policy actions by the Federal Reserve (monetary policy) or the national government (fiscal policy) or as a result of other autonomous spending changes in the economy.

Monetary Policy   Figure 14.4 shows the effects of expansionary monetary policy on the aggregate demand curve. In this figure, the original equilibrium at point A on aggregate demand curve AD_1 corresponds to point A in Figure 14.3.

Suppose that the Federal Reserve engages in expansionary monetary policy by increasing the nominal money supply. This is represented by a rightward shift of the real money supply curve, which results in a lower interest rate for equilibrium in the money market. The lower interest rate from the expansionary monetary policy generates interest-sensitive investment and consumption spending and a higher equilibrium level of real income Y_2.

Note that this example assumes that only the nominal money supply changed from Federal Reserve action and that the price level (P_1) has not changed. Thus, point B in Figure 14.4 corresponds to income level Y_2 and price level P_1. It is clear that point B cannot lie on the original aggregate demand curve AD_1 because the point represents the same price level, but a larger level of real income. If this analysis is repeated for another initial equilibrium, we trace out a second aggregate demand curve, AD_2, in Figure 14.4. Thus, expansionary monetary policy by the Federal Reserve causes the aggregate demand curve to shift to the right, resulting in increased aggregate demand at any given price level. Similarly, contractionary monetary policy causes the aggregate demand curve to shift to the left with less aggregate demand at any price level.

Comparing Figure 14.3 with Figure 14.4, we can see that in both cases, there is a change in the real money supply. In Figure 14.3, there is a change in the price level, but we assume the nominal money supply is held constant. Because the interest rate changes and there is a change in interest-related expenditure and equilibrium income, there is a movement along the aggregate demand curve, AD. In Figure 14.4, the Federal Reserve increases the nominal money supply at the same price level. This change lowers the interest rate and increases equilibrium income, but results in a shift of the aggregate demand curve from AD_1 to AD_2 because the price level has not changed.

Fiscal Policy   Figure 14.4 also shows the effect of expansionary fiscal policy (increasing government spending or lowering taxes) on the aggregate demand curve. Starting at point A, expansionary fiscal policy results in a higher equilibrium level of income Y_2 at the same price level P_1 (point B).[6] We see that this point cannot lie on the same aggregate demand curve as point A because it represents a higher level of income at the same price level. Point B lies on a new aggregate demand curve, AD_2. Thus, expansionary fiscal policy results in a rightward shift of the aggregate demand curve. Likewise, contractionary fiscal policy (decreasing government spending or increasing taxes) causes a leftward shift of the aggregate demand curve.

Other Autonomous Spending Increases   Other autonomous spending increases in any sector of the economy will have the same effect on aggregate demand, as illustrated in Figure 14.4. These spending increases cause a rightward shift of the AD curve. Likewise, decreases in autonomous spending cause a leftward shift of the AD curve.

These factors are summarized in Equation 14.1, which gives the general AD relationship in terms of the variables influencing autonomous consumption, investment, government, export, and import spending.

$$14.1 \quad AD : Y = f(\underset{(-)}{P}, \underset{(-)}{T_p}, \underset{(+)}{CC}, \underset{(+)}{W}, \underset{(+)}{CR}, \underset{(-)}{D}, \underset{(-)}{T_B}, \underset{(+)}{PR}, \underset{(+)}{CU}, \underset{(+)}{G}, \underset{(+)}{Y^*}, \underset{(-)}{R}, \underset{(+)}{M_S})$$

where

Y = real income
P = price level
T_P = personal taxes
CC = consumer confidence
W = consumer wealth
CR = consumer credit
D = consumer debt
T_B = business taxes
PR = expected profits and business confidence
CU = capacity utilization
G = government spending
Y^* = foreign GDP or real income
R = currency exchange rate (foreign currency per dollar)
M_S = nominal money supply (influenced by Federal Reserve policy)

The relationship between the left-hand variable, Y, and the first right-hand variable, P, in Equation 14.1 shows the shape of the aggregate demand curve (downward sloping). Other right-hand variables cause the aggregate demand curve to shift either rightward (+) or leftward (−). Both fiscal policy tools (government spending, G, and taxes, T) and monetary policy tools (Federal Reserve control of the nominal money supply) are included as variables in Equation 14.1. Note, however, the large number of other variables in the equation that also influence aggregate demand, *but are not under the control of any policy maker*. Forecasting the effects of changes in these other variables in order to develop sound fiscal and monetary policies is the major challenge facing policy makers. Determining the impact of changes in all of these variables on a firm's competitive strategy is one of the major tasks of a manager.

---

[6]This result is based on the aggregate expenditure function and the multiplier effect (Chapter 12).

TABLE 14.1   Factors Causing Shifts in the *AD* Curve

AD CURVE SHIFTS OUT TO THE RIGHT	*AD* CURVE SHIFTS BACK TO THE LEFT
HOUSEHOLD CONSUMPTION SPENDING (C)	**HOUSEHOLD CONSUMPTION SPENDING (C)**
Decrease in personal taxes (T_P)	Increase in personal taxes (T_P)
Increase in consumer confidence (CC)	Decrease in consumer confidence (CC)
Increase in consumer wealth (W)	Decrease in consumer wealth (W)
Increase in consumer credit (CR)	Decrease in consumer credit (CR)
Decrease in consumer debt (D)	Increase in consumer debt (D)
BUSINESS INVESTMENT SPENDING (I)	**BUSINESS INVESTMENT SPENDING (I)**
Decrease in business taxes (TB)	Increase in business taxes (TB)
Increase in expected profits and business confidence (PR)	Decrease in expected profits and business confidence (PR)
Increase in capacity utilization (CU)	Decrease in capacity utilization (CU)
GOVERNMENT SPENDING (G)	**GOVERNMENT SPENDING (G)**
Increase in government spending (G)	Decrease in government spending (G)
FOREIGN SECTOR SPENDING (X, M)	**FOREIGN SECTOR SPENDING (X, M)**
Increase in the level of foreign GDP or real income (Y^*)	Decrease in the level of foreign GDP or real income (Y^*)
Decrease in the currency exchange rate (R)	Increase in the currency exchange rate (R)
FEDERAL RESERVE POLICY	**FEDERAL RESERVE POLICY**
Increase in the nominal money supply	Decrease in the nominal money supply

Table 14.1 summarizes the effects of all the variables in the model on the *AD* curve.

Fiscal and Monetary Policy Implementation

The shift of the aggregate demand curve in Figure 14.4 from fiscal and monetary policy makes it appear as though using fiscal and monetary policy tools to influence the level of economic activity is a very mechanical and precise process. Although this is the case in the models, nothing could be further from the truth in the real world.

Fiscal Policy Changes   Fiscal policy changes result from a complex political process involving the president, his administration, and the Congress. Because there are so many people involved in this process, any changes in government expenditure or taxes meant to stimulate or contract the economy may take weeks or months to be approved by both the Senate and the House of Representatives and then sent to the president for his signature. Discussion of tax and spending changes is often more related to the political philosophy of the Democratic and Republican parties than to specific macroeconomic goals. Debate also focuses on the issue of whose spending and taxes will be changed. In some cases, at the beginning of a new fiscal year, federal agencies are authorized to undertake spending only on a temporary basis because the president and Congress have not agreed on the desired level of spending.

Fiscal policy takes even longer to have an impact on the economy after the changes are passed by Congress and signed by the president. Newly appropriated expenditures have to become part of a federal agency's budget, contracts must be established, programs must be funded, and employees must be hired. The impact of federal income tax changes depends on whether withholding rates from paychecks are changed and rebates are mailed out to consumers during the year or whether individuals must wait until April of each year, when federal income taxes are due, to determine the impact of any tax law changes.

In February 2009, in response to the recession and financial crisis, Congress passed the American Recovery and Reinvestment Act (ARRA) that had numerous spending and revenue provisions grouped as follows: (1) providing funds to states and localities, including aid for education and support for transportation projects; (2) supporting people in need through measures such as extending unemployment benefits; (3) purchasing goods and services including construction and other investment activities; and (4) providing temporary tax relief for individuals and businesses. The various elements of the legislation had different impacts on the economy.[7] The Congressional Budget Office (CBO) used evidence from models and historical relationships to estimate multipliers for each of the different categories of spending and tax provisions, with each multiplier representing the estimated direct and indirect effects on the nation's GDP per dollar of a given policy. Lower-bound estimates of the multipliers ranged from 0.2 to 0.5, while upper-bound estimates ranged from 0.8 to 2.5. For the second quarter of 2012, the CBO estimated that ARRA's policies raised real GDP by between 0.1 and 0.8 percent compared with what would have occurred otherwise. The CBO estimated that the effects of ARRA on the country's output peaked in the first half of 2010 and decreased since that time.[8]

The other fiscal policy issue that concerned decision makers in the summer of 2012 was the impending "fiscal cliff," or the increases in taxes and spending reductions that were scheduled to take effect in 2013 unless Congress acted otherwise.[9] These changes included: (1) expiration of numerous provisions of the Tax Relief, Unemployment Insurance Reauthorization, and Job Creation Act of 2010, including provisions that extended reductions in tax rates and expansion of tax credits and deductions originally enacted in 2001, 2003, and 2009; (2) significant reductions in Medicare payment rates for physicians' services; (3) the enactment of automatic enforcement procedures established by the Budget Control Act of 2011 to restrain discretionary and mandatory federal government spending; and (4) expiration of extensions of emergency unemployment benefits and a reduction of 2 percentage points in the payroll tax for Social Security. The CBO estimated that the federal budget deficit would decrease to $641 billion in fiscal year 2013 with these and other policy changes contained in the current law, but that the current law would

---

[7]Congressional Budget Office. *Estimated Impact of the American Recovery and Reinvestment Act on Employment and Economic Output from April 2012 Through June 2012*, August 2012. Available at www.cbo.gov.

[8]The 2007–2009 recession and the ARRA stimulated a large amount of research on the size of government expenditure and tax multipliers that used different types of models. Macroeconomic forecasting models incorporate relationships among aggregate economic variables based on historical data and economic theory, while time-series models rely heavily on historical data with less emphasis on economic theory. Dynamic general equilibrium models place greater emphasis on economic theory and focus on how an economy evolves over time. These issues are summarized by Felix Reichling and Charles Whalen, *Assessing the Short-Term Effects on Output of Changes in Federal Fiscal Policies*, Congressional Budget Office Working Paper 2012-08, May 2012. Available at www.cbo.gov. See also: Valerie A. Ramey, "Can Government Purchases Stimulate the Economy?" *Journal of Economic Literature* 49 (2011): 673–85; Jonathan A. Parker, "On Measuring the Effects of Fiscal Policy in Recessions," *Journal of Economic Literature* 49 (2011): 703–18; John B. Taylor, "An Empirical Analysis of the Revival of Fiscal Activism in the 2000s," *Journal of Economic Literature* 49 (2011): 686–702; Alan J. Auerbach and Yuriy Gorodnichenko, "Measuring Output Responses to Fiscal Policy," *American Economic Journal: Economic Policy* 4 (2012): 1–27; and Gunter Coenen, Christopher J. Erceg, Charles Freedman et al., "Effects of Fiscal Stimulus in Structural Models," *American Economic Journal: Macroeconomics* 4 (2012): 22–68.

[9]Congressional Budget Office, *Economic Effects of Reducing the Fiscal Restraint That is Scheduled to Occur in 2013*, May 2012; Congressional Budget Office, *An Update to the Budget and Economic Outlook: Fiscal Years 2012 to 2022*, August 2012. Available at www.cbo.gov.

likely lead to a recession with real GDP declining by 0.5 percent between the fourth quarter of 2012 and the fourth quarter of 2013. Under alternative assumptions, including the provision that Congress extended all expiring tax provisions indefinitely and that the automatic spending reductions under the Budget Control Act did not occur, the CBO estimated that the federal deficit would total $1.0 trillion but that real GDP would grow by 1.7 percent between the fourth quarter of 2012 and the fourth quarter of 2013. Thus, all economic forecasts at that time were conditional on assumptions about what Congress did or did not do regarding the fiscal cliff.

Some aspects of federal expenditures and taxes act as **automatic stabilizers** for the economy. These features tend to automatically slow the economy during times of high economic activity and boost the economy during periods of recession. For example, certain expenditures, such as unemployment compensation and welfare payments, are **nondiscretionary expenditures**. These expenditures increase automatically during periods of economic downturn. For example, during a recession, as more individuals lose their jobs, unemployment compensation expenditures increase simply because more individuals qualify for the program. The CBO estimated that automatic stabilizers added $367 billion to the federal deficit in fiscal year 2011, or 2.3 percent of potential GDP. The size of the automatic stabilizers depends on both the amount of excess capacity in the economy and the tax structure.[10]

Spending on these programs differs from **discretionary expenditures**, such as spending on defense or education programs, where the government spending must be authorized by Congress and funds must be appropriated for the programs. The tax system can also act as an automatic stabilizer. The U.S. federal income tax system is a **progressive tax system**, where higher tax rates are applied to higher income. This means that in times of greater economic activity, more taxes will be collected, which has a restraining effect on the economy. Thus, federal spending and taxation both affect and are influenced by the overall level of economic activity.

Monetary Policy Changes   Monetary policy is considered to be a more precise tool than fiscal policy for influencing economic activity, given that most monetary policy changes result from FOMC operations (Chapter 13). Even though these open market operations can take place on a daily basis, this does not mean that there is a definitive impact on the economy from these changes. The role of the Federal Reserve has also changed significantly since the financial crisis of 2007–2008 and the subsequent recession (Chapter 13).

The Fed always has to react to other changes that are occurring in the economy. Therefore, any targeted federal funds rate may become outdated by other changes in the economy and around the world. Although monetary policy focuses on the federal funds rate, an entire structure of interest rates exists in the economy. Most consumers are much more affected by changes in mortgage and personal loan rates than by the federal funds rate. Managers are influenced by the prime rate and other rates on business loans. Although interest rates tend to move together, there is not a strict correlation between them. Interest rates on different securities depend on the risk of default (or risk structure) and the length of time to maturity (or term structure) of the security. Higher interest rates are generally charged on more risky investments and on securities that have longer maturities. Thus, interest rates on long-term bonds (20 or 30 years) are generally higher than those on short-term bonds (a few months to a few years). Traditional monetary policy focused on the federal funds and other short-term interest rates, with the understanding that there

---

Automatic stabilizers
Features of the U.S. federal government expenditure and taxation programs that tend to automatically slow the economy during times of high economic activity and boost the economy during periods of recession.

Nondiscretionary expenditures
Federal government expenditures, for programs such as unemployment compensation, that increase or decrease simply as a result of the number of individuals eligible for the spending programs.

Discretionary expenditures
Federal government expenditures for programs whose funds are authorized and appropriated by Congress and signed by the president, where explicit decisions are made on the size of the programs.

Progressive tax system
An income tax system where higher tax rates are applied to increased amounts of income.

---

[10]Congressional Budget Office, "Appendix C: Automatic Stabilizers," *The Budget and Economic Outlook: Fiscal Years 2012 to 2022*, January 2012. Available at www.cbo.gov.

will be similar effects on long-term rates. This outcome might not always occur. For example, if contractionary monetary policy causes short-term interest rates to rise to slow the economy, long-term interest rates might actually fall if investors think future inflation might be less than expected.[11]

Spending changes on real goods and services that result from changes in monetary policy may vary by sector and take time to move through the economy. The estimated impact of these policy changes is also influenced by the econometric methods used by researchers. One study found that industrial production began to fall five months after a contractionary monetary shock and reached its minimum after approximately two years. Inflation also responded but with a longer delay of two to four years.[12] A recent study that contrasted various estimation methods found medium-sized effects from monetary policy changes that influenced historical U.S. macroeconomic fluctuations.[13]

The implementation of monetary policy has also changed over time. In the past, the Fed targeted the size of the money supply (M1). However, the demand for money became less stable over time as financial markets were deregulated and more types of near money (M2) came into use. These changes made M1 a less useful target. Thus, Fed policy shifted to focus on the federal funds rate rather than the monetary aggregates.

Fed policy is often characterized as "leaning against the wind." To avoid serious policy mistakes, the Fed usually adopts a gradualist approach. In a recessionary situation, the Fed will typically not try to close the entire gap between current GDP and potential output. That way, policy will not overstimulate the economy. This was the dilemma facing the Federal Reserve as discussed in the opening case of this chapter.

The Fed can act quickly in special situations, as in the days following the terrorist attacks of September 11, 2001. Immediately after the attacks, the Fed announced that the Federal Reserve System was functioning normally and that the discount window was available to meet liquidity needs. Borrowing increased to a record $45.5 billion by the next day. To maintain liquidity in the system, the FOMC cut the targeted federal funds rate the following week and at each subsequent meeting through the end of 2001.[14]

When the financial crisis developed in 2007, the Fed acted quickly, first by cutting the discount rate and extending term loans to banks and then by lowering the targeted federal funds rate (Chapter 13). In December 2008, the Fed lowered the targeted rate to between zero and 0.25 percent, where it remained at the time of this writing. The Fed also engaged in the large-scale purchase of financial assets and attempted to lower long-term interest rates through its Maturity Extension Program (Operation Twist) (Chapter 13).[15]

---

[11]President Clinton's deficit-reducing budget of January 1993 reduced investors' fears of future budget deficits enough that lower long-term interest rates resulted in the bond market. This change helped stimulate the economy and offset the need for as much monetary expansion by the Fed to lower the federal funds rate. See Alan S. Blinder and Janet L. Yellen, *The Fabulous Decade: Macroeconomic Lessons from the 1990s* (New York: Century Foundation Press, 2001), 15–24.

[12]Christina D. Romer and David H. Romer, "A New Measure of Monetary Shocks: Derivation and Implications," *American Economic Review* 94 (September 2004): 1055–84.

[13]Oliver Coibion, "Are the Effects of Monetary Policy Shocks Big or Small?" *American Economic Journal: Macroeconomics* 4 (2012): 1–32.

[14]Board of Governors of the Federal Reserve System, *Monetary Policy Report to the Congress*, February 27, 2002.

[15]Ben Bernanke summarized Federal Reserve policy since 2007 in "Monetary Policy Since the Onset of the Crisis," *Remarks by Ben S. Bernanke, Chairman, Board of Governors of the Federal Reserve System at the Federal Reserve Bank of Kansas City Economic Symposium, Jackson Hole, Wyoming*, August 31, 2012. Available at www.federalreserve.gov.

Interaction of Monetary and Fiscal Policy The final level of interest rates and real income in the economy typically depends on the Federal Reserve's reaction to fiscal policy or other autonomous changes in spending, which, in turn, relates to the Fed's policy goals of maintaining full employment, stable prices, and smooth economic growth. For example, an increase in spending either from expansionary fiscal policy or from some other autonomous spending change in the consumer, business, or foreign sectors would result in a higher equilibrium level of real income and a higher interest rate. The latter occurs because the higher level of real income increases the demand for money, which increases the interest rate (Chapter 13).

If the Fed believes that the increase in real income is appropriate, given its policy goals, it holds the money supply constant. The end result is a higher interest rate and an increased level of real income. However, the Fed's goal might be to hold the interest rate constant, such as in a recessionary situation where the Fed is trying to stimulate the economy by maintaining a low targeted federal funds rate. In this case, the Fed needs to increase the money supply to lower the interest rate and further increase income by shifting the *AD* curve.

Crowding out

The decrease in consumption and investment interest-related spending that occurs when the interest rate rises as government spending increases.

There might also be a concern about **crowding out**, the decrease in interest-related spending of consumers and businesses that occurs when the interest rate rises from increased government spending. If government spending increases without an increase in taxes, the government must borrow funds in the financial markets, driving up interest rates that then impact consumer and managerial spending decisions. The Congressional Budget Office takes expected Fed policy and potential crowding out into account when deriving its multipliers for increased government spending. The CBO argued that crowding out did not have much impact on estimates of the increased spending from the American Recovery and Reinvestment Act through the second quarter of 2012, given the Fed policy since 2008 of holding the targeted federal funds rate to between 0 and 0.25 percent.[16]

The Fed's goal can also be to hold the level of income constant in response to a change in fiscal policy or a change in autonomous spending because it is concerned about inflationary pressures arising from the increased spending. In this case, the Fed engages in contractionary monetary policy, reducing the money supply and raising interest rates.

After the presidential election in 1992, President Bill Clinton became convinced that reducing the federal budget deficit through a combination of spending cuts and tax increases was a high priority due to the crowding-out effects of deficit spending and possible financial calamities that might result from continued high deficits. This contractionary policy, reflected in the budget Clinton proposed in February 1993, could have slowed the economy (a leftward shift of the *AD* curve). However, the bond market reacted favorably with lower long-term rates, and the Fed continued its policy of targeting a federal funds rate of 3 percent until February 1994. Because the inflation rate was around 3 percent during this period, the real federal funds rate was approximately zero percent, representing expansionary monetary policy. By February 1994, the Fed was convinced that the economy was growing above trend on its own and that an increase in the federal funds rate was needed to gradually slow the growth rate and prevent possible future inflation. Although President Clinton was upset that the Fed began raising targeted interest rates barely six months after his politically sensitive deficit reduction package passed Congress, he maintained a hands-off policy toward the Fed.[17]

---

[16]Reichling and Whalen, "Assessing the Short-Term Effects on Output of Changes in Federal Fiscal Policies;" Congressional Budget Office, *Estimated Impact of the American Recovery and Reinvestment Act on Employment and Economic Output from April 2012 Through June 2012.* Available at www.cbo.gov.
[17]Blinder and Yellen, *The Fabulous Decade*, 15–26.

The Aggregate Supply Curve

Up to this point, our analysis has focused solely on aggregate expenditure or the demand side of the economy. The simple multiplier, the equilibrium level of income, and the aggregate demand (*AD*) curve all illustrate spending decisions by the various sectors of the economy—the consumer, business, government, and foreign sectors. To complete the aggregate macroeconomic model, we now need to examine the supply side of the economy.

The **aggregate supply curve** shows the price level at which firms in the economy are willing to produce different amounts of real goods and services or real income. An aggregate supply curve can have different shapes depending on the time frame of the analysis and the underlying assumptions of various models. Aggregate supply curves are based on an underlying **aggregate production function** for the economy as a whole, which is similar to the production function for an individual firm (Chapter 5). The aggregate production function incorporates information on

1. The quantity and quality of resources used in production (labor, capital, raw materials, and so on)
2. The efficiency with which resources are used
3. The production technology that exists at any point in time

However, the aggregate production function reflects production or supply possibilities for the economy as a whole. At any point in time, there is a maximum amount of real goods and services that can be produced, given the above factors. This is called the level of **potential output (GDP)**, or the full-employment level of output (GDP). Given the circular flow model, there is a maximum level of real income corresponding to the level of potential output.[18]

The equilibrium level of real income and output and the price level that exist in the economy at any point in time are determined by the interaction of aggregate demand and aggregate supply, which we model as the intersection point of the aggregate demand and supply curves. This **aggregate demand–aggregate supply equilibrium** is stable unless forces cause either curve to shift. In real-world economies, the aggregate demand curve, in particular, shifts often, so this equilibrium can change fairly quickly.

The shape of the aggregate supply curve and the level of potential output will determine whether this aggregate demand–aggregate supply equilibrium is considered desirable by policy makers in terms of the macroeconomic policy goals for the economy: maintaining stable prices, a high level of employment, and smooth economic growth over time (Chapter 11). The equilibrium level of output may lie far enough below the level of potential output that policy makers will use expansionary fiscal and monetary policies to stimulate the economy to generate more output and employment. On the other hand, the equilibrium output may lie above the potential level of output, causing inflationary pressures. In this case, policy makers will use contractionary policies to slow the economy. Most macroeconomic policy making, therefore, is concerned with influencing the equilibrium level of real output and the rate of change in the price level (inflation).

The equilibrium level of output changes as both the economy's aggregate demand curve and its aggregate supply curve shift. Because aggregate supply changes much more slowly than aggregate demand, we first examine changing aggregate demand with differently shaped aggregate supply curves. This process is the short-run policy problem faced by Federal Reserve officials and by the president and his

Aggregate supply curve
The curve that shows the price level at which firms in the economy are willing to produce different levels of real goods and services and the resulting level of real income.

Aggregate production function
The function that shows the quantity and quality of resources used in production, the efficiency with which resources are used, and the existing production technology for the entire economy.

Potential output (GDP)
The maximum amounts of real goods and services or real income (GDP) that can be produced in the economy at any point in time based on the economy's aggregate production function.

Aggregate demand–aggregate supply equilibrium
The equilibrium level of real income and output and the price level in the economy that occur at the intersection of the aggregate demand and supply curves.

---

[18]Potential or full-employment output is the output level produced when unemployment is at the natural rate or the nonaccelerating inflation rate of unemployment (NAIRU) (Chapter 11). Remember that we use the terms *real GDP*, *output*, and *income* interchangeably because real GPD can be measured from either the expenditure/output or earnings/income approach.

administration, as was discussed in the case opening this chapter. The shape of the aggregate supply curve depends on the time frame of the model and the assumptions about how firms respond to price changes. Macroeconomists continue to debate these issues.[19]

Short-Run Aggregate Supply Curve (Horizontal and Upward Sloping)

Figure 14.5 presents the aggregate demand–aggregate supply (*AD–AS*) model using a **short-run aggregate supply curve** with a horizontal portion and an upward sloping portion. The horizontal portion of the short-run aggregate supply curve reflects production in a range substantially below potential or full-employment output (Y_f), where firms can change the level of output produced without a change in the absolute price level. The economy's resources are not fully employed, so firms can increase the amount of real output produced and real income generated without having to bid resources away from other uses. This means that firms can produce more real output without an increase in their unit costs; thus, they do not need to charge higher prices for their products. Firms supply all the output that is demanded by the different sectors of the economy at a constant price level. This horizontal portion of the short-run aggregate supply curve is often called the **Keynesian model** because it reflects the economic conditions of worldwide depression that existed when John Maynard Keynes developed his macroeconomic analysis in the 1930s.

The initial equilibrium occurs at point *A* in Figure 14.5 where aggregate demand curve AD_0 intersects the horizontal short-run aggregate supply curve with price level P_1 and real income level Y_0. We then illustrate an increase in aggregate demand from AD_0 to AD_1, which results from either a policy change or an autonomous spending increase. The new equilibrium, point *B*, occurs at the same price level, but a larger level of real income, Y_1. Thus, with a horizontal short-run aggregate supply curve, all changes in aggregate demand result in changes in real income and output with no change in the price level.

The concept of equilibrium in Figure 14.5 implies that if aggregate demand does not increase from AD_0 to AD_1, the level of income in the economy will remain at Y_0. For example, in the Great Depression of the 1930s, the equilibrium level of income was substantially below the level of potential income and output. Researchers have attributed the Great Depression in the United States to a series of shocks that shifted aggregate demand to the left. The depression began in mid-1929 as a result of the tight Federal Reserve monetary policy, which raised interest rates in order to dampen the speculation on the U.S. stock market (causing a shift to the

Short-run aggregate supply curve
An aggregate supply curve that is either horizontal or upward sloping, depending on whether the absolute price level increases as firms produce more output.

Keynesian model
A model of the aggregate economy, based on ideas developed by John Maynard Keynes, with a horizontal short-run aggregate supply curve in which all changes in aggregate demand result in changes in real output and income.

FIGURE 14.5
Aggregate Demand–Aggregate Supply Equilibrium with Short- and Long-Run Aggregate Supply Curves

An increase in aggregate demand with a horizontal aggregate supply curve results only in an increase in real output, while an aggregate demand increase with an upward sloping aggregate supply curve results in an increase in both real output and the price level.

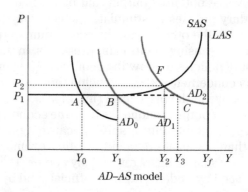

AD–AS model

[19]For a discussion of these debates and the models of aggregate supply that go beyond the scope of this chapter, see Robert J. Gordon, *Macroeconomics*, 12th ed. (Boston, MA: Addison-Wesley, 2012); and Andrew B. Abel, Ben S. Bernanke, and Dean Croushore, *Macroeconomics*, 7th ed. (Boston, MA: Addison-Wesley, 2011).

left of the *AD* curve). Interest-sensitive industries such as residential construction began to decline first. The stock market crash in October 1929 then led to a collapse in domestic consumption and investment spending as consumers and businesses became uncertain about the future and stopped purchasing durable goods (causing a further shift to the left of the *AD* curve). The decline in output in the first 18 months of the Great Depression was almost as large as in most previous and subsequent recessions combined.[20]

The short-run aggregate supply curve slopes upward as real income and output approach the economy's potential output. This upward sloping short-run aggregate supply curve occurs because firms' input costs rise when they have to bid resources away from competing uses, as most inputs are becoming fully employed. As input costs rise, firms charge higher prices for their products, and the absolute price level begins to increase. Firms will produce more real output only as the price level increases.

Figure 14.5 also illustrates the upward sloping aggregate supply curve. Starting at point *B*, we again show that expansionary fiscal policy or an autonomous spending increase causes a shift of the aggregate demand curve from AD_1 to AD_2. If the price level did not rise, equilibrium would be at point *C* at price level P_1 and income level Y_3.

However, in this case, the aggregate supply curve is upward sloping. The price level rises as output increases, given that the economy is approaching the full-employment level of output. The final equilibrium in Figure 14.5 is at point *F*, with price level P_2 and income level Y_2. Part of the increase in aggregate demand results in an increase in the price level rather than an increase in real output. This outcome occurs because the increase in the price level creates a smaller real money supply which causes the interest rate to rise. This increase in the interest rate chokes off some interest-related spending, thereby increasing real income only to Y_2 and not to Y_3.

The short-run aggregate supply curve can be expressed as Equation 14.2:

14.2   Short-run *AS*: $P = f(Y_f, $ Resource costs$)$
$$(0) \qquad (+)$$

where

$$P = \text{price level}$$
$$Y_f = \text{full-employment or potential output}$$
$$\text{Resource costs} = \text{costs of the resources or inputs of production}$$

Equation 14.2 shows that the price level is a function of the costs of the resources or inputs of production. Changes in these costs unrelated to overall demand will cause the short-run *AS* curve to shift up or down. If the cost of a major resource such as oil increases, a higher price level will be needed at every level of income to induce firms to supply that output. The level of potential or full-employment GDP (Y_f) does not change because the factors determining potential output (resources, efficiency, and technology) are fixed in the short run.

Long-Run Aggregate Supply Curve (Vertical)   Figure 14.5 also shows a **long-run aggregate supply curve**, which is vertical at the level of potential or full-employment output. This level of output is determined by the amount of resources, the efficiency with which they are used, and the level of technology in the economy. Because these factors are constant in the short run, the full-employment level of output represents a constraint on increases in aggregate demand. As aggregate demand increases beyond AD_2 in Figure 14.5 (and the short-run *AS* curve slopes

Long-run aggregate supply curve
A vertical aggregate supply curve that defines the level of full employment or potential output based on a given amount of resources, efficiency, and technology in the economy.

[20]Christina D. Romer, "The Nation in Depression," *Journal of Economic Perspectives* 7 (Spring 1993): 19–39.

upward and approaches the long-run *AS* curve), any increases in spending will result in smaller increases in real output and larger increases in the price level. With a vertical aggregate supply curve, any further increases in aggregate demand result only in a higher price level and no increase in real output.[21]

This figure, therefore, illustrates the ongoing policy dilemma of the Federal Reserve. If the Fed uses monetary policy to shift aggregate demand and increase output and employment, it may stimulate the economy too much, setting off an inflationary spiral. The Fed also needs to judge what changes in private-sector behavior would cause aggregate demand to increase on its own, reducing the need for further monetary intervention.

The long-run aggregate supply curve is defined in Equation 14.3:

$$\textbf{14.3} \quad \textbf{Long-run } AS\text{: } Y_f = f(P, \textbf{Resources}, \textbf{Efficiency}, \textbf{Technology})$$
$$\qquad\qquad\quad (0) \qquad (+) \qquad\quad (+) \qquad\qquad (+)$$

where

$\quad Y_f$ = full-employment or potential output

$\quad P$ = price level

Resources = amount of inputs in the economy used to produce final goods and services

Efficiency = means by which resources are combined to minimize the cost of production

Technology = state of knowledge in the economy on how to produce goods and services

Equation 14.3 implies that the long-run aggregate supply curve is vertical and not influenced by the price level. It can be shifted right or left over time by changes in the amount of resources available to produce final goods and services, by increased efficiency in minimizing the costs of production, or by the development of new technologies for producing goods and services.

Shifting Aggregate Supply   The policy dilemma of the Federal Reserve discussed above is made more complicated because both the short- and the long-run aggregate supply curves can shift.

Shifts in Short-Run Aggregate Supply   The short-run aggregate supply curve will shift as a result of productivity changes and changes in the costs of the inputs of production that are independent of overall demand changes. These changes have to be widespread throughout the economy, such as the oil price increases caused by the OPEC oil embargo during the 1970s, to have an influence on the absolute price level. We illustrate such a supply-side shock to the economy

---

[21]Remember that the focus of this text is explaining short-run fluctuations in income, output, and price level. In the long-run analysis of the economy, it is assumed that firms produce at their maximum sustainable output, so that the economy operates at its potential level of output. It is also assumed that prices are completely flexible in the long run. Therefore, any changes in aggregate demand in the long run can result only in changes in the price level, not in the level of real output and income. This model is called the Classical model because it reflects the beliefs about the economy held by the classical economists before John Maynard Keynes. These economists believed that any deviations of real output from potential output were only temporary because prices would adjust to bring the economy back to potential output. For example, if aggregate demand decreased and was insufficient to generate the full potential level of output at the current price level, classical economists believed the price level would fall sufficiently that the economy would return to that level of output. Likewise, if aggregate demand increased and exceeded potential output, the price level would rise sufficiently to bring the economy back to the level of potential output and income.

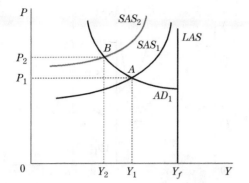

FIGURE 14.6
Change in Short-Run Aggregate Supply
The short-run aggregate supply curve shifts up due to major increases in the costs of production unrelated to demand, such as increases in the price of oil, resulting in a higher price level and a lower level of real output.

in Figure 14.6. In this figure, assume that the original equilibrium is at point A, the intersection of the AD_1 and SAS_1 curves, with income level Y_1 and price level P_1. We represent the oil price increase by the shift of the aggregate supply curve from SAS_1 to SAS_2. Firms' unit costs have increased, and they charge higher prices to cover those costs. Because these increases are widespread throughout the economy, the absolute price level rises to P_2. Given aggregate demand curve AD_1, the level of real income is reduced to Y_2 at point B. The higher price level and increased prices (inflation), when combined with lower real output and income (stagnation), are called **stagflation**.

Stagflation represents a major dilemma for policy makers. To deal with the problem of inflation, policy makers would need to use contractionary monetary or fiscal policy to shift the aggregate demand curve to the left. However, this policy would result in a still lower level of real income and output even further from potential output. If the policy goal is to focus on the stagnation problem, expansionary monetary or fiscal policy would be needed. However, expansionary policy would shift the aggregate demand curve to the right and would result in a higher price level and possible inflation. Thus, in the case of stagflation, policy makers are forced to choose between alternative policy goals. In the late 1970s, the Federal Reserve implemented a deliberate contractionary monetary policy to decrease the inflation generated by the oil price shocks earlier in the decade. This action resulted in recessions in 1980 and 1981, but a lower inflation rate was also achieved.[22]

Stagflation
Higher prices and price increases (inflation) combined with lower real output and income (stagnation), resulting from a major increase in input prices in the economy.

Shifts in Long-Run Aggregate Supply   The long-run aggregate supply curve can also shift over time if there are increases in the amount of inputs (labor, land, capital, and raw materials) in the economy and increases in technology and efficiency. These increases in long-run aggregate supply are favorable to the economy, as shown in Figure 14.7.

The original equilibrium in Figure 14.7 is at the intersection of aggregate demand curve AD_1 and short-run aggregate supply curve SAS_1 (point A, with price level P_1

[22]There were seven occasions in the post–World War II era when the Fed deliberately engaged in restrictive monetary policy to reduce the level of inflation. Industrial production declined 9.6 percent between 1979 and 1982 due to the monetary shocks of August 1978 and October 1979. However, production would have risen 9.3 percent in the absence of those shocks. The Fed had little mandate to fight the peacetime inflation of the 1970s by inducing a recession until the end of the decade, when there were increased fears about the costs of inflation. See Christina D. Romer, "Changes in Business Cycles: Evidence and Explanations," *Journal of Economic Perspectives* 13 (Spring 1999): 23–44; J. Bradford De Long, "America's Peacetime Inflation: The 1970s," in *Reducing Inflation: Motivation and Strategy*, ed. Christina D. Romer and David H. Romer (Chicago: University of Chicago Press, 1997), 247–280; and Charles L. Weise, "Political Pressures on Monetary Policy During the US Great Inflation," *American Economic Journal: Macroeconomics* 4 (2012): 33–64.

FIGURE 14.7
Change in Long-Run Aggregate Supply
Shifts in the long-run aggregate supply curve result from changes in the quantity and quality of resources and the introduction of new technology. Any increase in aggregate demand will result in a larger increase in real output and a smaller increase in the price level if the long-run aggregate supply curve also shifts out.

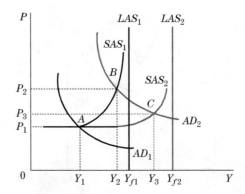

and income level Y_1). Given that the SAS_1 curve begins to slope upward because the economy is nearing the full-employment output, Y_{f1}, an increase in aggregate demand to AD_2 results in an increase in the price level to P_2 and an increase in real output and income to only Y_2.

However, if the long-run aggregate supply curve shifts and the full-employment level of output increases from Y_{f1} to Y_{f2}, given increases in the quantity and quality of the economy's productive resources and new technology, output can expand farther along short-run aggregate supply curve SAS_2 at a constant price level P_1 before the price level again begins to rise as Y_{f2} is approached. With this increase in long-run aggregate supply, the increase in aggregate demand from AD_1 to AD_2 results in an equilibrium at point C, at a lower price level, P_3, and a larger real output and income level, Y_3. Thus, increases in long-run aggregate supply can assist the Fed in reaching its policy goals. Much of the macroeconomic policy debate in the late 1990s centered on understanding the reasons why aggregate demand kept increasing, pushing unemployment lower without generating sustained inflation. Many analysts attributed these desirable outcomes to the increased productivity in the economy from computers and other electronic technology, or the new economy effect.

Some research on this new economy effect has focused on measuring the changes in the natural rate of unemployment, or the nonaccelerating inflation rate of unemployment (NAIRU) (Chapter 11). Decreases in the NAIRU represent a rightward shift of the long-run aggregate supply curve because the economy can produce more output and reach a lower level of unemployment without incurring an increase in the rate of inflation. These studies have shown that the NAIRU started at approximately 5.4 percent in 1960, increased up to a peak of 6.8 percent in 1979, and then declined to approximately 4.9 percent in 2000.[23] Various factors contributed to this trend. The proportion of the labor force aged 16 to 24 increased from 17 percent in 1960 to 24 percent in 1978 and then fell back to 16 percent in 2000. These changes in the composition of the labor force could have impacted the NAIRU because younger workers have higher unemployment rates than older workers. Increasing incarceration rates and more generous disability insurance payments may have also caused individuals with higher unemployment rates to leave the labor force, making the trade-off with inflation more favorable.

---

[23]Laurence Ball and N. Gregory Mankiw, "The NAIRU in Theory and Practice," *Journal of Economic Perspectives* 16 (Fall 2002): 115–36; Robert J. Gordon, "Foundations of the Goldilocks Economy: Supply Shocks and the Time-Varying NAIRU," *Brookings Papers on Economic Activity* 2 (1998): 297–333; Douglas Staiger, James H. Stock, and Mark W. Watson, "Prices, Wages, and the U.S. NAIRU in the 1990s," in *The Roaring Nineties: Can Full Employment Be Sustained?* eds. Alan B. Krueger and Robert Solow (New York: Sage Foundation and Century Foundation Press, 2001), 3–60.

While these trends explained much of the decline in the NAIRU up to 1995, subsequent decreases were probably related to increases in productivity in the economy resulting from the increased use of computers and the Internet. Given these productivity gains, firms were able to respond to workers' wage increases without raising prices. Average annual growth in output per hour of work was 1.5 percent over the period 1974–1995, but increased to 2.6 percent between 1996 and 2000.[24]

Stephen Oliner and Daniel Sichel have estimated that of the 1 percentage point acceleration in labor productivity that occurred between the periods 1991–1995 and 1996–1999, 0.45 percentage point was attributed to the growing use of information technology (IT) capital throughout the nonfarm business sector of the economy. Rapidly improving technology for producing computers contributed another 0.26 percentage point to the acceleration. However, the growth in other capital services per hour explained almost none of the acceleration. These researchers concluded that IT had been the primary factor behind the sharp increase in productivity growth in the late 1990s.[25]

More recent productivity estimates show that IT played a less important role in productivity growth after 2000 than it did in the 1990s. Researchers estimated that productivity growth from 2007 to 2017 might average 2.4 percent per year, a rate that was relatively rapid for the United States from a historical perspective but below average for the decade after 1995. These analysts noted that there was little likelihood that the U.S. economy would revert to the lower rates of productivity growth that existed in the 1970s and 1980s.[26] The sources of growth from 2000 to 2007 occurred in the IT-using industries rather than in the IT-producing industries. The leaders in innovation in the IT-using sector, wholesale and retail trade, included firms such as Wal-Mart and Cisco that have integrated supply chains around the world.[27]

The natural rate of unemployment was estimated to increase about one percentage point to 6.0 percent following the recession of 2007–2009.[28] This increase could have resulted from a mismatch between the characteristics of job openings and the skills of the unemployed, the availability of extended unemployment insurance benefits, and uncertainty about economic conditions. Researchers argued that the role of the first factor was limited, while the influence of the latter two were likely temporary, so that the natural rate was likely to return to its prerecession level of around 5 percent when the economy fully recovered from the recession.

[24]Ball and Mankiw, "The NAIRU in Theory and Practice."
[25]Stephen D. Oliner and Daniel E. Sichel, "The Resurgence of Growth in the Late 1990s: Is Information Technology the Story?" *Journal of Economic Perspectives* 14 (Fall 2000): 3–22. See also Erik Brynjolfsson and Lorin M. Hitt, "Beyond Computation: Information Technology, Organizational Transformation and Business Performance," *Journal of Economic Perspectives* 14 (Fall 2000): 23–48; Robert J. Gordon, "Does the 'New Economy' Measure Up to the Great Inventions of the Past?" *Journal of Economic Perspectives* 14 (Fall 2000): 49–74; and Blinder and Yellen, *The Fabulous Decade.*
[26]Dale W. Jorgenson, Mun S. Ho, and Kevin J. Stiroh, "A Retrospective Look at the U.S. Productivity Growth Resurgence," *Journal of Economic Perspectives* 22 (Winter 2008): 3–24.
[27]Dale W. Jorgensen, Mun S. Ho, and Jon D. Samuels, "Information Technology and U.S. Productivity Growth: Evidence from a Prototype Industry Production Account," *Journal of Productivity Analysis* 36 (2011): 159–75. For discussions of productivity changes over longer periods of time, see Robert J. Gordon, "Revisiting U.S. Productivity Growth over the Past Century with a View to the Future," *National Bureau of Economic Research Working Paper #15834*, March 2010; and Robert J. Gordon, "Is U.S. Economic Growth Over? Faltering Innovation Confronts the Six Headwinds," *National Bureau of Economic Research Working Paper #18315*, August 2012. Available at www.nber.org.
[28]This discussion is based on Mary C. Daly, Bart Jobijn, Aysegul Sahin, and Robert G. Valletta, "A Search and Matching Approach to Labor Markets: Did the Natural Rate of Unemployment Rise?" *Journal of Economic Perspectives* 26 (Summer 2012): 3–26.

Using the Aggregate Model to Explain Changes in the Economy from 2007 to 2008 and from 2011 to 2012

Managers can use the aggregate macroeconomic model we have developed to analyze changes in the macro environment in any time period (Chapters 11–14).[29] We now illustrate the use of the model to examine changes in the U.S. economy from 2007 to 2008 and again from 2011 to 2012.

Figure 14.8a illustrates the impact of these factors for 2007–2008 using the AD–AS model. Point A is the initial equilibrium determined by the intersection of the AD_{07} and SAS_{07} curves in Figure 14.8a with price level P_{07} and real income level Y_{07}. The full-employment level of output is given by Y_{f07}. The impact of changes in the above variables is shown by the curves labeled "08" in Figure 14.8a and in Table 14.2. All of these changes are derived from our aggregate macro model.

We can see in Table 14.2 that the variables influencing the AD curve have conflicting impacts. Some cause the AD curve to shift to the right, while others cause it to shift to the left. Thus, the final location of the curve and the final impact on the price level and the level of real output and income depend on the magnitude of the changes in the variables, which is what managers need to forecast.

Changes from 2007 to 2008   Macroeconomic conditions in the 2007–2008 period reflected the concern about whether the economy was headed into a recession, and there was also speculation about stagflation.

The major changes occurring in the economy over this period, illustrated in Table 14.2, were as follows:

- A decrease in home prices and consumer wealth
- Decreased consumer and business confidence
- A credit crisis in the financial markets
- Slower rate of growth in federal government spending
- A continuous increase in the money supply to lower interest rates
- A decrease in the value of the dollar
- Growth in foreign economies

The effect of these changes on aggregate demand and supply are shown in Figure 14.8a.

The negative effects of the decrease in housing prices that impacted consumer wealth, the loss of consumer and business confidence, and the decrease in residential

FIGURE 14.8

Using the Aggregate Model

The changes in the economy from 2007 to 2008 and from 2011 to 2012 are illustrated in the AD–AS model.

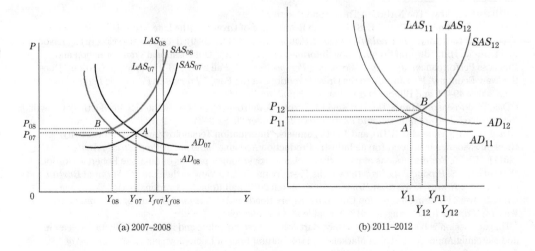

(a) 2007–2008

(b) 2011–2012

---

[29]Both the general and specific equations of the aggregate macro model are summarized in Appendix 14A.

TABLE 14.2 Impact of Changes in the Aggregate Model

CURVE	VARIABLE	SPENDING COMPONENT(S)	SHIFT OF CURVE
AD_{08}	1. Housing wealth decreases	1. Consumption decreases	1. Left
	2. Confidence decreases	2. Consumption and investment decrease	2. Left
	3. Credit crisis in financial markets	3. Residential investment decreases	3. Left
	4. Government spending slows	4. Government spending slows	4. Left
	5. MS increases	5. Lower interest rates increase consumption/investment	5. Right
	6. Dollar decreases in value	6. Exports increase; imports decrease	6. Right
	7. Foreign GDP increases	7. Exports increase	7. Right
AS_{08}	8. Employment costs increase	8. —	8. Short-run up
	9. Energy/commodity prices increase	9. —	9. Short-run up
	10. Productivity increases	10. —	10. Long-run right
AD_{12}	11. Housing wealth increases slowly	11. Consumption increases	11. Right
	12. Confidence increases from lows, but uneven changes; business caution	12. Consumption and investment increase	12. Right
	13. Increase in credit, but tight lending conditions	13. Residential investment increases slowly	13. Right
	14. Government spending decreases	14. Government spending decreases	14. Left
	15. MS increases (almost zero federal funds rate and asset purchases)	15. Lower interest rates but tight mortgage lending standards	15. Right
	16. Dollar increases in value	16. Exports decrease; imports increase	16. Left
	17. Some foreign GDP increases (Canada, Mexico); Europe flat or decreasing	17. Exports increase	17. Right
AS_{12}	18. Employment costs slight increase	18. —	18. Short run: negligible impact
	19. Energy/commodity prices increase, then decrease	19. —	19. Short run: negligible impact
	20. Small productivity increases	20. —	20. Long run: right

investment due to the collapse of the subprime mortgage market and tightening credit standards are all summarized in the leftward shift of the aggregate demand curve. We have shown these changes as a decrease in real income from 2007 to 2008. Real GDP growth was negative in the first, third, and fourth quarters of 2008.[30] Countering these trends were the decline in the value of the dollar, which increased U.S. exports and decreased imports, and the continued growth in foreign economies that strengthened exports. U.S. imports decreased due to the slowing U.S. economy. From August 2007 to December 2008, the Federal Reserve was actively engaged in open market operations and other nontraditional steps to lower interest rates to stimulate consumption and investment spending and to strengthen the financial institutions operating in the housing and mortgage markets to restore confidence and increase lending.

Although the economy held up well in the first half of 2007, the strains in the housing and financial markets began to have their effect in the fourth quarter.[31]

---

[30]U.S. Department of Commerce, Bureau of Economic Analysis, Table 1.1.1, Percentage Change from Preceding Period in Real Gross Domestic Product. Available at www.bea.gov.
[31]This discussion is based on Board of Governors of the Federal Reserve System, *Monetary Policy Report to the Congress*, February 27, 2008.

The decline in residential investment reduced the annual growth rate of real GDP in the second half of 2007 by more than 1 percentage point. Overall consumption spending in 2007 was sustained first by the lagged effects of the increases in household wealth in 2005 and 2006. However, the effects of the decreases in housing prices, declines in stock prices, and the sharply higher energy prices on consumption became apparent by the end of the year.

The external sector provided significant support to the U.S. economy in the second half of 2007. Net exports added approximately 1 percentage point to U.S. GDP growth during that period. Exports expanded at about an 11 percent annual rate, while imports growth decreased to about 1.5 percent in 2007 from a 3.75 percent increase in 2006.

Productivity in the nonfarm business sector rose to 2.5 percent in 2007, up from a 1.5 percent annual rate in the preceding three years. This is the reason that we show a small rightward shift in the *LAS* curve in Figure 14.8a. The employment cost index for private industry workers increased 3 percent in 2007. This increase, combined with the increases in energy and commodity prices, is represented by the leftward shift of the *SAS* curve in Figure 14.8a. The final equilibrium for 2008 at point *B* shows the potential for stagflation that existed in early 2008.

The downturn in economic activity continued throughout 2008. Real GDP decreased in the third quarter of 2008 due to decreases in personal consumption expenditure, residential fixed investment, and equipment and software. These changes were partially offset by positive contributions from federal government spending, private inventory investment, exports, nonresidential structures, and state and local government spending. Decreased import spending also had a slight positive effect on growth. Although the Fed had lowered its targeted interest rate to almost zero percent, it was also attempting to loosen credit by lending to damaged financial market institutions and by purchasing mortgage-backed securities. Concerns over stagflation had dissipated by this time as consumer prices posted their second straight monthly drop in November 2008.[32]

Changes from 2011 to 2012   As noted in the opening case for this chapter, in 2012 the Federal Reserve was concerned about the slow pace of the recovery from the recession of 2007–2009. The reasons for this slow pace are shown in Table 14.2, and the results are illustrated in Figure 14.8b.

Real GDP growth was only 2.0 percent in the first half of 2012, and the unemployment rate continued to hover at 8.1 to 8.3 percent.[33] Real consumption spending increased at this same rate of 2.0 percent. Household net worth increased in the first quarter of 2012, reflecting increases in both housing and equity prices. The ratio of household net worth to income had been on a slow upward trend since 2009, although it was far below the levels in the years immediately preceding the recession. Sales of new and existing homes rose in the first half of 2012, although demand was still constrained by consumer concerns about future income and employment and tight mortgage financing conditions.

Levels of consumer confidence had increased from their lowest values in 2009, but had not yet returned to prerecession levels. Businesses were still cautious, given uncertainty about the economic situation in Europe and about the possible "fiscal cliff" in the United States.

Consumer credit increased at an annual rate of 6.25 percent in the first half of 2012, driven primarily by automobile and student loans. Interest on consumer loans generally decreased in the first half of the year. Although mortgage rates had

[32]U.S. Bureau of Economic Analysis, News Release, November 25, 2008; Jon Hilsenrath, "Fed Cuts Rates Near Zero to Battle Slump," *Wall Street Journal*, December 17, 2008.
[33]This discussion is based on Board of Governors of the Federal Reserve System, *Monetary Policy Report to the Congress*, July 17, 2012.

declined to historically low levels, many creditworthy borrowers still had difficulty obtaining mortgages or refinancing due to tight standards and lending terms. Credit quality for mortgages still reflected strains on homeowners facing depressed home values and high unemployment.

Real federal government expenditure as measured in the national income and product accounts decreased at an annual rate of 6 percent in the first quarter of 2012. Defense spending contracted more than 8 percent, while nondefense spending decreased slightly. State and local government purchases fell at an annual rate of about 2.75 percent in the first quarter of 2012. Real construction expenditure by these governments fell sharply in the first quarter after lesser decreases in the latter half of 2011, and state and local governments were still reducing employment by 3,000 jobs per month on average. Federal aid to state and local governments had declined as funds from the American Recovery and Reinvestment Act had been almost completely phased out.

The Federal Reserve continued its policy of targeting the federal funds rate at between zero and 0.25 percent and had noted that it expected this policy to continue through late 2014. In June 2012, the Fed decided to continue its Maturity Extension Plan (Operation Twist) through the end of 2012 rather than completing the program at the end of June as previously scheduled. The Fed was also considering whether to undertake another large-scale asset purchase program.

The foreign exchange value of the dollar increased about 4.25 percent against a broad set of currencies since its low value in February 2012, with most of the appreciation occurring in May. The dollar appreciated against most currencies but depreciated against the Japanese yen for most of the period. These changes tended to decrease exports and increase imports. Both real exports and imports grew moderately in the first quarter of 2012. U.S. export growth was supported by relatively strong foreign economic growth, particularly in Canada and Mexico. However, growth in Europe was essentially flat in the first quarter of 2012 following a contraction in late 2011. Real GDP continued to fall in the United Kingdom in early 2012.

The net effect of these changes as shown in Figure 14.8b was a rightward shift of the aggregate demand curve, an increase in real income or GDP, and a slight increase in the price level. Excluding food and energy, consumer prices rose at a rate of about 2 percent during the first half of 2012. This was consistent with the Fed's goal of maintaining a stable price level.

The distance between Y_{11} and Y_{f11} in Figure 14.8b denotes the slack in the economy and the unemployment rate of over 9 percent that existed for most of 2011. The distance between Y_{12} and Y_{f12} reflects the slight decrease in the unemployment rate in 2012, but the substantial gap between the current GDP and the full-employment GDP still remained. The short-run aggregate supply curve was shown as stable from 2011 to 2012, given the slight increases in employment costs. Oil prices, which might have caused a shift in the curve, increased in the first quarter of 2012 but then more than reversed their previous increases. The long-run aggregate supply curve shifted slightly to the right, given modest productivity increases.

In 2012, the Congressional Budget Office predicted that the gap between actual and potential GDP would close in 2018.[34] Forecasts for years after 2017 were based not on estimates of cyclical movements in the economy but on the long-run factors discussed previously: the size of the labor force, the stock of productive capital, and the productivity of those factors. Potential GDP was expected to grow at an average annual rate of 2.2 percent for the entire period 2012 to 2018 and at 2.4 percent from 2018 to 2022. These growth rates were substantially below the average rate of 3.3 percent since 1950. Growth in the potential labor force was expected to slow, given the rise in baby boomers' retirements. Research has also shown that

---

[34]This discussion is based on Congressional Budget Office, *An Update to the Budget and Economic Outlook.*

economic downturns following financial crises tend to last longer than other downturns and the return to high employment tends to be slower.[35] These types of recessions decrease investment, raise the rate and average duration of unemployment, and reduce the number of hours that employees work. The effect is to reduce the economy's potential to produce output even after all resources are productively employed. The CBO estimated that the 2007–2009 recession lowered future potential output through a smaller labor supply, a smaller capital stock, and reduced total factor productivity.

Impact of Macro Changes on Managerial Decisions

The macro changes from 2007 to 2008 and from 2011 to 2012 discussed in the previous section had different impacts on various firms and industries, which we now illustrate. In all cases changes in the macroeconomic environment affect individual firms and industries through the microeconomic factors of demand, production, cost, and profitability (Chapter 11). Firms develop new strategies to respond to these macro changes, and their responses depend on the market environment in which they operate.

The decline in economic activity in 2007 and 2008 caused many firms to reevaluate their competitive strategies to determine how best to deal with the slowing economy.[36] J.C. Penney Co. announced that it expected declining sales in both March 2008 and for the entire first quarter. The company was assessing its new American Living line of apparel and home goods created by Polo Ralph Lauren Corp. because these products cost more than other similar items at Penney's and comparable products at Kohl's.

Many retailers also felt the impact of the slowing economy in late 2007 and early 2008. Stores reported poor retail sales in January 2008, and many chains announced plans to close hundreds of units and cut thousands of jobs.[37] These trends continued throughout 2008 with retail sales falling 5.5 percent in November and 8.0 percent in December compared with a year earlier. Even large price discounting could not offset the decline in overall consumer spending. During the holiday season, many retailers changed their advertising strategies to focus on loyal customers rather than attempting to attract new ones to their stores.[38]

For some companies that were already struggling, the economic slowdown only made managerial decisions more complex. Sears and Kmart had faced declining sales and profits as they struggled to distinguish themselves from Kohl's, J.C. Penney, Target, and Wal-Mart Stores. These rivals had been chipping away at Sears' clothing, appliance, and home-products businesses with better selection, shopping experiences, and prices. Sears' share of major U.S. appliance sales declined both from the increased competition and from the collapse of the housing market.[39]

By December 2008, the Big Three United States automobile makers, General Motors, Ford, and Chrysler, had all appealed to Congress for $34 billion in loans or lines of credit to help them survive the recession and the car-industry downturn. The political debate centered over whether government assistance would help the companies avoid collapse or whether structured bankruptcies would be the better

---

[35]Carmen M. Reinhart and Kenneth S. Rogoff, "The Aftermath of Financial Crises," *American Economic Review* 99 (May 2009): 466–72.

[36]Sudeep Reddy, Cheryl Lu-Lien Tan, and Neal Boudette, "Personal Spending Up Mere 0.1%, But Inflation Pressures Are Muted," *Wall Street Journal*, March 29, 2008.

[37]Amy Merrick and Kevin Kingsbury, "Retail Squeeze Felt Far Beyond Malls," *Wall Street Journal*, February 8, 2008.

[38]Emily Steel, "Marketers Reach Out to Loyal Customers," *Wall Street Journal*, November 26, 2008; Ann Zimmerman, Jennifer Saranow, and Miguel Bustillo, "Retail Sales Plummet," *Wall Street Journal*, December 26, 2008.

[39]Gary McWilliams, "Why Sears Must Engineer Its Own Makeover," *Wall Street Journal*, January 15, 2008.

course of action. In November 2008, United States new-vehicle sales fell 37 percent from the previous month.[40] In his final weeks in office President George W. Bush approved a lifeline for General Motors and Chrysler, while the Obama administration in March 2009 approved an additional $30 billion in loans bringing the total aid to close to $50 billion. General Motors and Chrysler went through structured bankruptcies and engaged in substantial cost cutting. By 2012, all three major U.S. automobile companies had regained profitability.[41]

In 2011 and 2012, the behavior of many companies reflected the uneven recovery from the 2007–2009 recession and the uncertain global outlook we have discussed in this chapter. Companies that survived the recession by laying off workers and cutting costs were earning increased profits, but weak demand and the uncertain outlook made many of them unwilling to increase hiring and production. Hoffer Plastics Corp., an Illinois-based producer of injection-molded parts for cars, packaging, and appliances, expected a 4 percent rate of growth in 2012 and was producing near capacity but was unwilling to hire additional workers, given fears that customers would not accept higher prices.[42] Sybesma's Electronics in Holland, Michigan, found that many business customers placed orders only to cancel them after sales turned out to be less than expected.[43]

Some parts of the manufacturing sector were recovering in Spring 2012. Bomco Inc., a Gloucester, Massachusetts, maker of metal parts for aerospace and industrial equipment, increased production in response to greater demand for products ranging from commercial jets to natural-gas turbines. The company added a second shift and planned to open a new 17,000 square foot manufacturing facility. United Technologies saw an unexpected upturn in its North American residential air-conditioning sales in March, given increased consumer sentiment. Honeywell International, Inc. and Eaton, a Cleveland-based maker of electrical and hydraulic equipment, also saw increased demand for their products.[44]

One Indiana steel mill, Burns Harbor, was revived by "twinning" it with an ultra-modern mill in Gent, Belgium. The parent company flew 100 U.S. engineers and managers to Belgium in 2008 to copy their manufacturing techniques. Burns Harbor, originally built by Bethlehem Steel in 1964, could not compete with low-cost Asian imports in the 1980s and 1990s and went bankrupt in 2000. The "twinning" process resulted in the plant using software developed in Belgium, increased use of robots, and record output in 2012.[45]

An International Paper Co. mill in Virginia was closed in 2009 due to decreased demand for copy paper during the recession. However, the mill was reopened in 2012 to produce fluff pulp, the soft, white absorbent used in diapers, personal hygiene products, and some medical bandages. This change was driven by increased demand for these products from the growing middle classes in China, India, and other Asian countries. The mill was able to take advantage of Asia's growing demand for the fluff pulp because the product can be made only from the

---

[40]John D. Stoll, Matthew Dolan, Jeffrey McCracken, and Josh Mitchell, "Big Three Seek $34 Billion Aid," *Wall Street Journal*, December 3, 2008; Gregg Hitt and Matthew Dolan, "Detroit Bailout Hits a Bumpy Road," *Wall Street Journal*, December 5, 2008.

[41]Sharon Terlep, "Target at Post-Bailout GM: Earning $10 Billion a Year," *Wall Street Journal (Online)*, February 6, 2012.

[42]Ben Casselman and Josh Mitchell, "Recovery Doesn't Feature Typical Snapback in Growth," *Wall Street Journal (Online)*, January 27, 2012.

[43]Conor Dougherty and Ben Casselman, "Economy Notches Fitful Gains," *Wall Street Journal (Online)*, August 17, 2012.

[44]Ben Casselman, "American Manufacturers Pick Up the Pace," *Wall Street Journal (Online)*, April 2, 2012; James R. Hagerty and Kate Linebaugh, "Manufacturers Regain Swagger with Rosy Earnings," *Wall Street Journal (Online)*, April 24, 2012.

[45]John W. Miller, "Indiana Steel Mill Revived with Lessons from Abroad," *Wall Street Journal (Online)*, May 21, 2012.

long, coarse fibers of the loblolly pine, a fast-growing tree that is prevalent in the southern part of the United States.[46]

FedEx Corp. announced in September 2012 that declining manufacturing activity, particularly in China, was expected to reduce its future profits. Global air freight volume decreased 3.2 percent in July from a year earlier and increased just 0.1 percent from the previous month. FedEx said that the weak global economy constrained growth more than anticipated in its Express business that handled international parcels. Many analysts view FedEx as an economic bellwether, given its international reach.[47]

Measuring Changes in Aggregate Demand and Supply

Both policy makers and managers use a variety of economic data to assess the future direction of the economy. Many of these variables give conflicting views on where the economy is headed. Forecasting is made more difficult by the differences in collection and benchmarking among the various data series.[48] For example, payroll statistics are derived from business and government reports that are checked once a year against unemployment insurance records. The statistics for the number of employed people are derived from a sampling of households that is benchmarked with the Census only once a decade. Data reporting for some series is voluntary, and it may be difficult to persuade new companies to participate in the process. Reported income data are much more reliable for wages and profits than for other forms of income.[49]

Over the years, The Conference Board, a leading economic research group, has developed a series of economic indicators that it uses to monitor the tendency of the economy to move from upward expansion to downward recession and then back again.[50] **Leading indicators**, such as manufacturing, employment, monetary, and consumer expectation statistics, are economic variables that generally turn down before a recession begins and turn back up before a recovery starts. **Coincident indicators**, including employment, income, and business production statistics, tend to move in tandem with the overall phases of the business cycle. **Lagging indicators**, such as measures of inflation and unemployment, labor costs, and consumer and business debt and credit levels, turn down after the beginning of a recession and turn up after a recovery has begun.

These leading, coincident, and lagging indicators are based on the concept that expectations of future profits are the driving force of the economy. If business executives are confident that sales and profits will rise, they will expand production of goods and services and investment in structures and equipment. These actions generate increased economic activity overall. Negative expectations about profits will cause the reverse effects and are likely to cause the economy to experience a downturn. The components of the different indicators are shown in Table 14.3.

Most of these indicators correspond to variables we have already discussed in our analysis of either the market for real goods and services or the money market. The role of these indicators in predicting recessions or expansions is not precise. Of the six recessions from 1969 to 2001, real time data gave no notice of a downturn

Leading indicators
Economic variables, such as manufacturing, employment, monetary, and consumer expectation statistics, that generally turn down before a recession begins and turn back up before a recovery starts.

Coincident indicators
Economic variables, including employment, income, and business production statistics, that tend to move in tandem with the overall phases of the business cycle.

Lagging indicators
Economic variables, including measures of inflation and unemployment, labor costs, and consumer and business debt and credit levels, that turn down after the beginning of a recession and turn up after a recovery has begun.

---

[46]Cameron McWhirter, "New Lifestyles Abroad Save U.S. Mill," *Wall Street Journal (Online)*, August 13, 2012.

[47]Bob Sechler, Doug Cameron, and Kristin Jones, "FedEx Warns of Slowdown," *Wall Street Journal (Online)*, September 5, 2012.

[48]Daniel Altman, "Data in Conflict: Why Economists Tend to Weep," *New York Times*, July 11, 2003.

[49]These data and forecasting problems were even more severe before the development of the National Income and Product Accounts in the 1930s. Even in the late 1920s, most of the country's leading economists were unable to forecast the Great Depression of the 1930s, largely due to the lack of current, standardized data on the U.S. economy. See Cynthia Crossen, "Pre-Depression Indicators Forecasted Rosy Economy," *Wall Street Journal*, August 6, 2003.

[50]This discussion is based on Norman Frumkin, *Tracking America's Economy*, 4th ed. (Armonk, NY: M.E. Sharpe, 2004), 325–47; Bernard Baumohl, *The Secrets of Economic Indicators*, 3rd ed. (Upper Saddle River, NJ: FT Press, 2013), 196–203; and U.S. Business Cycle Indicators, www.conference-board.org.

TABLE 14.3   Leading, Coincident, and Lagging Economic Indicators

Leading indicators	1. Average weekly hours, manufacturing
	2. Average weekly initial claims for unemployment
	3. Manufacturers' new orders, consumer goods, and materials
	4. ISM index of new orders
	5. Manufacturers' new orders, nondefense capital goods
	6. Building permits, new private housing units
	7. Stock prices, 500 common stocks
	8. Leading credit index
	9. Interest rate spread, 10-year Treasury bonds less federal funds
	10. Average consumer expectations for business conditions
Coincident indicators	1. Employees on nonagricultural payrolls
	2. Personal income less transfer payments (constant dollars)
	3. Industrial production
	4. Manufacturing and trade sales (constant dollars)
Lagging indicators	1. Average duration of unemployment
	2. Inventories to sales ratio, manufacturing and trade (constant dollars)
	3. Labor cost per unit of output, manufacturing (monthly change)
	4. Average prime rate charged by banks
	5. Commercial and industrial loans outstanding (constant dollars)
	6. Consumer installment credit outstanding to personal income ratio
	7. Consumer price index for services (monthly change)

Source: Bernard Baumohl, *The Secrets of Economic Indicators*, 3rd ed. (Upper Saddle River, NJ: FT Press, 2013), 196–203; U.S. Business Cycle Indicators, www.conference-board.org.

in three cases, three months' notice in two cases, and ten months' notice in one case. Revised data available in subsequent years showed advanced indications of 6–15 months before a downturn in five of the six recessions.[51]

In August 2012, the Conference Board announced that the Leading Economic Index increased 0.4 percent in July following a 0.4 percent decline in June and a 0.3 percent increase in May.[52] This change indicated a slow expansion in economic activity for the rest of the year and was consistent with the mixed signals on the economy we have discussed in this chapter.

We have noted that the Federal Reserve Open Market Committee bases its monetary policy decisions on the economic data in its Beige Book, which the district banks collect from businesses and other contacts (Chapter 13). Managers may also develop their own company-specific indicators. For example, the Kohler Company was surprised when the economic downturn hit in fall 2000 because the company's leading indicator had been its sales of bathroom and kitchen fixtures, which traditionally began to fall six months before the economy slowed.[53] This decrease in sales did not occur before this downturn. Rather, the first impact of the slowdown in economic activity appeared not in any of the company's 43 factories, but in the two luxury hotels the company operated in Kohler, Wisconsin, where business meeting reservations were cancelled.

---

[51]Frumkin, *Tracking America's Economy*, 4th ed.

[52]The Conference Board, News Release: The Conference Board Leading Economic Index (LEI) for the U.S. Increases, August 17, 2012. Available at www.conference-board.org.

[53]Louis Uchitelle, "Thriving or Hurting, U.S. Manufacturers Brace for the Worst," *New York Times*, March 2, 2001.

Managerial Rule of Thumb

Judging Trends in Economic Indicators

Managers need to be able to react to both policy changes and other aggregate spending changes in order to determine the optimal strategies for their firms and industries. They need to examine and make judgments about the trends in a variety of economic indicators. This process is made more complex because, at any point in time, different indicators may give conflicting signals as to the future direction of the economy. Many business and financial publications and Web sites provide data and analyses that can help managers develop their own forecasts of future economic activity. ■

Summary

This chapter has brought together and integrated the variables and relationships managers need to understand for the determination of income, output, interest rates, and the price level in the aggregate demand–aggregate supply (*AD–AS*) model of the economy. This model integrates spending decisions on real goods and services with the monetary side of the economy and then incorporates price-level and supply-side changes. We examined the effects of both fiscal and monetary policy changes and shifts in autonomous expenditures on the level of interest rates, prices, and real income in the economy. We also discussed the major issues involved in implementing fiscal and monetary policy, the impact of macro environment changes on different firms and industries, and the problems both managers and forecasters face in using various economic indicators to predict future economic changes.

Although we have integrated export and import spending and currency exchange rates into our aggregate demand–aggregate supply model, we need to examine the determination of currency exchange rates and the factors affecting other international financial flows (Chapter 15). After we have discussed these international economic issues, we will again use the aggregate macro model to develop case studies that further illustrate how changes in the macro environment influence managerial strategies (Chapter 16).

Appendix 14A Specific and General Equations for the Aggregate Macro Model

Specific Equation	General Equation
PERSONAL CONSUMPTION EXPENDITURE	**PERSONAL CONSUMPTION EXPENDITURE**
$C = c_0 + c_1(Y - T_p) - c_2 r + c_3 CC + c_4 W + c_5 CR - c_6 D$	$C = f(Y, T_p, r, CC, W, CR, D)$
	$(+)(-)(-)(+)(+)(+)(-)$
where	*where*
C = personal consumption expenditure	C = personal consumption expenditure
c_0 = other factors influencing consumption	Y = real income
Y = real income	T_p = personal taxes
T_p = personal taxes	r = real interest rate
r = real interest rate	CC = consumer confidence
CC = consumer confidence	W = consumer wealth
W = consumer wealth	CR = consumer credit
CR = consumer credit	D = consumer debt
D = consumer debt	
c_1 to c_6 = coefficients for the relevant variables	

Specific Equation	**General Equation**

GROSS PRIVATE DOMESTIC INVESTMENT

$I = i_0 + i_1Y - i_2r - i_3T_B + i_4PR + i_5CU$

> where
>> I = investment spending
>> i_0 = other factors influencing investment spending
>> Y = real income
>> r = real interest rate
>> T_B = business taxes
>> PR = expected profits and business confidence
>> CU = capacity utilization
>> i_1 to i_5 = coefficients for the relevant variables

GOVERNMENT EXPENDITURE

$G = G_0$

> where
>> G = government expenditure
>> G_0 = autonomous government expenditure determined by public policy

EXPORT EXPENDITURE

$X = x_0 + x_1Y^* - x_2R$

> where
>> X = export expenditure
>> x_0 = other factors influencing export expenditure
>> Y^* = foreign GDP or income
>> R = currency exchange rate (units of foreign currency per unit of domestic currency)
>> x_1, x_2 = coefficients of the relevant variables

IMPORT EXPENDITURE

$M = m_0 + m_1Y + m_2R$

> where
>> M = import spending
>> m_0 = other factors influencing import spending
>> Y = real domestic income
>> R = currency exchange rate (units of foreign currency per unit of domestic currency)
>> m_1, m_2 = coefficients of the relevant variables

AGGREGATE EXPENDITURE

$E = C_0 + c_1Y + I_0 + i_1Y + G_0 + X_0 - M_0 - m_1Y$
$E = C_0 + I_0 + G_0 + X_0 - M_0 + c_1Y + i_1Y - m_1Y$
$E = E_0 + (c_1 + i_1 - m_1)Y$

> where
>> E = aggregate expenditure
>> C_0 = autonomous consumption expenditure
>> Y = real income
>> I_0 = autonomous investment expenditure
>> G_0 = autonomous government expenditure
>> X_0 = autonomous export expenditure
>> M_0 = autonomous import expenditure
>> E_0 = sum of all autonomous expenditure components
>> c_1 = marginal propensity to consume
>> i_1 = marginal propensity to invest
>> m_1 = marginal propensity to import

REAL MONEY SUPPLY

$RLMS = M_S/P$

> where
>> M_S = nominal money supply
>> P = price level

GROSS PRIVATE DOMESTIC INVESTMENT

$I = f(Y, r, T_B, PR, CU)$
$\quad (+)(-)(-)(+)(+)$

> where
>> I = investment spending
>> Y = real income
>> r = real interest rate
>> T_B = business taxes
>> PR = expected profits and business confidence
>> CU = capacity utilization

GOVERNMENT EXPENDITURE

$G = f(Y, policy)$
$\quad (0) \ (+)$

> where
>> G = government expenditure
>> Y = real income
>> Policy = public policy determining autonomous expenditure

EXPORT EXPENDITURE

$X = f(Y, Y^*, R)$
$\quad (0)(+)(-)$

> where
>> X = export expenditure
>> Y = real income
>> Y^* = foreign GDP or income
>> R = currency exchange rate (units of foreign currency per unit of domestic currency)

IMPORT EXPENDITURE

$M = f(Y, R)$
$\quad (+)(+)$

> where
>> M = import spending
>> Y = real domestic income
>> R = currency exchange rate (units of foreign currency per unit of domestic currency)

AGGREGATE EXPENDITURE

$E = f(Y, T_p, r, CC, W, CR, D, T_B, PR, CU, G, Y^*, R)$
$\quad (+)(-)(-)(+)(+)(+)(-)(-)(+)(+)(+)(+)(-)$

> where
>> E = aggregate expenditure
>> Y = real income
>> T_p = personal taxes
>> r = real interest rate
>> CC = consumer confidence
>> W = consumer wealth
>> CR = consumer credit
>> D = consumer debt
>> T_B = business taxes
>> PR = expected profits
>> CU = capacity utilization
>> G = government spending
>> Y^* = foreign GDP or real income
>> R = currency exchange rate

REAL MONEY SUPPLY

$RLMS = f(r, \text{FR Policy or } M_S, P)$
$\quad (0) \quad (+) \quad (-)$

> where
>> $RLMS$ = real money supply
>> r = real interest rate
>> FR Policy or M_S = nominal money supply controlled by the Federal Reserve
>> P = price level

(continued)

Specific Equation	General Equation
REAL MONEY DEMAND	**REAL MONEY DEMAND**
$RLMD = M_D/P = d_0 - d_1 r + d_2 Y$	$RLMD = M_D/P = f(r, Y)$
	$(-)(+)$
where	*where*
$RLMD$ = real money demand	$RLMD$ = real money demand
M_D = nominal money demand	M_D = nominal money demand
P = price level	P = price level
d_0 = other factors influencing money demand	r = real interest rate
r = real interest rate	Y = real income
Y = real income	
d_1, d_2 = sensitivity of money demand to the real interest rate and real income	

AGGREGATE DEMAND CURVE

$AD: Y = f(P, T_P, CC, W, CR, D, T_B, PR, CU, G, Y^*, R, \text{FR Policy})$
$(-)(-)\ (+)(+)\ (+)(-)(-)(+)(+)(+)(+)(-)\ \ (+)$

where

$\quad Y$ = real income
$\quad P$ = price level
$\quad T_P$ = personal taxes
$\quad CC$ = consumer confidence
$\quad W$ = consumer wealth
$\quad CR$ = consumer credit
$\quad D$ = consumer debt
$\quad T_B$ = business taxes
$\quad PR$ = expected profits and business confidence
$\quad CU$ = capacity utilization
$\quad G$ = government spending
$\quad Y^*$ = foreign GDP or real income
$\quad R$ = currency exchange rate (units of foreign currency per dollar)
FR Policy = Federal Reserve policy (the nominal money supply)

Key Terms

aggregate demand–aggregate supply
  equilibrium, p. 397
aggregate demand curve, p. 388
aggregate production function, p. 397
aggregate supply curve, p. 397
automatic stabilizers, p. 394
coincident indicators, p. 410

crowding out, p. 396
discretionary expenditures, p. 394
Keynesian model, p. 398
lagging indicators, p. 410
leading indicators, p. 410
long-run aggregate supply curve, p. 399
nondiscretionary expenditures, p. 394

potential output (GDP), p. 397
progressive tax system, p. 394
short-run aggregate supply curve,
  p. 398
stagflation, p. 401

Exercises

Technical Questions

1. Explain why the aggregate demand curve represents a series of equilibria.
2. Explain how each of the following changes would shift the aggregate expenditure function (Chapter 12) and the aggregate demand curve (Chapter 14):
   a. An increase in personal taxes
   b. An increase in expected profits and business confidence

   c. A decrease in the level of foreign GDP or real income
   d. A decrease in the nominal money supply by the Federal Reserve

3. A change in the real money supply can result either from a change in the nominal money supply through Federal Reserve policy (holding the price level constant) or from a change in the price level (holding the nominal money supply constant). The

change in the nominal money supply causes a shift of the aggregate demand curve, whereas a change in the price level causes a movement along the aggregate demand curve. Explain.

4. Evaluate whether each of the following statements is true or false, and explain your answer:

a. The short-run aggregate supply (*SAS*) curve slopes upward because households spend more as their incomes increase.

b. The long-run aggregate supply curve can never shift.

c. Either a decrease in the nominal money supply by the Federal Reserve, all else held constant, or an increase in the price level, all else held constant, will shift the aggregate demand (*AD*) curve to the left.

d. The Keynesian portion of the short-run aggregate supply (*SAS*) curve would be relevant during a recessionary situation.

e. Stagflation occurs when the aggregate demand (*AD*) curve shifts out on the upward sloping portion of the short-run aggregate supply (*SAS*) curve.

5. In a closed (no foreign sector), mixed economy with stable prices, if we assume that consumption (*C*) and investment (*I*) spending do *not* depend on the interest rate (*r*), can we conclude that

a. The interest-related expenditure (*IRE*) function is vertical?

b. Monetary policy has *no* effect on real income and output? Explain your answers.

6. If the economy is operating on the upward sloping portion of the short-run aggregate supply (*SAS*) curve, show that an increase in aggregate demand (*AD*) from expansionary fiscal policy will result in an increase in both real income (*Y*) and the price level (*P*).

Application Questions

1. Describe how the following statements relate to the *AD–AS* model:

a. The Fed has bought more than $2 trillion of Treasury and mortgage bonds to stimulate the economy.

b. The above actions by the Fed may cause inflation to rise to levels that most would consider unacceptable.

c. The Fed expected a weaker dollar to help increase exports.

d. Businesses already have ample access to cheap credit and are reluctant to borrow, hire, and invest for other reasons.

2. Find one or more articles in the *Wall Street Journal* or other business publications that describe changes in fiscal and monetary policies in the United States. Discuss how these policies relate to the model of aggregate demand and aggregate supply and the issues involved in implementing the policies.

3. Find recent policy descriptions of the variables influencing aggregate demand drawn from the *Wall Street Journal* and other current business publications.

4. Using both the sources in this chapter and updated articles from the literature, discuss the debate over the rate of increase in productivity in the economy and the impact that productivity changes have on real GDP and the price level.

5. Find the most recent summary of the survey of economic forecasters in the *Wall Street Journal*. What are the predictions for changes in real GDP and its major components, inflation, and unemployment? Describe the degree of consensus among the various forecasters.

15

International and Balance of Payments Issues in the Macro Economy

We have been discussing international issues throughout the macroeconomic section of this text. For example, we introduced imports and exports as components of the circular flow (Chapter 11). We also discussed the determinants of import and export spending in the analysis of spending on real goods and services (Chapter 12). We have shown how changes in these variables cause the *AD* curve to shift, influencing the equilibrium level of income in the economy (Chapters 12 and 14).

We begin this chapter with a case that focuses on the slow growth among the world's economies in 2012 and how that relates to flows of imports and exports, currency exchange rates, and flows of financial assets. We then review the definition of exchange rates and examine their impact on imports and exports in more detail. Next we focus on the balance of payments accounts, the accounting system used to measure all international transactions. We present a simple model of foreign exchange markets that we use to show the impact of both flexible and fixed exchange rate systems. Finally, we present more complex, real-world examples of how these balance of payments issues influence the decisions of foreign and domestic policy makers and the competitive strategy of managers and firms responding to changes in the international economic environment.

Case for Analysis

Uncertainty in the World Economy in 2012

The uncertainty in the U.S. economy in 2012 as it struggled to recover from the recession of 2007–2009 was mirrored in the economies of countries around the world. In June 2012, the U.S. trade deficit with other countries decreased to $42.9 billion from $48 billion in the previous month, given that imports decreased while exports increased. Strong exports were reported almost everywhere except to Europe, which was facing a recession and a sovereign-debt crisis. Although the narrowing trade deficit would have a positive effect on U.S. economic growth, there was concern that an appreciating dollar, weaker demand in China, and the recession in Europe, along with the financial crisis in the euro zone, would continue to hamper the U.S. recovery.[1]

By October 2012, the World Trade Organization predicted that the global volume of trade in goods would increase only 2.5 percent in 2012 as compared with a 5 percent increase in 2011 and 14 percent in 2010. It appeared that the problems of many of the advanced economies were spreading around the world. The continuing recession in Europe caused Chinese exports to the European Union, its largest export market, to decrease 5 percent in 2012 through August, which then caused further slowdown in the Chinese economy, projected to grow only 7.5 percent in 2012, the smallest expansion since 1990. The weakening Chinese economy slowed exports to China from other Asian countries, including Singapore and Thailand.[2]

The Chinese economy had been exhibiting signs of weakness throughout 2012.[3] Although an 8.9 percent rate of growth was reported for the last quarter of 2011, analysts predicted a slowdown during 2012. The Chinese government had responded significantly to the recession of 2008 with a four trillion yuan ($586 billion) stimulus plan financed through lending by state-owned banks. Because this stimulus resulted in inflation, a real-estate bubble, and high levels of bad debts, analysts predicted that officials would respond more cautiously in 2012. By summer 2012 analysts also suspected that the slowdown might be greater than reported in official Chinese statistics. The effect of slowing export demand was magnified by weak domestic investment. Although the Chinese government attempted to prevent a real-estate price bubble through restrictions on apartment purchases, this policy hindered real-estate investment and also slowed factory output. By September 2012 the government approved an estimated $156 billion investment in new subways, highways, and other infrastructure, a stimulus move that many considered belated.

Europe's economy continued to worsen in fall 2012. Manufacturing activity in the euro-zone decreased for the fourteenth straight month in September 2012, and unemployment hit a new record high in August. Analysts estimated that it could take years for Southern Europe to recover from the damaging effects of the debt crisis. However, there were stark differences among the economies of the European countries. Reports indicated that 55 percent of Greeks under 25 years and 52.9 percent of young Spaniards were unemployed compared with just over 8 percent of the Germans.[4]

In response to these weak economic conditions, central banks around the world took steps to ease monetary policy and stimulate their economies.[5] The European Central Bank (ECB), the U.S. Federal Reserve, and the Bank of Japan all announced policies to purchase financial assets to drive down interest rates and potentially lower the value of their currencies, which would stimulate the country's exports. When the U.S. Federal Reserve engaged in this policy in November 2010, it caused concern in emerging countries in Asia and Latin America, whose economies were strong at that time. Low interest rates in the United States caused capital to flow to these emerging markets, increasing inflationary pressures and appreciation of their currencies, which would hurt their exports. Central banks in emerging markets at that time increased interest rates to prevent inflation from increasing but also instituted currency-intervention programs and capital flow restrictions to dampen capital inflows. In 2012, emerging-market countries faced slowing economies, given the impact of the European recession and the slowing Chinese economy on their exports. Most central banks lowered interest rates to stimulate economies around the globe, which modified the impact of currency flows.

---

[1]Conor Dougherty and Alex Frangos, "U.S. Bucks Export Slowdown," *Wall Street Journal (Online)*, August 10, 2012.
[2]Sudeep Reddy and Alex Frangos, "Trade Slows Around World," *Wall Street Journal (Online)*, October 1, 2012.
[3]This discussion is based on Tom Orlik and Bob Davis, "China's Growth Engine Declines," *Wall Street Journal (Online)*, January 17, 2012; Tom Orlik and Aaron Back, "Deeper Slowdown Suspected in China," *Wall Street Journal (Online)*, July 12, 2012; Tom Orlik and Aaron Back, "In China, New Cause for Worry on Growth," *Wall Street Journal (Online)*, August 10, 2012; Aaron Back, "Beijing Plans Infrastructure Binge," *Wall Street Journal (Online)*, September 7, 2012; Aaron Back and Tom Orlik, "China Economy Shows More Frailty," *Wall Street Journal (Online)*, September 10, 2012.

[4]Alex Brittain and Brian Blackstone, "Europe's Economic Outlook Worsens," *Wall Street Journal (Online)*, October 1, 2012.
[5]Tom Lauricella, Sudeep Reddy, and Erin McCarthy, "Central Banks Flex Muscles," *Wall Street Journal (Online)*, September 20, 2012; Alex Frangos, "Fed Move Could Aid Emerging Markets," *Wall Street Journal (Online)*, September 30, 2012.

Exchange Rates

In the opening case for this chapter, we have discussed imports and exports, the value of one country's currency relative to another, financial flows around the world, and the slowdown in most of the world's economies in 2012. All of these factors are interrelated. We will first discuss exchange rates and then expand the analysis to include the other factors.

Because companies and individuals in the United States trade with countries having different currencies, we need some way to compare these currencies. Japanese producers want to receive yen when selling their products abroad, while U.S. firms want to be paid in dollars. Thus, how much one currency is worth in terms of another is an additional factor affecting a firm's competitive strategy.

Currency exchange rate
How much of one currency can be exchanged for another or the price of one currency in terms of another.

The simplest definition of the **currency exchange rate** is how much of one currency can be exchanged for another (e.g., how many Japanese yen you can exchange for one U.S. dollar) (Chapter 12). This definition can also be stated as the price of one currency in terms of another—that is, how much one currency costs in terms of another.

How exchange rates are described is often a source of confusion. In some sources, the exchange rate is defined as units of foreign currency per dollar, whereas other sources define it as dollars per unit of foreign currency. Sometimes units on the vertical axis of a graph showing exchange rates are inverted, depending on the definition used. In this text, we define the exchange rate, R, as the number of units of foreign currency per unit of domestic currency or, from the U.S. perspective, per U.S. dollar. Therefore, $1/R$ is the number of dollars per unit of foreign currency. This definition has the most intuitive appeal because we define an appreciation in the domestic currency as an increase in R and a depreciation as a decrease in R.

Trade-weighted dollar
An index of the weighted exchange value of the U.S. dollar versus the currencies of a broad group of major U.S. trading partners.

The first two rows of Table 15.1 show exchange rates for the U.S. dollar compared to the euro and the Japanese yen in January 2009 and June 2009. The third row presents the **trade-weighted dollar**, an index of the weighted exchange value of the U.S. dollar versus the currencies of a broad group of major U.S. trading

TABLE 15.1   Exchange Rates

CURRENCY	R (UNITS OF FOREIGN CURRENCY PER $)		1/R ($ PER UNIT OF FOREIGN CURRENCY)	
	January 2009	June 2009	January 2009	June 2009
Euro (E)	0.76	0.71	1.32	1.40
Japanese yen (¥) ($/100¥)	90	97	1.11	1.03
Trade-weighted $ ($/100 units)	109	105	0.92	0.95
	January 2008	January 2009	January 2008	January 2009
Euro (E)	0.68	0.76	1.47	1.32
Japanese yen (¥) ($/100¥)	108	90	0.93	1.11
Trade-weighted $ ($/100 units)	99	109	1.01	0.92

Source: Federal Reserve Statistical Release, *Foreign Exchange Rates (Monthly)*. Available at www.federalreserve.gov/releases/g5.

partners. The currencies included in the trade-weighted or broad index are those of economies whose bilateral shares of U.S. imports or exports exceed 0.5 percent. Trade with these economies accounts for over 90 percent of total U.S. imports and exports.[6]

The bold numbers in Table 15.1 use our definition of the exchange rate, R (the foreign currency price of domestic currency or foreign currency units per dollar). In January 2009, $1 could be exchanged for 90 yen; in June 2009, $1 could be exchanged for 97 yen. Thus, between these two dates, the dollar appreciated against the yen (a dollar *will buy more* yen; a dollar *can be exchanged for more* yen; the dollar *is more expensive in terms of* the yen; the dollar *has strengthened against* the yen). Using our definition of the exchange rate, as R increases, the domestic currency *appreciates* (referred to as **currency appreciation**). However, the table also shows that the dollar depreciated against the euro and the currencies of the United States' major trading partners over this period.

The bottom half of Table 15.1 shows that the dollar depreciated against the yen between January 2008 and January 2009 (a dollar *will buy less* yen; a dollar *can be exchanged for fewer* yen; the dollar *is cheaper in terms of* the yen; the dollar *has weakened against* the yen). Thus, using our definition of the exchange rate, as R decreases, the domestic currency depreciates (referred to as **currency depreciation**). Note that during this time period, the dollar appreciated against the euro and the trade-weighted currencies.

The nonbold numbers in Table 15.1 show the exchange rate values using the inverse of R ($1/R$, the domestic price of foreign currency or dollars per foreign unit). The numbers show that from January 2009 to June 2009, the yen *depreciated* against the dollar (it cost *less* in terms of the dollar), while the yen *appreciated* against the dollar (they now cost *more* in terms of the dollar) between January 2008 and January 2009. Thus, when the dollar appreciates against the yen, by definition, the yen depreciates against the dollar, and vice versa.[7]

Table 15.2 shows the effect of dollar appreciation and depreciation on a hypothetical example of U.S. exports and imports. Technically, this relationship involves the **real exchange rate**, e^*, which is the **nominal exchange rate**, R (or the value at which one currency can be exchanged for another), times the ratio of the domestic price level to the foreign price level or $e^* = R(P_d/P_f)$. If we assume that the foreign price level is constant and we set the price level indices so that $P_d = P_f = 1$, then $e^* = R$. Movements in the nominal exchange rate, R, are reflected in the real exchange rate, e^*. We use this simplifying assumption throughout the analysis.[8]

As you can see in Table 15.2, as the dollar appreciates against the yen, U.S. exports such as computers become more expensive in terms of the number of yen required to pay the domestic price in dollars, while U.S. imports such

Currency appreciation
One currency can be exchanged for more units of another currency or the value of R increases.

Currency depreciation
One currency can be exchanged for fewer units of another currency or the value of R decreases.

Real exchange rate
The nominal exchange rate times the ratio of the domestic price level to the foreign price level.

Nominal exchange rate
The value at which one currency can be exchanged for another, or R.

---

[6]Mico Loretan, "Indexes of the Foreign Exchange Value of the Dollar," *Federal Reserve Bulletin* (Winter 2005): 1–8.

[7]In the Federal Reserve Statistical Release of monthly foreign exchange rates, most data are in the form of currency units per U.S. dollar. However, data for the euro, the Australian and New Zealand dollars, and the U.K. pound are reported as U.S. dollars per currency unit. See www.federalreserve.gov/releases/g5.

[8]For most of the last 30 years, the U.S. inflation rate did not vary substantially from the average inflation rate of its major trading partners. Thus, the real and nominal exchange rates moved together. See Charles Schultze, *Memos to the President: A Guide Through Macroeconomics for the Busy Policymaker* (Washington, DC: Brookings Institution, 1992), 101–103; and Imad A. Moosa, *Exchange Rate Regimes: Fixed, Flexible or Something in Between?* (New York: Palgrave Macmillan, 2005). Moosa reports correlations of 0.96, 0.88, and 0.65 between the nominal and real exchange rates for the U.S. dollar and the Canadian dollar, the Japanese yen, and the British pound for the period 1974–2004.

TABLE 15.2   Effect of Dollar Appreciation and Depreciation on U.S. Exports and Imports

$R = ¥/\$$	DOMESTIC PRICE	JAN 09: $R = 90$	JUNE 09: $R = 97$	EFFECT ON EXPORTS (X) AND IMPORTS (M)
U.S. exports: Computers	$10,000	¥900,000	¥970,000	X decreases
U.S. imports: Japanese cars	¥2,000,000	≈ $22,200	≈ $20,600	M increases
		JAN 08: $R = 108$	JAN 09: $R = 90$	
U.S. exports: Computers	$10,000	¥1,080,000	¥900,000	X increases
U.S. imports: Japanese cars	¥2,000,000	≈ $18,500	≈ $22,200	M decreases

as cars become cheaper in terms of the number of dollars required to pay the Japanese price in yen. This result implies that as R increases, the volume of exports (X) decreases, while the volume of imports (M) increases, all else held constant. The opposite case holds for a dollar depreciation. As the dollar depreciates against the yen, each dollar trades for fewer yen, so it takes more dollars to pay for Japanese cars that are priced in yen. However, fewer yen are needed for U.S. exports priced in dollars. This means that as R decreases, the volume of exports (X) increases, while the volume of imports (M) decreases, all else held constant.

Figure 15.1 shows the effect of the exchange rate on net exports (exports minus imports), or the **balance of trade**, from 2000 to 2012. The exchange rate is measured on the right axis as the weighted exchange value of the U.S. dollar versus the currencies of a broad group of major U.S. trading partners (R or units per dollar). The left axis shows the balance of trade, or exports minus imports. Figure 15.1 depicts the relationship between changes in the value of the dollar and net exports. An appreciating or strong dollar has a positive effect on U.S. imports and a negative effect on U.S. exports. This causes the balance of trade, or net exports, to become

Balance of trade
The relationship between a country's export and import spending, which can be positive if there is a trade surplus (exports exceed imports) or negative if there is a trade deficit (imports exceed exports).

FIGURE 15.1
Balance of Trade and the Exchange Rate
An appreciating dollar typically causes the balance of trade or net exports to become more negative, while a depreciating dollar has the opposite effect.
Source: Federal Reserve Economic Data (FRED II), *Economic Research*, Federal Reserve Bank of St. Louis. Available at http://research.stlouis-fed.org/fred2/.

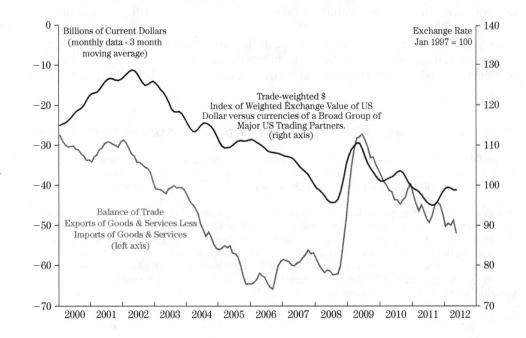

TABLE 15.3   Determinants of Exports and Imports

EXPORTS	IMPORTS	NET EXPORTS
$X = f(Y, Y^*, R)$	$M = f(Y, R)$	$F = f(Y, Y^*, R)$
$(0)(+)(-)$	$(+)(+)$	$(-)(+)(-)$

---

more negative (2000–2002). Net exports become less negative when the value of the dollar declines for an extended period (2006–2008) because exports increase while imports decrease.

These relationships are summarized in Table 15.3

> *where*
> X = export spending
> M = import spending
> F = net export spending (export minus import spending $= X - M$)
> Y^* = income in the rest of the world
> Y = income in the United States
> R = exchange rate as defined above (units of foreign currency per dollar)

The notation is read as follows: Exports (imports, net exports) "are a function of" the variables inside the parentheses. The positive and negative signs show whether the variables in the parentheses are directly $(+)$ or inversely $(-)$ related to the variable on the left. U.S. exports are not related to the level of U.S. income, but are directly or positively related to the level of income in the rest of the world and inversely or negatively related to the exchange rate. U.S. imports are directly or positively related to both the level of U.S. income and the exchange rate. Therefore, net exports (exports minus imports) are

1. Negatively related to income in the United States (an increase in U.S. income causes imports to increase, but has no effect on exports and, therefore, causes net exports to decrease)
2. Positively related to income in the rest of the world (an increase in foreign income has no impact on U.S. imports, but causes U.S. exports to increase and, therefore, net exports to increase)
3. Negatively related to R (an increase in R will cause exports to decrease, imports to increase, and, therefore, net exports to decrease)

Each of these relationships is defined assuming all else is held constant, as we have done throughout this text.

Managerial Rule of Thumb

Currency Exchange Rates

Managers are influenced by currency exchange rates because these exchange rates influence the prices of both the firm's inputs and its outputs if the firm sells its products or purchases its inputs abroad. An increase in a country's exchange rate hurts domestic firms that export to other countries, but helps firms that import their inputs from abroad. ∎

Equilibrium in the Open Economy

Before discussing how international transactions are measured, we'll review the concept of the equilibrium level of income and output as applied to a mixed, open economy. These relationships are expressed in Equations 15.1 through 15.4:

15.1 $E = Y$

15.2 $C + I + G + X - M = C + S + T$

15.3 $I + G + X = S + T + M$

15.4 $X - M = (S - I) + (T - G)$

where

E = aggregate expenditure
Y = real income
C = consumption expenditure
I = investment expenditure
G = government expenditure
X = export spending
M = import spending
S = saving
T = total taxes

Trade surplus

Occurs when a country's export spending exceeds the spending on its imports.

Capital outflow (k_o)

A lending of a country's savings that occurs when the country has a trade surplus and its citizens purchase real and financial assets from abroad.

Trade deficit

Occurs when a country's import spending exceeds the spending on its exports.

Capital inflow (k_i)

Borrowing from another country that occurs when the country has a trade deficit and its citizens sell real and financial assets to foreigners.

Net capital flow ($K_N = k_i - k_o$)

The difference between capital inflows and outflows, which must match the trade balance, or export spending minus import spending.

Drawing on the circular flow relationships we have developed, planned aggregate expenditure in the economy must equal aggregate income in equilibrium (Equation 15.1) (Chapters 11 and 12). Aggregate expenditure (E) represents the sum of consumption (C), investment (I), government (G), and export (X) minus import (M) spending. Households use aggregate income (Y) for consumption spending (C), saving (S), or taxes (T) (Equation 15.2). Simplifying and rearranging terms in Equation 15.2 leads to Equation 15.3, which shows injections to and leakages from the circular flow of U.S. economic activity. In a mixed, open economy, injections are investment, government, and export spending, while leakages are saving, taxation, and import spending.

In Equation 15.4, we have rearranged the terms in Equation 15.3 to show net exports, or the trade balance, on the left side of the equation. The right side shows the relationship between saving and investment in the private sector (the level of private saving) and the relationship between government spending and taxation in the public sector (the level of public saving). Because Equation 15.4 is based on the previous equations and represents an equilibrium condition for the economy, the trade balance must equal the level of private and public saving in the country.

If there is a **trade surplus** ($X - M > 0$) in the United States, the net saving on the right side of Equation 15.4 must be positive. Individuals and institutions in the United States are *lending* these savings abroad. They do so by purchasing foreign real and financial assets. This process represents a **capital outflow (k_o)** from the United States to the rest of the world. Likewise, if there is a **trade deficit** ($X - M < 0$), the net saving on the right side of Equation 15.4 must be negative. Individuals and institutions in the United States are *borrowing* from abroad. They do so by selling real and financial assets to foreigners. This process represents a **capital inflow (k_i)** to the United States. The **net capital flow ($K_N = k_i - k_o$)**

must, therefore, match the trade balance $(X - M)$.[9] If exports just equal imports, there are no net capital flows between the United States and the rest of the world.[10]

U.S. International Transactions in 2011 (Balance of Payments)

U.S. international transactions are reported in the **balance of payments (BP) accounting system**, a record of *all* transactions between residents of the reporting country and residents of the rest of the world over a period of time, usually one year. This is an accounting system similar to the GDP accounts for a given country. GDP measures the market value of all *currently produced* final goods and services in a country for a given year (Chapter 11). Because export and import spending flows are for currently produced goods and services in the United States and other countries, these expenditures are included in the GDP accounts. They are also included in the *BP* accounts because they are international transactions. However, there are capital flows between countries that reflect the buying and selling of *existing* real and financial assets. These transactions do not represent current production and are not included in the GDP accounts, but they are included in the *BP* accounts.

Table 15.4 shows the U.S. *BP* accounts for 2011 (all figures are measured in billions of dollars). A receipts item, which represents a flow of income to the United States, is listed as a positive number, whereas a payment item, which represents a flow from the United States to the rest of the world, is listed as a negative number. The *BP* accounts are divided into two sections: the current account and the financial account.[11]

The Current Account

The **current account** measures the current flows of goods, services, investment income, and unilateral transfers between the United States and the rest of the world. U.S. exports of goods and services are listed as a positive amount because they generate income flowing to the United States, while imports are listed as a negative amount because income flows from the United States to the rest of the world to pay for imported goods and services. The trade balance (net exports or exports minus imports) was –$559.5 billion in 2011.

The second major category in the current account is **net investment income**, which is the difference between the interest income or receipts earned on investments in the rest of the world by U.S. residents and the payments to foreigners on the investments they have made in the United States.[12] As you can see in Table 15.4, net investment income was $221 billion in 2011. **Unilateral transfers** represent flows of goods, services, and financial assets in which nothing of significant

Balance of payments (BP) accounting system
A comprehensive measure of all economic activity between a country and the rest of the world.

Current account
A measure of the current flows of goods, services, investment income, and unilateral transfers between a country and the rest of the world.

Net investment income
The difference between the interest income or receipts earned on investments in the rest of the world by the residents of a given country and the payments to foreigners on investments they have made in the given country.

Unilateral transfers
Flows of goods, services, and financial assets, such as foreign aid, from one country to another in which nothing of significant economic value is received in return.

[9]This relationship can also be seen with the alternative definition of equilibrium: $Y = E$. It follows that $Y = (C + I + G) + (X - M)$ or $Y - (C + I + G) = (X - M)$. If $(X - M) > 0$, then $Y > (C + I + G)$. Additional expenditures are needed for equilibrium. These are obtained by U.S. households and institutions purchasing real and financial assets from abroad (capital outflow). If $(X - M) < 0$, then $Y < (C + I + G)$. In this case, additional income is needed for equilibrium. This income is achieved by the sale of U.S. real and financial assets to foreigners (capital inflow).

[10]We use K_N to represent net financial capital flows in the macro model of this text. This is distinct from the use of K to represent the capital input in a production function (Chapters 5 and 6). K in the production function refers to real physical capital inputs in a production process that change as a result of investment spending by firms. K_N refers to the buying and selling of existing real and financial assets in response to differential rates of return and other factors.

[11]The Bureau of Economic Analysis calls these statistics the *International Transactions Accounts* (ITAs). See www.bea.gov.

[12]The current account includes the income on these financial investments. The dollar amounts of the actual investments in the United States and the rest of the world are included in the financial account below.

TABLE 15.4   U.S. Balance of Payments, 2011 (billion $)

CURRENT ACCOUNT TRANSACTIONS

Exports of goods and services	$2,105.1	
Imports of goods and services	−2,665.0	
Trade balance		−$559.9
Receipts on U.S. assets abroad	738.7	
Payments on foreign assets in United States	−517.7	
Net investment income		221.0
Unilateral transfers		−134.5
Current account balance		−473.4

FINANCIAL ACCOUNT TRANSACTIONS

Change in U.S. holdings of foreign assets (k_o)		−396.4
Change in foreign holdings of U.S. assets (k_i)		783.7
Financial derivatives	6.8	
Capital account transactions, net	−1.2	
Statistical discrepancy	80.5	
Net capital flows to United States		$473.4

Source: Sarah P. Scott and Alexis N. Chaves, "U.S. International Transactions Fourth Quarter and Year 2011," *Survey of Current Business* (April 2012): 22–31. Available at www.bea.gov/international.

economic value is received in return. These include government military and non-military transfers, such as foreign aid, private and government pensions to U.S. citizens living abroad, and gifts sent abroad by individuals and nonprofit organizations. These amounts totaled $134.5 billion in 2011 and were recorded as a negative item because they represented payments abroad. The net balance on the current account in 2011 was –$473.4 billion.

The Financial Account

Financial account
A measure of the change in the stock of real assets (buildings, property, etc.) and financial assets (bank deposits, securities, etc.) held by a country's residents in foreign countries and by foreigners in the given country.

The **financial account** measures changes in the stock of assets held by U.S. residents in foreign countries and by foreigners in the United States. The financial account includes both financial assets (bank deposits, securities, etc.) and real assets (buildings, property, etc.). In the international economy, financial account transactions or capital *flows* result from changes or differences in interest rates among countries or in rates of return among various types of financial and/or real assets as residents adjust their *stocks* of assets in search of the highest returns. If interest rates are higher in the United States than in the rest of the world, financial capital flows to the United States. There will be capital outflows from the United States if U.S. interest rates are lower than those in the rest of the world.[13]

As noted above, capital inflows (k_i) arise when U.S. residents sell real and financial assets to residents of the rest of the world; capital outflows (k_o) occur when U.S. residents buy real and financial assets from residents of the rest of the world. As you can see in Table 15.4, the change in foreign holdings of U.S. assets (a capital

[13]Capital flows are also affected by other factors, such as the political stability in different countries, profit potential, and credit conditions. For example, capital flows to and from the United States were much greater in the first half of 2007 than in the second half of the year, given the disruptions in the U.S. financial markets at that time. See Christopher L. Bach, "U.S. International Transactions in 2007," *Survey of Current Business* (April 2008): 22–47. Available at www.bea.gov/international.

inflow or positive number) was greater than the change in U.S. holdings of foreign assets (a capital outflow or negative number) by $387.3 billion. For simplicity, we also put net financial derivatives and net capital account transactions under the financial account transactions. Statistics on financial derivatives are a recent addition to the International Transactions Accounts to close a gap in coverage and to capture an area of financial activity that has grown rapidly over the past decade. The capital account transactions consist of capital transfers, such as changes in financial assets of migrants as they enter or leave the United States and U.S. government debt forgiveness.[14]

This positive balance on the financial account ($392.9 billion) is equal to the negative balance on the current account with the exception of the statistical discrepancy ($80.5 billion) noted in Table 15.4 and discussed later in the chapter. This equality did not happen by chance. It *must* hold for equilibrium in the balance of payments. If the current flows of goods and services, investment income, and unilateral transfers are greater from the United States to the rest of the world than vice versa (a negative balance on the current account), there must be an offsetting positive balance on the financial account, representing a net capital inflow into the United States. Thus, a negative balance of trade, which represents the largest component of the current account, must be financed by U.S. borrowing from the rest of the world (an increase in foreign holdings of U.S. assets).

Revenue or T-Account

It may be easier to understand these balance of payments relationships by reorganizing the data in Table 15.4 into a **revenue or T-account**. All international transactions can be classified in one of two ways. Either they generate receipts (income) to U.S. residents, or they generate payments (expenses) by U.S. residents. These transactions can be listed in a revenue or T-account (shown in Table 15.5), which, following the accounting concept of the income statement, records international transactions as either expense-generating items (listed on the left-hand or debit side) or income-generating items (listed on the right-hand or credit side).

Because the *BP* account records *all* transactions between U.S. residents and residents of the rest of the world, the left-hand side of the *BP* T-account must equal the right-hand side (total expenditures must equal total income). Table 15.6 puts the 2011 balance of payments information from Table 15.4 into the revenue or T-account form. This T-account approach combines elements from the *BP* current and financial accounts into import-type transactions or payments to the rest of the world (debits) and export-type transactions or receipts from the rest of the world (credits). Items that had a negative value in the 2011 balance of payments accounts (Table 15.4) are recorded in Table 15.6 on the payments or debit side of the T-account, whereas items that had a positive value in the *BP* accounts are recorded here on the receipts or credit side of the T-account.

As we noted earlier in the chapter, the totals on both sides of Table 15.6 must be equal. The **statistical discrepancy (*SD*)** arises from the fact that data collection

Revenue or T-account
An accounting statement that shows expense-generating items on the left-hand or debit side and income-generating items on the right-hand or credit side.

Statistical discrepancy (*SD*)
The imbalance between the financial and current accounts in the balance of payments statement or between payments and receipts in the revenue or T-account that arises from inefficient data collection.

TABLE 15.5   Revenue or T-Account for Balance of Payments

DEBIT (−)	CREDIT (+)
U.S. residents' payments (expenses) to residents of the rest of the world	U.S. residents' receipts (income) from residents of the rest of the world

---

[14]U.S. Department of Commerce, *Bureau of Economic Analysis, International Transactions Accounts*. Available at www.bea.gov.

TABLE 15.6   Revenue or T-Account for 2011 Balance of Payments (billion $)

PAYMENTS		RECEIPTS	
(IMPORT-TYPE TRANSACTIONS: DEBIT [−])		(EXPORT-TYPE TRANSACTIONS: CREDIT [+])	
Imports of goods & services	$2,665.0	Exports of goods & services	$2,105.1
Payments on foreign assets in United States	517.7	Receipts on U.S. assets abroad	738.7
		Financial derivatives	6.8
Unilateral transfers	134.5	Change in foreign holdings of U.S. assets	783.7
Capital account transfers	1.2		
Change in U.S. holdings of foreign assets	396.4	Statistical discrepancy	80.5
Total	$3,714.8	Total	$3,714.8

TABLE 15.7   T-Account Summary of 2011 Balance of Payments (billion $)

PAYMENTS (EXPENDITURE)		RECEIPTS (INCOME)	
Imports (*M*)	$3,318.4	Exports (*X*)	$2,850.6
Capital outflows (k_o)	396.4	Capital inflows (k_i)	864.2
Total expenditure	$3,714.8	Total income	$3,714.8

is not perfectly efficient. We cannot account for every single transaction between U.S. residents and residents of the rest of the world. Because the discrepancy is usually attributed to short-term capital flows, we can include an *SD* value of 80.5 under the heading of "Change in foreign holdings of U.S. assets."

Generalizing the transactions in Table 15.6 results in Table 15.7. In this table and the examples that follow, we assume that there is perfectly efficient data collection or that the statistical discrepancy equals zero. In Table 15.7, total expenditure is the sum of imports and capital outflows ($M + k_o$), while total income is the sum of exports and capital inflows ($X + k_i$). Because income equals expenditure, income minus expenditure equals zero. Substituting the components gives us Equation 15.5, while rearranging the terms gives Equation 15.6. Equation 15.6 is simply the equation for net exports ($F = X - M$) plus the equation for net capital flows ($K_N = k_i - k_o$). Thus, the balance of payments is the sum of the balance on the current account plus the balance on the financial account, or $BP = F + K_N = 0$. These balances must be equal and offsetting so that their sum equals zero. The balance of payments equation (15.6) and the balance of payments account in Table 15.4 separate the above transactions into flows affecting current income or current GDP (trade flows) and flows involving existing assets (capital flows).[15]

---

[15]For a discussion of the issues surrounding the size of the U.S. trade deficit, see Catherine L. Mann, *Is the U.S. Trade Deficit Sustainable?* (Washington, DC: Institute for International Economics, 1999); Catherine L. Mann, "Perspective on the U.S. Current Account Deficit and Sustainability," *Journal of Economic Perspectives* 16 (Summer 2002): 131–52; and Masaru Yoshitomi, "Global Imbalances and East Asian Monetary Cooperation," in *Toward an East Asian Exchange Rate Regime*, eds. Duck-Koo Chung and Barry Eichengreen (Washington, DC: The Brookings Institution, 2007), 22–48. For a discussion of the current account versus larger global financial flows, see Maurice Obstfeld, "Does the Current Account Still Matter?" *American Economic Review: Paper & Proceedings* 102 (2012): 1–23.

15.5 $(X + k_i) - (M + k_o) = 0$

15.6 $BP: (X - M) + (k_i - k_o) = 0$

Deriving the Foreign Exchange Market

Given the importance of exchange rates in influencing exports, imports, and GDP, we show how exchange rates are determined using concepts from the *BP* accounts. We use a simple two-country model of the United States and Japan to derive the foreign exchange market, and we use the revenue or T-account approach to show the quantity supplied and quantity demanded of both dollars ($) and yen (¥). This is similar to the microeconomic demand and supply analysis for specific products (Chapter 2). However, in the foreign exchange market, the commodity is a currency, and the price is the exchange rate between two currencies.

The Demand for and Supply of Dollars in the Foreign Exchange Market

We start with the income side of the international transactions revenue account (see Table 15.7). To pay for U.S. goods and services—both newly produced goods and services (U.S. exports, X) and existing real and financial assets (U.S. capital inflows, k_i)—Japanese residents *demand* $ by supplying their own currency, ¥, to the foreign exchange market. They sell ¥ and buy $. Alternatively, U.S. residents receive ¥ when they sell their goods to Japanese residents. Because yen are not U.S. currency, U.S. residents take their ¥ to the foreign exchange market and exchange them for $ (i.e., they buy $ with ¥). The income side of the revenue account shows the quantity demanded of dollars (see Table 15.8).

A similar analysis holds for the expense or payments side of the revenue account in Table 15.7. To pay for Japanese goods and services—both newly produced goods and services (U.S. imports, M) and existing real and financial assets (U.S. capital outflows, k_o)—U.S. residents need ¥. They *supply* $ to the foreign exchange market in exchange for ¥. Alternatively, Japanese residents receive $ when they sell their goods to U.S. residents and take these $ to the foreign exchange market to acquire their own currency, ¥. Either way, these transactions give rise to a quantity supplied of dollars (see Table 15.9).[16]

TABLE 15.8   Demand for Dollars in Foreign Exchange Market

UNITED STATES SELLS TO JAPAN	IF JAPAN PAYS IN $	IF JAPAN PAYS IN ¥	RESULT
In foreign exchange market	Japan sells ¥ to buy $	United States sells ¥ to buy $	$Q^d_\$$

TABLE 15.9   Supply of Dollars in Foreign Exchange Market

UNITED STATES BUYS FROM JAPAN	IF UNITED STATES PAYS IN $	IF UNITED STATES PAYS IN ¥	RESULT
In foreign exchange market	Japan sells $ to buy ¥	United States sells $ to buy ¥	$Q^s_\$$

---

[16]Note that this discussion includes the supply of and demand for $ and ¥ only in the foreign exchange market, not the domestic money market.

TABLE 15.10   T-Account, Supply of and Demand for Dollars

$Q^s_{\$}$	$Q^d_{\$}$
M	X
k_o	k_i

These results can be summarized in the following demand and supply functions (Equations 15.7 and 15.8) for dollars in the foreign exchange market:

15.7 $Q^d_{\$} = f(X, k_i)$

15.8 $Q^s_{\$} = f(M, k_o)$

Equation 15.7 states that the quantity of dollars demanded in the foreign exchange market is a function of the level of the receipts- or income-side factors in Table 15.7 (i.e., the amount of exports and the level of capital inflows). The quantity of dollars supplied in the foreign exchange market (Equation 15.8) is a function of the payments- or expenditure-side factors in Table 15.7 (i.e., the amount of imports and the level of capital outflows). These relationships are also shown in T-account form in Table 15.10. The determinants of exports, imports, and capital flows were developed above and are expressed in Table 15.11.

U.S. exports are positively related to the level of income in Japan and negatively related to the exchange rate. U.S. imports are positively related to both the level of U.S. income and the exchange rate. The last two relationships in Table 15.11 show the influence of differences in interest rates on U.S. capital inflows and outflows. Capital inflows occur if U.S. interest rates are higher than those in Japan; outflows occur when Japanese interest rates exceed those in the United States.[17]

Substituting these relationships into the dollar demand and supply equations (15.7 and 15.8) gives us Equations 15.9 and 15.10:

15.9 $Q^d_{\$} = f(R, Y_{Japan}, r_{US} > r_{Japan})$
$\quad\quad\quad\quad (-)\ (+)\quad\ \ (+)$

15.10 $Q^s_{\$} = f(R, Y_{US}, r_{US} < r_{Japan})$
$\quad\quad\quad\quad (+)\ (+)\quad\ \ (+)$

If we make the simplifying assumptions that interest rates in both countries are equal ($r_{US} = r_{Japan}$) and that incomes are constant in the United States and Japan, we can use all of these relationships to derive a *hypothetical* foreign exchange (or dollar) market (see Figure 15.2), where R is the price of $ in terms of ¥ (measured on the vertical axis) and $Q_{\$}$ is the quantity of dollars (measured on the horizontal axis).[18]

TABLE 15.11   Determinants of Exports, Imports, and Capital Flows

$X = f(Y_{Japan}, R)$	$M = f(Y_{US}, R)$	$k_i = f(r_{US} > r_{Japan})$	$k_o = f(r_{US} < r_{Japan})$
$(+)\ (-)$	$(+)\ (+)$	$(+)$	$(+)$

---

[17]This notation shows capital inflows and outflows as positive numbers and focuses on interest rate differentials between countries.

[18]Other factors, including the political environment in different countries and speculation by currency traders, can also influence the supply of and demand for various currencies. We ignore these factors in these simple models, but will discuss them in policy examples later in the chapter.

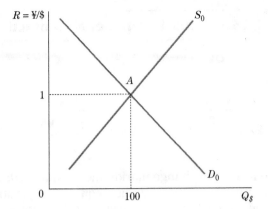

FIGURE 15.2
Foreign Exchange Market-Initial Equilibrium
Equilibrium in the foreign exchange (dollar) market is achieved at that exchange rate where the quantity demanded of dollars equals the quantity supplied of dollars.

As we discussed when first introducing demand functions, the demand for dollars is a function of the price, *holding all else constant*. The demand curve for dollars in the foreign exchange market is downward sloping. In Figure 15.2, a movement *down along* the D_0 curve shows the quantity of dollars demanded increasing as the exchange rate, R, decreases. As the exchange rate decreases and the dollar depreciates, U.S. exports become cheaper for Japanese residents. A greater demand for exports creates an increase in the quantity of dollars demanded to purchase those exports. Likewise, an increase in the exchange rate, R, all else held constant, makes U.S. exports more expensive for Japanese residents and results in a smaller quantity of dollars demanded to pay for those exports.

Changes in the other variables in Equation 15.9 cause a *shift* in the demand curve for dollars. With a higher level of Japanese income, there is a greater demand for U.S. exports and, thus, a greater demand for U.S. dollars at every exchange rate, R. This causes the demand curve, D_0 in Figure 15.2, to shift to the right. If interest rates in the United States are greater than those in Japan, there are higher capital inflows to the United States. This also creates a higher demand for U.S. dollars at every exchange rate, causing the demand curve, D_0, to shift to the right.

In the same way, the supply curve for dollars in the foreign exchange market is upward sloping. As the exchange rate increases and the dollar appreciates, all else held constant, imports become less expensive because more yen are obtained for each dollar. Thus, a movement *upward along* the S_0 curve shows the quantity of dollars supplied increasing because imports are becoming less expensive and more dollars are being supplied to the market to purchase those imports.

Changes in the other variables in Equation 15.10 result in a *shift* of the supply curve. If U.S. income increases, there is a greater demand for imports at every exchange rate. This results in an increased supply of dollars at every R to purchase those imports and, thus, a rightward shift of the supply curve in Figure 15.2. Similarly, if Japanese interest rates are higher than those in the United States, there are increased capital outflows to purchase Japanese financial instruments. This also causes an increased supply of dollars at every exchange rate and results in a rightward shift of the supply curve for dollars in Figure 15.2.

Equilibrium in the Foreign Exchange Market

Equilibrium in the foreign exchange market occurs at point A in Figure 15.2, at the price or exchange rate $R = 1$, where $Q^d_\$ = Q^s_\$ = 100$. The balance of payments effects of this equilibrium in the dollar foreign exchange market in Figure 15.2 can be summarized in Equation 15.11 and Table 15.12.

$$15.11 \quad BP = (X - M) + K = (100 - 100) + 0 = 0$$

TABLE 15.12   U.S. International Transactions

$Q^s_\$$		$Q^d_\$$	
M	100	X	100
k_o	0	k_i	0
	100		100

Equilibrium in the foreign exchange market means that at the price or exchange rate $R = 1$, the quantity demanded of dollars equals the quantity supplied of dollars. In this simplified example, we have assumed that interest rates are equal in the United States and Japan, so there are no capital flows between the countries ($k_i = k_o = 0$). Therefore, $100 is demanded in the foreign exchange market to finance $100 worth of exports. This is exactly matched by the $100 supplied to the foreign exchange market to finance $100 worth of imports. The exchange rate or price necessary to equate the quantities demanded and supplied in this example is $R = 1$. As shown in both Equation 15.11 and Table 15.12, the balance of payments accounts are in equilibrium because export spending equals import spending and there are no capital flows. Thus, equilibrium in the foreign exchange market implies a balance of payments equilibrium.

Managerial Rule of Thumb

The Foreign Exchange Market

The foreign exchange market operates in the same manner as a competitive market for other goods and services. There are demand and supply factors for each currency, and the resulting price in the market is the currency exchange rate. Because the foreign exchange market is very competitive, exchange rates are constantly changing. These changes influence the costs of production and the prices of products for firms that buy and sell in international markets. ∎

Exchange Rate Systems

Figure 15.2, Equation 15.11, and Table 15.12 all show equilibrium in the foreign exchange market and the balance of payments accounts. Yet this equilibrium is easily disturbed when there are changes in the factors influencing the demand for and supply of currencies in the foreign exchange market. If we continue our simple two-country example with the United States and Japan and assume that interest rates are equal in both countries, changes in the demand for dollars will result primarily from changes in Japanese income (which influence the amount of U.S. exports), and changes in the supply of dollars will result primarily from changes in U.S. income (which influence the amount of U.S. imports). These changes in demand and supply result in *shifts* of the curves, not movements along the curves. In any market, with a shift of a demand or supply curve, there will be a new equilibrium price if the market is allowed to operate freely.

There are two major types of exchange rate systems that countries can use: flexible and fixed. In a **flexible exchange rate system**, the exchange rate is determined strictly by the interaction of the supply of and the demand for currencies. This means that a payments imbalance (a net surplus or a net deficit) cannot arise in the overall balance of payments accounts. The equilibrium price will always be

Flexible exchange rate system
A system in which currency exchange rates are determined strictly by the forces of demand for and supply of the currencies and there is no intervention by any country's central bank in order to influence the level of exchange rates.

established in the foreign exchange markets, which results in equilibrium in the balance of payments accounts.[19] Under a flexible exchange rate system, there is no intervention by the central bank of any country in order to influence the level of the exchange rate.

Countries may not always want their exchange rates to be subject to the forces of demand and supply for various political and economic reasons. Because an exchange rate influences the levels of a country's imports and exports, which are components of aggregate demand, domestic policy makers may want to hold that rate at a particular level or within a certain range to achieve given domestic policy goals related to the level or growth of GDP. The unpredictable volatility of a floating exchange rate may reduce international trade and investment, given the difficulty of writing contracts, and may cause firms and workers hurt by exchange rate swings to demand tariffs, quotas, and other forms of import protection from their governments. It is often believed that an announcement of a fixed exchange rate may also help governments resist political pressures for overly expansionary macroeconomic policies.[20]

Thus, countries may operate under a **fixed exchange rate system**, which applies either to a **gold standard**, where central banks agree to buy or sell gold to keep the exchange rates at a certain level, or to a **managed float**, where central banks buy and sell foreign currencies in the foreign exchange market to maintain or stabilize the exchange rate. In either of these cases, payments imbalances can arise in the balance of payments accounts because there is disequilibrium in the foreign exchange markets. External forces are attempting to alter exchange rates through shifts in the demand for and supply of currencies, while policy makers are attempting to hold the exchange rates constant.

The **International Monetary Fund (IMF)** and the **World Bank**, the two major international organizations focusing on international financial and development issues, were created at the Bretton Woods conference in 1944. The countries participating in the conference also established a system of fixed exchange rates under which their currencies were tied to the U.S. dollar, which was directly convertible to gold at a price of $35 per ounce. This system, which lasted until 1971, when the United States abandoned the gold standard, then led to a system of more flexible exchange rates, in which countries let the value of their currencies float in given ranges.[21]

As of 1995, only a small number of countries had maintained or pegged a tightly fixed exchange rate against any currency for five years or more. The fixed rate countries were primarily small tourism economies, oil sheikdoms, and politically dependent principalities. These countries typically subordinated their monetary policies to, rather than coordinating them with, the monetary policies of their partner countries. Data from 1991 to 1999 for the IMF's member countries indicate that the percentage of countries with "hard pegs" increased from 16 to 24 percent and those with floating currencies increased from 23 to 42 percent, while those with intermediate or "soft pegs" decreased from 62 to 34 percent. Hard pegs include currency boards, which are formal mechanisms for fixing exchange rates, and situations where countries are part of a currency union or have formally adopted the currency of another

Fixed exchange rate system
A system in which the central banks of various countries intervene in the foreign exchange market to maintain or stabilize currency exchange rates.

Gold standard
A fixed rate system in which central banks agree to buy and sell gold to keep exchange rates at a given level.

Managed float
A fixed rate system in which central banks buy and sell foreign currency to maintain exchange rates at a given level.

International Monetary Fund (IMF)
An international financial organization created at the Bretton Woods conference in 1944 that helps coordinate international financial flows and can arrange short-term loans between countries.

World Bank
An international financial organization created at the Bretton Woods conference in 1944 that helps developing countries obtain low-interest loans.

---

[19]Any deficit in the current account must be matched by a corresponding surplus in the financial account, and vice versa.

[20]Maurice Obstfeld and Kenneth Rogoff, "The Mirage of Fixed Exchange Rates," *Journal of Economic Perspectives* 9 (Fall 1995): 73–96; Guillermo A. Calvo and Frederic S. Mishkin, *The Mirage of Exchange Rate Regimes for Emerging Market Countries*, Cambridge, MA.: National Bureau of Economic Research, NBER Working Paper Series, No. 9808, June 2003.); Moosa, *Exchange Rate Regimes*, 63–89.

[21]For a nontechnical discussion of the gold standard and fixed exchange rates, see Board of Governors of the Federal Reserve System, *The Federal Reserve and the Financial Crisis: Chairman Bernanke's College Lecture Series, Origins and Mission of the Federal Reserve, Lecture 1.* Available at www.federalreserve.gov/newsevents/lectures/about.htm.

country. Soft pegs include situations where the exchange rate is allowed to shift gradually over time or within a rate band, which may also shift over time.[22]

Flexible Exchange Rate System

We illustrate the differences between flexible and fixed exchange rate systems by building on the simplified two-country example of the United States and Japan developed in Figure 15.2, Equation 15.11, and Table 15.12. Assume for simplicity that U.S. decision makers use expansionary fiscal and monetary policies to raise domestic income *while maintaining prices and interest rates at their current levels*.[23] Also assume that no policy action is taken in Japan in response to this U.S. action (everything else is held constant). Thus, we are assuming that interest rates continue to be equal between the two countries, so that there are no capital flows between them. However, with increased income, U.S. residents will increase their demand not only for domestically produced goods and services (consumption expenditures), but also for foreign goods and services (import spending). This larger U.S. income increases the demand for U.S. imports *at every exchange rate*. At each exchange rate (R), U.S. residents want to supply a larger amount of dollars to exchange for yen to purchase these imports.

In Figure 15.3, this change in behavior is shown as a rightward shift of supply curve S_0 to supply curve S_1. As noted above, the supply curve for dollars in the foreign exchange market is drawn assuming a given level of U.S. income. We are illustrating an increase in U.S. income from a domestic economic policy change, which causes the demand for imports to increase and results in a rightward shift in the supply curve for dollars, given the above assumption of a constant interest rate and prices. The same result would occur with changes in any of the other variables affecting real spending (Chapter 14).

In Figure 15.2, at the original exchange rate, $R = 1$, the demand for dollars equals the supply of dollars because desired exports equal desired imports. In Figure 15.3, assume the demand for imports increases to $150 due to increased U.S. income. This causes a balance of payments deficit in the United States because imports equal $150, while exports equal $100, or $BP = (X - M) = (\$100 - \$150) = -\$50$. In the dollar or foreign exchange market, the U.S. balance of payments deficit is represented by the distance AB, an excess supply of dollars ($Q^s_\$ = 150 > 100 = Q^d_\$$). More dollars are supplied to the market at every exchange rate to purchase these

[22]Obstfeld and Rogoff, "The Mirage of Fixed Exchange Rates"; Stanley Fischer, "Distinguished Lecture on Economics in Government—Exchange Rate Regimes: Is the Bipolar View Correct?" *Journal of Economic Perspectives* 15 (Spring 2001): 3–24. There are numerous definitional problems involved with these classifications. Based on data from the 2003 IMF *Annual Report on Exchange Arrangements and Exchange Restrictions*, Moosa reports that 48 percent of countries have fixed exchange rates, 44 percent have flexible exchange rates, and 8 percent have intermediate regimes. However, these classifications are based on what countries report to the IMF, which may not be what they actually do. Many developing countries that report floating rates may actually have rather rigid rates. See Moosa, *Exchange Rate Regimes*, 21–23. For an analysis of countries that have moved to more flexible systems, see Inci Otker-Robe and David Vavra, and a team of economists, *Moving to Greater Exchange Rate Flexibility: Operational Aspects Based on Lessons from Detailed Country Experiences* (Washington, DC: International Monetary Fund, 2007). A recent analysis concludes that fixed exchange rate regimes apply to a large number of countries but a small proportion of global GDP and market activity, and that switches in exchange rates are becoming rare. Countries that fix exchange rates include oil exporters, offshore financial centers, sub-Saharan Africans, and former French colonies, while countries that target inflation rates, former Soviet Bloc members, and large rich economies have flexible rates. See Andrew K. Rose, "Exchange Rate Regimes in the Modern Era: Fixed, Floating, and Flaky," *Journal of Economic Literature* 49 (2011): 652–72.

[23]Using the aggregate macro model, these changes are represented by an increase in aggregate demand from the fiscal policy change, which results in a higher level of equilibrium income and interest rate combined with an increase in the money supply by the Federal Reserve so that the final interest rate remains unchanged. The scenario also assumes that the SAS curve is horizontal so that the price level does not change.

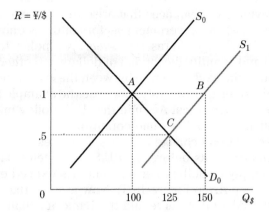

FIGURE 15.3
Foreign Exchange Market, Increase in U.S. Income
An increase in U.S. income, all else held constant, results in an increased supply of dollars in the foreign exchange market. Under a flexible exchange rate system, this increased supply of dollars results in a lower exchange rate or a depreciation of the dollar.

imports, resulting in a shift of the supply curve for dollars. The demand curve for dollars does not shift because we assume that Japanese income has not changed.

Under a flexible exchange rate system, this disequilibrium situation means that market pressures will force the exchange rate down (the dollar will depreciate or be worth less). At $R = 1$, the quantity supplied of dollars is greater than the quantity demanded of dollars. As R falls, the effect on U.S. exports is shown as a movement along the D_0 curve from point A to C. As the translated price of U.S. goods decreases, Japanese residents increase the quantity of dollars demanded to purchase the now-cheaper exports. Also, as R falls, the effect on U.S. imports is shown as a movement along the new supply curve, S_1, from point B to C. As R falls, the translated price of Japanese goods increases, thereby cutting off some of the increase in quantity of dollars supplied resulting from the increase in U.S. income. The final equilibrium is at point C in the foreign exchange market at a lower exchange rate, $R = 0.5$. Because this is an equilibrium exchange rate, the quantity of dollars demanded again equals the quantity supplied. This result also means that the balance of payments accounts are in equilibrium, with imports and exports equal at $125. Thus, flexible exchange rates automatically eliminate a balance of payments disequilibrium. These results are summarized in Equation 15.12 and Table 15.13.

$$15.12 \quad BP = (X - M) + K = (125 - 125) + 0 = 0$$

Fixed Exchange Rate System

Under a fixed exchange rate system, the central banks of different countries intervene in foreign exchange markets to maintain exchange rates between the countries at a given level or within a predetermined range. To do so, they must use their **reserve assets**, which include gold certificates, special drawing rights, the reserve position in the IMF, and holdings of foreign currencies. Changes in this account are labeled as "Changes in Official Reserve Assets" in the international transactions and balance of payments accounts. The function of this account is to

Reserve assets
Assets, including foreign currencies and gold certificates, that central banks use to maintain exchange rates between countries at a given level or in a predetermined range.

TABLE 15.13   U.S. International Transactions, Increase in U.S. Income

POINT A			POINT A–B			POINT C		
M 100		X 100	M 150		X 100	M 125		X 125
k_o 0		k_i 0	k_o 0		k_i 0	k_o 0		k_i 0
100		100	150		100	125		125

accommodate any payments imbalances that arise from autonomous transactions of the household, business, and government sectors of the economy, excluding the actions of central banks. Changes in reserve assets are a policy tool used to equate the quantity supplied and quantity demanded of dollars and other currencies, so as to maintain or influence the exchange rate between these currencies.[24]

To illustrate a fixed exchange rate system, we use the example from the previous section on flexible exchange rates. Assume that U.S. policy makers use domestic expansionary policies under the same conditions as in the previous example (U.S. income increases with no change in prices or interest rates and no Japanese policy response). This leads, as before, to a U.S. balance of payments deficit of $50 (i.e., an excess supply of dollars because imports exceed exports by $50, as illustrated by the distance AB in Figure 15.3). Now assume that the central banks of these countries, the Federal Reserve and the Bank of Japan, want to maintain the exchange rate at $R = 1$ for domestic policy reasons. They must intervene in the foreign exchange market to counter the market forces that are exerting downward pressure on the exchange rate, as shown in Figure 15.3. Distance AB in Figure 15.3 represents a disequilibrium situation. To maintain the exchange rate at $R = 1$, the Federal Reserve must change this to an equilibrium situation.

Because the distance AB in Figure 15.3 represents an excess supply of dollars or a balance of payments deficit, with expense transactions (imports) exceeding receipts transactions (exports), the Federal Reserve needs to generate receipts (income) of $50 in order to restore equilibrium. To do so, it *sells* reserve assets (RA), gold or yen (foreign currency), for dollars. At every exchange rate, the Federal Reserve increases the demand for dollars by supplying yen from its reserve assets to the foreign exchange market. This action is shown in Figure 15.4, as the original D_0 curve shifts to the right to intersect point B at $R = 1$ and $Q_\$ = 150$. Note that the shift from S_0 to S_1 resulted from the increase in U.S. income, an autonomous increase from the perspective of the Federal Reserve (even though it resulted from domestic U.S. economic policy). The shift from D_0 to D_1 results from the sale of reserve assets by the Federal Reserve, an accommodating increase resulting from a direct policy action by the Federal Reserve.[25]

Balance of payments equilibrium is restored through this policy action, as illustrated in Equation 15.13 and Table 15.14.

$$15.13 \quad BP = (X - M) + K + RA = (100 - 150) + 0 + 50 = 0$$

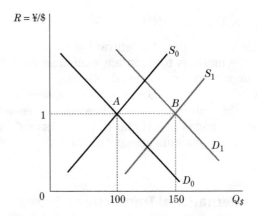

FIGURE 15.4

Federal Reserve Intervention

To maintain a fixed exchange rate in response to an increased supply of dollars, the Federal Reserve must increase the demand for dollars by selling its reserve assets for dollars.

---

[24]Reserve assets are included in the financial account numbers in Table 15.4. Because they are so small compared to the other flows, they essentially round to zero.

[25]This change might also result because the Bank of Japan does not want the yen to appreciate (as the dollar depreciates), so it buys dollars on the foreign exchange market.

TABLE 15.14 U.S. International Transactions, Federal Reserve Intervention

POINT A		POINT A–B		POINT B	
M 100	X 100	M 150	X 100	M 150	X 100
k_o 0	k_i 0	k_o 0	k_i 0	k_o 0	k_i 0
					RA 50
100	100	150	100	150	100

In the case of a fixed exchange rate system, the balance of payments equilibrium is restored not from a change in the exchange rate, but from a policy action by the central bank. The selling of reserve assets by the Federal Reserve creates an increased demand for dollars, which maintains the exchange rate at $R = 1$ in Figure 15.4, instead of allowing it to fall to $R = 0.5$, as shown in Figure 15.3. Both Equation 15.13 and Table 15.14 show the effect of the change in reserve assets in restoring balance of payments equilibrium. The selling of reserve assets by the central bank to buy dollars is an income- or receipts-generating transaction and is, therefore, included on the right-hand side of the revenue account in Table 15.14.

The Effect on the Money Supply

With a fixed exchange rate system, such as a gold standard, a central bank's intervention in the foreign exchange market will have certain effects on the country's domestic money supply. If the United States and Japan are on a gold standard (assume, for simplicity, $\$1 = ¥1 = 1$ oz. gold), gold is the central banks' reserve asset that backs bank reserves, which, in turn, back the money stock. With the U.S. balance of payments deficit, the Federal Reserve will buy back the excess supply of dollars from the Bank of Japan with gold. Therefore, gold flows out of the United States to Japan. As the United States is losing gold, the domestic money supply will decrease based on the money multiplier. The reverse process occurs in Japan (i.e., the money stock increases with the inflow of gold). The important point is that a continual balance of payments deficit in any country can be sustained only as long as the country's gold reserves hold out. This is one of the reasons that countries around the world eventually abandoned the gold standard.

In terms of a managed float, where the Federal Reserve uses holdings of foreign currencies to influence the exchange rate, the same effect on the money stock *may* occur. The previous conclusion will also hold: With a fixed exchange rate, continual balance of payments deficits can be sustained only as long as a country's foreign currency reserves hold out. Although a central bank's reserve assets include both gold and foreign currencies, in the modern banking system the money stock is no longer backed by gold. Government securities are the main source of bank reserve funds.

Sterilization

In the previous section, we noted that a country's money stock *may* decrease as a result of a balance of payments deficit. This will not be the case if the Federal Reserve sterilizes the effects of the balance of payments deficit. The previous example discussed a nonsterilized intervention, where the Federal Reserve allowed the country's balance of payments position to affect the domestic money stock. This may not be desirable, given domestic economic goals. Under a **sterilized intervention**, the Federal Reserve takes action to offset the balance of payments

Sterilized intervention
Actions taken by a country's central bank to prevent balance of payments policies from influencing the country's domestic money supply.

deficit's (or surplus's) effect on the domestic money stock through open market operations. In the case of a loss of reserves due to foreign exchange market operations, which would decrease the domestic money supply, the Federal Reserve can buy securities in the open market to increase the domestic money supply. This is the same type of operation it would follow if it wanted to increase the money supply for purely domestic reasons. Sterilized interventions typically result in only modest, if any, effects on exchange rates, given that relative money supplies are not changed with these procedures.[26]

Policy Examples of International Economic Issues

We now discuss several policy examples that illustrate the use of fiscal, monetary, and balance of payments policies with flexible and fixed exchange rate systems. We focus on

1. The U.S. economy from 1995 to 2000, from 2007 to 2008, and from 2010 to 2012
2. Policies regarding the euro from 1999 to 2003 and from 2010 to 2012
3. The impact of currency devaluations and the collapse of the economies of Southeast Asian countries in 1997
4. The debate over the weak Chinese yuan from 2003 to the present

Unlike in our previous discussion of fixed and flexible exchange rates in the simplified U.S.–Japan model, we will focus on all the variables influencing the demand for and supply of various currencies including political factors and speculation. We also discuss the impact of these international macro changes on managerial strategies.

The U.S. Economy, 1995–2000

From 1995 to 2000, the U.S. economy experienced relatively high GDP growth with low inflation and decreasing unemployment. This period has been called the "Goldilocks economy" and the "fabulous decade" because real GDP growth rates averaged 4.0 percent over the period, productivity increases were twice as high as in the 1973–1990 period, unemployment declined to 4.1 percent in 2000, and inflation averaged 2.9 percent over the period.[27] Much of this growth was driven by the wealth effect of the stock market on consumption spending and by productivity increases, which stimulated business investment spending. During the 1995–1997 period, the Fed kept the targeted federal funds rate at approximately 5.5 percent, given that the productivity increases were allowing the economy to grow without increasing inflationary pressures. The Fed actually lowered the targeted rate in 1998 to deal with the fallout from the Southeast Asian financial crisis (discussed below) and did not begin raising rates to restrain the economy until 1999.

The United States essentially followed a flexible exchange rate policy during this period. We model this situation in the foreign exchange market in Figure 15.5. We illustrate the foreign exchange market with the dollar versus the euro so that we can discuss the euro in more detail in the next section.

---

[26]Obstfeld and Rogoff, "The Mirage of Fixed Exchange Rates." For details of sterilization procedures, see Board of Governors of the Federal Reserve System, *The Federal Reserve System Purposes & Functions* (Washington, DC: Board of Governors, 2005).

[27]Alan S. Blinder and Janet L. Yellen, *The Fabulous Decade: Macroeconomic Lessons from the 1990s* (New York: Century Foundation Press, 2001), v–vi.

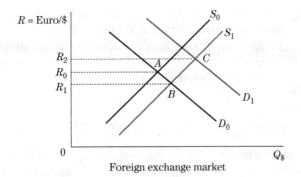

FIGURE 15.5
Exchange Rates and Aggregate Expenditure: The U.S. Economy, 1995–2000
Downward pressure on the value of the dollar from increased imports is represented by the shift of the supply curve from S_0 to S_1. This trend was more than offset by the increased capital inflows shifting the demand curve from D_0 to D_1.

In Figure 15.5, the initial equilibrium in the foreign exchange market is at point A with exchange rate R_0. The increase in consumption and investment spending from 1995 to 2000 results in a higher equilibrium level of real income and a higher interest rate.[28] If we assume that the U.S. interest rate was originally equal to that in the rest of the world, the U.S. interest rate is now higher than that of other countries. The increase in real income has two effects in the foreign exchange market.[29] As we discussed in our earlier example (Figure 15.3), an increase in U.S. income results in an increase in import spending. This means that U.S. residents are supplying more dollars to the foreign exchange market, placing downward pressure on the exchange rate. This change is modeled as a shift of the supply curve from S_0 to S_1 in Figure 15.5 with a decrease in the exchange rate to R_1 (point B). However, the new higher interest rate in the United States now causes capital inflows as investors search for the highest returns, resulting in an increase in the demand for U.S. dollars, which drives up the exchange rate.

In the 1995–2000 period, the net effect of these two forces in the U.S. economy was an increase in the exchange rate or a "strong dollar," represented by R_2 in Figure 15.5 (point C). This increase in R in turn causes imports to increase and exports to decrease, restraining the growth in income. Thus, the effect of the strong dollar at this time was to help hold back the economy in the face of the strong private-sector spending increases. This exchange rate effect actually made the job of the Fed easier because it was unnecessary for the Fed to increase the targeted federal funds rate as quickly to restrain the economy. Many U.S. policy makers, including Secretary of the Treasury Lawrence Summers, announced their support for a strong dollar policy during this period.[30] This example shows the feedback effects of the exchange rate on real spending in the economy.

Although the example presented here focused on increased spending from the private sector, the same outcome would occur if the spending increase resulted from expansionary fiscal policy. Expansionary fiscal policy also causes an increase in real income and the interest rate. Suppose that the domestic interest rate is greater than that in the rest of the world and that capital is mobile, so there are large flows. This interest rate change increases capital inflows, which pushes up

---

[28]In the absence of a change in monetary policy, an increase in spending generates a higher level of income, which results in a higher interest rate due to the increased demand for money to finance the transactions at the higher level of income (Chapters 13 and 14).

[29]Using r_{Europe} and Y_{Europe} to represent the interest rate and income level in Europe, we can restate Equations 15.9 and 15.10 for the demand for and supply of dollars:

$$Q_\$^d = f(R, Y_{Europe}, r_{US} > r_{Europe}) \text{ and } Q_\$^s = f(R, Y_{US}, r_{US} < r_{Europe})$$
$$\quad (-) \quad (+) \qquad (+) \qquad\qquad\qquad (+) \quad (+) \quad (+)$$

[30]Joseph Kahn and Edmund L. Andrews, "Major Central Banks Step In to Shore Up the Ailing Euro," *New York Times*, September 22, 2000.

the exchange rate. A higher exchange rate (increased imports, decreased exports) then partially offsets the expansionary fiscal policy. If capital is less sensitive to interest rate changes and, therefore, less mobile, the effect of expansionary fiscal policy is felt through the increased income, which increases import spending. This change puts downward pressure on the exchange rate, which causes a further increase in income.

The U.S. Economy, 2007–2008 and 2010–2012

The macroeconomic events in the U.S. economy in 2007 and 2008 and their impact in the international sector were almost the exact opposite of what we just described for the period 1995 to 2000. The collapse of the housing market and the credit crisis in the financial markets that began in 2007 caused consumers and businesses to pull back on their spending. This decrease in autonomous expenditure resulted in a lower level of real income and a lower interest rate, given the decreased demand for money at the lower level of income.[31]

The lower level of real income had two effects on the currency exchange rate. With lower income, there were fewer imports, which decreased the quantity of dollars supplied to the foreign exchange market, shifting the supply curve to the left and causing the exchange rate, R, to rise. If the original U.S. interest rate was equal to that in the rest of the world, the new lower interest rate resulted in increased capital outflows to the rest of the world in search of higher returns. This caused an increase in the supply of dollars to the foreign exchange market to finance these outflows, which would lower the exchange rate. In addition, as we have noted, the Federal Reserve began increasing the money supply in September 2007 to lower interest rates and achieve a targeted federal funds rate of 2 percent in April 2008. The domestic goal was to stimulate the economy, but the international effect of the lower interest rates was to generate further capital outflows, which also put downward pressure on the currency exchange rate. Throughout much of 2007, foreign economies had remained strong, which generated more U.S. exports, increased the demand for dollars in the foreign exchange market, and put upward pressure on the exchange rate. Although these were countervailing impacts on the exchange rate, the overall effect was that the exchange rate decreased and the dollar depreciated. The dollar had been declining gradually since 2003, but the decline became more pronounced in 2007 and 2008.

The overall effect of the lower value of the dollar was to decrease U.S. imports and increase U.S. exports. This development had a positive effect on the U.S. trade deficit and the balance of payments. U.S. exports increased at about an 11 percent annual rate in 2007, while the growth in imports decreased to about 1.5 percent. These changes in exports and imports combined with somewhat higher net investment income made the current account deficit decline on an annual basis in 2007 for the first time since 2001.[32] Although there is always concern that a lower value of the dollar may increase inflation due to higher import prices, this effect had become less pronounced due to the fact that foreign exporters often lower their prices to keep them constant after the currency effect to maintain U.S. market share. Although a 10 percent decline in the value of the dollar might be expected to increase import prices by 10 percent, the actual pass-through is 25 percent or less. This lower pass-through rate, which declined from a high of 50 percent in the mid-1970s to the 1990s, means that the Federal Reserve can stimulate the U.S. economy through lower interest rates with less concern about inflation from higher import

---

[31]This is the exact opposite of the process we described in footnote 28.

[32]Board of Governors of the Federal Reserve System, *Monetary Policy Report to the Congress*, February 27, 2008.

prices. How a depreciated dollar affects imports always depends on the specific product. Prices of luxury products often stay relatively constant as manufacturers accept lower profits, while airlines, which operate on smaller margins, are more likely to raise prices. Price increases of raw materials, such as steel and other commodities, tend to be passed through at a 90 percent rate or more because they are priced in global markets.[33]

Japan was particularly affected by the "weak" dollar and the resulting "strong" yen during this period, given that more than half of its 2.1 percent growth in 2007 was derived from exports. Expectations for a strong recovery from its long economic decline decreased, and investors' lack of confidence in the Japanese economy caused its stock market to decline 19 percent from January to March 2008.[34] Toyota Motor Corp. announced that the lower value of the dollar had caused its group operating profit to decline by 20 billion yen ($194 million) in the fourth quarter of 2007. Larger losses were expected for the first quarter of 2008.[35]

By fall 2008, most European countries had fallen into recession. The combined economies of the 15 countries using the euro shrank 0.2 percent in the third quarter for a second straight quarterly decline. The IMF estimated that global economic growth would increase just 2.2 percent in 2009, a rate the IMF traditionally considered to be a recession. Much of the decline resulted from the credit crisis that began in the United States. The Fed's lowering of its target interest rate to almost zero in December 2008 put more downward pressure on the value of the dollar as investors received little return for investments denominated in dollars. This change benefited the United States economy by making exports cheaper, but caused concern in both Japan and Germany regarding their recessions.[36]

Even though the U.S. recession officially ended in 2009, the slow recovery thereafter meant that the Federal Reserve undertook expansionary monetary policy using both traditional and nontraditional tools at the time of this writing in 2012 (Chapters 13 and 14). In addition to keeping short-term interest rates close to zero, the Fed engaged in quantitative easing or large-scale purchases of financial assets over this period to lower longer-term interest rates.

As noted in the opening case for this chapter, the quantitative easing in 2010 caused substantial concerns in emerging market economies that had recovered from the recession more quickly than the advanced economies.[37] Under a fully flexible exchange rate system, financial capital would flow from the United States and other advanced economies to the emerging market economies, given the higher interest rates in the latter economies. This would lead to currency appreciation in

[33]Sudeep Reddy, "The Weak Dollar Isn't the Inflation Driver It Once Was," *Wall Street Journal*, November 19, 2007.
[34]Yuka Hayashi and JoAnna Slater, "Dollar's Swift Decline Threatens Europe, Japan," *Wall Street Journal*, March 14, 2008.
[35]Yuka Hayashi and Laura Santini, "Japan Inc. Pays Price for Weak Dollar; Reliance on Exports Crimps Profit Growth and the Nikkei Index," *Wall Street Journal*, March 5, 2008.
[36]Joellen Perry, Alistair MacDonald, and Sudeep Reddy, "Global Push to Beat Economic Downturn," *Wall Street Journal*, November 7, 2008; David Gauthier-Villars and Michael M. Phillips, "Europe Tips into Recession," *Wall Street Journal*, November 15, 2008; Joanna Slater, "With Rates Near 0%, Dollar Is Dumped," *Wall Street Journal*, December 17, 2008; Joanna Slater, "Weaker Dollar Worries Japan, Germany," *Wall Street Journal*, December 29, 2008.
[37]This discussion is based on *Board of Governors of the Federal Reserve System*, "Rebalancing the Global Recovery. Remarks by Ben S. Bernanke, Chairman of the Board of Governors of the Federal Reserve System at the Sixth European Central Bank Central Banking Conference, Frankfurt, Germany," November 19, 2010; and *Board of Governors of the Federal Reserve System*, "Global Imbalances: Links to Economic and Financial Stability. Remarks by Ben S. Bernanke, Chairman of the Board of Governors of the Federal Reserve System at the Banque de France Stability Review Launch Event, Paris, France," February 18, 2011. Available at www.federalreserve.gov.

those economies that would reduce net exports (decrease exports and increase imports) and decrease current account surpluses. These changes would help slow these rapidly growing economies, a process similar to what we previously described in the section "The U.S. Economy, 1995–2000." Increased imports to the emerging market economies would also add to export demand in the advanced economies. However, many emerging market economies were reluctant to let their currencies appreciate at that time, given that currency undervaluation had been part of a long-term export-led strategy for growth and development. We also noted in the opening case that the emerging market response to the 2012 quantitative easing was much more muted, given that many of these economies were also using expansionary monetary policy to stimulate growth, given weakness in their exports due to the European recession. With most of these economies attempting to lower interest rates, there was much less impact on capital flows and currency exchange values.[38]

The overall decline of the dollar and appreciation of the yen continued from 2008 to 2012. This meant that Japanese automobile makers continued to struggle to compete with their U.S., German, and South Korean rivals. Toyota, Nissan Motor Co., and Honda Motor Co. had all shifted production abroad, given the yen's rise. Toyota also attempted to expand its share of the Japanese market to compensate for the shifts abroad. Given that 41 percent of its global production was manufactured in Japan, Toyota was more exposed to currency risk than its competitors Honda (28 percent) and Nissan (35 percent).[39]

Effects of the Euro in the Macroeconomic Environment

There has been major policy discussion regarding the value of the euro, the common European currency, since its introduction by the European Union on January 1, 1999. Debates about the euro during this initial period focused on its value relative to other currencies, particularly the U.S. dollar; trade imbalances and capital flows between the United States and Europe; the interaction between the value of the euro and other economic events, such as increasing oil prices; and political and psychological factors related to the value of the euro. Since the global recession of 2007–2008, the sustainability of the euro as a single currency has come into question with the convergence of three crises: a banking crisis, a sovereign debt crisis, and a growth crisis.[40] We first discuss the issues in the early years of the euro using the balance of payments and foreign exchange models developed in this chapter. We then summarize the three crises and discuss how they are interrelated. We will also examine how managers and firms have responded to these international macroeconomic issues in terms of their competitive strategies and profitability.

Most discussions of the euro take the perspective of Europe as the domestic economy and define the exchange rate, R, as dollars per euro. In this chapter, we have used the United States as the domestic economy and defined the exchange rate as units of foreign currency per dollar. We can easily modify Equations 15.9 and 15.10 and Figure 15.2 to the European perspective, as shown in Equations 15.14 and 15.15 and Figure 15.6. The exchange rate, R, in this discussion is now units of foreign currency per unit of domestic currency, or dollars per euro. Thus, the

[38]Lauricella, Reddy, and McCarthy, "Central Banks Flex Muscles"; and Frangos, "Fed Move Could Aid Emerging Markets."

[39]Chester Dawson and Yoshio Takahashi, "Strong Yen Dings Japan Car Exports," *Wall Street Journal (Online)* June 25, 2012.

[40]Jay C. Shambaugh, "The Euro's Three Crises," *Brookings Papers on Economic Activity* (Spring 2012): 157–211.

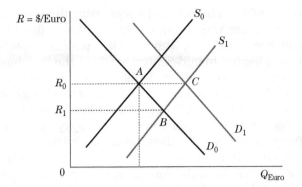

FIGURE 15.6
Euro Market
The euro market is usually analyzed from the European perspective. The exchange rate, defined as dollars per euro, is determined by the demand for and supply of euros. Downward pressure on the value of the euro is shown by the shift of the supply curve from S_0 to S_1. The intervention to hold up the value of the euro is shown by the shift of the demand curve from D_0 to D_1.

foreign exchange model in this chapter can be applied to any economy, provided the perspective taken in the demand and supply equations and graphs is that of the domestic economy and currency.

15.14 $Q^d_{Euro} = f(R, Y_{US}, r_{Europe} > r_{US})$
                 $(-)(+)$ $(+)$

15.15 $Q^s_{Euro} = f(R, Y_{Europe}, r_{Europe} < r_{US})$
                 $(+)\ (+)$ $(+)$

Equations 15.14 and 15.15 show the factors affecting the demand for and supply of euros: the exchange rate, income in the United States and Europe, and interest rate differentials. Figure 15.6 shows an initial equilibrium in the euro foreign exchange market at point A. The policy concern in Europe had been the long decline in the value of the euro after it was introduced on January 1, 1999.

The major factor causing this decline was the interest rate differential between the United States and Europe.[41] The higher U.S. interest rates and the attractive investment opportunities from the booming stock market in the late 1990s resulted in huge capital outflows from Europe to the United States. As shown in Equation 15.15 and Figure 15.6, higher interest rates and better investment opportunities in the United States caused the supply curve for euros to shift to the right from S_0 to S_1 as investors supplied euros to the foreign exchange market in exchange for dollars for U.S. financial capital transactions. This resulted in downward pressure on the value of the euro in dollar terms (exchange rate R_1 at point B). The fact that the U.S. economy was growing faster than the European economies created more U.S. investment opportunities for European investors and contributed to the capital flows from Europe to the United States. This inflow of foreign financial investment to the United States is consistent with the discussion of the balance of trade deficit and equilibrium in the open economy, as noted in Equation 15.6. The continuing U.S. balance of trade deficit must be financed by capital inflows from abroad.[42]

The European Central Bank (ECB) attempted to intervene in the foreign exchange markets in order to bolster the value of the euro. The lower value of the euro put

[41] This discussion is based on the following sources: Michael R. Sesit and G. Thomas Sims, "Sagging Euro Puts Upward Pressure on Inflation by Fueling Price Raises," *Wall Street Journal*, October 26, 2000; David Wessel, "Foreign Purchasing of U.S. Securities Fell in Quarter, but Remains Healthy," *Wall Street Journal*, September 19, 2000; Michael M. Phillips and G. Thomas Sims, "U.S. Joins Europe in Intervention to Help Support Faltering Euro," *Wall Street Journal*, September 25, 2000; and Jacob M. Schlesinger and Craig Karmin, "No Safe Haven: Dollar's Slide Reflects Wariness About U.S.," *Wall Street Journal*, June 3, 2002.
[42] Remember that the United States had a current account deficit and a financial account surplus, while the European countries had a current account surplus and a financial account deficit.

upward pressure on inflation in Europe by increasing the price of imported goods, particularly oil. Thus, there was an attempt to maintain a fixed or at least a higher exchange rate with the U.S. dollar, with all of the associated problems that we discussed earlier in the chapter. In mid-September 2000, the ECB began selling foreign currencies and buying euros. The United States joined Europe in an intervention to increase the value of the euro in late September 2000. This intervention occurred at the initiative of the ECB, even though the United States had been pursuing a "strong-dollar" policy, which had benefited that country by keeping imports cheap and attracting financial inflows to offset the trade deficit, as discussed previously in the chapter. The intervention was undertaken quickly and secretly in order to have maximum effectiveness in the foreign exchange markets. We represent this intervention in Figure 15.6 by the shift of the demand curve from D_0 to D_1, with a new equilibrium at point C.

By 2002, changes in the U.S. economy had caused the dollar to decrease in value against the euro and other currencies. Given the recession and the corporate scandals in the United States, foreign investors began searching for investment opportunities elsewhere. With a decreased demand for investment in the United States, foreign investors demanded fewer dollars, causing the value of the dollar to decrease against the euro and the yen.

In 2012, there was speculation about whether the euro could survive as a single currency for the euro-zone area, given a banking crisis, a sovereign debt crisis, and an economic growth crisis.[43] Banks in the euro area faced a capital shortfall, liquidity between banks was constrained, and future losses were uncertain. At least one country, Greece, was unlikely to be able to pay its debts in full, and other countries were likely to be in the same situation. Slow economic growth and a lack of competitiveness added to the burden of many of the indebted nations. All of these crises were interrelated. Many euro-area banks held so much sovereign debt of the countries in financial distress that failure of the countries to pay their debts would make the banking system insolvent. Fiscal austerity measures to relieve the sovereign stress problems slowed economic growth and increased the debt crisis problems. Any bank failures would negatively affect the countries supporting the banks, and reduced bank lending would have a further negative impact on growth.

Many of these problems arose from the use of a single currency by sovereign nations in a monetary union, which requires that all countries have the same monetary policy and the same basic interest rate. The single currency also means a fixed exchange rate within the monetary union and the same exchange rate relative to all other currencies even if differences in exchange rates would benefit individual countries. Thus, some of the tools that countries use to address their economic problems were eliminated by the monetary union, and boundaries that used to keep problems in one country were erased. For example, a balance of trade deficit in one country could be eased by a devaluation of its currency, but that is not possible with a currency union. Countries within the union also differ in their degrees of competitiveness, which influences their ability to respond to financial crises.

[43]There is a huge literature on the euro zone crisis. For comprehensive summaries, see Shambaugh, "The Euro's Three Crises"; Martin Feldstein, "The Failure of the Euro: The Little Currency That Couldn't," *Foreign Affairs* 91 (January/February 2012): 105–16; Philip R. Lane, "The European Sovereign Debt Crisis," *Journal of Economic Perspectives* 26 (Summer 2012): 49–68; Barry Eichengreen, "Europe's Vicious Spirals," *Project Syndicate*, January 11, 2012. Available at www.project-syndicate.org/commentary/europe-s-vicious-sprials; Iain Begg, "The EU's Response to the Global Financial Crisis and Sovereign Debt Crisis," *Asia Europe Journal* 9 (2012): 107–24; Philip Arestis and Malcolm Sawyer, "The Ongoing Euro Crisis," *Challenge* 54 (November/December 2011): 6–13; and International Monetary Fund, *World Economic Outlook: Growth Resuming, Dangers Remain*, April 2012. Available at www.imf.org.

The banking system in the euro area is large with total assets equivalent to over 300 percent of euro-area GDP in 2007 compared with less than 100 percent in the United States, Thus, when housing prices declined and securities based on their value became questionable, banks in both the United States and Europe faced large losses and difficulties in borrowing. Although the ECB stepped in to help the banks, it did not purchase assets as significantly as did the Federal Reserve in the United States. Also, European banks held significant amounts of securities of the nations' facing a debt crisis, which contributed to their financial problems.

In 2012, the ECB approved a plan for the bank to make unlimited purchases of the bonds of struggling members of the euro area.[44] The goal was to restore stability to the government debt markets of Spain and Italy and to increase private investment. The bank had begun buying Greek, Spanish, and Portuguese bonds in 2010 and continued in fits and starts over the next two years. Germany, the strongest economy in the euro area, continued to be skeptical of the effectiveness of such a program and feared that it could be inflationary. Greece continued to suffer from the austerity conditions forced upon it as part of its financial rescue in 2010. The restructuring of its debt still left the country with a large level of debt and a mandate to decrease government spending and force down wages and prices to make the country more competitive.[45] At the time of this writing, there was a continued question of whether Greece would exit the euro.

In October 2012, the IMF estimated that the risks of a global recession were intensified.[46] The euro zone was still of particular concern, given that the issues discussed above were not resolved. The IMF argued that the euro zone needed continued progress toward banking and fiscal union combined with short-term demand support and crisis management.

Euro Macro Environment Effects on Managerial Decisions

The European financial crisis and uncertainty about the euro created major challenges for managers and firms doing business in Europe.[47] Although most multinational companies agreed that the impact of a Greek withdrawal from the euro area was impossible to predict, they rehearsed for multiple contingencies including a possible civil breakdown in Greece or a broader breakup of Europe's common currency. Companies anticipated that if Greece reverted to its former currency, any remaining euros would be converted to less-valuable drachmas and that Greece might impose capital controls to keep the currency in the country. Dutch-brewer Heineken moved spare cash out of Greece and the euro area altogether and into the U.S. dollar and British pound. Some Greek companies drew on credit lines from foreign banks, while European tour operators developed plans to protect customers and assets in the event of Greek unrest. A German consulting firm advised clients to stipulate in contracts what currency or exchange rate would be used if Greece left the euro.

---

[44]Brian Blackstone and Alex Brittain, "Europe Outlook Dims as Bank Meets," *Wall Street Journal (Online)*, September 5, 2012; Brian Blackstone, "Europe Readies Bond Buying," *Wall Street Journal (Online)*, October 4, 2012.

[45]Marcus Walker, "How a Radical Greek Rescue Plan Fell Short," *Wall Street Journal (Online)*, May 10, 2012.

[46]International Monetary Fund, *World Economic Outlook: Coping with High Debt and Sluggish Growth*, October 2012. Available at www.imf.org; Sudeep Reddy and Bob Davis, "Global Recession Risk Rises," *Wall Street Journal (Online)*, October 8, 2012.

[47]This discussion is based on Vanessa Fuhrmans and Dana Cimilluca, "Business Braces for Europe's Worst," *Wall Street Journal (Online)*, June 1, 2012.

In spring 2012, General Electric Co. announced that the company would focus less on Europe in the future. GE's sales in Europe accounted for only 11 percent of its revenue in 2011 compared with 45 percent in the previous half-decade. Weak European growth of airline spare parts sales was expected to slow the growth of GE Aviation. As with other companies, GE did contingency planning regarding the breakup of the euro.[48]

Many Asian companies also felt the impact of Europe's crisis. Manufacturers of electronics devices in Taiwan reported decreased orders from companies such as Dell, Lenovo, and Nokia. Sony Corp., which had generated about 20 percent of its revenues in Europe, was bracing for a downturn. There was much diversity among the economies in terms of their exposure to Europe. Exports to the euro area accounted for 16.3 percent of China's total exports in 2011, but only 4.2 percent of its GDP, given its large domestic market. Euro-area exports represented 8.9 percent of all exports and 2.1 percent of GDP in Indonesia. However, euro exports were 9.0 and 7.7 percent of Hong Kong's and Singapore's exports and 15.9 percent and 12.2 percent of their GDPs.[49]

Some European companies expected to benefit from the weaker euro resulting from the European crisis if they had strong exposure to international markets. These companies include European Aeronautic Defence Co., Pernod Ricard SA, and auto maker BMW. A weak euro translated into higher revenue in euros for sales generated internationally in non-euro denominated currencies.[50]

Southeast Asia: An Attempt to Maintain Fixed Exchange Rates

Although the Southeast Asian financial crisis of 1997 resulted from a number of factors, it presents a vivid illustration of the difficulty, or impossibility, of maintaining fixed exchange rates in the face of speculation and other downward pressures on the value of a country's currency in the foreign exchange market. We discuss these issues with reference to Thailand, where the 1997 crisis began when the baht, the Thai currency, came under speculative attack and the markets lost confidence in the economy.[51] Similar developments then occurred in Korea, Indonesia, and Malaysia. The resulting recession in these crisis countries spread to Hong Kong, Singapore, the Philippines, and Taiwan. By 1998, there was evidence of a worldwide growth slowdown, with the IMF estimating world growth at only 2 percent compared with 4.3 percent anticipated one year earlier. As noted above, the Federal Reserve in the United States responded by lowering the federal funds rate target to help prevent both a global and a domestic crisis

Thailand had experienced high growth rates throughout much of the 1990s, driven by strong increases in consumption and investment spending. However, there were a number of warning signals that developed before 1997. To maintain

---

[48]Kate Linebaugh, "GE: Best Approach for Continent is to Pull Back," *Wall Street Journal (Online)*, May 31, 2012.

[49]Kathy Chu, Surabhi Sahu, and Patrick Barta, "Asia Strains Under Euro Crisis," *Wall Street Journal (Online)*, May 31, 2012.

[50]Marietta Cauchi, "Euro Loss is Europe Multinational Gain," *Wall Street Journal (Online)*, July 25, 2012.

[51]This section is based on Morris Goldstein, *The Asian Financial Crisis: Causes, Cures, and Systemic Implications* (Washington, DC: Institute for International Economics, June 1998); Giancarlo Corsetti, Paolo Pesenti, and Nouriel Roubini, "What Caused the Asian Currency and Financial Crisis?" *Japan and the World Economy* 11 (1999): 305–73; IMF, *Recovery from the Asian Crisis and the Role of the IMF—An IMF Issues Brief* (Washington, DC: IMF, June 2000); and Nouriel Roubini and Brad Setser, *Bailouts or Bail-Ins? Responding to Financial Crises in Emerging Economies* (Washington, DC: Institute for International Economics, 2004).

the high growth rates, there were public guarantees to many private investment projects through government control and subsidies. Given the climate of political favoritism, the markets came to believe that high returns on investment were "insured" against adverse changes in the economy. Investment expectations came to be based on unreal expectations about the growth of long-run output. A weak banking sector with lax supervision and weak regulation compounded this situation. There was much international lending to unsound financial institutions, such as finance and securities companies, particularly in real-estate markets. Domestic banks borrowed from foreign banks in order to lend to domestic investors who were not necessarily creditworthy.

The Thai government also ran a large current account deficit, averaging 6 percent of GDP in each year over the 1990s. As discussed throughout this chapter, a current account deficit needs capital inflows to be sustained. The size of a current account deficit that can be sustained depends on both a country's willingness to pay and its creditors' willingness to loan. Although there were signs that the profitability of many of these investments was low, lending continued over much of the period.

The nominal exchange rate of the Thai baht was fixed at 25.2 to 25.6 to the U.S. dollar during the period 1990–97, largely to provide the stability necessary to encourage the external financing of domestic projects. However, the U.S. dollar appreciated, particularly after spring 1995, so the real exchange rate of the baht also appreciated. This appreciation, which had a negative effect on exports and a positive influence on imports, resulted in slower growth in the Thai economy in 1995–1996 and an increase in the current account deficit to 8.5 percent of GDP. Much of the foreign investment in Thailand was in volatile short-term debt rather than more stable long-term foreign direct investment.

In June 1997, Thai officials discovered that the stock of international reserves effectively available to support the currency was a tiny fraction of that officially stated. These reserves were insufficient to maintain the value of the baht and prop up the fragile banking and finance system. Speculators lost confidence and began to sell off the baht, resulting in a decrease in its value of 25 percent by the end of July, compared with the beginning of the year, and 34 percent by the end of August. The Thai government was forced to announce a managed float of the baht. The real-estate bubble collapsed, bankrupting many finance companies who were further hurt by the depreciation of the baht because they had borrowed in foreign currency. Although the initial reaction of Thai authorities was not to contract the money supply and raise interest rates because they were concerned about the impact of high interest rates on the fragile banking and financial system, this policy was not sustainable. High interest rates to attract foreign investment and prevent further currency attacks and reform of the banking system were two key conditions for IMF assistance, which began in August 1997. These higher interest rates, combined with limited exports to a weak Japanese economy, forced Thailand into a recession. The competitive devaluations and recessions in the other Asian crisis countries then started to spread farther around the world, as noted above.

The changes in the Thai economy are modeled in Figure 15.7, where the targeted exchange rate for the baht is represented by R_0 at the initial equilibrium point A with baht demand and supply curves D_0 and S_0. The downward pressure on the value of the baht, first from the role of imports and the large current account deficit and then from the massive selling of baht by speculators in 1997, is represented by the shift of the supply curve from S_0 to S_1 and the decrease in the exchange rate to R_1 (point B). To maintain the fixed exchange rate, R_0, Thai officials first used their foreign exchange reserves to increase the demand for the baht from D_0 to D_1 (point C). This policy proved insufficient in the face of the speculation, and as a condition for IMF assistance, the central bank was forced

FIGURE 15.7

Illustration of Thailand Financial Crisis

Downward pressure on the Thai baht is represented by the shift of the supply curve from S₀ to S₁. The effect of the intervention and the contractionary monetary policy is shown by the shift of the demand curve from D₀ to D₁.

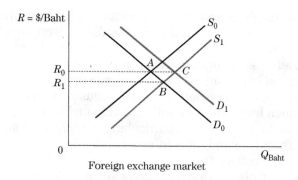

Foreign exchange market

to use contractionary monetary policy and raise interest rates in order to attract foreign investment. As noted above, this policy forced the country into recession.

Thailand and other East Asian countries, Indonesia, South Korea, Malaysia, the Philippines, and Singapore, experienced a V-shaped recovery with a very deep trough in 1998.[52] The average growth rate for the six precrisis years was higher than that for the seven postcrisis years. Although growth rates recovered to reasonable levels, the lost output of 1998 was never recovered. In hindsight, it has been argued that the IMF did not provide a recovery package sufficient to prevent further depreciation of the baht. This failure to provide sufficient resources might have resulted from criticism of the IMF for its earlier bailout of Mexico, but the policy meant that the IMF recommendations for tight macroeconomic policy and strict bank restructuring had significant negative impacts. Many Asian countries continued to resent the IMF's handling of this currency crisis because they believed that the negotiation process was politically humiliating and that the IMF handled subsequent crises more moderately, even though the macroeconomic fundamentals in these countries were worse.

Macro and Managerial Impact of the Chinese Yuan Since 2003

In 2003, the value of the Chinese yuan relative to the dollar became both an economic and a political issue in the United States.[53] The policy of the Chinese Central Bank was to keep the yuan at 8.28 to the dollar through the tightly controlled Shanghai foreign exchange market. Although there was a high level of foreign investment in China, which tended to push up the value of the yuan, the central bank sold enough yuan to keep it stable against the dollar. The value of the yuan stimulated Chinese exports and hurt imports into the country, thus impacting U.S. manufacturers. For example, the Iowa-based family-owned Shine Brothers Corporation blamed the low value of the yuan and Chinese subsidies for a deterioration in its scrap-metal recycling business. Although many U.S. manufacturers lobbied the Bush administration to pressure China to let its currency rise, these attempts were initially rebuffed by Chinese officials.

---

[52]This discussion is based on Takatoshi Ito, "Asian Currency Crisis and the International Monetary Fund, 10 Years Later: Overview," *Asian Economic Policy Review* 2 (2007): 16–49; and Takatoshi Ito, "Can Asia Overcome the IMF Stigma?" *American Economic Review: Papers & Proceedings* 102 (2012): 198–202.

[53]Peter Wonacott and Leslie Chang, "As Fight Heats Up over China Trade, Business Is Split," *Wall Street Journal*, September 4, 2003; Peter Wonacott and Michael M. Phillips, "China Won't Let Currency Rise, Quickly Rebuffing U.S. Request," *Wall Street Journal*, September 3, 2003.

However, not all U.S. businesses were expected to gain from a stronger yuan. For example, the New Balance Athletic Shoe Company made 60 percent of the 40 million pairs of shoes it sold each year in China. An increase in the value of the yuan would increase the cost of labor and raw materials used in producing the shoes. Large companies, such as Wal-Mart Stores, Inc., and Johnson & Johnson, that invested, manufactured, and financed businesses in China and other foreign countries also expected to be adversely affected by a rise in the value of the yuan. Thus, the strategies of large multinational companies do not always coincide with the interests of workers in their home countries or with those of smaller companies that market only domestically.

Since this period, China's economy has continued to be stimulated by domestic and foreign investment and by exports and a trade surplus. China's trade surplus in 2007 was equivalent to about 8 percent of its GDP compared with 2 percent at the beginning of the decade. Although the Chinese government traditionally promoted exports, it announced in late 2007 that it would start encouraging imports as well by imposing taxes on exports of several types of products, such as refined metals, and speeding up the appreciation of the yuan. The currency rose 6.9 percent against the U.S. dollar in 2007 compared with a 3.5 percent gain in 2006. Still, the country was concerned with the slowdown in U.S. economic growth in 2007 and 2008. Manufacturers in Shengzhou, a city south of Shanghai that claims to make 40 percent of the world's neckties, noted the declining U.S. orders and worried that the rising yuan would price them out of the market.[54]

Early in 2012, the IMF reviewed whether China's currency should still be considered "substantially undervalued," a term that had been used for the previous half-decade.[55] At that time, the U.S. Treasury Secretary argued that the yuan remained undervalued although it had been appreciating. Although China's central bank still set a daily reference rate for its currency, in April 2012 the bank widened the trading range around that rate from 0.5 to 1.0 percent in either direction. This policy shift began to change the expectations of both companies and investors who had long assumed that the yuan was undervalued. Some companies began to invest in financial derivatives that would protect them against both a rise and fall in the value of the yuan.

In the summer of 2012, there was some evidence that China was again trying to weaken the value of the yuan against the dollar to stimulate exports, given its slowing economy and the fallout from Europe's continuing debt crisis.[56] It was not clear whether this trend would continue, particularly because China had $3.24 trillion in foreign-exchange reserves, an amount sufficient to promote the rise of the yuan, if needed. At this time, the IMF noted that China's current account surplus had declined sharply from a high of 10.1 percent of GDP in 2007 to 2.8 percent of GDP in 2011. The IMF argued that the value of the yuan was close to equilibrium or, at most, slightly undervalued.

[54]Andrew Batson, "World Economy Threatens China Growth," *Wall Street Journal*, January 12, 2008; JoAnna Slater, "Weak Dollar Feels New Stress," *Wall Street Journal*, March 11, 2008; Marcus Walker, James Hookway, John Lyons, and James T. Areddy, "U.S. Slump Takes Toll Across Globe," *Wall Street Journal*, April 3, 2008.
[55]This discussion is based on Ian Talley, "IMF Reviews China Currency's Value," *Wall Street Journal (Online)*, January 30, 2012; and Lingling Wei, "China Loosens Grip on Yuan," *Wall Street Journal (Online)*, April 16, 2012.
[56]Bob Davis and Lingling Wei, "China Shifts Course, Lets Yuan Drop," *Wall Street Journal (Online)*, July 25 2012; International Monetary Fund, *People's Republic of China 2012 Article IV Consultation*, IMF Country Report No. 12/195, July 2012. Available at www.imf.org.

Policy Effectiveness with Different Exchange Rate Regimes

The previous examples point out several important issues regarding the role of monetary and fiscal policies in the open economy. In an open economy with global capital markets and mobile capital, which flows to countries with the highest interest rates, a country has control over either its domestic money supply or the exchange rate, *but not both variables*.[57] To maintain a fixed exchange rate, a country loses control over its domestic money supply. For example, most central banks can find the foreign exchange reserves to fight a devaluation of their currency brought about by currency speculators if these banks are willing to make this task the primary goal of their monetary policy. Using foreign exchange reserves to bolster the value of a currency ("defending the dollar" is the term often used in the United States) results in decreases in the domestic money supply and higher interest rates, which then can have a negative impact on consumption, investment, and aggregate demand. To offset a speculative attack against a fixed exchange rate, a country has to make a credible commitment to this policy, regardless of the consequences to the economy. Speculators know that most governments are not willing to do this and that the central banks will typically abandon a fixed exchange rate, as was the case in Thailand.[58]

If the exchange rate is allowed to vary, monetary policy is effective in stimulating the economy. Expansionary monetary policy results in an increase in income that increases imports and lowers the exchange rate. This change has a further expansionary effect on real spending (a shift of the *AD* curve). Expansionary monetary policy also lowers domestic interest rates, which results in less capital inflow and a decreased demand for domestic currency. This change also lowers the exchange rate. Indeed, in comparing the fiscal and monetary policy examples, we can see that monetary policy is more effective than fiscal policy in stimulating the economy under a flexible exchange rate system, whereas monetary policy is not effective under a fixed exchange rate system. The effects of the different exchange rate regimes on achieving equilibrium in the open economy are summarized in Table 15.15.[59]

TABLE 15.15   Effects of Exchange Rate Systems

FLEXIBLE	FIXED	
The exchange rate automatically adjusts to eliminate *BP* disequilibrium ($Q_s = Q_d$).	The domestic money supply automatically adjusts to eliminate *BP* disequilibrium (through flows of gold or currency).	
	The Fed does nothing, allowing *MS* to adjust.	The Fed sterilizes (through open market operations) and maintains *BP* disequilibrium

---

[57]This problem is often characterized as the "inconsistent trinity" or the "open-economy trilemma." A country cannot simultaneously maintain fixed exchange rates, have an open capital market, and use monetary policy to pursue domestic policy goals. See Maurice Obstfeld, "The Global Capital Market: Benefactor or Menace," *Journal of Economic Perspectives* 12 (Fall 1998): 9–30.

[58]Obstfeld and Rogoff, "The Mirage of Fixed Exchange Rates."

[59]For a detailed presentation of the arguments for and against both fixed and flexible exchange rates, see Moosa, *Exchange Rate Regimes*, 63–89; Rose, "Exchange Rate Regimens in the Modern Era: Fixed, Floating, and Flaky."

Summary

In this chapter, we extended our discussion of international and open economy issues. We first developed a model of the open economy and defined balance of payments concepts. We then presented a model of the foreign exchange market to show the factors influencing currency exchange rates and the impact of fixed and flexible exchange rate policies.

At the end of the chapter, we discussed the impact of currency value changes on both national economies (in the United States, Europe, and Southeast Asia) and the competitive strategies of different types of firms. Managers need to understand the impact of international economic events on the level of economic activity in the domestic economy and in those countries where they have substantial markets. Managers must also be able to analyze the implications of these changes for the competitive strategies of their own firms and those of their major competitors.

Appendix 15A Specific and General Equations for the Balance of Payments

Specific Equation	**General Equation**
EXPORT EXPENDITURE	**EXPORT EXPENDITURE**
$X = x_0 + x_1 Y^* - x_2 R$	$X = f(Y, Y^*, R)$
where	$\quad(0)\,(+)\,(-)$
$\quad X$ = export expenditure	where
$\quad x_0$ = other factors influencing export expenditure	$\quad X$ = export expenditure
$\quad Y^*$ = real foreign GDP or income	$\quad Y$ = real domestic income
$\quad R$ = currency exchange rate (units of foreign currency per unit of domestic currency)	$\quad Y^*$ = real foreign GDP or income
$\quad x_1, x_2$ = coefficients of the relevant variables	$\quad R$ = currency exchange rate (units of foreign currency per unit of domestic currency)
IMPORT EXPENDITURE	**IMPORT EXPENDITURE**
$M = m_0 + m_1 Y + m_2 R$	$M = F(Y, R)$
where	$\quad(+)\,(+)$
$\quad M$ = import expenditure	where
$\quad m_0$ = other factors affecting import expenditure	$\quad M$ = import expenditure
$\quad Y$ = real domestic income	$\quad Y$ = real domestic income
$\quad R$ = currency exchange rate (units of foreign currency per unit of domestic currency)	$\quad R$ = currency exchange rate (units of foreign currency per unit of domestic currency)
$\quad m_1, m_2$ = coefficients of the relevant variables	
NET EXPORT EXPENDITURE	**NET EXPORT EXPENDITURE**
$F = X - M$	$F = f(Y, Y^*, R)$
$F = x_0 + x_1 Y^* - x_2 R - m_0 - m_1 Y - m_2 R$	$\quad(-)\,(+)\,(-)$
$F = F_0 + x_1 Y^* - m_1 Y - (x_2 + m_2)R$	where
where	$\quad F$ = net export expenditure
$\quad F$ = net export expenditure	$\quad Y$ = real domestic income
$\quad X$ = export expenditure	$\quad Y^*$ = real foreign GDP or income
$\quad M$ = import expenditure	$\quad R$ = currency exchange rate (units of foreign currency per unit of domestic currency)

(continued)

Specific Equation	General Equation

x_0 = other factors influencing export expenditure

Y^* = real foreign GDP or income

R = currency exchange rate (units of foreign currency per unit of domestic currency)

x_1, x_2 = coefficients of the relevant variables

m_0 = other factors affecting import expenditure

Y = real domestic income

m_1, m_2 = coefficients of the relevant variables

$F_0 = x_0 - m_0$ = other factors influencing net export expenditure

NET CAPITAL FLOW

$K = k(r - r^*)$

where
K = net capital flow
k = interest sensitivity of capital flows
r = domestic interest rate
r^* = interest rate in the rest of the world

NET CAPITAL FLOW

$K = k_i - k_o$
$k_i = f(r > r^*)$
$(+)$
$k_o = f(r < r^*)$
$(+)$

where
K = net capital flow
k_i = capital inflows
k_o = capital outflows
r = domestic interest rate
r^* = interest rate in the rest of the world

Key Terms

balance of payments (BP) accounting system, p. 423
balance of trade, p. 420
capital inflow (k_i), p. 422
capital outflow (k_o), p. 422
currency appreciation, p. 419
currency depreciation, p. 419
currency exchange rate, p. 418
current account, p. 423
financial account, p. 424

fixed exchange rate system, p. 431
flexible exchange rate system, p. 430
gold standard, p. 431
International Monetary Fund (IMF), p. 431
managed float, p. 431
net capital flow ($K_N = k_i - k_o$), p. 422
net investment income, p. 423
nominal exchange rate, p. 419
real exchange rate, p. 419

reserve assets, p. 433
revenue or T-account, p. 425
statistical discrepancy (SD), p. 425
sterilized intervention, p. 435
trade deficit, p. 422
trade surplus, p. 422
trade-weighted dollar, p. 418
unilateral transfers, p. 423
World Bank, p. 431

Exercises

Technical Questions

1. Show the effect of dollar appreciation and depreciation with the euro on the price of U.S. exports and imports by updating Table 15.2, as shown in the updated table.

2. Evaluate whether the following statements are true or false, and explain your answer:

   a. A trade deficit occurs when the government spends more than it receives in tax revenue.

   b. In an open, mixed economy, the equilibrium level of GDP occurs when planned saving equals planned investment.

   c. An increase in interest rates in the rest of the world will lead to a stronger dollar.

   d. Under a fixed exchange rate system with global capital flows, monetary policy is ineffective. However, under a flexible exchange rate system, monetary policy is typically more effective than fiscal policy in increasing real GDP.

TABLE 15.2 (updated)   Effect of Dollar Appreciation and Depreciation on U.S. Exports and Imports

R = EURO/$	DOMESTIC PRICE	JAN 09: R = 0.76	JUNE 09: R = 0.71	EFFECT ON EXPORTS (X) AND IMPORTS (M)
U.S. exports: Televisions	$1,000			
U.S. imports: European cars	Euro 25,000			
		JAN 08: R = 0.68	JAN 09: R = 0.76	
U.S. exports: Televisions	$1,000			
U.S. imports: European cars	Euro 25,000			

3. If the U.S. economy is operating near full employment and the exchange rate increases (the dollar appreciates), explain why the Federal Reserve will be *less inclined* to raise interest rates.
4. In a flexible exchange rate system, explain why a country whose income grows faster than that of its trading partners can expect its exchange rate to fall, or the value of its currency to depreciate.
5. Using the simple model of Table 15.12, explain why there is a balance of payments equilibrium when export spending equals import spending. What is the more general condition for equilibrium in the balance of payments?
6. In the foreign exchange market, explain which variables cause a movement along the demand for dollars curve and which variables cause the curve to shift. Repeat the exercise for the supply of dollars curve.

Application Questions

1. In current business publications or on the Bureau of Economic Analysis international accounts Web page (www.bea.doc.gov/bea/international), find the latest statistics on the balance of payments (both the current and the financial accounts). How do the balance of payments figures compare with those for 2011 in Table 15.4?
2. On the Bureau of Economic Analysis international accounts Web page, find statistics on the current direct foreign investment in the United States. What are the categories of this investment, and how have they changed in recent years?
3. Based on the discussion in this chapter, update the controversy over the value of the Chinese yuan in foreign currency markets. Is China still using central bank foreign exchange policy to maintain the value of the yuan? What is the current policy of the United States on this issue?
4. What is the current value of the euro relative to the U.S. dollar? What macro policies are the countries in the European Union following regarding their economies, and how do these policies affect the value of the euro?
5. Find examples in current news publications similar to those in this chapter of the strategic responses of individual businesses to changes in currency exchange rates. Are these firms adapting to the changing international environment, or are they engaged in political action to try to modify that environment?

16

Combining Micro and Macro Analysis for Managerial Decision Making

I n this chapter, we draw on both microeconomic analysis and macroeconomic analysis to analyze the challenges to managerial decision making arising from changes in the business environment.

We begin this chapter with the case, "Strong Headwinds for McDonald's," which discusses the challenges that McDonald's Corp. faced in 2011 and 2012 as it dealt with new forms of competition from other firms in the fast-food industry and the global economy that was still struggling to recover from recession. We will highlight how quickly changes in both microeconomic and macroeconomic factors in the economy can impact the strategy of even a huge industry player such as McDonald's. We will discuss how McDonald's faced market challenges in the past, and we will focus on how the company expanded its operations in China over the years.

We will then discuss how recent actions by McDonald's major rivals, Burger King, Wendy's, and Subway, have influenced McDonald's strategies. We will also examine how public health policies, such as the posting of calorie counts and concerns over increasing obesity, particularly among children, have created challenges for all players in the fast-food industry.

We end the chapter by emphasizing the major theme of this text: *Changes in the macro environment affect individual firms and industries through the microeconomic factors of demand, production, cost, and profitability.* Firms can either try to adapt to these changes or undertake policies to try to modify the environment itself.

Case for Analysis

Strong Headwinds for McDonald's

In November 2012, McDonald's Corp. reported the first decrease in monthly same-store sales in nine years.[1] The company had already reported declines in second and third quarter earnings, but the decline in sales was larger than expected with a decrease in the United States and Europe of 2.2 percent and in the Asia/Pacific, Middle East, and Africa division of 2.4 percent. This trend had become apparent in summer 2012 when second quarter earnings declined and second quarter same-store sales increased 3.7 percent, down from a 7.3 percent increase in the first quarter of 2012. At that time McDonald's Chief Executive Don Thompson noted that the headwinds facing the company included both macroeconomic factors, such as declining consumer sentiment, and microeconomic factors, such as strategic decisions regarding the company's value menus and how new technology was implemented.

The slowly recovering and still uncertain global economy limited consumers' ability to eat at restaurants, particularly among young people who tend to eat fast food. The global economy and rising commodity prices limited McDonald's ability to lower its prices. The company also acknowledged that it placed too much emphasis on its Extra Value Menu that included items priced higher than a dollar and that it needed to reemphasize its Dollar Menu. The company added value menus in Australia and Japan but acknowledged that it had little room to raise prices in the United States and Europe.

Europe was of particular concern because it accounted for approximately 40 percent of McDonald's revenue and operating profit. The company operated more than 1,400 restaurants in Germany and more than 1,200 in France. Business in Europe weakened in spring 2012 and even declined in July of that year. In response, the company offered coupons for buy-one-and-get-one-free Big Macs and Chicken McNuggets, and it implemented the "Eurosaver" menu. Although similar discounts had been offered in the past, this effort was broader and was not the usual limited-time promotion.

In addition to the global macroeconomic influences, McDonald's faced increased competition from rivals that were revising their own strategies. Burger King Worldwide Inc. began offering new sandwiches and promoting discounts, while Wendy's Co. also offered coupons, upgraded restaurants, and added fresh menu items. In Germany, Burger King introduced its "King des Monats" or "King of the Month" deal with rotating sandwiches, large fries, and a drink. McDonald's managers urged U.S. franchisees and managers to move beyond the lackluster October 2012 performance and not give competitors a chance to steal market share. Franchisees were urged to ensure that restaurants were open through the holidays and to heavily promote the new cheddar bacon onion sandwiches, specialty coffee drinks, and the complete line of holiday drinks. McDonald's had also implemented a new "dual-point" ordering system where customers placed an order at one area of the counter and picked up food at another end when their order number was displayed on a screen.

The headwinds facing McDonald's arose after a long period of strong growth even during the U.S. recession of 2007–2009 and the ensuing period of global economic uncertainty.[2] Even in the third and fourth quarters of 2011, the company's growth barely slowed, and its revenue and profits exceeded analysts' expectations. Analysts estimated that McDonald's captured nearly 17 percent of the limited-service restaurant industry in the United States in 2011, nearly as much as the next four restaurants in that category combined—Subway, Starbucks, Burger King, and Wendy's. The average free-standing McDonald's restaurant in the United States generated $2.6 million in sales in 2011, a 13 percent increase since 2008. The company's annual advertising budget was estimated to exceed $2 billion. The company modernized its restaurants all over the world with Wi-Fi, colorful chairs, and flat-screen TVs. It expanded restaurant hours and added double-lane drive-throughs. The company also engaged "mom bloggers," who wrote about the company and who helped push for improvements in the nutritional content of Happy Meals. McDonald's reduced the size of the french fries and put apple slices in each meal nationally in March 2012.

McDonald's also focused heavily on emerging markets such as China for new-restaurant growth. In late 2011, the company's Asia/Pacific, Middle East, and Africa division reported the strongest same-store sales growth of all its business units. The company offered more drive-through restaurants and motorbike delivery of food in countries such as China, Egypt, and South Korea.

---

[1]The following discussion is based on Julie Jargon, "McDonald's Is Feeling Fried," *Wall Street Journal (Online)*, November 8, 2012; Julie Jargon and Laura Stevens, "McDonald's, Feeling Heat in Europe, Serves Up Deals," *Wall Street Journal (Online)*, October 10, 2012; Annie Gasparro and Chelsea Stevenson, "McDonald's Sales Faltered in July," *Wall Street Journal (Online)*, August 8, 2012; and Annie Gasparro, "McDonald's Loses Some Momentum," *Wall Street Journal (Online)*, July 23, 2012.

[2]The following discussion is based on Julie Jargon, "How McDonald's Hit the Spot," *Wall Street Journal (Online)*, December 13, 2011; and Keith O'Brien, "How McDonald's Came Back Bigger Than Ever," *The New York Times (Online)*, May 4, 2012.

Microeconomic and Macroeconomic Influences on McDonald's and the Fast-Food Industry

Managers in firms with market power can develop competitive strategies that focus either on consumer demand and the revenue derived from the sale of its products or on production technology and the costs of production. Increases in revenue and decreases in costs both help managers increase a firm's profits (the difference between total revenue and total cost). Unlike those who manage perfectly competitive firms, which cannot influence the price of the product, such as many farmers (Chapter 7), managers in firms with market power typically develop strategies that involve both the demand and the supply sides of the market.

As noted in the opening case, managers also face challenges arising from the overall macroeconomic environment. The U.S. economy entered into a recession in March 2001 and again in December 2007 (Chapter 14). These downturns in economic activity forced all the fast-food companies to develop new strategies as discussed below.

Shifting Product Demand

For much of 2001 and 2002, McDonald's faced a demand curve that shifted against its business for a number of reasons. Consumer tastes and preferences had been changing as more individuals became concerned about the high fat content of most fast foods. Activists claimed that the industry contributed to obesity and other health conditions in the population, such as heart disease and high blood pressure. The industry was also under competitive threat from the emergence of "quick-casual" restaurants, such as Cosi and Panera Bread, which had no table service, but served higher-quality foods, such as sandwiches and salads, and charged higher prices. Although industry analysts expected that most quick-casual customers would be middle-aged baby boomers who could afford the higher prices, 37 percent of the quick-casual customers were 18–34 years old, the population segment that typically consumed the most fast food.[3]

This change in fast-food demand is shown in the demand curve shift in Figure 16.1, which is based on the analysis we have previously developed (Chapters 2 and 3). With the original demand curve, D_1, in Figure 16.1, quantity Q_1 is demanded at price

FIGURE 16.1

Change in Demand in the Fast-Food Industry

To counter the decrease in demand from D_1 to D_2, fast-food managers must either try to shift the demand curve back out or lower price to increase quantity demanded. McDonald's and other fast-food companies have used both strategies.

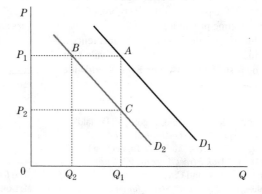

[3]Shirley Leung, "Fast-Food Chains' Price Cuts Only Get a Yawn from Diners," *Wall Street Journal,* November 11, 2002.

P_1. If the demand curve shifts to D_2 as a result of changing tastes and preferences, only quantity Q_2 will be demanded at price P_1, the situation described above. To restore the quantity demanded to Q_1, McDonald's can try to shift the demand curve to the right by influencing different variables in the demand function, by lowering the product price to increase the quantity demanded along demand curve D_2, or by using a combination of these strategies. The effectiveness of any strategy will depend on the consumer responsiveness or elasticity of the different variables in the demand function.

The Dollar Menu strategy of offering eight items for $1 each, which McDonald's undertook in fall 2002, was based on the assumption or hope that the price elasticity of demand was elastic or that the percentage change in quantity demanded is greater than the percentage change in price. In this situation, a price decrease actually results in an increase in total revenue (Chapter 3). The initial reaction to this strategy in early 2003 was that it was not working as expected. Some franchise owners reported that profits were declining from selling the discount items. Thus, demand for those items may actually have been inelastic, so that a decrease in price resulted in a decrease in total revenue. When McDonald's officials reported a fourth-quarter loss in 2002, the first quarterly loss in 38 years as a publicly traded company, they indicated they were reviewing the policy of keeping some of the big sandwiches, such as the Big 'N Tasty, on the Dollar Menu, given that these discounted items were decreasing sales of full-priced burgers, such as the Big Mac. Various industry and financial analysts argued that the Dollar Menu should be dropped or revised substantially because the discounting hurt not only McDonald's financial condition, but also that of the entire fast-food sector. However, an unconfirmed memo to franchisees indicated that McDonald's intended to allocate approximately 20 percent of its 2003 domestic advertising budget to the Dollar Menu in spite of the decrease in sales during the previous year, especially during the fourth quarter when the Dollar Menu was advertised extensively.[4]

Given rising costs, McDonald's announced in November 2008 that it was pulling its double cheeseburger off its Dollar Menu and replacing it with a McDouble burger, which had one slice of cheese instead of two. This change was estimated to save six cents per burger. McDonald's kept the double cheeseburger on its regular menu and raised the suggested price to $1.19.[5]

Oligopolistic Behavior

McDonald's Corp. operates in a market structure with many competitors and substitute foods. However, it engages in oligopolistic behavior with its major fast-food competitors, especially Burger King and Wendy's.[6] McDonald's held 43.1 percent of the U.S. burger market in 2002, followed by Burger King (18.5 percent) and Wendy's (13.2 percent). As noted in the opening case, McDonald's had 17 percent of the U.S. limited-service restaurant industry in 2011, nearly as much as that of Subway, Starbucks, Burger King, and Wendy's combined. Although the chains say they do not focus on each other as the main competition, their actions are definitely those of oligopolists. McDonald's introduction of its 8-item Dollar Menu with a $20 million

[4]Amy Zuber, "McD Plots Turnaround," *Nation's Restaurant News*, January 6, 2003, 1, 75.
[5]Janet Adamy, "McDonald's to Raise Burger's Price," *Wall Street Journal*, November 26, 2008; Janet Adamy, "McDonald's Sales Keep Growing," *Wall Street Journal*, December 9, 2008.
[6]This discussion is based on Leung, "Fast-Food Chains' Price Cuts Only Get a Yawn"; and Shirley Leung, "Burger Wars Are Yielding Ground to Bigger Shakeups," *Wall Street Journal*, December 16, 2002.

advertising campaign in 2002 was followed by Burger King's offering of a menu of 11 items at 99 cents each. Burger King claimed it lost customers to McDonald's because the Big 'N Tasty and McChicken sandwiches on the Dollar Menu were twice as large as any sandwich on Burger King's 99-cent menu. Meanwhile, both chains were fighting the obesity issue. In September 2002, McDonald's announced it would use a different oil to reduce the trans-fatty acid in its fried foods, while Burger King introduced a veggie burger in the same year.

The companies matched each other on price cuts, cooking styles, and menu variety for many years. In 1998, McDonald's introduced its "Made for You" campaign, which involved a costly redesign of its kitchens to emulate Burger King's "Have It Your Way" style of assembling sandwiches to order. Previously, McDonald's had made batches of burgers and microwaved them at the time of a customer order. The company spent $181 million on this change, while franchisees spent an average of $30,000 on each restaurant. Although this kitchen change was designed to produce hotter and fresher food and more customized service, many franchisees found the kitchens too complicated, often requiring an increase in staff, which added to costs.

Thus, the strategic question for McDonald's managers is whether consumers care more about convenience, taste, or price. This is a question of the sensitivity of different variables in the consumer demand function. We will address this question again later in the chapter when examining public health legislation regulating the fast-food industry.

In 2008, the fast-food rivals competed with new coffee strategies. Wendy's introduced a line of iced coffees and a new drink called Frosty-cino in August 2008. McDonald's rolled out its McCafe coffee drinks in more than 3,000 of its 14,000 U.S. locations. Based on focus group results, the company also began experimenting with new types of hot and cold drinks that were not made with coffee, designed for people who liked the idea of coffee drinks but not the actual taste. At McDonald's, all drinks tended to have higher profit margins than food items.[7]

All the rivals also experimented with their menus and pricing. Wendy's, which was acquired by Triarc Cos., which also owned Arby's, planned to focus on customers aged 24 to 49, change its value menu in light of higher ingredient and labor costs, and improve its french fries, sandwich buns, and bacon. Wendy's also attempted to break into the breakfast business, which McDonald's had long dominated. Burger King tested a smaller $1.00 Whopper Jr. in response to higher ingredient costs.[8] In the opening case of the chapter we discussed more recent oligopolistic behavior regarding new sandwich options and the use of discounts and coupons by all of the fast-food rivals. Thus, in the third quarter of 2012 as McDonald's announced its decrease in same-store sales, Wendy's announced that its same-store sales in North America increased 2.7 percent at company-owned restaurants and 2.9 percent at franchised restaurants, while Burger King's sales increased by 1.4 percent.[9]

Higher ingredients costs from the drought in the summer of 2012 put competitive pressures on all the fast-food rivals.[10] The price per pound of chicken wings was estimated to be up 86 percent from a year earlier. Fast-food firms had to decide whether to try to pass the increasing costs onto consumers or to hold prices steady

[7]Janet Adamy, "Wendy's Raises Its Coffee Profile," *Wall Street Journal*, September 8, 2008; Janet Adamy, "McDonald's Coffee Strategy Is Tough Sell," *Wall Street Journal*, October 27, 2008.

[8]Janet Adamy and Julie Jargon, "Burger King Battles Costs with Smaller Whopper Jr." *Wall Street Journal*, August 22, 2008; Janet Adamy, "Wendy's Comes Up with a New Strategic Recipe," *Wall Street Journal*, September 30, 2008.

[9]Julie Jargon, *Wall Street Journal (Online)*, November 8, 2012.

[10]Julie Jagon and Laura Stevens, "McDonald's, Feeling Heat in Europe, Serves Up Deals."; Julie Jargon, "Soaring Food Prices Put Restaurants in a Bind," *Wall Street Journal (Online)*, August 28, 2012.

while emphasizing low-cost menu items. Analysts argued that fine and casual-dining restaurants could better tolerate ingredient price increases, given their higher-priced menus and ability to adjust portion sizes. High gasoline prices also meant that fast-food restaurants competed more with home cooking.

Strategies to Offset Shifting Demand

McDonald's has engaged in a variety of strategies to counter shifting demand. Sales of Happy Meals to children declined 6 to 7 percent over 2001 and 2002. This decline was critical to the company because at that time Happy Meals accounted for 20 percent of the U.S. transactions, or approximately $3.5 billion in annual revenue.[11] Happy Meals also generated increased sales to adults. In some restaurants, the average adult order with a Happy Meal was 50 percent larger than those orders without a Happy Meal. McDonald's has dominated the market for children with its introduction of the Happy Meal in 1976 and in-store playgrounds in subsequent years. Burger King launched its Kids Meals only in 1990, and children's meals remain an insignificant business for Wendy's, Pizza Hut, KFC, and Taco Bell.

To counter this declining Happy Meal trend, McDonald's considered offering a "Mom's Meal," with a gift for the mother who bought the Happy Meal for the child. Competitive strategy also focused on the toy that came with the meal. In 2002, McDonald's began increasing the quality of its toys and adding toys with a greater appeal to children. Part of the problem was that the chain had signed a 10-year agreement with Walt Disney Company that prohibited McDonald's from featuring promotions involving any Disney competitors. Thus, the lack of success of some Disney movies had a negative impact on Happy Meal sales. McDonald's officials were also concerned that children were becoming bored with traditional toys at an earlier age. The chain considered offering more interactive toys with the meals and installing Nintendo videogame stations in some markets. To counter parents' concerns about fast foods and childhood obesity, McDonald's considered offering a variety of menu additions, such as apple slices, fruit juices, peanut butter and jelly sandwiches, and carrot sticks.

We noted in the opening case that in 2012 McDonald's reduced the size of the french fries and put apple slices in each Happy Meal to increase the nutritional content. At this time it also appeared that Happy Meals were losing their appeal to children and their parents.[12] Visits to fast-food restaurants in which kids meals were purchased had declined every year since 2007. A number of cities, including San Francisco, enacted regulations regarding the nutritional content of fast-food kids meals. There was even a proposed class action suit seeking to ban the sale of Happy Meals in California. Although some of this change was related to consumer education, income, and changing tastes and preferences, the availability of cheaper burgers and fries on dollar menus also likely influenced this behavior shift.

In 2001 and 2002, McDonald's tried to improve the quality of its service by hiring mystery shoppers to evaluate service, cleanliness, and food quality in more than 13,000 U.S. restaurants, using a single set of standards and measurements. Burger King used a similar type of grading system.[13] The question regarding this strategy

---

[11]The following discussion is based on Shirley Leung and Suzanne Vranica, "Happy Meals Are No Longer Bringing Smiles to McDonald's," *Wall Street Journal*, January 31, 2003.

[12]This discussion is based on Emily Bryson York, "Appetite Wanes for Fast-Food Kids Meals," *Los Angeles Times (Online)*, April 21, 2012.

[13]Shirley Leung, "McDonald's Hires Mystery Eaters to Find Out What Ails Food Sales," *Wall Street Journal*, December 17, 2001; Amy Zuber, "Slow Economy Feeds Fast-Food Fight," *Nation's Restaurant News*, January 21, 2002, 28–29; Shirley Leung, "Kindler, Gentler Fast Food? Testing New Service Pushes," *Wall Street Journal*, January 7, 2003.

was, again, the relative importance to the customer of service and cleanliness compared with price and the variety of menu items. A mystery shopper survey by the *Wall Street Journal* in 2001 found that the overall score for McDonald's was 81.9 percent compared with 80.1 percent for Burger King, 80.7 percent for Wendy's, and 77.1 percent for Taco Bell. Thus, customers may not be able to distinguish among the rival chains on the basis of this characteristic. It was also unclear what the impact on sales would be if the rating increased from 80 to 90 percent.

Cost-Cutting Strategies

To cut costs in the face of declining demand and increased competition, many fast-food restaurants have focused on reducing paper napkin costs.[14] Some restaurants overstuffed the dispensers, making it difficult for customers to grab more than one napkin. Others placed the dispensers near cashiers so they could be monitored. Most fast-food chains have cut the size of their napkins from a standard 13 by 17 inches to 13 by 12 inches, reducing costs by 10 to 12 percent. Fast-food napkins have also gotten approximately 10 percent thinner in the past decade. McDonald's reduced the size of its napkins three times from 1997 to 2002 and began testing a 6.5-by-8.4-inch napkin. As with other input changes, there is always a balance between cutting costs and influencing demand. Napkins typically account for approximately 1 percent of a fast-food restaurant's total expenses, but they may impact 10 to 20 percent of customer-satisfaction scores. Making napkins more difficult to grab out of a dispenser may actually result in more consumption as consumers end up grabbing wads of napkins instead of one or two. One study found that customers typically ended up grabbing 9.25 napkins from the hard-to-pull dispensers.

Innovations for Different Tastes

Given varying tastes around the world, McDonald's has implemented a different strategy with its restaurants in France than in the United States.[15] French managers were convincing consumers to linger over their meals by installing chic interiors and music videos and by adding menu items such as a hot ham and cheese sandwich. While the chain was closing restaurants worldwide, it opened a new outlet in France every six days in 2002. French customers typically spent $9 per visit compared with $4 in the United States, even though the price of a Big Mac was approximately the same in Paris as in New York City. McDonald's also designed its restaurants in France to blend in with the local architecture. Thus, the French strategy was contrary to McDonald's history of consistency in the design of its restaurants and food offerings.

More recent managerial debates have focused on whether this French concept can be transferred to the United States. The question is whether McDonald's customers are primarily interested in quick service and cheap food, perhaps obtained mostly through a drive-through window, or whether more customers

---

[14]Shirley Leung, "Napkins Get Smaller and Scarcer as Fast-Food Places Trim Costs," *Wall Street Journal*, May 2, 2002.

[15]Shirley Leung, "McHaute Cuisine: Makeover Boosts McDonald's in France," *Wall Street Journal*, August 30, 2002; Carol Matlack and Pallavi Gogoi, "What's This? The French Love McDonald's? Gallic Twists Are Luring Crowds—and Giving the Parent a Boost," *Business Week*, January 13, 2003, 50.

would respond to a comfortable setting and higher-quality food. In France and elsewhere in Europe, McDonald's has pushed its "Premier" line of sandwiches, priced 30 percent higher than the standard burger. The strategic issue is whether new customers can be attracted without alienating the old ones. Although Burger King pulled out of France in 1998, McDonald's restaurants have faced increased competition from chains serving fresh baguettes with ham and brie in a bistro setting.

In 2012, McDonald's began offering the McBaguette, a burger served on a baguette topped with French-made Emmental cheese and mustard.[16] Market research had shown that 65 percent of the two billion sandwiches sold each year in France were baguette-based. The company also devised 20 locally tailored menus in 14 European countries, including Finland, where it offered the Rye McFeast, a burger on a rye bun, and two new sandwiches in Italy, the Adagio and the Vivace. In September 2012, McDonalds announced plans to open vegetarian-only restaurants in India in 2013.[17] The company had already dropped beef and pork from its menus in India and divided its kitchens into separate sections for cooking vegetarian and nonvegetarian food. McDonald's restaurants offered numerous vegetarian versions of its American burgers including the McVeggie burger, the McSpicy Paneer, and the McAloo Tikki burger based on a spicy potato patty.

Drawing on Previous Experience

McDonald's has in the past faced challenges similar to the ones described above.[18] The environmental impact of the company's use of polystyrene foam packages for its products became a major issue in the late 1980s. Even though McDonald's sponsored waste reduction campaigns and polystyrene foam recycling programs, the company continued to be on the defensive regarding environmental issues. In 1990, the company announced it was phasing out foam packaging in the United States, a move that would eventually save each restaurant approximately $2,000 per year. That year McDonald's also developed a partnership and a comprehensive solid-waste-reduction action plan with the Environmental Defense Fund. These changes helped McDonald's turn a strategic problem into a competitive advantage.

The company also realized in the early 1990s that price and value were key strategic variables that needed greater attention. This change in strategy was brought about by both the recession of 1990–1991 and price discounting by competitors such as Taco Bell, again showing the interaction of macro and micro influences on a firm's competitive strategy. McDonald's had traditionally viewed price discounting as a local market tactic and not part of a national marketing strategy. In 1991, McDonald's introduced several low-price menu leaders and its combination Extra Value Meals, supported by a $47 million advertising campaign. The company found that it could still be profitable with the lower prices by also focusing on cost reduction. The company began using a new filter powder to extend the life of the shortening used to cook french fries, which saved

---

[16]Marion Issard, "To Tailor Burgers for France, McDonald's Enlists Baguette," *Wall Street Journal (Online)*, February 24, 2012.

[17]Annie Gasparro and Julie Jargon, "In India, McDonald's Plans Vegetarian Outlets," *Wall Street Journal (Online)*, September 5, 2012.

[18]This discussion is based on John F. Love, *McDonald's: Behind the Arches*, rev. ed. (New York: Bantam, 1995).

each restaurant $2,800 annually. Changing from a company-sponsored insurance program to eight approved insurance companies gave restaurant operators the flexibility to control costs through competitive bidding and resulted in an annual decrease in property and casualty insurance costs of $4,000 per restaurant. These two programs, combined with the savings from shifting to paper packaging, saved more than $80 million per year when applied to the more than 9,300 U.S. restaurants.

McDonald's was also able to lower the total average development cost of a U.S. restaurant by more than 27 percent from 1990 to 1993 by using better methods to determine the optimum size of the buildings and more cost-effective construction methods. The company developed the Series 2000 building, which is half the size of a traditional restaurant, but has a kitchen engineered to produce almost as much volume as a standard kitchen. These "mini" restaurants cost 30 percent less to build in 1991, but could handle 96 percent of the volume of a full-sized restaurant. The lower costs of these smaller units also opened up market niches in small towns and other areas that could not support traditional restaurants. As McDonald's expanded globally, it was able to achieve even greater economies of scale by purchasing supplies from around the world at the least cost. New Zealand cheese was flown to South America, while beef from Uruguay was distributed in Malaysia. The United States supplied potatoes for Hong Kong and Japan, while the sesame seeds for the buns were produced in Mexico. The company was often able to avoid currency problems through barter arrangements, as when it shipped Russian pies to Germany in return for packaging, lobby trays, and cleaning materials.

2012 and Beyond: A Focus on China and Other Emerging Markets

McDonald's developed its competitive strategy in China by focusing on the changing lifestyles and the new automobile-driven culture of Chinese consumers. Although the company opened its first restaurant in China in 1990, it developed the drive-through concept there only more recently, opening its first drive-through in 2005 as a major part of its strategy to compete with Yum Brands Inc.'s KFC fried-chicken chain. Yum Brands operated 3,700 KFC and 626 Pizza Hut outlets in China in 2012 compared with McDonald's 1,400 restaurants. McDonald's opened 200 stores in China in 2011, planned 250 in 2012, and expected to have 2,000 restaurants in China by the end of 2013. McDonald's was adding 100 new dessert kiosks in 2012, and 40 percent of its stores were planned to be drive-throughs.[19]

However, there was a period of adjustment for the drive-through innovation in China. Customers had to be taught how to use the drive-through window. Many outlets had customers place their orders through a person rather than a speaker to demystify the procedure.[20] In the United States, McDonald's pioneered the use of call centers to further increase efficiency in the drive-through process. Thus, the amount of cost-cutting technical innovation that can be introduced into a production process is a function not only of the technology itself but also of consumer acceptance.

McDonald's confronted a number of other major issues regarding consumer tastes and acceptance in this market. One of the most important issues has been

---

[19]This discussion is based on Gordon Fairclough and Geoffrey A. Fowler, "Drive-Through Tips for China," *Wall Street Journal (Online)*, June 30, 2006; and Laurie Burkitt, "McDonald's to Tout Quality in China," *Wall Street Journal (Online)*, February 29, 2012.
[20]Gordon Fairclough and Geoffrey A. Fowler, *Wall Street Journal (Online)*, June 30, 2006.

whether to adapt its products to the Chinese market or to keep a U.S.-based menu. The company tested a "rice burger," and it sold a range of foods made specifically for the Chinese, including triangle wraps of beef or chicken and vegetables and rice wrapped in a tortilla. However, by September 2006 when the company introduced the Quarter Pounder in China, it shifted strategy to emphasize traditional American hamburgers as opposed to specialties for the Chinese market.[21] The company discontinued the rice burgers and triangle wraps as it began pushing the Quarter Pounder. However, the Chinese Quarter Pounder was not identical to the U.S. version because it used cucumbers rather than pickles and tomatoes and a spicy sauce more appealing to the Chinese. These changes resulted from tests of more than 16 variations on consumers, emphasizing the importance of the techniques to determine consumer preferences (Chapter 4).

The Quarter Pounder introduction was supported by an advertising campaign that focused on beef as luxurious, healthy, and even sexy. Billboard ads featured a close-up of a woman's lips, while door ads showed a woman running her hands over a man's flexed biceps. TV commercials were even racier. "In one spot, a man and a woman eat Quarter Pounders, and close-up shots of the woman's neck and mouth are interspersed with images of fireworks and spraying water. The actors suck their fingers. The voice-over says: 'You can feel it. Thicker. You can taste it. Juicier.'"[22]

This campaign was important in a country with China's population, particularly given the fact that half of McDonald's sales in China had been of chicken products with beef making up only 35 percent. Beef typically costs more in China, and customers view it as a luxury good. However, market research and successful promotions for the Big Mac convinced McDonald's executives of the need for a change in strategy.

This changing strategy was part of a move to reverse a sliding market share for McDonald's in China and to compete more vigorously with Yum Brands' KFC, which focused more on foods specifically designed for the Chinese market. Average sales per McDonald's restaurant in China had been about half of what they were in the United States. Although McDonald's managers still made some concessions to local tastes, such as adding a corn cup and eliminating Diet Coke, which was not selling, these changes involved tweaking and adding side dishes rather than reshaping McDonalds's core menu. As incomes increased in China, beef consumption increased more rapidly than that of pork or chicken. These trends, combined with consumer research, convinced McDonald's executives that the company should emphasize its American roots.[23] In 2011 and 2012, McDonald's launched a new advertising campaign arguing that the company had the best quality among fast-food competitors. Ads featured "100% fresh beef" on the chopping block, farmers picking tomatoes, and chickens eating high-quality feed. Chinese customers typically believed that Western food chains used safe ingredients.[24]

Chinese customers traditionally did not favor take-out food and preferred to sit down for leisurely meals. Restaurants were often places for family gatherings and appointments with friends. McDonald's and KFC have both capitalized on this social aspect of the Chinese restaurant experience. Due to the Cultural Revolution, most restaurants in the 1970s looked similar inside and out, had a canteen mentality in management, and offered poor service and unpleasant dining experiences. When KFC and McDonald's opened their outlets in Beijing, customers were

---

[21]Gordon Fairclough and Janet Adamy, "Sex, Skin, Fireworks, Licked Fingers—It's a Quarter Pounder Ad in China," *Wall Street Journal*, September 21, 2006.
[22]Ibid.
[23]Ibid.
[24]Laurie Burkitt, "McDonald's to Tout Quality in China."

impressed by their beautiful appearances and brightly lit, climate-controlled interiors. Years of economic reform and improved living standards meant that many Chinese now had discretionary income. Dining out became a popular form of entertainment, and the cleanliness of the McDonald's and KFC outlets became an important issue.[25]

Other social issues were also important. There is pressure within Chinese culture for people holding banquets at restaurants to compete with neighboring tables on the basis of offering the guests the most expensive dishes and alcoholic beverages. To avoid competition and potential embarrassment, people would pay extra fees to reserve a private room. McDonald's became a good alternative for consumers with lower incomes because the menu was limited and all items were of similar value. McDonald's also evolved into a setting where people could define themselves as part of the middle class. Surveys and interviews showed that young professionals came to McDonald's in small groups or with their significant others and would spend an hour or more in the restaurant. Studies also indicated that women were more likely than men to eat at fast-food restaurants because they enjoyed ordering their own food and participating in conversation while dining. In formal Chinese restaurants, men ordered food for their female companions and controlled the conversation.[26]

McDonald's has traditionally been popular among Chinese children. The Chinese policy of one child per family has had the effect of turning single children into "fussy little emperors" who are the center of attention of their parents and relatives, so McDonald's actively marketed to children. Restaurants typically had a public relations staff available to answer questions. There were often several female receptionists who were called "Aunt McDonald" by children who knew Ronald McDonald as Uncle McDonald. The Aunt McDonalds learned the names of regular customers, chatted with families at the restaurants, and established relationships with the children. They would record information about the children in their "Book of Little Honorary Guests," send them birthday wishes, and visit their schools. Research interviews indicated that parents would often bring their children to McDonald's even if they themselves did not like the food or could barely afford it. One mother explained that, as an investment for the future, she wanted her daughter to learn English and brought her to McDonald's to experience American culture.[27]

Economic and Political Issues

McDonald's had to confront both technical and political issues with its production decisions in its entry into China. Entry into Beijing was accomplished through an equity joint venture with the Beijing General Corp. of the Agriculture Industry and Commerce United Co. (Beijing's Department of Agriculture). This investment, begun in 1991, was to last 20 years. McDonald's chose this partner because it was controlled by the Chinese government, which enabled the company to receive agricultural subsidies. McDonald's used the Department of Agriculture's connections to cope with barriers concerning agricultural products, but also for other supplier relationships and distributional channels. These relationships helped

[25]Yunxiang Yan, "McDonald's in Beijing: The Localization of Americana," in *Golden Arches East: McDonald's in East Asia* (2nd ed.), James L Watson (ed.) (Stanford: Stanford University Press, 2006); Yunxiang Yan, "Of Hamburger and Social Space: Consuming McDonald's in Beijing," in *The Consumer Revolution in China*, Deborah S. Davis (ed.) (Berkeley: University of California Press, 2000).
[26]Yan, "McDonald's in Beijing;" 2006; Yan, "Of Hamburger and Social Space," 2000.
[27]Yan, "McDonald's in Beijing;" Yadong Luo, *How to Enter China: Choices and Lessons* (Ann Arbor, MI: The University of Michigan Press, 2001).

McDonald's overcome entry barriers that the Chinese government placed on foreign companies acquiring natural resources within the country. McDonald's typically relied on independent suppliers who were required to meet and maintain the company's standards and specifications. As early as 1983, it began using apples from China to supply its restaurants in Japan. Thereafter, it began building up distribution and processing facilities in northern China. McDonald's also worked with Chinese farmers to teach them how to grow potatoes that could be used to make their french fries.[28]

There are many other examples of the political risk that McDonald's encountered with its entry into China. In 2004, Meng Sun became the first McDonald's franchisee in China. As noted previously, most McDonald's and KFC restaurants were company-owned or operated in joint ventures with local companies. As part of the conditions for entry into the World Trade Organization, China was required to set up a framework for everything from the recruitment and vetting of prospective entrepreneurs to the protection of brand and property rights. Western companies traditionally thought they could lose control of their trade secrets and brands by offering franchises in China, which offered few legal protections. New government rules made franchises more enticing to Chinese business people. Approximately 60 percent of McDonald's outlets outside the United States are franchised. Potential owners have to spend at least a year working at virtually every post in a restaurant. In 2001, McDonald's opened a Hong Kong branch of its Hamburger University to teach management practices.[29] McDonald's has, of course, been a primary target among several multinational corporations of anticorporation, anticapitalist, and antiobesity campaigns. In August 2002, two New York teenagers sued McDonald's for making them fat. Although the judge dismissed the suit, many trial lawyers, nutritionists, and anticorporate activists have since argued that purveyors of food should be held responsible for the long-term health consequences of their products, just as tobacco firms were called to account for cigarette damage. The Center for Science in the Public Interest has asked the FDA to put tobacco-style warning labels on sugary beverages. Similar antiobesity campaigns have spread to Korea and Hong Kong.[30] To respond to this backlash around the world, McDonald's entered a partnership with Chinese educational authorities to give nutrition classes in elementary schools. The company created a Ronald McDonald clown show for schools that combined encouragement of physical activity with educational materials about nutrition. These shows were presented in thousands of Chinese schools.[31]

Food safety and other health issues are always problems for firms in this sector of the economy. In 2003, McDonald's raised the price of its Big Mac in China as much as 4 percent, but denied a report that suggested the price increase was to cover expenses related to severe acute respiratory syndrome (SARS). Restaurants had suffered from the SARS outbreak as people avoided public places, especially in Beijing.[32] One of the reasons that food prices surged in China in late 2007 and early 2008 was the increased price of pork after pig herds were hit by porcine "blue ear" disease in 2007.[33]

---

[28]Luo, *How to Enter China*; Yan, "Of Hamburger and Social Space."

[29]Steven Gray and Geoffrey A. Fowler, "China's New Entrepreneurs: McDonald's and KFC Race to Recruit More Franchisees as Rules Are Standardized," *Wall Street Journal*, January 25, 2005.

[30]James L. Watson, "McDonald's as a Political Target: Globalization and Anti-globalization in the Twenty-First Century," in *Golden Arches East: McDonald's in East Asia*, 2nd ed., James L. Watson (ed.) (Stanford, CA: Stanford University Press, 2006).

[31]Geoff Dyer, "Ronald Helps McDonald's Head Off China Backlash," *Financial Times*, London, November 25, 2006.

[32]"Food Brief: McDonald's Corp." *Wall Street Journal*, June 10, 2003.

[33]"China Economy: Price Surge," *The Economist*, The Economist Intelligence Unit, March 11, 2008.

Multinational corporations always confront local legislation and institutions in terms of hiring and employment practices. McDonald's announced it was raising wages for restaurant crews 12 to 56 percent above China's minimum wage guidelines as of September 1, 2007. The All-China Federation of Trade Unions had accused the company of violating labor laws by underpaying part-time workers in Guangzhou. The company was absolved of wrongdoing, but it received negative publicity over the incident. McDonald's was able to offset these costs by lowering other costs, such as for paper, through increased economies of scale resulting from its expansion over time.[34]

In reaction to the implementation of the new labor law legislation in January 2008, many small- and medium-sized companies asked lawmakers to reconsider clauses regarding casual labor, which would allow them more flexibility in hiring temporary workers. The Labour Resources Intermediary Association argued that these companies helped keep unemployment rates under control by acting as intermediaries in providing employment for migrants. The association's chairman noted that if the law were strictly enforced, "there is a risk that some 30 percent of this labour force, or 15 million workers, would be left without jobs."[35]

McDonald's planned a major promotional effort regarding the Summer Olympics in China in 2008. The plan involved global advertising to showcase the company's history of feeding athletes and competitions in 30 countries to select 200 children for trips to the games.[36] At that time, this strategy was seen as a balancing act between the increased exposure from the games versus any negative fallout from the protests against the Chinese government that began when the Olympic flame traveled around the world in March 2008.[37] The lack of major protests at the games greatly benefited the company. McDonald's reported an 8.5 percent increase in August 2008 global same-store sales with its gain in the United States boosted by the Olympic-themed Southern Style Chicken Sandwich. The company's 10 percent growth in the Asia-Pacific, Middle East, and African regions was driven by extended hours and Olympic-related marketing.[38]

Responses of Other Fast-Food Competitors

Although McDonald's retained leadership in the fast-food industry, Wendy's passed Burger King in terms of sales by the end of 2011.[39] Wendy's became the number two burger chain and number four overall behind McDonald's, Subway, and Starbucks. Wendy's gained on Burger King without opening more restaurants. The chain had approximately 5,800 stores compared with 7,200 for Burger King, while McDonald's continued to have more U.S. restaurants than Wendy's and Burger King combined. Wendy's upgraded its menu, stopped using iceberg lettuce in its salads, and introduced new salads with different greens, apples, pecans, and asiago cheese. The chain also began using only Russet potatoes with the skin on for its french fries, and it switched to a looser grind of beef for thicker

[34]Mei Fong, "McDonald's Aims to Boost China Image with Wage Rise," *Wall Street Journal*, August 7, 2007.

[35]"China Regulations: Labour-Law Worries," *The Economist Intelligence Unit*, February 13, 2008.

[36]Emily Bryson York, "What's on McDonald's Olympic-Marketing Menu," *Advertising Age*, March 3, 2008.

[37]"China Politics: Political Risk Takes Centre Stage," *The Economist*, The Economist Intelligence Unit, March 14, 2008; "China Politics: Tibet Dilemma," *The Economist*, The Economist Intelligence Unit, March 17, 2008.

[38]Shara Tibken, "McDonald's Olympic Offerings Help Boost Same-Store Sales," *Wall Street Journal*, September 9, 2008.

[39]The following discussion is based on Julie Jargon, "Wendy's Stages a Palace Coup," *Wall Street Journal (Online)*, December 21, 2011; Tiffany Hsu, "Wendy's Dethrones Burger King; Chains Swap Spots Behind McDonald's as the No. 2 and No. 3 Burger Joints by Sales," *Los Angeles Times (Online)*, March 20, 2012; and Anupreeta Das and Mark Peters, "Burger King Goes Public Again," *Wall Street Journal (Online)*, April 4, 2012.

and juicier burgers. In response to consumer feedback, the company even reformulated its traditional square burgers with softer edges.

Analysts argued that Burger King suffered from a series of management and ownership changes, a lack of menu upgrading, and too-great reliance on young adult customers. Burger King became a public company again in April 2012 and had gone public–private many times since 2002. Trying to expand beyond its target market of men in their early twenties, Burger King phased out its mascot of a king in the summer of 2011 and announced an expanding menu of salads, fruit smoothies, and chicken snack wraps in the spring of 2012.

In 2012, all of the fast-food chains expanded their hours of operation.[40] Nearly 40 percent of McDonald's were open 24 hours per day, an increase from 30 percent seven years earlier. Burger King had several hundred restaurants open around the clock, while Dunkin' Donuts doubled the number of 24-hour restaurants in the past 10 years with one-third of its 7,000 U.S. restaurants open all the time. This was a strategy to generate more sales from existing restaurants, given estimates that one-fifth of all employed Americans worked primarily in the evening.

As noted above, all of the fast-food chains have been expanding their presence in emerging markets, particularly in China and India. In early 2012, Dunkin' Donuts announced plans to open its first restaurant in India, while Starbucks was to follow a month later.[41] Both of these chains were expected to face competition from other coffee chains and from native Indian doughnut shops, such as Mad Over Donuts that offered a cheese and corn combination with a sprinkle of chaat masala, a spicy sweet-and-sour flavor. Although Indians typically prefer tea, analysts argued that the joint effort by both companies might open up the coffee market in India. Starbucks also planned to triple the size of its workforce and restaurants in China over the next three years.[42] The plan was to increase the number of stores from 500 in 2012 to over 1,500 in 2015. The China Coffee Industry Association estimated that Chinese consumers drank only three cups of coffee per year compared with the world average of 240 cups, indicating a large potential market.

As all of the fast-food chains have moved into emerging markets, they have had to face the question of how much to adapt to local tastes. When Pizza Hut entered the Chinese market, it introduced Pizza Hut Casual Dining that resembled a Cheesecake Factory in terms of menu and design. However, Domino's Pizza decided to continue with traditional pizza delivery, its strategy in the United States.[43] Although this strategy worked in India, where the company had 440 locations and 21 percent same-store growth over the previous five years, the question was whether it would work in China, Malaysia, and Turkey with greater competition and less consumer demand for pizza. In China, McDonald's, Pizza Hut, and KFC were already offering delivery service for their products, a fact that could either help or hurt Domino's entry.

Calorie Counts on Menus

In September 2012, McDonald's announced that it would post calorie counts for all items on its menus in all of its restaurants and drive-throughs nationwide.[44] The company had already undertaken this policy in major cities such as New York and

[40]Julie Jargon, "Late-Night Sales on a Roll for U.S. Fast-Food Outlets," *Wall Street Journal (Online)*, January 25, 2012.

[41]Rumman Ahmed, "Dunkin', Starbucks to Duke it Out in India," *Wall Street Journal (Online)*, February 22, 2012.

[42]Rose Yu, "Starbucks to Brew a Bigger China Pot," *Wall Street Journal (Online)*, April 1, 2012.

[43]Annie Gasparro, "Domino's Sticks to Its Ways Abroad," *Wall Street Journal (Online)*, April 17, 2012.

[44]Schuyler Velasco, "McDonald's Adds Calorie Counts. Will Other Chains Follow? Yes," *The Christian Science Monitor (Online)*, September 13, 2012.

Philadelphia and in the entire state of California. New York City passed the first law mandating calorie counts on menus in 2008. Subway and Panera Bread Company had already been posting calorie counts. Given the oligopolistic behavior in the fast-food industry, it was likely that Wendy's and Burger King would follow with the same policy. McDonald's, however, gained the advantage in terms of being the leader among the largest chains.

Both the competitors in the fast-food industry and public health advocates concerned about the impact of fast food on nutrition and obesity are interested in knowing the impacts of posting calorie counts and other regulations on the fast-food menus. The provision of additional nutritional information would help consumers purchase healthier food. However, particularly in fast-food restaurants, consumers may care much more about convenience, price, and taste than nutritional content. The impact of these policies and strategies relates back to the microeconomic factors influencing the demand for a product (Chapters 2 and 3).

Bryan Bollinger, Phillip Leslie, and Alan Sorensen did a comprehensive analysis of calorie posting in a case study of Starbucks restaurants.[45] These authors obtained a data set containing every transaction at Starbucks company stores in New York City from January 1, 2008 to February 28, 2009. Mandatory calorie posting began in NYC on April 1, 2008. To control for other factors influencing consumer behavior, the authors also obtained data on every transaction in Starbucks outlets in Boston and Philadelphia where there was no calorie posting. For further insights on consumer behavior, the authors obtained a large sample of data on anonymous Starbucks cardholders both inside and outside NYC that they tracked over the same time period, and they analyzed a set of in-store surveys performed both before and after the introduction of a calorie posting law in Seattle on January 1, 2009.

The authors concluded that calorie posting influenced consumer behavior at Starbucks, decreasing average calories per transaction by 6 percent, from 247 to 232 calories per transaction. These effects lasted over the entire period that data were collected or 10 months after the calorie posting was introduced. Almost all of the effect was related to food, and not beverage, purchases. Three-quarters of the reduction in calories per transaction resulted from consumers buying fewer items, while the remaining effect resulted from the substitution to lower calorie items.

Calorie posting did not cause any significant change in Starbucks revenue overall. The authors estimated that Starbucks revenues increased 3 percent at stores located within 100 meters of a Dunkin Donuts store. Thus, customers may have preferred Starbucks compared with Dunkin Donuts as a result of the calorie posting. These behavior changes were derived under a policy that required all chain restaurants to post calorie information. The authors noted that the competitive effects would have been much different with voluntary posting by a single restaurant chain.

Consumers with higher income and education appeared to reduce calories more than others. Consumers reported placing more emphasis on calories as they purchased fast food after seeing the calorie posting. However, the choices of Starbucks cardholders who made purchases both in and outside NYC were influenced even at nonposting stores outside NYC.

The authors made only a rough estimate of the impact of this legislation on obesity. Assuming that 25 percent of the average consumer's calorie consumption was derived from chain restaurants, that calorie consumption was reduced by 6 percent at all chain restaurants, and that this reduction was not offset by

---

[45]This discussion is based on Bryan Bollinger, Phillip Leslie, and Alan Sorensen, "Calorie Posting in Chain Restaurants," *American Economic Journal: Economic Policy* 3 (February 2011): 91–128.

increases at other meals, the authors estimated a 1.5 percent decrease in total calorie consumption, or approximately 30 calories per day. This result was not expected to have a major impact on obesity across the country. However, the authors noted that this impact on consumer behavior might induce the fast-food chains to offer more low-calorie items in the future as part of their competitive strategy. Based on a small phone survey, they found that the probability of a restaurant introducing a low-calorie option was 0.71 based on posting and 0.45 for those not posting calorie counts.

In the appendix to this chapter, we present the results of an earlier statistical study of the fast-food industry that also analyzed the various factors influencing the demand for fast food.

Macroeconomic Influences on the Fast-Food Industry in 2011 and 2012

We noted in the opening case and in the earlier discussion the significant impact of the uncertainty in the global economy on all the competitors in the fast-food industry. This uncertainty was highlighted by the International Monetary Fund (IMF) in its *Global Economic Report* in October 2012.[46] The IMF noted that the global economy had deteriorated further since its last projections in July 2012, and that downside risks were judged to be more elevated than in previous reports in April 2012 and September 2011. Forecasts depended on how U.S. and European policy makers responded to their short-term economic challenges.

The IMF reported that its indicators of economic activity and unemployment showed increasing and broad-based sluggishness in the first half of 2012 with no significant improvement in the third quarter. Global manufacturing had slowed sharply with many countries in the European Union experiencing significant declines in economic activity. The United States and the United Kingdom were still struggling to recover from their recessions with labor markets and consumption failing to increase as hoped. GDP growth in emerging markets and developing economies had slowed from about 9 percent in late 2009 to 5.25 percent in 2012, a factor noted throughout the opening case of this chapter. In 2012, the IMF forecast only a modest reacceleration of economic activity, much of which depended on continued monetary policy accommodation, a gradual easing of financial conditions, and reduced policy uncertainty in the European Union and the United States.

Summary: Macro and Micro Influences on the Fast-Food Industry

McDonald's Corp. and its competitors in the fast-food industry were influenced by the global downturn in economic activity in 2001 and 2002. However, many of their problems and strategies were influenced by microeconomic changes affecting this particular industry. Traditional fast food was under attack by competing "casual-quality" substitutes and by consumer concerns over the health impacts of the products. These factors would affect McDonald's competitive strategies

---

[46]International Monetary Fund, *World Economic Outlook October 2012: Coping with High Debt and Sluggish Growth*, 2012. Available at www.imf.org.

even in the absence of an economic downturn. McDonald's and its competitors, who operate in an oligopolistic environment, must try to determine which variables—for example, price, quality, health concerns, convenience, speed of delivery, and ambiance of the restaurants—have the greatest influence on consumer demand.

The economic slowdown of 2007 and 2008 and the continued macroeconomic uncertainty up to 2012 had similar impacts on McDonald's and the fast-food industry. In March 2008, the company reported the first decline in U.S. same-store sales in five years, although there was a rebound in April driven by menu variety, enhanced convenience, and value pricing.[47] The profit margins of many McDonald's franchisees were being squeezed by higher food and paper costs. As always, the impact on consumer behavior was a major factor influencing decisions about menus and pricing in response to these cost factors. These same factors influenced managerial decision making in 2011 and 2012.

We noted in the opening case that McDonald's Chief Executive Don Thompson argued that the headwinds facing the company in 2011 and 2012 included both macroeconomic factors, such as declining consumer sentiment, and microeconomic factors, such as strategic decisions regarding the company's value menus and how new technology was implemented. Thus, his comments emphasized the major theme of this text: *Changes in the macro environment affect individual firms and industries through the microeconomic factors of demand, production, cost, and profitability.* Firms can either try to adapt to these changes or undertake policies to try to modify the environment itself.

Appendix 16 Statistical Estimation of Demand Curves

We have contrasted the marketing approach of understanding consumer behavior and demand—by, for example, using expert opinion, consumer surveys, and test markets and pricing experiments—with the economic approach of statistically estimating a demand function (Chapter 4). In this chapter we described McDonald's attempts to learn about consumer behavior using these marketing methods. The company has used knowledge gained from observing consumers and experimenting with different demand variables to develop new competitive strategies, not all of which were successful. The statistical estimation of demand functions can give managers added insights on the role of the different variables influencing consumer demand.

The fast-food industry has long recognized that the convenience of its restaurants is a major factor influencing sales and consumer demand. Consumers want a consistent and standardized product, but it must be accessible in easily reached locations. Mark Jekanowski, James Binkley, and James Eales analyzed the role of accessibility versus other variables in an econometric study of fast-food demand in 1992.[48] These researchers based the study on the concept that consumers react to the "full price" of purchasing fast food, which consists of both the money price and the value of time spent in acquiring the food.

[47]"McDonald's Reports Rise in Same-Store Sales," *Wall Street Journal*, May 9, 2008.

[48]This discussion is based on Mark D. Jekanowski, James K. Binkley, and James Eales, "Convenience, Accessibility, and the Demand for Fast Food," *Journal of Agricultural and Resource Economics* 26 (July 2001): 58–74.

Using data on a cross-section of 85 metropolitan areas from the Census of Retail Trade and the decennial population census, these researchers used multiple regression analysis to estimate a fast-food demand function in which per capita fast-food consumption was assumed to be a function of market characteristics, prices and income, demographic characteristics, and regional indicators.

The market characteristic variables measure access to both fast-food outlets and competitor restaurants, which were subdivided into inexpensive (under $7 per check) and expensive restaurants. Food (grocery) store density was also included, as these stores compete with fast-food restaurants through their deli counters and prepared take-out meals. Gasoline consumption per capita and population density were included as proxies for travel distance and cost. The average fast-food price was based on the hamburger, pizza, and chicken outlets in the study areas. Prices of the substitute products, grocery store food and inexpensive and expensive restaurant meals, were also incorporated in the analysis. The female labor force participation rate was included as a measure of the opportunity cost of time, as consumption of food away from home is generally greater in households where the female family member works outside the home. Age variables were added to measure the targeting of fast food to children and differential consumption by other age groups. The effect of household size, educational background, and cultural differences among two minority groups were also tested in the analysis.

The statistical results showed that the coefficient of the fast-food outlet density variable was positive and significant, indicating that in 1992, restaurant accessibility was an important factor influencing the demand for fast food, independent of price and the other variables in the equation. The lack of statistical significance of the other density variables indicated that neither other types of restaurants nor food stores competed directly with fast-food restaurants on the basis of travel costs. For food purchased in grocery stores, the time involved in preparing that food for meals, which was not measured in the study, was probably a more important factor affecting fast-food demand than the time spent purchasing the food. The results also suggested that inexpensive restaurants were a poor substitute for fast-food outlets in terms of convenience. Gasoline consumption did not affect fast-food demand, perhaps because this variable focused on a single type of transportation. The sign and significance of the population density variable suggest that fast-food consumption might be negatively affected by the inconvenience associated with mobility in densely populated areas.

The fast-food price variable was significant and had its expected negative sign. However, none of the other price or income variables in this analysis was statistically significant. These results suggest that convenience, more than price, drives the demand for fast food. Other types of restaurants may provide the same or higher-quality food, even at similar prices. However, if consumers place a high value on their time and restaurant convenience, the full price of fast-food outlets is always lower.

The price elasticity of demand was estimated to be elastic, and the size of this elasticity estimate increased from 1982. This increased sensitivity to price could have resulted from the fact that product price became a larger proportion of the full price of consuming fast food, as travel costs decreased due to increased customer accessibility to fast-food outlets. The larger price elasticity could also have resulted from an increase in the number of substitute products from 1982 to 1992, especially microwaveable foods and prepared meals in grocery stores.

The income elasticity of demand was estimated to be inelastic, although the variable was not statistically significant in the analysis. Other studies of the consumption of food away from home have also shown an inelastic income variable, indicating that consumption of these foods is not greatly affected by changes in income. These results support the above discussion, indicating that the problems of the fast-food industry are associated more with microeconomic demand and market changes than with changes in income arising from the overall macroeconomic environment.

How can these statistical results help McDonald's managers make better decisions? This study confirms fast-food managers' strategies of focusing on convenience as a major variable influencing consumer demand for their product. The results also suggest that fast-food restaurants are not in direct competition with table service restaurants in the same price range, but may face more competition from prepared meals in grocery stores. Fast-food managers should consider increasing the number of restaurants in minority-populated areas. The results also indicate differences in fast-food consumption by geographical area, which means that managers should attempt to discover the reasons for these differences through marketing approaches designed to increase understanding of consumer behavior. Given the available data, this study was not able to evaluate many of the specific McDonald's strategies and problems discussed previously in the chapter, such as the changing of the toys in the Happy Meals and the increasing consumer concerns about the quality of fast food. However, more recent and more detailed data would allow marketers and economists to incorporate these factors into the types of models discussed here. Combining both approaches to understanding consumer behavior can help managers develop better competitive strategies.

Exercises

Technical Questions

1. Describe the macroeconomic factors that caused headwinds for McDonald's in 2012.
2. Give examples of oligopolistic behavior among the rivals in the fast-food industry.
3. Regarding the discussion of when McDonald's introduced its Dollar Menu strategy in the fall of 2002, why was the company assuming or hoping that the demand for its products was elastic? Did this appear to be the case?
4. Based on the discussion in this chapter, how did McDonald's development of its mini-restaurants improve its overall profitability?

Application Questions

1. Discuss how the examples in this chapter illustrate the major theme of this text: *Changes in the macro environment affect individual firms and industries through the microeconomic factors of demand, production, cost, and profitability.* Drawing on current business publications, find some updated facts for each case that support this theme.
2. Compare and contrast the fast-food chains' strategies in emerging markets.
3. What role did the policies of various governments play in influencing the international expansion strategies of McDonald's?
4. What variables other than price appear to have the biggest impact on the demand for McDonald's products? How much influence does the company have over these variables?
5. In recent business publications, find a case study in which changes in the macro environment play a major role in influencing a firm's competitive strategy. Contrast this with a second case in which micro factors play a more important role.

Solutions to Even-Numbered Problems

Chapter 1

Technical Questions

2. Outputs are the final goods and services that firms and industries sell to consumers. Consumers create a demand for all of these goods and services. Inputs are the resources or factors of production that are used to produce the final outputs. Inputs include land, labor, capital, raw materials, and entrepreneurship. Firms' use of these inputs is related to the demand for their products.

4. In the model of perfect competition, firms are price-takers because it is assumed there are so many firms in each industry that no single firm has any influence on the price of the product. Each firm's output is small relative to the entire market, so the market price is determined by the actions of all suppliers and demanders. In the other market models, firms have an influence over the price. If they raise the price of the product, consumers will demand a smaller quantity; if they lower the price, consumers will increase the quantity demanded.

6. Fiscal policies are implemented by the national government and involve changing taxes (T) and government expenditure (G) to stimulate or slow the economy. These decisions are made by the political institutions in the country. Monetary policies are implemented by a country's central bank—the Federal Reserve in the United States. These policies focus on changing the money supply in order to influence interest rates, which then affect real consumption, investment spending, and the resulting level of income and output.

Application Questions

2. a. This is a description of a perfectly competitive market. It discusses factors influencing the demand and supply of corn, where the focus is on the price and quantity in the entire market, not the decisions of individual producers. The drought decreased the supply of corn in the U.S., which caused prices to increase. Countries such as China, Japan, and South Korea then turned to find substitute sources of corn in Argentina and Brazil.

   b. Staples, OfficeMax, and Office Depot operate in an oligopoly market with interdependent behavior. All these companies have been forced to close stores, downsize their existing stores, and increase their online operations.

   c. This discussion describes the attempt by the U.S. wireless telecommunications industry to gain monopoly or market power through mergers of independent firms. The federal government prohibited T-Mobile from merging with AT&T, given concerns over the market power of that combined firm. T-Mobile then announced a merger with its smaller rival, MetroPCS, that would still allow it to cut costs and expand its operations.

   d. Chinese restaurants represent monopolistic competition. There are 36,000 Chinese restaurants, most of them small, family operations. No national chain dominates these restaurants, largely due to the use of the wok for cooking. Specialized stoves and chefs are required for this type of cooking, which has limited the expansion of these firms into large-scale production.

4. Examples of these types of strategies are discussed in Chapter 14. Firms looked for ways to increase productivity and cut costs. Many also developed new pricing strategies to increase their profits or minimize their losses.

Chapter 2

Technical Questions

2. a. Supply increases.
   b. Supply decreases.
   c. There is a decrease in the quantity supplied of computers (and no change in the supply curve).
   d. Supply decreases (because costs of production have increased).
   e. There is no change in supply, as consumer incomes are a determinant of demand.

4. a. X and Z are complements in production. We know this because there is a positive relationship between the price of good Z and the supply of good X (thus, as the price of Z rises, producers produce more X).
   b. $Q_S = -200 + 20P_X - 5P_I + 0.5P_Z$
      $= -200 + 20P_X - 5(10) + 0.5(20)$
      $= -240 + 20P_X$

   c.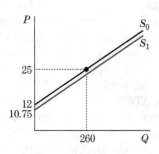

   d. Set $Q_S = 0$. The minimum price is $12.00.
   e. $Q_S = -240 + 20(25) = 260$.
   f. $Q_S = -200 + 20P_X - 5(5) + 0.5(20)$
      $= -215 + 20P_X$.

6. a. Demand increases (the price of a substitute has risen); equilibrium price and quantity rise.

   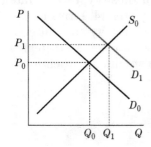

b. Supply decreases (the price of an input has risen); equilibrium price rises and quantity falls.

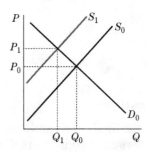

c. Demand increases; equilibrium price and quantity rise.

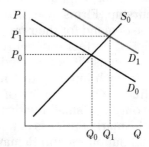

d. Supply increases; equilibrium price falls and quantity rises.

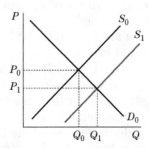

e. Demand decreases; equilibrium price and quantity fall.

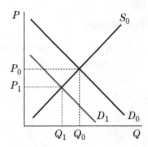

8. a. Because hamburger is an inferior good, demand will increase as incomes decrease, causing the price to rise (rightward shift of demand curve). The improvement in technology that lowers production costs causes supply to increase and tends to lower price (rightward shift of supply curve). With no further information, we know that the equilibrium quantity will rise, but the effect on price cannot be determined.

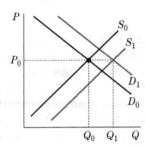

   b. The decrease in consumer incomes will cause demand to increase (for an inferior good), which will cause the price to rise, all other things held constant. If this effect is smaller than the effect of the improvement in technology (which will increase supply and cause the price to fall), then we may now be able to conclude that the equilibrium price of hamburger is likely to fall.

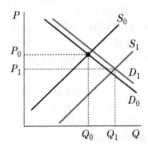

Application Questions

2. In February 2013, copper futures prices were at their highest level in nearly four months. This change was another sign that the U.S. economy was growing stronger. Increased manufacturing and construction activity appeared to be increasing the demand for copper and supporting higher prices. Consumers were also demanding more phones, laptops, and air conditioners, all of which use copper as an input.[1]

4. a. The hot summer and the lack of rain caused a significant decrease in the supply of peanuts. This caused a leftward shift in the supply curve that increased the price of peanuts.
   b. Because peanuts are an input to the production of peanut butter, the increase in peanut prices shifted the supply curve of peanut butter to the left, thus increasing its price. Peanut butter producers worried about the impact of price increases on their customers, so they tried to find ways to cut other costs, such as shipping and warehousing, to offset the increase in peanut prices.
   c. The supply of peanuts also decreased due to the high price of cotton. Farmers shifted some of their land from peanut to cotton production.
   d. The heat also influenced the quality of the peanut plants. Because many plants were scorched, the supply of peanuts used for peanut butter decreased, while the supply for peanut oil increased.

---

[1]See Tatyana Shumsky, "Copper Settles 1.4% Higher," *Wall Street Journal (Online)*, February 1, 2013.

Chapter 3

Technical Questions

2. a. Price elasticity $= -1$ (unitary elasticity)
   b. Price elasticity $= -3.0$ (elastic)
   c. Price elasticity $= -0.33$ (inelastic)

4. a. $P_X = 250 - 1/2Q$
   $$TR = PQ = (250 - 1/2Q)Q = 250Q - 1/2Q^2$$

   b.

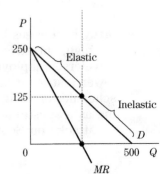

c. At $Q = 250$, $MR = 0$, and, thus, revenue is maximized. At that point, $P = \$125$, and, thus, $TR = \$31,250$.

d. The midpoint of the demand curve is at $Q = 250$, $P = \$125$. Above that point, demand is elastic, and below that point, demand is inelastic.

6. Demand is inelastic (and, thus, revenues will rise if you increase the price and fall if you lower it). Your good is a normal good and is income inelastic (or a necessity good). The related good is a substitute because a rise in the price of the other good causes an increase in demand for your product; the goods are fairly good substitutes as the demand for your product is elastic with respect to the price of the other good.

Application Questions

2. We can use the facts in the question to make inferences about the price elasticity of demand for walk-up, unrestricted business airfares.

a. On the Cleveland–Los Angeles route, the decrease in fare resulted in about the same revenue as the higher fare. This implies a consumer price elasticity of demand around -1.00. At unit elasticity, any change in price results in no change in total revenue. On the Cleveland–Houston route, the decrease in price resulted in less revenue, but greater market share. Demand was inelastic on this route because quantity demanded increased as the price was lowered, but total revenue decreased. Demand was price elastic on the Houston–Oakland route because the lower airfares resulted in increased total revenue for Continental on this route.

b. Consumer behavior differs on the three routes, but is also different from prior expectations. As discussed in the chapter, the airlines typically assumed that demand for business travel was inelastic, while demand for leisure travel was elastic. Under this assumption, airline companies did not decrease business fares because they believed they would have lost revenue in doing so.

c. Many businesses have gotten tired of paying the high, unrestricted fares for their business travelers. Employees began searching for lower restricted fares that would meet their schedules or using videoconferencing or driving as a substitute for air travel. The terrorist attacks on September 11, 2001, also had a major impact on the airline industry, with many employees refusing to fly in the months following the attacks and with business only slowly recovering in the following years. All of these factors resulted in major changes in business traveler behavior and a probable increase in their price elasticity of demand. The above market tests show that business demand is actually price elastic in certain markets.

4. A price elasticity of demand for urban transit between -0.1 and -0.6 means that demand is inelastic for transit users. Thus, increased fares will result in higher revenue for local governments and transit authorities. This is the economic argument for raising transit fares. However, there may be political constraints on raising fares. The inelastic demand may result from the low income levels and lack of automobiles and other substitute forms of travel of transit riders. Voters may perceive increased fares as placing an unfair burden on these low-income riders. Transit authorities often obtain voter approval for new transit systems by promising not to raise fares for a certain number of years. Governmental decisions are typically based on many factors other than economic arguments.

6. The price elasticity of demand for the product of an individual firm is typically greater than the price elasticity for the product overall because the individual firm competes with all the other producers of the same product. There are more substitutes for the product of an individual firm than for the product overall. This outcome is most clearly shown in Table 3.7 for agricultural products. The demand for many of the products in the table is inelastic for the product overall, while the table shows a price elasticity of demand for individual producers ranging from -500 to $-21,000$ (extremely elastic). The price elasticity of demand for individual physicians is also much larger than that for medical or dental care as a commodity. The demand for dental care may be inelastic, while the demand for care from any given dentist is price elastic, given the number of other dentists providing similar care.

8. The U.S. Postal Service raised Priority Mail rates by 16 percent, and Bear Creek Corporation reduced its package shipping by 15 to 20 percent. The implied price elasticity of demand ($\%\Delta Q/\%\Delta P$) ranges from $-15/16 = -0.94$ to $-20/16 = -1.25$. If this response is typical for all Postal Service

customers, revenues will either remain approximately the same or decrease, given that the price elasticity of demand is approximately unitary or price elastic. Particularly if the demand is elastic, the Postal Service will not be able to reduce its deficit by this strategy because revenues will decrease. Consumers will use Federal Express or UPS instead of the Postal Service to ship their packages.

Chapter 4

Technical Questions

2. The plotted data are simply price and quantity combinations for each of the 10 years. Although the data appear to indicate a downward sloping demand curve for potatoes, many factors other than the price of potatoes changed over this period. These factors included consumer incomes, the prices of other vegetables that could be substituted for potatoes, the introduction of packaged dried potatoes in grocery stores, and the changing tastes for french fries at fast-food outlets. Thus, each data point is probably on a separate demand curve for that year, and the data points in the figure result from shifts in those demand curves. To derive a demand curve from this time-series data, a multiple regression analysis should be run that includes other variables, such as income and the prices of substitute goods. Once these other variables are held constant statistically, the regression results can be used to plot the relevant demand curve showing the relationship between price and quantity demanded, all else held constant.

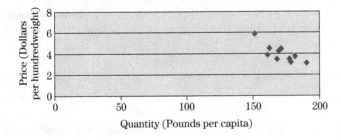

Application Questions

2. Test marketing and price experiments can be established so that consumer characteristics in addition to price, such as income and other demographics, can be varied in the different settings. Thus, consumer reaction to price can be measured while holding income constant in one setting and changing it to another level in a different setting. Individuals of various backgrounds can be specifically selected for different focus groups and laboratory experiments. Thus, test marketing, price experiments, focus groups, and laboratory experiments can be constructed to vary one characteristic (usually price), while holding other factors constant. Multiple regression analysis accomplishes this same task statistically. When variables are entered into a multiple regression analysis equation, their effects are statistically held constant. Each estimated coefficient shows the effect on the dependent variable of a one-unit change in an independent variable, holding the values of all other variables in the equation constant.

4. The estimating equation included variables measuring the monetary price of the cars as well as variables measuring the search costs of subsequent visits to a dealer and whether a consumer repurchases the same brand of vehicle (which lowers search costs). Because these variables, as well as the monetary price variable, were statistically significant in the analysis, they indicate that consumers do consider the full price of purchasing an automobile and not just the monetary price.

Chapter 5

Technical Questions

2. a.

Capital (K)	Labor (L)	Total Product (TP)	Average Product (AP)	Marginal Product (MP)
10	0	0	—	—
10	1	25	25	25
10	2	100	50	75
10	3	220	73	120
10	4	303	76	83
10	5	357	71	54
10	6	392	65	35
10	7	414	59	22
10	8	424	53	10
10	9	428	48	4
10	10	429	43	1

b.

TP

TP

MP_L, AP_L

AP_L

MP_L

b.

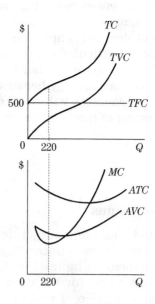

c. After the third worker (or output of 220), there are diminishing marginal returns.
d. Average product is maximized at an output level of 303.

4. a. Accounting profit is total revenue less explicit costs = $150,000 − [25,000 + 12,000 + 30,000 + 20,000] = $150,000 − 87,000 = $63,000.
   b. Economic profit = total revenue − explicit costs − implicit costs = $150,000 − 87,000 − 50,000 − 5,000 = $8,000.

6. a.

K	L	MP/TP	TFC	TVC	TC	AFC	AVC	ATC	MC
10	0	—/0	500	0	500	—	—	—	—
10	1	25/25	500	20	520	20	0.80	20.80	0.80
10	2	75/100	500	40	540	5	0.40	5.40	0.27
10	3	120/220	500	60	560	2.27	0.27	2.54	0.17
10	4	83/303	500	80	580	1.65	0.26	1.91	0.24
10	5	54/357	500	100	600	1.40	0.28	1.68	0.37
10	6	35/392	500	120	620	1.28	0.31	1.59	0.57
10	7	22/414	500	140	640	1.21	0.34	1.55	0.91
10	8	10/424	500	160	660	1.18	0.38	1.56	2.00
10	9	4/428	500	180	680	1.17	0.42	1.59	5.00
10	10	1/429	500	200	700	1.16	0.47	1.63	20.00

c. Average total cost is minimized at an output level of approximately 414 (or average total cost of $1.55). Average variable cost is minimized at an output level of approximately 303 (or average variable cost of $0.26).

8. An improvement in technology lowers (shifts rightward) marginal cost and all other cost curves (except fixed cost, which is not affected by marginal product). The minimum points on the average total and average variable cost curves will be at higher outputs and lower costs.

Application Questions

2. a. There will be diminishing returns in the drug manufacturing process because much of the testing for quality, gauging of dryness, and testing for bacterial contamination is done by hand. There are bottlenecks in terms of the fixed inputs—batches of chemicals that must be dried, the use of microscopes to count organisms. Adding more workers to the production process without increasing the fixed inputs will result in diminishing returns.
   b. The FDA allowed firms to maintain these types of production processes to maintain the quality and safety of the drugs. Pursuing this goal made the pharmaceutical companies very hesitant to

change the production process and adopt new technologies because any change would require new FDA approval. The time and paperwork involved would probably put the company at a competitive disadvantage.

4. A change in a firm's total fixed costs of production will shift its average total cost (*ATC*) curve

because $ATC = AFC + AVC$ and $AFC = TFC/Q$. Thus, an increase in total fixed cost will shift up the average total cost curve. Fixed costs do not influence the marginal costs of production. $MC = \Delta TC/\Delta Q = \Delta TVC/\Delta Q$. Marginal cost is influenced only by the variable costs, as fixed costs, by definition, do not change.

Chapter 6

Technical Questions

2.

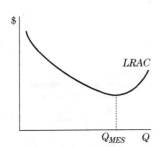

4 a. The minimum efficient scale should be at a high level of output.

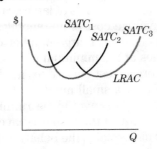

b. The minimum efficient scale should be at a low level of output.

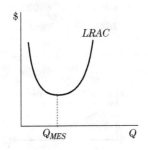

6. a.

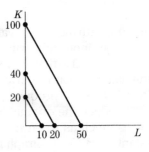

b.

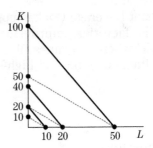

8. a. In the short run, with fixed capital, the firm cannot change its input mix because capital is fixed. Thus, the firm must employ exactly the same inputs if it wishes to produce the same quantity of output. However, the total cost of production will increase (new isocost line).

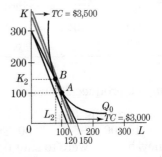

b. The firm's short-run cost curves will increase (shift leftward).

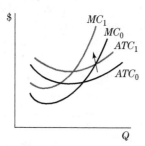

c. In the long run, with all factors variable, the firm will switch to an input mix with less labor and more capital. (Note also that the rise in costs may reduce the quantity that the firm wishes to produce.) The total cost of production will increase in order to produce the original level of output, but not by as much as when the input mix was held constant (part a). See graph for part a.

Application Questions

2. Sunny Delight Beverage Co. has upgraded five of its U.S. juice factories. Improvements include a "filler room" where machines fill four flavors of juice simultaneously on one high-speed line. In the past, flavors were filled on separate lines with each line requiring its own operator. The new combined line requires only two people to operate it. The company also plans to use automated vehicles to replace the current fleet of forklifts and drivers. The German company Stihl has opened a Virginia Beach factory for making chain-saw guide bars that uses 120 robots that run around the clock with only seven workers on each shift.[2]

4 Economies of scale suggest that large-scale production is cheaper than small-scale production or that the long-run average cost curve slopes downward. However, this large-scale production is cheaper only if a large amount of output is produced and sold. The huge fixed costs of large-scale production lower the average cost of automobiles only if they are spread out over a large number of autos. The plant that lies at the minimum point of a U-shaped long-run average cost curve does not have the lowest costs if only a small number of autos are produced. Automakers would be running plants at unprofitable rates if they did not have a large market share. This explains the behavior in the quote.

[2]See Timothy Aeppel, "Man vs. Machine, a Jobless Recovery," *Wall Street Journal (Online)* January 17, 2012.

Chapter 7

Technical Questions

2. a.

Number of Worker Hours	Output (Q)	Fixed Cost (TFC)	Variable Cost (TVC)	Total Cost (TC)	Marginal Cost (MC)	Average Variable Cost (AVC)	Average Total Cost (ATC)
0	0	15,000	0	15,000	—	—	—
25	100	15,000	575	15,575	5.75	5.75	155.75
50	150	15,000	900	15,900	6.50	6.00	106.00
75	175	15,000	1,100	16,100	8.00	6.28	92.00
100	195	15,000	1,275	16,275	8.75	6.53	83.46
125	205	15,000	1,400	16,400	12.50	6.82	80.00
150	210	15,000	1,500	16,500	20.00	7.14	78.57
175	212	15,000	1,585	16,585	42.50	7.47	78.23

b. The firm will produce 205 units.

c. The firm's profit is $[(12.50)(205)] - 16,400 = 2,562.50 - 16,400 = -\$13,837.50$. The firm is losing money, but if it were to shut down, it would lose $15,000 (its fixed costs); thus, the loss-minimizing choice is to stay in business in the short run (as $P > AVC$).

d.

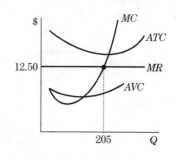

4. Supply curve S_2 is more elastic than supply curve S_1. We can infer this because, for a given change in price, the change in quantity supplied is far greater on supply curve S_2 (in other words, a given percentage change in price leads to a larger percentage change in quantity supplied).

6. a. The decrease in demand causes the price to fall to P_2. Thus, marginal revenue falls for the firms, and they will produce less and make a loss (as $P < ATC$).

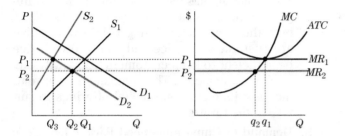

   b. Losses will induce firms to exit the industry, given enough time. Thus, industry supply will decrease, causing equilibrium price to rise and quantity to fall. This continues until the price rises to the original price, at which firms just break even, and there is no further incentive for exit. There will be fewer firms in the new long-run equilibrium, but each firm will produce the original quantity (q_1) and make zero economic profit.

Application Questions

2. a. The greater number of uses for cranberries increases the demand for the product, resulting in higher prices and greater profitability for cranberry producers.

   b. The factors creating a smaller crop of cranberries cause the supply curve to shift to the left, resulting in higher prices. We can infer from the statement that the demand for cranberries is probably inelastic, resulting in higher total revenue with the higher prices. Thus, profits decline by a smaller percent than the decrease in cranberry production.

   c. All of these health-related factors associated with consuming cranberries will increase the demand for the product, resulting in higher prices and profitability.

   d. Ocean Spray has been using the health benefits of cranberries to develop and promote a wider variety of cranberry drinks.

4. Overall, the statement is false. Information about a perfectly competitive firm's fixed costs is not needed to determine the profit-maximizing level of output. Profit maximization occurs at that level of output where marginal revenue equals marginal cost. In perfect competition, this is also the point where price equals marginal cost. Because marginal cost shows the change in total cost as output changes, it does not incorporate fixed costs. Fixed costs are relevant to determining the level of profit earned at that level of output. The relationship between price and average total cost determines whether profits are positive, zero, or negative. Because $ATC = AFC + AVC$, fixed costs are relevant for determining the level of profit.

Chapter 8

Technical Questions

2.

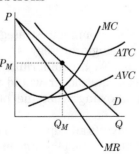

The ATC curve must be above the demand curve at all points.

4.

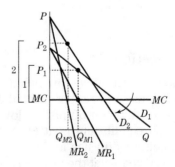

For simplicity, assume that marginal cost is constant. Persuasive advertising makes demand more inelastic (shifts from demand curve D_1 to D_2), and as elasticity decreases, the markup over marginal cost (and, thus, market power) is greater. However, advertising also increases fixed costs, and, thus, whether profit rises depends on the effectiveness of advertising relative to its cost.

6. a. The three-firm concentration ratio for Industry C is 75, whereas it is 95 for Industry D. In both industries, the four-firm concentration ratio is 100 because these firms account for the entire market.

  b. The HHI in Industry C is 2,500. The HHI for Industry D is 6,550.

  c. Although the four-firm concentration ratios are the same, the three-firm ratios and the HHI show that Industry D would be of more concern to antitrust authorities. The HHI is far higher due to the presence of one very large firm, which undoubtedly has more market power than any of the four equally sized firms in the other industry. Three firms control 95 percent of the market for Industry D and only 75 percent for Industry C.

8. Effective advertising may increase demand and make it more inelastic. But it also increases costs. Thus, advertising may lengthen the period during which the firm is able to make a positive profit, but with demand decreasing due to the entry of other firms and costs rising, in the long run, profits must be zero.

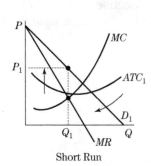

Short Run

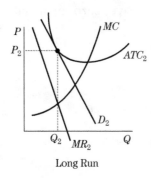

Long Run

Application Questions

2. a. As with Eastman Kodak Co. in the opening case of the chapter, American Greetings Corp. has faced declining market power from changing consumer preferences for new technology. Many customers who sent physical holiday greeting cards in the past are now using the Internet and mobile phones to express their feelings. This change has caused a long-term decline in the greeting card industry.

  b. The company has used discount pricing strategies to increase sales of greeting cards. However, the question for managers is how sensitive are customers to price and will a lower price be sufficient to keep customers from switching to electronic media. The company may have to increase its e-card and digital offerings to survive in the future.

4. a. Demand in China influenced Parker Pen Co.'s strategies through both income and consumer preferences variables. Household income in China had increased, which gave consumers greater ability to pay for both inexpensive and expensive pens. China's gift-giving culture created a demand for expensive pens as a status symbol. The latter factor, in particular, differed from consumer behavior in North America and Europe where many persons no longer used pens of any form.

  b. Parker already faces competition in the expensive-pen market, which will increase if profits continue to grow. This could erode the company's market power and force it to develop new strategies to adapt to the Chinese market.

Chapter 9

Technical Questions

2. a. The dominant strategy for each firm is to price low (because no matter what the other firm does, you are better off pricing low).

  b. The Nash equilibrium is at (100, 100). At this point, neither firm has an incentive to change strategy, given what the other firm is doing.

  c. The firms would be collectively better off pricing high, but that is not an equilibrium. They are collectively worse off pricing low, and that is the only equilibrium of the game.

4. a. There is no dominant strategy in this game because no single strategy is better in all cases.

  b. There is no Nash equilibrium in this game. In every case, one player would want to change strategy, knowing what the other player had chosen.

  c. All of the payoffs add up to zero (or to a constant sum). Whatever one player gains, the other loses, and, thus, there is no way for everyone to win.

6. a. If the entrant has already come in, the monopolist gets 20 if he prices high and five if he prices

low. It is not rational to price low once the entrant is in, and, thus, it is not a credible threat.

b. The Nash equilibrium is (20, 10), where the entrant comes in and the monopolist prices are high.

c. The monopolist would have to make it more desirable to price low, even if the entrant comes in, perhaps by building a large plant or contracting to supply large amounts of output.

8. a. The total marginal cost curve is the horizontal sum of the two marginal costs.

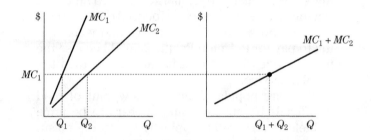

b.

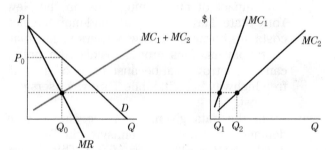

c. If each firm views the cartel price as fixed, then MR (for the firm) $> MC$, and each firm wishes to expand output. (Of course, if they do, the price must fall.)

Application Questions

2. Home Depot and Lowe's are the leaders in the home improvement industry, so their behavior is interdependent. Each company has developed similar strategies to compete in the flowering plant business, which is an important source of revenue each year. They both try to obtain exclusive rights to sell the most popular plant varieties to limit the market power of their rival. Each company uses a similar strategy to gather information on consumer preferences for various blooms.

4. Google and Amazon invaded each other's markets to increase their market power. Both companies are so large that their behaviors are interdependent. Google attempted to challenge Amazon's fast-shipping programs, while Amazon increased its product searches and online advertising. Both companies were responding to consumer demand for online purchases combined with fast and low-cost shipping.

6. Oligopoly theory predicts that cartels are inherently unstable. This result was clearly illustrated in the European laundry detergent price-fixing case. The companies engaged in all types of secret behavior to fix prices. However, monitoring the agreements became extremely difficult over time. As soon as one company decided to cheat, others quickly followed with the same behavior.

Chapter 10

Technical Questions

2. a. $m = -1/[1 + (-15)] = 1/14$ or 7%
   b. $m = -1/[1 + (-8)] = 1/7$ or 14%
   c. $m = -1/[1 + (-3)] = 1/2$ or 50%

4. a. $Q = 6 - P$ or $P = 6 - Q$,
   $MR = 6 - 2Q$,
   $MC = AC = 1$
   $MR = MC$
   $6 - 2Q = 1$
   $Q = 2.50$
   $P = \$3.50$
   $\pi = TR - TC = (\$3.50)(2.50) - (1)(2.50)$
   $= \$8.75 - 2.50 = \$6.25$

b. If $P = MC = AC = 1$, $Q = 5$ slices of pizza. The firm earns nothing on these slices because price equals AC. However, the firm can charge a fixed price for this option up to the maximum amount of the consumer surplus at $P = 1$. This is the area of the triangle under the demand curve and above $P = 1$. Consumer surplus is $(0.5)(5)(6-1) = (0.5)(5)(5) = \$12.50$. If the firm charges a fixed price greater than $\$6.25$, but less than $\$12.50$, it will increase its profit with this two-part pricing strategy.

6. In the business market, the markup (over marginal cost) will be $-1/[1 + (-2)] = 100\%$. In the vacation market, the markup will be $-1/[1 + (-5)] = 25\%$. Thus, the ratio of weekday to weekend prices will be 100/25, or 4. Weekday prices will be four times higher than weekend prices.

8.

	Sports Package	Kids Package
Parents	10	50
Sports fans	50	10
Generalists	40	40

a. With the package option of any one package for $50 or the combined bundled package for $70, parents will buy the Kids package, sports fans will buy the Sports package, and generalists will buy both. (Note that generalists will not be willing to buy either package separately.)

b. The level of profits depends, in general, on the number in each group and the value that each group places on each package, but this type of pricing exploits the value that certain consumers place on particular items and, at the same time, attracts more revenue by inducing others (the generalists) to buy the products, too.

Application Questions

2. a. Timken's strategy changed as a result of the recession in 2001 and the slow recovery thereafter, as well as of the increase in imports. More customers also began to demand the bundled products, so Timken responded in order to maintain their market position.

b. The chapter discussion showed how bundling can increase a firm's revenues if it attracts customers who would not have purchased the individual components. Bundling is also successful if it reduces the dispersion in willingness to pay. The case presented additional factors, such as the change in production

methods and the education of customers, necessary to make bundling a successful strategy. The case also showed that Timken engaged in political action as part of its competitive strategy.

4. Both of these cases are examples of versioning, developing specific products to meet the needs of different customers. In the Wildeck case, the "lite" version of the product attracted price-conscious customers who might have purchased it from its competitor. However, many of these customers ended up purchasing the original product, helping Wildeck maintain its market share. The Union Pacific "blue streak" service focused on those customers who wanted faster service and were willing to pay for it. Union Pacific gained because the new service did not cost it much more than the regular service.

6. a. Tolls are popular from the viewpoint of road officials because demand appears to be price inelastic. There are typically few good substitutes for travel on interstate toll roads. As the toll increases, total revenue to the operating agency increases also.

b. The impact of maintaining tolls on the New York State Thruway is that road-maintenance costs are borne by Thruway users rather than all taxpayers. This cross-subsidization policy can be controversial because users of the toll-free highway benefit, while Thruway users pay the cost.

c. From the data given, the price elasticity of demand for use of the Pennsylvania Turnpike is $\%\Delta Q/\%\Delta P = -1\%/43\% = -0.023$. This is very inelastic demand.

Chapter 11

Technical Questions

2. Of the three choices given, only the purchase of a new house is considered to be an investment when calculating GDP. Investment refers to business purchases of tangible capital goods and software; all construction purchases, both residential and nonresidential; and changes in inventories in the national income accounts. The purchase of an automobile for private, nonbusiness use is treated as consumption spending. The purchase of corporate bonds represents the transfer of ownership of existing assets.

4. U.S. GDP measures the total market value of all final goods and services produced in the economy

in one year. Imports are subtracted from exports when calculating GDP because they do not entail production in the United States.

6. Calculations are shown in Table 11.E1. Nominal GDP and real GDP are the same ($50) in the 2010 base year. Case 1 shows an increase in prices with no increase in quantities. Nominal GDP increase to $95, while real GDP is constant at $50. Case 2 shows an increase in quantities with no change in prices. Both real GDP and nominal GDP increase to $95. Case 3 shows an increase in both prices and quantities. Both real GDP and nominal GDP increase, although the increase in nominal GDP is much greater.

TABLE 11.E1 Nominal Versus Real GDP

YEAR	COFFEE (CUPS)		MILK (GALLONS)		GDP
2010	Price	Quantity	Price	Quantity	
	$1.00	10	$2.00	20	
Expenditure	$10		$40		$50 (nominal)
					$50 (real)
2011 (Case 1)	Price	Quantity	Price	Quantity	
	$1.50	10	$4.00	20	
Expenditure	$15		$80		$95 (nominal)
					$50 (real)
2011 (Case 2)	Price	Quantity	Price	Quantity	
	$1.00	15	$2.00	40	
Expenditure	$15		$80		$95 (nominal)
					$95 (real)
2011 (Case 3)	Price	Quantity	Price	Quantity	
	$1.50	15	$4.00	40	
Expenditure	$22.50		$160		$182.50 (nominal)
					$95 (real)

Application Questions

2. The changes are shown in the following table:

Variable (billions $)	1970	1980	1990	2000	2010
Real GDP	$4,266.3	$5,834.0	$8,027.1	$11,216.4	$13,088.0
Consumption	$2,738.9 (64.2%)	$3,764.5 (64.5%)	$5,313.7 (66.2%)	$7,604.6 (67.8%)	$9,220.9 (70.5%)
Investment	$473.4 (11.1%)	$715.2 (12.3%)	$989.9 (12.3%)	$1,963.1 (17.5%)	$1,714.9 (13.1%)
Government	$1,233.7 (28.9%)	$1,358.8 (23.3%)	$1,864.0 (23.2%)	$2,097.8 (18.7%)	$2,556.8 (19.5%)
Exports	$175.3 (4.1%)	$351.4 (6.0%)	$599.7 (7.5%)	$1,187.4 (10.6%)	$1,663.2 (12.7%)
Imports	$236.4 (5.5%)	$344.5 (5.9%)	$672.6 (8.4%)	$1,638.7 (14.6%)	$2,085.0 (15.9%)

The percentage change in real GDP over each decade is:

1970–1980	36.7%
1980–1990	37.6%
1990–2000	39.7%
2000–2010	16.7%

Consumption spending has remained roughly constant over the 40-year period, varying from 64 to 70 percent of GDP. Investment spending increased to 17 percent of GDP in 1990 but then fell back to 13 percent in 2010, given the effect of the recession. Government spending was a smaller percent of GDP in 2010 than in 1970, 1980, and 1990. Export and import spending have become larger percentages of GDP over the period.

4. Advance estimates of GDP are fairly reliable. Studies have shown that initial estimates of real GDP successfully indicated the direction of change in GDP approximately 98 percent of the time; the direction of change in major GDP components about 88 percent of the time; whether GDP was accelerating or decelerating 75 percent of the time; and whether GDP growth was above, near, or below trend 80 percent of the time. The mean revision between the advance estimate and the latest estimate was only 0.4 percentage point over the 1983–2006 period.[3]

[3]See J. Steven Landefeld, Eugene P. Seskin, and Barbara M. Fraumeni, "Taking the Pulse of the Economy: Measuring GDP," *Journal of Economic Perspectives* 22 (Spring 2008): 193–216; Dennis J. Fixler and Bruce T. Grimm, "The Reliability of the GDP and GDI Estimates," *Survey of Current Business* 88 (2008): 16–32; U.S. Department of Commerce, Bureau of Economic Analysis, *Concepts and Methods of the U.S. National Income and Product Accounts* (Chapters 1–9), November 2011. Available at http://www.bea.gov/methodologies/index.htm#na.

6. The following table shows the labor force data: The percent of the population in the labor force has increased from 60 percent in 1969 to more than 66 percent in 1992 and later years. The unemployment rate was very low during the booming periods of the late 1960s and the late 1990s. It increased substantially during the recessions of 1982 and 1991. The "jobless recovery" from the 2001 recession is evidenced by the relatively high unemployment rate in 2003. Although the 2007 figures had not yet shown the impact of the slowing economic activity in 2007 and 2008, the impact of the recession from 2007 to 2009 is shown in the 8.9 percent unemployment rate in 2011.

8. The article should focus either on changes in taxes and government spending (fiscal policy) or on changes in the money supply in order to influence interest rates (monetary policy). The minutes and press releases issued following meetings of the Federal Open Market Committee contain a clear statement of the goals of price stability, full employment, and adequate economic growth and the Fed's assessment of future economic conditions.

	Civilian Noninstitutional Population (thousands)	Civilian Labor Force (thousands) (% of population)	Number Employed (thousands)	Number Unemployed (thousands)	Unemployment Rate (%)
1969	134,355	80,734 (60.1)	77,902	2,832	3.5
1982	172,271	110,204 (64.0)	99,526	10,678	9.7
1992	192,805	128,105 (66.4)	118,492	9,613	7.5
2000	212,577	142,583 (67.1)	136,891	5,692	4.0
2003	221,168	146,510 (66.2)	137,736	8,774	6.0
2007	231,867	153,124 (66.0)	146,047	7,078	4.6
2011	239,618	153,617 (64.1)	139,869	13,747	8.9

Chapter 12

Technical Questions

2. The currency exchange rate (R) is defined as the number of units of foreign currency per dollar. As R increases, U.S. imports become cheaper and exports become more expensive, so that import spending increases and export spending decreases. The opposite happens when R decreases. U.S. imports become more expensive and exports become cheaper, so that import spending decreases and export spending increases.

4. a. False. The multiplier measures the change in real income that results from a change in autonomous expenditure. The effect of an initial change in autonomous expenditure is multiplied because the expenditure becomes an additional round of income, of which households spend a certain amount, depending on the marginal propensity to consume. This expenditure generates subsequent declining rounds of income, of which households spend a fraction. The size of the multiplier depends on the marginal propensities to consume, invest, and import.

b. False. An increase in government expenditure (G) represents an injection into the circular flow, or expansionary fiscal policy. This is an increase in autonomous expenditure that causes the aggregate expenditure function to shift up. An increase in taxes (T) represents a leakage out of the circular flow and causes a downward shift of the aggregate expenditure function.

c. From the perspective of the national income accounts, real income always equals real expenditure, given the definition of the circular flow. We can measure economic activity either by the expenditure/output approach or by the income/earnings approach. This measurement identity does not mean that the economy is always in equilibrium. Equilibrium is achieved when the desired aggregate expenditure just equals the level of income and output produced and there are no unplanned inventory changes. If the economy is in disequilibrium and there are unplanned inventory changes, the accounting identity between income and expenditure still holds because inventory changes are counted as investment.

6. $C = 800 + 0.8(Y - T_P), I = 200, G = T_P = 200,$
$X = M = 0$

a. $Y = C + I + G$

$Y = 800 + 0.8(Y - 200) + 200 + 200$

$Y = 800 + 0.8Y - 160 + 400$

$Y = 1{,}040 + 0.8Y$

$0.2Y = 1{,}040$

$Y = 5{,}200$

b. $G = 300$

$Y = 1{,}140 + 0.8Y$

$0.2Y = 1{,}140$

$Y = 5{,}700$

Y increased by 500, while G increased by 100, so $m = 5$.

$m = 1/(1 - MPC) = 1/(1 - 0.8) = 1/(0.2) = 5$

c. $Y = 800 + 0.8(Y - 300) + 200 + 300$

$Y = 800 + 0.8Y - 240 + 500$

$Y = 1{,}060 + 0.8Y$

$0.2Y = 1{,}060$

$Y = 5{,}300$

Y increases by 100, so the equilibrium level of income increases even though $\Delta G = \Delta T_P$.

Application Questions

2. a. A greater sensitivity of interest-related consumption and investment expenditure to changes in the interest rate would make the IRE function flatter and result in a larger amount of interest-related expenditure for a given change in the interest rate. This would result in a larger change in equilibrium income.

b. A larger multiplier in the aggregate expenditure model would result in a higher level of equilibrium income for any given increase in interest-related expenditure.

4. A recession is the falling phase of a business cycle, in which the direction of a series of economic indicators turns downward (Chapter 11). Real GDP typically falls for at least two quarters. The recession of 2001 caused a lack of consumer demand for many businesses, resulting in declining profits and employee layoffs. The fact that the dollar remained strong did not provide any relief for businesses producing in the United States and competing with foreign companies. The strong dollar decreased the price of U.S. imports and increased the price of exports. U.S. manufacturers had to look to other solutions, such as developing new methods to produce and sell their products, in order to counter the negative macroeconomic trends.

6. Check articles in the *Wall Street Journal* and other business publications and the web pages for the Bureau of Economic Analysis (www.bea.gov), the Bureau of Labor Statistics (www.bls.gov), and the Board of Governors of the Federal Reserve System (www.federalreserve.gov)

Chapter 13

Technical Questions

2. A fractional reserve banking system is one in which banks are required to keep only a fraction of their deposits as reserves in the bank or on deposit with the Federal Reserve. This system allows them to use the excess reserves to make loans, which provide income to the bank. If these loans are redeposited in the banking system, the

overall money supply is expanded. The size of the expansion relates to the size of the reserve requirement. The central bank, or Federal Reserve, influences the amount of reserves in the system, which changes the size of the money supply and prevailing interest rates.

4. The three tools are open market operations, the reserve requirement, and the discount rate. Open market operations, the most important tool, are the buying and selling of government securities, which influences the amount of reserves in the banking system and the federal funds rate that banks charge each other to borrow reserves. With expansionary monetary policy, the Federal Reserve buys securities, which increases the amount of reserves in the system and drives down the federal funds rates. Other short-term interest rates follow the federal funds rate. This stimulates interest-related consumption and investment expenditure and increases real income. Open market operations are the most flexible tool of monetary policy because they can be used on a daily basis. The Fed can also change the reserve requirement, regulating how much of their deposits banks must hold as reserves, and the discount rate, the rate the Fed charges banks to borrow reserves from the Fed. These are less-flexible tools that are not changed as frequently; they are used more for their announcement effects than as major tools of monetary policy.

6. a. True. If the real quantity of money demanded is greater than the real quantity of money supplied, individuals want to hold more of their assets in the form of money instead of bonds. They sell bonds to obtain money, which drives the price of bonds down and the interest rate up. As the interest rate rises, households want to hold less money, and equilibrium in the money market is obtained at a higher interest rate. When the quantity of money demanded exceeds the quantity of money supplied, equilibrium is reached only at a higher interest rate.

b. False. The central bank, or the Federal Reserve, is the institution that controls the money supply and influences interest rates in the United States. The Federal Reserve is not part of the federal government (Congress and the administration). It was designed to be insulated from the political system in this country. The monetary policy of the Federal Reserve is used more than the fiscal policy of the federal government (taxes and expenditure) because it is a more flexible tool that can better deal with changing economic conditions.

c. False. A decrease in the reserve requirement increases the money supply because banks have more excess reserves to loan out. These excess reserves create further deposits, a fraction of which can also be loaned out. If the reserve requirement is 0.2, the simple deposit multiplier is $1/0.2 = 5$. If the reserve requirement decreases to 0.1, the simple deposit multiplier becomes $1/0.1 = 10$. This change results in a greater expansion of the money supply.

d. False. This statement is closer to a description of the interest-related expenditure and the aggregate expenditure functions that show the relationship between the interest rate and spending on real goods and services (Chapter 12). The real money demand curve shows the quantity of money balances individuals wish to hold at different interest rates.

e. True/false. An increase in the nominal money supply by the Federal Reserve shifts the real money supply curve to the right. This change results in an increase in the real money supply. An increase in the price level causes a decrease in the real money supply, which shifts the real money supply curve to the left.

Application Questions

2. The statements that the FOMC makes after its meetings are becoming increasingly important indicators of future changes in monetary policy. Investors and forecasters analyze the wording of the statements to detect even subtle changes in policy. The "Parsing the Fed" feature for the August 1, 2012 FOMC press release noted that the statement was largely unchanged from the press release for the June 2012 meeting. The biggest change was that the August statement said that the Fed "will provide additional accommodation as needed" compared to the June statement where it said that it was "prepared" to take further action. See Phil Izzo, "Parsing the Fed: How the Statement Changed," *Wall Street Journal (Online)*, August 1, 2012.

4. The minutes provide a detailed account of the factors influencing FOMC decisions.

Chapter 14

Technical Questions

2. a. An increase in personal taxes shifts the aggregate expenditure function down and the aggregate demand curve to the left.

   b. An increase in expected profits and business confidence shifts the aggregate expenditure function up and the aggregate demand curve to the right.

   c. A decrease in the level of foreign GDP or real income shifts the aggregate expenditure function down and the aggregate demand curve to the left.

   d. A decrease in the nominal money supply by the Federal Reserve causes a decrease in the real money supply, which increases interest rates and lowers interest-related consumption and investment expenditure. This causes a downward shift in the aggregate expenditure function and a leftward shift of the aggregate demand curve.

4. a. False. The short-run aggregate supply curve slopes upward as real income and output approach the economy's potential output. This upward sloping short-run aggregate supply curve occurs because firms' input costs rise when they have to bid resources away from competing uses, as most inputs are becoming fully employed. As input costs rise, firms charge higher prices for their products, and the absolute price level begins to increase. Firms will produce more real output only as the price level increases.

   b. False. The long-run aggregate supply curve can also shift over time if there are increases in the amount of inputs (labor, land, capital, and raw materials) in the economy and increases in technology and efficiency.

   c. True and false. A decrease in the nominal money supply by the Federal Reserve, all else held constant, does shift the aggregate demand (AD) curve to the left. This policy change causes the real money supply to decrease, resulting in a higher interest rate, which decreases interest-related expenditure and results in a lower equilibrium level of income at the same price level. An increase in the price level, all else held constant, results in an upward movement along a given AD curve. The increase in the price level decreases the real money supply, which results in a higher interest rate and a lower level of real income. This results in a movement along a given AD curve, as the nominal money supply is held constant and there is no change in Federal Reserve policy.

   d. True. The Keynesian portion of the short-run aggregate supply (SAS) curve is the horizontal portion. The assumption is that real output can change from increases or decreases in spending (aggregate demand) without the price level changing. This would be most relevant in a recessionary situation, where there is significant unemployment and excess capacity. Increases in aggregate demand could result in increases in real output because there would be little tendency for wages and prices to rise in this case.

   e. False. Stagflation occurs when there is an upward shift in the short-run aggregate supply (SAS) curve resulting from a supply shock, such as an increase in the price of oil. With a given aggregate demand (AD) curve, the resulting equilibrium is at a higher price level and a lower level of real output. The economy can both have inflation and be stagnating at a lower level of real output and employment.

6. With an upward sloping SAS curve, an increase in AD from expansionary fiscal policy results in both an increase in real income (Y) and an increase in the price level (P). There will be a smaller increase in real income than if the price level did not rise. This outcome occurs because the increase in the price level creates a smaller real money supply, which causes the interest rate to rise. This increase in the interest rate chokes off some interest-related spending, thereby increasing real income by a smaller amount.

Application Questions

2. Fiscal policy changes relate to decisions by the president and Congress on federal government spending and taxation. The president releases the proposed federal budget every January. Other fiscal policy changes may be proposed, such as the economic stimulus bill in February 2009. Monetary policy changes typically relate to

ongoing decisions by the Federal Open Market Committee and are discussed regularly in all business publications.

4. Economists continue to debate the size and duration of the productivity increases from the investment in information technology (IT) that occurred in the late 1990s. The consensus appears to be that investments in information technology played a lesser role in productivity increases after 2000 than they did in the 1990s. It is always difficult to measure productivity changes due to problems in measuring changes in the quality of many goods and services. It can also be difficult to determine whether productivity changes are transitory or more permanent. See the research of Robert J. Gordon, Stephen Oliner and Daniel Sichel, Erik Brynjolfsson, Dale Jorgenson, and Kevin Stiroh.

Chapter 15

Technical Questions

2. a. False. A trade deficit occurs when import spending exceeds export spending. There is a government budget deficit when the government spends more than it receives in tax revenue. The two deficits often move together because government deficit spending stimulates the economy, which increases import spending.

b. False. The equality of planned saving and investment determines equilibrium in a closed (no foreign sector), private (no government sector) economy. This is a balance of leakages and injections in the economy. In an open, mixed economy, equilibrium occurs when $I + G + X = S + T + M$. In this chapter, we rewrote this condition as follows: $(X - M) = (S - I) + (T - G)$. This condition implies that the trade balance must equal the level of private and public saving in the country.

c. False. An increase in interest rates in the rest of the world leads to a weaker dollar. U.S. investors supply dollars to the foreign exchange market to purchase euros and yen in order to make financial investments in those countries with the higher interest rates. The increased supply of dollars drives down the value of the dollar in foreign exchange markets.

d. True. Under a fixed exchange rate policy with global capital flows, a country loses control of its money supply to maintain that exchange rate. To fight a devaluation of its currency, a country's

central bank has to use its foreign exchange reserves to bolster the value of its currency. This typically results in a decreased domestic money supply and higher interest rates. Countries cannot usually make a credible commitment to this policy regardless of the consequences to the economy. Under a flexible exchange rate system, monetary policy is typically more effective than fiscal policy in increasing real GDP. Expansionary monetary policy increases real income, which increases import spending and lowers the exchange rate. This change has a further expansionary effect on real spending. Expansionary monetary policy also lowers domestic interest rates, which decreases the demand for domestic currency and lowers the exchange rate. While expansionary fiscal policy stimulates the economy and increases imports, which may lower the exchange rate, it also increases domestic interest rates, attracts financial capital, and increases the value of the currency. If this effect dominates (as it did in the late 1990s), the higher exchange rate will slow the growth in the economy.

4. If income in the United States grows faster than income in its major trading partners, U.S. imports will increase faster than exports. U.S. households and institutions will supply more dollars to the foreign exchange market to purchase those imports. The increase in the supply of dollars will drive the exchange rate down. If the economies of the trading partners begin to grow faster, that will increase the demand for U.S. exports, which will tend to drive up the demand for dollars and the currency exchange rate.

6. A change in the currency exchange rate (R) causes a movement along the demand curve for dollars. If R increases, imports become cheaper and exports more expensive. There is a smaller quantity of dollars demanded to purchase those exports, so the dollar demand curve slopes downward. The level of foreign income and the interest rate differential between the United States and the rest of the world cause the demand curve for dollars to shift. An increase in foreign income creates a greater demand for dollars at every exchange rate and shifts the demand curve to the right. If interest rates in the United States are higher than those in the rest of the world, there are higher capital inflows to the United States, creating an increased demand for dollars. The supply of dollars curve slopes upward. As the exchange rate increases, imports become cheaper. As import spending increases, the quantity of dollars supplied to the

market increases, so there is a larger quantity supplied at a higher exchange rate. The supply of dollars curve shifts to the right if U.S. income increases. This increases import spending, so more dollars are supplied to the foreign exchange market at every exchange rate. If interest rates are higher in the rest of the world than in the United States, the supply of dollars in the foreign exchange market also increases as U.S. households and institutions purchase those foreign financial investments. This also shifts the supply of dollars curve to the right.

Application Questions

2. The direct foreign investment statistics on the Bureau of Economic Analysis Web page can be broken down by country and area of the world and by industry sector in the United States. Students should find data on how this investment differs by these categories.

4. The value of the euro and the macro policies of the European Union countries are discussed in the *Wall Street Journal* and other current business publications.

Chapter 16

Technical Questions

2. The companies have matched price cuts, cooking styles, and menu innovations for many years. They all began competing on coffee strategies in 2008, and they have all had to consider whether to adapt to local tastes when expanding to emerging markets. Under threat of legislation and as a marketing strategy, the rivals have all begun posting calorie counts on their menus.

4. McDonald's mini-restaurants cost 30 percent less to build in 1991, but could handle 96 percent of the volume of a full-sized restaurant. This is an example of a decision based on incremental costs and revenues. The lower costs of these smaller units also opened up market niches in small towns and other areas that could not support traditional restaurants.

Application Questions

2. All of the fast-food chains increased the number of their outlets in emerging markets and expanded the use of drive-throughs and delivery. McDonald's had realized that there was a period of adjustment for the drive-through innovation in China. Both Dunkin Donuts and Starbucks planned to open restaurants in India, while Starbucks attempted to expand the coffee market in China. Unlike some of its competitors, Domino's Pizza planned to continue with its U.S. strategy of traditional pizza delivery in emerging markets.

4. McDonald's has focused on changing tastes and preferences by developing more healthy alternatives on its menus. It developed Happy Meals and in-store playgrounds to appeal to children. The company has tried to improve the quality of its service by hiring mystery shoppers to evaluate service, cleanliness, and food quality. McDonald's has developed different menus and restaurant designs in various countries around the world. More recently, the company increased the nutritional content of its Happy Meals and began posting calorie counts on its menus.

Glossary

Absolute price level: A measure of the overall level of prices in the economy using various indices to measure the prices of all goods and services.

Accounting profit: The difference between total revenue and total cost where cost includes only the explicit costs of production.

Adjusted R^2 statistic: The coefficient of determination adjusted for the number of degrees of freedom in the estimating equation.

Advertising elasticity of demand: The percentage change in the quantity demanded of a good relative to the percentage change in advertising dollars spent on that good, all other factors held constant.

Aggregate demand curve: The curve that shows alternative combinations of the price level (P) and real income (Y) that result in simultaneous equilibrium in both the real goods and the money markets.

Aggregate demand–aggregate supply equilibrium: The equilibrium level of real income and output and the price level in the economy that occur at the intersection of the aggregate demand and supply curves.

Aggregate expenditure: The sum of consumption, investment, government, and net export spending on the total amount of real output produced in an economy in a given period of time, which equals the income generated from producing and selling that output.

Aggregate expenditure function: The relationship between aggregate expenditure and income, holding all other variables constant.

Aggregate production function: The function that shows the quantity and quality of resources used in production, the efficiency with which resources are used, and the existing production technology for the entire economy.

Aggregate supply curve: The curve that shows the price level at which firms in the economy are willing to produce different levels of real goods and services and the resulting level of real income.

Antitrust laws: Legislation, beginning with the Sherman Act of 1890, that attempts to limit the market power of firms and to regulate how firms use their market power to compete with each other.

Arc price elasticity of demand: A measurement of the price elasticity of demand where the base quantity or price is calculated as the average value of the starting and ending quantities or prices.

Automatic stabilizers: Features of the U.S. federal government expenditure and taxation programs that tend to automatically slow the economy during times of high economic activity and boost the economy during periods of recession.

Autonomous consumption expenditures: Consumption expenditures that are determined by factors other than the level of real income in the economy.

Average fixed cost: The total fixed cost per unit of output.

Average product: The amount of output per unit of variable input.

Average revenue: Total revenue per unit of output. Average revenue equals the price of the product by definition.

Average revenue function: The functional relationship that shows the revenue per unit of output received by the producer at different levels of output.

Average total cost: The total cost per unit of output, which also equals average fixed cost plus average variable cost.

Average variable cost: The total variable cost per unit of output.

Balance of payments (BP) accounting system: A comprehensive measure of all economic activity between a country and the rest of the world.

Balance of payments issues: Issues related to the relative value of different countries' currencies and the flow of goods, services, and financial assets among countries.

Balance of trade: The relationship between a country's export and import spending, which can be positive if there is a trade surplus (exports exceed imports) or negative if there is a trade deficit (imports exceed exports).

Barriers to entry: The structural, legal, or regulatory characteristics of a firm and its market that keep other firms from producing the same or similar products at the same cost.

Barter system: A system in which goods and services are exchanged directly without a common unit of account.

Beige Book: A publication of the Federal Reserve System that includes information on current economic conditions gathered from the Federal Reserve banks' staff and interviews with business contacts, economists, market experts, and other sources.

Best practices: The production techniques adopted by the firms with the highest levels of productivity.

Budget surplus/deficit: The relationship between federal government revenue and expenditure with a surplus indicating revenue greater than expenditure and a deficit indicating revenue less than expenditure.

Bundling: Selling multiple products as a bundle where the price of the bundle is less than the sum of the prices of the individual products or where the bundle reduces the dispersion in willingness to pay.

Business cycles: The periodic increases and decreases in overall economic activity reflected in production, employment, profits, and prices.

Business fixed investment: Spending on the structures, equipment, and software that provide the industrial capacity to produce goods and services for all sectors of the economy.

Capacity utilization rates (*CURs*): The ratio of production to capacity calculated monthly for the manufacturing, mining, and electric and gas utilities industries and used as an indicator of business investment spending on structures and equipment.

Capital flows: The buying and selling of existing real and financial assets among countries.

Capital inflow (k_i): Borrowing from another country that occurs when the country has a trade deficit and its citizens sell real and financial assets to foreigners.

Capital outflow (k_o): A lending of a country's savings that occurs when the country has a trade surplus and its citizens purchase real and financial assets from abroad.

Capital-intensive method of production: A production process that uses large amounts of capital equipment relative to the other inputs to produce the firm's output.

Cartel: An organization of firms that agree to coordinate their behavior regarding pricing and output decisions in order to maximize profits for the organization.

Change in demand: The change in quantity purchased when one or more of the demand shifters change, pictured as a shift of the entire demand curve.

Change in quantity demanded: The change in quantity consumers purchase when the price of the good changes, all other factors held constant, pictured as a movement along a given demand curve.

Change in quantity supplied: The change in amount of a good supplied when the price of the good changes, all other factors held constant, pictured as a movement along a given supply curve.

Change in supply: The change in the amount of a good supplied when one or more of the supply shifters change, pictured as a shift of the entire supply curve.

Changes in business inventories: Changes in the amount of goods produced, but not sold in a given year.

Circular flow model: The macroeconomic model that portrays the level of economic activity as a flow of expenditures from consumers to firms, or producers, as consumers purchase goods and services produced by these firms. This flow then returns to consumers as income received from the production process.

Coefficient of determination (R^2): A measure of how the overall estimating equation fits the data, which shows the fraction of the variation in the dependent variable that is explained statistically by the variables included in the equation.

Coincident indicators: Economic variables, including employment, income, and business production statistics, that tend to move in tandem with the overall phases of the business cycle.

Compensation of employees: The wages and salaries and the fringe benefits paid by employers to employees.

Complementary goods: Two goods, X and Y, are complementary if an increase in the price of good Y causes consumers to *decrease* their demand for good X or if a decrease in the price of good Y

causes consumers to *increase* their demand for good X.

Concentration ratios: A measure of market power that focuses on the share of the market held by the X largest firms, where X typically equals four, six, or eight.

Confidence interval: The range of values in which we can be confident that the true coefficient actually lies with a given degree of probability, usually 95 percent.

Conjoint analysis: An approach to analyzing consumer behavior that asks consumers to rank and choose among different product attributes, including price, to reveal their valuation of these characteristics.

Consumer Confidence Index (CCI): An index, based on a mail survey of 5,000 households conducted by the Conference Board, that measures households' perceptions of general business conditions, available jobs in the households' local area, and expected personal family income in the coming six months.

Consumer Price Index (CPI): A measure of the combined price consumers pay for a fixed market basket of goods and services in a given period relative to the combined price of an identical basket of goods and services in a base period.

Consumer Sentiment Index (CSI): An index, based on a telephone survey of 500 households conducted by the University of Michigan, that measures households' attitudes regarding expected business conditions, personal financial conditions, and consumer confidence about purchasing furniture and major household appliances.

Consumer surplus: The difference between the total amount of money consumers are willing to pay for a product rather than do without and the amount they actually have to pay when a single price is charged for all units of the product.

Consumption function: The fundamental relationship in macroeconomics that assumes that household consumption spending depends primarily on the level of disposable income (net of taxes) in the economy, all other variables held constant.

Contractionary monetary policy: Federal Reserve policy to decrease the rate of growth of real GDP by decreasing the amount of bank reserves in the system and raising the federal funds and other interest rates.

Cooperative oligopoly models: Models of interdependent oligopoly behavior that assume that firms explicitly or implicitly cooperate with each other to achieve outcomes that benefit all the firms.

Core rate of inflation: A measure of absolute price changes that excludes changes in energy and food prices.

Corporate profits: The excess of revenues over costs for the incorporated business sector of the economy.

Cost function: A mathematical or graphic expression that shows the relationship between the cost of production and the level of output, all other factors held constant.

Cross-price elasticity of demand: The percentage change in the quantity demanded of a given good, X, relative to the percentage change in the price of good Y, all other factors held constant.

Cross-sectional data: Data collected on a sample of individuals with different characteristics at a specific point in time.

Crowding out: The decrease in consumption and investment interest-related spending that occurs when the interest rate rises as government spending increases.

Currency appreciation: One currency can be exchanged for more units of another currency or the value of R increases.

Currency depreciation: One currency can be exchanged for fewer units of another currency or the value of R decreases.

Currency exchange rate: The rate at which one nation's currency can be exchanged for that of another, which is determined in foreign exchange markets.

Current account: A measure of the current flows of goods, services, investment income, and unilateral transfers between a country and the rest of the world.

Deflation: A sustained decrease in the price level over time.

Degrees of freedom: The number of observations (n) minus the number of estimated coefficients (k) in a regression equation.

Demand: The functional relationship between the price of a good or service and the quantity demanded by consumers in a given time period, *all else held constant.*

Demand curve: The graphical relationship between the price of a good and the quantity consumers demand, with all other factors influencing demand held constant.

Demand deposits: Another name for checking accounts or checkable deposits, one of the major components of the M1 measure of the money supply.

Demand elasticity: A quantitative measurement (coefficient) showing the percentage change in the quantity demanded of a particular product relative to the percentage change in any one of the variables included in the demand function for that product.

Demand shifters: The variables in a demand function that are held constant when defining a given demand curve, but that would shift the demand curve if their values changed.

Depository institutions: Institutions that accept deposits from individuals and organizations, against which depositors can write checks on demand for their market transactions and that use these deposits to make loans.

Direct consumer surveys: An approach to analyzing consumer behavior that relies on directly asking consumers questions about their response to prices, price changes, or price differentials.

Discount rate: The interest rate the Federal Reserve charges banks that borrow reserves at the Fed's discount window.

Discouraged workers: Persons 16 years of age and over who are not currently seeking work because they believe that jobs in their area or line of work are unavailable or that they would not qualify for existing job openings.

Discretionary expenditures: Federal government expenditures for programs whose funds are authorized and appropriated by Congress and signed by the president, where explicit decisions are made on the size of the programs.

Diseconomies of scale: Incurring higher unit costs of production by adopting a larger scale of production, represented by the upward sloping portion of a long-run average cost curve.

Disposable income: Personal household income after all taxes have been paid.

Dominant strategy: A strategy that results in the best outcome or highest payoff to a given player no matter what action or choice the other player makes.

Durable goods: Commodities that typically last three or more years, such as automobiles, furniture, and household appliances.

Earnings or income approach: Measuring overall economic activity by adding the earnings or income generated by selling the output produced in the economy.

Economic profit: The difference between total revenue and total cost where cost includes both the explicit and any implicit costs of production.

Economies of scale: Achieving lower unit costs of production by adopting a larger scale of production, represented by the downward sloping portion of a long-run average cost curve.

Elastic demand: The percentage change in quantity demanded by consumers is greater than the percentage change in price and $|e_P| > 1$.

Employed: Persons 16 years of age and over who, in the survey week, did any work as an employee; worked in their own business, profession, or farm; or worked without pay at least 15 hours in a family business or farm.

Equilibrium level of income and output: The level of income or, equivalently, the aggregate output where the desired spending by all sectors of the economy just equals the value of the aggregate output produced and the income received from that production.

Equilibrium point for the perfectly competitive firm: The point where price equals average total cost because the firm earns zero economic profit at this point. Economic profit incorporates all implicit costs of production, including a normal rate of return on the firm's investment.

Equilibrium price: The price that actually exists in the market or toward which the market is moving where the quantity demanded by consumers equals the quantity supplied by producers.

Equilibrium quantity (Q_E): The quantity of a good, determined by the equilibrium price, where the amount of output that consumers demand is equal to the amount that producers want to supply.

Expansion: The rising phase of a business cycle, in which the direction of a series of economic indicators turns upward.

Expansionary monetary policy: Federal Reserve policy to increase the rate of growth of real GDP by increasing the amount of bank reserves in the system and lowering the federal funds and other interest rates.

Expenditure or output approach: Measuring overall economic activity by adding the expenditure on the output produced in the economy.

Expert opinion: An approach to analyzing consumer behavior that relies on developing a consensus of opinion among sales personnel, dealers, distributors, marketing consultants, and trade association members.

Explicit cost: A cost that is reflected in a payment to another individual, such as a wage paid to a worker, that is recorded in a firm's bookkeeping or accounting system.

Export spending (X): The total amount of spending on goods and services currently produced in one country and sold abroad to residents of other countries in a given period of time.

Federal Deposit Insurance Corporation (FDIC): The government regulatory institution that supervises the activities of depository institutions in the United States and provides depositors with accounts up to a certain amount (currently $250,000) with a guarantee that they will receive their funds even in the event of a bank failure.

Federal funds market: The private financial market where banks borrow and loan reserves to meet the minimum reserve requirements.

Federal funds rate: The interest rate that commercial banks charge each other for loans of reserves to meet their minimum reserve requirements.

Federal Open Market Committee (FOMC): The Federal Reserve body that has the primary responsibility for conducting monetary policy.

Federal Reserve System (Fed): The central bank in the United States that implements monetary policy and helps regulate and operate the country's financial system.

Final goods and services: Goods and services that are sold to their end-users.

Financial account: A measure of the change in the stock of real assets (buildings, property, etc.) and financial assets (bank deposits, securities, etc.) held by a country's residents in foreign countries and by foreigners in the given country.

First-degree price discrimination: A pricing strategy under which firms with market power are able to charge individuals the maximum amount they are willing to pay for each unit of the product.

Fiscal policy: Changes in taxes and spending by the executive and legislative branches of a country's national government that can be used to either stimulate or restrain the economy.

Fixed exchange rate system: A system in which the central banks of various countries intervene in the foreign exchange market to maintain or stabilize currency exchange rates.

Fixed input: An input whose quantity a manager cannot change during a given period of time.

Flexible exchange rate system: A system in which currency exchange rates are determined strictly by the forces of demand for and supply of the currencies and there is no intervention by any country's central bank in order to influence the level of exchange rates.

Fractional reserve system: A banking system in which banks are required to keep only a fraction of their deposits as reserves.

F-statistic: An alternative measure of goodness of fit of an estimating equation that can be used to test for the joint influence of all the independent variables in the equation.

Functional relationship: A relationship between variables, usually expressed in an equation using symbols for the variables, where the value of one variable, the independent variable, determines the value of the other, the dependent variable.

Game theory: A set of mathematical tools for analyzing situations in which players make various strategic moves and have different outcomes or payoffs associated with those moves.

GDP deflator: A measure of price changes in the economy that compares the price of each year's output of goods and services to the price of that same output in a base year.

Gold standard: A fixed rate system in which central banks agree to buy and sell gold to keep exchange rates at a given level.

Government consumption expenditures and gross investment (G): The total amount of spending by federal, state, and local governments on consumption outlays for goods and services, depreciation charges for existing structures and equipment, and investment capital outlays for newly acquired structures and equipment in a given period of time.

Gross domestic product (GDP): The comprehensive measure of the total market value of all currently produced final goods and services within a country in a given period of time by domestic and foreign-supplied resources.

Gross private domestic investment spending (I): The total amount of spending on nonresidential structures, equipment, software, residential structures, and business inventories in a given period of time.

Group pricing: Another name for third-degree price discrimination, in which different prices are charged to different groups of customers based on their underlying price elasticity of demand.

Herfindahl-Hirschman Index (*HHI*): A measure of market power that is defined as the sum of the squares of the market share of each firm in an industry.

Historical cost: The amount of money a firm paid for an input when it was purchased, which for machines and capital equipment could have occurred many years in the past.

Horizontal summation of individual demand curves: The process of deriving a market demand curve by adding the quantity demanded by each individual at every price to determine the market demand at every price.

Horizontal summation of marginal cost curves: For every level of marginal cost, add the amount of output produced by each firm to determine the overall level of output produced at each level of marginal cost.

Imperfect competition: Market structures of monopolistic competition, oligopoly, and monopoly, in which firms have some degree of market power.

Implicit cost: A cost that represents the value of using a resource that is not explicitly paid out and is often difficult to measure because it is typically not recorded in a firm's accounting system.

Import spending (*M*): The total amount of spending on goods and services currently produced in other countries and sold to residents of a given country in a given period of time.

Imputed value: An estimated value for nonmarket transactions, such as the rental value of owner-occupied housing, included in GDP.

Income elasticity of demand: The percentage change in the quantity demanded of a given good, *X*, relative to a percentage change in consumer income, assuming all other factors constant.

Increasing marginal returns: The results in that region of the marginal product curve where the curve is positive and increasing, so that total product increases at an increasing rate.

Individual demand function: The function that shows, in symbolic or mathematical terms, the variables that influence the quantity demanded of a particular product by an individual consumer.

Individual supply function: The function that shows, in symbolic or mathematical terms, the variables that influence the quantity supplied of a particular product by an individual producer.

Induced consumption expenditures: Consumption expenditures that result from changes in the level of real income in the economy.

Industry concentration: A measure of how many firms produce the total output of an industry. The more concentrated the industry, the fewer the firms operating in that industry.

Inelastic demand: The percentage change in quantity demanded by consumers is less than the percentage change in price and $|e_P| < 1$.

Inferior good: A good for which consumers will have a smaller demand as their incomes increase, all else held constant, and a greater demand if their incomes decrease, other factors held constant.

Inflation: A sustained increase in the price level over time.

Injections: Any supplement to consumer spending that increases domestic aggregate output and income.

Inputs: The factors of production, such as land, labor, capital, raw materials, and entrepreneurship, that are used to produce the outputs, or final goods and services, that are bought and sold in a market economy.

Input substitution: The degree to which a firm can substitute one input for another in a production process.

Interest-related expenditure (*IRE*) function: The function that shows the inverse relationship between planned consumption and investment spending and the real interest rate, all else held constant.

Intermediate goods and services: Goods and services that are used in the production of other goods and services.

International Monetary Fund (IMF): An international financial organization created at the Bretton Woods conference in 1944 that helps coordinate international financial flows and can arrange short-term loans between countries.

Investment spending function: The functional relationship between investment spending and income, holding all other variables that influence investment spending constant.

Joint profit maximization: A strategy that maximizes profits for a cartel, but that may create incentives for individual members to cheat.

Keynesian model: A model of the aggregate economy, based on ideas developed by John Maynard Keynes, with a horizontal short-run aggregate supply curve in which all changes in aggregate demand result in changes in real output and income.

Kinked demand curve model: An oligopoly model based on two demand curves that assumes that other firms will not match a firm's price increases, but will match its price decreases.

Labor force: Those individuals 16 years of age and over who are working in a job or actively seeking employment.

Labor-intensive method of production: A production process that uses large amounts of labor relative to the other inputs to produce the firm's output.

Lagging indicators: Economic variables, including measures of inflation and unemployment, labor costs, and consumer and business debt and credit levels, that turn down after the beginning of a recession and turn up after a recovery has begun.

Law of diminishing marginal returns or law of the diminishing marginal product: The phenomenon illustrated by that region of the marginal product curve where the curve is positive, but decreasing, so that total product is increasing at a decreasing rate.

Leading indicators: Economic variables, such as manufacturing, employment, monetary, and consumer expectation statistics, that generally turn down before a recession begins and turn back up before a recovery starts.

Leakages: Any uses of current income for purposes other than purchasing currently produced domestic goods and services.

Lean production: An approach to production pioneered by Toyota Motor Corporation in which firms streamline the production process through strategies such as strict scheduling and small-batch production with low-cost flexible machines.

Learning by doing: The drop in unit costs as total cumulative production increases because workers become more efficient as they repeat their assigned tasks.

Lerner Index: A measure of market power that focuses on the difference between a firm's product price and its marginal cost of production.

Limit pricing: A policy of charging a price lower than the profit-maximizing price to keep other firms from entering the market.

Linear demand function: A mathematical demand function graphed as a straight-line demand curve in which all the terms are either added or subtracted and no terms have exponents other than 1.

Linear supply function: A mathematical supply function, which graphs as a straight-line supply curve, in which all terms are either added or subtracted and no terms have exponents other than 1.

Liquidity: The ability of a financial asset to be used to immediately make market transactions.

Lock-in and switching costs: A form of market power for a firm in which consumers become locked into purchasing certain types or brands of products because they would incur substantial costs if they switched to other products.

Long-run aggregate supply curve: A vertical aggregate supply curve that defines the level of full employment or potential output based on a given amount of resources, efficiency, and technology in the economy.

Long-run average cost (*LRAC*): The minimum average or unit cost of producing any level of output *when all inputs are variable.*

Long-run production function: A production function showing the relationship between a flow of inputs and the resulting flow of output, where all inputs are variable.

Luxury: A good with an income elasticity greater than 1, where the expenditure on the good increases more than proportionately with changes in income.

Macroeconomics: The branch of economics that focuses on the overall level of economic activity, changes in the price level, and the amount of unemployment by analyzing group or aggregate behavior in different sectors of the economy.

Managed float: A fixed rate system in which central banks buy and sell foreign currency to maintain exchange rates at a given level.

Managerial economics: Microeconomics applied to business decision making.

Marginal benefit: The valuation that a consumer places on each additional unit of a product, which is measured by the price of that product.

Marginal cost: The additional cost of producing an additional unit of output, which equals the change in total cost or the change in total variable cost as output changes.

Marginal product: The additional output produced with an additional unit of variable input.

Marginal propensity to consume (*MPC*): The additional consumption spending generated by an additional amount of real income, assumed to take a value less than 1.

Marginal propensity to save (*MPS*): The additional household saving generated by an additional amount of real income, which equals $1 - MPC$.

Marginal revenue for the perfectly competitive firm: The marginal revenue curve for the perfectly competitive firm is horizontal because the firm can sell all units of output at the market price, given the assumption of a perfectly elastic demand curve. Price equals marginal revenue for the perfectly competitive firm.

Marginal revenue: The additional revenue that a firm takes in from selling an additional unit of output or the change in total revenue divided by the change in output.

Marginal revenue function: The functional relationship that shows the additional revenue a producer receives by selling an additional unit of output at different levels of output.

Market demand function: The function that shows, in symbolic or mathematical terms, the variables that influence the quantity demanded of a particular product by all consumers in the market and that is thus affected by the number of consumers in the market.

Market power: The ability of a firm to influence the prices of its products and develop other competitive strategies that enable it to earn large profits over longer periods of time.

Markets: The institutions and mechanisms used for the buying and selling of goods and services. The four major types of markets in microeconomic analysis are perfect competition, monopolistic competition, oligopoly, and monopoly.

Market supply function: The function that shows, in symbolic or mathematical terms, the variables that influence the quantity supplied of a particular product by all producers in the market and that is thus affected by the number of producers in the market.

Markup pricing: Calculating the price of a product by determining the average cost of producing the product and then setting the price a given percentage above that cost.

Microeconomics: The branch of economics that analyzes the decisions that individual consumers, firms, and industries make as they produce, buy, and sell goods and services.

Minimum efficient scale (*MES*): That scale of operation at which the long-run average cost curve stops declining or at which economies of scale are exhausted.

Mixed economy: An economy that has both a private (household and firm) sector and a public (government) sector.

Monetary base: Currency plus reserves (both required and excess), a variable controlled by central bank policy.

Monetary policies: Policies adopted by a country's central bank that influence the money supply, interest rates, and the amount of funds available for loans, which, in turn, influence consumer and business spending.

Money: The stock of financial assets that can easily be used to make market transactions and that serves as a medium of exchange, a unit of account, and a store of value.

Money multiplier: The money multiplier, mm—which is usually smaller than the simple deposit multiplier, d—reflects individuals' decisions to hold some of their assets in cash rather than deposit them in a checking account and banks' decisions to hold excess reserves.

Money supply: Currency plus checkable accounts or demand deposits (M1).

Monopolistic competition: A market structure characterized by a large number of small firms that have some market power as a result of producing differentiated products. This market power can be competed away over time.

Monopoly: A market structure characterized by a single firm producing a product with no close substitutes.

Multiple regression analysis: A statistical technique used to estimate the relationship between a dependent variable and an independent variable, *holding constant the effects of all other independent variables.*

Multiplier: The multiple change in income and output that results from a change in autonomous expenditure.

Nash equilibrium: A set of strategies from which all players are choosing their best strategy, given the actions of the other players.

National income accounting system: A system of accounts developed for each country, based on the circular flow, whose purpose is to measure the level of economic activity in that country.

National income: Income that is generated from the sale of the goods and services that are produced in the economy and that is paid to the individuals and businesses who supply the inputs or factors of production.

National Income and Product Accounts: The U.S. national income accounting system, operated by the Bureau of Economic Analysis (BEA) in the U.S. Department of Commerce.

Natural rate of unemployment: The minimum level of unemployment that can be achieved with current institutions without causing inflation to accelerate.

Necessity: A good with an income elasticity between 0 and 1, where the expenditure on the good increases less than proportionately with changes in income.

Negative (inverse) relationship: A relationship between two variables, graphed as a downward sloping line, where an increase in the value of one variable causes a decrease in the value of the other variable.

Negative marginal returns: The results in that region of the marginal product curve where the curve is negative and decreasing, so that total product is decreasing.

Net capital flow ($KN = k_i - k_o$): The difference between capital inflows and outflows, which must match the trade balance, or export spending minus import spending.

Net export expenditure: The difference (F) between export spending (X) on domestically produced goods and services by individuals in other countries and import spending (M) on foreign-produced goods and services by domestic residents in a given period of time or $F = X - M$.

Net interest: The interest private businesses pay to households for lending money to the firms minus the interest businesses receive plus interest earned from foreigners.

Net investment income: The difference between the interest income or receipts earned on investments in the rest of the world by the residents of a given country and the payments to foreigners on investments they have made in the given country.

Network externalities: A barrier to entry that exists because the value of a product to consumers depends on the number of consumers using the product.

Nominal exchange rate: The value at which one currency can be exchanged for another, or R.

Nominal GDP: The value of currently produced final goods and services measured in current year prices.

Nominal interest rate: The real interest rate plus the expected rate of inflation, which may differ substantially from the real interest rate during periods of inflation.

Nominal money supply (M_S): The money supply (M1), controlled by the Federal Reserve, which is defined in dollar terms.

Nominal terms: Measuring expenditures and income with the price level allowed to vary, so that changes in these values represent changes in the actual amount of goods, services, and income; changes in the price level; or a combination of both factors.

Noncooperative oligopoly models: Models of interdependent oligopoly behavior that assume that firms pursue profit-maximizing strategies based on assumptions about rivals' behavior and the impact of this behavior on the given firm's strategies.

Nondiscretionary expenditures: Federal government expenditures, for programs such as unemployment compensation, that increase or decrease simply as a result of the number of individuals eligible for the spending programs.

Nondurable goods: Commodities that last less than three years and may be consumed very quickly, such as food, clothing, and gasoline.

Normal good: A good for which consumers will have a greater demand as their incomes increase, all else held constant, and a smaller demand if their incomes decrease, other factors held constant.

Oligopoly: A market structure characterized by competition among a small number of large firms that have market power, but that must take their rivals' actions into account when developing their own competitive strategies.

Open economy: An economy that has both domestic and foreign sectors.

Open market operations: The major tool of Fed monetary policy that involves the buying and selling of government securities on the open market in order to change the money supply and influence interest rates.

Opportunity cost: The economic measure of cost that reflects the use of resources in one activity, such as a production process by one firm, in terms of the opportunities forgone in undertaking the next best alternative activity.

Outputs: The final goods and services produced and sold by firms in a market economy.

Panel data: Cross-sectional data observed at several points in time.

Perfect competition: A market structure characterized by a large number of firms in an industry, an undifferentiated product, ease of entry into the market, and complete information available to participants.

Perfectly (or infinitely) elastic demand: Infinite elasticity of demand, illustrated by a horizontal demand curve, where the quantity demanded would vary tremendously if there were any changes in price.

Perfectly inelastic demand: Zero elasticity of demand, illustrated by a vertical demand curve, where there is no change in quantity demanded for any change in price.

Personal consumption expenditures (C): The total amount of spending by households on durable goods, nondurable goods, and services in a given period of time.

Personal income: Income received by households that forms the basis for personal consumption expenditures.

Personalized pricing: Another name for first-degree price discrimination, in which the strategy is to determine how much each individual customer is willing to pay for the product and to charge him or her accordingly.

Point price elasticity of demand: A measurement of the price elasticity of demand calculated at a point on the demand curve using infinitesimal changes in prices and quantities.

Positive (direct) relationship: A relationship between two variables, graphed as an upward sloping line, where an increase in the value of one variable causes an increase in the value of the other variable.

Potential GDP: The maximum amount of GDP that can be produced at any point in time, which depends on the size of the labor force, the number of structures and the amount of equipment in the economy, and the state of technology.

Predatory pricing: A strategy of lowering prices below cost to drive firms out of the industry and scare off potential entrants.

Price discrimination: The practice of charging different prices to various groups of customers that are not based on differences in the costs of production.

Price elasticity of demand (e_P): The percentage change in the quantity demanded of a given good, X, relative to a percentage change in its own price, all other factors assumed constant.

Price experiments: An approach to analyzing consumer behavior in which consumer reaction to dif-

ferent prices is analyzed in a laboratory situation or a test market environment.

Price leadership: An oligopoly strategy in which one firm in the industry institutes price increases and waits to see if they are followed by rival firms.

Price-cost margin (PCM): The relationship between price and costs for an industry, calculated by subtracting the total payroll and the cost of materials from the value of shipments and then dividing the results by the value of the shipments. The approach ignores taxes, corporate overhead, advertising and marketing, research, and interest expenses.

Prices: The amounts of money that are charged for goods and services in a market economy. Prices act as signals that influence the behavior of both consumers and producers of these goods and services.

Price-setter: A firm in imperfect competition that faces a downward sloping demand curve and must set the profit-maximizing price to charge for its product.

Price-taker: A characteristic of a perfectly competitive firm in which the firm cannot influence the price of its product, but can sell any amount of its output at the price established by the market.

Prime rate: The interest rate that banks charge on loans to their best customers.

Producer Price Index (PPI): A measure of the prices firms pay for crude materials; intermediate materials, supplies, and components; and finished goods.

Production function: The relationship between a flow of inputs and the resulting flow of outputs in a production process during a given period of time.

Profit: The difference between the total revenue that a firm receives for selling its product and the total cost of producing that product.

Profit maximization: The assumed goal of firms, which is to develop strategies to earn the largest amount of profit possible. This can be accomplished by focusing on revenues, costs, or both.

Profit-maximizing rule: To maximize profits, a firm should produce the level of output where marginal revenue equals marginal cost.

Progressive tax system: An income tax system where higher tax rates are applied to increased amounts of income.

Promotional pricing: Using coupons and sales to lower the price of the product for those customers willing to incur the costs of using these devices as opposed to lowering the price of the product for all customers.

Proprietors' income: The income of unincorporated businesses, such as medical practices, law firms, small farms, and retail stores.

Real exchange rate: The nominal exchange rate times the ratio of the domestic price level to the foreign price level.

Real GDP: The value of currently produced final goods and services measured in constant prices, or nominal GDP adjusted for price level changes.

Real interest rate: The nominal interest rate adjusted for expected inflation, which is the rate that influences firms' investment decisions.

Real money demand: The demand for money in real terms, which is a function of the real interest rate and the level of real income.

Real money supply (M_S/P): The nominal money supply divided by the price level, which expresses the money supply in terms of real goods and services and which influences behavior.

Real terms: Measuring expenditures and income with the price level held constant, so that any changes in these values represent changes in the actual amount of goods, services, and income.

Recession: The falling phase of a business cycle, in which the direction of a series of economic indicators turns downward.

Relative prices: The price of one good in relation to the price of another, similar good, which is the way prices are defined in microeconomics.

Rental income: The income households receive from the rental of their property.

Reserve assets: Assets, including foreign currencies and gold certificates, that central banks use to maintain exchange rates between countries at a given level or in a predetermined range.

Reserve requirement: Required reserves kept in banks' vaults or as deposits at the Federal Reserve divided by demand deposits or the fraction of deposits banks are required to keep as reserves.

Residential fixed investment: Spending on newly constructed housing units, major alterations of and replacements to existing structures, and brokers' commissions.

Revenue or T-account: An accounting statement that shows expense-generating items on the left-hand or debit side and income-generating items on the right-hand or credit side.

Saving (S): The amount of disposable income that households do *not* spend on the consumption of goods and services.

Second-degree price discrimination: A pricing strategy under which firms with market power charge different prices for different blocks of output.

Services: Noncommodity items, such as utilities, public transportation, private education, medical care, and recreation.

Short-run aggregate supply curve: An aggregate supply curve that is either horizontal or upward sloping, depending on whether the absolute price level increases as firms produce more output.

Short-run average total cost ($SATC$): The cost per unit of output for a firm of a given size or scale of operation.

Short-run cost function: A cost function for a short-run production process in which there is at least one fixed input of production.

Short-run production function: A production process that uses at least one fixed input.

Shutdown point for the perfectly competitive firm: The price, which equals a firm's minimum average variable cost, below which it is more profitable for the perfectly competitive firm to shut down than to continue to produce.

Simple deposit multiplier: The amount by which the money supply can be increased in a fractional reserve banking system, which equals ($1/rr$), where rr is the reserve requirement.

Simple regression analysis: A form of regression analysis that analyzes the relationship between one dependent and one independent variable.

Stagflation: Higher prices and price increases (inflation) combined with lower real output and income (stagnation), resulting from a major increase in input prices in the economy.

Standard error: A measure of the precision of an estimated regression analysis coefficient that shows how much the coefficient would vary in regressions from different samples.

Statistical discrepancy (SD): The imbalance between the financial and current accounts in the balance of payments statement or between payments and receipts in the revenue or T-account that arises from inefficient data collection.

Sterilized intervention: Actions taken by a country's central bank to prevent balance of payments policies from influencing the country's domestic money supply.

Strategic entry deterrence: Strategic policies pursued by a firm that prevent other firms from entering the market.

Substitute goods: Two goods, X and Y, are substitutes if an increase in the price of good Y causes consumers to *increase* their demand for good X or if a decrease in the price of good Y causes consumers to *decrease* their demand for good X.

Supply: The functional relationship between the price of a good or service and the quantity supplied by producers in a given time period, *all else held constant.*

Supply curve: The graphical relationship between the price of a good and the quantity supplied, with all other factors influencing supply held constant.

Supply curve for the perfectly competitive firm: The portion of a firm's marginal cost curve that lies above the minimum average variable cost.

Supply curve for the perfectly competitive industry: The curve that shows the output produced by all perfectly competitive firms in the industry at different prices.

Supply shifters: The other variables in a supply function that are held constant when defining a given supply curve, but that would cause that supply curve to shift if their values changed.

Tacit collusion: Coordinated behavior among oligopoly firms that is achieved without a formal agreement.

Targeted marketing: Selling that centers on defining different market segments or groups of buyers for particular products based on the demographic, psychological, and behavioral characteristics of the individuals.

Technical factors: Other influences on the commercial banking system's reserves that are unrelated to Fed monetary policy.

Test marketing: An approach to analyzing consumer behavior that involves analyzing consumer response to products in real or simulated markets.

Third-degree price discrimination: A pricing strategy under which firms with market power separate markets according to the price elasticity of demand and charge a higher price (relative to cost) in the market with the more inelastic demand.

Time-series data: Data collected on the same observational unit at a number of points in time.

Total benefit: The total amount of money consumers are willing to pay for a product rather than go without the product

Total cost: The sum of the total fixed cost plus the total variable cost.

Total fixed cost: The total cost of using the fixed input, which remains constant regardless of the amount of output produced.

Total product: The total quantity of output produced with given quantities of fixed and variable inputs.

Total revenue: The amount of money received by a producer for the sale of its product, calculated as the price per unit times the quantity sold.

Total revenue function: The functional relationship that shows the total revenue (price times quantity) received by a producer as a function of the level of output.

Total variable cost: The total cost of using the variable input, which increases as more output is produced.

Trade balance: The relationship between a country's exports and imports, which may be either positive (exports exceed imports) or negative (imports exceed exports).

Trade deficit: occurs when a country's import spending exceeds the spending on its exports.

Trade surplus: Occurs when a country's export spending exceeds the spending on its imports.

Trade-weighted dollar: An index of the weighted exchange value of the U.S. dollar versus the currencies of a broad group of major U.S. trading partners.

Transfer payments: Payments that represent the transfer of income among individuals in the economy, but do not reflect the production of new goods and services.

t-test: A test based on the size of the ratio of the estimated regression coefficient to its standard error that is used to determine the statistical significance of the coefficient.

Two-part pricing: Charging consumers a fixed fee for the right to purchase a product and then a variable fee that is a function of the number of units purchased.

Underground economy: Economic transactions that cannot be easily measured because they are not reported on income tax returns or other government economic surveys.

Unemployed: Persons 16 years of age and over who do not currently have a job, but who are actively seeking employment.

Unilateral transfers: Flows of goods, services, and financial assets, such as foreign aid, from one country to another in which nothing of significant economic value is received in return.

Unitary elasticity (or unit elastic): The percentage change in quantity demanded is exactly equal to the percentage change in price and $|e_P| = 1$.

Unplanned inventory decrease: An unexpected decrease in inventories that occurs when desired aggregate expenditure exceeds the level of output currently produced.

Unplanned inventory increase: An unexpected increase in inventories that occurs when desired aggregate expenditure is insufficient to purchase the level of output currently produced.

Value-added approach: A process of calculating the value of the final output in an economy by summing the value added in each stage of production (i.e., raw materials to semifinished goods to final products).

Variable input: An input whose quantity a manager can change during a given period of time.

Versioning: Offering different versions of a product to different groups of customers at various prices, with the versions designed to meet the needs of the specific groups.

World Bank: An international financial organization created at the Bretton Woods conference in 1944 that helps developing countries obtain low-interest loans.

X-inefficiency: Inefficiency that may result in firms with market power that have fewer incentives to minimize the costs of production than more competitive firms.

Index

Autonomous expenditures, 332, 348, 348–351
Average costs, 129–132
Average fixed cost, 129
Average product, 118–121
Average revenue, 57
Average revenue function, 57
Average total cost, 129
Average variable cost, 129

B

Balance of payments (BP) accounting system, 423
Balance of payments issues, 316
Balance of payments issues in macroeconomic
    environment, 440–441
  equations for, 449–450
  equilibrium in open economy, 422–427
  exchange rates, 418–421
  foreign exchange market, 427–436
  policy examples of, 436–448
  summary, 449
  U.S. dollar valuation, 418–419
Balance of trade, 420–421
Bank of Japan, 417, 434, 435
Bank reserves, market for, 383
Barnes & Noble, 210, 213, 225
Barriers to entry, 8, 199, 201–210
Barter system, 362
Bear Stearns Company, 376
Beer, demand elasticity and, 69–70
Beige Book, 367
Beijing General Corp. of the Agriculture Industry, 462
Bernanke, Ben, 321, 361, 366, 372
Best practices, 150
BHP Billiton, 203
Binkley, James, 468
Blinder, Alan, 135, 137, 284
Board of Governors, 367, 371
Book of Little Honorary Guests, 462
Bookstores, monopolistically competitive, 225–226
Borden, 107
Borders Group Inc., 212–213
Boston Scientific Corp., 325
Brand loyalties, 208
Brand-specific training, 209
Bretton Woods conference (1944), 431
Bricks-and-mortar prices, 76, 212
Broiler chicken industry, competition and, 184–185
Budget constraints, 79–80
Budget line, 79–80
Budget surplus/deficit, 341
Bundling, 279, 281
Burger King, 115, 452, 453–459, 464–466
Burns, Harbor, 409
Bush, George W., 325, 409, 446
Business activities, in fast-food industry, 458–459

Business confidence, 336–337
Business cycles, 297
Business fixed investment, 300–301
Business inventories, changes in, 301
Business investment spending, 332–334, 392
Business pricing strategies, 264–265
Business taxes, 335–336

C

Cablevision Systems Corp, 87
California Milk Processor Board, 187
Campbell's, 234
Capacity utilization rates (CURs), 337
Capital flows, 316, 424
Capital inflow, 422
Capital-intensive method of production, 144
Capital outflow, 422
Capper-Volstead Act, 171
Cardinal Health, 224
Cargill, 186
Caribou, 234
Carlsberg AS, 203
Carnation Coffee-mate case study, 107–108
Carnation Evaporated Milk case study, 108–109
Cartels, 245–250
Cattleman's Collection, 186
Celler-Kefauver Act of 1950, 217
Census, analysis of, 91
Census of Manufactures, 185
Census of Retail Trade, 469
Center for Science in the Public Interest, 463
Central Bank. *See* Federal Reserve
Cephalon Inc., 206
Change in demand, 25–26, 38
Change in quantity demanded, 25–26
Change in quantity supplied, 31–32
Change in supply, 31–32, 38–39
Changes in business inventories, 301
Chapter 11 Bookstore, 225
Chavez, Hugo, 249
Cheating, in cartels, 247
Chicken products, demand elasticity and, 68–69
China
  agriculture industry in, 123
  auto producers, 4
  copper market, 17–18, 41
  economic activity in 2012, 344, 410, 417
  as emerging market, 37, 387
  foreign investment, 446–447
  imports to U.S., 30
  iPhone in, 143
  KFC in, 115
  McDonald's in, 453, 460–464
  middle class economy in, 409
  per capita GDP, 297